ROMAN FRUGALITY

Roman Frugality offers the first-ever systematic analysis of the variants of individual and collective self-restraint that shaped ancient Rome throughout its history and had significant repercussions in post-classical times. In particular, it does justice to the complexity of a phenomenon that is situated at the interface of ethics and economics, self and society, and the real and the imaginary, and which touches upon thrift and sobriety in the material sphere, but also modes of moderation more generally, not least in the spheres of food and drink, sex and power. Adopting an interdisciplinary approach drawing on ancient history, philology, archaeology and the history of thought, the volume traces the role of frugal thought and practice within the evolving political culture and political economy of ancient Rome from the archaic age to the imperial period and concludes with a chapter that explores the reception of ancient ideas of self-restraint in early modern times.

INGO GILDENHARD is a Reader in Classics and the Classical Tradition at the University of Cambridge and a Fellow of King's College. His publications include *Paideia Romana* (2007) and *Creative Eloquence* (2011) and, with M. Silk and R. Barrow, *The Classical Tradition* (2013).

CRISTIANO VIGLIETTI is an Associate Professor of Roman History at the University of Siena. He is the author of *Il limite del bisogno. Antropologia economica di Roma arcaica* (2011).

CAMBRIDGE CLASSICAL STUDIES

General editors

J. P. T. CLACKSON, W. M. BEARD, G. BETEGH,
R. L. HUNTER, M. J. MILLETT, S. P. OAKLEY,
R. G. OSBORNE, T. J. G. WHITMARSH

ROMAN FRUGALITY

Modes of Moderation from the Archaic Age to the Early Empire and Beyond

Edited by

INGO GILDENHARD
University of Cambridge

CRISTIANO VIGLIETTI
Università degli Studi, Siena

CAMBRIDGE
UNIVERSITY PRESS

University Printing House, Cambridge CB2 8BS, United Kingdom

One Liberty Plaza, 20th Floor, New York, NY 10006, USA

477 Williamstown Road, Port Melbourne, VIC 3207, Australia

314–321, 3rd Floor, Plot 3, Splendor Forum, Jasola District Centre,
New Delhi – 110025, India

79 Anson Road, #06–04/06, Singapore 079906

Cambridge University Press is part of the University of Cambridge.

It furthers the University's mission by disseminating knowledge in the pursuit of
education, learning, and research at the highest international levels of excellence.

www.cambridge.org
Information on this title: www.cambridge.org/9781108840163
DOI: 10.1017/9781108879088

© Faculty of Classics, University of Cambridge 2020

This publication is in copyright. Subject to statutory exception
and to the provisions of relevant collective licensing agreements,
no reproduction of any part may take place without the written
permission of Cambridge University Press.

First published 2020

Printed in the United Kingdom by TJ International Ltd, Padstow Cornwall

A catalogue record for this publication is available from the British Library.

Library of Congress Cataloging-in-Publication Data
NAMES: Gildenhard, Ingo, 1970– editor. | Viglietti, Cristiano, editor.
TITLE: Roman frugality : modes of moderation from the archaic age to the early
empire and beyond / [edited by] Ingo Gildenhard, Cristiano Viglietti.
DESCRIPTION: 1 Edition. | New York : Cambridge University Press, 2020. |
SERIES: Cambridge classical studies | Includes bibliographical references and index.
IDENTIFIERS: LCCN 2020000927 (print) | LCCN 2020000928 (ebook) |
ISBN 9781108840163 (hardback) | ISBN 9781108793834 (paperback) |
ISBN 9781108879088 (epub)
SUBJECTS: LCSH: Thriftiness–History.
CLASSIFICATION: LCC HG179 .R6326 2020 (print) | LCC HG179 (ebook) |
DDC 330.937–dc23
LC record available at https://lccn.loc.gov/2020000927
LC ebook record available at https://lccn.loc.gov/2020000928

ISBN 978-1-108-84016-3 Hardback

Cambridge University Press has no responsibility for the persistence or accuracy
of URLs for external or third-party internet websites referred to in this publication
and does not guarantee that any content on such websites is, or will remain,
accurate or appropriate.

CONTENTS

List of Figures	*page* vii
List of Contributors	viii
Acknowledgements	ix
Note on Translations	xi
List of Abbreviations	xii

Introduction: Frugality in Theory and History   1
INGO GILDENHARD AND CRISTIANO VIGLIETTI

1 'Frugality', Economy and Society in Archaic Rome
(Late Seventh to Early Fourth Century BCE)   127
CRISTIANO VIGLIETTI

2 From Licinius Stolo to Tiberius Gracchus: Roman
Frugality and the Limitation of Landholding   159
JOHN RICH

3 Frugality as a Political Language in the Second
Century BCE: The Strategies of Cato the Elder
and Scipio Aemilianus   192
LAURE PASSET

4 Smallholding, Frugality and Market Economy in
the Gracchan Age   213
MATTIA BALBO

5 *Frugalitas*, or: The Invention of a Roman Virtue   237
INGO GILDENHARD

6 Frugality, Building, and Heirlooms in an Age of
Social Mobility   347
JOHN R. PATTERSON

v

Contents

7 From Poverty to Prosperity: The Recalibration
of Frugality   372
CHRISTOPHER J. BERRY

Index Locorum   400
General Index   409

FIGURES

Chart 1   Possible model of a 2-*iugera* field in a
system of crop rotation in early
republican Rome.   *page* 147

CONTRIBUTORS

MATTIA BALBO is Assegnista di Ricerca at the Università degli Studi di Torino, Dipartimento di Studi Storici.

CHRISTOPHER J. BERRY is Honorary Professorial Research Fellow in the School of Social & Political Sciences at the University of Glasgow.

INGO GILDENHARD is Reader in Classics and the Classical Tradition in the Faculty of Classics, University of Cambridge.

LAURE PASSET is Professeure agrégée at the Lycée La Saulaie de Saint-Marcellin (Isère).

JOHN R. PATTERSON is Senior Lecturer in the Faculty of Classics, University of Cambridge.

JOHN RICH is Emeritus Professor in the Department of Classics at the University of Nottingham.

CRISTIANO VIGLIETTI is Professore Associato in the Dipartimento di Filologia e critica delle letterature antiche e moderne at the Università di Siena.

ACKNOWLEDGEMENTS

We are profoundly grateful to the Marie Skłodowska-Curie Fellowship Programme (FP7-PEOPLE-2011-IEF) of the European Commission, which funded a two-year stay of Cristiano Viglietti at the University of Cambridge (project ECO-FRUGAL: *The Economics of Frugality between Ancient Rome and Contemporary Western Society*). The present volume is one of the outcomes of the ensuing international collaboration, which stretches far beyond this particular output and its contributors. We are equally beholden to the Faculty of Classics, University of Cambridge, and King's College Cambridge for liberal support and hospitality during the various workshops in which the authors of the chapters collected here as well as numerous other scholars (notably Jean-Jacques Aubert, Luigi Capogrossi Colognesi, Gabriele Cifani, Stefano Ferrucci, Rebecca Flemming, Peter Garnsey, Alessandro Launaro, Jérôme Maucourant, Neville Morley, Stephen Oakley and Andrew Wallace-Hadrill) shared their thoughts on Roman frugality. During the editorial process we benefited greatly from the advice and generosity of our contributors and other colleagues, in particular Rebecca Flemming, Neville Morley, Robin Osborne and Andrew Wallace-Hadrill. The readers for *Cambridge Classical Studies* provided us with bracing feedback on an early draft that forced us to rethink and reshape the volume in fundamental ways. As editors we did not always concur with their criticisms, but we hope that the final product shows how seriously we engaged with the feedback provided.

We are profoundly grateful to the Staatliche Antikensammlungen und Glyptothek München for providing us with our cover image ('Relief depicting a rural scene: farmer with cow on his way to the market') free of charge. We are also very much indebted to David Hemsley for his meticulous copy-

Acknowledgements

editing of the manuscript and to the marvellous support, efficiency and speed of Hal Churchman and, in particular, Michael Sharp at CUP, who managed to transform our ms. into a book in record time.

The editors

NOTE ON TRANSLATIONS

Citations from works in languages other than English (whether Greek, Latin or a modern vernacular) that occur in the body of the text are accompanied by a translation. Contributors have adopted a more selective approach in the footnotes, esp. when the passage in question is paraphrased in the discussion and/or is cited primarily for lexical reasons.

ABBREVIATIONS

Abbreviations for Greek and Latin authors and texts by and large follow the conventions of H. G. Liddell and R. Scott, *A Greek-English Lexicon*, the *Oxford Latin Dictionary* or (for later Latin authors) the *Oxford Classical Dictionary*. Exceptions – such as specific titles for Seneca's *Dialogi* (differentiated only by number in the *OLD* and *OCD*) – ought to be self-explanatory. Where possible, abbreviations for journals follow the practice of *L'Année Philologique*. Note in addition the following:

ANRW	*Aufstieg und Niedergang der römischen Welt.* Berlin and New York, 1972–.
CIL	*Corpus Inscriptionum Latinarum.* Berlin, 1862–.
FRHist	T. J. Cornell et al. *The Fragments of the Roman Historians.* Oxford, 2013.
ILLRP	A. Degrassi (ed.) *Inscriptiones Latinae Liberae Rei Publicae*, 2 vols. Florence, 1957–1963.
ILS	H. Dessau (ed.) *Inscriptiones Latinae selectae*, 3 vols. Berlin, 1892–1916.
ORF	E. Malcovati, *Orationum Romanorum Fragmenta.* Turin, 1953, ³1967, ⁴1976.
RE	*Paulys Realencyclopädie der classischen Altertumswissenschaft*, 83 vols. Stuttgart, 1893–1980.
TLL	*Thesaurus Linguae Latinae.* Munich, 1900–.

xii

INTRODUCTION

Frugality in Theory and History

INGO GILDENHARD AND CRISTIANO VIGLIETTI

Roman Frugality: Stories of Decline and Fall

Concern with frugal conduct (or lack thereof) has a pervasive presence in our ancient sources and registers with particular force in the literary record of late-republican and early imperial Rome. In the story that many a text from this period tells, frugality was a characteristic attitude to wealth on the part of Rome's ancestral aristocracy – or indeed the populace as a whole. Roman historiographers frequently convey the impression that 'the Romans' (suitably reified) lived in simple self-sufficiency throughout the first five or six centuries of their city's history, beholden to a set of values (not least *frugalitas*) that encouraged self-restraint, material sobriety and prudent husbandry and disowned greed and ambition alongside those professions that were deemed to promote a luxurious style of life. But in the years after the Second Punic War, military conquest and the transition to a Mediterranean-wide empire, which coincided with the adoption of foreign customs and the embrace of 'Eastern' luxury, fatally weakened this frugal ethos and ushered in the unchecked pursuit of material enrichment and the spendthrift enjoyment of new-found wealth – leading to moral corruption and, ultimately, the downfall of the republican commonwealth.[1] The adoption of a profligate lifestyle by

---

[1] See Lintott 1972 for a critical discussion of the ancient sources that link imperial expansion to moral decline. For the (gendered) link between luxury and autocracy in ancient thought involving the concepts of *truphe/luxuria* and *hubris/superbia* see Dench 1998: 124: '*Hybris* is a trait attendant on successes which are not controlled by moderation, and in consequence those in possession of absolute power and of empire are particularly prone to it: the immoderation of *hybris* associates it closely with the feminine traits of decadent behaviour, or *tryphe*.'

I

Ingo Gildenhard and Cristiano Viglietti

a significant segment of the Roman population also triggered the rise of a nostalgic discourse among the more prudent or economically disadvantaged that lamented the decline and eventual loss of the ancestral outlook that had long prevailed in Roman society and enabled its rise to imperial greatness. This discourse ensured that even as Rome lost its frugal ways and succumbed to the vices of greed, ambition and luxury, her seemingly exemplary commitment to material sobriety during the heydays of the republic was able to endure as a model of inspiration and emulation for later ages with similar ambitions to moral and military grandeur.

From the seventeenth to the early nineteenth century, scholars writing on Roman history were by and large content with replicating variants of the historical plot the ancient moralists constructed, with a similar ideological emphasis: they approved of frugality and rebuked luxury. Austere management of material resources tended to be understood in positive terms, as a key reason for Rome's political stability and military success. Peasant discipline in the form of economic thrift and moral fibre was thought to have ensured that republican Rome rested on solid foundations.[2] Conversely, disregard for ancestral customs was perceived to be the cause of a moral as well as political and economic downturn during the empire.[3] Yet this 'classical' paradigm gradually went out of fashion as the notion of luxury and economic phenomena more generally underwent a process of 'demoralisation' in the early modern period.[4] In the wake of Bernard Mandeville (1670–1733) and others, who radically re-evaluated the significance of 'private vices' by turning them into a source for 'public benefits', the correlation of morality and economic productivity in ancient Rome equally underwent fundamental reassessment.[5] From the

---

[2] Representatives of this school of thought include Montesquieu 1734; Dureau de la Malle 1840; and Sirago 1995.

[3] See e.g. Meursius 1605: 1–3; Constant 1819; Dureau de la Malle 1840: 491–2; Zumpt 1841: 70–5.

[4] Berry 1994 (and Chapter 7 in this volume) reconstructs this story.

[5] On the debate between Mandeville and Shaftsbury and its implications for the study of Roman history see Wallace-Hadrill 2008: 320–9.

Introduction

late eighteenth century to more recent times, a considerable number of social and economic historians came to endorse the view that Rome's avowed commitment to frugality constitutes evidence of an essentially pre-modern (a.k.a. 'primitive') mindset insofar as it inhibited economic enterprise and hence needlessly stymied prosperity.

For this school of thought the frugal habitus that has often been taken to characterise the ancient Romans tout court presented an obstacle to the development of an economic system akin to our modern one, based as it is on growth, investment of capital, unfettered consumption and the theoretically unlimited expansion of the market. The alleged traditional mentality of the republican aristocracy was thus deemed to impede economic progress; conversely, the apparent crisis of traditional values in the imperial age received re-evaluation as a positive development that temporarily helped to improve the Roman economy, at least according to such performance indicators as accelerated growth and the production of surplus. The novel opportunities that arose under the principate and ensuing changes in attitude and outlook were thought to have provided a stimulus for commercial activities and, more generally, the emergence of a more profit- and investment-oriented culture, alongside the rise of social groups that lived off those activities. In this story, the prosperity of the Roman Empire resulted at least in part from the breakdown of Rome's traditionally frugal ethos.[6] The Romans thereby matured into an ancient variant of the *homo oeconomicus* (the term was coined by Maffeo Pantaleoni in his *Principii di economia pura*, 1889) who populates certain forms of modern economic theory that consider the satisfaction of as many wants as possible and the desire for capital accretion omnipresent factors of economic activity – trans-historical universals as it were, limited only by the respective state of technological progress and

---

[6] See e.g. Mengotti 1787: vii; Gibbon 1782; Friedländer 1964: 180, 307; Earl 1967: 31–2. For discussion see Finley 1985: 60–1; Garnsey and Saller 1987: 43; Morris 1999: xx–xxiii; Hitchner 2005; Harris 2007: 538.

Ingo Gildenhard and Cristiano Viglietti

varying socio-political circumstances.[7] Certain aspects of Roman history – sustained imperial expansion, the ruthless exploitation of conquered territories or the unrestrained indulgence in the pleasures of consumption fuelled by the windfalls of military aggression – seem indeed to attest that ancient Rome provides another case study in the arguably universal human desire to accumulate and use wealth to the fullest possible extent.

But scholarly interest in ancient modes of (economic) self-restraint and their alleged disappearance in the imperial age anyway peaked some time ago. More recent work on the Roman economy tends to bracket preoccupation with frugality altogether.[8] Whether the focus is on craftsmen or trade – on, to cite some representative titles, 'the world of the *fullo*', 'Roman artisans and the urban economy', 'urban craftsmen and traders in the Roman world', 'the economics of the Roman stone trade', 'the Romans and trade' or on settlement and urbanisation, agriculture, *ager publicus* and landownership, material sobriety and self-restraint have seemingly become irrelevant in our efforts to analyse and explain data.[9] Likewise, recent attempts to 'quantify the Roman economy' have been as uninterested in frugality as studies on 'Rome's economic revolution', 'the Roman market economy' and 'globalisation and the Roman world'.[10]

While scholars no longer ponder the enabling or inhibiting impact of Rome's allegedly frugal ethos, the question of how to study ancient economic practice has remained controversial. The respective strengths and weaknesses of approaches that are

---

[7] See e.g. Jongman 2007: 598.

[8] Exceptions include Passet 2011 and Viglietti 2011: 139–224.

[9] See, respectively, Flohr 2013; Hawkins 2016; the papers in Wilson and Flohr 2016; Russell 2013; Tchernia 2011/2016. On settlement and demographics, agriculture and the exploitation of natural resources (of the sea and the land) in the Roman world see Marzano 2013; the papers in Bowman and Wilson 2011 and 2013b; and the papers in Erdkamp, Verboven and Zuiderhoek 2015; on *ager publicus* in Italy during the republican centuries (396–89 BCE) Roselaar 2010; on commerce and trade the papers in Wilson and Bowman 2018 (cf. Bresson 2016 for a comparable study of the Greek world).

[10] See the papers in Bowman and Wilson 2009; Kay 2014; Temin 2013; and the papers in Pitts and Versluys 2015.

Introduction

'primitivist' and/or 'substantivist' in orientation vis-à-vis those that are 'modernist' and/or 'formalist'[11] have remained the subject of debate – not least as part of concerted efforts to move beyond what has always been a somewhat artificial binary.[12] Many studies now put the emphasis on detail, specificity and heterogeneity and take into consideration social context and the potential impact of noneconomic values, certainly on the attitudes, to some extent also on the conduct, of specific individuals or groups – while emphasising the importance of economic rationality and financial self-interest as key, yet often neglected factors in history.[13] But frugality, however defined, is not a variable that registers much (if at all). The same is true of contemporary accounts of Roman military expansion and imperial exploitation as well as their domestic repercussions:[14] such studies unceremoniously dispense with the plot of the ancient moralisers who considered imperial success a main reason for the weakening of frugal values insofar as it enabled the influx of 'Eastern' luxury and thereby caused moral decadence and, more generally, societal decline (while conveniently overlooking the awkward fact that Rome smashed much of the Mediterranean world and Northern Europe to pieces at the same time it succumbed to supposedly effeminising luxury).[15]

---

[11] The terms are taken from Scheidel 2012b: 7–8. He glosses them as follows: 'Put in a highly simplified manner, formalist positions stress similarities between ancient and modern economies by emphasizing the putative significance of price-setting markets, comparative advantage, and capitalist ventures, whereas substantivists emphasize discontinuities by focusing on how status concerns mediated economic behavior and generated specific dynamics that reflected elite preference for rent-taking and landownership and disdain for commercial enterprise that reinforced the fusion of political and economic power and marginalized independent merchants.' For a summary of the debate, see Scheidel, Morris and Saller 2007; Viglietti 2018: 216–24.

[12] See e.g. Harris 1993 and Saller 2005.

[13] See e.g. Morley 2004a: 48–50; the papers in Bang, Ikeguchi and Ziche 2006 and Droß-Krüpe, Föllinger and Ruffing 2016; or Manning 2018: 15: 'analysis of "the ancient economy" must be located between the "static traditional economy" and a "fluid market economy".' (The quotation marks seem designed to indicate scepticism of reifying 'the ancient economy' (single and unchanging) in favour of a plurality and heterogeneity of (local) economies, with significant change over time.)

[14] See e.g. Erskine 2010; Lavan 2013; the papers in Hoyos 2013; Harris 2016.

[15] Already Cicero, in his anti-austerity speech *pro Murena*, called the bluff: see below 66.

Ingo Gildenhard and Cristiano Viglietti

In short, over time, 'frugality' has morphed from a key factor into a non-factor in our endeavours to understand the world(s) of ancient Rome. Historians now tend to treat frugality not primarily as a habitus that regulated economic behaviour, but as a discursive phenomenon of scant economic or socio-political import – a reaction by certain members of the Roman elite to societal changes brought about by unparalleled levels of consumption in the wake of Rome's imperial expansion in Southern Italy and the wider Mediterranean. The current indifference to modes of (material) sobriety and (economic) self-restraint as variables in Roman history suggests that the scholarly discussion has simply moved on. From the point of view of much modern scholarship, Rome's supposed commitment to frugality in the days of yore has by and large dwindled into a discursive reflex in authors of the late republic and early imperial period without significant purchase on economic, cultural or socio-political practice: it has become 'a curious accretion to be ignored by those in pursuit of the real matter in Roman texts'.[16] Stories of the decline and fall of Roman frugality thus have a counterpart in the decline and fall of Roman frugality as a historical phenomenon worth studying.

Roman Frugality Rethought

Arguably, however, the history of scholarship on Roman frugality is a case of the baby getting thrown out with the bathwater – without the infant receiving the courtesy of prior in-depth examination. For despite its prominent place in the cultural imaginary of late-republican and early imperial Rome, frugality has received little direct, let alone systematic attention even in those quarters where its existence and importance were taken for granted, at least in comparison and contrast to the interest generated by related concepts such

---

[16] Edwards 1993: 2, who is critical of this outlook. Cf. Gibbon 1782: 62; Salvioli 1929: 12–13; Lintott 1972: 626–7, 638; Courtney 1980: 255.

Introduction

as luxury or poverty.[17] If at all, it tends to register as an ancillary concern: in most of the scholarly literature, whatever its overall approach and underlying premises, frugality figures primarily as an unexamined given to be asserted, denied or ignored for arguments whose focus lies elsewhere. Neither the concept nor the phenomenon has ever been at the centre of a sustained cross-disciplinary investigation that explores the limits and possibilities of detecting modes of frugality in Roman society and offers genealogical soundings into Roman practices of, and reflections on, (material) moderation – let alone the largely unexplored impact this body of thought has had on later historical periods. Part of the reason is that Roman frugality tends to be understood in narrowly moral–economic terms. Yet while the interface of the moral and the economic constitutes an important aspect of Roman frugality, this interface is more complex than is generally assumed and the phenomenon as a whole much broader in scope, as already indicated by the variety of 'equivalents' the Latin term *frugalitas* has attracted in English translations – including 'thrift', 'sobriety', 'moderation', 'self-restraint' (esp. concerning food and drink, but also sex and power), 'healthy diet', 'uprightness' or 'honesty'. With its complex semantics and adventurous history, *frugalitas* is not *just* an antonym of luxury – it is also only one of the concepts of relevance here.

Hence the aim of our volume: in and through this introduction and the subsequent case studies, it tries to rethink the place and function of (appeals to) thrift, self-restraint (material) sobriety and, more generally, 'the morality of needs and wants', as well as the associated Latin terms and discourses from the archaic period to early imperial times and beyond. Our approach is historical and genealogical in Foucault's

---

[17] Interest in Roman luxury dates back to Meursius 1605; see also Baudrillart 1881; De Marchi 1895. More recent work includes Clemente 1981; Ampolo 1984; Edwards 1993; Goddard 1994; Dalby 2000; Bottiglieri 2002; Fulminante 2003; Coudry 2004; Weeber 2006; 2007; Dubois-Pelerin 2008; Wallace-Hadrill 2008; Arena 2011; Zanda 2011; Casinos Mora 2015; Andreau and Coudry 2016. On poverty, see the papers in Atkins and Osborne 2006 and Corbo 2006 (focusing on late antiquity); cf. Townsend 1979; 1985.

Ingo Gildenhard and Cristiano Viglietti

sense of the term:[18] the objective is to identify the factors – the economic circumstances, socio-political dynamics and discursive opportunities – that, at certain moments in time, rendered it attractive for specific social groups or individuals to engage in, or at least endorse and encourage, modes of frugality and thereby to explain the workings of Roman notions and practices of moderation with reference to their wider socio-political settings and cultural contexts. Our point of departure is the suspicion that we might miss the cultural logic that informed and governed the strategies and choices of historical agents if we consider Roman frugality as just a discursive construct or as the product of a greatly civilised society or of a primitive people: much recent scholarship in social history and anthropology has emphasised the importance of describing the conceptual and social worlds of communities differently from those of the modern observer.[19] (Nowadays this includes critical reflection on the ways in which we inevitably project our own categories and common sense onto historical realities and recognition of the risk that the search for historical specificity may turn into a reification of difference.[20])

Such a project, of course, cannot simply turn back the clock. Certain gambits that in times past endowed frugality with inherent significance and explanatory value are dead for good reasons and should remain buried. Grand narratives that explain the historical record by appealing to the mentality of 'a people' have run their course. Claims that 'the Romans' of old were somehow naturally frugal are now as antediluvian as attempts to interpret the absence of significant literary activities in Rome before the middle of the third century BCE with

---

[18] Foucault 1980.

[19] Geertz 1973: 5–30; 2000: 36–72; Sahlins 1985: vii–xviii; 1995: 5–14; Roller 2010: 236–41; Bettini and Short 2018.

[20] Cf. James Hynes' satiric take on the debate between Marshall Sahlins and Gananath Obeyesekere in *Publish and Perish: Three Tales of Tenure and Terror* (1997), who reappear as Joe Brody, 'a stubborn old Irishman who argued that the Hawaiians murdered Cook because they mistook him for the god Lono' and Stanley Tulafale, 'a massive, soft-spoken Samoan who bristled eloquently on behalf of Third Worlders everywhere at the imputation that level-headed Hawaiians could mistake a bad-tempered Yorkshireman for their god of renewal' (104).

Introduction

reference to a 'national character' or the uninspiring Italian climate.[21] Any rethinking of Roman frugality has to resist the reifications so prevalent in earlier scholarship, where 'frugality' often figured as a defining characteristic of 'the Romans' – a mental outlook, born and bred into their bones in legendary times.

Likewise, the stories of decadence told by ancient authors and the attendant celebration of frugality have ceased to compel as explanatory accounts of the causes and consequences of developments in Roman history. This material does not amount to a critical discourse with inbuilt analytic value, but is itself a historical phenomenon in need of analysis and explication. By definition, the assertion of frugal norms allegedly upheld by the ancestors or the diagnosis of contemporary socio-political pathologies in narratives of moral disintegration are first and foremost acts of rhetoric and authorial self-fashioning (not least since the authors tended to exempt themselves from the general malaise they diagnosed all around them) and need to be treated as such.[22] The notion of a turning point in Roman history, for instance, when the floodgates of luxury opened and swept away the ancestral culture of frugality that dominates many a historiographical text from the late republic seems to be a figure of thought that first emerged towards the end of the second century BCE, arguably in response to the Gracchan crisis and its aftermath.[23] Conversely, of course, the fact that ancient sources which nostalgically evoke frugal times and lament their disappearance have a precise set of enabling conditions and a specific historical context does not mean that they are not worth studying as revealing forms of Roman self-description. This is more generally true of Roman reflections on modes of material sobriety, whatever their relation to economic and socio-political practice. As Andrew Wallace-Hadrill has recently maintained, the elaborate controversies, and the

---

[21] These ideas dominate in Latin literary histories until the middle of the twentieth century.

[22] See e.g. Morley 2004b and Biesinger 2016. [23] Lintott 1972.

Ingo Gildenhard and Cristiano Viglietti

juridical provisions, vis-à-vis the good and bad uses of material possessions that register at various moments in Roman history, 'rather than representing a failure to confront the more "real" social and economic issues, [...] may prove to be antiquity's way of expressing them. [...] We need [...] to listen to [the ancient Romans'] discourse more attentively.'[24]

The point of departure for a historical-genealogical study of frugality has to be the recognition that Roman frugality 'as such' does not exist. There might be considerable 'categorical continuity' of *parsimonia-frugalitas*/frugality or related notions and their overwhelmingly (but not exclusively) positive connotations across Roman history.[25] Yet the limits of what was judged ethically, socially and legally commendable in the material sphere (or, conversely, unbecoming) show a 'substantive discontinuity' throughout different phases in Roman history:[26] the boundaries of acceptable behaviour regarding the consumption and use of wealth changed considerably over time – and often with great velocity. The same is true of vernacular cultures.[27] We are, then, dealing with a complex and multifaceted phenomenon, in which socio-political and economic practices and institutions interlock with moral codes around behaviours and attitudes concerned with the accumulation and strategic deployment of material resources not least in the pursuit of power – across a time-span of almost a millennium. Like related phenomena or concepts such as 'luxury', 'wealth', 'conspicuous consumption' and expenditure (*sumptus*) or 'poverty', frugality does not possess an ahistorical essence: it needs to be studied contextually and diachronically.[28] The distinction between discursive assertions and enacted norms is as important here as due attention to which

---

[24] Wallace Hadrill 2008: 329. See also the papers in Andreau, France and Pittia 2004; in Andreau and Coudry 2016; and in Beck, Jehne and Serrati 2016. Cf. Clemente 1981: 14; Arena 2011: 464.

[25] Clemente 1981: 10–13; cf. Dubois-Pelerin 2008: 13.

[26] On luxury, Edwards 1993: 140–72; Berry 1994: 241; cf. Coudry 2004: 160–1. Dubois-Pelerin 2008: 43; cf. more generally the other items cited in note 17.

[27] See in particular Berry 1994; Kovesi Killerby 2002; Muzzarelli and Campanini 2003.

[28] See Bottiglieri 2016: 14 on changing conceptions of *sumptus*.

Introduction

individuals or social groupings (or subsections thereof, perhaps in explicit contrast to a deviant majority or minority) decided to embrace frugal habits and/or invest in a rhetoric of frugality – and when. Societies do not march in step: the insistence on a 'frugal ethos' by some may well – or perhaps is even bound to – coexist with the 'excessive' pursuit of wealth and power by others.

Complexity already registers at the level of the Latin lexicon. For the early period literary sources are either absent or late, containing only few nuggets of reliable information, which are, moreover, difficult to identify as such.[29] And when they start to become more plentiful – from the late third century BCE onwards – the evidence is by no means straightforward. The Romans evolved a wide-ranging terminology to refer to the management of material resources and self-restraint in the accumulation and use of wealth and, more generally, the morality of needs and wants. Nouns or phrases such as *abstinentia, continentia, diligentia, disciplina, industria, integritas, moderatio, modestia, modus, parsimonia, simplicitas, sobrietas, temperantia* and *tenuitas uictus* (to list a few) often have a similar range of meanings, yet are not exactly synonyms. And they all have distinct histories of usage – on their own, in combination with each other and in conjunction with related terms (such as *paupertas*). They play off a variety of antonyms, in particular those to do with (excessive) expenditure (e.g. *largitio, liberalitas, licentia, luxuria/luxuries/luxus*[30] and *sumptus*), unrestrained desire (especially for power and wealth) and the indulgence in pleasures, not least those of the table and the bedroom (*ambitio, auaritia, cupiditas/cupido, libido, uoluptas*), but also notions that have a more strictly moralising focus (such as *improbitas* or *nequitia*).[31] This terminology found application in diverse cultural spheres, ranging from farming and agriculture to the consumption of

---

[29] For a recent case study see Richardson 2019.
[30] '[A] rare and artificial variant for *luxuria*': Adam 1974: 57 (cited by Woodman and Martin 1996: 379, with further statistics on the preferences of individual authors).
[31] Lexically oriented studies include Scheidle 1993 and Viglietti 2011.

Ingo Gildenhard and Cristiano Viglietti

food and drink (not least during banquets staged by members of the socio-political elite), from the possession and display of expensive items of clothing, furniture, jewellery and precious metal, in particular silver including expensive tableware[32] to the sexual (mis-)conduct of people in power, from the management of public revenues by office-holders (and the deployment of personal resources for political gains) to aesthetics and literary criticism. Take *tenuitas (uictus)*, for example, and related phrases. Cicero employs the expression in conjunction with *continentia* and links it to the name of an exemplary ancestor, M'. Curius Dentatus.[33] In Horace and the satirical tradition the sense of frugality that the attribute *tenuis* can carry is employed to imbricate aesthetics and food consumption.[34] In a historical retrospect by Aulus Gellius *tenuitas uictus* joins forces with *parsimonia* to express the commitment of 'the ancient Romans' to maintain discipline in both the domestic and the civic sphere, and be it through legal sanctions.[35] And the phrase has continued to resonate down the centuries.[36]

Curiously, the set of Latin concepts that capture aspects of frugal conduct initially did not seem to have included one lexeme that would proceed to have a stellar career within European vernaculars and as such features in the title of this volume, i.e. *frugalitas* itself. Cato the Elder is a case in point:

---

[32] For the importance of silver in the Roman discourse on luxury see most recently Bernard 2018b and Chapter 6 (Patterson).

[33] *Parad.* 1.12: *quid continentia C. Fabrici, quid tenuitas uictus M'. Curi sequebatur?*

[34] Mette 1961 (on *genus tenue* and *mensa tenuis* in Horace) and Bramble 1974: 162–3. Cf. Perry 2000 on *diligentia* as a term of Roman art criticism.

[35] Gel. 2.24.1 (*De uetere parsimonia deque antiquis legibus sumptuariis*): *parsimonia apud ueteres Romanos et uictus atque cenarum tenuitas non domestica solum obseruatione ac disciplina sed publica quoque animaduersione legumque complurium sanctionibus custodita est* ('On ancient frugality and on early sumptuary laws: frugality among the early Romans and moderation in food and entertainments were secured not only by observance and training at home, but also by public penalties and the inviolable provisions of numerous laws' – trans. J. C. Rolfe/ Loeb).

[36] See e.g. Amm. Marc. 25.4.4 (on the emperor Julian's frugality at table): *uictus . . . mensarumque tenuitas* and 27.3.15: *tenuitas edendi potandique parcissime* with den Boeft et al. 2009: 75–6; or Alain de Lille, *Liber poenitentialis* 2.7: *asperitas habitus contra vanam gloriam* [sc. *remedium est*], *tenuitas victus contra crapulam.*

12

Introduction

one would not wish to deny the censor the 'Mr Frugal' badge, and he indeed aggressively broadcasts his commitment to a frugal way of life in his writings – and yet he did not use *frugalitas* (or indeed *frugi* or *frugaliter*) in those parts of his *oeuvre* that have survived. When he references modes of material sobriety or self-discipline he opts instead for *diligentia, disciplina, parsimonia* or *industria*. Indeed, of our four surviving Roman agronomists, i.e. Cato the Elder, Varro, Columella and Palladius, only Varro and Columella use the term *frugalitas* – rarely.[37] As it turns out, the noun does not come into its own as a Roman value concept until Cicero, who furnishes the lexeme with special ideological texture at particular moments in his career. His conceptual creativity prepared the ground for those authors of the early imperial period who elaborate on the idea that *frugalitas* is a quintessential Roman virtue and provide it with the requisite ancestral pedigree, in particular Valerius Maximus, Seneca the Younger and Pliny the Younger.[38] These considerations are a useful reminder of how perilous it is to reconstruct Roman (linguistic) realities of the archaic period and the early and middle republic on the basis of late-republican and early imperial texts: however inviting it might seem to use an author such as Valerius Maximus and his cast of exemplary characters to infer something about linguistic registers or the Roman 'national character' in the days of yore, the temptation to do so should be resisted: *exempla* and their discursive matrices evolve – just as value terms. The rise to prominence of the *lexeme frugalitas* in

---

[37] See Var. *R.* 3.3.6 (as part of a discussion of three types of enclosures for the keeping of fowls, game and fish): *omnibus tribus his generibus sunt bini gradus, superiores, quos frugalitas antiqua, inferiores, quos luxuria posterior adiecit* and Col. 1.9.4 (where *frugalitas* means something akin to 'honesty' on the part of slaves); 10 praef. 1 (a reference to the *parcior frugalitas* to be found *apud priscos*); 11.1.19 (a good *uilicus* should set a *frugalitatis exemplum* to those under his command when it comes to consumption of food and drink). On frugality and Roman economic thinking in Varro's *Res rusticae* see the excellent paper by Morley 2018; further Diederich 2007 who discusses expert knowledge, literary ambition and ideology as key coordinates of Roman handbooks on agriculture.

[38] Cicero, as we have seen, praises M'. Curius Dentatus for his *tenuitas uictus* (*Parad.* 12); Valerius Maximus turns him into *exactissima norma Romanae frugalitatis idemque fortitudinis perfectissimum specimen* (4.3.5).

13

Ingo Gildenhard and Cristiano Viglietti

late-republican and early imperial times, which prepared the stage for its career in neo-Latin and the European vernaculars, is part of the story our volume sets out to tell – though one should of course not presuppose straightforward semantic continuity between a Latin lexeme and its vernacular derivatives.[39]

Enquiry into the histories of the concepts that express aspects of frugality is of course only one angle of approach. Notoriously, discourse and practice do not neatly map onto one another. And for long stretches of Roman history literary sources are anyway absent or extremely sparse – and archaeological evidence happens to be our principal window into the past. To capture the shifting place of and preoccupation with frugality over the course of Rome's societal evolution therefore calls for broad frames of reference as well as a combination of archaeological, historical, literary and philological perspectives, to say nothing of constant methodological reflection on the limits and possibilities of our source material – of what the available data might (and what they might not) be able to tell us. To arrive at a methodologically sound, theoretically informed and historically more nuanced understanding of Roman modes of moderation, it might be helpful to distinguish roughly between the following, often decidedly interrelated, spheres in which frugal thought and action register with particular force: (i) the lived realities and the husbandry of small-scale farmers and the discursive reflection (and inflection) of peasant conditions in other settings; (ii) 'the frugal subaltern': slaves and freedmen and their economic interests and acumen, as well as 'the thrifty wife'; (iii) Rome's political culture, in particular its political economy, i.e. the interface of wealth and power; (iv) the (literary/rhetorical) projects of specific individuals, not least those who invested in virtue signalling and shows of self-restraint as salient aspects of their self-promotion and/or authorial self-fashioning.

---

[39] See e.g. Dubois-Pelerin 2008: 17–24, noting important differences between the modern idea of luxury and Latin *luxuria*.

Introduction

Husbandry

The original setting for frugal action in Roman history (and Rome's cultural imaginary) was the sphere of agriculture and transhumance farming:[40] owners of small farmsteads (and most farmsteads in archaic Rome *were* small) had to practise a special degree of material sobriety to ensure subsistence and survival and, perhaps, the production of a modest surplus.[41] The association of frugality with peasant conditions seems straightforward, but in fact raises several interesting questions.

To begin with, the distinction between outright destitution and prudent husbandry is particularly difficult to ascertain from archaeological evidence alone – not least since the boundaries are fluid and (calorific) needs and wants vary significantly throughout history and from one society to the next. In a daily struggle for survival at (or close to) subsistence level, extreme austerity in the use of material resources may simply be a bare necessity – a mode of living imposed by external circumstances to ensure survival.[42] This 'enforced frugality' stands in contrast to situations where practices of material sobriety involve an element of choice – beyond, that is, eschewing death by starvation. If thrift and self-restraint are optional, their moral value arguably increases.[43] Rome's *exempla*-discourse knows both types, i.e. frugality enforced by poverty and characters that consciously embrace a frugal way of life, abstaining from possible pleasures or available enrichment opportunities.

Secondly, the distinction between necessity and choice when it comes to thrift and moderation enables a conception of

---

[40] For transhumance see Chapter 4 (Balbo), further Corbier 2016, who emphasises the complementary nature of agriculture and the cultivation of livestock; Marcone 2016; and Grelle 2016, all with further bibliography.

[41] For the (changing) size of land allotments and their 'nutritional value' see further Chapter 1 (Viglietti), Chapter 2 (Rich) and Chapter 4 (Balbo).

[42] Cf. Quint. *Decl.* 298, which rehearses the case of the small-scale farmer who disowns his parasite son and notes at one point that his family property would yield enough not only for frugality but also for some surplus to be enjoyed – if, that is, it were cultivated by two owners: *mihi rus paternum erga labores gratissimum, non frugalitati tantum suffecturum sed et delectationi, si coleretur a dominis duobus* (4).

[43] At least according to Pacatus Drepanius: 97–8 below.

Ingo Gildenhard and Cristiano Viglietti

frugality that focuses on an internal disposition towards wants and desires quite independent of the material resources a given person might have at their disposal. Seneca the Younger, for instance, a multi-millionaire himself writing for others similarly well endowed, defines *frugalitas* as *paupertas <u>uoluntaria</u>* ('*voluntary* poverty').[44] There is of course no need to adopt his idiosyncratic definition, motivated as it is by his philosophical project. Yet at some level, it *is* helpful to differentiate between outright poverty and frugality understood as self-moderation that might be compatible with considerable affluence.

Thirdly – and relatedly – it is equally difficult to reconstruct the (strategic) reasons why members of a society exercise frugal discipline by deliberately living below their means or abstaining from producing greater surplus and accumulating more wealth than would in theory be possible. Thrift or self-restraint might be motivated by a variety of reasons – such as satisfaction with one's circumstances of existence, self-abnegation in the present in the hope of improving one's situation in the future, a special interest in protecting and increasing the patrimony, the desire eventually to transform frugally accumulated wealth into socio-political capital or moral imperatives within a cultural logic that discourages the (unfettered) pursuit of riches. Not all of these factors are mutually exclusive. At the same time, it is important to recognise that 'frugality' paradoxically encompasses approaches to material resources and the generation of wealth that are 'satisficing' as well as those that are 'maximising': thrifty living and prudent resource management might be *either* the result of contentment with one's lot *or* a strategy to accumulate wealth motivated by the keen desire for enrichment, perhaps driven by socio-political ambition (*ambitio*). We also need to reckon with the phenomenon of (elite) observers of peasant realities turning what are *homines oeconomici* doing their best to improve their lot within restrictive circumstances into *homines suo contenti*, who are not particularly interested in strategies

---

[44] *Ep.* 17.5. See further below Chapter 5 (Gildenhard): 321–2.

16

Introduction

that generate a surplus or maximise profit.[45] And modes of satisficing (rhetoric) and maximising (practice) may well coexist in intricate and intriguing ways. Cato the Elder is, as so often, a case in point. He claimed kudos for growing up in conditions of hard manual labour at subsistence level, implicitly advocating the moral benefits of a satisficing style of life, whereas in his treatise on agriculture *de Agri Cultura* he promoted strategies of enrichment through prudent estate-management. And while he chose to focus on farming as the principal and preferred source of income in his *writings*, in *practice* he also operated as a venture-capitalist, engaging in profitable commerce via middle men and pursuing a smart policy of risk-distribution.[46]

And finally, as the example of Cato the Elder shows, the satisficing farmer, while rooted in the lived realities of near-subsistence husbandry, also began to lead an imaginary existence within various rhetorical agendas. As a generic type and an exemplary figure, who ploughed his fields, roasted his turnips and served up humble meals in dishes of clay (while conquering Latium, Italy and the world), he became an integral component of Rome's political culture and literary discourse. When and why this happened is far from obvious. Indeed, in a society where 'power and wealth depended almost directly on the area and fertility of the land which each individual possessed' and 'land-holdings were the geographical expression of social stratification', celebration of satisficing seems at variance with the factors constitutive of the economic and hence socio-political elite:[47] given the strongly positive connotations of wealth, the correlation of degrees of wealth with socio-political rank and the concomitant ideology that the rich deserve their good fortune in part because they are also superior in other respects such as morals, the appeal of the small-scale farmer as living an ideal form of existence is *prima facie* surprising. His prominence in Rome's cultural imaginary

---

[45] See Osborne 2006: 103 for the terms 'satisficing' and 'maximising' and the tendency of elite discourse to model peasants as being content with 'satisficing'.

[46] See D'Arms 1981 and Chapter 3 (Passet).   [47] Quotations from Hopkins 1978: 8.

17

is the result of a complex set of factors, including decisive interventions by resourceful authors such as Cato the Elder who gave this figure discursive shape – not least (but not only) in prose writings *De Re Rustica*.[48] It is, at any rate, important to identify the socio-political place of literary-rhetorical eulogies of 'self-sufficiency' in a society that in other ways rendered the production of a surplus and the accumulation of wealth desirable and rewarding – at least from the point of view of the individual (as opposed, perhaps, to that of the larger group or community).

The Frugal Subaltern: Slaves, Freedmen, Wives

Etymologically speaking, agriculture (the cultivation of crops and the production of *fruges*) is the primordial sphere of frugality. But next in line is slavery: the adjective *frugi* ('useful', 'thrifty') occurs most prominently as an attribute of profitable and/or upright slaves and economically prudent freedmen.[49] Frugality played a key role in Rome's slave discourse: a *seruus frugi* was a slave who benefited his master economically (was 'good value'); and the Roman institutions of *peculium* and manumission ensured that many slaves had also significant motivations to act with economic prudence and due subservience on their own behalf: if they saved enough money and pleased their master in other ways, they might be

---

[48] The ideology also informs poetry (such as Virgil's *Georgics*) and extends to fiction where poverty and contentment often go hand in hand with a privileged form of morality and sense of religion: see e.g. Ovid's tale of Philemon and Baucis at *Met.* 8.611–724, who enact the frugal piety Augustus himself was keen on. See below 75–9, further Gildenhard and Zissos 2004: 67–9. White 1970: 14–46 offers a survey of our ancient sources on Roman agriculture; Hollander 2019: 1–4 discusses the problematic concept of 'self-sufficiency', with reference to such passages as Cato *Agr.* 2.7, Var. *R.* 1.22 or Plin. *Nat.* 18.41 and lists abundant further bibliography on the Roman ideology of self-sufficiency at 16 n. 4. Rhetoric and reality do not necessarily match, of course.

[49] As the dative of the noun *frux, frugis* (f.), *frugi* seems to have originally occurred in such phrases as '*esse frugi bonae*', i.e. 'to be capable of giving a good crop' or (when applied to persons) 'to be reliable and useful'. Over time, the predicative final dative also became a self-standing attribute in its own right; and 'eventually *bonae frugi* was abbreviated to *frugi*, which functioned as an indeclinable adjective': Palmer 1988: 70.

Introduction

allowed to buy their freedom.[50] *Liberti*, too, had many incentives to remain committed to the values of thrift and sobriety as they pursued wealth to establish themselves in society, often as successful entrepreneurs; as such they retained the attribute *frugi*. The distinction between free/slave was absolutely fundamental for Roman self-definitions; yet esteem for material sobriety and economic prudence crosses this divide[51] – and can be found in distinctive forms across the entire social hierarchy at Rome, from the lowest to the highest echelons (which, however, would not necessarily use the attribute *frugi* self-referentially). A similar point concerns gender: in funerary epitaphs, thriftiness, as expressed through the attribute *frugi* and the noun *frugalitas*, registers as one of the qualities that Roman men valued highly in their spouses.[52] And continence and moderation in one sphere (household economics) were thought to coincide with restraint in other respects as well, such as sexual desire.[53]

The social stigma of slavery and the prevailing patriarchal ideology raise the question of how a notion strongly associated with slaves and freedmen and (though less strongly)

---

[50] On the *peculium* see du Plessis 2015: 96; on freedmen Mouritsen 2011. The importance of self-interest in the management of material resources (specifically the exercise of thrift) registers in Quint. *Decl.* 261, which imagines a scenario of tyrannically imposed communism (*aequatio patrimoniorum*). In such a situation, everyone would be incentivised to splurge since they would do so not with their own but with common property: *nam et frugalitatem eorum qui seruaturi sunt imminuet et luxuriae eorum qui consumpturi sunt prospiciet: cur enim quisquam seruet, tam perditurus aliena luxuria quam sua, cur enim non quisque abutatur?* (6).

[51] For *libertas* see Arena 2012, with further bibliography.

[52] See e.g. *CIL* 6.26192 = *ILS* 8398: *hic est illa sita pia frug. casta | pudic. Sempronia Moschis, | cui pro meriteis ab coniuge | gratia relatast; CIL* 6.11602 = *ILS* 8402: *hic sita est Amymone Marci optima et pulcherrima, | lanifica pia pudica frugi casta domiseda; CIL* 8.11294 = *ILS* 8444: *Postumia Matronilla inconpa|rabilis coniux, mater bona, avia | piissima, pudica religiosa laborio|sa frugi efficaxs vigilans sollicita | univira unicuba [t]otius industriae et fidei | matrona, vixit annis n. LIII mensibus n. V diebus tribus;* and *CIL* 8.9520 = *ILS* 8445: *Tadiae Fortuni coniugi, | cum qua vita iucunda, | conversatio religiosa, | frugalitas honesta, | fides cum disciplina exacta est. | L. Caecilius Honoratus | signo Thaumanti,* with Gardner and Wiedemann 1991: 52: 'Funeral epitaphs do not necessarily reveal the virtues that women thought important, but they certainly show us what men hoped to find in women.'

[53] Cf. Shelton 2013: 111 (in a discussion of Plin. *Ep.* 4.19, in which he praises the *frugalitas* and chastity of his third wife Calpurnia): 'Thriftiness was associated with temperance and sexual restraint; extravagance with promiscuity.'

Ingo Gildenhard and Cristiano Viglietti

women fit into elite male discourse and self-perceptions. If the image of the frugal and disciplined farmer raises compatibility issues with standard elite ideology, the mismatch is even more acute where slaves, freedmen and women are concerned – though one strategy to solve or at least diminish the problem was to differentiate at the lexical level by avoiding the attribute *frugi* while linking a distinct idiom of moderation to elite maleness. As we already had occasion to note, Cato the Elder stays clear of **frug–* terminology: in contrast to *homines frugi*, such as profitable slaves or enterprising freedmen, or the *frugi* wife, the ideal farmer of his imagination was a free *agricola* and as such a *uir bonus* who combined economic prudence with commitment to peasant values, superior moral qualities and a distinctly masculine gender identity that ensured, above all, military prowess: as a *uir* he is also a *miles*.[54]

Political Culture and Political Economy[55]

The concept of political culture broadens the focus from livelihood and economic enterprise to the broader societal matrix. It refers to the ways in which a civic community organises itself – including such matters as elite formation and their inner workings and hierarchies; the terms of interaction between elites and the wider populace (e.g. rituals, performances, elections); civic institutions, the set of norms and values and legislative measures that regulate public life and the exercise of power; and the expression of these processes and

---

[54] See further Chapter 3 (Passet) and Chapter 5 (Gildenhard), which explores how the social ambit of the attribute *frugi*, which remained firmly grounded in the slave/freedman milieu throughout Roman history, also managed to rise further up the social scale.

[55] Approaches to Roman history that emphasise aspects of the political economy (e.g. Brunt 1971; 1988; Wiseman 2002; Crawford 2008; 2011; Harris 2003; 2011; 2016) are at times contrasted with those that emphasise political culture (e.g. Meier 1966/ 1980; Hölkeskamp 2017): see most recently Harris 2019, in his review of Hölkeskamp 2017 and Mouritsen 2017. For conscious attempts at analysing the political economy and the political culture of Republican Rome as interrelated see e.g. the papers in Beck, Jehne and Serrati 2016; Tan 2017; Bernard 2018a; 2018b.

Introduction

practices in symbolic form, both in discourse and visually, through art and architecture or status symbols.[56] For our concerns, one key dimension of Rome's evolving political culture are the equally fluid terms of its political economy – in other words, how the Romans throughout their history negotiated the interface of wealth and power. Unlike the exigencies experienced by relatively poor peasants on their small-scale farmsteads or the financial dealings of those otherwise oppressed or disadvantaged (slaves and freedmen; wives), here the emphasis falls on the economic activities and sociopolitical dynamics of more or less well-off elites within a larger societal whole and the ways in which they constructed and negotiated their collective identity, both internally and vis-à-vis other segments of the population. It includes such phenomena as the 'economics of status', in particular competition for rank and standing through forms of conspicuous consumptions and other material investments;[57] the distribution of resources within and between specific groups as well as society at large and attendant processes of differentiation and social mobility upwards and downwards;[58] and fiscal regimes, including issues to do with taxation and public revenues more generally, monetisation, the relation between communal resources and private fortunes or the terms of imperial exploitation involving spoils and so-called 'tax farming'.[59]

[56] See e.g. Hölkeskamp 2010; 2017; 2019 all with ample further bibliography.

[57] For the concept see Jehne 2016. Since it is of crucial importance for the present volume, his explication of it with regard to republican Rome deserves to be cited in full: 'In contrast to legal status, social status is not something which you simply have and keep ... If a senator was ambitious and wanted to advance his career in order to become a leading *princeps in re publica* he had to cope with the ever increasing competition and had to seek opportunities of status enhancement. Since economic assets are only one factor in the game the handling of economic capital in status struggles is often uneconomic: no *homo oeconomicus* in the idealized form of former economic theory who exclusively focused on material profit would have succeeded in Roman status struggles. To put it bluntly: the economics of status is not focused on economic gain, but on gain in status. Even if economic fortune and income was the foundation of status in Rome, there was always a symbolic or cultural surplus which had to be earned in arenas other than business' (191).

[58] For senatorial wealth see Shatzman 1975 and, more recently, Tan 2017.

[59] For a definition of fiscal regimes see Monson and Scheidel 2015: 7; for the fiscal regimes of the Roman republic Tan 2015 and 2017; for that of the early principate

Socio-political elites, which embrace superior wealth as a source of privilege and status, are not an immediately obvious place to go to in search of frugality. Yet societies tend to manifest a keen interest in the interface of wealth and power, more specifically the transformation of the former into the latter (and vice versa): if wealth as such was not considered problematic, some of its political implications certainly were. Ancient Rome is no exception – in part, and seemingly paradoxically, precisely because it formalised the correlation between degrees of affluence and modes of participation in the public life of the civic community through the institution of the census.[60] This official correlation inevitably produced repercussions for individual psychology and group dynamics that brought aspects of frugality to the fore. By formally endowing wealth with political significance, the census incentivised frugal conduct even further. It encouraged those already in possession of the requisite level of wealth for full participation in the political life of their community to maintain their privileged status through prudent husbandry and the protection of patrimony; conversely, for those assessed to fall into one of the lower classes it held out the prospect of rising up the socio-economic ranks by acquiring the necessary degree of wealth.[61] As such, and given the vicissitudes of fortune, over time an institution such as the census must have generated mismatches between traditional family status and degrees of affluence or indigence of more recent vintage. This in turn raises the question of how the established elite dealt with upward and downward mobility – a live issue throughout Roman history. What were those in power to do when persons

---

Scheidel 2015; on tax farming Badian 1972 and Tan 2017, with a review of the earlier literature. Rowan 2013 offers an interesting case study of the interrelation of economic exploitation and cultural values with regard to silver, suggesting that the ethos of the republican political elite prevented it from exploiting certain imperial opportunities to the full at the state level.

[60] On different aspects of the census and its development over time see e.g. Mattingley 1937; Wiseman 1969; Lo Cascio 1988; 2016; Gargola 1989; Rathbone 1993; Pittia 2007; Humm 2015; Tan 2017: 21 (discussing the 'demise' of the institution in the late republic); Gauthier 2019.

[61] Jehne 2016: 190.

Introduction

of lower rank punched at the same economic level or even outperformed their socio-political betters because of hard work and material sobriety – in short, by being *frugi*? Had, for instance, those sons of freedmen who, benefiting from their fathers' and their own frugality, managed to meet the census requirement, the right to be included in the senate? Or did they have the material wealth but were deemed to lack the moral worth?[62]

Similar problems arise if in addition to regulating access to the ruling elite by means of fiscal criteria, there is further competition *within* it, involving the investment of wealth in the economics of status. Such investment can take different forms depending on how the political system works – from conspicuous consumption (in many ways at variance, of course, with the logic of the census) to more oblique ways of using material resources to enhance socio-political rank and standing – such as liberal gifts to the voting public (a.k.a. bribery) when advancement requires election to offices. Competition sharpens the problems attendant on social mobility by generating obvious winners and downright losers.[63] And the experience of getting ahead or losing ground in a competitive environment is ever relative to the starting position: someone whose family background places them at or very near the top of the socio-political hierarchy might feel that their status is under threat for different reasons (partly because of a greater sense of inherited entitlement) from those who start lower down the pecking order and have further room for upward advancement. Again, such competition has inevitable repercussions for individual psychology, perhaps even resulting in

---

[62] The issue flared up at the end of the fourth century BCE: see Cornell 2000: 84 on the *lectio senatus*: 'The procedure was severely tested in 312 BC, when the censor Appius Claudius outraged conservative opinion by including sons of freedmen in the Senate. These men were unquestionably rich and well-to-do, and Claudius no doubt believed that they deserved to be included under the heading *optimus quisque ex omni ordine*' and 85: 'The issue of sons of freedmen in the Senate was finally settled in 304 BC, when the censor Q. Fabius Rullianus excluded them, and established the rule for the future that such men were not worthy to be enrolled in the Senate.'

[63] On losers, see now the excellent set of papers in Beck and Hölkeskamp 2018 and, for the imperial period, Klingenberg 2011.

the opposite of prudent husbandry: if the stakes are high in a zero-sum game, the desperate and the daring might just be tempted to roll the dice and take their chances, playing fast and loose with their patrimony.[64] Conversely, some who would have the requisite economic resources to compete in the economics of socio-political status might for a variety of reasons decide not to do so.[65]

All this goes to show that elite competition involving the use of material and other resources can prove socially divisive and expensive. Communities therefore frequently invest significant efforts to manage the interface of wealth and competition for status and power. The most obvious index of such efforts are legislative measures, which render it evident that certain groups had an interest in setting limits and trying to impose restraint – however ineffectual some of these laws will have been in achieving their objective.[66] Even if unenforced or unenforceable, such laws still bear witness to a prevalent perception that influential individuals were in the business of pursuing status in ways that were deemed detrimental to the well-being of the group or community and testify to widespread interest in the desirability of moderation (of course evincing at the same time that a considerable number did not so moderate themselves). Laws designed to regulate the use of wealth for socio-political purposes amount to what one could label 'legislated frugality' insofar as they try to impose restrictions on the behaviour of certain groups in the context of the political economy.

[64] The annual rotation of public office might also have resulted in a risk-prone habitus of Rome's political elite, not least in military contexts. The magistrate in charge only had a few months to make the most of his time in office: and who could resist a shot at gaining the right to triumph if the opportunity presented itself, and hence acquire immortality in the memory of his family and the wider civic community – whatever the odds might have been? See Walter 2017b for discussion.

[65] Roman *equites* had options: they could try to pursue a political career and compete for entry into and advancement on the *cursus honorum*; or they could invest their time otherwise, e.g. in efforts to acquire wealth, socio-economic and/or cultural distinction. (Atticus is a case in point.) Arguably, those *equites* who decided to enter politics imported an outlook into the governing elite shaped by economic considerations and experiences: Märtin 2012: 183–92, with further bibliography.

[66] See Walter 2017a on *leges publicae* as one (often rather ineffectual) instrument among others within Roman political culture to shape individual conduct.

Introduction

Legislated frugality is widespread in pre-modern societies. Ancient Rome was no exception, though the pervasive presence of the phenomenon is easy to overlook: radical changes in political economy and fiscal regimes over the course of Roman history meant that laws to do with (the acquisition of) wealth and its *political* use appear in various guises and under a variety of labels, from the time of the Twelve Tables, a law code that includes our oldest evidence for legally imposed moderation at Rome (arguably codifying oral laws dating back to c. 600 BCE; see Chapter 1: Viglietti) right down to the early principate. Yet the diversity of names and articulations ought not to obfuscate a consistent unity of purpose: to regulate the interface of wealth and power by imposing limits – limits on the use of wealth as investment in the economics of status in such settings as the funeral or the *conuiuium* or to do with the display of wealth, not least by women (*leges sumptuariae, leges cibariae*);[67] limits on usury (*leges fenebres*); limits on the amount of landed wealth that members of the ruling elite may hold in their possession; limits on the ways and means by which senators were allowed to accumulate wealth; limits on the degree of wealth those in charge of administering Rome's overseas domains may extract from their provinces in the context of imperial exploitation (*leges de repetundis*); or limits on the (material) means

---

[67] The *leges sumptuariae* have attracted attention from the eighteenth century onwards: see e.g. Platner 1752; Wolffhard 1737; Boxmann 1818; Pennink 1826; Houwing 1883; Giraudias 1910; Kübler 1931; Savio 1940 – surveyed briefly by Sauerwein 1970 1–2. Sauerwein himself offers a grand historical sweep, setting the *leges sumptuariae* in relation to other institutions and tracing their efforts of social control in correlation with historical developments: I. Die Aufwandsbestimmungen der Frühzeit und die Sittenaufsicht der Zensoren; II. Die auf die Gesamtheit des Staates gerichtete Politik des Senats and der Versuch einer einheitlichen Lebensführung mit Hilfe der leges sumptuariae; III. Die leges sumptuariae der Revolutionszeit und die grossen Reformversuche im ersten Jahrhundert. However, he remains rather beholden to the views of our sources, seeing the legislation primarily as an effort to fight the corrupting impact of Eastern luxury on the traditional Roman way of life that supposedly threatened to 'effeminise' the Roman polity. More recent scholarship includes Clemente 1981; Baltrusch 1989; Edwards 1993; Coudry 1998; 2004; 2012; Bottiglieri 2002; Dauster 2003; Venturini 2004; 2016; Zanda 2011; El Beheiri 2012; Andreau and Coudry 2016.

Ingo Gildenhard and Cristiano Viglietti

by which candidates for office go about canvassing support (*leges de ambitu*).[68]

The rationale for a group or civic community to resort to 'legislated moderation' varies. Such laws might be designed to safeguard patrimony by disallowing irresponsible dissipation of accumulated wealth and thereby enhance family cohesion and genealogical continuity; they might be intended to increase feelings of solidarity across (steep) divides in wealth, status, power, influence and prestige by enforcing elites to adopt modes of public display and consumption more in line with the life-experiences of ordinary citizens; they might be motivated by a more general concern with the perceived status of the socio-moral order in times of crisis or change; or they could be passed to protect cohesion within the ruling class by establishing norms on how much or by what means its members could acquire wealth or transform economic into socio-political capital: measures to cap the escalation of competitive expenditure could help to keep the playing field reasonably level and safeguard against downward mobility of those stretched to compete – what Daube has labelled 'protection of the non-tipper'.[69] Restraint legislation to do with the acquisition and deployment of wealth on the part of the politically active elite thus sits aside other legislative efforts designed to maintain a level playing field, such as measures to ensure distribution of opportunities to hold prestigious offices.[70] The positive rhetoric of moderation as a virtue that tends to accompany such legislation has a counterpart in

---

[68] At the same time, the Romans struggled to legislate certain activities effectively that attracted significant levels of conspicuous expenditure such as public games or gladiatorial contests. See Zanda 2011 and below 44–5.

[69] See Daube 1969: 124: 'the protection of the non-tipper is an aim of most anti-luxury measures; it definitely played an enormous part in the Roman ones which got under way towards the end of the third century BC ... there was at work the wish to put down the prodigals whose style set the tone and forced their parsimonious brethren to emulate them or be out of the swim. Many people's lives (among the upper crust) were overshadowed by the fear of being thought a miser, to judge by the frequent mention of it in literature. Lavish spending would be a way out; but a cheaper one was to have laws which, by prohibiting lavishness, made the miser undetectable.'

[70] Examples from Rome include certain stipulations of the *leges Liciniae* (367 BCE), the *Lex Genucia* (342 BCE) and the *Lex Villia Annalis* (180 BCE).

Introduction

negative emotions: the restraints that a group imposed upon its members through acts of 'collective abstention' often imply the envy and distrust of peers, anxieties over the potential success of others and fears of losing ground in the competition for rank and standing.[71]

In addition to legislative measures, Rome's political culture evolved other features that betoken a concern with boundaries and the desirability of a certain degree of self-restraint within the political economy. Examples include the institution of the censorship (and its imperial variant, the *praefectura morum* of the *princeps*), especially in the way it evolved over time with an expansion of its remit from the assessment of wealth to determine voting status, tax levels and army service to responsibility for the *lectio senatus* and the exercise of the so-called *regimen morum*.[72] Its very existence 'helped to reinforce the sense of identity, the social values, and the coherence of the Roman aristocracy' – above and beyond its potential as a weapon 'used against corruption and the abuse of power' that found its most striking articulation in those instances (relatively few) when the censors removed individuals from the senatorial roll.[73] The censorship institutionalised a collective investment in certain norms that applied in particular to the behaviour of members of the ruling elite, not least those to do with economic prudence (as a quality that helped protect patrimony) and moderation in the arena of conspicuous consumption, i.e. the transformation of wealth into socio-political influence.[74]

Legislated frugality and the threat of a censorial *nota* are negative instruments insofar as they recognise that for many members of the community the imposition of limits and the expectation of moderation would have been unwelcome – such measures codify and formalise norms that the community

---

[71] For the notion of 'collective abstention' see Tan 2017: 63.

[72] Suolahti 1963; Astin 1988; Cornell 2000; Kunkel and Wittmann 1995: 391–473; for the *praefectura morum* of the emperor also Klingenberg 2011: 96–109.

[73] Astin 1988, with quotations from pages 34 and 33.

[74] To what degree this institution was effective in ensuring compliance with a socially expected code of conduct is an open question. And the civic ideology that informed the censorship did of course not necessarily prevent individuals from pursuing blatantly partisan agendas while in office.

Ingo Gildenhard and Cristiano Viglietti

overall considers important, but specific individuals wanted to transgress or circumvent in the pursuit of personal advantage. In addition to punitive strictures the Romans also developed and celebrated frugality as an ideal – as embodied by the figure of the satisficing and self-sufficient farmer. This ideal finds its most striking and explicit articulation in the *exempla*-discourse, which included such figures as Cincinnatus or M'. Curius Dentatus, legendary for their material sobriety and self-restraint. From one point of view, those figures give a positive embodiment to negative emotions such as social envy by enabling pride in parsimony and allowing for the coincidence of humility and honour. It is, at any rate, important to ask what purpose and ideological agendas such figures were supposed to serve, which may well have changed significantly over time – in addition, that is, to complementing in a positive key the negative forms of legislated and censorial frugality. When did they acquire traction and appeal, why and for whom? In a society that correlated wealth and socio-political status their function, to say nothing of their efficaciousness as role models, is (again) not immediately obvious.

Frugality as Personal Style and Literary Theme

The habits and ideologies of groups or entire cultures and the posturing and practices of specific persons are mutually implicated: the strategic choices of historical agents are conditioned by the circumstances in which they operate and *vice versa*. For two reasons, it nevertheless makes sense to differentiate between, on the one hand, elite frugality as a group phenomenon and society-wide efforts at placing a limit on the pursuit of wealth and power (explored in the previous section) and, on the other, the rhetorical self-fashioning and the literary projects of specific individuals who resort to frugal ideologems to negotiate their position and identity in socio-political and cultural space.

First, the focus on individuals highlights personal choice and thus gets away from the notion that the Romans were naturally born or socially conditioned automata, who had all

Introduction

internalised frugal standards of living as a matter of course and moderated themselves in the quest for riches and political office and influence. For any member of Rome's socio-political elite, regardless of the depth of his cultural conditioning, there was room to decide for himself which aspect of legislated frugality and related cultural norms of moderation he would abide by and which he would ignore, try to circumvent or outright violate. A spectrum of options was available, ranging from extreme endorsement of frugal habits in all spheres of life to various degrees of disregard – with every shade of compromise and conflict between rhetoric and practice in-between. The same applies to the 'style' or 'image' that emperors adopted to give their imperial persona a distinctive profile.[75] The reasons why individuals restrain themselves, deliberately (posturing as) going for less satisfaction of personal wants and fulfilment of desires than would be possible, again vary, but tend to involve self-promotion, which may include attack on others *lacking* in commonly valued moderation and sobriety. The performance (or at least projection) of self-restraint in certain situations or, more generally, style of life almost inevitably stands in contrast to obnoxious individuals, objectionable social types or irritating groups less beholden to frugal ideals (greedy peers, immoderate emperors, the tasteless *nouveaux riches*), whom those who endorse frugality as one of their values can then brand as revolting and depraved. There is no reason to assume great consistency across career and occasion: opportunistic individuals could easily wax lyrical about the virtues of frugality one day and fly into an anti-austerity rage the next.[76]

Secondly, the emphasis on individuals helps to ensure proper recognition of the importance of Rome's 'literary revolution' for (our understanding of) Roman frugality and its continuing resonance within the context of the classical tradition. The term 'literary revolution' captures the curious fact that before the second half of the third century BCE – i.e. at a

---

[75] See 72–100 below.   [76] Cicero comes to mind: see below 65–72.

time when Greek literary production had been in full swing for almost half a millennium – literary texts that can be attributed to specific authors hardly existed at Rome;[77] but from c. 250 BCE onwards, the Romans began to domesticate a wide range of Greek genres for a wide variety of purposes: literary efforts acquired prominence as innovative means of political self-promotion and novel media of reflection and commentary on contemporary society and culture.[78] The implications of this development for Roman frugality are profound but tend to be underappreciated. Consider for example the following passage (our italics):[79]

Yet in Rome, the ideology connecting virtue and frugality was especially strong. Republican *exempla*, told and retold with a strong recommendation to imitate the ancestors, were filled with stories about heroes who lived in humble surroundings but who were always available for service to the fatherland. Cincinnatus is the prime example, M'. Curius Dentatus is another one, but *even* the elder Cato *still* constructed an image of himself as a farmer willing to work with his own hands.

The passage nicely pinpoints the massive watershed in Roman cultural history that we labelled 'literary revolution' – but does so unwittingly: it begins with a reference to anonymous discourse ('*exempla*, told and retold') and ends with a named individual: Cato the Elder. The smooth transition from oral tradition to a literary author suggests that the difference is not important. In fact, Cato here gets assimilated to what came before instead of being recognised as the trend-setter for what followed: the words 'even' and 'still' imply that he operated within and perpetuated a long-standing tradition that was at the point of weakening or petering out: as Roman aristocrats became increasingly removed from their agricultural roots and humble origins, so the assumption seems to be, aristocratic self-fashioning adapted to novel circumstances and ceased to

---

[77] The first 'author' whom we can capture as such is Appius Claudius Caecus, c. 340–273 BCE.

[78] A much-studied phenomenon: see most recently Feeney 2016; Gildenhard, Gotter, Havener and Hodgson 2019.

[79] Jehne 2016: 189. We pick on this section from an otherwise excellent paper somewhat unfairly, *exempli gratia*.

Introduction

invoke the (imagined) realities of ancient history – though *even* someone whose *floruit* falls into the first half of the second century BCE was *still* keeping this tradition alive. There are, however, two fundamental problems with this picture.

First, Cato the Elder spearheaded Rome's literary revolution in the area of Latin prose writing.[80] There is considerable evidence that he not only 'constructed an image *of himself*' but also the images of those Romans of old whom he, the *homo nouus*, elected as his notional ancestors (often in the form of an anonymous collective: the *maiores*) – in an effort to construct a virtual genealogy of excellence to rival the kinship genealogies of former office-holders cultivated by the noble *gentes*.[81] That our earliest writer of Latin prose is such an idiosyncratic figure should send shivers of methodological scruple down the spine of anyone relying on Catonian and post-Catonian evidence for the reconstruction of Roman cultural practice and discourse in the previous centuries. As recent scholarship has shown, even the rise of M'. Curius Dentatus to prominence in Roman discourse is in large part due to the role he plays in the self-promotion of his 'fellow Sabine' Cato.[82]

---

[80] Gotter 2001; 2003a; 2009; Sciarrino 2011. See further Chapter 3 (Passet).

[81] One cannot be cautious enough when projecting a long tradition of exemplary discourse into the Roman past even though (or precisely because) our ancient sources do this as a matter of routine whatever the evidence. At *S. Rosc.* 50, for instance, Cicero makes reference to 'that famous Atilius' whom emissaries found tilling his own fields' (... *illum Atilium, quem sua manu spargentem semen, qui missi erant, conuenerunt* ...), implying a long-standing tradition. But as Dyck 2010: 119 points out 'he is mentioned here for the first time in extant Latin' – and 'given the absence of historical context in our sources [also *Sest.* 72 and V. Max. 4.4.5], it is hard to say which of the consular Atilii is in question.' He notes that 'the anecdote is meant to explain the cognomen Serranus/Saranus [from *sero*, to sow] borne by a branch of the Atilii.' Yet agriculturally based *cognomina* could function as (initial) slurs just as much as badges of honour: see Chapter 5 (Gildenhard) on Piso Frugi.

[82] Dench 1998: 139 who notes that Cato is the first to invest the Sabines with 'positive austerity'. See also Pasco-Pranger 2015; Berrendonner 2001; Reay 2005 – though Ennius also knows the anecdote of M'. Curius roasting turnips and rejecting the Samnites' offer of gold (fr. 456 Skutsch); as Skutsch 1985: 613 notes with his usual caution: 'The admiration of Cato, who considered Curius the greatest Roman (Plu. *Cato Mai.* 2), may to some extent be responsible for the later rhetorical accounts of Curius' virtues, which resemble those of his contemporary Fabricius; but it need not be thought to have influenced Ennius here.' Catonian influence can of course not be excluded here either.

Ingo Gildenhard and Cristiano Viglietti

Secondly, the (imaginary) heydays of frugality enacted are not necessarily the heydays of frugality reflected. Whatever the economic circumstances and living conditions of Rome's socio-political elites in the regal period and the early centuries of the republic, the rhetorical point and profile of the satisficing farmer and, more generally, ancestral austerity arguably increase the more this imaginary style of life contrasts with contemporary realities. In that case, use of this figure as exemplary acquired *ever greater* prominence and appeal in the course of Roman history. It enabled someone like Cato to assert a rupture in customs that he sets out to repair, as one of the few individuals who embody the ancestral virtues in an otherwise decadent society.[83] Indeed, before Cato the Elder there is actually rather little evidence that abiding by the alleged frugality of the ancients formed a particularly prominent part of the *mos maiorum* – a point that the cited passage rather glosses over with a rhetoric of plenitude even for the centuries before Cato ('Republican *exempla* ... were *filled* with stories ...').

More generally, in producing literary texts on the basis of Greek models, authors such as Cato the Elder codified and reconfigured Rome's cultural knowledge, while also endowing their vision with special coherence and permanence. Their texts became points of reference for similar efforts later on; and the ensuing intertextual dialogue ensured that anyone writing afterwards viewed the 'pre-literary (not pre-literate) centuries' at least in part through the lens of his predecessors. Roman literary self-definitions and rhetorical in(ter)ventions began to contribute their share to constituting a more or less imaginary past (of self-sufficiency, of a peasant lifestyle, of

---

[83] The exemplarity of a Cincinnatus or Dentatus presupposes that already in their own lifetime their commitment to sobriety was somehow special – otherwise, they would not have stood out as extraordinary. (Paradoxically, an *exemplum* requires a *unique* degree of distinction, for better or worse.) Their later invocations often gloss over this point and turn them into representatives of an entire period, which is then upheld as 'exemplary'. Such a move, however, in turn diminishes the splendour of individual figures whose excellence emerges as average and ordinary for the period they lived in. Cicero reflects on this paradox at *Ver.* 2.1.56. See Gildenhard 2011b: 72–3.

Introduction

humble and temperate aristocrats) and keeping it present – as a continuous point of reference and source of positive value that individuals could tap into if they thought it expedient to do so.

Moreover, the import of Greek genres – such as various forms of historiography – opened up novel ways of thinking, also about such issues as material sobriety and its opposite. As Benjamin Biesinger has shown, the plot of decadence and decline as a result of *luxuria* that gained such traction in late-republican Rome had no place in the conception of history built into the memorial culture of the nobility but found a congenial medium of expression in written narratives.[84] Furthermore, literary texts also facilitate the circulation and domestication of foreign bodies of thought and thus intercultural dialogue. For our concerns, it is noteworthy that many philosophical schools advocated more or less extreme forms of frugality – from the radical austerity of the Cynics to the Stoics, with their teachings about the self-sufficiency of virtue for a happy life (and the ensuing unimportance of creature comforts) to the Epicureans who embraced the principle of pleasure but sought it in a community of likeminded adepts who embraced a frugal style of existence. Authors such as Bion of Borysthenes (335–245 BCE) gave philosophical variants of frugality an entertaining rhetorical form and influenced similar literary efforts at Rome.[85] Self-restraint and prudence grounded in philosophical principles merged with historical traditions and cultural knowledge that valued moderation for socio-political reasons. Inspiration for individual projects might come from the commitment to an (idealised) past and its frugal values or philosophical doctrine and its frugal values – or indeed both, as authors generated philosophically inflected historical visions with a contemporary thrust. Unsurprisingly, literary discourse

---

[84] Biesinger 2016. We come back to this point in more detail below 45–6.

[85] See Kindstrand 1976 and for the tradition of Menippean satire from antiquity until early modern times Weinbrot 2005. It is important to emphasise that the Roman engagement with Greek philosophy was a two-way process: see e.g. Asmis 2004, who argues that Philodemus' views in *On Household Economics* depart from the 'orthodoxy' of Epicurus and Metrodorus to align Epicurean thought better with the circumstances of Roman aristocrats. (We are grateful to Ian Du Quesnay for the reference.)

Ingo Gildenhard and Cristiano Viglietti

of this kind often homed in on areas of cultural practice that also attracted legislative attention, such as gastronomic immoderation: 'There developed a whole sub-genre of literature, largely but not exclusively satirical, devoted to the depiction of extravagant banquets'.[86] When it comes to frugality, Latin literature thus presents a peculiar amalgam of Greek conceptual thought and abstract ethics and (imaginary) Roman historical experiences.[87]

If we now step back and take stock, collecting key words from each of the spheres just surveyed, the ensuing list might include the following: *allotment size* (bina *or* seven *iugera*); *calorific needs and nutrition – demographics – enforced frugality?: exigencies and options – husbandry (cultivation of crop and rearing of livestock) – peasants and poverty – the real and the imaginary – scarcity of resources, subsistence and self-sufficiency, survival and surplus – satisficing and maximising strategies | slaves and freedmen – the ideal wife | census – conspicuous consumption – economics of status – elite and people – exempla discourse – fiscal regimes, public revenues and imperial exploitation – group dynamics: competition and consensus, differentiation and cohesion within/between groups and society at large – legislated frugality – norms and values – political culture – preservation of patrimony and risk-management – political economy – social mobility | authorial self-fashioning – critique: tales of decadence and decline – historical invention – imperial styles – Greece and Rome –*

---

[86] Woodman and Martin 1996: 377, with reference to Hor. *S.* 2.8; Sal. *Hist.* 2.70; Cael. *ap.* Quint. *Inst.* 4.2.123–4; Petr. (*Cena Trimalchionis*); Juv. 5 and 11. See further Gowers 1993; Richardson-Hay 2009; Zanda 2011.

[87] For the influence of Greek philosophy on Roman poetry more generally see the papers in Garani and Konstan 2014. The co-presence of Greek and Roman elements does of course not prevent individual authors from comparing and contrasting the two cultures in an effort to re-inscribe distinctions – indeed it encourages them to do so. See e.g. Keulen 2009: 183 (on Aulus Gellius): 'In Gellius' ethical and cultural landscape, there is a significant discrepancy between the Greek discipline and moderation of the individual philosopher symbolised by Socrates, which is termed *labor uoluntarius* and *exercitium corporis* (2, 1, 1), and traditional Roman frugality, moderation and training, which is not only a private, voluntary attitude but also a public duty, secured by the law' (with reference to 2.24.1).

Introduction

literary revolution – luxury – masculinity and moralising – nostalgia – past and present – philosophy (and other discursive genres) – virtue signalling and invective. The range seems dizzying. Yet despite the centrifugal pull of the relevant data, the ideal of material sobriety and a concern with limits (and the attendant notion of moderation, especially in the pursuit of riches and power) endow the phenomenon of frugal thought and practice at Rome with an underlying coherence and ensured its relevance throughout the city's history, from its earliest phases down to imperial times – even though the precise terms of 'Roman frugality' of course changed over time, in line with evolutions and revolutions in Rome's political system, its economy and its culture. And this phenomenon is worth studying in its own right – not least since frugality broadly conceived occupies a distinctive position within ancient discourses on and responses to the material conditions of human existence often in defiance of prevailing ideologies: it thereby opens up suggestive ambiguities and productive paradoxes. Most importantly, frugality challenges the binary between the rich and the poor, the haves and the have-nots.[88] It is a genuine *tertium quid* that is implicated in discourses of both poverty and wealth, but reconfigures the significance of material resources on its own terms.[89] As a conclusion to this section, some of the consequences are worth highlighting:

First, frugality offers an alternative to the strict correlation of wealth and social status. Appreciation of frugality in the sense of contentment with little, material sobriety and prudent husbandry with scarce resources as virtuous destabilises the idea that anyone who is *not* wealthy cannot possibly belong

---

[88] On poverty in ancient Greece (with a focus on Athens) see recently Cecchet 2015: esp. 185–26 ('*KALOS KAI PENÊS*: The Rhetoric of Good Poverty') and Taylor 2017: esp. 31–67 ('Poverty and Poverty Discourses'); for Rome see e.g. the papers in Atkins and Osborne 2006 and Harris 2011: Ch. 2 ('Poverty and Destitution in the Roman Empire'). Osborne 2006: 15 questions whether a discourse of poverty existed at all (as opposed to one of wealth).

[89] Roman frugality has an interesting comparandum in ancient Sparta and its reputation for self-control, collective discipline and proud commitment to physical regimen and an austere way of life, which, for these reasons, also served as a source of inspiration for disciplinarian regimes and apostles of sobriety and self-restraint down the centuries: Rawson 1969.

Ingo Gildenhard and Cristiano Viglietti

among 'the best'. The strong nexus between frugality and virtue and the insistence that the acquisition and use of wealth calls for moderation and limits invite qualification of the widespread notion that wealth was an *unqualified* good in ancient Rome (and elsewhere).[90] Certain conceptions of frugality offer a powerful platform for critique of the aristocratic conceit that affluence, family pedigree and superior morals necessarily coincide. The image of (say) the Roman farmer-soldier living in self-sufficiency at near-subsistence level subverts the assumption that to be impecunious is to be bad, that poverty is the result of idleness or some other failing, that lack in one area coincides with lack in other areas. And certain figures of Rome's *exempla* discourse who are celebrated for their relative poverty, simplicity and the benefits of a humble lifestyle in agricultural labour illustrate that – despite the logic of the census and elite pride in wealth – affluence is in principle no prerequisite for moral worth and socio-political esteem.[91] This disjunction could be tapped into for self-promotional purposes: the imaginary frugality enacted by the free, self-sufficient and satisficing farmer offers a suggestive source of positive associations for those interested in obfuscating differentials in wealth and power by demonstrating commitment to self-restraint – such as members of the ruling elite interacting with the wider populace or emperors communicating with the senate.

---

[90] See e.g. Cornell 2000: 80: '... in Rome (and in ancient societies generally) wealth was morally good and automatically implied the possession of other qualities. In fact there is little point in asking whether in the present context it refers to moral character, high birth, or wealth; to a Roman mind these three attributes naturally coalesced in the "best" people', with reference to Finley 1985: 35–40.

[91] Certain variants of frugal ideology deliberately highlight the inverse correlation of wealth and political status: see e.g. V. Max. 4.4.11 on men of little means achieving the highest possible distinction in the service of the commonwealth: *nullum aut admodum parui ponderis argentum, paucos seruos, septem iugera aridae terrae, indigentia domesticae impensae funera, inopes dotum filias, sed egregios consulatus, mirificas dictaturas, innumerabiles triumphos cernimus* ('We see a very small weight of silver or none at all, few slaves, seven *iugera* of parched land, funerals indigent in private expenditure, daughters without dowries – yes, but outstanding Consulships, marvellous Dictatorships, countless triumphs' – trans. D. R. Shackleton Bailey/ Loeb).

Introduction

Secondly, and conversely, wealth and frugality (unlike wealth and poverty) are not mutually exclusive – quite the contrary. By comprising diverse and potentially countervailing modes of moderation, including the specifically economic value of thrift, i.e. the careful use of resources for further enrichment, frugality may well be a significant driver of wealth.[92] While restraint legislation targeting members of the ruling elite speaks to a communal interest in status- and context-specific limits in acquiring, spending and investing capital in the competition for political rank and standing, those individuals who were either excluded from holding public office because of their low social status (slaves, freedmen, the poor) or those who, despite having the status- and property-qualification to do so, decided not to enter a political career could pursue riches to their heart's content and still (or indeed for that very reason) be considered *frugi*.[93] The seemingly paradoxical possibility that frugality and affluence can coincide in turn enabled the rich to 'perform' frugality without (excessive) hypocrisy – such as (again) elite politicians in communication with the people broadcasting commitment to hard labour and self-denying discipline or a Stoic philosopher like Seneca who equated a frugal outlook not with poverty but indifference to material circumstances.

Thirdly, the grounding of frugal virtues in the sphere of agriculture challenges a one-sided contrast between the city as a centre of civilisation and the countryside as a sphere of doltish and unenlightened brutishness. Cicero's speech *pro Roscio Amerino* offers evidence for the countervailing discourses of value that revolved around *urbanitas* and *rusticitas*.

---

[92] There are affinities here with the idea in moralising literature that 'wealth' is relational: Xenophon, for instance, contrasts the insatiability of the rich (and in particular the tyrant) who never have enough to satisfy their needs with the self-sufficiency and contentment of the seemingly poor who, despite their limited resources, still have enough to pay for what they want. But this view simply inverts the relative valence of wealth and poverty – whereas the notion of frugality advocates values that are not strictly related to specific degrees of indigence or affluence.

[93] This is one of the reasons why senators often used freedmen (preferably those who were *frugi* in the sense of useful and thrifty) as middlemen for their commercial interests and investments: D'Arms 1981.

37

Ingo Gildenhard and Cristiano Viglietti

If the prosecution tried to establish a quasi-causal link between the rural background of the defendant (whom they call a 'wild and uncultivated person', a *homo ferus atque agrestis: S. Rosc.* 74 with Dyck 2010: 140), his paternally enforced exile in the countryside and the savage act of parricide, Cicero invests in an alternative point of view: a rural way of life, he insists, teaches thrift (*parsimonia*), industry (*diligentia*) and justice (*iustitia*) and is therefore in and of itself an argument in favour of innocence (*innocentia*); by contrast, the city engenders extravagance (*luxuries*), *luxuria* produces greed (*auaritia*), *auaritia* entails recklessness (*audacia*) and *audacia* fosters crimes of every sort (*omnia scelera ac maleficia*).[94] That Cicero could peddle these lines of reasoning shows that at least in part Rome's urban elite remained committed to the notion that the countryside nourishes a certain frugal and upright disposition free from desires and depravities, such as greed for money to be spent on a luxurious style of life.[95]

Fourth, as the foregoing discussion has already shown, the remit of frugality extends significantly beyond the narrowly economic. In the specific sense of 'thrift' its primary focus may be on the prudent handling of material resources; but from there Roman ideas of frugality branch out to include other modes of moderation – on the basis of the cultural logic that continence in one area testifies to the same quality in other areas. Frugality in the moral sense of self-control and uprightness speaks more generally to the ways in which humans relate to or regulate their needs, wants and desires – not just in the sphere of material goods and wealth, but also others, in particular those of food and drink, sex and power.

In all, then, the inbuilt complexities of Roman frugality ensured the phenomenon a pervasive presence throughout Roman history and across genders and social strata, from the very bottom (slaves, freedmen) to the very top (members of the

---

[94] *S. Rosc.* 75.

[95] See Dyck 2010: 109–12, 140–1 on Cic. *S. Rosc.* 37–9 and 75, further Vasaly 1993: 157–92 (on stereotypes of city vs. country) and, for the continuity of the theme in the Augustan period, Eigler 2002 and below 75–7.

Introduction

governing classes, including emperors) though in different ways, depending on emphasis (economic thrift or other modes of moderation) and sphere of activity (economy, politics, their intertwining in the political economy and the economics of status or moral discourse).

Towards a History of/Case Studies in Roman Frugality (and its Reception)

This final part of the introduction traces the evolution of frugal thought and practice at Rome from the archaic age to the early imperial period – and beyond. As goes without saying, we here paint with a very broad brush: the aim is to single out a few facts and figures, dynamics and developments within Rome's societal evolution that have shaped preoccupation with moderation – as frame and backdrop for the case studies to follow, which are here summarised as well. They, too, range from archaic to early imperial times, with the final Chapter 7 (Berry) broadening out into the post-classical by considering the changing perceptions of (Roman) frugality in the early modern period.[96]

The Archaic Period

The suitably vague label 'archaic' here comprises the time-span from the earliest foundations of the city down to c. 367/6 BCE, i.e. including the royal period and the first three of Flower's thirteen 'republican' segments, which cover the period after the end of monarchy but before the so-called Rome of the nobility had fully come into its own.[97] These early centuries are of course precisely those phases in Roman history for which the amount of existing information is particularly scarce and the available textual evidence invariably

[96] For the tricky business of periodisation in Roman history see most recently Flower 2010.
[97] See Flower 2010: 33 (c. 509–494; 494–451/0; 450–367/6).

39

Ingo Gildenhard and Cristiano Viglietti

late and often highly controversial. Yet for many authors of the late republic and early imperial period, frugality was a cultural trait particularly manifest during the early phases in the city's history. With them as guides, it is easy to envision a regal period in which rustic Romans joined Romulus in his hut, to share in a meal of emmer served in dishes of clay. The picture sketched by later re-imaginings, however, is by no means uniform. For Sallust, the prosperity and power of the early city, which derived from the *concordia* of the citizen community, triggered the envy of neighbouring kings and peoples (... *inuidia ex opulentia orta est* ...) who resorted to warfare to get a piece of the pie.[98] And Valerius Maximus in places characterises the time of 'the ancients' (*antiqui*) as one of affluence or even opulence.[99] But the historical fictions of historiographers and antiquarians are anyway by and large worthless as sources for scholars trying to reconstruct the material conditions and the socio-political arrangements that applied in archaic Rome.

To make headway here, the principal point of reference is our growing archaeological data, which suggest that we can continue to improve upon our understanding of archaic Roman culture and society – and the place of frugal attitudes within it.[100] With the requisite methodological scruple and caution it remains possible to reconstruct some of the coordinates and parameters, socio-political dynamics and political economy of archaic Rome. Some sense of the specific forms of frugality traceable in those early centuries would at any rate help put in perspective what happens in the better documented subsequent phases of Roman history, by enabling us to gauge in what ways later developments relate to earlier habits and institutions and how the moralising discourse of late-republican Rome

---

[98] Sal. *Cat.* 6.3.   [99] V. Max. 1.1.1b.

[100] For recent discussions of the evidence available for the study of early Rome, spanning the spectrum from sceptics to believers, see Cornell 1995: 1–30; Carandini 2000 and Carandini and Cappelli 2000 with Wiseman 2001; Smith 2006; Cifani 2008; the papers in Richardson and Santangelo 2014 (with the editors' introduction); Drogula 2015: 8–181; Armstrong 2016: 18–46.

Introduction

(re-)invented or (mis-)represented practices of moderation and material sobriety in the archaic city.[101]

In Chapter 1: '"Frugality", Economy and Society in Archaic Rome (Late Seventh to Early Fourth Century BCE)', Cristiano Viglietti accordingly begins by acknowledging the methodological challenges involved in identifying how material resources were managed in a period and by a society for which there is hardly any textual evidence. Relying primarily on archaeological data, he notes that, in funerary contexts, we have to reckon with the practice of conspicuous consumption in the archaic period – which in itself blows a hole in the narrative of the ancient moralists who claimed that the Romans 'of old' were consistently averse to the use of wealth for purposes of ostentatious self-promotion. Rather, throughout the city's history, frugal modes of managing resources emerged (and disappeared) in response to demographic and socio-political stimuli. In his attempt to map out the dynamic intersections of wealth and power in archaic Rome, Viglietti identifies the introduction of the census as playing a crucial role in shifting the display of wealth from funerary settings to housing, or, put differently, from the dead to the living. As an institution, the census governed rank and standing in Roman society by serving as a basis for the allocation of a higher degree of political influence and power to the richest citizens – but to remain among this elite now required a certain degree of economic prudence. It at once bestowed privileges of rank to land ownership (and an associated lifestyle) and required the elite to perform to high economic standards in order to maintain their status.

The existence of census mechanisms implies a set of moral and practical caveats to do with the management of a citizen's patrimony within a cultural logic favourable to wealth as an indispensable prerequisite for rank ascension and/or preservation and for obtaining magistracies.[102] But the transformation

---

[101] Clemente 1981: 2–3; Andreau and Coudry 2016.
[102] Nicolet 1976; Clemente 1981: 1–2; Bottiglieri 2002: 175–8; 2016; Pina Polo 2016: 170–3; Jehne 2016: 189, 195.

Ingo Gildenhard and Cristiano Viglietti

of wealth into forms of socio-political display also seems to have had limits. The archaeological evidence suggests some glass ceiling for the degree to which the living could magnify their visual presence in the political centre of the archaic Roman community. In the final part of the chapter, Viglietti's focus shifts to the lower end of the social scale: there is evidence of legal arrangements designed to protect individuals from the dissipation of their patrimony and to encourage the prudent management of resources to guarantee subsistence or even generate a surplus (however small). A complex equation involving factors such as yield rates and comparative data suggests that Roman farmers could manage to eke out a living on rather small allotments.

The Rome of the Nobility (I)[103]

The proto-republican decades that followed the end of monarchy at Rome remain particularly difficult to reconstruct. What seems reasonably certain is that a group of influential families tried to concentrate power in their own hands by employing the criterion of hereditary status to exclude others from communal positions of power: for some time, only so-called 'patricians' could act in certain civic and religious capacities.[104] This system, however, soon came under pressure. In a period of transition, often referred to as the struggle of the orders, which seems to have included debt crises, military revolts and successions of the plebs, a compromise was reached, consisting of 'the plebeian success in breaking [patrician] monopolies' and 'patrician success in remaining central to the Roman state'.[105] The emerging elite, the so-called 'patricio-plebeian nobility', regulated access to public magistracies

---

[103] Flower splits the years 450–60 BCE into six republics. Other divisions suggest themselves, depending on focus. Tan 2017, for instance, whose concern is with Rome's political economy, divides the period into roughly two halves with the Second Punic War as watershed.

[104] The oligarchy of early modern Venice offers a comparandum.

[105] Smith 2006: 280. See also the papers in Raaflaub (1986/2005); Linke 1995; and most recently Crooks 2019, a thesis that explores the origins and growth of civic identity at Rome from the mid-seventh to the mid-fourth century BCE.

42

Introduction

differently. In particular, it now involved an element of competition in the form of election, open to Roman citizens with the requisite level of wealth, which over time evolved into a *cursus honorum* with formalised procedures and institutions.[106] In the new system access to positions of power was thus no longer a matter of hereditary privilege (patrician status) alone. A new economics of status evolved, in which success in public elections to various magistracies, in particular those that included responsibility for commanding an army and ideally resulting in the celebration of a triumph, came to constitute the most prestigious form of socio-political distinction.

Over time, the presence of magistrates in the family tree evolved into a special type of symbolic capital that the established families cultivated in the public eye through various media of commemoration, such as little shrines on display in the atrium containing the wax-masks (*imagines*) of former office-holders, together with *tituli* that summarised their career and *stemmata* that placed them within the wider lineage of other successful members of the family as a means of facilitating further electoral success – the 'logic' being that past achievement would guarantee similarly stellar service by other members of the family in the present and future.[107] This symbolic capital disadvantaged newcomers since it partially cancelled out two assets on which upstarts often relied: wealth and individual talent. Wax masks of former office-holders (unlike, say, votes ...) were not for sale nor could they be acquired quickly – they constituted a hereditary form of capital, acquired in competition, accumulated over time and passed down as part of the family's patrimony. Similarly, *imagines* implied that excellence runs in families across the generations (though not necessarily from father to son) – a notion with purchase not just on the electorate but also, and perhaps even more forcefully, on many a scion from a noble

---

[106] See e.g. Hölkeskamp 1987; Beck 2005; the papers in Beck, Duplá, Jehne and Pina Polo 2011; Bernard 2018a.

[107] See Flaig 1995; 2003a: 49–98; 2015; Flower 1996 (with appendices of ancient sources).

family who considered a successful public career his birth-right. They had at any rate every incentive to give vying for office their best shot: only entry into and advancement on the *cursus honorum* ensured a specific type of recognition and prestige (*honores, dignitas*) and survival within the memory of one's family and hence the *res publica* at large (*gloria*).[108]

The novel economics of status significantly altered the way in which wealth was invested to enhance rank and standing – not least in funerary contexts. A form of funeral celebrated for those who had achieved election to one of the higher magistracies developed into a striking occasion for the presentation of a family's accumulated symbolic capital to the larger public. The family of the deceased hired actors to impersonate its other former office-holders and form a procession that marched the corpse to the forum where the son or another close relative delivered the funeral eulogy, praising each of the successful ancestors in turn down to the one who had just died for what they had achieved in the service of the state. The funeral thus retained its function as a prime setting for elite display. But unlike in archaic times, a family now put on show not conspicuous affluence but conspicuous achievement. The currency that counted was not wealth but accomplishments. Among other things, this shift transformed the emotional key of the occasion. Given the emphasis on historical deeds (rather than wealth) and the celebration of success (rather than the tragedy of death), many of the sumptuary strictures that we find in the Twelve Tables with regard to the conduct of aristocratic funerals – concerning such practices as conspicuous display of expensive clothing or precious metal or the performance of grief by women in attendance – lost their point and purpose. Alongside the core elements of the funeral, however, the ruling elite found new modes of conspicuous consumption designed

---

[108] As Flaig 2003a: 61 puts it: 'Ob man *imagines* besaß oder nicht, man litt unter ihnen' – *homines noui* resented the advantage a distinguished set of ancestors afforded candidates from established families in the competition for office, whereas scions of impressive lineage faced the challenge to live up to high standards of ancestral achievement or be considered a family failure.

Introduction

to recommend those incurring the expenditure to the larger populace, such as the sponsorship of gladiatorial games from 264 BCE onwards. As a form of personal piety and civic generosity, such *munera* did not attract legislative strictures and provided an essentially unregulated arena of elite competition that saw massively escalating outlays over time.[109]

With a view towards the rise of moralising historiography at Rome from the end of the third century BCE onwards, which has played such a powerful role in shaping our perception of Roman *parsimonia* and *luxuria* also for the earlier centuries, several features of the conception of history built into the memorial culture of the nobility are worth emphasising. Storage of the historical data was notably decentralised: each family celebrated its historical superstars, if within the wider context of the *res publica*. While the families kept records of their successful members and their achievements and had them on permanent display in their *atria*, the enactment of this memory in the public spaces of the city during funeral celebrations was ephemeral and polycentric: in each individual instance, the time in the public spotlight was brief and passed from family to family. Moreover, the displays or enactments featured what we might call a 'selectively annalistic' outlook: each family could only hope to commemorate a subsection of the former magistrates and their deeds that made up the story of the Roman commonwealth. No family, not even the most powerful one, could lay claim to an uninterrupted sequence of annual office-holders.[110] Finally, and for our purposes most importantly, this system did not – could not – easily articulate a coherent notion of societal decline.[111]

To begin with, the means and media of aristocratic self-promotion do not construe the present as in any way worse than the past: while the ancestors set standards, new generations vied to reach a degree of distinction that excelled the

---

[109] See Edmondson 2016. The table on page 39 nicely illustrates the 'fairly steady increase in their scale' over the years 264–160 BCE.

[110] The paragraph recapitulates Gildenhard et al. 2019: 13. It is based above all on Flaig 1995.

[111] The following draws on Biesinger 2016.

ancestral benchmark. Each family was invested in cultivating a story of success. And in the context of inner-aristocratic competition, the accumulation of more officer-holders over time would indeed improve the rank and standing of the family vis-à-vis other families. Moreover, the individuals chosen for commemoration were only those who had prospered: family losers, defined as those who never served as magistrates of the *res publica*, were not awarded a wax-mask, did not march impersonated in the funeral procession and did not have their names displayed in the atrium. The memory of the past that each family put on display was therefore inevitably one of achievement and success stretching into an open future. If the procession was relatively small, this might either signal the family's fairly recent arrival within the ruling elite or obscurity over stretches in the past – but the very fact that the family celebrated a procession in the here and now reconfirmed its contribution to the triumphant vibrancy of the Roman commonwealth. Likewise, even if some families fell on hard times, this inevitably meant that others had taken their place and were excelling in the present: so any oscillation in family fortune did not affect the present prosperity and power of the societal whole. In short, at its core the memorial culture of the nobility had no truck with nostalgia. Within the historical consciousness it fostered, the belief that the past was inevitably better than the present had no place. Conversely, the modes of commemoration that the Romans invested in before the advent of literary historiography could not even properly articulate the idea that the Roman community had somehow fallen into decadence and decline.

Where, then, can we detect concern with thrift and moderation within this political system? Two (countervailing) modes stand out: (a) the 'symbolic frugality' collectively enacted and projected by the ruling elite; and (b) elite disquiet over wealth skewing competition for public office (but not necessarily harbouring royal ambition).[112] If the former was an element of the

---

[112] In some quarters, there is still the tendency to see the republic as haunted by the fear of monarchy with each high magistrate a potential Tarquinius Superbus Rediuiuus. But evidence for a virulent *anti-regnum* discourse during the years of

Introduction

interaction between the ruling elite and the people, the latter primarily concerned dynamics within the ruling elite.

(a) The political system of the Roman republic placed a premium on achieving success in elections for magistracies of the commonwealth and prowess in warfare. As we had occasion to note, only success in these fields of civic and military endeavour ensured entry into the collective memory of the family and the commonwealth and thereby ensured a specific form of highly desirable prestige and future immortality. The politically active segment of Rome's socio-economic elite therefore had every reason to cultivate and advertise those qualities that enhanced their chances in competition for office. A political culture evolved in which the ruling elite found it expedient to engage in a style of self-representation that aligned with the interests and the ideological preferences of ordinary citizens, revolving around hard physical labour in the service of the commonwealth. Symbolic 'gestures of joviality' downplayed differences in wealth and emphasised shared experiences, common commitments and reciprocal ties and responsibilities.[113]

Conversely, the elite tended to eschew exclusive cultural practices that would have highlighted discrete levels of prosperity.[114] As such, the modes of self-promotion that the Roman nobility adopted comprised an element of collective moderation and self-denial in the form of abstention from activities that would have reinforced exclusive aristocratic distinction, such as cultivation of the body through dancing

---

the middle republic is scarce – apart from some concerns about an unusual concentration of power (e.g. in the institution of the dictatorship; Russo 2015) or various *exempla mala* (also beyond the classical trio of *affectatores regni* Sp. Cassius, Sp. Maelius and Manlius Capitolinus: as a group and category 'a modern myth': Neel 2015; see further Chassignet 2001; Vigourt 2001a; 2001b; or Flower 2006: 44–50) who did not rein in their ambitions as opposed to the *exemplum bonum* of Cincinnatus, a paragon of self-moderation: the satisficing farmer content with his lot is the perfect counter-image to the arrogant aristocrat secretly desiring omnipotence. The discourse of tyranny did not really come into its own in Rome until the second half of the second century BCE, with senatorial opposition to Tiberius Gracchus: Pina Polo 2006.

[113] For 'gestures of joviality' see Jehne 2000.

[114] This and the following paragraph are based on Flaig 1993.

Ingo Gildenhard and Cristiano Viglietti

and athletic exercises in the gymnasium or drinking parties informed by the culture of *mousikê* (to name some such possibilities well known from the Greek world). Instead of expending precious time on matters only of relevance to a tiny number of fellow-aristocrats – and elite time is a resource that tends to be in short supply[115] – Roman nobles highlighted their full commitment to the concerns of the civic community in their role as *patresfamilias* and patrons, senators and magistrates. The ramifications of this approach to elite self-fashioning are broad and manifest themselves not least in visual culture. Roman veristic portraiture, with its care-worn countenances marked by physical labour, emphasises individual recognisability and projects the values of self-discipline, hard work and sacrifice – just like the scarred bodies that aristocrats would at times disclose as a means of symbolic communication with the people.[116] Put differently, Rome's ruling elite ended up building aspects of the frugal and disciplined farmer-soldier (husbandry, *grauitas*, *labor*, *disciplina*, self-restraint, material sobriety, physical sacrifice) into the image it projected to the electorate, individually to woo voters and collectively to justify their leading position in the community.

This system also had the benefit of generating two cultural resources that Rome, constantly at war, desperately needed (or put the other way around: the need to generate these two resources helped the system to evolve in the way it did): an elite focused on politics and warfare on behalf of the community; and a wider populace willing to follow their leaders with a profound degree of obedience despite steep hierarchies in wealth and power.[117] Indeed, military clashes between Rome and its neighbours constitute the setting in which legendary

---

[115] Flaig 2002.

[116] Flaig 2003a: 123–36 ('Auf Narben verweisen – Zur Kritik kultureller Semantik').

[117] The same logic seems to have informed the passing of sumptuary legislation in situations of military crisis such as the *Lex Oppia* of 215 BCE, which restricted in particular the display of wealth by women. Moderation of aristocratic display of socio-economic distinctions was one way of enhancing societal solidarity and cohesion.

Introduction

figures of conspicuous austerity first appear: belief in such qualities as relative poverty, incorruptibility and civic solidarity helped the Romans to explain to themselves and others why they outperformed their adversaries on the battlefield, according to the logic that the masculine virtues of tough, frugal living and self-control trump the feminine vices of luxury and indulgence. Superiority in terms of masculine moral fibre entails, explains and justifies military triumph.[118] Austerity as a style of self-promotion also enabled the charge of 'luxury' against opponents in domestic politics. Thus Aulus Gellius reports that the censor Fabricius Luscinus expelled his rival P. Cornelius Rufinus from the senate in 275 BCE for owning ten pounds of silver plate, which 'suggests ... that quantified metallic wealth continued to expose individuals to possible moral polemics' – and served as a foil for the pronounced austerity of Fabricius himself or Curius Dentatus.[119]

(b) Rank and standing within the formalised hierarchies of the patricio-plebeian governing class rested on success in competitive election, not wealth, though wealth remained a crucial variable and not just as a minimum entry requirement in the form of the census. While affluence could not guarantee a successful outcome, individuals could increase their chances by wooing the voting public with acts of civic generosity (*liberalitas*), such as *munera*, the construction of temples (perhaps funded through the proceeds of booty) and other public building projects or spectacular games, paid for in part by the public purse, which the magistrate in charge could supplement with personal funds or borrowed money. A candidate for office could of course also resort to illegal means, such as bribing the electorate. As in archaic times, the interface of

---

[118] See Dench 1998: 137–8, who argues for 'the intensity of Roman promotion of images of their own austerity in the middle Republic' and identifies M'. Curius Dentatus, conqueror of Sabines and Samnites, as the most famous example, 'whose legendary austerity seems to have been reinvented in a number of generations.' (Unfortunately, of course, we only have access to the reinventions, from Cato the Elder onwards.)

[119] Bernard 2018b: 13, citing Gel. 4.8. But cf. Keulen 2009: 183–9 for a rhetorical analysis of Gellius' text, suggesting that its value as a reliable historical source for the third century BCE is perhaps not as straightforward as one might wish.

wealth and power thus remained highly sensitive. Even though the evidence for the early centuries is thin, efforts to keep the playing field level by imposing legal limits on the use of wealth in the pursuit of political power register in our sources meagre as they are. Some measures against *ambitus* (electoral bribery) are already on record for 432 BCE (Liv. 4.25.13) and 358 BCE (*Lex Poetelia de ambitu*).[120] And laws were passed that imposed a measure of moderation also on the acquisition of wealth. The most famous is arguably the *Lex Licinia de modo agrorum* (367 BCE), which is the subject of Chapter 2: 'From Licinius Stolo to Tiberius Gracchus: Roman Frugality and the Limitation of Landholding' by John Rich.

The chapter has a wide chronological range – from the early fourth to the late second century BCE, with a focus on the key issue of land use and ownership. It confronts head-on the methodological problem that Roman historiographers tend to adopt a synoptic view of the past, often conflating discrete historical moments from a presentist perspective. Thus in later sources the laws promulgated by Licinius Stolo and Tiberius Gracchus play off each other in ways difficult to untangle. Rich therefore revisits the juridical, political and economic issues surrounding Tiberius Gracchus' agrarian law of 133 BCE, which reasserted an older law that limited the amount of land a man might hold to 500 *iugera*. After sketching out the history of scholarly controversy and identifying three alternative explanations (i.e. the orthodox position of Niebuhr that both the pre-Gracchan and Gracchan limits applied only to public land; Rathbone's recent suggestion that both applied just to private land; and the theory of Huschke – recently revived – that the earlier limit applied to all landholding, but Gracchus restricted it to public land), Rich reconsiders the sources, which, on his reading, provide powerful evidence that Huschke's position is correct: whereas the pre-Gracchan limit applied to all landholding (not just public land), Gracchus, who was interested in reclaiming public land for distribution

---

[120] Adamietz 1989: 23–7 surveys *ambitus*-legislation from the archaic to the early imperial period, with further bibliography.

Introduction

(rather than putting a limit on elite wealth), revived the earlier limit, but applied it only to public land. The subsequent section argues for identifying the pre-Gracchan legislation with a law carried by the tribune C. Licinius Stolo in 367 BCE, in response to the substantial land confiscations and allotments of the early fourth century – and in the belief that the concentration of too much land in the hands of particular individuals was potentially problematic for the civic community. Rich thus identifies one of the main reasons for the 'ethos of frugality' in mid-republican Rome in the desire of the oligarchic elite to prevent individual members from accumulating excessive material resources.

The final part of his chapter traces the history of the tension between the pursuit of personal enrichment and the interest of the wider community to keep such pursuits in check – an endeavour rendered increasingly difficult given Rome's foreign conquests. But the existence of legislation that tried to control the amassing of wealth (not least in the form of landed property) facilitated the effort of imaginative individuals like Cato the Elder to attack the perceived 'greed' of some of their contemporaries as being at variance with ancestral values.

The Rome of the Nobility (II)

Rome's increasing dominion over Middle Italy, Magna Graecia and the wider Mediterranean world (a milestone in this respect occurred in 241 BCE at the end of the First Punic War, when Sicily became Rome's first overseas province) did not just enable aristocrats to amass land. The process of imperial expansion resulted in other sources of income acquiring ever greater import within Rome's political economy, such as warfare and commerce.

Successful generals by and large controlled the economic windfall of a successful campaign[121] – even though debates

---

[121] Flaig 2003a: 32–48 ('Der Triumph. Individuelle Aneignung kollektiver Leistung'); further Holz 2009: 195 and, more generally, the other papers in Coudry and Humm 2009. For Roman cultural appropriation (or 'plunder') in the context of

over the proper handling of war spoils raged throughout the republican centuries.[122] They decided how much of the booty to give to their soldiers, how much to put into the state coffers and how much to keep for themselves – and what to do with it. Individual generals disposed of booty in different ways, according to background and personal inclinations.[123] But the basic dynamic of how victory on the battlefield and the captured spoils were funnelled into the material and symbolic economy at Rome remained the same: military success often led to a significant amount of disposable income, which could be invested to enhance visibility and prestige of the commanding general as a means of enhancing his and his family's rank and reputation. Escalating competition put significant stress on the cohesion of Rome's ruling elite, but despite intense debates it never managed to impose a meaningful degree of moderation in this particular area. The failure to regulate the consequences of military victory successfully was arguably one key factor in the downfall of the republican commonwealth.[124]

Military expansion also opened up novel commercial opportunities, and the *plebiscitum Claudianum* of c. 218 BCE, prohibiting the ownership of trading vessels of a certain size by senators and their sons, arguably ought to be seen in this context. The measure might have been motivated in part by the desire to protect senators from risking their patrimony through hazardous maritime trade;[125] but it is equally an index of Rome responding to changes in the economy brought about by an ever-expanding empire, with inevitable repercussions for

---

imperial expansion see now the introduction and papers in Loar, MacDonald and Padilla Peralta 2018.

[122] See e.g. Cato the Elder's speech *uti praeda in publicum referatur* (= fr. 98 *ORF*³) where he argues that statues of gods brought to Rome as spoils of war ought to be exhibited in a public setting and not in a private property.

[123] For a possible example see Bernard 2018b: 12–13, who compares and contrasts the handling of *spolia* by the two *triumphatores* L. Papirius Cursor and Spurius Carvilius Maximus in 293 BCE, arguing that 'while Papirius used his spoils to emphasise inherited authority within the aristocratic community, Carvilius, as a *nouus homo* and without illustrious ancestors, promoted the individual aspects of his accomplishment ...' (13).

[124] Flaig 2003b.   [125] Gabba 1988: 89–106; Zanda 2011: 54.

Introduction

the economics of status:[126] those who knew how to exploit new enrichment prospects would have gained a competitive advantage over those who for whatever reason did not.[127] Acts of 'collective abstention' such as the *plebiscitum* partly counterbalanced the pressure novel forms of wealth put on the cohesion of the ruling elite.[128]

The tension between the desirability of accumulating as much wealth as possible and a collective interest in keeping the self-enrichment of politically active individuals within reasonable limits also registers in the summary of the funeral oration that Q. Caecilius Metellus delivered for his father L. Metellus (*cos.* 251, *cos.* II 247 BCE) in 221 BCE.[129] As we had occasion to note, the core data that the nobility remembered in various media revolved around achievements, such as offices held or triumphs celebrated. The *laudatio funebris* afforded the opportunity to pad out such facts rhetorically, with reference to forms of excellence not easily captured in *tituli* and *imagines* alone. Metellus *filius* identified the following ten areas of competitive interest for a Roman aristocrat with brains, in all of which the *laudandus* is said to have excelled: to be the foremost warrior (*primarius bellator*) and bravest general (*fortissimus imperator*), to have the greatest deeds (*maximas res*) performed under his auspices (*auspicio suo*), to enjoy the greatest honour (*maximo honore uti*), to epitomise supreme wisdom (*summa sapientia*), to be considered the best senator (*summus senator*), to have accumulated a significant amount of wealth by honourable means (*pecuniam magnam bono modo inuenire*), to father many

---

[126] See e.g. Tchernia 2011: 199–228; Venturini 2009; and, in particular, Prag 2016, who takes the plebiscite to point forward to the *leges de repetundis* of the mid-second century BCE: see further below.

[127] Cf. the problems attendant on monetisation, another process that played itself out in the fourth and third centuries BCE. As Bernard 2018b: 3 notes, 'coinage arose alongside acquisitive and market-oriented economic behaviours relating to the acquisition of wealth outside of existing Roman social networks; increased engagement in such activities dramatically shifted the balance of transactional orders and therefore stimulated a moralised discourse concerning wealth and aristocratic identity'. See also Coffee 2017 with the critical review by von Reden 2019.

[128] For collective abstention see above 26–7.

[129] As transmitted by Plin. *Nat.* 7.139–40.

children and be the most famous (*clarissimus*) in the entire commonwealth.

The catalogue focuses exclusively on just a few areas of activity. Renown in the community (cf. *clarissimus*) derives above all from superlative achievements in warfare (*bellator, imperator, auspicium, res gestae*), then also from contributions to domestic politics (*honor, sapientia, senator*) and family planning and lineage continuity in the form of patrimony and children (*pecunia magna, multi liberi*). Eulogy is not a genre that encourages moderation, and Metellus *pater* and *filius* went for the maximum, both in deeds and their rhetorical elaboration – with one notable exception: whereas the immoderate superlative reigns in every other respect (*primarius, fortissimus, maximas, maximo, summa, summus, clarissimus*), praise of Metellus' enrichment activities is doubly qualified: the amount of wealth (*pecunia*) he accumulated is not *maxima*, only *magna*; and he went about doing so in socially approved ways (*bono modo*).

The downgrading from the superlative to the positive is either apologetic (Metellus just was not particularly successful in enriching himself and his family, so his son had to resort to a morally contrived form of praise) or a lie (he was extraordinarily successful but societal conventions required his son to spin the truth to make his enrichment record praiseworthy). The emphasis on *bono modo*, a phrase that glosses and explains the otherwise unimpressive positive *magna* and turns the apparent failure to reach maximum distinction in this one area into a badge of honour, triggers similar reflections: it implies that many of his peers (perhaps even Metellus himself) went about enriching themselves *malo modo*, i.e. in ways that were disreputable or indeed illegal – and that, for this very reason, moderation in this area was considered notable and praiseworthy.[130] The change in rhetorical register suggests that the audience of the oration, i.e. the wider civic community, would

---

[130] Again, whether Metellus exercised such self-restraint is impossible to ascertain: what else would Metellus *filius* say about his father in the context of a *laudatio funebris*? *De mortuis* . . .

Introduction

have deemed a certain amount of self-restraint in the acquisition of wealth laudable (but also noteworthy!) in a member of the political elite – whereas no such expectation to rein in ambition applied elsewhere. We capture here the desire to maximise wealth while paying attention (or at least lip service) to communally approved limits – which is tantamount to a modicum of praiseworthy moderation: otherwise the speech swells with the rhetorical assertion of superlative excellence.

Delivered in 221 BCE, at the eve of the Second Punic War (218–201 BCE), Metellus' eulogy of his father belongs to a period just before certain developments that had long been accumulating momentum magnified exponentially. Shortly after Rome was almost brought to her knees by Hannibal, the dynamics of imperial expansion took off for good, with significant consequences for the political system at all levels – generating a situation that was rather unique for a pre-industrial society, i.e. a society 'whose very small surplus production is bespoken, embedded, routinely used for the same purpose year after year':[131]

But Roman society, because the fruits of conquest were being heaped into Italy, temporarily escaped from some of these limitations. It had massive resource availability, for which there was no traditional allocation in society. These resources were 'free-floating.' Romans therefore faced the new and bewildering problem of how these resources were to be used, and for whose benefit. We know one answer: the rich grew richer.

In the decades after the Second Punic War, possibilities for a select group of individuals to enrich themselves skyrocketed – while the struggle to get elected to one of the few magistracies

---

[131] Hopkins 1978: 90, cited by Tan 2017: xviii. See also Crawford 1977 for a survey of the different modes of exploitation and wealth extraction Rome practised in conquered territories – from the imposition of tributes to acquisition of land to slaves – and the behavioural consequences of imperial expansion, i.e. 'an increase in the number of junior magistracies, without any corresponding increase in the number of consuls; this led inevitably to increased competition, the growth of bribery and the need for wealth' (51). Whether or not this wealth was acquired *bono modo* or not was a secondary consideration: 'extortion by provincial governors of the Republic is so notorious as to need no discussion' (ibid.); self-restraint meant losing out to peers less encumbered by personal scruples.

Ingo Gildenhard and Cristiano Viglietti

further intensified.[132] Profitable provincial commands were considered both a return for prior investment in the steep climb up the *cursus honorum* and as platform for the acquisition of further wealth for renewed investment in the competition for office as well as an opportunity to acquire further immaterial goods, such as priceless *gloria* in the memory of one's family and the community at large. Rome's war machine generated a tremendous amount of resource that could be poured into competition within the economics of status: members of the ruling elite vied for prestige and recognition and, ultimately, votes through staging spectacular games, celebrating memorable triumphs, hosting lavish dinner parties or expanding their networks of friends and clients through acts of material generosity and other means.[133] In this context, extravagance, novelty and the extraordinary counted – immoderation was the name of the game. Emulative transgression of existing modes or measures in such areas as public spectacles and triumphal displays became the norm.[134] Increased competition required higher levels of investment, which forced candidates to take greater financial risks (e.g. in terms of taking out loans) and resulted in more pronounced ways of winning and losing. The higher the stakes, the more extreme forms of conduct emerged.

The influx of wealth, not least in the form of plunder and Greek cultural resources, also resulted in increased societal differentiation.[135] Likewise certain types of activity often of Greek provenance emerged or gained in prominence that operated according to their own logic of distinction but

---

[132] See e.g. Märtin 2012: 179–83 ('Die Magistratswahlen als Austragungsort erbitterter Konkurrenz') or Beck 2016: 136–9.

[133] Tac. *Ann.* 3.55.2–3; Beck 2016: 149–50; Jehne 2016: 195–9; Dubois-Pelerin 2008: 43; Bottiglieri 2016. This situation ended up ruining several, often old and renowned, Roman families: La Penna 1990: 284.

[134] Veyne 1990: 208–10. Historiographers like to single out notable victories as pivotal for setting in motion decadence and decline. See e.g. Liv. 39.6, who fingers the return of Manlius Vulso's army from the Greek East in 187 BCE as the catalyst for the spread of luxury in Rome.

[135] Märtin 2012.

Introduction

interlocked with the economics of status.[136] Rome's elite understood the benefits of training in rhetoric, began to appreciate the potential of a range of literary genres for self-promotion or promotion by others, such as poets, who could offer a certain form of textual immortality in addition to the traditional media of commemoration and realised the spectacular impact they could achieve with acts of civic generosity suitably enhanced by Greek cultural imports, such as theatrical performances based on sophisticated literary scripts.[137] Imperial exploitation generated wealth of such magnitude that the civic community could, in 167 BCE, even do away with the *tributum* – a radical change in Rome's fiscal regime that had been in place for centuries: *prima facie* this decision ensured that all of the civic community benefited from the proceeds of empire – but it also meant that a significant and influential segment of the population that had previously supported Rome's war efforts financially lost political leverage, with unforeseen ramifications for the dynamics of elite competition and the interactions between the elite and the wider populace.[138]

The seismic tremors that went through Rome's political economy and their impact on the economics of status

---

[136] For the dynamics and complexities of 'Greece in Rome' see e.g. Gruen 1990; 1992; Flaig 1999; and esp. Gotter 2000; 2001; 2003b; 2008; further Bernard 2018b: 9–10, who discusses monetisation as an early form of Hellenisation, emphasising more generally the essential point that 'for Romans as for others, Greek cultural elements provided local elites with a political tool for intra-community competition'. This is an important insight: when elite Romans refer to elements of Greek culture, more often than not the point at issue was not Greece 'as such' but tussles *within* Rome's political elite: what 'Greece' or 'the Greeks' were made to signify in Roman discourse – from expression of Philhellenism to fits of xenophobia – was primarily a matter of strategic choice and pragmatic expedience, shaped above all by how a particular Roman wanted to position himself vis-à-vis his fellow Romans. This fact also explains how aristocrats who eagerly embraced Greek cultural resources at one level could at the same time speak out against Greek influence at Rome at another: Cato the Elder, with his innovative use of Greek genres and ideas (not flagged up as such, of course) on the one hand and his vitriol against the allegedly corrosive influence of Greek figures and culture on the other, is a case in point.

[137] See further Gildenhard 2003 (on epic as a new medium of immortality); 2010 (on Greek-inspired dramatic performances).

[138] See Tan 2017.

Ingo Gildenhard and Cristiano Viglietti

provoked counter-reactions that tried to enforce or at least encourage (a minimum of) moderation. In the first half of the second century, preoccupation with material sobriety intensified in line with the hike in available resources. It is the phase in Roman history when debates over the nature and boundaries of consumption and expenditure reached their acme.[139] Insistence on (imaginary) ancestral *mores* in contradistinction to the corrupting influence of foreign wealth and the indulgence in luxuries begins to play a distinctive role in the self-promotion of certain members of Rome's senatorial elite. This period also saw a host of legislative measures designed to rein in the acquisition of wealth and its use within the economics of political rank and standing. Prominent targets included conspicuous consumption (sumptuary laws), illegal vote buying (*de ambitu*) or extreme forms of provincial exploitation (*de repetundis*).[140] Banquets attracted special attention, perhaps because they could be perceived as a form of private indulgence and were thus particularly vulnerable to moralising caveats.[141] None of these measures had much, if anything to do with economic thrift per se – though they either explicitly or implicitly appealed to alleged ancestral self-restraint (whether enforced or voluntary) as a normative benchmark to promote or enforce moderation in the use of material resources, above all by members of the senatorial elite.[142]

Newly domesticated literary genres offered media for reflection on what was happening and produced genre-specific

---

[139] La Penna 1990; Coudry 2004; Dubois-Pelerin 2008; Nichols 2010; Venturini 2016.

[140] See Coudry 2012: 512–13: Annexe. Tableau récapitulatif des lois somptuaires, a chronological survey from the *Lex Orchia* of 182 BCE to the *Lex Julia* of 18 BCE, with brief indications of the proposer, our sources and the content (and abrogation). For further bibliography, see note 67 above. Venturini 2004: 582 rightly notes 'una certa convergenza funzionale tra la stessa legislazione de ambitu e quella de repetundis'.

[141] Coudry 2004: 152–7. On the originality of Roman sumptuary laws, see Coudry 2004: 137–40; 2016; Venturini 2016. It remains a matter of debate to what extent legislation targeting private banquets affected elite customs and reconfigured forms of food consumption.

[142] Clemente 1981: 4–11; Coudry 2004: 144–8 and 159–60; 2016; Dubois-Pelerin 2008: 86–91; 2016; Arena 2011: 464, 470–4; Tchernia 2011: 205–17; Andreau and Coudry 2016; Beck 2016: 132–6, 139–43; Jehne 2016: 192–4; Venturini 2016.

58

Introduction

participant observers across all social strata, from the low (Plautine comedy) to the high (senators writing history). Awareness of – and fun with – (changing) *mores* is co-extensive with Greek-inspired Latin literature, as a famous passage from Plautus' comedy *Trinummus* illustrates (1028–45):[143]

STA: utinam ueteres homin<um mor>es, ueteres parsimoniae
 potius <in> maiore honore hic essent quam mores mali!
CHAR: di immortales, basilica hicquidem facinora inceptat loqui!   1030
 uetera quaerit, uetera amare hunc more maiorum scias.
STA: nam nunc mores nihili faciunt quod licet nisi quod lubet:
 ambitio iam more sancta est, libera est a legibus;
 scuta iacere fugereque hostis more habent licentiam:
 petere honorem pro flagitio more fit.   1035
CHAR: morem improbum!
STA: strenuiores praeterire more fit.
CHAR: nequam quidem!
STA: mores leges perduxerunt iam in potestatem suam,
 magisque is sunt obnoxiosae quam ... parentes liberis.
 eae miserae etiam ad parietem sunt fixae clauis ferreis,
 ubi malos mores affigi nimio fuerat aequius.   1040
CHAR: lubet adire atque appellare hunc; uerum ausculto perlubens
 et metuo, si compellabo, ne aliam rem occipiat loqui.
STA: neque istis quicquam lege sanctum est: leges mori seruiunt,
 mores autem rapere properant qua sacrum qua publicum.
CHAR: hercle istis malam rem magnam moribus dignum est dari.   1045

STA: I wish people's old customs and their old thriftiness were in greater honour here rather than bad customs!
CHAR: (aside) Immortal gods, he's beginning to talk about matters of state! He's looking for the old ways, you can see that he loves the old ways according to our forefathers' customs.
STA: Yes, customs nowadays don't care for what's allowed, only for what's pleasurable: bribery is now sanctioned by custom and free from the laws; through custom people think they have the freedom to throw their shields away and flee from the enemy. Through custom, public office is sought as a reward for criminal behaviour.

---

[143] We cite the text and translation of W. de Melo in the Loeb Classical Library. For discussion see e.g. Earl 1960: 237–8; Blösel 2000: 29–35 and Richlin 2017: 342, who notes that 'the long rant ... on the degenerate morals of today is undercut by the fact that [the slave Stasimus] is drunk, and by his eavesdropping owner's pious interjections'. On the notions of *mos, mores* and *mos maiorum* more generally see e.g. Bettini 2000; Blösel 2000; Hölkeskamp 2004.

Ingo Gildenhard and Cristiano Viglietti

CHAR: (aside) An indecent custom!
STA: Through custom it happens that they don't elect their betters.
CHAR: (aside) Awful!
STA: Customs have now brought the laws into their power, and the laws are more under their thumb than ... parents are under that of their children. Those wretched laws are even fastened to the walls with iron nails, where it would have been much fairer to fasten bad customs.
CHAR: (aside) I wish to approach and address him; but I listen to him with great pleasure and I'm afraid that if I address him, he'll begin talking about something else.
STA: Nothing is laid down as binding by law for them. The laws are slaves to custom, while customs hurry to carry off everything both sacred and profane.
CHAR: (aside) Those customs really ought to be given a big thrashing.

The passage works the difference between ancestral and modern customs, the former invariably good, the latter depraved, and contrasts the thriftiness allegedly cherished in the past (*parsimonia*) with the desire or licence (*licentia*) in the pursuit of pleasure or political ambition (*ambitio*) rampant now. While Plautus' plays are located in a Greek milieu, the passage also offers a sly take on the contemporary situation at Rome. Members of the ruling elite also engaged in various forms of literary commentary. Historiographical genres in particular afforded a perfect medium to plot historical developments on a large chronological scale as background for reflections on current affairs – and many senators began both to immortalise themselves and their deeds and to moralise about the present state of Roman society, taking turns in identifying the moment in time when the floodgates of luxury truly opened.[144] The option to pattern Roman history as a story of decline found many takers – suggesting such stories appealed to a reasonably large readership. Lament about the present and invocation of a better past will no doubt have sounded particularly plausible and attractive to those who were experiencing anxiety and disquiet over perceived threats to their relative rank and standing.

---

[144] See Edwards 1993: 176–8 for a survey of possibilities.

Introduction

As we already had occasion to note, for the history of Roman frugality Cato the Elder proved to be a uniquely inventive and influential trendsetter, in both discursive and institutional terms. Moderation in the transformation of wealth into power was a central aspect of his self-fashioning;[145] and he tried his best to rally support for acts of collective abstention as well. In his public oratory, notably the speech in defence of the Rhodians, he argued passionately for a policy of imperial self-restraint, warning of the dangers of arrogance (*superbia*).[146] He got involved in debates over sumptuary legislation as in his opposition to the repeal of the *Lex Oppia* in 195 BCE;[147] and he used his stint as censor for high-profile interventions.[148] In his writings, Roman frugality also experienced a strategic geographical displacement: deeming Rome itself to have become a morass of Greek-inspired luxury and immorality, Cato looked to the surrounding ethnicities for proper discipline and, lo and behold, found it in the countryside where he himself grew up:[149]

In the work of the Elder Cato, we have ... the tentative beginnings of the long history of the location of moral excellence within the Sabine countryside. Defeated and subsequently enfranchised by Rome, the Sabines came to lose their barbarian, luxurious aspect in Roman eyes. Their remaining hint

---

[145] See e.g. Cat. *orat.* 173 M³: *numquam ego pecuniam neque meam neque sociorum per ambitionem dilargitus sum.*

[146] Cat. *orat.* 163 M³.

[147] In his reimagination of this speech Livy aligns Cato's argument for self-restraint with patriarchy (34.4–7). More generally, one of the reasons that rendered the invective trope of luxury (and the corresponding ideal of frugality and hard work) so compelling was that it fed into models of identity and self-definition that operated with satisfyingly simple binaries and relied on widespread preconceptions and prejudices about such binaries as past | present, ideal | real, self | other, West | East, norm | transgression, stability | change, order | chaos, virtue | vice, male | female. See further Zanda 2011: 4: 'if luxury makes a man effeminate it is because luxury is feminine and a threat to what is proper and masculine: strength and simplicity.'

[148] Astin 1978. It is worth noting, though, that during his time in office he used public revenues to immortalise himself in Rome's cityscape.

[149] Dench 1998: 139. In addition, Cato endowed his specifically Roman–Sabine frugality with a broader ethnic significance by differentiating his (ideal) Romans from the Greeks (building on the similar contrast between Romans and Samnites). See Petrocheilos 1974: 57: 'The standard of *mores antiqui*, with its insistence on frugality and its rejection of luxury, is thus the basis of the distinction which the Romans draw between their own national character and that of the Greeks.'

of distinctness and outsider quality no longer a threat, they were treated within Roman ideology as a sub-group of Rome within which moral excellence could conveniently be located. Already in a fragment of a speech by Cato the Elder, the Sabine landscape had been converted into an unequivocally rough one, a suitable environment for *parsimonia, duritia*, and *industria*.

Cato, then, deserves to be recognised for giving frugality a prominent place in efforts to redefine what it is to be Roman in the fast-paced decades after the Second Punic War. He made the need for individual and collective self-restraint a key element in a new political language, as Laure Passet argues in Chapter 3: 'Frugality as a Political Language in the Second Century BCE: The Strategies of Cato the Elder and Scipio Aemilianus'. In her contribution, Cato emerges as the 'inventor' not of frugality per se, but a novel ethos of principled thrift and pride in peasant parsimony that responds to the specific historical circumstances at the time, defined as they were by the massive and unprecedented influx of war spoils and other riches into Rome. Passet explores how Cato turned aspects of prudent and parsimonious husbandry as allegedly practised by earlier generations of Roman peasants into a normative benchmark for all Romans, and in particular members of the senatorial elite and endowed his vision with authoritative and exemplary force by projecting it back into an unspecified past. For the first time, he proceeded with the help of literary genres made in Greece that enabled entirely new levels of nuance and sophistication and gave his views a permanent presence in Roman public discourse. But his reconfiguration of material moderation as an ancestral ideal also met with fierce resistance: as Passet points out, his adversaries branded the degree of austerity he advocated as over the top, a paradoxical form of 'excessive self-restraint' indicative of the repellent outlook of a miser and the vice of greed; but it also opened up novel modes of aristocratic self-promotion that operated in both elective affinity and deliberate contrast to those of Cato. Specifically, Passet analyses how P. Cornelius Scipio Aemilianus aligns himself in some respects with the Catonian persona but distances himself from it in others, not

Introduction

least in his explicit if partial embrace of Greek culture – or rather those aspects of Greek culture that could be presented as compatible with Roman tradition.[150]

The way in which frugal values were brought into play on both sides of an ideological tussle over the nature of Rome's political economy attest to their continuing force also in subsequent decades. In the speeches addressed to the censors and the people upon his return from Sardinia (124 BCE), Gaius Gracchus was keen to promote himself as the physical embodiment of self-restraint, both at home and on campaign, in matters to do with money and matters to do with sex, as a way of signalling that he always placed the people and the public interest before his personal ambitions and desires; his rhetoric contrasts aristocratic self-interest and indulgence with an ideology of moderation and public service.[151] And yet, when he proposed his agrarian legislation, his opponents branded him as a spendthrift maverick intent on wasting public money to advance his political ambitions. His adversaries thus also found it expedient to march under the banner of frugality, none more so than L. Calpurnius Piso Frugi who adopted the very attribute as his *agnomen*.[152] Thrift and self-restraint were values that individuals of various political persuasions wished to claim for themselves, even if they meant different things – an ideological rift also detectable in the contested notion of *libertas*.[153]

The developments within Rome's political economy in the decades after the Second Punic War also had profound

---

[150] See now also Harders 2017. The contrastive styles of Cato the Elder and Scipio Aemilianus offer the possibility for creative syntheses, an opportunity taken up, above all, by Cicero. See van der Blom 2010: 230–3.

[151] C. Graccus frs. 23 (= Plu. *CG* 23.6–10) and 26–8 (= Gel. 15.12.1–4) *ORF*[3].

[152] With this act of inventive nomenclature, *frugi*, hitherto used almost exclusively with reference to persons of low social status (in particular slaves and freedmen), for the first time entered into the upper echelons of Roman society: see Chapter 5 (Gildenhard). For the clash between Gracchus and Frugi within Rome's political economy see Tan 2017: 166. Roth 2019 discusses how the Gracchan land reforms may have affected local elites. Grain distribution remained a live-wire issue in the following decades. See most recently Rising 2019 on P. Clodius' *lex frumentaria* of 58 BCE.

[153] Arena 2012.

Ingo Gildenhard and Cristiano Viglietti

repercussions on economic activity broadly conceived, perhaps even triggering an 'economic revolution'.[154] In Chapter 4: 'Smallholding, Frugality and Market Economy in the Gracchan Age', Mattia Balbo reconsiders the transformation of smallholding in the late second century BCE. His discussion focuses chiefly on landholding during the years dominated by the Gracchi (133–120 BCE), with a specific emphasis on the recurrence of frugal ideals in the political debate arising from the Gracchan reforms and the role of smallholdings in the face of significant changes brought about by the emergence of large market-oriented estates and related developments, such as the rise in the price of land, increase in the number of slaves, the consequences of imperial plunder and tax-farming and the management of the grain supply and subsidies. Importantly, the chapter pays equal attention to the ideological framework that defined smallholding in the Gracchan age and its practical consequences.

The Rome of the Nobility (III)

As the chapters by Rich, Passet and Balbo demonstrate, by the end of the republic a complex discourse had evolved over different kinds of wealth and expenditure. Public speakers clashed over the (excessive) use of private resources for private pleasure, the (inordinate) use of public resources by magistrates and the use of (lavish) private resources for either the benefit of the wider civic community or to gain an illegal advantage in the competition for political status (or both). Yet precisely what counted as *luxuria*, what as *liberalitas* and what as *largitio/ambitus* depended on the political position and ideological preferences of the observer.[155] And if already the

---

[154] Kay 2014.

[155] Cf. Edwards 1993: 200–4: 'The distinction between prodigality and liberality was not always easy to draw', though this phrasing implies that the possibility to draw such a distinction 'objectively' in principle existed. In our sources, however, these terms are always heavily contested, and what one aristocrat would peddle, without difficulty, as *liberalitas*, another would brand just as easily as *luxuria* or *largitio*. The question of who was 'right' was frequently resolved in court, where the best spinner won (see below) – and also registers in rhetoric liable to incite violence:

64

Introduction

opposition between luxury and self-restraint is far from self-evident, the contrast between *liberalitas* and self-restraint is even more difficult to negotiate: both are values – and potentially at variance with one another. This situation enabled resourceful individuals to either wave the banner of *liberalitas* or fly the frugality flag as the occasion demanded. The ensuing complexities – nicely illustrated by Cicero – are worth exploring in some detail since they continue to shape Rome's cultural imaginary also in imperial times.

When L. 'Sleaze' Murena, one of the designated consuls for 62 BCE, was accused of electoral bribery, i.e. of violating restraint requirements in his desire to achieve political success: a case of excessive *ambitio* crossing over into illegal *ambitus*, Cicero came to his aid with an anti-austerity diatribe. Speaking as part of the defence, he faced the awkward situation that the prosecution, which featured Sulpicius Rufus, known above all for his juridical expertise, and also included Mr. Political Morality himself, Cato the Younger, stood for exemplary self-restraint, ancestral virtue and law-abiding citizenship. Cato, in fact, was frugality squared: as a descendant of Cato the Elder, *parsimonia* was born and bred into his DNA, which he fortified further by adopting the dogmatic austerity of Stoic philosophy on top. Yet rather than ceding the moral high ground to the prosecution, Cicero tackles the problem head-on, arguing that his esteemed opponents labour under a fundamental and embarrassing misconception of how moderation works at Rome. By lambasting both (excessive) austerity and (excessive) indulgence, he puts a limit on luxury *and* sobriety in staking out a complex middle ground for the use of wealth within the cultural and socio-political dynamics of the city. With this golden mean as benchmark, his client emerges not just as whitewashed of any wrongdoing but as a true Roman upholding the *mos maiorum*, whereas Cato the Younger's self-righteous parsimony stands unexpectedly revealed as alien and perverse.

C. Fannius (*cos.* 122), for instance, rebukes what he considers *largitio* on the part of C. Gracchus as the hallmark of a tyrant (*ORF*[3] Fannius fr. 6 and 7).

The strategy runs through the entire speech, culminating in paragraphs 74–6 where Cicero transmogrifies the frugality of Cato the Younger from a virtue into a vice. Several conceptual ploys underwrite this remarkable sleight of hand. First, picking up on and inverting Cato's line of attack that canvassing of votes through the provision of pleasures and public entertainment violates the dignity of the consulship and the Roman people, he fingers the position adopted by his opponent as foreign in origin and outlook, imported from Sparta – and utterly out of line with Roman practice, customs and civilisation itself.[156] Greece, as is well known, is a country of excess. Yet if elsewhere it tends to be associated with excessive indulgence in pleasure, here it is made to stand for excessive austerity. But neither the Spartans, whom Cato has unwisely chosen as his model in life and speech (*Mur.* 74: *Lacedaemonii, auctores istius uitae atque orationis*) nor the similarly austere Cretans proved a match to the Romans on the battlefield. The Romans, then, are the civilisation that knows best how to administer its public affairs, not least by dividing time between pleasure and work (*Mur.* 74: *Romani homines qui tempora uoluptatis laborisque dispertiunt …*)! Put differently, Cicero here dismisses the causal link between degrees of austerity and degrees of (martial) *uirtus* or sound government to which the theorists of decadence are so beholden: despite the fact that the Romans are less severe and self-denying than the Spartans, they nevertheless run a superior *res publica* and army.

Once he has painted Cato into a Greek corner he keeps him there. In a second line of attack, he brings into play the *exemplum* of Tubero, as another member of Rome's Greek Frugality Club. When asked to provide coverings for the couches used during the funeral banquet Q. Fabius Maximus Allobrogicus was giving to the Roman people in honour of his renowned uncle Publius Africanus, Tubero misguidedly took this as an opportunity to broadcast his dedication to the frugal principles of Stoicism: he covered the Punic couches with

---

[156] *Mur.* 74: *horribilis oratio! sed eam usus, uita, mores, ciuitas ipsa respuit.*

Introduction

shabby goat skins and opted for Samian crockery that would have been more suited to the burial of the Cynic Diogenes than the funeral of the great Scipio Africanus, conqueror of Carthage. Cicero disapproves for the same reason Cato objected to Murena's alleged vote-buying: such austerity lowers the majesty of Rome. The Roman empire and those who created it deserve a certain degree of splendour, and the people, so Cicero asserts in a populist vein, were none too pleased, making Tubero pay for his *peruersa sapientia*. Despite the fact that he was a 'most upright person' (*homo integerrimus*) and an 'excellent citizen' (*ciuis optimus*) with fabulous family pedigree (just like Sulpicius, of course), he lost the election to the praetorship because of his meanness.[157] Cicero explains (*Mur.* 76):

> odit populus Romanus priuatam luxuriam, publicam magnificentiam diligit; non amat profusas epulas, sordis et inhumanitatem multo minus; distinguit rationem officiorum ac temporum, uicissitudinem laboris ac uoluptatis.

> The Roman people hate private luxury but love public splendour. They do not like extravagant banquets, but much less do they like meanness and lack of civility. They understand the rationale of obligations and circumstances and the alternation of work and pleasure.

In Rome, there was something of a 'sliding scale' between 'public' and 'private' (in our understanding of these terms). Very little an aristocrat did was devoid of political significance: not holding public office, i.e. the technical sense of Latin *priuatus* in republican time, was not the same as being politically inactive.[158] Networking (not least through banquets) and canvassing for the next *honor* on the *cursus* never stopped. For that very reason, advocates of ancestral virtues such as Cato the Elder insisted on asserting the same code of conduct across all spheres of activity, *negotium* and *otium*, whether as magistrate or *priuatus*; they did not confine the remit of thrift and self-restraint to private affairs – indeed, they would not have recognised the distinction between *publice* and *priuatim* as

---

[157] The causal link between Tubero's frugality and his electoral loss that Cicero here asserts is most likely his own invention: see Chapter 6 (Patterson): 349–50.

[158] See Russell 2016: 8–9 with further literature listed in n. 18.

Ingo Gildenhard and Cristiano Viglietti

meaningful in the first place, opposing self-aggrandising or self-indulgent expenditure tout court. *Pace* Russell et al., however, Cicero here wilfully ignores this 'sliding scale' between public and private and draws a sharp distinction that splits the phenomenon of significant expenditure into a good, public (*publica magnificentia*) and a bad, private (*priuata luxuria*) variant. What turns one into a vice and the other into a virtue are the setting and the audience: Cicero contrasts lavish outlays for personal gratification with significant investment of resources for the benefit of the wider populace.[159] It is important to stress that this distinction does not concern 'public over private wealth'.[160] The notion of *priuata luxuria* (which does not signify 'wealth' per se, but extravagant expenditure of wealth) is in fact a deliberate red herring: the question under negotiation, after all, was not Murena's self-indulgence (on which there were no legal restrictions) but whether his financial investments in the public sphere – '*publica luxuria*' as it were – for purposes of political self-promotion amounted to illegal *ambitus*. Irrelevant to the case at hand, the notion of *priuata luxuria* serves Cicero to obfuscate the real issue: the (illicit) use of *personal* resources for *political* advantage. Put differently, despite appearances the crime hides in the positive element of the binary, i.e. *publica magnificentia*.

Cicero continues his game of misdirection by proceeding to indicate 'extravagant banquests' (*profusae epulae*) as an example of *priuata luxuria*, falsely implying that lavish hospitality by candidates were of no political consequence; and instead of balancing this faux-instance of *priuata luxuria* with an example of *publica magnificentia* (as one might expect), he asserts that what the people dislike *even more* than private luxury is un-Roman meanness and lack of civility – *inhumanitas*, in particular, carries connotations of 'foreign', 'barbaric', 'savage'. This surprising move generates a staggered sequence of public preferences consisting of (a) *publica magnificentia*,

---

[159] For discussion see Adamietz 1989: 226–9; La Penna 1989: 18–23; Berno 2014: 370–2.
[160] *Pace* Harrison 2017: 177.

68

Introduction

(b) *priuata luxuria*, (c) *sordes et inhumanitas*: the people love (a), hate (b) and loathe (c). The introduction of the third term reconfigures the initial contrast in two ways. First, it qualifies the negative value of (b): excessive and immoderate indulgence (*luxuria*) is bad, but excessive and immoderate parsimony (*sordes et inhumanitas*) is worse. And secondly, there is a telling blind spot in his scheme: Cicero does not identify a positive counterpart to *publica magnificentia* for the private sphere. Where *frugalitas* might have figured, there gapes a conceptual void. Instead, he implies that the *sordes et inhumanitas* he mentions amount to vices that cover *both* the public and the private sphere.[161] The following table illustrates Cicero's conceptual scheming:

	Positive	Negative
Public	*magnificentia*	*sordes et inhumanitas*
Private		*luxuria < sordes et inhumanitas*

That the Roman people object to members of the governing class indulging in the (excessive) pursuit of private pleasure is only reasonable: they feel that the available resources ought also to be of benefit to the wider public – in line with ancestral tradition, as Cicero goes on to state (*Mur.* 77):[162]

qua re nec plebi Romanae eripiendi fructus isti sunt ludorum, gladiatorum, conuiuiorum, quae omnia maiores nostri comparauerunt, nec candidatis

---

[161] For present purposes he characterises the latter as a sphere of non-political *otium*, dedicated to relaxation and pleasure (*uoluptas*), in contrast to *labor* (*negotia*).

[162] Of the three forms of *publica magnificentia* that Cicero lists in § 76, i.e. *ludi*, gladiatorial *munera* and *conuiuia*, the first tended to be paid for by a specified amount from the state coffers, further supplemented by the private resources of the presiding magistrate, the second and third entirely by the individual in charge. As Zanda 2011: 13 notes: 'it was not the duty of a single magistrate to organise games, but of the college as a whole; on the other hand each magistrate could contribute financially as he wished … It was indeed the popularity of the games among electors that made them political acts and therefore a field for strong competition among the aristocrats.' The reference to public banquets might be a dig at Cato the Younger's ancestor, Cato the Elder, who imagined the Roman forbears at *conuiuia*.

ista benignitas adimenda est quae liberalitatem magis significat quam largitionem.

For this reason, the Roman people ought not to be robbed of the enjoyment of games, gladiatorial contests and banquets, all of which our ancestors put in place, and candidates ought not to be prevented from engaging in civic generosity, which indicates liberality rather than bribery.

If in other contexts Cicero can be absolutely scathing about popular amusements, here he is keen to label the provision of enjoyment for the Roman people a virtue (*liberalitas*) rather than a vice, let alone a crime (*largitio*) – a particularly Roman form of euergetism sanctioned by ancestral custom, which the Roman people reward with success at elections. He is of course quite right: this kind of reciprocity – material investments for immaterial returns – is indeed a key element of Rome's political culture. But once more he only skirts the actual issue at stake, namely that *liberalitas* has legally defined limits. And he blithely ignores that the imposition of such limits is also backed by ancestral tradition: *liberalitas* and the need for its moderation are two sides of the same coin, a Tweedle-dum and Tweedle-dee of Roman republican history. This brazenly skewed perspective enables him to present Tubero, Sulpicius Rufus and Cato the Younger, all with a massive chip on their shoulders about ancestral *mos*, as un-Roman: far from upholding tradition, their outlook on politics and life, so Cicero mischievously suggests, is unorthodox and alien, indeed – *horribile dictu!* – Greek. Resembling Diogenes the Cynic, they are beholden to an unnatural form of foreign wisdom, which encourages them to exercise (and to expect of others) extreme degrees of austerity in private *and* public life that lower practitioners to the level of uncivilised savages or even beasts (cf. *in-humanitas*), while yielding no apparent advantage for the military capacity of the community.

The *pro-Murena* passage thus illustrates several salient points. First, it shows that rhetorically elevated dedication to frugal living constituted a potential source of prestige in late-republican Rome – as a discursive complement to restraint legislation it was a 'political language', defined (if not invented) by such individuals as Cato the Elder, available both

70

Introduction

to his descendants (Cato the Younger) and other senators with similar inclinations (Tubero) and aligning well with the outlook of certain philosophical schools. Secondly, and conversely, austerity in the use of material resources and self-restraint in the pursuit of pleasure was potentially at variance with other values, in particular *liberalitas*, that promised greater electoral rewards. Thirdly, individuals clashed over the definition of generosity and moderation – of where to draw the line between *liberalitas* and *largitio/ambitus* or between *moderatio* and *sordes/inhumanitas*. *Exempla* are always open to contestation, and Cicero here rebukes 'frugality all the way' as an extremist position, out of line with ancestral norms: Tubero, elsewhere an exemplary specimen of venerable parsimony, here emerges as a wrong-headed deviant, led astray by the perversities of dubious Greek dogma. Fourth, this contestation frequently involves (as here) endeavours to define what it is to be Roman. For Cicero, Rome is the epitome of a *manly* civilisation – a cultural configuration that combines supreme martial prowess (*uirtus*; witness the Cretans and Spartans, conquered despite their austere discipline) with urbanity and splendour and a proper appreciation of a work–life balance (*labor* and *uoluptas*). Others (and Cicero elsewhere) offered alternative definitions, operating with 'Greece' and *luxuria* in various combinations as ciphers of difference.[163] And last but not least, the foregoing analysis shows up the complexity, often underestimated, of some of our source material. In the statement that the Roman people hate private luxury and love public splendour, which is often cited as a self-evident truism about Roman attitudes towards wealth, each individual category (*luxuria, magnificentia, priuatus, publicus*), their pairing and the phrase as a whole are implicated in Ciceronian spin and contribute to court-room polemics designed to address the exigencies of the legal case at hand, while in oblique ways engaging with, and taking a partisan position

---

[163] In many ways the more orthodox approach: Petrocheilos 1974. Cicero's stance in the *pro Murena* is unusual in this respect. For the complexities of the 'Greece/Rome' interface see the bibliography cited above n. 136.

Ingo Gildenhard and Cristiano Viglietti

on, the wider political economy, social dynamics and political culture of late-republican Rome.

While Cicero adopted an anti-austerity posture in the *pro Murena* as demanded by the occasion, elsewhere he promoted sobriety and self-restraint. In fact, as Ingo Gildenhard argues in Chapter 5, '*Frugalitas*, or: The Invention of a Roman Virtue', Cicero catalysed the ascent of the *lexeme frugalitas* to the status of a quintessential Roman virtue in the first place. The chapter looks into the absence of *frugalitas* in earlier authors (the noun does not register in our sources before the first century BCE) and traces the reasons for its rise to prominence in Cicero. This involves consideration of the adjective *frugi*: primarily used of slaves and freedmen, it was adopted, as we already had occasion to note, by Lucius Calpurnius Piso Frugi as an *agnomen*. Piso's integration of *frugi* into his nomenclature 'ennobled' the attribute and thereby facilitated Cicero's investment in the abstract noun: at two specific moments in his career, here analysed in depth, namely the speeches against Verres and the *Tusculan Disputations* (along with the speech on behalf of king Deiotarus), he found it opportune to promote *frugalitas* as a key Roman virtue, thereby setting the stage for its stellar career in imperial times and later centuries. The chapter concludes with a brief survey of the use select authors of the early empire (Horace, Valerius Maximus, Seneca the Elder, Petronius, Seneca the Younger, Quintilian and Pliny the Younger) made of *frugi, frugaliter* and *frugalitas*.

Early Empire

Rome's ruling elite ultimately failed to keep the playing field level; the concentration of extraordinary degrees of wealth and power in the hands of a few individuals generated a situation in which some could operate as 'quasi-states' (to use Michael Crawford's striking formulation).[164] Eventually, the last one

---

[164] Crawford 2008.

Introduction

of these quasi-states left standing merged with the actual state – and the Roman *res publica* became recentred in the *domus Caesaris*. The change in political regime from republic to autocracy had profound repercussions at every level, including Rome's political economy, political culture, economics of status and cultural imaginary. But the need of the emperor to cooperate with the suitably redefined senatorial collective (which constituted itself *as* a collective vis-à-vis the *princeps*)[165] also ensured significant lines of continuity with the republican centuries. The tension between the desire for self-aggrandisement through the ostentatious use of wealth and a normative discourse that frowned upon practices of material extravagance in particular for members of the senatorial elite, which defined the last two centuries of the republic, thus remained very much in force during the early empire, and in Chapter 6: 'Frugality, Building, and Heirlooms in an Age of Social Mobility' John Patterson analyses the debates over and constraints on luxury and encouragement of frugality with respect to building projects and expensive heirlooms (not least those made of silver) from the late republic to the early imperial period. His chronologically and thematically wide-ranging chapter foregrounds in particular the enhanced social mobility that civil war and autocracy introduced into Roman society, including a discussion of why provincial newcomers such as Tacitus and Pliny the Younger affected particular enthusiasm for frugality and disapproved of luxury, as a way of positioning themselves as new arrivals within the ruling class of Rome.

In many ways, members of the governing elite of the imperial period remained as fiercely competitive as they had been in republican times, continuing to vie with each other as senators and patrons in the arena of civic *liberalitas* – similar to, yet inevitably on smaller scale than, the *publica magnificentia* of the patron of the *res publica* as a whole, i.e. the emperor.[166] In addition to this unregulated form of competition they also competed with each other for positions and offices within the

---

[165] Russell 2019 with further bibliography.   [166] Eck and Heil 2005.

Ingo Gildenhard and Cristiano Viglietti

imperial hierarchy.[167] In this field, success was ultimately up to the emperor. Thus instead of contending with each other in front (and for the favour) of the people as in republican times, those with political ambition contended with each other in front (and for the favour) of the *princeps*, which meant that the forms of soliciting favour changed – from canvassing to currying, from shows of generosity to shows of loyalty. (To phrase the point cynically, to defeat a rival no longer involved bribing the electorate, but informing on him to the *princeps*.) The imperial period also saw a rise in importance of belonging to a specific status-group, visualised by means of status symbols.[168]

To some extent the various types of competition were interrelated: success or failure in the competition for official rank and standing in the imperial regime inevitably impacted on the capabilities of senators to function as patrons in their own right and vie for status in the field of conspicuous consumption. At the same time, investment in civic euergetism in Rome or elsewhere could also be a means of compensating for failure to advance in the imperial hierarchy. For these and other reasons, 'by the first century AD, conspicuous consumption and private luxury – especially in the form of feasting, housing, jewellery, collecting artworks, clothing and funerary monuments – had developed into a dominant model of status advertisement ... Prestige goods (in the widest sense) and all forms of conspicuous leisure became socially charged and gained the significance of unofficial status symbols, flouting the order of formal rank and its attendant insignia.'[169] And the banquet retained or even increased its significance within the economics of status of the imperial senate: 'There are good grounds for supposing that the entertainment of one's peers became increasingly important under the principate, as, in practice, senior magistrates came to be chosen by their fellow

---

[167] See Wallace-Hadrill 2008: 353 (and passim).
[168] Social status of senators and knights: Duncan-Jones 2016.
[169] Kuhn 2015a: 22–3.

74

Introduction

senators and the emperor, rather than by assemblies of the Roman people.'[170]

The two systems did not always align: those of the highest rank or social prestige did not necessarily have the most money to spend. The impoverished senator and the *nouveau riche* are two social types that haunt the cultural imaginary of imperial Rome – as members of the traditional elite tried to maintain the level of expenditure expected of their status and ended up ruining themselves (a phenomenon Juvenal labels *ambitiosa paupertas*: 3.182–3[171]) and the new institutional setting of the imperial court, the recruitment mechanisms for the senate and the imperial economy offered unprecedented career and enrichment opportunities for people with obscure and undistinguished backgrounds, from *homines noui* to freedmen.

For Augustus himself, strategic investment in modes of moderation helped to endow the legitimising fiction of a 'commonwealth restored' with credibility: it was a key element in the ideology of the *princeps ciuilis*, at the core of which stood the paradox of 'self-restrained omnipotence'.[172] What distinguishes the *princeps ciuilis* from the tyrant is precisely *moderatio* – deliberate abstention from *possible* indulgence in the pleasures of consumption and the *abusive* exercise of power. Augustus practised his own variant of what one could label, in the terms of Cicero's speech *pro Murena*, *publica magnificentia*, boasting that he had found a city built in brick and left it adorned in marble, as the dignity of the empire demanded (*pro maiestate imperii*).[173] Yet whereas he spent lavishly on behalf of the community in the best tradition of civic *liberalitas* (easily outperforming all other public benefactors: *Res Gestae* 15–23), he practised ostentatious self-restraint

---

[170] Edwards 1993: 202. On the Roman *conuiuium* see further Stein-Hölkeskamp 2005 and Schnurbusch 2011.

[171] Kuhn 2015a: 23, listing instances from the *Satires* where Juvenal illustrates the phenomenon with cases in point (Pollio: 9.6–8, 11.43; Ruilus: 11.1–26; Caetronius: 14.86–95). See more generally Klingenberg 2011 and Hartmann 2016: 173–8 ('Die Nöte der traditionellen Elite').

[172] Wallace-Hadrill 1982; for the importance of *moderatio* and *modestia* see further Klodt 2000.

[173] Suet. *Aug.* 28.3.

Ingo Gildenhard and Cristiano Viglietti

in his own personal style, both in terms of living conditions and his approach to governance, in the best tradition of Cato the Elder. Thus Suetonius, after a balanced account of Augustus' vices – he was in general chaste but could not resist deflowering virgins; he hated extravagance but had a passion for gambling – praises the emperor as a paragon of self-restraint, citing the view as consensual that in all other details of his life he was most temperate (*continentissimum*) and above suspicion of any fault (*sine suspicione ullius uitii*), deliberately choosing to live below his means in relatively modest quarters with rooms that, unlike the city itself, did not feature marble decorations or handsome pavements (*Aug.* 72.1).[174] It is thus tempting to resort to the trope of paradox to describe Augustan Rome:

> The projection of images of imperial Rome in the early empire involved a complex combination of two different modes of advertising success and superiority – flamboyance and self-control. ... Just as the combined flamboyance and austerity of Augustus himself could be seen to embody both models of superiority and success traditionally enacted by elite Roman males, so Augustan Rome itself embodied both the flamboyance and *urbanitas* ascribed to the Etruscans, and the moral rectitude ascribed to the Samnites.[175]

Ancestral frugality was not just part of Augustus' personal style; it also became an important aspect of his novel conception of history. Republican historiography, in both its annalistic and Sallustian incarnations, told stories of decadence and decline, of moral chaos and civil bloodshed: it was critical of its times and often pessimistic to boot. Augustus' conception

---

[174] Not everyone in his household appreciated the frugal norms he adopted and encouraged: anecdotally, his daughter Julia, advised to take the *exemplar paternae frugalitatis* to heart, retorted with a witticism that would have made Caligula proud: 'He forgets that he is Caesar, but I remember that I am Caesar's daughter.' (Macr. 2.5.8: *item cum grauem amicum audisset Iulia suadentem melius facturam si se composuisset ad exemplar paternae frugalitatis, ait, 'ille obliuiscitur Caesarem se esse, ego memini me Caesaris filiam.'*)

[175] Dench 1998: 145–6. See also Eigler 2002: 290 who notes the paradox of 'Der Prinzeps im bäuerlichen Hausrock als Initiator eines gewaltigen rein stadtbezogenen Bauprogramms in Glanz und Marmor' and goes on to explore the tension in Augustan literature, both poetry and prose, between the value of *rusticitas* in a new age of gold and urban splendour.

Introduction

of history offered an optimistic counter-vision, without denying the chaos of the recent past: after all its resolution made a vital contribution to the legitimacy of his autocratic regime. Three scripts in particular, which came with the inbuilt advantage of being compatible with the stories of decadence and decline told by moralising republican historiographers, helped Augustus to position himself and his regime in time: the notion of a historical caesura, which generated a simple binary between the civil war chaos of the recent past and the Augustan present, with internal peace and constitutional order re-established; the investment in foreign conquest and an ever-expanding empire as the true mission of the Roman people, which got temporarily derailed by moral decline leading to internal discord but had now been put back on track; and the autocratic and teleological reconfiguration of the aristocratic competition that defined Rome's ruling elite during republican times but had now found its unsurpassable endpoint in the nonpareil achievements of the *princeps*.[176]

The key quality that enabled the local community to become a global powerbroker was fierce commitment to military discipline – a constant throughout Roman history, seemingly unaffected by decadence and decline.[177] It is a plot already fully articulated by late-republican authors, in particular Cicero.[178] All Augustus had to do is to identify himself as the ultimate protagonist of the process, who overcame the temporary aberrations of the recent past.[179] As we already had occasion to note, investing in empire had the advantage of picking up on a real contradiction in the story of decline

---

[176] See Biesinger 2019; Gildenhard et al. 2019b: 27–8; Gotter 2019; Havener 2019.

[177] In his statue galleries of *summi uiri* on display in the Forum he celebrates all those who contributed to Rome's imperial expansion – even those who subsequently fought against each other in civil war: Biesinger 2019; Gotter 2019.

[178] See e.g. *S. Rosc.* 50.

[179] For early imperial variants see e.g. V. Max. 2.8 *praef.* or Sen. *Contr.* 1.6.4. In *Contr.* 2.1, Porcius Latro links *paupertas* to internal peace and stability and wealth and luxury to civil discord (2.1.1: *quietiora tempora pauperes habuimus; bella ciuilia aurato Capitolio gessimus*) and Arellius Fuscus Senior extols the virtue of poverty with reference to the fact that the people that have conquered the world venerate a lowly hut on the Capitol Hill (2.1.5: *colit etiamnunc in Capitolio casam uictor omnium gentium populus*).

told by moralising moaners: despite what some of the historiographers claimed on the premise that *luxuria* enfeebles and emasculates, there is no evidentiary basis for a causal connection between the influx of wealth and the loss of martial prowess: the period in which Rome supposedly succumbed to Eastern luxury coincided with the addition of vast swathes of conquered territory.

For various reasons Augustus and his ideologues endowed archaic Rome with special significance. To begin with, the return to the very beginning and the choice of Romulus as one of the emperor's historical alter egos (alongside the other foundational figure of Aeneas) generated a compelling plot that linked the point of departure and the final destination of the teleology that had Rome rise from humble beginnings to world empire under Augustus. Secondly, the focus on the archaic period helped to keep rustic modes of moderation relevant for an age of blissful abundance: in a quickly changing world, what remained the same was a set of 'peasant values', in particular military discipline, material sobriety and self-restraint. The frugal rusticity of Rome's foundational period thus offered both continuing inspiration for, but also an important contrast to, the present (may the virtues continue to thrive, while the original city, with its humble huts and muddy marshes, has been transformed into a proper world capital of imperial splendour), a combination that resonates in various keys across the literature of the period. And thirdly, pushing the 'age of thrift' back from 'the republic of the ancestors' to include the foundation period further marginalised the republican centuries when the now disenfranchised nobility had its heydays and the family of the *princeps* remained obscure.[180]

Combining the celebration of golden age abundance and imperial success with a celebration of domestic discipline and self-restraint also helped to address the need to hammer out a *modus uiuendi* between the emperor and members of the traditional ruling elite. Ostentatious moderation on the part of the

---

[180] See variously Eigler 2002; Gildenhard 2007; Price 2019.

Introduction

emperor facilitated interaction between him and the senate – and found ritual expression in the performance of *recusatio*, i.e. the rejection of honours offered.[181] Since in principle the *princeps* can do anything, his embrace of limits had to be self-motivated – whereas his very presence 'moderated' other members of the ruling elite: this was part of his *raison d'être*. Many of course will have harboured the desire to become *princeps* themselves, as the long list of attempts at usurpation throughout the imperial period shows;[182] but such exceptional circumstances apart (important as they are in revealing the socio-political dynamics of the imperial regime), in everyday practice the new autocratic normal imposed a glass ceiling on senatorial ambition and on how high a senator could rise in the economics of status, whether through emulative expenditure or other means.

Different emperors adopted different policies in their interaction with the senatorial elite. Beyond advertising his own commitment to thrift and self-restraint, Augustus took a pro-active approach in helping to define the identity and enhance the group cohesion of the upper classes and in particular the senate. He helped individuals who had fallen on rough times and were no longer able to meet the census requirement by allowing them to preserve their status nevertheless; he assumed the office of *praefectus morum*, the imperial variant of the censorship;[183] and he passed pieces of restraint legislation, perhaps in the tradition of Sulla.[184] Augustus even extended the remit of such measures to areas that had been considered off-limits during the republic: the frosty reception of his *Lex Iulia et Papia Poppaea*, which struck below the belt, demonstrates that his target audience did not always appreciate his efforts.[185]

Tiberius, for one, cottoned on to the fact that an emperor's legislative insistence on senatorial moderation could well be considered an *im*moderate use of imperial power. At various

---

[181] See e.g. Huttner 2004; Freudenburg 2014.
[182] For the phenomenon and its enabling conditions see Flaig 1992.
[183] See above n. 72. [184] Baltrusch 1989: 93–6.
[185] See Zanda 2011: 60–9 for a discussion of this measure as a sumptuary law.

Ingo Gildenhard and Cristiano Viglietti

moments in his reign, we capture programmatic attempts to imitate and emulate Augustan moderation, to show that he was even more *ciuilis* than his predecessor, starting with the way he ascended to the throne. The drama that unfolded in the senate in 16 CE, when Tiberius, after having already secured the full support of the imperial army, initially refused to accept the emperorship and explored various forms of power-sharing, can be read as an attempt to re-enact and outdo the grandiose moment in 27 BCE when Octavian ceded all power to the senate only to have it returned to him with the honorary title of Augustus on top.[186] His decision to do away with sumptuary legislation seems to have followed a similar logic.[187] Whatever noble motives might inform such legal measures, they nevertheless constituted a form of autocratic encroachment on senatorial freedom (and be it the freedom to ruin themselves). Paradoxes ensue: by not imposing restraints on others, Tiberius exercised self-restraint (yet in competitive emulation of his illustrious predecessor), even though he thereby enabled members of the elite to spend *im*moderately, for all they are worth, up to and including the destruction of their patrimony. But then again, by not putting a cap on one type of senatorial competition (conspicuous consumption), he simultaneously moderated another type: informing on those in breach of the law as a way of demonstrating loyalty to the *princeps* in return for imperial favours. Tacitus notes that one of the reasons why Tiberius refused to pass sumptuary legislation was his unwillingness to deal with accusers who were licking their chops at the prospect of denouncing transgressions and concedes that Tiberius, by not criminalising luxury, exercised *moderatio*.[188]

If Tiberius embraced *parsimonia* and *moderatio* in an attempt to garner credit for *ciuilitas*, his successor vaunted deliberate transgression and defiance of proto-republican norms to celebrate the boundless nature of imperial power.

---

[186] Tac. *Ann.* 1.4–15.
[187] Tac. *Ann.* 3.52.2–54.5; Suet. *Tib.* 28; 42–4 with Wallace-Hadril 2008: 330–3, to whose brilliant analysis this paragraph is much indebted.
[188] Tac. *Ann.* 3.56.1: *Tiberius, fama moderationis parta, quod ingruentis accusatores represserat, mittit litteras ad senatum ...*

80

Introduction

Calling a spade a spade, Caligula is said to have used an aspect of Rome's frugality discourse to draw a sharp distinction between himself and everyone else, the emperor and his subjects – in particular in the area of lavish expenditure and conspicuous consumption (Suet. *Cal.* 37.1):[189]

nepotatus sumptibus omnium prodigorum ingenia superauit, commentus nouum balnearum usum, portentosissima genera ciborum atque cenarum, ut calidis frigidisque unguentis lauaretur, pretiosissima margarita aceto liquefacta sorberet, conuiuis ex auro panes et obsonia apponeret, aut frugi hominem esse oportere dictitans aut Caesarem.

In reckless extravagance he outdid the prodigals of all times in ingenuity, inventing a new sort of baths and unnatural varieties of food and feasts; for he would bathe in hot or cold perfumed oils, drink pearls of great price dissolved in vinegar, and set before his guests loaves and prepared dishes of gold, declaring that a man ought either to be frugal or Caesar.

Caligula's pronouncement, in its implied opposition of *luxuria* and *frugalitas*, recognises the semantic expansion of *frugi* initiated by L. Calpurnius Piso Frugi (*cos.* 133 BCE), which involved an ideology of aristocratic self-restraint. But he gives this a malicious twist by reaffirming the original association of *frugi* with slaves. From his perspective, the only social distinction that truly matters runs between the emperor, who lives according to his own rules (the most basic being that there aren't any) and everyone else, who are notionally subservient to the *princeps* and ought accordingly abide by a slave code of conduct.[190] The extreme forms of power-play, subjection and notional enslavement supposedly practised by Caligula could hardly be outdone.[191] Caligula's brutal frankness renders it

---

[189] For passages from Suetonius we cite the translation of J. C. Rolfe in the Loeb Classical Library, at times adjusted.

[190] The nexus between the power to command, to do what one sees fit, and a particular conception of freedom (and its opposite) has tradition in Rome. In one of his speeches Scipio Aemilianus articulated a republican variant of the link between *imperium* and *libertas*, though he still saw fit to embed the exercise of power within a legitimising ethics: *ex innocentia nascitur dignitas, ex dignitate honor, ex honore imperium, ex imperio libertas* (*ORF*[3] fr. 32).

[191] For the question of what accounts for Caligula's behaviour – was it method or madness? – see Winterling 2011, who identifies the method in the apparent madness.

81

Ingo Gildenhard and Cristiano Viglietti

apparent that elite self-restraint was not just a voluntary choice in imperial times but inevitably involved an element of (autocratic) compulsion.

Claudius, who, before becoming *princeps*, had virtually no opportunities to distinguish himself in the economics of status, unsurprisingly returned to the modes of moderation pioneered by Augustus[192] – an approach to imperial self-promotion that earned him the deftly paradoxical label *iactator ciuilitatis*, i.e. someone boastfully conceited about his self-restrained omnipotence.[193] At the same time, he seems to have looked into re-establishing the traditional role of the *princeps* as offering guidance to other members of the elite: he revived the censorship;[194] and developed a finely scaled 'currency of honour' across all segments of Roman society that had its centre in loyalty to the emperor.[195]

With Nero, the pendulum swung again: he pursued a politics of theatrical extravagance and embraced elements of Greek culture (especially mythology) in his imperial image-making that looked (or could be made to look) luxurious and decadent especially in retrospect: hostile commentators spotted signs of tyrannical incontinence in desperate need of *moderatio*.[196] In his 'plausible and well-constructed invective', Suetonius nastily suggests that Nero found inspiration for what he rebuked as unhinged profligacy in the precedent set by his uncle Caligula (*Nero* 30.1):[197]

diuitiarum et pecuniae fructum non alium putabat quam profusionem, sordidos ac deparcos esse quibus impensarum ratio constaret, praelautos uereque magnificos qui abuterentur ac perderent. laudabat mirabaturque

---

[192] Kuhn 2015b: 211: 'Unter dem Eindruck der Despotie des Caligula gegenüber der Senatsaristokratie war es ein Gebot der Stunde, an die augusteische Praxis der *recusatio* und *civilitas* wieder anzuknüpfen und Ideale wie *moderatio, modestia* und *comitas* zu verkörpern, um sich nicht des Verdachts herrscherlicher Überheblichkeit auszusetzen.'

[193] Suet. *Cl.* 35.1.

[194] Suet. *Cl.* 16. See Hurley 2001: 127–8 with further bibliography.

[195] Kuhn 2015b. The phrase 'currency of honour' is from Lendon 1997 (cited by Kuhn 2015b: 227).

[196] For the positive rationale of Nero's imperial style, which in the early phases of his reign made him one of the most popular emperors, see Champlin 2003.

[197] Barton 1994: 58.

82

Introduction

auunculum Gaium nullo magis nomine, quam quod ingentis a Tiberio relictas opes in breui spatio prodegisset.

He thought that there was no other way of enjoying riches and money than by riotous extravagance, declaring that only stingy and niggardly fellows kept a correct account of what they spent, while the fine and genuinely magnificent wasted and squandered. Nothing in his uncle Gaius so excited his envy and admiration as the fact that he had in so short a time run through the vast wealth which Tiberius had left him.

Galba, Otho and Vitellius, despite the brevity of their reigns, also managed to flaunt distinctive takes on the protocols of imperial moderation – or so Suetonius suggests. He portrays Galba as nothing if not inconsistent already before he ascended to the throne and then on it;[198] and his inability to find the proper *modus* manifested itself in excessive *seueritas* and the vices of savagery (*saeuitia*) and greed (*auaritia*) – as well as pointless parsimony (12–13), a niggardly haughtiness that ultimately cost him the loyalty of the legions when he denied the soldiers their expected donative (16).[199] Otho is said to have shown remarkable *moderatio* and *abstinentia* during his ten-year stint as quaestor in the province of Lusitania, which also marked his approach to the exercise of power.[200] Conversely, Vitellius is imagined to have used his time on the throne to establish himself as the physical embodiment of excess in the tradition of Nero (cf. Suet. *Vit.* 11.2), appointing a freedman with the telling name of Asiaticus as 'master of ceremonies' (12.1). His two greatest vices are said to have consisted in *luxuria* and *saeuitia*, and Suetonius pictures him spending his days alternating between feasting at the table and feasting his eyes on executions.[201]

---

[198] Suet. *Gal.* 9.1: *per octo annos uarie et inaequabiliter prouinciam rexit, primo acer et uehemens et in coercendis quidem delictis uel immodicus* and 14.2: *modo acerbior parciorque, modo remissior ac neglegentior quam conueniret principi electo atque illud aetatis.*

[199] For Galba's approach to imperial governance, by which he managed to alienate all the other constituencies in the Roman field of power, see Flaig 1992: 293–6.

[200] Suet. *Otho* 3.2.

[201] Suet. *Vit.* 13–14, esp. 14.2: ... *quendam ... coram interfici iussit, uelle se dicens pascere oculos.* Cf. Plin. *Nat.* 35.163; Tac. *Hist.* 1.62; 2.62, 95.

Nero's cultivation of a certain degree of spectacular extravagance and Vitellius' reputation for debauched cruelty set the stage for Vespasian, who was all but forced to tap into the prestige of frugality as a source of political authority owing to his obscure and 'humble' background: 'The Flavian dynasty faced formidable challenges at its inception, stemming in no small part from its relative *ignobilitas*.'[202] Vespasian chose Augustus as his model but went even further in terms of validating material sobriety and peasant values: he consciously highlighted his common background as an index of virtue, not least in the visual sphere.[203] If the first *princeps* opted for an eternally youthful classicism, Vespasian adopted a different visual idiom that embraced the lack of public recognition his family had historically achieved by associating humble origins and modest means with the experience of manual labour, distinguished public service and peasant discipline.[204] Vespasian's endorsement of frugal values (in the tradition of *homines noui*, especially those of Sabine background!) contrasts with the ostentatious display and moral depravity of the last scion of the Julio-Claudian dynasty: in him, we get the imperial variant of Cato the Elder's self-promotion. As all emperors, Vespasian of course continued the tradition of imperial *liberalitas*, most spectacularly with the construction of the Colosseum on the same site where portions of Nero's Golden House had stood. By replacing one type of building that could easily be stigmatised, in the terms of Cicero's *pro Murena*, as the petrified version of *priuata luxuria*, by another type that through its very purpose broadcast *publica magnificentia*, he wove his imperial ideology, which combined personal parsimony with civic generosity, into the very fabric of the city.[205]

In his excursus on luxury at *Annals* 3.55, Tacitus stops his historical survey with the novel restraint introduced by

---

[202] Tuck 2016: 109. On the public image of the Flavians, see also the other chapters in Zissos 2016, esp. Wood 2016.
[203] For Vespasian's *imitatio Augusti* see Rosso 2009.
[204] Tuck 2016 with further bibliography.
[205] For buildings (in particular the *Domus Aurea*) and 'the rhetoric of imperial degeneracy' see Elsner 1994.

Introduction

Vespasian, but includes a gesture to his own times, within general musings about historical processes.[206] While he consistently paints black in black when chronicling the decline and fall of the Julio-Claudian dynasty, his tone suddenly brightens in his glimpse forward – very much in the spirit of the preface to his *Histories*, where he hails the principate of Nerva and Trajan for having re-established proto-republican freedom. It is also the time of a seemingly new variant of emperorship where any excellent citizen is an adoption away from the throne – including (perhaps above all?) those *noui homines* from the *municipia*, the colonies and the provinces who brought their virtuous lifestyle, their *domestica parsimonia* with them into the imperial senate – like Tacitus himself.[207] To what extent we are dealing with an actual 'change in Roman manners and society' is a matter for debate – but doubts are in order, and not just because of the blatant self-interest by which Tacitus identifies the group he happens to be a member of as a positive force in history.[208] Frugality in the form of *parsimonia* (Tacitus) or *frugalitas* (Pliny the Younger) certainly offered ambitious and literary gifted members of the

---

[206] On this important passage see further Chapter 6 (Patterson): 365–6.

[207] Cf. Tac. *Ann.* 3.56.3.

[208] Rutherford 1989: 78, cited with cautious approval by Woodman and Martin 1996: 401. One should also consider the possibility that Tacitus here reworks Plin. *Pan.* 44–6, which operates with the same cluster of ideas. Pliny too argues that the emperor is more effective in changing the *mores* of his subjects for better (or worse) by setting an example rather than using compulsion: in particular for a *princeps* who prides himself on being *ciuilis*, it is much preferable to use his life as a form of censorship, in the sense of setting an exacting and observable benchmark of excellence for others to emulate, than to assume the office of the censor or the *praefectura morum* and impose punitive sanctions. (Compare, for instance, *Pan.* 46.1: *et quis terror ualuisset efficere quod reuerentia tui effecit?* with *Ann.* 3.55.4: *obsequium inde in principem et aemulandi amor ualidior quam poena ex legibus et metus*, using the methodology for the study of Latin prose intertextuality developed by Whitton 2019, which encourages us to notice lexical reminiscences, such as *ualuisset* ~ *ualidior*, synonym substitutions, such as *reuerentia tui* ~ *obsequium ... in principem* or *terror* ~ *metus* and the chiastic inversion of spelling out the negative and the positive approach.) If Tacitus composed this part of his text in dialogue with Pliny's *Panegyricus* – selling his sequel (he follows Pliny) as a prequel (Pliny's Trajan follows his Vespasian; what his literary rival talks up as radically new is in fact ancient history) – this would seem to cast further doubt on the value of this passage as a source for diagnosing large-scale historical change as opposed to testimony for ingenious literary polemics.

Ingo Gildenhard and Cristiano Viglietti

senatorial elite under Trajan an idiom to stake out a position that aligned their own values with those they saw in (or saw fit to project onto) those in power, be it a former or the reigning *princeps*.[209] It is one element of a larger effort to represent the reigns of Nerva's and Trajan's predecessors (in particular that of Domitian) as defined by a despotic incontinence that infested society, fractured truth and freedom and crushed literary talent; by way of contrast, their own present emerges as a time of *felicitas* and *libertas* after a dark period of tyranny that enables literary *ingenia* to shine anew.[210]

If senators could never hope to rival the emperor in terms of *publica magnificentia*, even though the competition between the *princeps* and the senators continued, they could subscribe to self-restraint and moral rectitude and, in this particular area, even outperform the emperor. The most extreme case of self-restraint on such an imperial scale that it outclasses a *princeps* who is himself eulogised as the living embodiment of modesty and moderation is arguably Pliny the Younger.[211] As he suggests in *Epistle* 2.1, the *moderatio* of his venerable patron Verginius Rufus, who turned down the emperorship twice, and of himself (who surely would have been Verginius' adopted successor of choice, in the same vein in which Nerva adopted Trajan) outdoes even that of Trajan by literally rendering the pair overqualified for the throne.[212]

Outlook

Some scholars let the story of Roman preoccupation with material sobriety and the desirability of limits not least on

---

[209] See Chapter 5 (Gildenhard): 333–6. Pliny's fondness for **frug–* words stands in striking contrast to the strict avoidance of *frugi* and *frugalitas* by Tacitus, who never uses the terms – perhaps in conscious imitation of his republican heroes Cato the Elder and Sallust, in whose (surviving) *oeuvre* the words are also absent. Tacitus' preferred label for a frugal disposition is the same as Cato the Elder's: *parsimonia*. Genre of course also matters here.

[210] The plot of Tac. *Hist.* 1.1: see Geisthardt and Gildenhard 2019: 266–9; on the retrospective recoding of Domitian across a range of genres see the papers in Bönisch-Meyer et al. 2014; Cordes 2017; Schulz 2019.

[211] *modestia* (used 16 times) and *moderatio* (15) are leitmotifs in Pliny's *Panegyricus*.

[212] For the full argument see Gildenhard 2019.

Introduction

the part of those in power come to an end in the first century CE. The seemingly uninhibited practice of conspicuous consumption during the high empire, alongside the apparent loss of any appreciation of frugal values during a time when emperors wore precious crowns studded with jewels and strutted about in garments of purple, often figure as elements within a broader historical dynamic that pushed Rome towards 'an oriental conception of power' in the 'absolute monarchy' of late antiquity.[213] But the sweeping (and orientalising) plot that takes us from the Principate to the Dominate, from an ideology of imperial self-restraint to one of unabashed immoderation, hardly does justice to the evidence and has come under significant critical pressure.[214]

To begin with, an 'oriental conception of power' is, as a polemic concept, part and parcel of Roman political discourse from the late republic onwards, when creative individuals began to experiment with aspects of Hellenistic kingship ideology.[215] Every emperor from Caesar onwards, who was assassinated on the eve of his departure for 'the Orient', was potentially an 'oriental despot' – and was expected to establish his credibility as a *princeps ciuilis*, not least in cultivating modes of moderation in interaction with the senate, such as the ritual rejection or at least reluctant acceptance of certain honours proffered. Given the easy analogies that existed between immoderation in the spheres of power, wealth, sex, food and drink, especially in invective discourse, a reputation for debauched licence and disrespect for the protocols of *ciuilitas* frequently go hand in hand in transforming the *princeps*

---

[213] Bottiglieri 2016: 18: 'Dopo Vespasiano la questione del lusso non viene più ripresa. ... ci si avvicina sempre di più alla concezione orientale del potere. Il monarca assoluto esprime la propria potenza anche attraverso i simboli; egli compare in pubblico con un diadema e con la veste intessuta di fili d'oro e pietre preziose e il mantello di porpora: nessuno, in tale contesto, proporrebbe più di limitare le ostentazioni di ricchezza.'

[214] See e.g. Ando 2009; further Flower 2013: 37–40, with specific discussion of the *Panegyrici Latini* (and Pliny's place within the collection).

[215] Imperial panegyric has intriguing precedents in such Ciceronian speeches as the *pro lege Manilia* and the *pro Marcello*: see Morton Braund 2012 and below 91–2.

87

Ingo Gildenhard and Cristiano Viglietti

into a tyrant.[216] As Chapter 5 (Gildenhard) and Chapter 6 (Patterson) show, the Roman discourses on luxury and tyranny and their opposites continue to register powerfully in our sources well into the second century CE. And the temporary disappearance of distinctive (literary) views on frugality and extravagance after Martial, Tacitus, Pliny the Younger, Suetonius and Juvenal have arguably more to do with the socio-political and cultural dynamics that enabled powerfully idiosyncratic (and massively self-interested) authorial voices and/or the vagaries of transmission than a general indifference to limiting excess and extravagance during the high empire.

In fact, the imperial biographies of the *Historia Augusta* suggest that playing the 'ancient frugality' card in the sense of self-restraint in the use of (public) wealth and in the exercise of power remained an attractive option within the repertory of imperial self-promotion and/or retrospective endeavours to fix the image of an emperor for posterity, be it in a panegyric or an invective vein.[217] Antoninus Pius (*r.* 138–161), for instance, is praised for his *diligentia* in administering public affairs and his *parsimonia* in matters of the table, his prudent handling of the state finances, his generous deployment of private resources for public benefit and his deliberate avoidance of excessive public expenditure for government activities such as travel.[218] Upon the death of Antoninus Pius, Marcus Aurelius (*r.* 161–180) is said to have been 'forced by the senate to assume the government of the state' in a scenario reminiscent of Tiberius' ascension to the throne, though the transition drama of imperial *moderatio* will presumably have been better staged, with all actors knowing their parts, not least since the

---

[216] See Morton Braund 2012 for the protreptic element of panegyric and the papers in Börm 2015 for anti-monarchic discourse in antiquity.

[217] For a recent discussion of date and authorship, with review of the previous literature, see Cameron 2011: 743–82, who argues for single authorship in the early 380s by a 'frivolous, ignorant person', whose political views boil down to 'utopian fantasies such as good emperors respecting the senate and choosing the best men to succeed them' (781).

[218] SHA *Ant. Pius* 7. Unlike many a royal throughout the ages, Antoninus Pius realised that imperial travel, even if conducted in an over-frugal manner, was a burdensome matter for those required to host his entourage (7.11: ... *dicens grauem esse prouincialibus comitatum principis, etiam nimis parci*).

88

Introduction

occasion also involved nomination of his brother Verus (*r.* 161–169) as joint *princeps*.[219] Marcus may have come to regret the decision to share power since not even a campaign against the Parthians taught his 'middling' brother the *parsimonia* that behooves a good emperor: he is said to have splurged enormous public resources on luxurious banquets, much to the horror of his civic-minded brother.[220]

Pertinax (*r.* January–March 193), too, is presented as having cultivated ostentatious, perhaps even excessive parsimony in deliberate contrast to the extravagant expenditures of Commodus (*r.* 180–192),[221] whereas enemies of his successor Didius Julianus (*r.* March–June 193) tried to besmear his reputation by spreading rumours of extravagant banquets in deliberate defiance of the frugal fare of his predecessor Pertinax's board in whose death they accused Didius Julianus to have connived. The biography of Didius, however, assures us that his *parsimonia* was such that he made the gift of a suckling pig or a hare 'last for three days' and even when there was no religious reason was often 'content with a vegetarian diet of cabbages and beans' (*nulla exsistente religione holeribus leguminibusque contentus sine carne cenauerit*).[222] Living up to their names, Septimius Severus (*r.* 193–211) attracted the cognomen Pertinax on account of his frugal ways,[223] whereas Aurelius Severus Alexander (*r.* 222–235), again in contrast to the seemingly lavish extravagance of previous emperors, was

---

[219] SHA *M. Ant.* 7.5: *post excessum diui Pii a senatu coactus regimen publicum capere fratrem sibi participem in imperio designauit.*

[220] SHA *Verus* 1.4 (*quem constat non inhorruisse uitiis, non abundasse uirtutibus*) and 5.6–7 (on the banquet). The biographer goes on to note that this all took place after the Parthian War, to which Marcus had sent his brother either to hide his debaucheries from the public eye, to teach him thrift (*parsimonia*), to shock him into some sense through exposure to war or to make him realise what being an emperor ought to entail.

[221] SHA *Pert.* 8.9–11 (arguably causing economic depression among those who made a living in the supply chain that kept the imperial larder luxuriously stocked) and 12.2–6, where the biographer suggests that his immoderate parsimony, which involved serving lettuce and edible thistles at his banquets in half portions before he ascended to the throne, made him look *illiberalis ac prope sordidus* (resembling Tubero and Cato the Younger of Cicero's *pro Murena*).

[222] SHA *Did. Jul.* 3.7–10.   [223] SHA *Sev.* 17.6: *ex morum parsimonia.*

89

Ingo Gildenhard and Cristiano Viglietti

sparing with handing out presents to those who entertained the people during public spectacles.[224]

As these examples show, the biographies situate their subjects on a familiar spectrum, which ranges from the vice of excessive severity and parsimony (*illiberalitas, sorditas*) on the one end to excessive indulgence in luxury and wasteful expenditure (*luxuria*) on the other. The golden mean they employ as a normative benchmark to assess (or better: to construct) the personality and conduct of the emperor under consideration consists in a combination, in the right measure, of personal *moderatio* with civic *liberalitas*. Given the discursive rules of panegyric and invective discourse – 'a world of "virtual reality", where illusion creates substance' – and 'the powers of invention' and the 'genuine talent for fiction' on display in the collection, we should be cautious in using these texts as reliable accounts of the actual gastronomic and fiscal policies adopted by the various emperors.[225] Any imperial portfolio of activities was up for polemic grasp and under negotiation in the law court of public opinion or literary hindsight, in the spirit of Cicero's *pro Murena*: 'facts' could be forged and what the *princeps* and his propagandists might have advertised as an outflow of civic generosity (*publica magnificentia*), hostile observers could easily inveigh against as immoderate and excessive acts of (*priuata*) *luxuria* or *sumptus*. Why someone found himself situated on a specific point of the above spectrum in biographical or historiographical retrospect depended on a variety of factors, including the specific style of an emperor's image-making (which lent itself more or less to invective distortion) and the availability of gifted litterateurs (or, as the case may be, uninspired hacks) who used their writings to shape the image of emperors for posterity, denigrating some and elevating others – and be it to signal loyalty to a new regime.

---

[224] SHA *Alex. Sev.* 37.1: *spectacula frequentauit cum summa donandi parsimonia, dicens et scaenicos et uenatores et aurigas sic alendos quasi seruos nostros aut uenatores aut muliones aut uoluptarios.*

[225] Citations from Barton 1994: 58 (first) and Cameron 2011: 778 (second and third).

Introduction

Even the *Panegyrici Latini, prima facie* not a corpus of texts that promises rich hunting grounds for modes of moderation, contain intriguing engagements with the Roman discourse of frugality.[226] The overriding tendency of the genre is, of course, 'to lay it on with a trowel';[227] and the *Panegyrici Latini* abound in effusive praises of an emperor's divinity, the divine support he receives (*felicitas*) and the charismatic military prowess that renders him 'ever invincible' (*semper inuictus*) or even 'supremely invincible' (*inuictissimus*). Yet as we have noted, ever since the dying years of the republic, encomia of strongmen at Rome combined efforts to make the *laudandus* look larger than life with a respect for limits: at least a modicum of moderation and self-restraint proves the crucial difference between the good king and the vicious despot – even though in panegyric and invective discourse the difference is of course primarily rhetorical, with the victor often carrying the spoils.[228] Archetypes of this panegyric protocol can again already be found in Cicero's speeches *pro lege Manilia*, in which he turns Pompey into the physical embodiment of the *summus imperator*, including charismatic *felicitas* and divinity in the eyes of Eastern subjects, while assuring his Roman audience that Pompey's *humanitas* and *temperantia*, among other qualities implying moderation, will nevertheless prevent him from becoming a second Sulla Felix; and *pro Marcello*, where he argues that however great Caesar's military victories might be, the victory he won over victory itself on account of his self-control, which facilitated his pardon of one of his most inveterate enemies, was even greater.[229] The opening formulation *tantum in summa potestate rerum omnium modum* (*Marc.* 1: 'such supreme moderation by someone in full possession of autocratic power') epitomises the concept of 'self-restrained

---

[226] For the *Panegyrici Latini* we cite the translation of C. E. V. Nixon and B. S. Rodgers 1994. For the current state of scholarship see Ware 2019.

[227] The formulation is from Dewar 1994.

[228] Omissi 2018: 301–6: 'Those made tyrants by the victory of others', further Flower 2013 on how bishops weighed in on the assessment of imperial power, esp. as regards emperors they regarded as heretical.

[229] Gildenhard 2011a: 255–72 (*Man.*) and 351–64 (*Marc.*).

Ingo Gildenhard and Cristiano Viglietti

omnipotence', which should remain the defining feature of the *princeps ciuilis* (though on the level of rhetoric, as Cicero's prose shows, even the aspect of self-restraint tends to get extolled immoderately).

The Latin panegyrists, too, are keen to stress that the unmatched martial *uirtus* of their *laudandi* has a counterpart in qualities that temper the exercise of power – such as pietas;[230] *misericordia* towards the vanquished and *iustitia* in protecting the rights of the dispossessed;[231] *continentia, fortitudo, iustitia, prudentia* and rejection of all sexual promiscuity, lusts and pleasures in the observance of modesty (*uerecundia*);[232] or *clementia, pietas, grauitas, lenitas, uerecundia* and *iustitia*.[233] Eumenius' oration for the Restoration of the Schools contains a pitch for the importance of the study of literary texts as the foundation for all the virtues, insofar as they teach *continentia, modestia, uigilantia* and *patientia*, which properly cultivated at an early age remain important later in life even during military service (IX.8.2). In their role as benevolent and divinely graced rulers emperors act as guardians of virtue, keeping in check not least the vices of luxury and sexual licence.[234] These qualities contrast with the traits of the tyrant, though only Nazarius in his *Panegyric of Constantine* (IV) and Pacatus Drepanius in his *Panegyric of Theodosius* (X) actually use the lexemes *tyrannus* and *tyrannis*. Still, most of the orations feature topoi of anti-tyranny

---

[230] Maximian Augustus receives praise for his *pietas*, i.e. reverence for the gods and the affection for his brother that informs the fraternal, power-sharing harmony of the Dyarchs, which the orator elevates above manifestations of the emperor's military might in what he calls a *noua dicendi lex* (XI.5.4) – even though already Cicero used a similar ploy in the *pro Marcello*: Nixon and Rodgers 1994: 90 n. 39.

[231] VI.6.1. Cf. also IV.3.3: *diuina uirtus et eius misericordia comes.*

[232] VII.3.4–4.1 (Constantine, at the occasion of his wedding to Fausta, the daughter of Maximian, and his promotion to the rank of Augustus; he is also praised for his handsome appearance). Cf. VI.16.3 on *continentia*.

[233] VIII.19.3.

[234] IV.31.3: *Scelus domitum, uicta Perfidia, diffidens sibi Audacia et Importunitas catenata. Furor uinctus et cruenta Crudelitas inani terrore frendebant; Superbia atque Adrogantia debellatae, Luxuries coercita et Libido constricta nexu ferreo tenebantur.* Cf. already 8.2; 9.5; 15.3.

Introduction

discourse – as usurpers become emperors and need to construct their legitimacy.[235]

Likewise, when the panegyrists turn to matters of the political economy and fiscal policy familiar themes recur, with many opting for an idiom of infinity to capture the generosity of an emperor's *liberalitas, benignitas* or *indulgentia*.[236] For the most part, they are uninterested in exploring where the money for such bounteous benevolence comes from – with one exception. After waxing lyrical about the new golden age of rich abundance that dawned under Julian (*r.* 360–363), which the emperor facilitated by injecting vast amounts of wealth into rebuilding an empire he found in lamentable condition (III.10.1–2), Claudius Mamertinus poses the rhetorical question of how Julian managed to gain hold of the material resources that he lavishes on everybody given that his extraction of taxes was moderate – and singles out Julian's lifestyle, more specifically his parsimony, in his answer (III.10.3):

> maximum tibi praebet parsimonia tua, Auguste, uectigal. quidquid enim alii in cupiditates proprias prodigebant, id omne nunc in usus publicos reseruatur.

> Your frugality, Augustus, affords you your greatest source of income, for whatever others used to squander on their own desires is now all reserved for public uses.

Mamertinus proceeds to rail against the *sumptus* practised by Julian's predecessors and their wasteful splurging on buildings ('with variegated marble inlays and paneled ceilings of solid gold'), courtiers and banquets: by contrast the present emperor is praised for sleeping on the bare ground under the open sky

---

[235] Omissi 2018. Cf. e.g. the striking syncrisis between Constantine Augustus and Licinius, the son of Maximian, opposing *pietas* and *impietas*, *clementia* and *crudelitas*, *pudicitia* and *libido* (XII.4.4).

[236] IV.35.1. The splendour he bestowed upon the city was such that by comparison the things that hitherto looked magnificent now were deemed to betray 'the unseemly parsimony of the ancients': ... *sed illa ipsa quae antehac magnificentissima putabantur nunc auri luce fulgentia indecoram maiorum parsimoniam prodiderunt* (IV.35.4). The orator who rendered thanks to Constantine in 311 CE praised him for his *indulgentia* (V.1.3, 8.3, 10.4, 11.2, 12.1, 12.6, 13.4) and *liberalitas* (V.14.1) for his generous approach to taxation that saved many from financial ruin.

Ingo Gildenhard and Cristiano Viglietti

for the greater part of the year while on campaign with his legions, content with as much food as is necessary to keep going, which he consumes standing in the company of the odd servant and washes down with whatever drink happens to be at hand (III.11.1–4).[237] Julian's seemingly counterintuitive embrace of self-directed parsimony and other-directed generosity leaves Mamertinus dumbfounded (III.12.1):

Sed inter haec mirari satis nequeo quod tam seuere parcus in semet in ciues suos tam liberalis est ac remissus, laborum asperrima sibi sumens ut nos quietis rebus agitemus ...

But in the midst of this I cannot be sufficiently amazed that being so strictly frugal toward himself he is so generous and indulgent toward his citizens, taking upon himself the harshest of labors that we might spend our time in quiet pursuits ...

Put in Ciceronian terms, Julian is hailed for rejecting *priuata luxuria* and endorsing *priuata frugalitas/parsimonia*, which in turn enables *publica magnificentia/liberalitas*.[238] The emperor himself seems to have encouraged this strategy: other contemporary sources, such as Libanius or Ammianus Marcellinus, confirm that Mamertinus picked up on an important element of Julian's image-making, including his own writings.[239] Julian pronounced himself much taken by the philosophy of Diogenes the Cynic, in which he saw realised 'independence, self-sufficiency, justice, temperance, religious reverence, gratitude and diligent attention not to do anything without purpose, at random or irrationally' – all qualities he incorporated in his personal style.[240]

---

[237] The contrast seems generic rather than grounded in reality. See Nixon and Rodgers 1994: 411 n. 79: 'his predecessor ... was not one who overindulged his appetites' with reference to Amm. Marc. 21.16.5–6.

[238] On the private lives of the public figures praised in the *Panegyrici* see further Rees 2004.

[239] See Amm. Marc. 25.4.4 (with reference to the frugal lifestyle adopted by Julian): *hoc autem temperantiae genus crescebat in maius iuuante parsimonia ciborum et somni, quibus domi forisque tenacius utebatur*; Libanius *Or.* 18.174–81, 276; 13.44; 12.94–95; 17.27; further Nixon and Rodgers 1994: 410–13.

[240] Jul. *or.* 6 (to the uneducated cynics): πρότερον μέντοι τὴν Διογένους ἡμῖν ἐπιδειξάμενος εὐμάθειαν καὶ τὴν ἀγχίνοιαν καὶ τὴν ἐν τοῖς ἄλλοις ἅπασιν ἐλευθερίαν, αὐτάρκειαν, δικαιοσύνην, σωφροσύνην, εὐλάβειαν, χάριν, προσοχήν, ὡς μηδὲν εἰκῇ μηδὲ μάτην μηδὲ

Introduction

Within the corpus of the *Panegyrici Latini*, Mamertinus' praise of Julian paves the way for Pacatus Drepanius' eulogy of Theodosius (*r.* 379–395) – an oration that, while being the last chronologically, is closest in spirit to Pliny the Younger's *Panegyricus* in the celebration of the *laudandus* as a *princeps ciuilis* and his frugal ways. The arrangement of the speeches in the edited collection, most likely the work of Pacatus himself, reinforces the special affinities between the two texts, the two panegyrists and the two emperors: the *laudatio* of Theodosius features right after Pliny's *Panegyricus*, which heads the corpus.[241] The arrangement implies that the most recent speech approximates the generic archetype most closely – and that the ideal of the *princeps ciuilis* that Pliny celebrates has reappeared in the person of Theodosius – prefigured to some extent by Julian, whose panegyric by Mamertinus, the penultimate in terms of chronology, the editor (Pacatus?) placed third. Indeed, what Pacatus arguably does in the familiar dynamics of *imitatio* and *aemulatio* is to 'update' the figure of the ideal emperor he found in Pliny and to present his modern variant as superior to the archetype.[242] The analogy and inequality (Pliny : Trajan < Pacatus : Theodosius) finds geopolitical confirmation in their shared origins. Both hail from Spain – the jewel of the Roman Empire, a land abundant in material and human resources, 'the mother of emperors' (II.4.5). Pacatus mentions '*Traianum illum*' and Hadrian before identifying Theodosius as their divine equivalent[243] – superior even to Jupiter and his

---

ἀλόγως ποιεῖν· ἐπεὶ καὶ ταῦτα τῆς Διογένους ἐστὶ φιλοσοφίας οἰκεῖα (202a). See also Julian *Mis.* 340b–c; 341c–d; further García Ruiz 2018.

[241] Nixon and Rodgers 1994: 3–8; Pichon (2012/1906).

[242] See Rees 2018: 314 for 'the characterisation of Theodosius as neo-Trajanic'; he points out that both Pliny and Pacatus operate with a tyrant-figure (Domitian and Maximus, respectively) as foil for their favourite emperor.

[243] Lippold 2012/1968 finds it remarkable 'that no greater emphasis is given to Trajan elsewhere in the speech' 'in that the tale of Theodosius' direct descent from this emperor, who had acquired exemplary status in the fourth century more than ever before, may already have been widespread c. 389' (with reference to [Aur. Vict.] *Epitome* 48.1; Them. *Or.* 34. 450 and contorniate coins) (363), yet concedes that, with the exception of Pliny's panegyric, 'none of the other speeches included in the *Panegyrici Latini* collection mentions Titus, Trajan and Hadrian' (375 n. 77). (Pliny's) Trajan *is* special (even though the laws of the anxiety of influence ensure that the significance is hidden in the intertextual interstices).

95

Ingo Gildenhard and Cristiano Viglietti

mythic birthplace of Crete or Hercules and his supposed city of origin, Thebes: 'We do not know whether to credit the stories we have heard, but Spain has given us a god whom we can actually see' (II.4.5: *fidem constare nescimus auditis; deum dedit Hispania quem uidemus*).[244]

This superiority manifests itself not just in terms of ontological status but also in a lack of imperial ambition, exemplary self-restraint and material sobriety (as usual, a frugal disposition entails moderation in all walks of life, including the desire for power). Like Pliny's Trajan, Pacatus' Theodosius had all the qualities to become emperor – yet did nothing to obtain the throne (II.10.4). And whereas Pliny presents Trajan's appointment as Nerva's successor as a simple matter of obeying the order of the emperor – and orders need to be obeyed[245] – Pacatus tops this imperial modesty with an elaborate account of Theodosius' *recusatio imperii* (II.11–12), arguing that his variant of ritual refusal (for once not feigned!) outdid all those before him: Theodosius became Augustus very much against his will (II.12.1–2: *inuitus*). 'The Principate suffers a rebuff': 'it is the one aim of the candidate not to be elected'.[246] The degree of humility on display gets hailed as

---

[244] While Pliny is cagey about Trajan's *diuinitas* (*Pan.* 2.7: *quid nos ipsi? diuinitatem principis nostri, an humanitatem, temperantiam, facilitatem, ut amor et gaudium tulit, celebrare uniuersi solemus?*), Pacatus elevates Theodosius ontologically into a *praesens deus*. (For 'ontological elevation and divine favouritism' (and its discontents) in 'classical' Roman panegyric see Levene 1997–8; Gildenhard 2011a: 255–99.) The assimilation of a mortal to a god would seem to be even more problematic in a Christian context – but Christian and non-Christian 'identities' in this period were notoriously fluid and the dynamic of immoderation inherent in panegyric continued to ignore the boundary between the mortal and the immortal even once Christianity had reclaimed genuine divinity for God alone and the interface between the divine and the human, *diuinitas* and *humanitas*, that classical panegyric explores in the tradition of Hellenistic *Gottmenschentum* had become the exclusive domain of his son Jesus Christ: Rodgers 1986; Cameron 2011: esp. 227–30.

[245] Cf. Plin. *Pan.* 9: one of Trajan's claims to moderation (9.1: *moderatio*) consists in the fact that in becoming emperor he simply obeyed the order of an emperor – despite the fact that his background and standing in the imperial hierarchy and with the legions would have enabled him to make a pitch for the throne. And orders by those empowered to issue them have to be followed: *ubi deinde disciplina, ubi mos a maioribus traditus, quodcumque imperator munus iniungeret, aequo animo paratoque subeundi?*

[246] II.12.2: *repulsam patitur principatus, et unus est ambitus candidati ne declaretur.*

Introduction

utterly unprecedented, unique in every respect, impossible to rival, which posterity will be hard put to believe (II.12.3): in terms of 'competitive moderation' Theodosius stands supreme – a *primus sine paribus*.

Pacatus achieves a similar elevation of Theodosius by casting him as the avatar of those Romans of old, the Curii, the Coruncanii, the Fabricii, who alternated between city and country, public service and private farming, wielding swords in triumphant battle and ploughshares to eke out a living (II.9.5). But what elevates Theodosius above these ancient *exempla* is the fact that he embraced his agricultural existence out of his own free will. The legendary figures were forced to labour the soil out of bare necessity – and this element of compulsion (*necessitas*) diminishes the praiseworthiness of their actions: poverty (*inopia*) simply did not leave them any other choice.[247] In other words, Theodosius' spotless record of voluntary frugality is historically unique[248] – and Pacatus makes the most of it (II.13):[249]

(1) Quin ubi primum te imperio praestitisti, **non contentus** ipse ultra **uitia** recessisse, aliorum **uitiis** corrigendis curam adiecisti, idque *moderate*, ut *suadere potius honesta* quam **cogere** uidereris. (2) et quia uel longo **Orientis** usu uel multorum retro principum **remissione** tantus quosdam **luxus** infecerat ut adulta consuetudo **lasciuiae** haudquaquam facile uideretur *obtemperatura* medicinae, ne quis se pati iniuriam putaret, a te uoluisti incipere *censuram*, et **impendia palatina** *minuendo*, nec solum **abundantem** *reiciendo* **sumptum** sed uix *necessarium usurpando dimensum*, quod natura difficillimum est, emendasti uolentes. (3) an quis ferret moleste ad principis semet *modum* coerceri? aut subtractum sibi doleret **priuata luxuria**, cum uideret imperatorem rerum potentem, terrarum hominumque dominum, *parce contenteque uiuentem*, *modico et castrensi cibo ieiunia longa solantem*; (4) ad hoc aulam omnem Spartanis gymnasiis *duriorem, laboris patientiae frugalitatis exemplis*

---

[247] II.9.7: *detrahit laudem patientiae inopia; maioris exempli est labor sine necessitate.* This idea might come from the chapter on poverty in V. Max. (4.4), even though his *exempla* and his concluding catalogue at 4.4.11 (*Publicolas Aemilios Fabricios Curios Scipiones Scauros*) does not include Coruncanius.

[248] 'Spotless' in contrast to some virtuous Romans whose CV is blemished by occasional indulgence in luxury. See II.7.3: *an non clarissimos nominis Romani uiros (Sullas Catulos Scipiones loquor) aliquantisper sibi luxuria uindicauit?*

[249] The terms speaking to frugality are in *italics*, those speaking to luxury in **bold**; *non contentus* (13.1) and *abundantem* (13.4) are in italics and bold since they speak to both.

Ingo Gildenhard and Cristiano Viglietti

abundantem; neminem unum inueniri qui auderet ad penum regiam flagitare **remotorum litorum piscem, peregrini aeris uolucrem, alieni temporis florem**?

Indeed when you first took command of the State, you were *not content* that you yourself were far removed from **vice**: in addition you took pains to correct the **vices** of others, and that *moderately*, so that you might seem *to be encouraging* rather than **compelling** *honorable behavior*. And because either through long experience of **the East** or through the **laxity** of many of your imperial predecessors some men were so given up to the **extravagant living** that it seemed by no means an easy task *to restrain* their inveterate practice of **self-indulgence** by any remedy, you wished the *moral reform* to begin with yourself, lest anyone consider that he was suffering an injustice; and by *reducing* **palace expenditures**, not only *by doing away with* **superfluous expenses**, but also *by subjecting necessaries to a strict budget*, you corrected men with their consent, which is in the nature of things a very difficult task. For who could take it ill that he was being confined to *the limits* of a ruler, or be grieved that something was being subtracted from his **private luxury**, when he saw his Emperor, ruler of the world, master of lands and men, *living frugally and contentedly, relieving long fasts with the simple meals of a soldier*, or, in addition to this, the whole court, *sterner* than the Spartan gymnasia, *abounding in examples of toil, endurance and frugality*; or that not one man could be found to dare to demand at the palace table **fish from remote shores, fowl from foreign climes, a flower that was out of season**?

Pacatus operates with familiar binaries. On the one side, we get the good emperor Theodosius – an epitome of moderation, self-restraint and contentment, who revives the spirit of the censorship by applying the principles of the *regimen morum* to himself, reduces unnecessary expenditure at court, sees to the disciplined use of even those material resources that constitute bare necessities, and embraces a style of life that is deliberately Spartan in simplicity, dedicated to hard work (*labor*) willingly endured (*patientia*) and virtuous sobriety (*frugalitas*).[250] On the other side, we get an image of what living under the regime of a bad emperor is like: vice is rampant; Oriental luxury infests the community and the court; extravagant expenditures of the imperial palace skyrocket; general indulgence in pleasures weakens the moral fabric of society; private luxury festers away; and the carbon footprint of the feasts is off the scale.

---

[250] The lexeme occurs in no other speech included in the *Panegyrici Latini* but is a key virtue in Pliny's *Panegyricus*: see Chapter 5 (Gildenhard): 333–6.

Introduction

In his subsequent description of gluttony, Pacatus does a good imitation of the satiric spirit of a Petronius or a Juvenal: the *luxus mensae* that Theodosius is said to have brought to an end included delicacies from the most far-flung corners of the empire (esp. those situated in the East) and beyond – for decadent feasts designed to titillate the palates of 'foppish and effeminate fellows' (II.14.1: *delicati illi ac fluentes*). What a contrast to what gets served at Theodosius' table, i.e. fresh seasonal produce, locally sourced – more frugal in fact than the meals of common people. Pacatus argues that this commitment to material sobriety at the top has welcome repercussions across society: it has made everyone else ashamed of luxury (*luxuria*) and led to the cultivation of thrift (*parsimonia*) – especially since Theodosius did not enforce this change in outlook through disciplinary actions such as laws, but by encouraging private repentance spurred on by his own exemplary conduct.[251]

Pacatus concludes the paragraph by reiterating the general pedagogic principle, which is already prominent in the previous paragraph, that Theodosius achieves the moral improvement of his subjects not by means of compulsion but by providing a benchmark of excellence: 'That is the way of the world, that is the way it is: men are irritated when commanded to reform; the most persuasive form of direction is by example' (*sic est enim, sic est: exasperat homines imperata correctio, blandissime iubetur exemplo*). As we had occasion to note, this principle has a precedent in Pliny (and Tacitus' *Annals*):[252] already Trajan (and before him Vespasian) refused to assume the role of censor or take other punitive measures to improve morals.[253] He understood, so Pliny submits, that the best way to improve the general health of the community is to encourage everybody to imitate an exemplary emperor: his life constitutes a superior form of censorship.[254] Both Pliny and

---

[251] II.14.4: *tuae, imperator, epulae mensis communibus parciores locorum ac temporum fructibus instruuntur. hinc certatim in omnes luxuriae pudor, parsimoniae cultus inoleuit, et quiescentibus legum minis subiit quemque priuatim sui poenitentia.*
[252] See above 85.   [253] Plin. *Pan.* 45.4.   [254] Plin. *Pan.* 45.6.

Ingo Gildenhard and Cristiano Viglietti

Pacatus turn 'their' emperor into the perfect embodiment of self-moderation, which in turn underwrites such features as openness and approachability, affability and the cultivation of friendship.[255]

Pacatus' rivalry with the ancients continues to resonate in the remainder of the speech. At II.20.5–6 he imagines the scenario of Brutus the liberator returning to life for assessing the Roman Empire under Theodosius. He would see a blessed age 'imbued and overflowing with enthusiasm for virtue (*uirtus*), thrift (*parsimonia*) and humanity (*humanitas*), with no trace anywhere in the world of arrogance (*superbia*), lust (*libido*) or cruelty (*crudelitas*)'.[256] The principal reason for this perfect condition is the emperor himself whom Brutus would see 'living both in public and in private with the austerity of leaders of old, the chastity of pontiffs, the moderation of consuls and the affability of candidates for office'.[257] Given the perfect combination of *dignitas* and *libertas* on display, Brutus would change his mind and endorse kingship (*regnum*) as a desirable form of government, superior even to the republic – even though *bad* rulers such as Tarquin of course have to be removed, not least for the common good. As Pacatus argues at II.26–7, the political economy under a tyrannical regime sucks up all the riches of the realm like a whirring black hole – in contrast to the fiscal benevolence of the good ruler, the *munificus imperator* (II.27.5), who presides over a mutually enriching flow of wealth to and from the seat of power.

Pacatus' celebration of the figure of the *princeps ciuilis* and his frugal ways as figured by Pliny and other authors of the early imperial period nicely illustrates the potential for 'hypoleptic communication' inherent in literary traditions, i.e. the option to coopt and reactivate 'textually archived ideas' across temporal, spatial and cultural distances.[258] In addition to such idiosyncratic acts of re-novation, the lexicon of frugality also

---

[255] See Nixon and Rodgers 1994: 515 n. 168, with further literature.   [256] II.20.5.

[257] II.20.5: *qua publice qua priuatim cerneret priscorum duritia ducum, castitate pontificum, consulum moderatione, petitorum comitate uiuentem.*

[258] For the concept see Assmann 2011: 257–8.

Introduction

continued to undergo more subliminal changes. Ammianus' usage of *parsimonia* is a case in point. Of the eight instances of the lexeme in the surviving portions of his work only one carries the traditional meaning 'parsimony'.[259] All of the remaining seven appear in the negated form *sine (ulla) parsimonia* and refer to indiscriminate slaughter of humans or livestock, in the sense of 'without sparing', 'without compunction'.[260] This usage is rare before Ammianus.[261] It arguably developed in analogy to the semantic range of Greek φειδώ, which covers both the sparing use of material resources (the original meaning of *parsimonia*) and a lenient approach to 'human resources', and the corresponding adverb ἀφειδῶς, which can mean 'freely, lavishly' or 'without mercy'.[262]

More significantly, during imperial times a religious belief-system gradually rose to prominence, which comprised a revolutionary challenge to the ideologies of wealth that had hitherto prevailed in Greco-Roman antiquity: Christianity. Deploying the beyond as a site of radical inversion of what is commonly taken to matter in the here and now, Christianity invites us to fundamentally reassess the value of material riches and their social importance. The notion that it is easier for a camel to go through the eye of a needle than for a rich man to enter the kingdom of God (Mk 10:25; Lk 18:25; Mt 19:24) and that the poor are blessed because theirs *is* the kingdom of God (Lk 6:21–2), the belief that it is impossible to worship simultaneously God and Mammon (Mt 6:24) or, more generally, the prospect of an otherworldly revolution that uplifts the

---

[259] Amm. Marc. 25.4.4 (cited above n. 239). For the others see 15.8.10; 16.5.1–5; 21.9.2; 24.4.27; 25.2.2.

[260] 15.4.8, 17.10.6, 19.11.14, 25.3.10, 25.4.17, 29.6.8, 31.13.6.

[261] See *TLL* X.1, 489.68 (Plin. *Nat.* 12.62: *Alexandro ... sine parsimonia tura ingerenti aris*) and the passages from Seneca collected at 490.65–9: *Clem.* 1.1.3 (Seneca imagining Nero being proud of his *summa parsimonia uilissimi sanguinis*); *Ben.* 4.1.3 (the path of *uirtus* must be followed without sparing our own blood: *sine ulla sanguinis sui parsimonia*); and *Nat.* 5.18.9 (on the madness of humanity to wage war *sine ulla parsimonia nostri alienique sanguinis*).

[262] Cf. e.g. D.H. 8.79.3 on how Roman fathers treated their wayward sons: καὶ ἄλλοι πολλοὶ πατέρες, οἱ μὲν ἐπὶ μείζοσιν αἰτίαις, οἱ δ᾽ ἐπ᾽ ἐλάττοσιν, οὔτε φειδὼ τῶν παίδων οὔτ᾽ ἔλεον ἔσχον ('And many other fathers, some for greater, others for lesser reasons, have shown neither mercy nor pity to their sons').

101

Ingo Gildenhard and Cristiano Viglietti

faithful abject (Mt 11:5–6: 'The blind receive their sight, and the lame walk, the lepers are cleansed, and the deaf hear, the dead are raised up, and the poor have the gospel preached to them. And blessed is *anyone*, whosoever shall not be offended in me') are difficult to reconcile with the socio-economic common sense of the Greco-Roman world – and go significantly beyond the enactments and celebrations of frugality in classical times.[263] With Christianity acquiring ever-greater reach and influence, its principles of faith also began to shape economic behaviour across a wider scale and at different levels of the socio-political hierarchy within a changing world.[264] New modes of 'conspicuous consumption' that were supposed to enhance prestige and standing in specifically Christian communities but also had God as ultimate addressee start to emerge, such as various forms of charity involving generous giving to the poor or acts of civic *liberalitas* for 'heavenly profits': 'Resources that had previously been allocated to the construction and restoration of traditional civic buildings were now spent on ecclesiastical buildings.'[265]

Frugality in the sense of material sobriety and moderation chimed well with core aspects of Christian doctrine, and church fathers unsurprisingly embrace *frugalitas* as a virtue. Jerome, for instance, uses the lexeme as a positive variant of (excessive) thrift (for which he uses *parcitas* or *parsimonia*) and an antonym of *luxuria*.[266] Augustine, too, employs *frugalitas* in the sense of (bracing) material sobriety and modest circumstances as a term that enables him to express Christian attitudes towards material wealth in his correspondence.[267]

---

[263] Rhee 2012. The exception are the cynics: Balch 2004.

[264] For economic change in late antiquity see e.g. Duncan-Jones 2004.

[265] Giardina 2007: 767, from Section IX: 'Heavenly Profits'. See further Brown 2002; Horden 2012.

[266] See *in Zachariam* 3.12, 187: *uia dextra, parcitas est, quam Graeci* φειδολίαν *uocant, sinistra, luxuries, media rectaque frugalitas*; *Dialogi contra Pelagianos* 3.11, 35: *quanto enim inter se distant pertinacia et perseuerantia, parsimonia et frugalitas, liberalitas et profusio, prudentia et calliditas, fortitudo et temeritas, cautela et timiditas?*

[267] See e.g. *Ep.* 36.23; 85.2 (where he rebukes his addressee Paulus for a lifestyle that is not just morally corrupt but economically unsustainable given the small income of his church: *. . . in ea professione uiuere dicaris, cui frugalitas ecclesiae tuae sufficere*

102

Introduction

In addition to such fairly orthodox applications of frugal idiom, the patristic material also contains more elaborate moments of conceptual creativity that pick up on idiosyncrasies in the classical sources, such as Cicero's experimental deployment of *frugalitas* as a superior Latin equivalent to Greek σωφροσύνη in *Tusculan Disputations* 3 and *pro rege Deiotaro* 26.[268] Augustine performs one such Christian 'update' of classical thought in his *De Beata Vita*[269] – a work designed to capture a discussion about the happy life that took place on his birthday 'after a dinner sufficiently modest so as not to weigh down intellectual endeavours' (1.6: *post tam tenue prandium, ut ab eo nihil ingeniorum impediretur*).

Frugality is thus on the menu from the start here, and the theme of felicitous nourishment dominates the entire dialogue, which programmatically oscillates between references to actual food and food for thought (or the soul), starting with the opening discussion of the human being as a composite of body and soul, each in need of a specific kind of sustenance.[270] When Augustine's point that the minds of the uneducated are starved of the fine arts (*bonae artes*) and hence famished runs into the objection that such minds are, on the contrary, 'full of defects and wickedness' (2.8: *plenos, inquit Trygetius, et illorum animos esse arbitror, sed uitiis atque nequitia*), he rejoins that

---

non possit ...); 189.7 (*ornet mores tuos pudicitia coniugalis, ornet sobrietas et frugalitas*); 211.9.
[268] Both texts are analysed in detail in Chapter 5 (Gildenhard).   [269] Barbone 1994.
[270] See e.g. *DBV* 2.9, where Augustine concedes that on his birthday he ought to dish up a more sumptuous dinner (*prandium paulo latius*) for both body and soul and his guests show themselves eager to devour whatever he might put on the table (*omnes se uultu ipso et consentiente uoce, quicquid praeparassem, iam sumere ac uorare uelle dixerunt*) or 2.13, where Augustine draws proceedings on this particular theme to a close so as not to overstuff the members of his party: in both real and intellectual feasts *luxuries* and over-indulgence is to be avoided: the right measure (*modus*) in terms of amount and speed of consumption is important for good health – though nobody says no to dessert and Augustine obligingly serves up a dainty polemic against the Academics (2.14–16, a portion of the text stuffed cloyingly full with food metaphors) as a concluding tidbit. The gavage continues in his account of what transpired on the following day, where Augustine does not even shy away from casting God as the purveyor of an unlimited amount of victuals for the soul (3.17); and at 3.20–1 yet another food-for-thought joke cracks up even Augustine's mum Monica. Satiety only kicks in at the very end (3.36), with God providing the ultimate *modus* for good measure.

103

Ingo Gildenhard and Cristiano Viglietti

this perverse form of plenitude is in itself 'a kind of sterility and starvation of the mind' (*quaedam sterilitas et quasi fames animorum*): 'for, as a body without food is generally full of diseases and sores, and these defects in it indicate starvation, so too the minds of such men are filled with diseases that reveal their lack of food.'[271] To shore up this analogy, Augustine, picking up on the notion of *nequitia* he gave as cue to Trygetius, invokes Cicero's antithesis of *nequitia* and *frugalitas* (2.8):

> Etenim ipsam nequitiam matrem omnium uitiorum ex eo, quod nec quicquam sit, id est ex eo, quod nihil sit, ueteres dictam esse uoluerunt. cui uitio quae contraria uirtus est, frugalitas nominatur. ut igitur haec a fruge, id est a fructu propter quandam animorum fecunditatem, ita illa ab sterilitate, hoc est a nihilo, nequitia nominata est. nihil est enim omne, quod fluit, quod soluitur, quod liquescit et quasi semper perit. ideo tales homines etiam perditos dicimus. est autem aliquid, si manet, si constat, si semper tale est, ut est uirtus. cuius magna pars est atque pulcherrima, quae temperantia et frugalitas dicitur.

> The ancients decided to call wickedness (*nequitia*) the mother of all defects because it is not anything (*nec quicquam*), that is, because it is nothing. And the virtue opposed to this defect is called fruitfulness (*frugalitas*). As the latter is derived from fruit (*frux*), that is, from produce (*fructus*), because of a kind of fecundity (*fecunditas*) of the mind, so the former is called wickedness from sterility, that is, from nothing. Nothing is whatever is flowing, dissolving, melting, and – so to speak – constantly perishing. Hence we call such persons lost (*perditos*). Something is, however, if it remains, stands firm, is always the same, as virtue is. And a great and most beautiful part of virtue is what is called temperance (*temperantia*) or fruitfulness (*frugalitas*).

The ancient who hides behind 'the ancients' is Cicero: several aspects of this passage are much indebted to *Tusculan Disputations* 3, where he moots *frugalitas* as the most appropriate translation of Greek σωφροσύνη (as an alternative to the standard *temperantia* and *moderatio*; *Tusc.* 3.16) and argues that *frugalitas* comprises all the other virtues (*Tusc.* 3.17: *reliquas etiam uirtutes frugalitas continet*; cf. Augustine's description of *nequitia* as 'the mother of all defects', which finds its complement in *frugalitas* as the 'mother of all virtues' at *DBV* 3.31),

---

[271] *DBV* 2.8. For the *DBV* we cite the translation by R. J. Teske, S. J. in *The Augustine Series, Volume VI: Trilogy on Faith and Happiness*, New York 2010.

Introduction

before identifying *nequitia* as its antonym on the basis of etymological play similar to the one offered here by Augustine.[272] However, the basic sense of *frugalitas* here undergoes a fundamental redefinition: instead of only referring to self-restraint and moderation as it does in Cicero, Augustine turns the lexeme also into a virtual synonym of *fecunditas* in the sense of 'fruitfulness' or 'plentiful nourishment' – quite unlike the sense he tends to presuppose in his correspondence. In other words, Augustine here does the same as Cicero, i.e. endow *frugalitas* with an unorthodox meaning. Both authors move the lexeme away from an exclusive focus on thrift and material sobriety (and related terms such as *parsimonia* or *sobrietas*) and turn it into a virtue that has affinities with the philosophical concept of temperance, with Augustine taking the further step of associating it with measured plenitude on the basis of its etymology.

The dialogue revisits this novel sense of *frugalitas* on the subsequent day after the group has reached the conclusion that 'neediness' (*egestas*) and 'folly' (*stultitia*) are virtual synonyms, insofar as every fool is in need and everyone in need is a fool (3.30). Augustine recapitulates the antithesis between *frugalitas* (associated with being) and *nequitia* (associated with non-being) established previously (3.30), before asking about the opposite of *egestas*. Trygetius moots 'wealth' (*diuitiae*) though concedes that its usual antonym is 'poverty' (*paupertas*). Insofar as *egestas* and *paupertas* are often thought of as one and the same thing, Augustine likes this suggestion but believes that a second positive term is needed alongside wealth to balance out the two negative terms of poverty and neediness. Licentius then proffers plenitude (*plenitudo*) and Augustine, with an apologetic gesture to Sallust, whose antonym of choice is *opulentia*, embraces this proposal and proceeds to intertwine the three pairs of antonyms now on the table: *nequitia* v. *frugalitas* ~ *egestas* v. *plenitudo* ~ *stultitia* v. *sapientia* (3.31). He then claims that 'many' have called *frugalitas* 'the mother of all virtues' before citing from Cicero's speech *pro rege Deiotaro*, where *frugalitas* is singled

[272] *Tusc.* 3.18.

Ingo Gildenhard and Cristiano Viglietti

out as the 'greatest virtue' (*uirtutem maximam*) and glossed with *modestia* and *temperantia*.[273]

Augustine gives this citation from Cicero the thumbs up, as it links *frugalitas* to 'fruit' and 'being'. He has to concede, however, against his historically unsustainable claim that Cicero is here agreeing with many others, that this particular sense of the term goes against common usage (*uulgarem loquendi consuetudinem*), where *frugalitas* means something akin to *parsimonia* – hence also the need for Cicero's double gloss, which Augustine goes on to consider in more detail (3.31). What he likes about *modestia* (from *modus*) and *temperantia* (from *temperies*) is their built-in sense of perfect balance, of the golden mean, of neither too much nor too little (*nec plus est quicquam nec minus*). This observation is the basis for establishing the superiority of *plenitudo* as an antonym to *egestas*, rather than, say, *abundantia*, which suggests overflowing excess and hence the lack of a limit. After thus configuring 'measured temperance' as an ideal, he launches into a series of quick-fire deductions: given that (a) wisdom is the opposite of folly, (b) folly is neediness and (c) neediness is the opposite of plenitude, it follows that wisdom (*sapientia*) is plenitude. And since plenitude has a limit (*modus*), the limit of the mind resides in wisdom (*modus igitur animi in sapientia est*).

In the concluding paragraphs, Augustine uses these deductions to turn to God: he contrasts a necessarily wretched, immoderate mind in incontinent search of worldly pleasures and desires with a mind in search of wisdom (*sapientia*), which, once it has succeeded, is perfectly happy – without any fear of immoderation (*immoderatio*), neediness (*egestas*) or unhappiness (*miseria*). Happiness consists of having reached *sapientia*, that is, one's limit (*modus*) and this limit, so Augustine establishes in a final move, is God as the highest limit (*summus modus*) that limits itself and contains within itself truth

---

[273] Cic. *Deiot.* 26; *DBV* 3.31: *merito etiam uirtutum omnium matrem multi frugalitatem esse dixerunt. quibus consentiens Tullius etiam in populari oratione ait: 'ut uolet, quisque accipiat; ego tamen frugalitatem, id est modestiam et temperantiam, uirtutem maximam iudico.'* The 'many' are a figment of Augustine's imagination: he is operating with Ciceronian material alone: see Chapter 5 (Gildenhard).

106

Introduction

(*ueritas*), i.e. the Son of God.[274] Put differently, Augustine uses Cicero's unorthodox rethinking of *frugalitas* as a Creative Commons licence to do something similar: in his own idiosyncratic redefinition of *frugalitas*, he co-opts the aspects of (a) ethical uprightness (as antonym to *nequitia*) and (b) prudent self-restraint (as a Latin equivalent to σωφροσύνη) from Cicero and combines it with (c) measured fecundity and satisfactory plenitude (via its etymological connection with *fruges*) in the course of ascending from a frugal birthday banquet to the Holy Trinity – the grand finale to the banquet of the mind that leaves everyone full and satisfied for now – yet hungry for more at a future point in time (3.36).

The contributions of *frugalitas* to the thematic economies of Pacatus' panegyric of Theodosius and Augustine's dialogue *De Beata Vita* testify to the powerful and unpredictable dynamic that one random act of conceptual creativity (in this case Cicero's, who inspired Pliny's play with *frugalitas* in his *Panegyricus*: see Chapter 5 for details) can develop in the history of thought. And these two distinct engagements with classical modes of moderation are only the tip of the iceberg. Unfortunately, here we can do little more than gesture to the high empire and late antiquity. A systematic exploration of the rich material from these periods is beyond the scope of our volume – it, too, has its limits. Yet we are keen to insist that the story of Roman frugality does not have a definitive end, certainly not in antiquity. The phenomenon, in particular as configured in late-republican and early imperial sources (and their re-imaginings of earlier phases in the city's history) continued to shape perception of Roman morality and its contemporary lessons more generally also in post-classical times and the emerging vernacular cultures.[275] In our final Chapter 7: 'From Poverty to Prosperity: The Recalibration of Frugality',

---

[274] *DBV* 3.34. Monica, of course, in her religious intuition had always already been there. Cf. 2.11 where she identifies the source of happiness of someone content with what he has not in the possessions themselves but the moderation of his mind (*. . . animi sui moderatione beatus est*).

[275] For an instance from the period of Renaissance Humanism see Chapter 5 (Gildenhard): 237–8 and 337.

107

Christopher Berry traces the incorporation of the ideal of *frugalitas* (in its sense of material sobriety, as devised especially by Cicero drawing upon the middle Stoa) into Christian thought and its subsequent 'demoralisation' by David Hume and Adam Smith on the grounds that luxury or opulence would enhance the overall material well-being of society. Nevertheless, the two Scottish philosophers partially re-incorporated 'frugality' in their system of thought as economic prudence directed to the acquisition of fortune as a way of sacrificing present advantage for greater return later.

Hume's and Smith's emphasis lies very much on the *economic* benefits of frugal resource management. In more recent times, arguments have been gaining traction that the very desire for the accumulation of every greater riches is deeply misguided, indeed self-destructive on a global scale – and that a world-wide commitment to a different conception of frugality, understood as an ethical and ecological ideal of deliberate self-restraint in the exploitation of natural resources, constitutes humanity's only hope to avert cataclysmic disaster.[276] The notion that an enacted ethics of sustainability, simplicity and perhaps also spirituality ought to be regarded as ultimately more satisfying as well as more prudent in terms of the common good (including nature, future generations and society as a whole) than materialism, especially in the form of consumer capitalism, is gaining in popularity across the globe. Within academia, the research project 'Spirituality and the Economics of Frugality' (www.eurospes.be) has tried to endow this outlook with historical pedigree by considering spiritual approaches advocating frugal conduct in Buddhist, Christian, Jewish, Islamic and philosophical traditions, including gestures to Epicurean ethics and Stoicism.[277]

---

[276] Monbiot 2019.

[277] See the papers in Bouckaert, Opdebeeck and Zsolnai 2008. They do not offer a systematic consideration of the Roman evidence, which would indeed not yield much of 'spiritual' value – with the exception, perhaps, of Seneca's Stoicism, whose notion of *frugalitas* covers the gamut from the question of what to have for supper to sublimity: see Chapter 5 (Gildenhard): 310–25. For the current revival of interest in frugality more generally see further Farrell 2009; Latouche 2011; Legrenzi 2014.

Introduction

Bibliography

Adam, J. N. (1974) 'The vocabulary of the later decades of Livy', *Antichthon* 8: 54–62.

Adamietz, J. (1989) *Cicero, Pro Murena*. Darmstadt.

Ampolo, C. (1984) 'Il lusso nelle società arcaiche: note preliminari sulla posizione del problema', *Opus* 2: 469–76.

Ando, C. (2009) 'Narrating Decline and Fall', in *A Companion to Late Antiquity*, eds. P. Rousseau with the assistance of J. Raithel. Chichester: 59–76.

Andreau, J. (1998) 'Cens, évaluation et monnaie dans l'Antiquité romaine', in *La monnaie souveraine*, eds. M. Aglietta and A. Orléan. Paris: 213–50.

(2004) 'Sur les choix économiques des notables romains', in *Mentalités et choix économiques des Romains*, eds. J. Andreau, J. France and S. Pittia. Paris: 71–85.

Andreau, J. and Coudry, M. (2016) 'Présentation', in *Le luxe et les lois somptuaires dans la Rome antique*, eds. J. Andreau and M. Coudry. (= *MEFRA* 128.1): 5–12.

Andreau, J., France, J. and Pittia, S. (eds.) (2004) *Mentalités et choix économiques des Romains*. Bordeaux.

Arena, V. (2011) 'Roman sumptuary legislation: three concepts of liberty', *European Journal of Political Theory* 10: 463–89.

(2012) *Libertas and the Practice of Politics in the Late Roman Republic*. Cambridge.

Armstrong, J. (2016) *War and Society in Early Rome: From Warlords to Generals*. Cambridge.

Asmis, E. (2004) 'Epicurean economics', in *Philodemus and the New Testament World*, eds. J. T. Fitzgerald, D. Obbink and G. S. Holland. Leiden and Boston: 133–76.

Assmann, J. (2011) *Cultural Memory and Early Civilization: Writing, Remembrance, and Political Imagination*. Cambridge.

Astin, A. E. (1978) *Cato the Censor*. Oxford.

(1988) '*Regimen Morum*', *JRS* 78: 14–34.

Atkins, M. and Osborne R. (eds.) (2006) *Poverty in the Roman World*. Cambridge.

Badian, E. (1972) *Publicans and Sinners: Private Enterprise in the Service of the Roman Republic*. Oxford.

Balch, D. L. (2004) 'Philodemus, "On Wealth" and "On Household Management": naturally wealthy Epicureans against poor cynics', in *Philodemus and the New Testament World*, eds. J. T. Fitzgerald, D. Obbink and G. S. Holland. Leiden and Boston: 177–96.

Baltrusch, E. (1989) *Regimen morum: Die Reglementierung des Privatlebens der Senatoren und Ritter in der römischen Republik und frühen Kaiserzeit*. Munich.

Ingo Gildenhard and Cristiano Viglietti

Bang, P. F., Ikeguchi, M. and Ziche, H. G. (eds.) (2006) *Ancient Economies, Modern Methodologies: Archaeology, Comparative History, Models and Institutions*. Bari.

Barbone, S. (1994) '*Frugalitas* in Saint Augustine', *Augustiniana* 44: 5–15.

Barton, T. (1994) 'The *inventio* of Nero: Suetonius', in *Reflections of Nero: Culture, History, & Representation*, eds. J. Elsner and J. Masters. Chapel Hill: 48–66.

Baudrillart, H. (1881) *Histoire du luxe privé et public depuis l'Antiquité jusqu'à nos jours*. Paris.

Beck, H. (2005) *Karriere und Hierarchie: Die römische Aristokratie und die Anfänge des cursus honorum in der mittleren Republik*. Berlin.

(2016) 'Wealth, power, and class coherence: the *ambitus* legislation of the 180s B.C.', in *Money and Power in the Roman Republic*, eds. H. Beck, M. Jehne and J. Serrati. Brussels: 131–52.

Beck, H., Duplá, A., Jehne, M. and Pina Polo, F. (eds.) (2011) *Consuls and Res Publica: Holding High Office in the Roman Republic*. Cambridge.

Beck, H. and Hölkeskamp, K.-J. (eds.) (2018) *Verlierer und Aussteiger in der 'Konkurrenz unter Anwesenden': Agonalität in der politischen Kultur des antiken Rom*. Stuttgart.

Beck, H., Jehne, M., and Serrati, J. (eds.) (2016) *Money and Power in the Roman Republic*. Brussels.

Bernard, S. (2018a) *Building Mid-Republican Rome: Labor, Architecture, and the Urban Economy*. Oxford.

(2018b) 'The social history of early Roman coinage', *JRS* 108: 1–26.

Berno, F. R. (2014) 'In praise of Tubero's pottery: a note on Seneca, *Ep*. 95.72–73 and 98.13', in *Seneca Philosophus*, eds. J. Wildberger and M. L. Colish. Berlin and Boston: 369–91.

Berrendonner, C. (2001) 'La formation de la tradition sur M'. Curius Dentatus et C. Fabricius Luscinus: un homme nouveau peut-il être un grand homme?', in *L'invention des grands hommes de la Rome antique*, eds. M. Coudry and T. Späth. Paris: 97–116.

Berry, C. J. (1994) *The Idea of Luxury: A Conceptual and Historical Investigation*. Cambridge.

Bettini, M. (2000) '*Mos, mores e mos maiorum*: L'invenzione dei "buoni costumi" nella cultura romana', in *Le orecchie di Hermes: Studi di antropologia e letterature classiche*. Turin: 241–92.

Bettini, M. and Short W. M. (2018) 'Introduction', in *The World Through Roman Eyes: Anthropological Studies of the Ancient World*, eds. M. Bettini and W. M. Short. Cambridge: 1–23.

Biesinger, B. (2016) *Römische Dekadenzdiskurse: Untersuchungen zur römischen Geschichtsschreibung und ihren Kontexten (2. Jahrhundert v. Chr. bis 2. Jahrhundert n. Chr.)*. Stuttgart.

(2019) 'Rupture and repair: patterning time in discourse and practice (from Sallust to Augustus and beyond)', in *Augustus and the Destruction*

Introduction

of History: The Politics of the Past in Early Imperial Rome, eds. I. Gildenhard et al. Cambridge: 81–96.

Blösel, W. (2000) 'Die Geschichte des Begriffes *mos maiorum* von den Anfängen bis Cicero', in *Mos Maiorum: Untersuchungen zu den Formen der Identitätsstiftung und Stabilisierung in der Römischen Republik*, eds. B. Linke and M. Stemmler. Stuttgart: 25–97.

Bönisch-Meyer, S. et al. (eds.) (2014) *Nero und Domitian: Mediale Diskurse der Herrscherrepräsentation im Vergleich*. Tübingen.

Börm, H. (ed.) (2015) *Antimonarchic Discourse in Antiquity*. Stuttgart.

Bottiglieri, A. (2002) *La legislazione sul lusso nella Roma repubblicana*. Naples.

(2016) 'Le leggi sul lusso tra repubblica e principato: mutamento di prospettive', in *Le luxe et les lois somptuaires dans la Rome antique*, eds. J. Andreau and M. Coudry *(= MEFRA* 128.1): 13–19.

Bouckaert, L., Opdebeeck, H., and Zsolnai, L. (2008) 'Why frugality', in *Frugality: Rebalancing Material and Spiritual Values in Economic Life*, eds. L. Bouckaert, H. Opdebeeck and L. Zsolnai. Oxford: 3–25.

Bowman, A, and Wilson, A. (2009) 'Quantifying the Roman economy: integration, growth, decline?', in *Quantifying the Roman Economy: Methods and Problems*, eds. A. Bowman and A. Wilson. Oxford: 3–84.

(eds.) (2011) *Settlement, Urbanization, and Population*. Oxford.

(2013a) 'Quantifying Roman agriculture', in *The Roman Agricultural Economy*, eds. A. Bowman and A. Wilson. Oxford: 1–32.

(eds.) (2013b) *The Roman Agricultural Economy: Organization, Investment, and Production*, Oxford.

Boxmann, A. (1818) *De legibus Romanorum sumptuariis*. Leyden.

Bramble, J. C. (1974) *Persius and the Programmatic Satire: A Study in Form and Imagery*. Cambridge.

Bresson. A. (2016) *The Making of the Ancient Greek Economy: Institutions, Markets and Growth in the City-States*. Princeton.

Brown, P. (2002) *Poverty and Leadership in the Later Roman Empire*. Hanover and London.

Brunt, P. A. (1971) *Italian Manpower 225 BC–AD 14*. Oxford.

(1988) *The Fall of the Roman Republic and Related Essays*. Oxford

Cameron, A. D. E. (2011) *The Last Pagans of Rome*. Oxford and New York.

Carandini, A. (2000) *Giornale di scavo: pensieri sparsi di un archeologo*. Turin.

Carandini, A. and Cappelli, R. (eds.) (2000) *Roma: Romolo, Remo e la fondazione della città*. Milan.

Casinos Mora F. J. (2015) *La restricción del lujo en la Roma republicana. El lujo indumentario*. Madrid.

Cifani, G. (2008) *Architettura romana arcaica*. Rome.

Cecchet, L. (2015) *Poverty in Athenian Public Discourse: From the Eve of the Peloponnesian War to the Rise of Macedonia*. Stuttgart.

III

Ingo Gildenhard and Cristiano Viglietti

Champlin, E. (2003) *Nero*. Cambridge, MA.

Chassignet, M. (2001) 'La "construction" des aspirants à la tyrannie: Sp. Cassius, Sp. Maelius et Manlius Capitolinus', in *L'invention des grands hommes de la Rome antique*, eds. M. Coudry and T. Späth. Paris: 83–96.

Clemente, G. (1981) 'Le leggi sul lusso e la società romana tra III e II secolo a.C.', in *Società romana e produzione schiavistica. III. Modelli etici, diritti e trasformazioni sociali*, eds. A. Giardina and A. Schiavone. Rome and Bari: 1–14.

Coffee N. (2017) *Gift and Gain: How Money Transformed Ancient Rome*. Oxford.

Constant, B. (1819) 'De la liberté des Anciens comparée à celle des Modernes (1819)', in *Œuvres politiques*. Paris 1874: 258–85.

Corbier, M. (2016) 'Interrogations actuelles sur la transhumance', *MEFRA* 128.2: 269–86.

Corbo, C. (2006) *Paupertas. La legislazione tardoantica*. Naples.

Cordes, L. (2017) *Kaiser und Tyrann: Die Kodierung und Umkodierung der Herrscherrepräsentation Neros und Domitians*. Berlin and Boston.

Cornell, T. (1995) *The Beginnings of Rome. Italy and Rome from the Bronze Age to the Punic Wars (c. 1000–264 BC)*. London.

Cornell, T. J. (2000) 'The *Lex Ovinia* and the emancipation of the senate', in *The Roman Middle Republic: Politics, Religion and Historiography c. 400–133 BC*, ed. C. Bruun. Rome: 69–89.

Coudry, M. (1998) 'Luxe et politique dans la Rome républicaine: les débats autour des lois somptuaires, de Caton à Tibère', in *Les petits-fils de Caton: attitudes à l'égard du luxe dans l'Italie antique et moderne*, ed. M. Coudry. Paris: 9–20.

   (2004) 'Loi et société: la singularité des lois somptuaires de Rome', *Cahiers du Centre Gustave Glotz* 15: 135–71.

   (2012) 'Lois somptuaires et *regimen morum*', in *Leges publicae: La legge nell'esperienza giuridica romana*, ed. J.-L. Ferrary. Pavia: 489–513.

   (2016) 'Lois somptuaires et comportement économique des élites de la Rome républicaine', in *Le luxe et les lois somptuaires dans la Rome antique*, eds. J. Andreau and M. Coudry (= *MEFRA* 128.1): 47–63.

Coudry, M. and Humm, M. (eds.) (2009) *Praeda: Butin de guerre et société dans la Rome républicaine/Kriegsbeute und Gesellschaft im republikanischen Rom*. Stuttgart.

Courtney, E. (1980) *A Commentary on the Satires of Juvenal*. London.

Crawford, M. (1977) 'Rome and the Greek world: economic relationships', *The Economic History Review* 30: 42–52.

   (2008) 'States waiting in the wings: population distribution and the end of the Roman Republic', in *People, Land, and Politics: Demographic Developments and the Transformation of Roman Italy 300 BC–AD 14*, eds. L. de Ligt and S. Northwood. Leiden and Boston: 631–44.

   (2011) 'Reconstructing what Roman Republic?', *BICS* 54.2: 105–14.

Introduction

Crooks, J. A. (2019) *When is Rome?: Developments in Roman Civic Identity during the Archaic Period (c. 650 – c. 350 BC)*. Doctoral thesis St. Andrews.

Dalby, A. (2000) *Empire of Pleasures: Luxury and Indulgence in the Roman World*. London and New York.

D'Arms, J. H. (1981) *Commerce and Social Standing in Ancient Rome*. Cambridge, MA.

Daube, D. (1969) *Roman Law: Linguistic, Social and Philosophical Aspects*. Edinburgh.

Dauster, M. (2003) 'Roman republican sumptuary legislation: 182–102', in *Studies in Latin Literature and Roman History XI*, ed. C. Deroux. Brussels: 65–93.

de Ligt, L. (2006) 'The economy: agrarian change during the second century', in *A Companion to the Roman Republic*, eds. N. Rosenstein and R. Morstein-Marx. Malden: 590–605.

den Boeft, J., Drijvers, J. W., den Hengst, D. and Teitler, H. C. (2009) *Philological and Historical Commentary on Ammianus Marcellinus XXVII*. Leiden and Boston.

Dench, E. (1998) 'Austerity, excess, success, and failure in Hellenistic and early imperial Italy', in *Parchments of Gender: Deciphering the Bodies of Antiquity*, ed. M. Wyke. Oxford: 121–46.

De Marchi, A. (1895) *Le leggi cibarie. Studio di antichi costumi romani*. Florence.

Dewar, M. (1994) 'Laying it on with a trowel: the proem to Lucan and related texts', *CQ* 44: 199–211.

Diederich, S. (2007) *Römische Agrarhandbücher zwischen Fachwissenschaft, Literatur und Ideologie*. Berlin and New York.

Drogula, F. K. (2015) *Commanders and Command in the Roman Republic and Early Empire*. Chapel Hill.

Droß-Krüpe, K., Föllinger, S. and Ruffing, K. (eds.) (2016) *Antike Wirtschaft und ihre kulturelle Prägung /The Cultural Shaping of the Ancient Economy*. Wiesbaden.

Dubois-Pelerin, E. (2008) *Le luxe privé à Rome et en Italie au Ier siècle ap. J.C.* Naples.

Duncan-Jones, R. P. (2004) 'Economic change and the transition to late antiquity', in *Approaching Late Antiquity: The Transformation from Early to Late Empire*, eds. S. Swain and M. Edwards. Oxford: 20–52.
(2016) *Power and Privilege in Roman Society*. Cambridge.

du Plessis, P. J. (2015) *Borkowski's Textbook on Roman Law*. Oxford.

Dureau de la Malle, A. J. C. (1840) *Économie politique des Romains*, 2 vols. Paris.

Dyck, A. R. (2010) *Cicero, Pro Sexto Roscio*. Cambridge.

Earl, D. (1960) 'Political terminology in Plautus', *Historia* 9: 235–42.
(1967) *The Moral and Political Tradition of Rome*. London.

113

Ingo Gildenhard and Cristiano Viglietti

Eck, W. and Heil, M. (eds.) (2005) *Senatores populi Romani: Realität und mediale Präsentation einer Führungsschicht.* Stuttgart.

Edmondson, J. (2016) 'Investing in death: gladiators as investment and currency in the late republic', in *Money and Power in the Roman Republic,* eds. H. Beck, M. Jehne and J. Serrati. Brussels: 37–52.

Edwards C. (1993) *The Politics of Immorality in Ancient Rome.* Cambridge.

Eigler, U. (2002) 'Urbanität und Ländlichkeit als Thema und Problem der augusteischen Literatur', *Hermes* 130: 288–98.

El Beheiri, N. (2012) *Das regimen morum der Zensoren: die Konstruktion des römischen Gemeinwesens.* Berlin.

Elsner, J. (1994) 'Constructing decadence: the representation of Nero as imperial builder', in *Reflections of Nero: culture, history, & representation,* eds. J. Elsner and J. Masters. Chapel Hill: 112–30.

Erdkamp, P., Verboven, K. and Zuiderhoek, A. (eds.) (2015) *Ownership and Exploitation of Land and Natural Resources in the Roman World.* Oxford.

Erskine, A. (2010) *Roman Imperialism.* Edinburgh.

Farrell C. (2009) *The New Frugality: How to Consume Less, Save More, and Live Better.* New York.

Feeney, D. C. (2016) *Beyond Greek: The Beginnings of Latin Literature.* Cambridge/MA.

Finley, M. I. (1985) *The Ancient Economy,* 2nd edn. London. [Originally published 1963.]

Flaig, E. (1992) *Den Kaiser herausfordern: Die Usurpation im Römischen Reich.* Frankfurt.

    (1993) 'Politische Lebensführung und ästhetische Kultur: Eine semiotische Untersuchung am römischen Adel', *Historische Anthropologie* 1: 193–217.

    (1995) 'Die *pompa funebris*: Adlige Konkurrenz und annalistische Erinnerung in der Römischen Republik', in *Memoria als Kultur,* ed. O. G. Oexle. Göttingen: 115–48.

    (1999) 'Über die Grenzen der Akkulturation: Wider die Verdinglichung des Kulturbegriffs', in *Rezeption und Identität: Die kulturelle Auseinandersetzung Roms mit Griechenland als europäisches Paradigma,* eds. G. Vogt-Spira and B. Rommel. Stuttgart: 81–112.

    (2002) 'Die umkämpfte Zeit: Adlige Konkurrenz und Zeitknappheit in der römischen Republik', in *Zeit und Geschichte: Kulturgeschichtliche Perspektiven,* eds. E. Chvojka, A. Schwarcz and K. Thien. Vienna and Munich: 72–84.

    (2003a) *Ritualisierte Politik: Zeichen, Gesten und Herrschaft im Alten Rom.* Göttingen.

    (2003b) 'Warum die Triumphe die römische Republik ruiniert haben – oder: Kann ein politisches System an zuviel Sinn zugrunde gehen?', in *Sinn (in) der Antike: Orientierungssysteme, Leitbilder und Wertkonzepte im Altertum,* eds. K.-J. Hölkeskamp et al. Mainz: 299–313.

Introduction

(2015), 'Prozessionen aus der Tiefe der Zeit: Das Leichenbegängnis des römischen Adels – Rückblick', in *Raum und Performanz: Rituale in Residenzen von der Antike bis 1815*, eds. D. Boschung, K.-J. Hölkeskamp and C. Sode. Stuttgart: 99–126.

Flohr, M. (2013) *The World of the Fullo: Work, Economy, and Society in Roman Italy*. Oxford.

Flower, H. I. (1996) *Ancestor Masks and Aristocratic Power in Roman Culture*. Oxford.

(2006) *The Art of Forgetting: Disgrace and Oblivion in Roman Political Culture*. Chapel Hill.

(2010) *Roman Republics*. Princeton.

Flower, R. (2013) *Emperors and Bishops in Late Roman Invective*. Cambridge.

Foucault, M. (1980) *Language, Counter-Memory, Practice: Selected Essays and Interviews*, ed. D. F. Bouchard. Ithaca, NY.

Freudenburg, K. (2014) '*Recusatio* as political theatre: Horace's Letter to Augustus', *JRS* 104: 105–32.

Friedländer, L. (1964) *Darstellungen aus der Sittengeschichte Roms: in der Zeit von Augustus bis zum Ausgang der Antonine*, vol. 2, 10th edn. Stuttgart.

Fulminante, F. (2003) *Le sepolture principesche del Latium Vetus*. Rome.

Gabba, E. (1988) *Del buon uso della ricchezza: Saggi di storia economica e sociale del mondo antico*. Milan.

Garani, M. and Konstan, D. (eds.) (2014) *The Philosophizing Muse: The Influence of Greek Philosophy on Roman Poetry*. Newcastle.

García Ruiz, M. P. (2018) 'Julian's self-representation in coins and texts', in *Imagining Emperors in the Later Roman Empire*, eds. D. P.W. Burgersdijk and A. J. Ross. Leiden: 204–33.

Gardner, J. F. and Wiedemann, T. (1991) *The Roman Household: A Sourcebook*. London and New York.

Gargola, D. J. (1989), 'Aulus Gellius and the property qualifications of the *proletarii* and the *capite censi*', *CP* 84: 213–34.

Garnsey, P. and Saller, R. (1987) *The Roman Empire: Economy, Society and Culture*. Berkeley and Los Angeles.

Gauthier, F. (2019) 'Remarks on the existence of a senatorial property qualification in the Republic', *Historia* 68: 285–301.

Gazzarri, T. (2018), '*Truculentus* and the abrogation of the *Lex Oppia*', *RhM* 161: 1–21.

Geertz, C. (1973) *The Interpretation of Cultures: Selected Essays*. New York.

(2000) *Local Knowledge: Further Essays in Interpretive Anthropology*, 2nd edn. New York.

Geisthardt, J. and Gildenhard, I. (2019) 'Trojan plots: conceptions of history in Catullus, Virgil and Tacitus', in *Augustus and the Destruction of History: The Politics of the Past in Early Imperial Rome*, eds. I. Gildenhard et al. Cambridge: 241–82.

Ingo Gildenhard and Cristiano Viglietti

Giardina, A. (2007) 'The transition to late antiquity', in *The Cambridge Economic History of the Greco-Roman World*, eds. W. Scheidel, I. Morris and R. Saller. Cambridge: 743–68.

Gibbon, E. (1782) *The History of the Decline and Fall of the Roman Empire*, vol. 1, 5th edn. London.

Gildenhard, I. (2003) 'The "annalist" before the annalists: Ennius and his *Annales*', in *Formen römischer Geschichtsschreibung von den Anfängen bis Livius*, eds. U. Eigler et al. Darmstadt: 93–114.

   (2007) 'Virgil vs. Ennius – or: the undoing of the Annalist', in *Ennius perennis: the Annals and beyond*, eds. W. Fitzgerald and E. Gowers. Cambridge: 73–102.

   (2010) 'Buskins and SPQR: the Roman reception of Greek tragedy', in *Beyond the Fifth Century: Interactions with Greek Tragedy from the Fourth Century BCE to the Middle Ages*, eds. I. Gildenhard and M. Revermann. Berlin and New York: 153–85.

   (2011a) *Creative Eloquence: The Construction of Reality in Cicero's Speeches*. Oxford.

   (2011b) *Cicero, Against Verres, 2.1.53–86: Latin Text with Introduction, Study Questions, Commentary and English Translation*. Cambridge.

   (2019) 'A wh(if)f away from the throne, or: Pliny the emperor', *Omnibus* 78: 30–2.

Gildenhard, I., Gotter, U., Havener, W. and Hodgson, L. (2019) 'Introduction', in *Augustus and the Destruction of History: The Politics of the Past in Early Imperial Rome*, eds. I. Gildenhard et al. Cambridge: 1–36.

Gildenhard, I and Zissos, A. (2004) 'Ovid's Hecale: Deconstructing Athens in the Metamorphoses', *JRS* 94: 47–72.

Giraudias, É. (1910) *Etudes historiques sur les lois somptuaires*. Thèse Poitiers.

Goddard, J. P. (1994) *Moral Attitudes to Eating and Drinking in Ancient Rome*. Diss. Cambridge.

Gotter, U. (2000) 'Akkulturation als Methodenproblem der historischen Wissenschaften', in *wir/ihr/sie. Identität und Alterität in Theorie und Methode*, ed. W. Eßbach. Würzburg: 373–406.

   (2001), *Griechenland in Rom? Die römische Rede über Hellas und ihre Kontexte (3.–1. Jh. v. Chr.)*, Habil. Freiburg.

   (2003a) 'Die Vergangenheit als Kampfplatz der Gegenwart: Catos (konter) revolutionäre Konstruktion des republikanischen Erinnerungsraums', in *Formen römischer Geschichtsschreibung von den Anfängen bis Livius: Gattungen, Autoren, Kontexte*, eds. U. Eigler et al. Darmstadt: 115–34.

   (2003b), 'Ontologie versus Exemplum: Griechische Philosophie als politisches Argument in der späten römischen Republik', in *Philosophie und Lebenswelt*, ed. K. Piepenbrink. Darmstadt: 165–85.

   (2008) 'Cultural differences and cross-cultural contact: Greek and Roman concepts of power', *HSCP* 104: 179–230.

Introduction

(2009) 'Cato's *Origines*: The historian and his enemies', in *The Cambridge Companion to the Roman Historians*, ed. A. Feldherr. Cambridge: 108–22.

(2019) 'The succession of empires and the Augustan *res publica*', in *Augustus and the Destruction of History: The Politics of the Past in Early Imperial Rome*, eds. I. Gildenhard et al. Cambridge: 97–110.

Gowers, E. (1993) *The Loaded Table: Representations of Food in Roman Literature*. Oxford.

Grelle, F. (2016), 'Allevamento equino, transumanza e agricoltura nella Puglia romana, fra quarto e primo secolo a. C.', *MEFRA* 128.2: 297–303.

Gruen, E. S. (1990) *Studies in Greek Culture and Roman Policy*. Leiden.

(1992) *Culture and National Identity in Republican Rome*. Ithaca.

Harders, A.-C. (2017) 'The exception becoming a norm – Scipio the Younger between tradition and transgression', in *La norme sous la République romaine et le Haut-Empire*, eds. T. Itgenshorst and P. Le Doze. Bordeaux: 241–52.

Harris, W. V. (1993) 'Between archaic and modern: some current problems in the history of the Roman economy', in *The Inscribed Economy: Production and Distribution in the Roman Empire in the Light of Instrumentum Domesticum: The Proceedings of a Conference Held at the American Academy in Rome on 10–11 January, 1992*, ed. W. V. Harris. Ann Arbor: 11–29 [= *Journal of Roman Archaeology*, Supplementary Series 6]

(2003), 'Roman governments and commerce, 300 B.C. – A.D. 300', in *Mercanti e politica nel mondo antico*, ed. C. Zaccagnini. Rome: 275–305.

(2007) 'The late republic', in *The Cambridge Economic History of the Greco-Roman World*, eds. W. Scheidel, I. Morris and R. Saller. Cambridge: 511–42.

(2011) *Rome's Imperial Economy: Twelve Essays*. Oxford.

(2016) *Roman Power: A Thousand Years of Empire*. Cambridge.

(2019) 'Review of Hölkeskamp 2017 and Mouritsen 2017', *Gnomon* 91: 524–35.

Harrison, S. (2017) *Horace, Odes Book II*. Oxford.

Hartmann, E. (2016) *Ordnung in Unordnung: Kommunikation, Konsum und Konkurrenz in der stadtrömischen Gesellschaft der frühen Kaiserzeit*. Stuttgart.

Havener, W. (2019) 'Augustus and the end of "triumphalist history"', in *Augustus and the Destruction of History: The Politics of the Past in Early Imperial Rome*, eds. I. Gildenhard et al. Cambridge: 111–132.

Hawkins, C. (2016) *Roman Artisans and the Urban Economy*. Oxford.

Hitchner, B. (2005) 'The advantages of wealth and luxury: the case for economic growth in the Roman empire', in *The Ancient Economy: Evidence and Models*, eds. I. Morris and J. Manning. Stanford: 207–22.

Ingo Gildenhard and Cristiano Viglietti

Hölkeskamp, K.–J. (1987) *Die Entstehung der Nobilität: Studien zur sozialen und politischen Geschichte der Römischen Republik im 4. Jhdt. v. Chr.* Stuttgart.

(2004) '*Exempla* und *mos maiorum*: Überlegungen zum kollektiven Gedächtnis der Nobilität', in *Senatus populusque Romanus: Die politische Kultur der Republik – Dimensionen und Deutungen.* Stuttgart: 169–98.

(2010) *Reconstructing the Roman Republic: An Ancient Political Culture and Modern Research*, trans. H. Heitmann-Gordon. Princeton.

(2017) *Libera Res Publica: Die politische Kultur des antiken Rom – Positionen und Perspektiven.* Stuttgart.

(2019) '"Cultural Turn" oder gar Paradigmenwechsel in der Althistorie? Die politische Kultur der römischen Republik in der neueren Forschung', *Historische Zeitschrift* 309.1: 1–35.

Hollander, D. B. (2019) *Farmers and Agriculture in the Roman Economy.* London and New York.

Holz, S. (2009) '*Praeda* and Prestige – Kriegsbeute und Beutekunst im (spät–)republikanischen Rom', in *Praeda: Butin de guerre et société dans la Rome républicaine/Kriegsbeute und Gesellschaft im republikanischen Rom*, eds. M. Coudry and M. Humm. Stuttgart: 187–206.

Hopkins, K. (1978) *Conquerors and Slaves.* Cambridge.

Horden, P. (2012) 'Poverty, charity, and the invention of the hospital', in *The Oxford Handbook of Late Antiquity*, ed. S. F. Johnson. Oxford: 715–43.

Houwing, J. F. (1883) *De Romanorum legibus sumptuariis.* Leyden.

Hoyos, D. (ed.) (2013) *A Companion to Roman Imperialism.* Leiden and Boston.

Humm, M. (2015) 'Census, classes censitaires et statuts civiques à Rome sous la République', in *Politica e religione: censo, ceto, professione. Il censimento come problema teologico-politico.* Brescia: 87–119.

Hurley, D. (2001) *Suetonius: Divus Claudius.* Cambridge.

Huttner, U. (2004) *Recusatio Imperii: Ein Politisches Ritual zwischen Ethik und Taktik.* Hildesheim and New York.

Jehne, M. (2000) 'Jovialität und Freiheit', in *Mos maiorum: Untersuchungen zu den Formen der Identitätstiftung und Stabilisierung in der römischen Republik*, eds. B. Linke and M. Stemmler. Stuttgart: 207–35.

(2016) 'The senatorial economics of status in the late republic', in *Money and Power in the Roman Republic*, eds. H. Beck, M. Jehne and J. Serrati. Brussels: 188–207.

Jongman, W. (2007) 'The early Roman empire: consumption', in *The Cambridge Economic History of the Greco-Roman World*, eds. W. Scheidel, I. Morris and R. Saller. Cambridge: 592–618.

Kay, P. (2014) *Rome's Economic Revolution.* Oxford.

Introduction

Keulen, W. H. (2009) *Gellius the Satirist: Roman Cultural Authority in Attic Nights*. Leiden and Boston.

Kindstrand, J. F. (1976) *Bion of Borysthenes*. Uppsala.

Klingenberg, A. (2011) *Sozialer Abstieg in der Römischen Kaiserzeit: Risiken der Oberschicht in der Zeit von Augustus bis zum Ende der Severer*. Paderborn.

Klodt, C. (2000) *Bescheidene Größe: Die Herrschergestalt, der Kaiserpalast und die Stadt Rom in literarischen Reflexionen monarchischer Selbstdarstellung*. Göttingen.

Kovesi Killerby, C. (2002) *Sumptuary Law in Italy: 1200–1500*. Oxford.

Kübler, B. (1931) 'Sumptus', *RE* 4, A.1: 901–8.

Kuhn, A. B. (2015a) 'The dynamics of social status and prestige in Pliny, Juvenal and Martial', in *Social Status and Prestige in the Graeco-Roman World*, ed. A. B. Kuhn. Stuttgart: 9–28.

(2015b) 'Prestige und Statussymbolik als machtpolitische Ressourcen im Prinzipat des Claudius', in *Social Status and Prestige in the Graeco-Roman World*, ed. A. B. Kuhn. Stuttgart: 205–32.

Kunkel, W. and Wittmann, R. (1995) *Staatsordnung und Staatspraxis der römischen Republik: Die Magistratur*. Munich.

La Penna, A. (1989) 'La leggitimazione del lusso privato da Ennio a Vitruvio: momenti, problemi, personaggi', *Maia* 41: 3–34.

(1990) 'La legittimazione del lusso privato da Ennio a Vitruvio', in *Contractus e pactum. Tipicità e libertà negoziale nell'esperienza tardo repubblicana*, ed. F. Milazzo. Naples: 251–85.

Latouche, S. (2011) *Vers une société d'abondance frugale*. Paris.

Lavan, M. (2013) *Slaves to Rome: Paradigms of Empire in Roman Culture*. Cambridge.

Legrenzi, P. (2014) *Frugalità*. Bologna.

Lendon, J. E. (1997) *Empire of Honor: The Art of Government in the Roman World*. Oxford.

Levene, D. (1997–98) 'God and man in the classical Latin panegyric', *PCPS* 43: 66–103.

Linke, B. (1995) *Von der Verwandtschaft zum Staat: Die Entstehung politischer Organisationsformen in der römischen Frühgeschichte*. Stuttgart.

Lintott, A. W. (1972) 'Imperial expansion and moral decline in the Roman empire', *Historia* 31: 626–38.

Lippold, A. (2012) 'The ideal of the ruler and attachment to tradition in Pacatus' Panegyric', in *Oxford Readings in Classical Studies: Latin Panegyric*, ed. R. Rees. Oxford: 360–86 [= 'Herrscherideal und Traditionsverbundenheit im Panegyricus des Pacatus', *Historia* 17, 1968, 228–50]

Loar, M. P., MacDonald, C. and Padilla Peralta, D. (eds.) (2018) *Rome, Empire of Plunder: The Dynamics of Cultural Appropriation*. Cambridge.

119

Ingo Gildenhard and Cristiano Viglietti

Lo Cascio, E. (1988) 'Ancora sui censi minimi delle cinque classi "serviani"', *Athenaeum* 66: 273–302.

(2016) 'Property classes, elite wealth, and income distribution in the late republic', in *Money and Power in the Roman Republic*, eds. H. Beck, M. Jehne and J. Serrati. Brussels: 153–64.

Manning, J. G. (2018) *The Open Sea: The Economic Life of the Ancient Mediterranean World from the Iron Age to the Rise of Rome*. Princeton and Oxford.

Manning, J. G. and Morris, I. (eds.) (2005) *The Ancient Economy: Evidence and Models*. Stanford.

Marcone, A. (2016) 'Il rapporto tra agricoltura e pastorizia nel mondo romano nella storiografia recente', *MEFRA* 128.2: 287–95.

Märtin, S. (2012) *Die politische Führungsschicht der römischen Republik im 2. Jh.v.Chr. zwischen Konformitätsstreben und struktureller Differenzierung*. Trier.

Marzano, A. (2013) *Harvesting the Sea: The Exploitation of Marine Resources in the Roman Mediterranean*. Oxford.

Mattingley, H. (1937) 'The property qualifications of the Roman classes', *JRS* 27: 99–107.

Meier, C. (1966/1980) *Res publica amissa: Eine Studie zu Verfassung und Geschichte der späten römischen Republik*. Wiesbaden.

Mengotti, F. (1787) *Del Commercio de' Romani*. Padua.

Mette, H. J. (1961) '*genus tenue* und *mensa tenuis* bei Horaz', *MH* 18: 136–9.

Meursius, J. (1605) *De luxu Romanorum*. The Hague.

Monbiot, G. (2019) 'For the sake of life on Earth, we must put a limit on wealth', *The Guardian*, 19 September, www.theguardian.com/commen tisfree/2019/sep/19/life-earth-wealth-megarich-spending-power-environ mental-damage (last accessed 9 February 2020).

Monson, A. and Scheidel, W. (2015), 'Studying fiscal regimes', in *Fiscal Regimes and the Political Economy of Premodern States*, eds. A. Monson and W. Scheidel. Cambridge: 3–27.

Montesquieu, C. L. (1734) *Considérations sur les causes de la grandeur des Romains et de leur décadence*. Paris.

Morley, N. (2004a) *Theories, Models and Concepts in Ancient History*. London.

(2004b) 'Decadence as a theory of history', *New Literary History* 35: 573–85.

(2018) 'Frugality and Roman economic thinking in Varro's *Rerum rusticarum*', *I Quaderni del Ramo d'Oro* 10: 41–54, www.qro.unisi.it/fron tend/node/215 (last accessed 9 February 2020).

Morris, I. (1999) 'Foreword', in M. I. Finley, *The Ancient Economy*, 2nd edn. Berkeley and Los Angeles: ix–xxvii.

Introduction

Morton Braund, S. (2012) 'Praise and protreptic in early imperial panegyric: Cicero, Seneca, Pliny', in *Oxford Readings in Classical Studies: Latin Panegyric*, ed. R. Rees. Oxford: 85–108.

Mouritsen, H. (2011) *The Freedman in the Roman World*. Cambridge.

(2017) *Politics in the Roman Republic*. Cambridge.

Muzzarelli, M. G. and Campanini, A. (eds.) (2003) *Disciplinare il lusso: La legislazione suntuaria in Italia e in Europa tra Medioevo ed Età Moderna*. Rome.

Neel, J. (2015) 'Reconsidering the *affectatores regni*', *CQ* 65: 224–41.

Nichols, M. (2010) 'Contemporary perspectives on luxury building in second-century BC Rome', *PBSR* 78: 39–61.

Nicolet, C. (1976) 'Le cens senatorial sous la République et sous Auguste', *JRS* 66: 20–38.

Nixon, C. E. V. and Saylor Rodgers, B. (1994) *In Praise of Later Roman Emperors: The Panegyrici Latini*. Berkeley, Los Angeles and Oxford.

Omissi, A. (2018) *Emperors and Usurpers in the Later Roman Empire: Civil War, Panegyric, and the Construction of Legitimacy*. Oxford.

Osborne, R. (2006), 'Introduction: Roman poverty in context', in *Poverty in the Roman World*, eds. M. Atkins and R. Osborne. Cambridge: 1–20.

Palmer, L. R. (1988) *The Latin Language*. Norman.

Pasco-Pranger, M. (2015) 'Finding examples at home: Cato, Curius Dentatus, and the origins of Roman literary exemplarity', *CA* 34: 296–321.

Passet, L. (2011) *Refuse du luxe et frugalité à Rome: Histoire d'un combat politique (fin du IIIe siècle av. J.-C. – fin du IIe siècle av. J.-C.)*. Doctoral thesis, Lyons.

Pennink, E. (1826) *De luxu et legibus sumptuariis ex oeconomica politica diiudicandis*. Leyden.

Perry, E. E. (2000) 'Notes on *diligentia* as a term of Roman art criticism', *CP* 95: 445–58.

Petrocheilos, N. (1974) *Roman Attitudes Towards the Greeks*. Athens.

Pichon, R. (2012/1906) 'The origin of the *Panegyrici Latini* collection', in *Latin Panegyric*, ed. R. Rees. Oxford: 55–74.

Pina Polo, F. (2006) 'The tyrant must die: preventative tyrannicide in Roman political thought', in *Repúblicas y ciudadanos: modelos de participación cívica en el mundo antiguo*, eds. F. M. Símon, F. Pina Polo and J. Remesal Rodríguez. Barcelona: 71–101.

(2016) '*Cupiditas pecuniae*: wealth and power in Cicero', in *Money and Power in the Roman Republic*, eds. H. Beck, M. Jehne and J. Serrati. Brussels: 165–77.

Pittia, S. (2007) 'L'invisible hiérarchie censitaire romaine', in *Vocabulaire et expression de l'économie dans le monde antique*, eds. J. Andreau and V. Chankowski. Bordeaux: 145–76.

Ingo Gildenhard and Cristiano Viglietti

Pitts, M. and Versluys, M. J. (eds.) (2015) *Globalisation and the Roman World: World History, Connectivity and Material Culture*. Cambridge.

Platner, F. (1752) *De legibus sumptuariis, 2*. Abhandlung. Leipzig.

Prag, J. R. W. (2016) '*Antiquae sunt istae leges et mortuae*: the *plebiscitum Claudianum* and associated laws', *MEFRA* 128.1: 65–76.

Price, H. (2019) 'Flooding the Roman Forum', in *Augustus and the Destruction of History: The Politics of the Past in Early Imperial Rome*, eds. I. Gildenhard et al. Cambridge: 189–222.

Raaflaub, K. A. (1986/2005) *Social Struggles in Archaic Rome: New Perspectives on the Conflict of the Orders*, expanded and updated edition. Malden and Oxford.

Rathbone, D. (1993) 'The "census" qualifications of the "assidui" and the "prima classis"', in *De agricultura: in memoriam Pieter Willem De Neeve*, eds. H. Sancisi-Weerdenburg et al. Amsterdam: 121–52.

Rawson, E. (1969) *The Spartan Tradition in European Thought*. Oxford.

Reay, B. (2005) 'Agriculture, writing, and Cato's aristocratic self-fashioning', *CA* 24: 331–61.

Rees, R. (2004) 'The private lives of public figures in Latin prose panegyric', in *The Propaganda of Power: The Role of Panegyric in Late Antiquity*, ed. M. Whitby. Leiden, Boston, Cologne: 77–101.

  (2018) 'Authorising freedom of speech under Theodosius', in *Imagining Emperors in the Later Roman Empire*, eds. D.P.W. Burgersdijk and A. J. Ross. Leiden: 289–309.

Rhee, H. (2012) 'Wealth, poverty, and eschatology: pre-Constantine Christian social thought and the hope for the world to come', in *Reading Patristic Texts on Social Ethics: Issues and Challenges for the Twenty-First Century*, eds. J. Leemans, B. J. Matz and J. Verstraeten. Washington, DC: 64–84.

Richardson, J. H. (2019) 'Some thoughts on *suffragium* and the practice of voting in archaic Rome', *Hermes* 147: 283–97.

Richardson, J. H. and Santangelo, F. (eds.) (2014) *The Roman Historical Tradition: Regal and Republican Rome*. Oxford.

Richardson-Hay, C. (2009) 'Dinner at Seneca's table: the philosophy of food', *G&R* 56: 71–96.

Richlin, A. (2017) *Slave Theater in The Roman Republic: Plautus and Popular Comedy*. Cambridge.

Rising, T. (2019) 'Bread and bandits: Clodius and the grain supply of Rome', *Hermes* 147: 189–203.

Rodgers, B. (1986) 'Divine insinuation in the *Panegyrici Latini*', *Historia* 35: 69–104.

Roller, M. B. (2010) 'Culture-based approaches', in *Oxford Handbook of Roman Studies*, eds. A. Barchiesi and W. Scheidel. Oxford: 234–49.

Roselaar, S. T. (2010) *Public Land in the Roman Republic: A Social and Economic History of Ager Publicus in Italy, 396–89 BC*. Oxford.

Introduction

Rosenstein, N. (2006) 'Aristocratic values', in *A Companion to the Roman Republic*, eds. N. Rosenstein and R. Morstein-Marx. Malden: 365–82.

Rosso, E. (2009) 'Le thème de la "Res publica restituta" dans le monnayage de Vespasien: pérennité du "modèle ausgustéen" entre citations, réinterprétations et dévoiements', in *Le principat d'Auguste: Réalités et représentations du pouvoir autour de la Res publica restituta*, eds. F. Hurlet and B. Mineo. Rennes: 209–42.

Roth, R. (2019) 'Sympathy with the allies? Abusive magistrates and political discourse in republican Rome', *AJP* 140: 123–66.

Rowan, C. (2013) 'The profits of war and cultural capital: silver and society in republican Rome', *Historia* 62: 361–86.

Russell, A. (2016) *The Politics of Public Space in Republican Rome*. Cambridge.

(2019) 'The Augustan senate and the reconfiguration of time on the Fasti Capitolini', in *Augustus and the Destruction of History: The Politics of the Past in Early Imperial Rome*, eds. I. Gildenhard et al. Cambridge: 157–86.

Russell, B. (2013) *The Economics of the Roman Stone Trade*. Oxford.

Russo, F. (2015) 'Roman discourses against the monarchy in the 3rd and 2nd century BCE: the evidence of Fabius Pictor and Ennius', in *Antimonarchic Discourse in Antiquity*, ed. H. Börm. Stuttgart: 153–80.

Rutherford, R. B. (1989) *The Meditations of Marcus Aurelius: A Study*. Oxford.

Sahlins, M. D. (1985) *Islands of History*. Chicago.

(1995) *How 'Natives' Think: About Captain Cook, for Example*. Chicago.

Saller, R. (2005) 'Framing the debate over growth in the ancient economy', in *The Ancient Economy: Evidence and Models*, ed. J. G. Manning and I. Morris. Stanford: 223–38.

Salvioli, L. (1929) *Il capitalismo antico: storia dell'economia romana*. Bari.

Sauerwein, I. (1970) *Die leges sumptuariae als römische Maßnahme gegen den Sittenverfall*. Hamburg.

Savio, E (1940) 'Intorno alle leggi suntuarie Romane', *Aevum* 1: 174–94.

Scheidel, W. (ed.) (2012a) *The Cambridge Companion to the Roman Economy*. Cambridge.

(2012b) 'Approaching the Roman economy', in *The Cambridge Companion to the Roman Economy*, ed. W. Scheidel. Cambridge: 1–21.

(2015) 'The early Roman monarchy', in *Fiscal Regimes and the Political Economy of Premodern States*, eds. A. Monson and W. Scheidel. Cambridge: 229–57.

Scheidel, W. and Friesen, S. J. (2009) 'The size of the economy and the distribution of income in the Roman empire', *JRS* 99: 61–91.

Scheidel, W., Morris, I. and Saller, R. (2007) 'Introduction', in *The Cambridge Economic History of the Greco-Roman World*, eds. W. Scheidel, I. Morris and R. Saller. Cambridge: 1–12.

Ingo Gildenhard and Cristiano Viglietti

Scheidle, K. (1993) *Modus optumum: die Bedeutung des 'rechten Maßes' in der römischen Literatur (Republik–frühe Kaiserzeit), untersucht an den Begriffen modus – modestia – moderatio – temperantia.* Frankfurt am Main.

Schnurbusch, D. (2011) *Convivium: Form und Bedeutung aristokratischer Geselligkeit in der römischen Antike.* Stuttgart.

Schulz, V. (2019) *Deconstructing Imperial Representation: Tacitus, Cassius Dio, and Suetonius on Nero and Domitian.* Leiden and Boston.

Sciarrino E. (2011) *Cato the Censor and the Beginnings of Latin Prose: From Poetic Translation to Elite Transcription.* Columbus, OH.

Shatzman, I. (1975) *Senatorial Wealth and Roman Politics.* Brussels.

Shelton, J.-A. (2013) *The Women of Pliny's Letters.* London and New York.

Sirago, V. A. (1995) *Storia agraria romana, Volume primo. Fase ascensionale.* Naples.

Skutsch, O. (1985) *The Annals of Quintus Ennius: edited with Introduction and Commentary.* Oxford.

Smith C. J. (2006) *The Roman Clan: The Gens from Ancient Ideology to Modern Anthropology.* Cambridge.

Stein-Hölkeskamp, E. (2005) *Das Römische Gastmahl: Eine Kulturgeschichte.* Munich.

Suolahti, J. (1963) *The Roman Censors: A Study on Social Structures.* Helsinki.

Tan, J. (2015) 'The Roman Republic', in *Fiscal Regimes and the Political Economy of Premodern States*, eds. A. Monson and W. Scheidel. Cambridge: 208–28.

(2017) *Power and Public Finance at Rome, 264–49 BCE.* Oxford.

Taylor, C. (2017) *Poverty, Wealth, & Well-Being: Experiencing Penia in Democratic Athens.* Oxford.

Tchernia A. (2011) *Les Romains et le commerce.* Naples. [= *The Romans and Trade*, trans. J. Grieve. Oxford 2016.]

Temin, P. (2013) *The Roman Market Economy.* Princeton and Oxford.

Townsend, P. (1979) *Poverty in the United Kingdom: A Survey of Household Resources and Standards of Living.* Berkeley and Los Angeles.

(1985) 'A sociological approach to the measurement of poverty', *Oxford Economic Papers* 37: 659–68.

Tuck, S. L. (2016) 'Imperial image-making', in *A Companion to the Flavian Age of Imperial Rome*, ed. A. Zissos. Chichester: 109–28.

van der Blom, H. (2010) *Cicero's Role Models: The Political Strategy of a Newcomer.* Oxford.

Vasaly, A. (1993) *Representations: Images of the World in Ciceronian Oratory.* Berkeley and Oxford.

Venturini, C. (2004), 'Leges sumptuariae', *Index* 32: 355–80. [= *Studi di diritto delle persone e di vita sociale in Roma antica*, Naples 2014, 553–82.]

Introduction

(2009), 'Senatori e navi dal plebiscito Claudio alla *lex Iulia repetundarum*: qualche rilievo', in *Scritti in onore di Generoso Melillo 3*, Napoli, 1459–71. [=*Studi di diritto delle persone e di vita sociale in Roma antica*, Naples 2014, 421–36.]

(2016) '*Leges sumptuariae*: divieti senza sanzioni?', in *Le luxe et les lois somptuaires dans la Rome antique*, eds. J. Andreau and M. Coudry (= *MEFRA* 128.1). Rome: 41–6.

Veyne, P. (1990) *Bread and Circuses: Historical Sociology and Political Pluralism*, trans. P. Pearce. London.

Viglietti, C. (2011) *Il limite del bisogno: Antropologia economica di Roma arcaica*. Bologna.

(2018) 'Economy', in *The World through Roman Eyes: Anthropological Approaches to Ancient Culture*, eds. M. Bettini and W. M. Short. Cambridge: 216–48.

Vigourt, A. (2001a) 'L'intention criminelle et son châtiment: les condamnations des aspirants à la tyrannie', in *L'invention des grands hommes de la Rome antique*, eds. M. Coudry and T. Späth. Paris: 271–88.

(2001b) 'Les adfectores regni et les normes sociales', *L'invention des grands hommes de la Rome antique*, eds. M. Coudry and T. Späth. Paris: 333–40.

von Reden, S. (2019) 'Review of Coffee 2017', *Gnomon* 91: 625–9.

Wallace-Hadrill, A. (1982) '*Civilis princeps*: between citizen and king', *JRS* 72:32–48.

(2008) *Rome's Cultural Revolution*. Cambridge.

Walter, U. (2017a) 'Legislation in the Roman republic: setting rules or just political communication?', in *La norme sous la République romaine et le Haut-Empire*, eds. T. Itgenshorst and P. Le Doze. Bordeaux: 533–40.

(2017b) '*Spes pro periculis praemiorum*: Risiko und Aktualität im politischen Agieren republikanischer Aristokraten', in *Politische Kultur und soziale Struktur der Römischen Republik: Bilanzen und Perspektiven* (= Akten der internationalen Tagung anlässlich des 70. Todestages von Friedrich Münzer, Münster, 18–20. Oktober 2012), eds. M. Haake and A.-C. Harders. Stuttgart: 361–80.

Ware, C. (2019) 'Review article: panegyric and the discourse of praise in late antiquity', *JRS* 109: 1–14 (first view).

Weeber, K.-W. (2006) *Luxus im alten Rom: Die öffentliche Pracht*. Darmstadt.

(2007) *Luxus im alten Rom: Die Schwelgerei, das süße Gift*, 2nd edn. Darmstadt.

Weinbrot, H. D. (2005) *Menippean Satire Reconsidered: From Antiquity to the Eighteenth Century*. Baltimore.

White, K. D. (1970) *Roman Farming*. London and Southampton.

Whitton, C. (2019) *The Arts of Imitation in Latin Prose: Pliny's Epistles/ Quintilian in Brief*. Cambridge.

125

Ingo Gildenhard and Cristiano Viglietti

Wilson, A. and Bowman, A. (eds.) (2018) *Trade, Commerce, and the State in the Roman World*. Oxford.

Wilson, A. and Flohr, M. (eds.) (2016) *Urban Craftsmen and Traders in the Roman World*. Oxford.

Winterling, A. (2011) *Caligula: A Biography*. Berkeley.

Wiseman, T. P. (1969) 'The census in the first century B.C.', *JRS* 59: 59–75.

(2001) 'Reading Carandini', *JRS* 91: 182–93.

(2002) 'Roman history and the ideological vacuum', in *Classics in Progress: Essays on Ancient Greece and Rome*, ed. T. P. Wiseman. Oxford and New York: 285–310.

Wolffhard, J. P. (1737) *De legibus cibariis post legem Fanniam*. Rinteln.

Wood, S. (2016) 'Public image of the Flavian dynasty: sculpture and coinage', *A Companion to the Flavian Age of Imperial Rome*, ed. A. Zissos. Chichester: 129–47.

Woodman, A. J. and Martin, R. H. (1996) *The Annals of Tacitus: Book 3, edited with commentary*. Cambridge.

Zanda, E. (2011) *Fighting Hydra–Like Luxury: Sumptuary Regulation in the Roman Republic*. Bristol.

Zissos, A. (ed.) (2016) *A Companion to the Flavian Age of Imperial Rome*. Chichester.

Zumpt, C. G. (1841) *Über den Stand der Bevölkerung und die Volksmehrung im Altertum*. Berlin.

Postscript: The authors would like to note that the Introduction has been a collaboration in the fullest sense of the word: they debated and developed the contents, the overall design and the details as the volume evolved. Their respective spheres of expertise helped to determine who produced the first version of specific sections and also account for slight differences in viewpoint. They would like to note that the initial draft of what became pages 1–38 was produced by CV; but both contributed to and stand behind the whole.

CHAPTER I

'FRUGALITY', ECONOMY AND SOCIETY IN ARCHAIC ROME (LATE SEVENTH TO EARLY FOURTH CENTURY BCE)

CRISTIANO VIGLIETTI

For Neville Morley

Frugality is founded on the principal that all riches have limits.
Edmund Burke (1780)

Were the Archaic Romans Frugal? Two-Odd Centuries of Debate (in a Nutshell)

In the history of scholarship on the ancient economy and society, the frugality of the Romans of the archaic period has long been taken for granted. Already in 1787, Francesco Mengotti's pioneering *Del commercio de' Romani* emphasised that

[ancient] historians glorify the rustic simplicity of the Romans of old. They say that the latter devoted themselves for five centuries to farming their small estates; ... that the likes of Camillus, Cincinnatus, Curius and Fabricius ... shifted from the plough to commanding legions. ... I admire these good customs, but what does this say about commerce? That there wasn't any.[1]

Some 50 years later, Adolphe Dureau De la Malle's *Économie Politique des Romains* sketched out the workings of the first six centuries of Rome's economy, arguing that this phase corresponds to

---

[1] Mengotti 1787: vii: 'Gli storici esaltano ... l'antica ed agreste semplicità de' Romani. Dicono ch'essi si applicarono per cinque secoli alla coltivazione de' loro piccioli poderi; ... che i Camilli, i Cincinnati, e i Curj, e i Fabrizi ... passavano dall'aratro a prendere il comando delle legioni. ... Io ammiro questi buoni costumi, ma che ne segue rispetto al commercio? Che non ve n'era alcuno.' Cf. also Machiavelli 1531: iii. 25.

Cristiano Viglietti

the time of austere habits, industrious poverty, and internal prosperity. …
The simplicity of the primitive customs allowed Rome to get by without arts
and commerce, … [which] were largely compensated for by the prosperous
condition of agriculture.[2]

Finally, a century after Dureau, a very similar outlook can
be traced in an article by Emanuela Savio, who stresses that

the fortunate wars that Rome had waged against Carthage, the Orient and
Asia revealed to the Romans – who were used to a thrifty life, to simple
furnishings, to frugal food – a world of refinement and luxury previously
unknown to them.[3]

Whether critical or complimentary of archaic Rome's frugality, all these scholars share the idea that frugality was
central to that social and historical context, and consisted of
a system of economic habits, attitudes and practices oriented
towards the thrifty farming of small self-sufficient estates
where, however, the low technological level constrained to a
certain degree the capacity of producing surpluses, and therefore of bringing about commercial activity and accumulating
wealth. This form of frugality is supposed to have characterised Rome not only in the *longue durée*, over her first five or six
centuries, but to have encompassed and involved the entire
Roman people, including high-ranking citizens like consuls
and dictators.[4]
The evidence on which these scholars relied in grounding
their interpretation of Rome's 'original' frugality was exclusively textual in nature, a body of written sources scarcely
homogeneous (in chronology, purpose or genre)[5] that, albeit
dealing with archaic times of Rome, are never actually

---

[2] Dureau de la Malle 1840: 491–2: 'C'est l'époque des mœurs austères, de la pauvreté laborieuse, de la prospérité intérieure. … La simplicité des mœurs primitives lui permettait de se passer facilement des arts et du négoce … [qui] étaient largement compensée par l'était prospère de l'agriculture.'
[3] Savio 1940: 174: 'Le guerre fortunate che Roma aveva condotto contro Cartagine, l'Oriente e l'Asia dischiusero ai Romani – abituati a una vita parca, a semplice mobilia, a cibo frugale – un mondo di raffinatezza e lusso fino ad allora loro ignoto.'
[4] Cf. Garnsey 1999: 77–9.
[5] E.g. Col. *Praef.* 1.1–20; Hor. *Carm.* 2.5; *Ep.* 1.1.54–66; 2.1.139; Liv. *Praef.* 11–12; Ov. *Fast.* 1.197–9, 3.179–98; Plin. *Nat.* 18.2.7, 5.27; Prop. 4.1.1–27; Juv. 11; cf. Wallace-Hadrill 2008: 315–19; Zanda 2011: 7–10.

128

'Frugality', Economy and Society in Archaic Rome

contemporary, and whose interpretation has been the object of intense debate.[6] This long-established interpretation of archaic Rome's frugality began to be questioned in the early decades of the twentieth century, after discoveries of archaeological remains dating back to the archaic age in Rome and in Latium Vetus. The excavations at Praeneste, for instance, brought to light the relics of some eighth and early seventh century BCE 'princely' tombs displaying an impressive number of refined gold, silver, ivory, iron, bronze and earthenware objects, sometimes imported even from distant areas of the Mediterranean – the opposite of Rome's primeval rustic simplicity as Giuseppe Salvioli pointed out in 1929:[7]

> Historians and moralists of the imperial period deliberately aimed to highlight moderation of desires, the frugal livelihood, the absence of any luxury. ... But as far as simplicity, the absence of comforts, the aversion to luxury are concerned, the historians' overstatement is belied by many relics that have emerged from the soil.[8]

For Salvioli, the contemporaneous archaeological evidence patently contradicts the later literary evidence. Frugal behaviours of the likes of Cincinnatus and other archaic aristocrats as reported by ancient authors should be regarded as nothing more than 'legends of political flavour',[9] while the economic history of the first centuries of Rome should be seen as a constant 'conquest of richness'[10] which, however, only a narrow minority would enjoy. Indeed, according to Salvioli, most Romans of the time lived in a condition better understood in terms of sheer poverty.

---

[6] Critical attitudes to the literary sources register since Perizonius 1685 and De Beaufort 1738; cf. in more recent times, Poucet 2000; Forsythe 2005; Richardson 2012. On the issue, Grandazzi 1991: 17–49; Cornell 1995: 1–30; Smith 2013.

[7] The 'princely tombs' at Praeneste were discovered between 1855 and 1876. On the complex history of their publication see Zevi 1976: 214–17; cf. Ross Holloway 1994: 156–60.

[8] Salvioli 1929: 12–13: 'Gli storici e i moralisti dell'epoca imperiale si proposero deliberatamente di porre in evidenza la moderazione nei desideri, il vivere parco, l'assenza di ogni lusso. ... Ma, per quanto riguarda la povertà, l'ignoranza di ogni comodo, l'avversione al lusso, l'esagerazione degli storici è smentita da tante reliquie affiorate dal suolo.'

[9] Salvioli 1929: 12: 'Leggende di sapore politico'.

[10] Salvioli 1929: 11: 'Conquista della ricchezza'.

129

Cristiano Viglietti

Other scholars concur with Salvioli, not least in the light of the discovery of further archaeological remains that seem to confirm his conclusions. For instance, Nicola Terrenato has recently argued that evidence of big aristocratic houses with stone foundations and tile roofs dating from the sixth to the early fifth century BCE, unearthed in the city of Rome and the surrounding countryside from the late 1980s,

> reinforces the impression that the contemporaries of Cincinnatus did not possess an ounce of his proverbial restraint, either in the city or in their country estates ... Shocking as this reconstruction may be for those who took later republican exaltations of pristine modesty at face value, we cannot but conclude at this point, on the strength of the archaeological evidence, that luxurious private residences ... existed, both in the city and outside it.[11]

In Terrenato's view, archaic Rome's elite appears as anything but frugal, and instead composed of refined lovers of luxury interested in relentlessly accumulating chattel goods or constructing opulent houses in durable materials sometimes connected to large estates.

The strength, and appeal, of this luxury-oriented reading of the archaic Romans' economic attitudes rests on two points. First, it is rooted in contemporary archaeological evidence rather than dubious later literary reconstructions of a past that the Romans themselves acknowledged was partly lost.[12] Secondly, this understanding of the material evidence is consistent with the widespread conviction in economic thinking that 'the purpose of all economic activity is to satisfy as many of our wants as possible'.[13] In this perspective, the archaeological evidence turns out to furnish proof of the fact that already in archaic Rome a number of more or less economically rational individuals aimed at – and largely succeeded in – satisfying increasing wants and desires, availing themselves of recent developments in technology of production and trade that boosted a not-so-backward economy.[14]

---

[11] Terrenato 2012: 71–2.   [12] E.g. Cic. *Rep.* 2.33; Liv. 6.1.1; cf. Cornell 1995: 15.
[13] Jongman 2007: 594. Cf. Hume 1740: 484; Robbins 1932: 15.
[14] Smith 1996: 120–2, 189. On the backwardness of the early Roman economy, cf. e.g. Momigliano 1989: 100; Schiavone 1989: 21–34.

'Frugality', Economy and Society in Archaic Rome

This chapter aims to re-frame the issue of frugality in archaic Rome, particularly for the period between the late seventh and the early fourth century BCE. Though sharing with Salvioli and Terrenato the conviction that any interpretation of economic conditions and behaviours in archaic Rome must be rooted as far as possible in contemporary evidence, I try to show moreover that the conclusions these scholars reach overlook some important pieces of evidence that allow us to reconstruct a society and economy at least partly invested in principles of frugality.

Hoc Plus ne Facito. **Archaic Rome's Elites from Conspicuous Consumption to the Sumptuary Laws**

As previously mentioned, archaeological excavations in Latium Vetus have provided evidence for the appearance – from the mid-eighth until the late seventh century BCE – of a number of aristocratic tombs, placed outside the city borders and characterised by the conspicuous consumption of refined, sometimes imported, chattel goods both as grave goods and ceremonial offerings.[15] Sometimes these goods are placed in equally sumptuous chamber (or pseudo-chamber) tombs.[16] This form of conspicuous consumption in a funerary context can be traced also in Etruria and other Mediterranean societies.[17] Most scholars agree that this phenomenon should be understood as one of the signs of an unfolding early urban society where the emerging aristocratic groups are now for the first time able to advertise their social superiority through the possession, display and extravagant consumption of a remarkable quantity of objects.[18] In particular, funerals represented a major opportunity for the members of the burgeoning elite

---

[15] Bartoloni, Cataldi Dini and Zevi 1982: 266–7; cf. Smith 1996: 79–89.

[16] Colonna 1988: 467–8; Ross Holloway 1994: 114–22, 156–60; cf. Bartoloni 1987: 157.

[17] Colonna 1988: 468; Smith 1998: 32–5; 2005: 102–4; Fulminante 2003: 21; Bartoloni 2010: 141–2.

[18] Cf. Smith 2005; Fulminante 2014. Social inequalities are *per se* a far older phenomenon: Fulminante 2003: 249–50; Smith 2006: 145.

131

Cristiano Viglietti

families to embark on a sort of competitive struggle where the capacity to dissipate valuable goods was likely intended as directly proportional to the social power of the parental group.[19] Competitive conspicuous consumption as traceable in mid-eighth to late seventh century BCE Latin society, despite not being a rational economic attitude in modern terms, can be understood as an aspect of an early consumer revolution closely tied to the increase in production, the concentration of power, greater wealth and the development of trade that enhanced the aristocrats' capacity to accumulate and expend wealth so as to devise and satisfy more and new wants.[20] It is therefore hard to relate these archaeological and social phenomena to the idea of frugality. Yet the interesting point for the purposes of this study is that the conspicuous consumption-oriented practices and attitudes characterising the early urbanisation of Rome and Latium came to an end relatively quickly. As of c. 620 BCE, in most Latium Vetus and definitely in Rome and the area likely under her control[21] the ostentatious destruction of wealth in aristocratic tombs – as well as in the building of tombs of large size – begins to decrease dramatically. Around 590 BCE grave goods practically disappear from most burials:[22] even when introduced, they are few, hardly in precious materials and almost never imported. This phenomenon, albeit present on a minor scale also elsewhere in the Mediterranean and in Italy,[23] takes on a quite radical dimension in Rome, where it will last until the second half of the fourth century BCE, when rich burials reappear.[24]

---

[19] Fulminante 2003: 239–42; cf. Smith 2005: 104.
[20] Smith 1998: 32–6; cf. Wallace-Hadrill 2008: 328.
[21] E.g. at Pratica di Mare, Fidenae and Lanuvium; outside the Roman domain, the archaeological phenomenon under consideration is absent in this phase: Bartoloni, Nizzo and Taloni 2009: 65; Bartoloni 2010: 142.
[22] Cornell 1995: 105–6; Fulminante 2003: xi.
[23] Ampolo 1984: 93–7; Toher 1986: 303–5; Colonna 1988: 489, 517–23; Bartoloni 2010: 141, 144, 147–8; Zanda 2011: 27–36.
[24] In some cases, the majestic seventh century BCE chamber tombs are re-utilised in the middle republic; Bartoloni 1987: 157.

132

'Frugality', Economy and Society in Archaic Rome

The first scholar who provided an interpretation of this remarkable phenomenon was the archaeologist Giovanni Colonna in 1977. Colonna argued that the abrupt reduction and impoverishment of grave goods and tombs in Rome is to be seen as a consequence of the enactment of an early, probably oral, version of the sumptuary norms aimed at reducing funerary expenses (*minuendi sumptus*) that were put into writing in the mid-fifth century BCE, in the tenth table of the Law of the Twelve Tables – a table that we know in detail thanks to a long fragment preserved in Cicero's *de Legibus*.[25] Following Colonna's work, Mark Toher and then Gilda Bartoloni noticed more recently that there is a certain discrepancy between funerary practices and the law in the sense that the former were carried out in a far stricter way than the requirements specified in the tenth table, according to which, for instance, citizens were not prevented from introducing imported or silver objects, or from having chamber tombs.[26] As the history of sumptuary laws in the Western world – and in Rome herself – shows, this is quite atypical: one of the most common traits of these laws is that they are constantly broken, discontinued or re-adapted by the states to keep up with the ways the citizens devised to circumvent them.[27] In the case under enquiry here, we have, on the contrary, the evidence of practices that were executed more rigorously than the legal requirements, and which remained effective and basically unchanged for over two-and-a-half centuries. For these reasons, Mark Toher regarded those laws as non-sumptuary;[28] but they evidently are. The tenth table commences with the intimidating caveat *hoc plus ne facito* ('do not do anything more than this')[29] and proceeds to list a long series of expenses, evidently possible only for richer citizens – hiring of professional flute players and wailers; anointing of corpse by slaves;

---

[25] Cic. *Leg.* 2.58, 62; cf. Tab. 10.1–10; Colonna 1977: 158–61; Ampolo 1984: 81–92; Viglietti 2011: 191–201.

[26] Toher 1986: 322–3; Bartoloni 1987: 144.

[27] E.g. Plin. *Nat.* 10.139; Tac. *Ann.* 3.52.2, 53.1–4; cf. Wallace-Hadrill 2008: 320–5, 329–31.

[28] Toher 1986: 306.   [29] Tab. 10.2.

Cristiano Viglietti

use of high-end wood for the funeral pyre; funeral banquets; sprinklings; introduction of gold objects, incense boxes, garlands, crowns or of an excessive number of veils and tunics in the tomb; duplication of the funeral itself – that were strictly forbidden on the occasion of funerals because, according to the law, they were considered excessive, too expensive (*sumptuosa*).[30]

The existence in archaic Rome of sumptuary laws inevitably brings into play the concept of frugality. Indeed, as most specialists of sumptuary laws have pointed out, these norms are based on a general, and characteristically pre-modern, principle according to which it is entirely acceptable that the central power and the community decide to socially and/or lawfully pry into, blame, restrain, punish certain (long-established, or flourishing) forms of possession and consumption of wealth that were considered excessive and socially destabilising.[31] In this perspective, the check on funerary expenses in archaic Rome can be understood as one of the measures through which the burgeoning city-state progressively curbed and controlled the possibly 'centrifugal' attitudes of some wealthier families – that, by means of the kin celebration through luxurious funerals and burials, might undermine the balance of public power – and promoted new socially acceptable values[32] which, as it happens, imply the thought-provoking idea that wants and desires can not only be fully met, but even *excessively* met.[33]

---

[30] Tab. 10.6a; cf. Smith 2006: 315; Viglietti 2018b: 239.

[31] Berry 1994: 85–7; Franceschi 2003: 167; Bartoloni 2010: 146; cf. Zanda 2011: 1. As Berry 1994: 201–17 subtly notes, in modern Western societies luxury is not punished, but simply governed by specific taxation aimed at redistributing wealth in the form of services. Cf. also Wallace-Hadrill 2008: 321.

[32] Ampolo 1984: 97–8; Torelli 1988: 252–7; Bartoloni 2010: 145; Zanda 2011: 32–6; Cifani 2016: 156. Smith 2006: 155–6 notes the instability of the Latial aristocracies as detectable from the eighth and seventh century BCE burials. The check of the city on funerary display might in a sense have been anticipated by the eighth–seventh century BCE push of conspicuous consumption in services outside the city boundaries: cf. Naglak and Terrenato 2019: 111.

[33] This kind of attitude evidently undermines the claimed universality of the postulate of scarcity; Sahlins 1972: 1–2; Xenos 1987: 225–7; cf. Morley 2018: 41–3.

'Frugality', Economy and Society in Archaic Rome

Houses, Census, *Res Mancipi* and The Boundaries of the Desirable

The marked frugality that the city demanded and expected of aristocratic funerary customs is not to be seen as the sign of the success of an anti-acquisitive and retrogressive culture or political philosophy in archaic Rome, however. Indeed, as mentioned apropos of Terrenato's position, the impoverishment of burials in Rome and in most of Latium Vetus is chronologically parallel with the appearance of private houses and public structures, sometimes impressive in size, in durable materials (tufa blocks for foundations and walls, earthenware for roof tiles and decorations), while imported chattel goods decrease in number and are often sacrificed in the votive deposits of temples.[34]

In 1996, Christopher Smith suggested that this patent reorientation of the uses of wealth by elite Roman society should in fact be considered a sign more of continuity than of change: in his view, aristocratic conspicuous consumption simply shifted from the underworld to the real world around 600 BCE.[35] On closer inspection, however, the uses of wealth for private houses in this phase can scarcely be defined as a new version of the preceding vogue for conspicuous consumption, both because – as we shall see later – houses were built to last (and to be passed on) and because some of them were connected to fields and incorporated productive parts aimed at processing (sometimes with impressive state-of-the-art implements) or storing farming yields.

Accordingly, the dramatic changes in the use of wealth from the end of the seventh century BCE onwards are rather to be understood as the upshot of a substantial institutional and cultural transformation that some scholars have recognised as slightly anticipating, and then overlapping with, one of the most important political and social changes in Roman history

---

[34] Cornell 1995: 225; Smith 1996: 228, cf. 2006: 315–16. The reduction of imports in sixth to mid-fourth century BCE is not to be understood as a sign of the exclusion of Rome from the Mediterranean trade of chattel goods: see Cifani 2016: 157–9.

[35] Smith 1996: 189. Smith changed his opinion in Smith 2006: 315–16.

Cristiano Viglietti

according to our written sources: the introduction of early forms of the census.[36] Even if it is likely that the early organisation of the census classes was simpler than, and overall rather different from, what Cicero, Livy and Dionysius maintain,[37] most scholars agree that from the sixth century BCE onwards Roman adult citizens began to be socially and militarily ranked according to an assessment of their visible, collectively recognisable wealth.[38] In such circumstances, conspicuous consumption in burials, quite apart from being prohibited legally, most likely also started to look 'irrational',[39] whereas the possession of durable houses, as well as estates and the instruments to farm them began to be indispensable for a citizen to obtain a place in the social and military ranks of the city.

At the same time, this institutionally, legally and culturally motivated re-orientation of economic habits based on the possession of census-valuable goods accounts for the impressive success of the early sumptuary laws and raises new questions related to the issue of frugality. Census is, in theory, a timocratic institution that tends to prize wealth and reward the rich(er) insofar as it encourages the accumulation of wealth as indispensable for social recognition and advancement; it may thus appear rooted in an ideology that supports greed and luxury. But the combination of contemporary material remains and (mostly contemporary) written evidence allows us to see that, despite appearances, frugality is actually an important component of archaic Rome's censitarian culture.

Archaeologically attested transformations beginning in the sixth century BCE, as well as some later written sources, strongly suggest that at least in the early days of the census only a relatively narrow category of possessions was important for

[36] Ampolo 1988: 218–31; cf. Cornell 1995: 108.
[37] Cic. *Rep.* 2.39; Liv. 1.43.1–9; D.H. 4.14–22; Humm 2001: 222–3; 2005: 283–308; cf. Viglietti 2018a: 147–8.
[38] Ampolo 1988: 221–28; Cornell 1995: 179–97; Andreau 1998: 239–42; Viglietti 2018a: 134–8; *contra* Armstrong 2016 (e.g. 126–8).
[39] Cf. Ampolo 1984: 97–8; Ross Holloway 1994: 170–1.

136

'Frugality', Economy and Society in Archaic Rome

the public assessment of one's status. These possessions – houses, estates and instruments to farm them, like cattle and slaves – belong to a characteristically local 'sphere of exchange'[40] that in all likelihood finds a legal definition in the later regal period, that is, *res mancipi*.[41] *Res mancipi* were purchased through a very complex and formal procedure called *mancipatio*, possible only between Roman citizens or between Romans and allies who had received *ius commercii*. Roman jurists considered *res mancipi* 'more prized things' (*res pretiosiores*), evidently because of their status-conferring capacity.[42]

Accordingly, the introduction of a census ideology does not encourage a generic acquisitive or luxury-oriented attitude. Instead, it promotes a selective pattern as to the possession and accumulation of things, where *res mancipi* – and the results of an extensive use of *res mancipi*, like farming outcomes – play a major role.[43] Furthermore, even within this peculiar framework some frugal caveats existed. One of these caveats concerned the appropriate management of one's patrimony, in which *res mancipi* normally played a central role. The two variants of norm 5.7c of the Law of the Twelve Tables as reported by Ulpian state the following:[44]

By the Law of the Twelve Tables a spendthrift is forbidden to exercise administration over his own goods. And this was introduced by customs from the beginnings (*moribus ab initio introductum est*).

The Law of the Twelve Tables ordains that a person, who – being insane or a spendthrift (*furiosum itemque prodigum*) – is prohibited from administering his own goods, shall be under the trusteeship of agnates.

---

[40] Bohannan and Dalton 1962: 3–8; cf. Viglietti 2011: 252–3.

[41] E.g. Capogrossi Colognesi 1988: 269–71; McClintock 2016: 83.

[42] Drummond 1989: 119. On *res mancipi* see Gaius *Inst.* 1.192. *Mancipatio* and *res mancipi* are often mentioned in the Twelve Tables: Tab. 5.2, 6.1, 6.5b. *Res mancipi* were distinguished from the *res nec mancipi*, which were bought through a far simpler sale (*traditio*) permitted among Romans and theoretically any foreign people: Tab. 7.11; Gaius *Res cottidianae* 2.3; Ulp. *Tituli ex corpore* 19.1 and 7; Catalano 1965: 65–78; Albanese 1982: 136–7.

[43] Drummond 1989: 118–20. The inappropriate maintenance of a field was punished by the censors: Cato, fr. 124 Malcovati; Plin. *Nat.* 18.3.11; Nicolet 1980: 79; Edwards 1993: 182; Viglietti 2011: 267–9. Cf. from a different perspective Humm 2005: 308–44.

[44] Ulp. *dig.* 27.19.1; *Tituli ex corpore* 12.2. Cf. Riccobono 1968: 40; Crawford 1996: 644 (variants h and j).

137

Cristiano Viglietti

The norm preventing spendthrift citizens from managing their patrimony – the existence of which in oral and customary form predates the mid-fifth century BCE according to Ulpian – reveals a social concern with the potential negative effects of extravagance or negligence on the social status of the spendthrift himself and his descendants. In this perspective, the Romans of the time considered the transferral of trusteeship to the group of agnates the best way to guarantee the preservation and transmission of patrimony, the possibility of maintaining census rank and the honour of the 'House'[45] for the spendthrift's family over time. The destabilising power of a prodigal citizen's behaviour for the balance of society is further accounted for by the juridical correlation of the latter with someone mentally insane.[46] Accordingly, the anxieties implied by the Twelve Tables show that in the phase under enquiry the social encouragement to accumulate stable possessions was embedded in an economic view promoting maximum carefulness and frugality in managing one's resources, in order to hand them down intact to the following generations.[47]

Other frugal caveats concerned the extent to which patrimony – specifically in the form of *res mancipi* – could be accumulated in accordance with law and custom. As mentioned earlier, the decades between the mid-sixth and the early fifth century BCE are characterised by important private building activities in the heart of Rome and in the countryside. Many of the houses built of durable materials in this phase in all likelihood belonged to prominent families, who began to inhabit bigger residences than those – already with durable components – of the early sixth century BCE or than the more ancient ones consisting of perishable materials.[48] The cause for this building activity, along with the technological

---

[45] On the concept of 'House' (as defined by Lévi-Strauss 1975) applied to archaic Rome, cf. Naglak and Terrenato 2019: 106–8; Smith 2019: 31–4.

[46] Cf. Diliberto 1984: 40, 120–3; Edwards 1993: 180–1.

[47] Cf. Dubois-Pelerin 2008: 19.

[48] On early sixth century BCE houses in Rome, Delfino 2014: 92; on eighth to seventh century BCE houses in Latium, Colonna 1988: 450–1, 471–2; Ross Holloway 1994: 51–60. On the case of Gabii, Naglak and Terrenato 2019: 106–13.

138

'Frugality', Economy and Society in Archaic Rome

improvements of the time,[49] likely has to do with the increase in the importance of the Forum area within the general institutional and monumental reorganisation of the late regal age, which prompted the local elite to strive for taking possession of the most strategic and visible areas near the political heart of the city.[50] What is interesting is that, after this housing boom, city buildings do not further increase in size (and likely in number) for quite a long time. Houses are sometimes reorganised or restored over time, but not enlarged before the middle/late fourth century BCE.[51] The supposed economic crisis of the fifth century BCE, that would affect also richer citizens, is a possible partial explanation for this, even though this form of restraint in housing sometimes continues until the late third century BCE, that is in a far more expansive phase of Rome's history. Another possible interpretation is that this archaeological phenomenon is the result of a sort of agreement among the relatively few dominant families of the late monarchy and early republic, who, once they had apportioned among themselves the physically limited spaces of the city centre, decided to be content with what they had and avoided expanding this indefinitely 'without it necessarily being the case that the economic power of the owners decreased'.[52] This form of space sharing and of self-imposed frugality from the early fifth century BCE at the same time expresses and reinforces the characteristic balance within the Roman elite families in this phase and its tendency 'towards the distribution of power rather than its concentration'.[53]

While aristocratic housing undergoes a long-lasting curb, the Roman elite appears interested in taking possession of another type of *res mancipi*, that is, cultivable lands in the

---

[49] Cifani 2008: 256–333 *passim*; 2016: 154; Viglietti 2020.

[50] Carafa 1995: 264–6; cf. Beck 2009: 361, 365–6.

[51] E.g. Carafa 1995: 253 (Domus 3 on the Palatine slope); cf. Smith 2006: 154.

[52] 'Senza che questo significhi necessariamente una contrazione della forza economica dei proprietari'; De Albentiis 1990: 58.

[53] Smith 2006: 315. This conclusion is partly compatible with Gaetano De Sanctis' (1907: 224–55) theory of the 'serrata del patriziato'; cf. Cornell 1995: 251–6; Smith 2011: 224; 2019: 36. Balance of power does not imply economic uniformity, though. Cf. in a different perspective Gabba 1981: 34.

Cristiano Viglietti

still-limited Roman territory. The developments of early villas (alongside smaller-size farms) and, in general, the noticeable increase in rural sites in the sixth and fifth century BCE account for this state of affairs.[54] Interestingly, also in this case villas do *not* grow in size after the early decades of the fifth century BCE;[55] and at a certain point in time, a limit on the amount of land controlled by individual aristocrats was imposed, in the form of the Licinian-Sextian law *de modo agrorum* of 367 BCE.[56] The legal threshold of 500 *iugera*, despite being quite a high limit for that time, accounts again for the presence of the idea in archaic Rome's culture that wealth, including socially acceptable forms of it, cannot be accumulated indefinitely lest the city's social and political balances be destabilised.[57] This characteristic mechanism of setting a social or legal limit to the accumulation even of *res mancipi* operates also for the *res nec mancipi*. Indeed, not only did the sumptuary laws restrain the exhibition and consumption of chattel goods during funerals; the Twelve Tables also imposed the *fenus unciarium* (one-twelfth of the capital) as a maximum interest, while other fourth-century laws suspended or further reduced the interest rate, keeping in check the possibility for a citizen to enrich himself through moneylending.[58] Also in this case, the law appears aimed at safeguarding social stability in a phase in which getting into debt was quite a common phenomenon with potentially dramatic consequences, by preventing creditors from demanding theoretically limitless interest that would eventually ruin the debtor.[59]

And it is precisely from the world of the debtor that we can observe another, final facet of frugality in archaic Rome.

---

[54] Carafa 2000; Cifani 2009. On the possible extent of the villa phenomenon in the early republic, Volpe 2012: 98, 106–7.

[55] E.g. De Davide 2006: 225 (Auditorium site); cf. Ricci 2006: 191.

[56] The historical reality of this law is now commonly accepted: Rich 2008: esp. 561–4; Balbo 2010: 305–11; Roselaar 2010: 105–12; Capogrossi Colognesi 2012: 77–83. For the debate on this topic, see Roselaar 2010: 95–105 and Chapter 2 (Rich) in this volume.

[57] Gargola 1995: 143–5; Rich 2008: 563–4. Cf. Smith 2011: 220–1, 225–7.

[58] Tab. 8.18a–b; cf. Andreau 1999: 90–1; Aubert 2004: 164–5; Cifani 2016: 155.

[59] Cornell 1995: 265–8, 280–3; Lerouxel 2015.

'Frugality', Economy and Society in Archaic Rome

Frugality of the Have-Nots: A Remedy Against Poverty

So far, we have addressed some frugality-oriented attitudes and institutional requirements that must have operated principally among the wealthier citizens of archaic Rome. Now we shall try to see whether it is possible to detect (and if so in what forms) frugal habits in the poorer sections of Roman society in the phase under enquiry. Investigating this topic is particularly hard – and of course more speculative – because the amount of information available is very small and mostly concerns the fifth and fourth centuries BCE. Yet owing to some recent discoveries, the available evidence, however scarce, offers some unexpected interpretive paths.

In his *Attic Nights* (20.1.45–7), Aulus Gellius quotes and comments on the norms of the Law of the Twelve Tables that regulated the behaviours of the creditor vis-à-vis a defaulting debtor incapable of finding a surety or unwilling to find a compromise (usually by becoming a *nexus*).[60] In these circumstances the debtor was *addictus* to the creditor. At this point the law states:

> The debtor if he shall wish may live on his own. If he does not live on his own, he (sc. the creditor) shall give him one pound of emmer for each day (*libras farris endo dies dato*). He may give more if he shall so desire.[61] Moreover, there was meanwhile the right of compromising, and unless they made a compromise debtors were held in bonds for sixty days. During that time [the *addicti*] were brought before the praetor's court in the *comitium* on three successive *nundinae* and the amount for which they were judged liable was announced; and on the third *nundinae* they suffered capital punishment or were delivered up for sale across the Tiber, abroad.[62]

The interesting point in this norm for the issue of the frugality of the have-nots in archaic Rome concerns the pound of emmer that a creditor was legally expected to give the *addictus* debtor. Even though the diet based on the *libra farris* was evidently meant to be punitive, it was also supposed to be not so harsh as to put the debtor's life at risk if after 60 days the latter could be sold as a slave on the Etruscan market. The energy value

---

[60] Cf. Drummond 1989: 213–17; Aubert 2004: 165–6; Viglietti 2011: 125–6.
[61] Tab. 3.4.   [62] Tab. 3.5; cf. Riccobono 1968: 32–3; Crawford 1996: 625–9.

141

Cristiano Viglietti

provided by a Roman pound (327 grams) of emmer corresponds to 1100–1150 kcal/day. This amount is c. 25–30 per cent less than the 1400/1500 kcal/day that a 40-year-old man, 160 cm (5.3 ft.) tall and weighing 60 kg – taken here as the standard 'archaic Roman poor'[63] – needs for his basal metabolic rate, that is the minimal rate of energy expenditure at complete rest, according to the current FAO human energy requirements.[64] The energy provided by a pound of emmer is furthermore c. 70 per cent inferior to the round figure of 2000 kcal/day today generally considered the standard for subsistence.[65]

This evident contradiction between the Twelve Tables and modern energy requirements can be resolved in two ways. First, if the FAO standards are considered universal – as they claim to be – the archaic law is to be interpreted as something between a blatant exaggeration and a terrorising caveat not corresponding to any reality since the *libra farris* would be 'inferior to the vital minimum'.[66] And secondly, if instead the Twelve Tables norms are taken to have been applied in practice, they offer an interesting indicator of the fact that the levels of consumption among the lower ranking Romans of the archaic age could have been lower than those that are reckoned to be the bare minimum today – and in fact also lower than those traceable in later Roman historical documents.[67]

This second alternative, if accepted, provides scope for positing the existence of 'frugal' norms in the social context under consideration. Economic historian Peter Temin has recently criticised the habit of numerous scholars of utilising

---

[63] Cf. Foxhall and Forbes 1982: 46; Garnsey 1989: 45; Jongman 2007: 607–9. Archaeology has shown that eighth–seventh century BCE Latin inhumed skeletons (likely of aristocrats) were relatively tall (avg. 168.3 cm; 5.6 ft.): Kron 2005: 72–5.

[64] FAO 2004: 37; cf. Viglietti 2018b: 230–3.

[65] Jongman 2007: 598–600; cf. Hopkins 1980: 118; 1996: 197 and n. 11; Campano and Salvatore 2006: 11.

[66] 'Inferiore al minimo vitale'; De Martino 1979: 6.

[67] For instance, at *Agr.* 56–8, Cato, writing around 160 BCE, recommended four modii/month (27 kg) of wheat (*triticum*) in the winter, and four-and-a-half modii/month (30.4 kg), that is 2700 to 3050 kcal/day as food for slaves employed for heavier works. Yet rations for the estate overseer (*uilicus*) and wife, for shepherds and guardians were definitely lower, three modii/month equivalent to 2040 kcal/day: cf. Foxhall and Forbes 1982: 63; Rathbone 2009: 314.

'Frugality', Economy and Society in Archaic Rome

modern standards of subsistence to reconstruct ancient levels of consumption, 'as if [subsistence] was a biological constant that had not changed in two millennia'. For Temin, subsistence is primarily 'a sociological construct, not a biological one'.[68] As social anthropology has shown, the levels and features of poverty and malnourishment differ markedly from one society to the next and in Temin's viewpoint it is incorrect to fix a threshold of universal value below which an individual or a community cannot fall. The economic historian of ancient Rome should try to inquire 'not whether ordinary Romans lived at subsistence level, but rather which kind of subsistence they experienced' in any given period.[69]

It is not hard to find proof for the difference between our levels of subsistence and those of other societies in either the ancient or the ethnographic record. For instance, Thucydides reports that for eight months the Athenian soldiers imprisoned after the defeat in Syracuse of 413 BCE were daily fed with two κοτύλαι of barley or wheat (σῖτος), equivalent to 1000 to 1200 kcal, and compelled to undergo hard labour. Only some of them died.[70] Furthermore, among the modern Samburu, a people of livestock herders of Northern Kenya, the high frequency of droughts has caused them to develop a famine diet based on the consumption of very modest quantities of food (basically a mixture of cow's milk and blood) for some months of every year, corresponding roughly to 1000–1100 kcal/day. Interestingly, anthropologist Jon Holtzman noticed that even in normal conditions the average number of calories ingested by Samburu men, although higher than in the drought period, nevertheless remains relatively low compared to our standards, and on average inferior to 2000 kcal/day.[71]

---

[68] Temin 2013: 215, 250. Temin draws especially on the results of Dasgupta 1993: esp. 412, 439–40. Interestingly, he reaches very similar conclusions to Pearson 1957: 325.

[69] Temin 2013: 250; cf. Horden and Purcell 2000: 271.

[70] Th. 7.87.1–3; Foxhall and Forbes 1982: 61–2.

[71] Holtzman 2009: 208. Their low levels of consumption apparently do not harm life expectancy. Paul Spencer 1965: 14 observed that 26 per cent of the Samburu he had surveyed were at least 57 years old.

Samburu practices of food consumption – along with the passage of Thucydides – cannot only help make sense of the reality of the *addictus* diet as indicated in the Twelve Tables and corroborate the possibility that Romans in the archaic age were capable of subsisting with little in unfortunate and short-term circumstance.[72] Their levels of consumption in ordinary times also provide some hint as to the possible normal standards of subsistence among the poor in archaic Rome.

The fact that the levels of consumption of lower ranking citizens in this phase were in general not high can be deduced from a quite important set of literary sources. Ancient writers tell us that between 504 and 329 BCE, Rome carried out seven land assignments, consisting of lots called *heredia*, two to three-and-a-quarter *iugera* in size (5040 to 8190 m² or 1.25 to 2.02 acres) and directed at poorer citizens or colonists. Still in 173 BCE an apportionment of three *iugera* is mentioned in a Latin colonisation of *ager Ligustinus et Gallicus*.[73]

Just as in the case of the *addictus* diet, some scholars have considered the information on the early republican *heredia* implausible because (so the argument goes) those few *iugera* of land would have been insufficient to feed a family.[74] Yet this position is based on assumptions that recently have been put into question – and insofar as possible this chapter would like to contribute to this process of reconsideration.

---

[72] Comparison here is only aimed at 'construire des analogies efficaces' (Detienne 2010: 21) that can help make sense of isolated and otherwise inscrutable pieces of evidence by putting them into a comparative perspective with the help of data from other cultures; but this does not imply that the cultures from which the evidence is taken belong to the same (evolutionary) stage even though they share comparable practices. Cf. Kluckhohn 1949; Bettini 2018.

[73] 504 BCE, distribution of two *iugera* in Rome (Plu. *Publ.* 21.10); 418 BCE, two *iugera* in the colony of Labici (Liv. 2.47.6); 385 BCE, two-and-a-half *iugera* in the colony of Satricum (Liv. 6.16.6–7); 369 BCE, two *iugera* in the colony of Velitrae (Liv. 6.36.11); 340 BCE, two-and-three-quarter *iugera* between Latin and Privernian territory and three-and-a-quarter *iugera* in Falernian territory (Liv. 8.11.14); 329 BCE, two *iugera* in the colony of Anxur (Liv. 8.21.11); on the three-*iugera* apportionment of 173 BCE, see Liv. 42.4.3–4. Cf. Roselaar 2010: 26–31; Chiabà 2011: 91–109. On the two-*iugera* plots see also Var. *R.* 1.10.2; Plin. *Nat.* 18.2.7; Fest. 47.1–2L; further Drummond 1989: 120–1; Viglietti 2014: 453.

[74] E.g. Ampolo 1980: 25–6; Crawford 1985: 24; Momigliano 1989: 100; Drummond 1989: 121; Torelli 2011: 28–9.

'Frugality', Economy and Society in Archaic Rome

Scholars who over the course of time have downplayed the historical value of the tradition of the few-*iugera* plots have maintained that there are two strictly connected reasons why those pieces of land would have been insufficient. First, they argue that in this phase yields were very low (only three or four times the sown seed), which means that relatively big areas of land would be needed for Roman farmers to subsist.[75] And secondly, they maintain that the meagre yields of those small lots of land were supposed to feed a quite extended number of recipients, that is a Roman *paterfamilias* and his *familia*, including wife, sons, daughters and eventual grandchildren.[76] This sceptical position was given an initial blow when experimental archaeology demonstrated that even with Iron Age implements and techniques it is possible to obtain relatively high yields of emmer or spelt – no less than seven to eight times the sown seed, or more[77] – provided that the farmer worked the field with 'productive capacity'.[78] Further weakening the case for scepticism towards the historical value of our sources for small early republican land assignments, Luigi Capogrossi Colognesi has demonstrated that the legal recipients of the few-*iugera* lots were not just *patresfamilias*, but all *uiri*, that is all the adult males of the family. This means that the small *heredia* were expected to satisfy the needs of not more than an adult man, a woman and their underage children, while a *pater* with male sons older than sixteen would get an extra plot for

---

[75] Ampolo 1980: 16–24; Pucci 1989: 371–2; Hermon 2001: 155 and n. 33. Cf. already Mommsen 1865: 190 n. On the history of scholarship on this theme, see Viglietti 2014: 454–9.

[76] Ampolo 1980: 25–6, according to whom at least seven *iugera* would be needed. Cf. De Martino 1979: 4.

[77] Reynolds 1981: 104–12; Viglietti 2014: 463. On emmer and spelt as the most archaeologically attested cereals in archaic Rome see Motta 2002: 74. Cf. Hollander 2019: 23–4. These relatively good outcomes make more sense of (i) the increase in population in sixth century BCE Latium as traceable by the boom in rural sites (Carafa 2000; Carandini 2006: 598–609; Cifani 2016: 159; cf. Fulminante 2003: 235–7); (ii) the history of Roman agriculture as characterised by more gradual improvements and not by a drastic passage from very low yields to the definitely good ones (ten to fifteen times the seed sown) reported by late-republican sources: Var. *R.* 1.44; cf. Cic. *Ver.* 2.3.112; Viglietti 2014: 460–1.

[78] Sahlins 1972: 82–94; cf. Chayanov 1966: 75–6.

145

Cristiano Viglietti

each of them.[79] Furthermore, it is worth stressing that the ancient sources on the topic consider the few *iugera* of land as necessary only for growing cereals (in particular emmer) and cultivable plants in general, and not as the only source of the owner's subsistence.[80] Wild fruits, herbs, wood and grazing lands for a few goats, sheep or pigs could be found elsewhere, on the public/common lands.[81] Finally, recent archaeological discoveries of very small (c. 25 m^2) farms in the Roman countryside dating from the mid-sixth century BCE, partly made of durable materials, account for the actual existence of low-ranking farmers that likely lived off small possessions of land.[82]

Once we take into consideration that these allotments were (a) capable of obtaining, according to the likely standards of the time, average yields definitely superior to three/four times the sown seed; (b) only meant to satisfy the needs of just a nuclear family in terms of cereals and plants; and (c) aimed at people whose caloric requirements were lower relative to ours, the clues from the Twelve Table norm on the treatment of the *addictus* by the creditor and from the Samburu diet can help make further sense of our sources for few-*iugera heredia*. As I have investigated elsewhere, from a moderately successful crop yield (eight times the sown seed) even the smallest plots (those of two *iugera*) would have been able to produce cereals, legumes, vegetables and fruits, which, once integrated with the milk of a goat and the meat of two pigs (living in a sty in the plot and grazing elsewhere) (**Chart I**), would have provided an average of c. 5000 kcal/day for the family.[83] The amount of 5000 kcal can be divided, for instance, into c. 1850 for the *uir*,[84] c. 1250 for his wife and c. 950 for each of two minor children. In the case of slightly bigger plots the overall quantity of kcal/day derived from the vegetables would increase and offer either the possibility of consuming more or, if the yield

[79] Capogrossi Colognesi 2006 (esp. 44); cf. Viglietti 2014: 470.
[80] Plin. *Nat.* 18.2.7, cf. 19.19.52; Paul. *Fest.* 89.1L; Crawford 1985: 24; Viglietti 2018b: 236–8.
[81] Capogrossi Colognesi 1988: 268–75; 2012: 61–83; Garnsey 1999: 36–41.
[82] Cifani 2009: 317–24; cf. Drummond 1989: 120–2.
[83] Viglietti 2014 (esp. 459–70); 2018b: 230–8.   [84] Cf. Garnsey 1998: 229.

146

'Frugality', Economy and Society in Archaic Rome

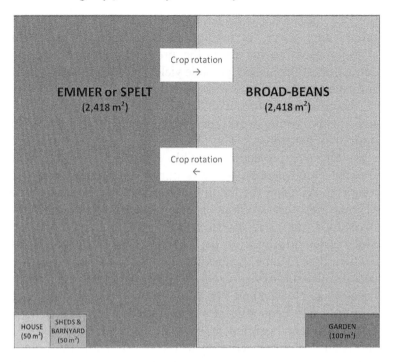

Chart 1 Possible model of a 2-*iugera* field in a system of crop rotation in early republican Rome.
Drawing by the author.

was a little less successful (seven times the sown seed), guarantee the family subsistence.

This reconstruction can provide some elements for a definition of the workings of frugality in the lower section of archaic Roman society. On the one hand, the Roman have-nots' frugality consists in the fact that, generally speaking, they had relatively low caloric requirements compared not only to ours, but also to those of the Romans of the late Republic and of the early empire, and in all likelihood also to those of wealthier contemporary citizens.[85] On the other hand,

---

[85] The height of eighth–seventh century BCE skeletons found in Latin aristocratic burials, impressive for that historical context, possibly reflects the rich and balanced diet of the local elite: see Kron 2005: 72–5 and cf. n. 63 above.

Cristiano Viglietti

precisely because a considerable number of Romans owned rather small pieces of land, they must have worked them skilfully so as to maximise the production and ensure the extraction of the highest possible yields in order to satisfy their subsistence requirements (however low).[86]

Accordingly, the formula 'low food requirements plus intensive, thrifty farming work' sums up the frugality of the Roman poor in archaic times.[87] This formula in fact turns out to be the most effective protection possible against poverty in those specific circumstances, but was hardly very effective in the long run. As again the literary evidence shows, after a couple of centuries the two/three-*iugera* system came to an end. Already in the early fourth century BCE at Veii, and then more systematically from the early third to the early second century BCE, Rome assigned bigger lots to colonists, usually between five and seven *iugera*.[88] This is in a sense no surprise because, as Horden and Purcell point out,[89] sheer subsistence is not a safe economic strategy: and the early republican system of land assignments was evidently very close to a subsistence politics according to the standards of the time.[90] In the long run, unpredictable factors like war, enemy raids or, more rarely, the vagaries of Mediterranean weather[91] ended up jeopardising this fragile arrangement, where safety surplus margins were very thin,[92] as the information on the relatively frequent food crises in this phase reveals.[93]

---

[86] On the importance of 'productive capacity' in farming societies, Sahlins 1972: 82–94; cf. Chayanov 1966: 75–6.

[87] On later phases, see Rathbone 2008.

[88] 396 BCE, seven *iugera* at Veii (Liv. 5.30.8–9); 290–275 BCE, c. seven *iugera* in Sabine territory (Col. 1, *Praef.* 14; V. Max. 4.3.5; Plin. *Nat.* 18.4.18); 273 BCE, six *iugera* at Cosa (Liv. *Per.* 14; Vell. 1.14.7); 184 BCE, six *iugera* at Potentia and Pisaurum (Liv. 39.44.10); 183 BCE, five *iugera* at Mutina, eight at Parma, ten at Saturnia (Liv. 39.55.7–9); 181 BCE, five *iugera* at Graviscae (Liv. 40.29.1–2); 177 BCE, six-and-a-half *iugera* at Luna (Liv. 41.13.4–5); cf. Cornell 1995: 328–9; Roselaar 2010: 41–3.

[89] Horden and Purcell 2000: 271–3.

[90] As Plin. *Nat.* 19.19.50–2 and Paul. *Fest.* 89.1L imply.

[91] The two (out of fourteen) early republican food crises caused by insufficient crops in years too rainy or too dry are those of 456 BCE (Liv. 3.31.1) and 392 BCE (Liv. 5.31.5; D.H. 13.4); Garnsey 1988: 169–71; Viglietti 2017a: 155.

[92] Cf. Sahlins 1972: 69–74, 101–2; Halstead 1989: 73.

[93] Virlouvet 1985: 11–13; Garnsey 1988: 167–81; Viglietti 2017a: 155–6.

'Frugality', Economy and Society in Archaic Rome

Conclusion: Rethinking the Boundaries of Frugality in Archaic Rome

This investigation has attempted to understand to what extent the concept of frugality can be a helpful tool for making sense of some important and peculiar aspects of the economic customs, laws and behaviours of the Romans in the archaic phase.

The available archaeological evidence has first of all shown that an aristocracy existed in archaic Rome that was characterised by the possession of definitely more wealth than the lower section of the Roman populace,[94] while institutions like the census promoted specific modes of material acquisition.[95] Therefore, the long-held notion that in the first centuries of the city's history the entire Roman people, including its elite, were poor and disdained any form of wealth is rather to be seen as the result of later – although already ancient – interpretations based on a teleological or evolutionary vision of the Roman past that only marginally has to do with historical reality.[96] However, the fact that wealth played an important role in the society of archaic Rome in the early phases of the city does not entail that the growing (and theoretically endless) satisfaction of wants and the acquisition and possession of ever more goods were socially promoted economic objectives in this context. Rather, the history of Rome from c. 620 BCE onwards reveals the presence of different and peculiar facets of what we would call frugality. In the first place, frugality involved habits and norms that controlled, restrained and punished some material behaviours potentially practised by richer citizens. Sumptuary laws are the clearest case in point. Yet, frugality in this historical context is not to be understood only as a restrained and institutionally controlled mode of *consumption*. Laws and customs over time also acted as frugal

---

[94] It is worth noting that the presence of mid-sized farms (about 100–120 m^2) in the sixth–fifth century BCE Roman countryside accounts for the existence of a relatively stratified society. Cf. Cifani 2009: 317–20.

[95] Cf. Harris 1979: 65–6.

[96] Garnsey 1999: 79; Viglietti 2017b: 243–5; cf. Zehnacker 1990: 325.

149

checks on forms of wealth *accumulation* that were considered problematic – as the selective fostering of the acquisition of *res mancipi*, the laws limiting the possibility of enrichment through usury and (later) the accumulation of land, and the peculiar attitude of aristocrats, who after the early fifth century BCE abstained for a long time from expanding their houses in the city and the countryside of Rome, testify. Finally, we have seen that the concept of frugality is also heuristically helpful for describing a potent and socially encompassing model for the *administration* and *production* of goods.[97] Indeed, the careful, thrifty and maximising management of one's possessions (regulated and prompted by the norms that forbade spendthrift citizens from administering their patrimony) and the importance of being in charge of one's own estate and its cultivation enabled citizens belonging to the higher echelons of society to keep, and possibly increase, their patrimony and status. Those same attitudes also enabled poorer citizens lower down the social scale to subsist and, at the same time, remain in control of the quantity of land that was required to have a role in the army and the voting assemblies.[98] We have also seen that, in the case of poorer Roman citizens, frugality in running their estates was likely complemented by a mode of food consumption involving relatively low caloric levels, which contributed to a more achievable subsistence in the politically unstable early republican phase.[99]

The historical presence and cultural pervasiveness of these peculiar cultural ingredients allow us to hypothesise that frugality played an important role in constructing the 'shared vision'[100] of the Roman community, especially after the important institutional watershed beginning in the late seventh/early sixth century BCE. It is also possible that different facets of archaic Roman frugality were to a certain extent

---

[97] Cf. Morley 2018, esp. 50–2.   [98] Crawford 1985: 24.
[99] Sahlins 1972: 1–2; cf. Viglietti 2011: 220–2.
[100] Smith 2006: 316; 2011: 227–28. Wallace-Hadrill 2008: 443 subtly criticises the widespread tendency to understand Roman culture only as an elite phenomenon: 'if culture is about the construction of identities, we cannot stop with the construction of elite identity.'

'Frugality', Economy and Society in Archaic Rome

consistent with each other as components of what the later sources call *parsimonia*, a concept that incorporates careful, thrifty, maximising, non-destructive practices and attitudes aimed at guaranteeing the family's subsistence and preserving or, if possible, increasing the patrimony[101] – as well as an anti-*luxuria* ethos meant to inspire behaviours and norms that by avoiding excess in the consumption or accumulation of (certain) material goods were thought to guarantee the preservation of the desired social order.[102]

Bibliography

Albanese, B. (1982) *Gli atti negoziali nel diritto privato romano*. Palermo.

Ampolo, C. (1980) 'Le condizioni materiali della produzione. Agricoltura e paesaggio agrario', *DArch* n.s. 2.1: 15–46.

(1984) 'Il lusso funerario e la città arcaica', *AION (archeol)* 6: 71–102.

(1988) 'La città riformata e l'organizzazione centuriata. Lo spazio, il tempo, il sacro nella nuova realtà urbana', in *Storia di Roma I. Roma in Italia*, eds. A. Momigliano and A. Schiavone. Turin: 203–39.

Andreau, J. (1998) 'Cens, évaluation et monnaie dans l'Antiquité romaine', in *La monnaie souveraine*, eds. M. Aglietta and A. Orléan. Paris: 213–50.

(1999) *Banking and Business in the Roman World*. Cambridge.

Armstrong, J. (2016) *War and Society in Early Rome: From Warlords to Generals*. Cambridge.

Aubert, J.-J. (2004) 'The Republican economy and Roman law: regulation, promotion, or reflection?', in *The Cambridge Companion to the Roman Republic*, ed. H. I. Flower. Cambridge: 160–78.

Balbo, M. (2010) 'La *lex Licinia de modo agrorum*: riconsiderazione di un modello storiografico', *RFIC* 138.3–4: 265–311.

Bartoloni, G. (1987) 'Esibizione di ricchezza a Roma nel VI e V secolo a.C.: doni votivi e corredi funerari', *Scienze dell'Antichità* 1: 143–59.

(2010) 'Il cambiamento delle pratiche funerarie nell'età dei Tarquini', in *La grande Roma dei Tarquini: atti del 17° convegno internazionale di*

---

[101] E.g. Cato, *orat.* 128 Malcovati; Cic. *Off.* 2.87. Accordingly, Roman frugality is in no sense opposite to richness *per se*. Cf. Garnsey 1999: 79.

[102] Pl. *Trin.* 1028–9; Gel. 13.24, the source of Cato, *orat.* fr. 174 Malcovati; Cic. *Parad.* 6.49, 51; Tac. *Ann.* 3.54.3. Cf. Smith 2006: 315; Wallace-Hadrill 2008: 318, 329, 333; Viglietti 2011: 176–216. On the life based on 'limited [economic] objectives' in Columella, see Garnsey 1999: 79. On the cultural and historical relativity of the concept of luxury, see Fulminante 2003: 22; Zanda 2011: 1–4.

Cristiano Viglietti

studi sulla storia e l'archeologia dell'Etruria, ed. G. M. Della Fina. Rome: 141–67.

Bartoloni, G., Cataldi Dini, M. and Zevi, F. (1982) 'Aspetti dell'ideologia funeraria nella necropoli di Castel di Decima', in *La mort, les morts dans les sociétés anciennes*, eds. G. Gnoli and J.-P. Vernant. Cambridge: 257–73.

Bartoloni, G., Nizzo, V. and Taloni, M. (2009) 'Dall'esibizione al rigore: analisi dei sepolcreti laziali tra VII e VI sec. a.C.', in *Tra Etruria, Lazio e Magna Grecia: indagini sulle necropoli*, eds. R. Bonaudo, L. Cerchiai and C. Pellegrino. Paestum: 65–86.

Beck, H. (2009) 'From Poplicola to Augustus: senatorial houses in Roman political culture', *Phoenix* 63.3–4: 361–84.

Berry, C. (1994) *The Idea of Luxury: A Conceptual and Historical Investigation*. Cambridge.

Bettini, M. (2018) 'Comparison', in *The World through Roman Eyes: Anthropological Approaches to Ancient Culture*, eds. M. Bettini and W. M. Short. Cambridge: 24–46.

Bohannan, P. and Dalton, G. (1962) 'Introduction', in *Markets in Africa*, eds. P. Bohannan and G. Dalton. Chicago: 1–26.

Campano, F. and Salvatore, D. (2006) *Income Distribution*. Oxford.

Capogrossi Colognesi, L. (1988) 'La città e la sua terra', in *Storia di Roma I. Roma in Italia*, eds. A. Momigliano and A. Schiavone. Turin: 263–89.

——— (2006) 'Curie, centurie ed *heredia*', in *Studi in onore di Francesco Grelle*, eds. M. Silvestrini, T. Spagnuolo Vigorita and G. Volpe. Bari: 41–9.

——— (2012) *Padroni e contadini nell'Italia repubblicana*. Rome.

Carafa, P. (1995) 'Interpretazione e cronologia', in *Palatium e Sacra via*, eds. A. Carandini and P. Carafa, *Bollettino di Archeologia* 32–33: 253–5.

——— (2000) 'Una nuova analisi archeologica per il settore settentrionale del Suburbio di Roma', *BCAR* 101: 185–96.

Carandini, A. (2006) 'La villa dell'Auditorium interpretata', in *La fattoria e la villa dell'Auditorium*, eds. A. Carandini, M. T. D'Alessio and H. Di Giuseppe. Rome: 559–610.

Catalano, P. (1965) *Linee del sistema sovrannazionale romano. I.* Turin.

Chayanov, A. V. (1966) *The Theory of Peasant Economy*. Homewood, IL.

Chiabà, M. (2011) Roma e le *Priscae Latinae Coloniae*. Trieste.

Cifani, G. (2008) *Architettura romana arcaica. Edilizia e società tra monarchia e repubblica*. Rome.

——— (2009) 'Indicazioni sulla proprietà agraria nella Roma arcaica in base all'evidenza archeologica', in *Suburbium II. Il suburbio di Roma dalla fine dell'età monarchica alla nascita del sistema delle ville (V-II secolo a. C.)*, eds. V. Jolivet et al. Rome: 311–24.

——— (2016) 'L'economia di Roma nella prima età repubblicana (V-IV secolo a. C.): alcune osservazioni', in *L'Italia centrale e la creazione di una koiné*

152

'Frugality', Economy and Society in Archaic Rome

culturale? I percorsi della 'romanizzazione', eds. M. Aberson et al. Bern: 151–82.

Colonna, G. (1977) 'Un aspetto oscuro del Lazio antico. Le tombe del VI-V secolo a.c.', *PP* 32: 131–65.

—— (1988) 'I Latini e gli altri popoli del Lazio', in *Italia omnium terrarum alumna*, dir. G. Pugliese Carratelli. Milan: 409–528.

Cornell, T. J. (1995) *The Beginnings of Rome: Italy and Rome from the Bronze Age to the Punic Wars (c. 1000–264 B.C.)*. London and New York.

Crawford, M. H. (1985) *Coinage and Money under the Roman Republic*. London.

Crawford, M. H. (ed.) (1996) *Roman Statutes. Volume II*. London.

Dasgupta, P. (1993) *An Inquiry into Well-Being and Destitution*. Oxford.

De Albentiis, E. (1990) *La casa dei Romani*. Milan.

De Beaufort, L. (1738) *Dissertation sur l'incertitude des premiers cinque siècles de l'histoire romaine*. Utrecht.

De Davide, C. (2006) 'Periodo 4. La villa ad atrio (225–80 a.c.)', in *La fattoria e la villa dell'Auditorium*, eds. A. Carandini, M. T. D'Alessio and H. Di Giuseppe. Rome: 224–38.

Delfino A. (2014) *Forum Iulium:* L'area del Foro di Cesare alla luce delle campagne di scavo 2005–2008. Oxford.

De Martino, F. (1979) *Storia economica di Roma antica*, vol. 1. Florence.

De Sanctis, G. (1907) *Storia dei Romani, I*. Turin.

Detienne, M. (2010) *L'identité nationale, une énigme*. Paris.

Diliberto, O. (1984) Studi sulle origini della *cura furiosi*. Naples.

Drummond, A. (1989) 'Rome in the fifth century I: the social and economic framework', in *The Cambridge Ancient History. Second Edition. Volume VII, part 2. The rise of Rome to 220 B.C.* Cambridge: 113–71.

Dubois-Pelerin, E. (2008) *Le luxe privé à Rome et en Italie au Ier siècle ap. J.C.* Naples.

Dureau de la Malle A. J. C. A. (1840) *Économie politique des Romains. Tome second*. Paris.

Edwards, C. (1993) *The Politics of Immorality in Ancient Rome*. Cambridge.

FAO (2004) *Energy and Protein Requirements: Report of a Joint FAO/WHO/UNU Expert Consultation*. Geneva.

Forsythe, G. (2005) *A Critical History of Early Rome*. Berkeley.

Foxhall, L. and Forbes H. A. (1982) 'Σιτομετρεία: the role of grain as a staple food in classical antiquity', *Chiron* 12: 41–90.

Franceschi, F. (2003) 'La normativa suntuaria nella storia economica', in *Disciplinare il lusso: La legislazione suntuaria in Italia e in Europa tra Medioevo ed età moderna*, eds. M. G. Muzzarelli and A. Campanini. Rome: 163–78.

Fulminante, F. (2003) *Le sepolture principesche nel Latium Vetus*. Rome.

Cristiano Viglietti

(2014) *The Urbanisation of Rome and Latium Vetus: From the Bronze Age to the Archaic Era.* Cambridge.

Gabba, E. (1981) 'Ricchezza e classe dirigente romana fra III e I sec. a.C.', *RSI* 93: 54–58 [reprinted in Gabba 1988: 27–44].

(1988) *Del buon uso della ricchezza: Saggi di storia economica e sociale del mondo antico.* Milan.

Gargola, D. (1995) *Lands, Laws & Gods: Magistrates & Ceremony in the Regulation of Public Lands in Republican Rome.* Chapel Hill.

Garnsey, P. (1988) *Famine and Food Supply in the Graeco-Roman World: Responses to Risk and Crisis.* Cambridge.

(1989) 'Food consumption in antiquity: towards a quantitative account', in *Food, Health and Culture in Classical Antiquity*, ed. P. Garnsey. Cambridge: 36–49.

(1998) *Cities, Peasants and Food in Classical Antiquity, Essays in Social and Economic History.* Cambridge.

(1999) *Food and Society in Classical Antiquity.* Cambridge.

Grandazzi, A. (1991) *La fondation de Rome: Réflexion sur l'histoire.* Paris.

Halstead, P. (1989) 'The economy has a normal surplus: economic stability and social change among early farming communities of Thessaly, Greece', in *Bad Year Economics. Cultural Responses to Risk and Uncertainty*, eds. P. Halstead and J. O'Shea. Cambridge: 68–80.

Harris, W. V. (1979) *War and Imperialism in Republican Rome, 327–70 BC.* Oxford.

Hermon, E. (2001) *Habiter et partager la terre avant les Gracques.* Rome.

Hollander D. B. (2019) *Farmers and Agriculture in the Roman Economy.* London and New York.

Holtzman, J. (2009) *Uncertain Tastes: Memory, Ambivalence and the Politics of Eating in Samburu, Northern Kenya.* Berkeley and Los Angeles.

Hopkins, K. (1980) 'Taxes and trade in the Roman Empire (200 B.C. – A.D. 200)', *JRS* 70: 101–25.

(1996) 'Rome, taxes, rents and trade', *Kodai* 6/7: 41–75 [reprinted in Scheidel and von Reden 2002: 190–230].

Horden, P. and Purcell, N. (2000) *The Corrupting Sea: A Study of Mediterranean History.* Oxford.

Hume, D. (1740) *A Treatise of Human Nature*, 2nd edn. London.

Humm, M. (2001) 'Servius Tullius et la censure. Élaboration d'un modèle institutionnel', in *L'invention des grands hommes de la Rome antique*, eds. M. Coudry and T. Späth. Paris: 221–43.

(2005) *Appius Claudius Caecus: la république accomplie.* Rome.

Jongman, W. (2007) 'The early Roman empire: consumption', in *The Cambridge Economic History of the Greco-Roman World*, eds. W. Scheidel, I. Morris and R. Saller. Cambridge: 592–618.

Kluckhohn, C. (1949) *Mirror for Man: The Relation of Anthropology to Modern Life.* Tucson, AZ.

'Frugality', Economy and Society in Archaic Rome

Kron, J. (2005) 'Anthropometry, physical anthropology, and the reconstruction of ancient health, nutrition, and living standards', *Historia* 54: 68–83.

Lerouxel, F. (2015) 'Bronze pesé, dette et travail contraint (*nexum*) dans la Rome archaïque (VIe s.–IVe s. a. C.)', in *La main-d'oeuvre agricole en Méditerranée archaïque*, ed. J. Zurbach. Bordeaux: 109–52.

Lévi-Strauss, C. (1975) *La voie des masques*. Paris.

Machiavelli, N. (1531) *Discorsi intorno alla prima deca di Tito Livio*. Florence.

McClintock, A. (2016) 'Giustizia senza dèi', in *Giuristi nati: Antropologia e diritto romano*, ed. A. McClintock. Bologna: 73–95.

Mengotti, F. (1787) *Del commercio de' Romani dalla prima guerra punica a Costantino*. Padua.

Momigliano, A. (1989) 'The origins of Rome', in *The Cambridge Ancient History. Second Edition. Volume VII, part 2. The rise of Rome to 220 B.C.* Cambridge: 52–112.

Mommsen, T. (1865) *Römische Geschichte, Erster Band*, 4th edn. Berlin.

Morley, N. (2018): 'Frugality and Roman economic thinking in Varro's *Rerum rusticarum*', *I Quaderni del ramo d'oro on-line* 10: 41–54, www.qro.unisi.it/frontend/sites/default/files/Morley%20QRO%2010.pdf (last accessed 6 February 2020).

Motta, L. (2002) 'Planting the seed of Rome', *Vegetation History and Archaeobotany* 11: 71–7.

Naglak, M., and Terrenato, N. (2019) 'A house society in Iron Age Latium? Kinship and state formation in the context of new discoveries at Gabii', in *La società gentilizia nell'Italia antica: Tra realtà e mito storiografico*, eds. M. Di Fazio and S. Paltinieri. Bari: 99–118.

Nicolet, C. (1980) *The World of the Citizen in Republican Rome*, trans. P. S. Falla. London.

Pearson, H. W. (1957) 'The economy has no surplus: critique of a theory of development', in *Trade and Market in the Early Empires*, eds. K. Polanyi, C. M. Arensberg and H. W. Pearson. Glencoe, IL: 320–41.

Perizonius, J. (1685) *Animadversiones Historicae*. Amsterdam.

Poucet, J. (2000) *Les rois de Rome: tradition et histoire*. Louvain.

Pucci, G. (1989) 'I consumi alimentari', in *Storia di Roma 4. Caratteri e morfologie*, ed. A. Schiavone. Turin: 369–88.

Rathbone, D. (2008) 'Poor peasants and silent herds', in *People, Land, and Politics: Demographic Developments and the Transformation of Roman Italy. 300 BC–AD 14*, eds. L. de Ligt and S. Northwood. Leiden and Boston: 305–22.

(2009) 'Earnings and costs: living standards and the Roman economy (first to third centuries AD)', in *Quantifying the Roman Economy*, eds. A. Bowman and A. Wilson. Oxford: 299–326.

Reynolds, P. (1981) 'Deadstock and livestock', in *Farming Practice in British Prehistory*, ed. R. Mercer. Edinburgh: 97–122.

155

Rich, J. W. (2008) 'Lex Licinia, Lex Sempronia: B.G. Niebuhr and the Roman limitation of landholding in the Roman republic', in *People, Land, and Politics: Demographic Developments and the Transformation of Roman Italy. 300 BC–AD 14*, eds. L. de Ligt and S. Northwood. Leiden and Boston: 519–72.

Richardson, J. H. (2012) *The Fabii and the Gauls: Studies in Historical Thought and Historiography in Republican Rome*. Stuttgart.

Ricci, G. (2006) 'Periodo 3. La Villa dell'Acheloo (300–225)', in *La fattoria e la villa dell'Auditorium*, eds. A. Carandini, M. T. D'Alessio and H. Di Giuseppe. Rome: 191–201.

Riccobono, S. (1968) (ed.) *Fontes Iuris Romani Anteiustiniani. Pars prima: Leges*. Florence.

Robbins, L. (1932) *Essay on the Nature and Significance of Economic Science*. London.

Roselaar, S. (2010) *Public Land in the Roman Republic*. Oxford.

Ross Holloway, R. (1994) *The Archaeology of Early Rome and Latium*. London and New York.

Sahlins, M. (1972) *Stone Age Economics*. Chicago.

Salvioli, G. (1929) *Il capitalismo antico. Storia dell'economia romana*. Bari.

Savio. E. (1940) 'Intorno alle leggi suntuarie romane', *Aevum* 14: 174–94.

Scheidel, W. and von Reden, S. (eds.) (2002) *The Ancient Economy*. Edinburgh.

Schiavone, A. (1989) 'La struttura nascosta. Una grammatica dell'economia romana', in *Storia di Roma 4. Caratteri e morfologie*, ed. A. Schiavone. Turin: 7–69.

Smith, C. J. (1996) *Early Rome and Latium: Economy and Society, c. 1000–500 B.C.* Oxford.

    (1998) 'Traders and artisans in archaic central Italy', in *Trade, Traders and the Ancient City*, eds. H. Parkins and C. J. Smith. London and New York: 31–51.

    (2005) 'The beginnings of urbanization in Rome', in *Mediterranean Urbanization. 800–600 BC*, eds. R. Osborne and B. Cunliffe. Oxford: 91–111.

    (2006) *The Roman Clan: The Gens from Ancient Ideology to Modern Anthropology*. Cambridge.

    (2011) 'Citizenship and community: inventing the Roman republic', in *State Formation in Italy and Greece: Questioning the Neoevolutionist Paradigm*, eds. N. Terrenato and D. C. Haggis. Oxford: 217–30.

    (2013) 'Methodology and historiography in the study of early Rome', in *Mediterranean Archaeology: a GID-EMAN training course. Rome 8–10 October 2012*, eds. L. Godart, E. La Rocca and P. Sommella. Rome: 23–38.

    (2019) 'Revisiting the Roman clan', in *La società gentilizia nell'Italia antica: Tra realtà e mito storiografico*, eds. M. Di Fazio and S. Paltinieri. Bari: 25–45.

'Frugality', Economy and Society in Archaic Rome

Spencer, P. (1965) *The Samburu: A Study of Gerontocracy in a Nomadic Tribe*. London.

Temin, P. (2013) *The Roman Market Economy*. Princeton.

Terrenato, N. (2012) 'The enigma of "Catonian" villas: the *De agri cultura* in the context of second-century BC Italian architecture', in *Roman Republican Villas: Architecture, Context and Ideology*, eds. J. A. Becker and N. Terrenato. Ann Arbor, MI: 69–93.

Toher, M. (1986) 'The tenth table and the conflict of the orders', in *Social Struggles in Archaic Rome: New Perspectives on the Conflict of the Orders*, ed. K. A. Raaflaub. Berkeley: 301–26.

Torelli, M. (1988) 'Dalle aristocrazie gentilizie alla nascita della plebe', in *Storia di Roma 1. Roma in Italia*, eds. A. Momigliano and A. Schiavone. Turin: 241–61.

(2011) *La forza della tradizione. Etruria e Roma: continuità e discontinuità agli albori della Storia*. Milan.

Viglietti, C. (2011) *Il limite del bisogno. Antropologia economica di Roma arcaica*. Bologna.

(2014) 'I *bina iugera* riconsiderati', in *La leggenda di Roma. Volume quarto*, ed. A. Carandini. Milan: 453–71.

(2017a) 'Les crises frumentaires dans la Rome alto-républicaine et la question des consommations alimentaires: entre croissance et limitation', *Topoi (Lyon)* 21: 151–72.

(2017b) 'L'"economia" di Publio Valerio Publicola: Condizione materiale e atteggiamenti etici, tra storia, letteratura e archeologia', *MEFRA* 129.1: 235–53.

(2018a) 'Ordini di cose e persone a Roma tra VIII e V secolo a.C.', in *Il valore delle cose e il valore delle persone*, ed. M. V. Vallerani. Rome: 129–52.

(2018b) 'Economy', in *The World through Roman Eyes: Anthropological Approaches to Ancient Culture*, eds. M. Bettini and W. M. Short. Cambridge: 216–48.

(2020) 'Investment and uses of wealth in archaic Rome and Latium (late 8th to early 4th century BC)', in *Capital, Investment and Innovation in the Roman World*, eds. P. Erdkamp, K. Verboven and A. Zuiderhoek. Oxford: 67–97.

Virlouvet, C. (1985) *Famines et émeutes à Rome des origines de la République à la mort de Néron*. Rome.

Volpe, R. (2012) 'Republican villas in the *Suburbium* of Rome', in *Roman Republican Villas: Architecture, Context, and Ideology*, eds. J. A. Becker and N. Terrenato. Ann Arbor, MI: 94–110.

Wallace-Hadrill, A. (2008) *Rome's Cultural Revolution*. Cambridge.

Xenos, N. (1987) 'Liberalism and the postulate of scarcity', *Political Theory* 15.2: 225–43.

Cristiano Viglietti

Zanda, E. (2011) *Fighting Hydra-like Luxury: Sumptuary Regulation in the Roman Republic*. Bristol.

Zehnacker, H. (1990) 'Rome: une société archaïque au contact de le monnaie (VIe–IVe siècle)', in *Crise et transformation des sociétés archaïques de l'Italie antique au Ve siècle av. J.C. Actes de la table ronde organisée par l'École Française de Rome. Rome 19–21 novembre 1987*. Rome: 307–26.

Zevi, F. (1976) 'Palestrina (*Praeneste*)', in *Civiltà del Lazio primitive*. Rome: 213–18.

CHAPTER 2

FROM LICINIUS STOLO TO TIBERIUS GRACCHUS: ROMAN FRUGALITY AND THE LIMITATION OF LANDHOLDING

JOHN RICH

The Controversy

One of the most remarkable outcomes of the Roman ethos of frugality was the passage in or around 367 BCE by the tribune C. Licinius Stolo of a law which limited the amount of land a man might hold by any form of tenure to 500 *iugera* (about 125 hectares). Over time the law came to be disregarded, but it remained nominally in place into the later second century. The agrarian law passed by Tiberius Gracchus in 133 enforced the older law, but with an important limitation: Gracchus' law applied only to holdings of public land, *ager publicus*. In this chapter I examine both the origins and character of the Licinian law and the subsequent developments, assessing their implications for the Roman frugality ethos. First, however, this interpretation of the law requires to be justified.

Until very recently it has been generally accepted that the pre-Gracchan law limiting landholding applied, like Gracchus' law, only to holdings of public land, and many scholars have held that the earlier law should be dated not to the fourth, but to the early second century. This consensus on the scope of the law goes back to Niebuhr in the early nineteenth century, but in the last few years it has come under challenge, and I and others have argued that the pre-Gracchan limit applied to all the land a man held, private as well as public. In what follows I shall briefly set out again the case for this view before going on to explore its implications.

The problem arises from an apparent conflict in our sources. A large number of Roman writers refer to the pre-Gracchan limit; most of these attribute it to a law passed by the tribune

159

John Rich

C. Licinius Stolo, and in the detailed narrative of Livy this is one of three laws carried in 367 BC by Stolo and his colleague L. Sextius after ten years of agitation. All these Roman writers speak of the law as limiting the amount of land a man was permitted to 'have' (*habere*) or 'occupy' (*possidere*); none of them gives any explicit indication that it applied only to *ager publicus*. We are less well informed about Tiberius Gracchus' land law, but our chief sources portray it as relating to *ager publicus*, and Appian and Plutarch speak of it as reasserting an earlier limit, although without mentioning Licinius or giving a clear indication of the earlier law's date.

From the sixteenth to the eighteenth centuries a wide range of writers – political thinkers like Machiavelli and Montesquieu, writers on Roman antiquities from Manuzio and Sigonio to Beaufort, and historians of Rome like Vertot, Hooke and Ferguson – struggled with this evidential puzzle and came up with various solutions, usually fudges. During the French Revolution it became a live political issue: some radicals, claiming Roman precedents, called for an 'agrarian law' which would redistribute all landed property in the interest of equality. For mainstream politicians this was anathema, and on 18 March 1793 the National Convention decreed the death penalty for anyone proposing the agrarian law.[1] Scholars too sought to show that Roman practice gave no support for such conceptions, arguing that both the Licinian and the Gracchan limits had applied only to public land which the Romans had acquired through conquest, not to private landholding: this was the view taken by Heyne in an oration at Göttingen given in 1793, a few days before the National Convention's decree, and in histories of the Gracchan 'disturbances' by Heeren and Hegewisch.[2]

In 1811–12, Niebuhr produced his great history of Rome down to the fourth century BCE, which offered a radically new

[1] For the sixteenth to eighteenth century controversy see Rich 2008: 527–38; Balbo 2010: 267–79.

[2] Heyne 1796: 362; Hegewisch 1801: 3–5, 28–9, 71–6; Heeren 1803: 178–82 (first published 1795). On these writers' contributions see Rich 2008: 535–8, and on Heeren's work see also Marcone 1989.

160

From Licinius Stolo to Tiberius Gracchus

way of interpreting early Rome and effectively inaugurated the modern study of Roman history, and at the end of his life he published a radically revised edition. Each version included a lengthy excursus on the Roman public lands, and Niebuhr insisted throughout that both the Licinian and the Gracchan limits had applied only to holdings of *ager publicus*. He represented this as a radical departure from older scholars' views, quite wrongly claiming that there had been a general consensus that both limits applied to private land ownership. However, he deemed it unnecessary to argue in detail for his view, on the grounds that it had already been proved by Heeren and Hegewisch.[3]

Like much else in his history, Niebuhr's conception of the Licinian limit gave rise to controversy. Two scholars – Hüllmann and, more fully, the jurist Huschke – proposed an alternative solution, namely that the Licinian limit applied to all landholding, private as well as public, but Tiberius Gracchus, when he revived the limit, restricted its application to public land.[4] For the next generation or so, the issue was vigorously debated. Writers on Roman law generally followed Huschke, while Puchta (1841: 202–4, 272–3; 1846) proposed a modification, namely that the Licinian limit applied only to private land. Historians, however, mostly sided with Niebuhr, and quite soon the tendency developed to take Niebuhr's view for granted.[5]

In the twentieth century, the controversy effectively became buried. Those who referred to it at all (with a few isolated exceptions) took Niebuhr's view as established. Most scholars did not even refer to it, but proceeded as though our sources

---

[3] Niebuhr's first treatment is at Niebuhr 1812: 349–51, 394–402, and his revised discussion at Niebuhr 1830: 146–50, 1832a: 13–23 (= Niebuhr 1832b: 129–32, 1842: 11–19). He also treated the topic in his posthumously published lectures (Niebuhr 1848: 191–3, 356). Niebuhr paid fulsome tribute to Heyne in his later statements, but never cited Heeren and Hegewisch by their names (supplied by his translators at Niebuhr 1832b: 132 n.). On Niebuhr's contribution see Rich 2008: 521–7, 538–41, with further bibliography.

[4] Hüllmann 1832: 272–6; Huschke 1835: 2–21.

[5] On the nineteenth century debate see Rich 2008: 542, with references, to which add Long 1864: 143–55. On Niebuhr's reception in Britain see Murray 2010.

161

John Rich

clearly speak of the Licinian limit as applying just to public land. Instead, scholars focused on a new controversy over the date at which holdings of *ager publicus* were limited to 500 *iugera*: some continued to date the limit to the fourth century; others, starting with Niese (1888), argued that such a limit on *ager publicus* was too high for the fourth century, and must instead have been introduced in the early second century; and there was also a good deal of support for the compromise position, developed most fully by Tibiletti (1948, 1949), that a limit on holdings of *ager publicus* was introduced by a fourth-century Licinian law, but raised to 500 *iugera* only in the late third or early second century.[6]

The first recent scholar to call the Niebuhr doctrine into question was Wolfgang Kunkel, who, in his massive, posthumously published study of the Roman magistracy, argued briefly that the pre-Gracchan limit applied to both private and public landholding (Kunkel 1995: 493–6). Next came Dominic Rathbone. In a brilliantly radical discussion of *ager publicus*, Rathbone (2003) argues, like Puchta, that the pre-Gracchan limit applied only to private land and proposes a novel solution for Tiberius Gracchus, namely that he made existing holdings of public land private, but allowed retention of private land only up to the now extended limit of 1000 *iugera*. My own contribution (Rich 2008) offers both an overview of the controversy from the sixteenth century to the present day and an extended presentation of the case for supposing that the pre-Gracchan limit applied to all landholding. This view has subsequently been followed by Mattia Balbo, Luigi Capogrossi Colognesi, Saskia Roselaar and Thibaud Lanfranchi.[7]

---

[6] For overviews of this controversy, with bibliography, see Forsén 1991: 13–28; Manzo 2001: 19–37; Oakley 1997–2005: 1.654–9; Rich 2008: 520–1.

[7] Balbo 2010; 2013: 73–83; 2014; and this volume; Roselaar 2010: 95–112, 293; Capogrossi Colognesi 2012: 77–83, 194; Lanfranchi 2015: 433–8. Capogrossi Colognesi had already inclined to this solution in his earlier response to Rathbone (2007: esp. 692–3). See also Kay 2014: 163–4; Gagliardi 2017; Tan 2017: 152 n. 37; Lomas 2018: 223.

162

From Licinius Stolo to Tiberius Gracchus

Thus there is now a choice between three alternatives, namely the orthodox Niebuhrian doctrine that both the pre-Gracchan and Gracchan limits applied only to public land; Rathbone's radical suggestion that both applied just to private land; or the recently revived theory of Huschke that the earlier limit applied to all landholding, but Gracchus restricted it to public land. To decide between these, it is necessary to take a closer look at the sources.

The Sources

Our earliest source for the pre-Gracchan land limit is the speech delivered by the Elder Cato in 167 BCE against a proposal that war be declared on the Rhodians in retribution for the stance they had taken during Rome's recent war with King Perseus of Macedon. We owe our knowledge of the speech mainly to Aulus Gellius' response (*NA* 6.3) to a critique by Cicero's secretary Tiro, which includes extensive citations both from the speech itself and from Tiro's observations. One of Gellius' citations from Cato runs as follows (Gel. 6.3.37 = Cato *ORF*[4] F 167, *FRHist* 5 F 90):

quid nunc? ecqua tandem lex est tam acerba quae dicat 'si quis illud facere uoluerit, mille minus dimidium familiae multa esto; si quis plus quingenta iugera habere uoluerit, tanta poena esto; si quis maiorem pecuum numerum habere uoluerit, tantum damnas esto'? atque nos omnia plura habere uolumus, et id nobis impune est.

What? Is there any law so harsh as to say: 'if anyone shall have wished to do that, let the fine be 1000 *asses*, less than half his property; if anyone shall have wished to have more than 500 *iugera*, let the penalty be so much; if anyone shall have wished to have a greater number of livestock, let the punishment be so much'? In fact, we wish to have more of everything, and we are not punished for it.

Cato's argument is that the Rhodians, like Roman citizens, should not be punished for a mere wish, but only for an act of transgression. He illustrates the point by citing the legal limit on landholding along with two other provisions which may be taken from the same law. The passage thus shows that the land limit was at least nominally in force in 167. Cato cites the limit

John Rich

as prohibiting anyone to 'have' (*habere*) more than 500 *iugera*, without any indication of land type. He does not name the law's author, but Tiro in his comment (which Gellius goes on to cite) attributes it to Licinius Stolo, while echoing Cato's wording of the prohibition.[8]

Licinius' law is cited in exactly the same terms by our next witness, Varro. One of the participants in his dialogue *De Re Rustica*, probably composed in 37 BCE, is his acquaintance C. Licinius Stolo, and Varro adduces as one of his qualifications for discoursing on agriculture that 'his ancestors carried the law about the limit of land – for that law which forbids a Roman citizen to have (*habere*) more than 500 *iugera* was Stolo's' (*Rust.* 1.2.9: *cuius maiores de modo agri legem tulerunt – nam Stolonis illa lex, quae uetat plus D iugera habere ciuem R.*).

Livy gives us our only detailed account of the extended agitation said to have been conducted by the repeatedly re-elected tribunes C. Licinius Stolo and L. Sextius (6.35–42), and refers to the landholding limit both there and later in his history. In all these references he uses the verb *possidere* ('occupy') rather than *habere*, but, like the earlier sources, speaks of the limit just as relating to land, without any specification of land type. In his account, the agitation of Licinius and Sextius began in 376, when they proposed the law enacting the land limit, along with two other laws, and was only resolved in 367, when all three laws were finally carried. Livy is the only source to credit the land law to Sextius as well as Licinius. He defines its terms when promulgated as 'about a limit on lands, that no one should occupy more than 500 *iugera* of land' (*de modo agrorum, ne quis plus quingenta iugera agri possideret*) (Livy 6.35.5).

Under the year 357, Livy recounts the probably apocryphal tale that Stolo was punished under the land law: 'C. Licinius Stolo was fined 10,000 asses by M. Popilius Laenas under his own law, because he occupied 1000 *iugera* of land with his son

---

[8] Gel. 6.3.40: ... *plus quingenta iugera habere uelle, quod plebiscito Stolonis prohibitum fuit.* ('Stolonis' is Bentley's emendation for the manuscripts' 'colonis').

164

From Licinius Stolo to Tiberius Gracchus

and by emancipating his son had fraudulently evaded the law' (7.16.9: *C. Licinius Stolo a M. Popilio Laenate sua lege decem milibus aeris est damnatus, quod mille iugerum agri cum filio possideret emancipandoque filium fraudem legi fecisset*).

Livy mentions the limit again under 298, reporting that 'in that year numerous men were prosecuted by the aediles, because they occupied more land than was permitted by law, and virtually none were acquitted' (10.13.14: *eo anno plerisque dies dicta ab aedilibus, quia plus quam quod lege finitum erat agri possiderent, nec quisquam ferme est purgatus*). This passage is one of Livy's bald notices of isolated administrative events, and so is likely to derive ultimately from an archival source, perhaps the Annales Maximi. It is thus decisive evidence that a limit on landholding was already in place by the beginning of the third century.

Since these passages of Cato, Tiro, Varro and Livy all speak just of a limit on the amount of land a man might 'have' or 'occupy', without specifying land type, it is natural to interpret them as implying that the pre-Gracchan limit applied to all of a man's landholding, both public and private. In Livy's case confirmation is provided by his repeated references to the law as a restraint on excessive 'greed' (*cupido*). When reporting the promulgation of Licinius' and Sextius' three laws, he describes them as threatening 'all the things for which there is an unlimited greed among mortals, land, money and honours' (6.35.6: *omnium ... rerum, quarum immodica cupido inter mortales est, agri, pecuniae, honorum*), and he appends to his notice of the convictions of 298 the authorial comment that thereby 'a huge check was placed on unlimited cupidity' (10.13.14: *uinculumque ingens immodicae cupiditati iniectum est*).[9] Later, in the speech he provides for Cato against the repeal of the *Lex Oppia* in 195, he represents him as asking 'What prompted the Licinian law about 500 *iugera* other than a huge greed for extending landholdings?' (34.4.8: *quid legem Liciniam excitauit de quingentis iugeribus nisi ingens cupido agros continuandi?*).

---

[9] For *cupiditati* in preference to the mss. reading *cupiditatis* see Oakley 1997–2005: 4.182.

165

John Rich

Livy could hardly have interpreted the law as checking greed if he envisaged it as applying only to one category of landholding, particularly if private landownership were excluded.

Further corroboration is provided by the numerous later sources which refer to the passage of Licinius' law and/or his condemnation under it, all of which speak of the law just as limiting the amount of land a man might have (*habere*) or occupy (*possidere*) without any specification of land type.[10] Some of these also, like Livy, speak of the law in moralising terms. Aulus Gellius cites it along with the Voconian law limiting women's inheritance rights and the sumptuary laws as instances of salutary ancient legislation eventually rendered obsolete by Roman opulence.[11] Columella and the Elder Pliny both adduce the law approvingly as evidence for the moderate size of landholdings in early times, and Columella attributes Licinius' violation of his own limit to 'unlimited lust for occupying' (*immodica possidendi libidine*).[12]

Niebuhr and his supporters have argued that the use of *possidere* and its cognates of the Licinian law by Livy and later writers implies, even without further qualification, that it only affected public land. However, although these terms were often used of holdings of *ager publicus* and could be so used without explicit reference where the context made it clear, they could also apply to private land. Under Roman law *possessio* denoted the control over land enjoyed by its occupier. For private land, the owner (*dominus*) was usually the *possessor*. For public land, the Roman people was the owner, but the occupier held *possessio*. Thus even where our sources speak of the pre-Gracchan limit as the amount of land a man was permitted to 'occupy' (*possidere*), normal usage implies, in

---

[10] Thus V. Max. 8.6.3 (from Livy, and using *possidere*); Vell. 2.6.3 and *vir. ill.* 20.3–4 (both using *habere*; the transmitted text of *vir. ill.* misstates the limit as 100 *iugera* and Licinius' holding as 150 *iugera*). Cf. Plu. *Cam.* 39.5–6, stating that the law fixed 500 *plethra* (= *iugera*) as the most a man was permitted κεκτῆσθαι (which cannot be pressed to imply ownership, rather than just landholding).

[11] Gel. 20.1.23 (*quid salubrius uisum est rogatione illa Stolonis iugerum de numero praefinito?*).

[12] Col. 1.3.11; Plin. *Nat.* 18.17. Both Columella and Pliny use *possidere*; if the ms. reading is correct, Columella gives the limit as 50 *iugera*.

166

From Licinius Stolo to Tiberius Gracchus

the absence of any contrary contextual indication, that this covered all his landholding, including both the private land in his ownership and public land held in *possessio*. Moreover, as we have seen, the term used by our earliest sources is not *possidere*, but *habere*, which is sometimes used of land as a synonym for *possidere* and sometimes to denote ownership, but never without appropriate qualification just for the occupation of public land.[13]

Livy's fifth-century narrative reports numerous proposed land allotment laws (*leges agrariae*), all thwarted, from that of Sp. Cassius in 486 BCE on. The land proposed for division is said to have included both public land recently confiscated from defeated enemies and land alleged to be public and wrongly occupied by private individuals, and, although Livy takes care not to confirm such claims in his own voice, he represents the champions of the *plebs* as frequently inveighing against the unjust occupation of public lands by such *possessores*.[14] It has been maintained that, in the light of what had gone before, Livy will have expected his readers to conclude that the Licinian law too applied specifically to public land. This is a misinterpretation. Whereas the earlier proposals were all described as *leges agrariae*, Livy, as we have seen, calls the Licinian measure a law 'about a limit on lands', *de modo agrorum*, and interprets it in his own authorial voice as a threat to unlimited desire for land. In his extensive account of Licinius' and Sextius' agitation, he reports them as accusing the patricians of 'seizing land' (6.37.2: *agros occupandi*) and denouncing 'unjust occupiers' (6.39.9: *iniustis possessoribus*), but they make no reference to public land, while their opponent Ap. Claudius is even made to insist that their law will expel owners (*domini*) from their property (6.41.11). This markedly different presentation must be significant. Livy is in effect indicating a change in the popular movement's strategy: whereas earlier tribunes had failed in all their attempts to

---

[13] See further Capogrossi Colognesi 2007: 683; Rich 2008: 552–4; Balbo 2010: 291–3; Roselaar 2010: 106–9.

[14] E.g. Liv. 2.41.2, 61.2; 4.51.5–6, 53.6; 6.5.4, 14.11.

John Rich

redistribute land they regarded as public, Licinius and Sextius now succeeded in imposing a limit on the overall amount of land a man might hold, private as well as public.

The texts we have considered thus constitute a very powerful body of evidence clearly implying that the pre-Gracchan limit applied to all landholding, not just public land. We must now turn to the well-known Gracchan narratives of Appian and Plutarch. Each of these writers introduces Tiberius Gracchus' land law with an account of problems relating to the public land to which it was a response (App. *BC* 1.7.26–8.34; Plu. *TG* 8.1–4). Both agree that, having disposed of some of the public land they had acquired through conquest, the Romans left the rest available for occupation for the benefit of the poor, but this land came to be misappropriated by the rich who worked it by slave labour, and the pre-Gracchan law was an unsuccessful attempt to check this development. The two accounts show some divergences, of which the most notable, Appian's characterisation of the intended beneficiaries as 'the Italians', is probably his own contribution.[15] However, as most scholars have recognised, they must derive from a common source: the most likely candidate for this source is perhaps Posidonius.[16]

Thus Appian and Plutarch, following their source, set both Gracchus' law and its predecessor in the context of the public land and the disputes relating to it. However, what they say about the application of the laws is less clear. Appian tells us that by the first law the Romans 'decided that no one was to have more than 500 *iugera* of this land' (8.33: ἔκριναν μηδένα ἔχειν τῆσδε τῆς γῆς πλέθρα πεντακοσίων πλείονα). The word τῆσδε is omitted in some inferior manuscripts; it should probably be retained, but omitting it would make little difference. Appian has previously (7.29) described the estates of the rich as built up partly from public land and partly from land bought or seized from the poor, so the implication could be that the limit was to apply to both forms of land, and so in

---

[15] On Appian's notorious presentation of the Italians in the opening chapters of his *Civil Wars* see especially Mouritsen 1998: 11–22.
[16] Cf. Rich 2015: 113.

168

From Licinius Stolo to Tiberius Gracchus

effect to all landholding. The same applies also to Gracchus' bill itself: Appian tells us that Gracchus 'proposed to renew the law that no one should have more than 500 *iugera*' (9.37: ἀνεκαίνιζε τὸν νόμον μηδένα τῶν πεντακοσίων πλέθρων πλέον ἔχειν). Further indications that Appian envisaged the limit as applying to all landholding, private as well as public, may be detected in his statements that, when the first law was passed, it was expected that land held above the limit would be sold to the poor (8.34), and that the complaints of the rich against Gracchus' bill included the claim that it would deprive them of payments they had made to their neighbours, evidently for land purchase (10.39). As for Plutarch, he is even more opaque: he simply describes the first law as 'forbidding anyone to have more than 500 *iugera* of land' (*TG* 8.2: οὐκ ἐῶν πλέθρα γῆς ἔχειν πλείονα τῶν πεντακοσίων), and does not clearly state the terms of Gracchus' law.

Appian and Plutarch thus do not provide the unequivocal support for Niebuhr's view which has often been supposed, and it is even less clear that their common source did so. However, even if that source did represent both laws' limits as applying just to public land, it would not necessarily follow that the writer was correct to do so. His account of the whole topic was patently presented from the standpoint of the Gracchan crisis itself. This resulted in some evident distortions, for example about the spread of slave-run *latifundia*, and could well have led to misrepresentation of the laws themselves.

The meagre remaining sources for Gracchus' law contain various confusions and contradictions: the limit is stated as 500 *iugera* by Velleius, 1000 *iugera* by the *Periocha* of Livy and the *De viris illustribus*, and 200 *iugera* by Siculus Flaccus, while Velleius bizarrely ascribes the law not to Tiberius Gracchus, but to his brother Gaius. Velleius, Siculus Flaccus, and the *De viris illustribus* all present the limit simply as a restriction on the amount of land a man might 'have' or 'occupy'.[17] However, these are unreliable writers, whose testimony carries little

---

[17] Vell. 2.6.3 (*C. Gracchus*) *uetabat quemquam ciuem plus quingentis iugeribus habere, quod aliquanto lege Licinia cautum erat*; Sic. Fl. 102.31–2 Campbell (*Gracchus*)

169

John Rich

weight and is in no way comparable to the numerous, authoritative sources for the pre-Gracchan limit. Moreover, there are several weighty indications that the Gracchan limit related just to holdings of *ager publicus*. The agrarian law of 111 refers back to the Gracchan limit in its opening provision, under which any existing holding of *ager publicus* is declared private, 'provided that its size be not greater than what it was lawful for one man to take or keep for himself according to statute or plebiscite'.[18] Cicero says that 'Tiberius and Gaius Gracchus established the *plebs* on public lands, which were formerly occupied by private individuals'.[19] The Livian *Periocha* states that Gracchus' law limited the amount a man might occupy 'from public land'.[20] There is no reason to doubt that a comparable statement was given by Livy himself: thus Livy specified that Gracchus' limit related to public land, as he had conspicuously avoided doing for the Licinian limit.

In the light of this examination of the sources, we should surely conclude that the Niebuhrian orthodoxy that the pre-Gracchan limit applied only to public land must be mistaken: a strong body of evidence makes it clear that the limit also applied to private landholding, and Appian and Plutarch afford no good reason for denying this. Nor is it attractive to suppose, with Puchta and Rathbone, that the limit only applied to the ownership of private land: the widespread use of the word *possidere* in respect of the limit suggests the contrary, and, as we shall see, Rathbone's claim that no significant amount of public land remained under occupation at the time the law was passed is unconvincing.[21] As for Gracchus' law, its purpose was clearly to reclaim public land for

---

legem tulit, nequis in Italia amplius quam ducenta iugera possideret; vir. ill. 64.2
(*Tiberius Gracchus*) legem tulit, ne quis plus mille agri iugera haberet.

[18] Crawford 1996, no. 2, line 2: *quod non modus maior siet, quam quantum unum hominem ex lege plebeiue sc(ito) sibei sumer[e relinquereue licuit].*

[19] Cic. *Agr.* 2.10 *Ti. et C. Gracchos plebem in agris publicis constituisse, qui agri a priuatis antea possidebantur.*

[20] Liv. *Per.* 58 *Tib. Sempronius Gracchus trib. pleb. cum legem agrariam ferret ... nequis ex publico agro plus quam mille iugera possideret ...*

[21] For further criticisms of Rathbone's thesis see Capogrossi Colognesi 2007; Rich 2008: 560; Roselaar 2010: 104–10.

From Licinius Stolo to Tiberius Gracchus

distribution, and Rathbone's suggestion that it did so by imposing a limit on private landholding seems an unappealing complication. So we should conclude, with Huschke, that Gracchus revived the earlier limit, but applied it only to public land. The fact that no source explicitly mentions this restriction to its application need not trouble us, in view of the poor quality of our sources on Gracchus' law.

The Licinian Law

The foregoing discussion has thus confirmed that the pre-Gracchan law imposed a limit of 500 *iugera* on a man's overall holding of land, private as well as public. We can now move on to consider the date, provisions, context and purpose of this law.

One of the great benefits of our conclusion about the scope of the pre-Gracchan limit is that it makes redundant the controversy over the dating of the 500-*iugera* limit, to which so much scholarly energy has been devoted. There is now no good reason to doubt that the limit was established in the fourth century BCE. Livy's notice of prosecutions in 298, as we have seen, probably derives ultimately from an archival source and so constitutes firm evidence that a limit on land-holding was already in place by that date. Appian, it is true, appears to locate the law imposing the limit relatively late in the process of rich slaveowners' misappropriation of the land, but the tendentious character of his account means that this can carry no weight; Plutarch's version places it earlier and in this respect may well be closer to their common source. The most weighty argument adduced in favour of a lower dating has been that 500 *iugera* would have been unrealistically high for a limit on the occupation of public land as early as the fourth century, but once it is recognised that the limit covered holdings of private as well as public land, this argument loses all its force. Although we have no information on the size of individual landholdings in the fourth century, it is wholly plausible that those of some members of the elite may have come close to or even exceeded 500 *iugera*, particularly when

John Rich

their occupation of *ager publicus* was added to the private land under their ownership.[22]

This conclusion is reinforced by recent archaeological discoveries close to Rome, in particular on the site of the new Auditorium in the northern suburb of Parioli. Here a modest earlier structure was replaced in the fifth century BCE by a villa complex built around a central courtyard on a scale comparable to that of the grand villas of the late Republic, and, with major modifications from the third century, the site continued in elite occupation down to the imperial period. At the time of its discovery, no rural sites of comparable scale had been identified before the late-Republican period. However, reconsideration of other sites like the Villa delle Grotte at Grottaferrata has suggested that the Auditorium site was not unique in the early Republic. These discoveries constitute remarkable evidence for rural landed wealth under the early Republic, in striking contrast to the conventional view of this period as marked by relative impoverishment.[23]

As we have seen, most of our sources attribute the law introducing the 500-*iugera* limit to C. Licinius Stolo, and Livy represents it as passed in 367 following extended agitation conducted by him and his fellow tribune L. Sextius, along with two other laws providing for debt relief and for the abolition of the consular tribunate and opening of the consulate to plebeians. Rathbone and Balbo regard the attribution of the 500-*iugera* limit to Licinius Stolo and its association with his constitutional agitation as a later invention and prefer instead to date it to the end of the fourth century, during the Samnite War period and shortly before the prosecutions attested for 298.[24] In my view, however, it is preferable to accept the traditional dating as at least approximately correct.

[22] Cf. Kunkel 1995: 495.

[23] On the significance of the Auditorium site and related developments see especially Terrenato 2001; 2012; Smith 2006: 153–5; Becker 2013: 314–16; Fulminante 2014: 143–7. Carandini, D'Alessio and Di Giuseppe 2006 provide full publication of the Auditorium site. For the Villa delle Grotte see Becker 2006; Terrenato and Becker 2009. For scepticism about the standard view of fifth century Rome as in economic recession as a result of incessant and largely unsuccessful warfare see Rich 2007a.

[24] Rathbone 2003: 146–9; Balbo 2010: 303–7, and see this volume, 217–18.

From Licinius Stolo to Tiberius Gracchus

A substantial body of sources from Tiro and Varro on attributes the limit to Licinius Stolo, and the reforming tribune is the only known bearer of that name until Varro's friend, whose branch of the Licinii probably revived the *cognomen* Stolo in the late Republic (Münzer 1927). Although Livy provides our only detailed account of the Licinio-Sextian agitation, the scrappier reports which survive in other sources differ from Livy only in details, for example Livy's unique attribution of the land law to Sextius as well as Licinius (6.35.4–5), for which either he himself or his immediate source may have been responsible.[25] It is true that this annalistic tradition on the tribunes' activity is distorted by numerous improbabilities, such as the tale of Licinius' jealous wife and the five years' anarchy, and, since there were some all-patrician colleges in the immediately following years, the law eventually carried cannot, as Livy implies, have reserved one consulship for a plebeian. However, the evidence of the Fasti does show that, for all its deficiencies, the tradition has a solid historical basis: from 367 (on the 'Varronian' chronology) the consular tribunate disappears and is replaced by a revived consulate open to plebeians, beginning in 366 with L. Sextius himself. It is therefore reasonable to conclude that this constitutional change was the product of agitation by Licinius and Sextius, and, in the absence of any conflicting tradition, that another of its outcomes was Licinius' law limiting landholding.[26]

---

[25] Two of the minor sources for the Licinio-Sextian agitation mention the land law (Plu. *Cam.* 39.5; *vir. ill.* 20.3), and the lack of explicit reference to it elsewhere, for example in what remains of Dio's account (fr. 29; Zonar. 7.24.7–13), is not significant. Although no mention of Licinius Stolo's land law survives in the fragments of Dionysius, his reference to Licinius' conviction and fine (14.12) shows that the law must have featured in his narrative.

[26] In general on the problems of the Licinio-Sextian agitation and the resulting legislation see von Fritz 1950; Billows 1989; Cornell 1995: 327–40; Oakley 1997–2005: 1.645–61; Forsythe 2005: 262–7; Pellam 2014; Armstrong 2017; Lomas 2018: 221–5. The references by Columella (1.3.10) and Pliny (*Nat.* 18.4.18) to allotments of seven *iugera* made 'after the expulsion of the kings', according to Columella by a tribune Licinius, are in no respect an alternative tradition to Licinius Stolo's much better attested 500-*iugera* limit, as claimed by Rathbone and Balbo (and cf. Wiseman 2009: 44–50). These passages must in fact be garbled from Varro's obscure statement that C. Licinius, tribune 345 years after the expulsion of the kings (= 145 BCE), 'led the people from the Comitium to the seven *iugera* of the Forum for

173

John Rich

We should accordingly accept that the 500-*iugera* limit was introduced by a law carried by the tribune C. Licinius Stolo in or around 367 BC, on the conventional 'Varronian' chronology.[27]

The only sanction for holding land in excess of the limit was prosecution by the aediles and, on conviction, the imposition of a fine. Niebuhr followed earlier scholars in supposing that the law, like that of Gracchus, provided for the distribution in allotments of land held in excess of the limit, but there is no trace of this in our sources, and, as has long been recognised, the law was simply a *lex de modo agrorum*, limiting landholdings, and not a *lex agraria* providing for land distribution.

The first of the three legal provisions cited by Cato in the fragment of his speech for the Rhodians, cited above, specified a fine of '1000 *asses*, less than half his property' (*mille minus dimidium familiae*). Comparable provisions in later laws show that this must mean a fixed fine of 1000 *asses* providing this came to less than half of the convicted person's estate.[28] If, as seems likely, Cato cited all three provisions from the same measure, it follows that Licinius Stolo's law specified this fixed fine for landholdings above the 500-*iugera* limit. When introduced in the 360s, well before the inception of Roman coinage, the fine will have been expressed in pounds of bronze. As Rathbone (2003: 147 n. 38) observes, it will have been 'a sharp but not heavy penalty for a rich man', perhaps a tenth of the

---

receiving laws', which, however it is to be explained (cf. Cic. *Amic.* 96), cannot relate to land distribution or regulation (Tibiletti 1950: 236–9; Rich 2008: 552 n. 94). Columella subsequently refers (1.3.11) to the limit imposed on landholding by C. Licinius (Stolo) and his condemnation under his own law only after he has mentioned Curius Dentatus' third-century land distribution, but this is merely awkwardly developed argument and should not be taken as evidence of a variant tradition on the dating of the Licinian limit (cf. Tibiletti 1948: 220).

[27] The 'Varronian' chronology runs four years too early since it includes the spurious 'dictator years', and dates in this period are at best only approximately reliable: see e.g. Cornell 1995: 399–402.

[28] So rightly Crawford 1996: 739 (suggesting the reading *mille <dum> minus dimidium familiae*); Balbo 2014: 80–1. For fines restricted to less than half an estate see Crawford 1996: nos. 7, line 12; 13, lines 12–13, 26–7, 35; 22, line 32; 46, line 12. Fronto's claim (*Ant.* 1.5.3, p. 93 van den Hout) that it was ancient practice to impose a fine of *mille minus dimidio* may be based on this passage of Cato.

174

From Licinius Stolo to Tiberius Gracchus

census qualification for the first class.[29] Balbo (2014: 82–4) has suggested that the 10,000 *asses* reported by Livy (7.16.9) as the fine imposed on Licinius Stolo for breaching his own law represents a conversion to later values of the 1000 *asses* specified in the law, but this overvalues Livy's evidence: 10,000 or 15,000 *asses* is the fine he specifies for numerous early trials, all of dubious historicity.[30]

Cato's third provision specifies a limit on the number of pasture animals a man might have, and Appian (*BC* 1.8.33) tells us that, in addition to limiting landholding, the pre-Gracchan law fixed a maximum number of animals for grazing. As we shall see, evidence that graziers were fined on various occasions from 296 on probably shows that a grazing limit was already in place by that date, and it is thus likely that Licinius Stolo's law included such a provision. If so, it will have applied to grazing on private as well as public land, and infringements were presumably liable to the fixed 1000-*asses* fine. However, Appian's claim that the maximum was fixed at 100 'larger animals' and 500 'smaller animals' is problematic. Tibiletti, using data from early twentieth century Lazio, calculated that at least 1800 *iugera* would have been required to pasture 600 such animals, and, although this estimate is open to question, it remains doubtful whether pasturing on such a scale would have been feasible for Roman citizens in the mid-fourth century, even allowing for the use of private as well as public land.[31] It is possible that the grazing limits were fixed at the level Appian specifies at a later date, perhaps in the early third century after the extensive land confiscations of the Samnite War period.[32] Alternatively, his grazing maxima may be a later invention.

---

[29] For 10,000 *asses* as the likely first class qualification before the devaluations of 217–211 BCE see Lo Cascio 1988; Rathbone 1993. For the Roman pre-coinage use of a pound of bronze (the *as*) as the fixed monetary unit, see Crawford 1985: 18–24.

[30] Liv. 3.31.6; 4.41.10, 44.10; 5.12.1, 29.7, 32.9; see Ogilvie 1965: 323–6, 369; Rathbone 1993: 134–5. Livy sometimes specifies the amount just as *aeris*, sometimes as *aeris gravis*, usually taken as denoting libral *asses*.

[31] See Tibiletti 1949: 9–12; Forsén 1991: 41; Roselaar 2010: 99. Skydsgaard 1974: 16–21 objects that Tibiletti's calculations do not allow for transhumance.

[32] Cf. Roselaar 2010: 111–12.

John Rich

Two further details about the pre-Gracchan law supplied by Appian (*BC* 1.8.33–4) are best seen as inventions reflecting the concerns of the Gracchan period. The alleged stipulation in the law that landholders should employ a stipulated 'number of free men, who would watch and report on what was going on' must echo Gracchan anxieties about slave-run farming in the light of the recent slave revolts. Although there was some chattel slavery in fourth century Rome, its scale cannot have been significant enough to have prompted such a provision. Such concerns were later addressed by the dictator Caesar, who ordained that those engaged in pasturage should employ free men for at least a third of their herdsmen (Suet. *Jul.* 42.1). The provision reported by Appian has sometimes been seen as an attempt by his source (direct or indirect) to provide a spurious precedent for Caesar's enactment, but Appian is unlikely to have been following so late a source at this point.[33]

Appian's claim that 'they swore to the law' is best interpreted as echoing the oaths required from magistrates and/or senators to various late second century laws. Provisions in the *Lex Agraria* of 111 (lines 40–2) show that such oaths had been demanded by legislators before that date, and Crawford's suggestion is attractive that the oath reported by Appian for the pre-Gracchan law limiting landholding may have been invented as a precedent for such a requirement in Gracchan legislation.[34]

Thus in (approximately) 367 C. Licinius Stolo passed his law limiting the amount of land (private and public) a man might hold and probably also the number of animals he might graze on pain of a substantial fine and at the same time also legislated, with his colleague L. Sextius, for constitutional and debt reform. Why had the issue of landholding gained such

---

[33] Invented precedent for Caesar: so Flach 1994: 294; Rathbone 2003: 144; Roselaar 2010: 112.

[34] Crawford 1996: 169. A less likely alternative is that Appian was portraying the pre-Gracchan law as an archaic *lex sacrata* (so Roselaar 2010: 101–2; Santalucia 2012: 132 n. 83); on *leges sacratae* see now Pellam 2015, showing that they did not necessarily include an oath, but made their violaters *sacer*.

From Licinius Stolo to Tiberius Gracchus

importance at this time, and why did Licinius' remedy take this form?

Many scholars have supposed that much land in archaic Rome was held not by individuals, but communally by clans (*gentes*), and this has often been linked with the supposed exclusion of the plebeians from public land. Capogrossi Colognesi has argued subtly that later sources' references to public land in early Rome are in fact anachronistic reinterpretation of *ager gentilicius*.[35] The enlargement of the Auditorium site and other developments in its vicinity have been taken as showing that 'at the beginning of the Republic a major established clan felt the need for asserting its control over the landscape' (Terrenato 2001: 17). However, such theories suffer from the lack of explicit attestation for clan landholding, and individual property-holding is presumed for the census and in the Twelve Tables, where a man's *gentiles* figure only as potential inheritors from the intestate (5.4–5).[36] The Auditorium villa may have been occupied by a wealthy individual owner rather than a clan leader, with the land worked by dependent labour in the form of clients or debt-bondsmen (*nexi*). If they had ever existed, it is unlikely that clan holdings of land were still in force by the 360s or had any bearing on the Licinian law.

Livy, as we saw above, reports numerous unsuccessful fifth-century attempts to pass agrarian laws providing for allotments from public land acquired by confiscation from enemy states or allegedly held by rich occupiers, often said to be patricians, starting with the law reportedly promulgated by the consul Sp. Cassius in 486 and continuing with proposals by successive tribunes. Similar accounts appear in Dionysius and other sources. Both the content of these laws and the grievances alleged by their proposers have evident Gracchan echoes, and how much truth, if any, there may be in this tradition has been hotly disputed since its authenticity was first

---

[35] See especially Capogrossi Colognesi 1980; 1983; 2012: 61–76; Hermon 2001.
[36] For critiques of the *gens* theory of land tenure see Smith 2006: 235–50; Cifani 2009; Roselaar 2010: 20–4; Lanfranchi 2015: 410–18.

John Rich

impugned by Niese (1888).[37] The amount of public land available for occupation in the fifth century may in fact have been quite small: little Roman expansion took place then, and how much of the territory which had been acquired in the regal period now counted as public land is quite uncertain.[38] Much of such public land as there was may have been held by patricians, as the sources allege. However, the only source antedating the Gracchan period which may bear on this point is the phrase *quicumque propter plebitatem agro publico eiecti sunt* ('whoever were ejected from public land because plebeian'), quoted by the lexicographer Nonius Marcellus from the mid-second century BCE historian Cassius Hemina: it is uncertain to what period the fragment relates or whether the implication is that men were expelled because they were plebeian or through poverty.[39]

The major Roman successes of the early fourth century BCE yielded substantial acquisitions of public land, namely all the territory of Veii and significant gains in the Pomptine area at the expense of the Volsci, and these gains at last permitted major land allotments. According to Livy, an allocation of seven *iugera* was made to each Roman citizen from the territory of Veii in 393, and loyal Veientines also received land in 390, while four new tribes were created for the settlers and new citizens in 387.[40] Some of Veii's land is likely to have remained public and so available for occupation, although estimates of its extent have varied widely.[41] Livy tells us that a commission was appointed to make land allocations in the Ager Pomptinus in 383, but warfare continued in the region in subsequent years, and the division of the land may not have been

---

[37] For optimistic assessments see Cornell 1995: 268–71; Oakley 1997–2005: 1.433–4; Lanfranchi 2015: 363–433.

[38] See Roselaar 2010: 20–31, arguing against Rathbone's view that no *ager publicus* was retained at this period.

[39] Nonius 217 L = Cassius Hemina *FRHist* 6 F 41, with J. Briscoe's commentary, and, on Hemina's date, *FRHist* 1.220–1. Sallust's statement (*Hist.* 1.11 M) that patrician oppression in the early Republic included driving plebeians from the land reflects the late-Republican perspective.

[40] Liv. 5.30.8, 6.4.4–5, 6.5.8; D.S. 14.102.4 (variant figures for the allotment size).

[41] See Cornell 1995: 329 and Roselaar 2010: 298–9, with further bibliography.

178

From Licinius Stolo to Tiberius Gracchus

completed much before 358, when the tribe Pomptina was created for the settlers.[42]

These substantial early fourth century land confiscations and allotments provide a plausible context for the emergence of the demand for a restriction on landholding which was eventually met by the passage of the Licinian law. Suspicions may have arisen, whether or not well founded, that significant amounts of these newly acquired public lands had come to be concentrated in the hands of a few patricians, whether as occupiers of land not included in the distributions or through acquisition of land allotted to others by purchase or by other means. Concerns of this kind, along with longer established resentment of elite landholders, may thus have been combined with other plebeian grievances to provide the ingredients on which the legislators Licinius and Sextius were able to draw.

Issues arising from the recent acquisition and distribution of large tracts of public land may thus have played a significant part in bringing about the Licinian law, and the law's proponents may well have hoped that the passage of the law would free up more public land for distribution or occupation as those who held land in excess of the limit gave up some of their holdings to bring themselves into compliance. However, these factors alone are not enough to explain the passing of a law which applied to all forms of landholding, private as well as public, whose only sanction was an aedilician fine, and which made no provision for subsequent land distribution. So formulated, the law must reflect a belief that the concentration of too much land in the hands of particular individuals was in itself not for the good of the community.

As we saw above, Livy, Columella and Aulus Gellius all speak of the Licinian law approvingly as a salutary check on excessive greed for landholding. These remarks show that in later times the law was often understood in moral terms, and this ethical conception of its purpose surely goes back to the time of its passage. Similar traditional ethical assumptions

---

[42] Liv. 6.21.4, 7.15.11; Roselaar 2010: 299–300.

John Rich

may also be reflected in statements disapproving of individuals occupying more land than they could cultivate through their own resources in Columella's reference to the Licinian and Siculus Flaccus' to the Gracchan restriction.[43]

As Gargola has argued, Licinius' law enforced a moral standard, like the later sumptuary laws.[44] His reform may reflect similar concerns to those underlying the funerary restrictions imposed by the tenth of the Twelve Tables.[45] It is certainly linked with other moral checks enforced by the aediles through prosecutions leading to fines, upholding both statutory regulations, as on usury, and customary norms, as against sexual misconduct.[46]

Another element which may perhaps have contributed to the movement for limiting landholding may have been beliefs about how land had been apportioned in Rome's past. Annalistic writers assume that there had been inequality of wealth at Rome since the foundation, and the alternative tradition found in technical writers that Romulus had distributed lands equally in tiny *heredia* of just two *iugera* is probably just a learned construction.[47] We can only conjecture what beliefs may have been held about this and other aspects of the Roman past as early as the fourth century. It is, however, striking that an equal distribution was made to citizens from the territory of Veii, and that the land allocations for some colonial foundations were very small, amounting to a mere two *iugera* at least at Tarracina in 329.[48] Some may well have held that large estates were contrary to Roman tradition.

It is thus likely that Licinius' law limiting landholding reflects a contemporary ethos of frugality. However, the

---

[43] Col. 1.3.11; Sic. Fl. 102.32–3 Campbell. Mantovani 1997 refutes the attempt of Tibiletti (1948: 219–25, 1949: 20–7) to deduce pre-Licinian customary restrictions on landholding from these texts, on which see further Balbo in this volume.

[44] Gargola 1995: 143–5; cf. Viglietti 2011: 206–7.   [45] But see Toher 2005.

[46] For aedilician prosecutions see Bauman 1974; Kunkel 1995: 490–504; Lintott 1999: 131–3; Oakley 1997–2005: 4.269–71.

[47] Gabba 1978. For the tradition see Var. *R.* 1.10.2; Plin. *Nat.* 18.7; Paul. Fest. 47; and the gromatic treatises (Campbell 2000: 51.29–31, 120.9–12). See also now Capogrossi Colognesi 2006; Viglietti 2011: 139–55; Lanfranchi 2015: 381–3, 391–5.

[48] Liv. 8.21.11; Oakley 1997–2005: 1.676–7.

From Licinius Stolo to Tiberius Gracchus

measure was not extremist, in striking contrast with the equal redistributions of property enacted in some Greek cities in the fourth and third centuries. At the time the law was passed, only a few Romans are likely to have had holdings in excess of the limit, and existing inequalities would thus have been left largely untouched. This is unsurprising, since Licinius' and Sextius' reforms constituted a package appealing to diverse interests, with, as our sources stress, the constitutional element promoting mainly well-to-do plebeians' opportunity for office.

From Licinius Stolo to Tiberius Gracchus

As we saw above, numerous sources report that Licinius Stolo himself was convicted under his own law (according to Livy, in 357) for holding twice the permitted amount of land and fraudulently seeking to evade the restriction by emancipating his son, and a further, certainly reliable, notice in Livy (10.13.14) records that in 298 numerous men were prosecuted by the aediles and convicted for occupying land above the limit.[49] Since Licinius' reported conviction coheres with our sources' claim that his own motivation as a reformer was just personal ambition and the motif of a legislator falling foul of his own law is widespread, it is likely that, as most scholars have supposed, the tale is an invention.[50] Some prosecutions may nonetheless have taken place in the years immediately following the passage of the law: the silence of our sources on prosecutions before 298 is not a counter-indication, since Livy only begins to report routine administrative items like aedilician prosecutions towards the end of his first decade.

Rome's successful warfare and expansion against the Samnites and others in the late fourth and early third centuries BCE brought ample opportunities for enrichment, particularly

---

[49] Sources for Licinius' conviction: Liv. 7.16.9; D.H. 14.12; V. Max. 8.6.3; Col. 1.3.11; Plin. *Nat.* 18.17; Plu. *Cam.* 39.6; *vir. ill.* 20.3–4. Both Valerius Maximus and the *de viris illustribus* assert that Licinius was the first to be convicted under his law.

[50] For defences of its possible authenticity see Münzer 1927: 469; Oakley 1997–2005: 2.183–4.

John Rich

for the new patricio-plebeian nobility. The Roman state acquired extensive new public lands by confiscation from defeated enemies, and, although much of this land will have been distributed in colonial and viritane allotments, much is likely to have been retained and so remained available for occupation.[51] More relatively large holdings are thus likely to have been formed in this period, from both private land and occupied public land, with some exceeding the Licinian limit. The abolition of *nexum* by the *Lex Poetelia* in 326 had removed one source of dependent labour, but, in their place, chattel slaves may now have begun to be exploited to work the land: these had been made relatively abundant by the large-scale enslavements in war, for which Livy gives detailed reports.[52]

The prosecutions of 298 were probably made in reaction to these developments. Further prosecutions for holdings in excess of the limit may have taken place in the same period: Livy's notices of aedilician prosecutions in Book 10 cannot be taken as comprehensive, and the loss of Livy's second decade means that we lack a detailed annalistic narrative for the years 292–219.

Livy also reports aediles' prosecution and conviction of 'graziers' (*pecuarii*) in 296 and 293, and a further such episode is reported for 241 or 238 by Ovid and Festus.[53] Livy does not report the graziers' offence, but it is most likely to have been contravention of a legal restriction on the number of animals to be grazed, probably, as we have seen, fixed by the Licinian law.[54] Although the restriction may have applied to all types of land, as for the limit on landholding, it will have been most easily policed on *ager scripturarius*, public land where a grazing toll was collected, a practice probably already in force

---

[51] See Roselaar 2010: 39–64.

[52] On Roman public and private enrichment in the Samnite War period see especially Harris 1979: 58–67; Cornell 1995: 380–94.

[53] Liv. 10.23.13, 47.4; Ov. *Fast.* 5.283–94; Festus 276 L. For the problematic date of the final episode see Broughton 1951: 220 n. 3.

[54] Skydsgaard 1974: 18–20; Botteri 1977; Roselaar 2010: 111–12; *contra*, Forsén 1991: 75–6. Ovid confusedly claims that grazing public pastures was itself an offence.

182

From Licinius Stolo to Tiberius Gracchus

by this time.[55] Thus these prosecutions too may reflect the new opportunities created by recent land confiscations from defeated enemies.

Tensions can be discerned within the elite arising from the new enrichment. Some will have been uninhibited in exploiting and displaying their wealth. One such may have been L. Postumius Megellus, whose notoriously arrogant actions are said to have included using 2000 soldiers under his command to clear woodland on his estate during his third consulship in 291.[56] Others are presented in the later tradition as models of high principle and antique *parsimonia*, notably C. Fabricius Luscinus and M'. Curius Dentatus, the latter, according to Valerius Maximus, 'both the consummate pattern of Roman frugality and the most perfect example of bravery' (4.3.5: *exactissima norma Romanae frugalitatis idemque fortitudinis perfectissimum specimen*). These plebeian new men held multiple consulships and were among the most successful commanders of the early third century, but figure in the tradition above all as the protagonists of a string of much adorned exemplary tales.[57] A good deal of what we are told about them can have little or no historical basis, and an important part in the working up of the legend is likely to have been played by the Elder Cato, who was fond of linking himself with Curius in particular. It may well have been Cato who began the surely unhistorical portrayal of Curius and Fabricius as living in contented poverty. However, at least one of the exemplary actions attributed to them is certainly historical: as censor in 275 Fabricius expelled P. Cornelius Rufinus, who had been twice consul, from the senate for possessing ten pounds weight of silver vessels, a signally

---

[55] Roselaar 2010: 135, against Rathbone 2003: 135, 166–71, who holds that there was little leasing of pasture until the later second century.

[56] D.H. 17/18.4.3; Liv. *Per.* 11; Dio fr. 36.32. The incident is also mentioned in a parchment fragment of Livy Book 11, where Gabii is probably to be restored as the location of the estate (Bravo and Griffin 1988; Gabrielli 2003).

[57] On the careers of Fabricius and Curius and the development of the exemplary traditions about them see Forni 1953; Berrendonner 2001; Vigourt 2001; Beck 2005: 188–216; Pasco-Pranger 2015.

John Rich

modest amount by the standards of later Roman luxury.[58] Rufinus was the first of only four ex-consuls to be expelled throughout the Republic, and Fabricius' action, later so celebrated, must have been shocking at the time. Rufinus was his personal enemy, but the ground on which Fabricius chose to act made a powerful assertion of the ethos of frugality.[59]

As consul in 290, Curius was responsible for one of the largest viritane distributions of confiscated enemy land, making allotments to Roman citizens following his Sabine conquests. Once again, the grants were of seven *iugera* each, as after the annexation of Veii. The story that Curius was voted a larger allotment but refused to take more than the standard share may be historical. If so, his declared reason will have been that ascribed to him by Valerius Maximus and others, that the worthy citizen should not seek a larger share than was being received by his fellows, rather than the more extreme version alleged by Pliny, that everyone should be satisfied with seven *iugera*.[60] Curius' stance reflected similar values to the passage and enforcement of the Licinian law.

By the early second century, the personal wealth of the Roman elite had greatly increased, as a result of continued Roman conquest and its further consequences for the Roman economy. By then, although individual farms will generally have been below this limit, the total holdings of many elite members must have exceeded 500 *iugera*.[61] The limits on grazing were still sometimes enforced: successful prosecutions are reported in 196 and 193.[62] Cato's reference in his speech for the Rhodians in 167 shows that the 500-*iugera* limit on individuals' landholdings remained notionally in force, but in

[58] Varro *ap.* Non. 745 L; Liv. *Per.* 14; D.H. 20.13; and many other sources, collected at Torelli 1978: 199–202.
[59] The enmity between the two is attested in the story of Fabricius' support for his second consulship (Torelli 1978: 192–3).
[60] V. Max. 4.3.5; Plin. *Nat.* 18.18. In agreement with V. Max.: Sen. *Ben.* 7.7.5; Col. 1.3.10; Fron. *Str.* 4.3.12. See also Plu. *Mor.* 194E, *Crass.* 2.9–10; Flor. 1.10.2-3; *vir. ill.* 33.5–6.
[61] On senatorial landholding in the period see Shatzman 1975: 11–18, 241–61; Kay 2014: 34–7.
[62] Liv. 33.42.10, 35.10.11–12.

184

From Licinius Stolo to Tiberius Gracchus

practice it will have become a dead letter. Too many were now in breach of the limit for enforcement to be a practical possibility, and, if, as Cato's reference suggests, the prescribed fine remained 1000 *asses*, the reduction of the *as* to the sextantal standard during the Second Punic War meant that it was no longer a significant penalty.[63] Nonetheless, many may still have paid lip service to the principle that excessive landholding was undesirable, and Cato and others who prided themselves on their antique virtue may have taken pains to remain within the limit: Cato would hardly have chosen to mention it in his speech if he did not. Plutarch's tale of Cato's varied investments (*Cato* 21.5–8) suggests strategies by which an enterprising but principled senator might enrich himself while respecting the Licinian prescription, as well as other constraints such as the *Lex Claudia* of 218 limiting senators' shipowning.

When Tiberius Gracchus promulgated his agrarian law in 133, he was impelled by developments in respect of land and manpower concerns (whether real or imagined) which were altogether different from those which the Licinian law *de modo agrorum* had sought to address.[64] Acting, as he believed, in the national interest, he boldly set out to enforce the Licinian limit, probably for the first time since the early third century. However, since his object was now not to limit landholding for its own sake, but to obtain land for distribution, he replaced the old procedure of aedilician prosecution by the new mechanism of the land commission.

Our sources indicate that Gracchus tried in various ways to sweeten the pill. Plutarch (*TG* 9.2, 10.4) speaks of an initial offer of compensation, later withdrawn, and Appian (*BC* 1.9.37, 11.46) tells us that, in addition to the 500-*iugera* entitlement, a further half allowance could be retained for each child, although the 1000 *iugera* specified for the limit by the Livian

---

[63] However, Livy's notices show that substantial sums were raised by the prosecution of graziers: in 196 fines from just three graziers paid for the building of the temple of Faunus.

[64] Recent surveys of these developments include Rich 2007b; Roselaar 2010: 146–220; Kay 2014: 131–83; Balbo 2013: 21–42 and this volume.

John Rich

Periocha and the *De viris illustribus* may indicate that this concession was limited to two children.[65] The most important concession was that the limit was to be applied, not, as the Licinian law had prescribed, to all landholding, but just to holdings of public land.[66] Gracchus' law may well have included a provision explicitly removing private land from the application of the limit.

In advocating his law, Gracchus will necessarily have laid emphasis on the public land, arguing that observance of the limit was especially appropriate there. This may have led him to make claims about the original purpose of the public lands and their occupation, explaining them in terms of the same concern for manpower which prompted his own law, and he may also have interpreted the earlier, Licinian measure in the same way. This interpretation is likely to have had a significant influence on subsequent historiography, and in particular on the account of agrarian developments and the Gracchan crisis given by the common source of Appian and Plutarch.

Gracchus and his supporters will have expected strong opposition, including a tribunician veto, but they could reasonably have hoped that, given the concessions that had been offered, and once popular enthusiasm had been mobilised and distinguished senators had deployed their authority in support, the vetoing tribune would back down, as had happened with the Cassian ballot law four years earlier.[67] Gracchus believed that the public interest required the passage of his law. Licinius Stolo had doubtless had the same belief, but Gracchus was seeking not to uphold frugality, but to assure manpower. However, Gracchus had underestimated his opponents'

---

[65] First suggested by Niebuhr in his lectures (1844: 328 = 1849: 281–2), and widely accepted, although, as Badian (1972: 702–3) observed, such a restriction would have been hardly consistent with Gracchus' declared aim of encouraging child-rearing. See further Roselaar 2010: 230–1. The alternative view ascribed to Niebuhr by Roselaar is in fact a comment added by G. Zeisz in his edition of Niebuhr's lectures (translated back into German from the English edition of L. Schmitz).

[66] For possible enforcement of the limit just on public land earlier in the second century see Balbo, this volume.

[67] See Badian 1972: 690–701.

186

From Licinius Stolo to Tiberius Gracchus

obduracy, and, whereas Licinius Stolo's reforms had helped to establish a new order, Gracchus' law set in train the Republic's disintegration.

Bibliography

Armstrong, J. (2017) 'The consulship of 367 BC and the evolution of Roman military authority', *Antichthon* 51: 124–48.

Badian, E. (1972) 'Tiberius Gracchus and the beginning of the Roman revolution', *ANRW* 1.1: 668–731.

Balbo, M. (2010) 'La *Lex Licinia de modo agrorum*: riconsiderazione di un modello storiografico', *RFIC* 138: 265–311.

(2013) *Riformare la Res Publica: Retroterra sociale e significato politico del tribunato di Tiberio Gracco*. Bari.

(2014) '*Lex tam acerba*: la sanzione per i trasgressori del *modus agrorum* nella Roma repubblicana', *RFIC* 142: 75–90.

Bauman, R. A. (1974) 'Criminal prosecutions by the aediles', *Latomus* 33: 245–64.

Beck, H. (2005) *Karriere und Hierarchie: Die römische Aristokratie und die Anfänge des cursus honorum in der mittleren Republik*. Berlin.

Becker, J. A. (2006) 'The Villa delle Grotte at Grottarossa and the prehistory of Roman villas', *JRA* 19: 213–20.

(2013) 'Villas and agriculture in Republican Italy', in *A Companion to the Archaeology of the Roman Republic*, ed. J. D. Evans. Malden: 309–22.

Berrendonner, C. (2001) 'La formation de la tradition sur M'. Curius Dentatus et C. Fabricius Luscinus: un homme nouveau peut-il être un grand homme?', in *L'Invention des grands hommes de la Rome antique*, eds. M. Coudry and T. Späth. Paris: 97–116.

Billows, R. (1989) 'Legal fiction and political reform at Rome in the early second century BC', *Phoenix* 43: 112–33.

Botteri, P. (1977) '*Pecuarius* et *scripturarius*', *REL* 55: 313–24.

Bravo, B. and Griffin, M. T. (1988) 'Un frammento del libro xi di Tito Livio', *Athenaeum* 66: 447–521 [partially repr. at M. T. Griffin, *Politics and Philosophy at Rome. Collected Papers*. Oxford, 2018: 187–208].

Broughton, T. R. S. (1951) *The Magistrates of the Roman Republic*, vol. 1. Cleveland, OH.

Campbell, B. (2000) *The Writings of the Roman Land Surveyors. Introduction, Text, Translation and Commentary*. London.

Capogrossi Colognesi, L. (1980) 'Alcuni problemi di storia romana arcaica: "ager publicus", "gentes" e clienti', *BIDR* 83: 29–65 [repr. in Capogrossi Colognesi 2000: 93–139].

(1983) '"Ager publicus" e "ager gentilicius" nella riflessione storiografica moderna', in *Studi in onore di Cesare Sanfilippo*. Milan: 3.73–106 [repr. in Capogrossi Colognesi 2000: 263–303].

187

John Rich

(2000) *Cittadini e territorio: consolidamento e trasformazione della 'civitas Romana'*. Rome.

(2006) 'Curie, centurie ed "heredia"', in *Studi in onore di Francesco Grelle*. Bari: 41–9.

(2007) 'Le radiche storiche della *Lex Licinia de modo agrorum*', in *Fides Humanitas Ius: Studii in onore di Luigi Labruna*. Naples: 2.677–95.

(2012) *Padroni e contadini nell'Italia repubblicana*. Rome.

Carandini, A., D'Alessio, M. T. and Di Giuseppe, H. (2006) *La fattoria e la villa dell'Auditorium*. Rome.

Cifani, G. (2009) 'Indicazioni sulla proprietà agraria a Roma in base all'evidenza archeologica', in *Suburbium II: il suburbio di Roma alla fine dell'età monarchica alla nascita del sistema delle ville (V–II secolo a. C.)*, eds. V. Jolivet et al. Rome: 311–24.

Cornell, T. J. (1995) *The Beginnings of Rome: Italy and Rome from the Bronze Age to the Punic Wars (c. 1000–264 BC)*. London.

Crawford, M. H. (1985) *Coinage and Money under the Roman Republic: Italy and the Mediterranean Economy*. London.

(1996) *Roman Statutes*. London.

Flach, D. (1994) *Die Gesetze der frühen römischen Republik*. Darmstadt.

Forni, G. (1953) 'Manio Curio Dentato uomo democratico', *Athenaeum* 31: 170–240.

Forsén, B. (1991) *Lex Licinia de modo agrorum – Fiction or Reality?* Helsinki.

Forsythe, G. (2005) *A Critical History of Early Rome from Prehistory to the First Punic War*. Berkeley, Los Angeles and London.

Fritz, K. von (1950) 'The reorganization of the Roman government in 366 BC and the so-called Licinio-Sextian Laws', *Historia* 1: 3–44.

Fulminante, F. (2014) *The Urbanisation of Rome and Latium Vetus from the Bronze Age to the Archaic Era*. Cambridge.

Gabba, E. (1978) 'Per la tradizione dell'*heredium* romuleo', *RIL* 112: 250–8 [repr. in *Roma arcaica: storia e storiografia*. Rome, 2000: 227–34].

Gabrielli, C. (2003) 'Lucius Postumius Megellus at Gabii: a new fragment of Livy', *CQ* 53: 247–59.

Gagliardi, L. (2017) 'Leges Liciniae Sextiae', in *Oxford Classical Dictionary* online, DOI: 10.1093/acrefore/9780199381135.013.8188.

Gargola, D. J. (1995) *Lands, Laws, and Gods: Magistrates and Ceremony in the Regulation of Public Lands in Republican Rome*. Chapel Hill and London.

Harris, W. V. (1979) *War and Imperialism in Republican Rome 327–70 BC*. Oxford.

Heeren, A. L. W. (1803) *Geschichte der Staatsunruhen der Gracchen*, in *Kleine Historische Schriften*. Göttingen: 1.145–254.

Hegewisch, D. H. (1801) *Geschichte der Gracchischen Unruhen in der römischen Republik*. Hamburg.

From Licinius Stolo to Tiberius Gracchus

Hermon, E. (2001) *Habiter et partager les terres avant les Gracques*. Rome.

Heyne, C. G. (1796) 'Leges agrariae pestiferae et execrabiles', in *Opuscula Academica* IV. Göttingen: 350–73.

Hüllmann, K. D. (1832) *Römische Grundverfassung*. Bonn.

Huschke, P. E. (1835) *Über die Stelle des Varros von den Liciniern (de re rust. 1.2.9), nebst einer Zugabe über Fest. v. Possessiones und Possessio: Zwei Abhandlungen aus dem Gebiete der Alterthumswissenschaft und Rechtsgeschichte*. Heidelberg.

Kay, P. (2014) *Rome's Economic Revolution*. Oxford.

Kunkel, W. (1995) *Staatsordnung und Staatspraxis der römischen Republik, 2: Die Magistratur*. Munich.

Lanfranchi, T. (2015) *Les tribuns de la plèbe et la formation de la République romaine 494–287 avant J.-C.* Rome.

Lintott, A. W. (1999) *The Constitution of the Roman Republic*. Oxford.

Lo Cascio, E. (1988) 'Ancora sui censi minimi delle cinque classi "Serviane"', *Athenaeum* 76: 273–302.

Lomas, K. (2018) *The Rise of Rome: From the Iron Age to the Punic Wars 1000—264 BC*. London.

Long, G. (1864) *The Decline of the Roman Republic*, vol. 1. London.

Mantovani, D. (1997) 'L'occupazione dell'*ager publicus* e le sue regole prima del 367 A.C.', *Athenaeum* 87: 575–98.

Manzo, A. (2001) *La Lex Licinia Sextia de modo agrorum. Lotte e leggi agrarie tra il V e il IV secolo a.C.* Naples.

Marcone, A. (1989) 'Gli echi della Rivoluzione francese a Göttingen: lo studio di A.H.L. Heeren sui Gracchi', *Critica storica* 26: 525–32.

Mouritsen, H. (1998) *Italian Unification: A Study in Ancient & Modern Historiography*. London.

Münzer, F. (1927) 'Licinii Stolones', *RE* 13: 464–71.

Murray, O. (2010) 'Niebuhr in Britain', in *Historiographie de l'antiquité et transferts culturels: Les histoires anciennes dans l'Europe des XVIIIe et XIXe siècles*, eds. C. Avlami and J. Alvar. Amsterdam and New York: 239–54.

Niebuhr, B. G. (1812) *Römische Geschichte*, vol. 2. Berlin.

(1830) *Römische Geschichte*, vol. 2, 2nd edn. Berlin.

(1832a) *Römische Geschichte*, vol. 3. Berlin.

(1832b) *The History of Rome*, vol. 2, trans. J.C. Hare and C. Thirlwall. London.

(1842) *The History of Rome*, vol. 3, trans. W. Smith and L. Schmitz. London.

(1844) *The History of Rome, vol. 4: The History of Rome from the First Punic War to the Death of Constantine, in a Series of Lectures*, ed. L. Schmitz. London: vol. 1.

(1848) *Lectures on the History of Rome from the Earliest Times to the Commencement of the First Punic War*, ed. M. Isler, trans. L. Schmitz. London.

189

John Rich

(1849) *Lectures on the History of Rome from the First Punic War to the Death of Constantine*, ed. L. Schmitz. London: vol. 1.

Niese, B. (1888) 'Das sogenannte Licinisch-Sextische Ackergesetz', *Hermes* 23: 410–23.

Oakley, S. P. (1997–2005) *A Commentary on Livy Books VI–X*. Oxford.

Ogilvie, R. M. (1965) *A Commentary on Livy Books 1–5*. Oxford.

Pasco-Pranger, M. (2015) 'Finding examples at home: Cato, Curius Dentatus and the origins of Roman literary exemplarity', *ClAnt* 34: 296–321.

Pellam, G. (2014) 'A peculiar episode from the "Struggle of the Orders"? Livy and the Licinio-Sextian Rogations', *CQ* 64: 280–92.

(2015) '*Sacer, sacrosanctus*, and *leges sacratae*', *ClAnt* 34: 322–34.

Puchta, G. F. (1841) *Cursus der Institutionen*. Leipzig: vol. 1.

(1846) 'Remarks on Professor Long's paper on the Licinian Law *de modo agri*', *Classical Museum* 3: 67–78.

Rathbone, D. W. (1993) 'The *census* qualifications of the *assidui* and the *prima classis*', in *De Agricultura: In Memoriam Pieter Willem de Neeve*, eds. H. Sancisi-Weerdenburg et al. Amsterdam: 121–53.

(2003) 'The control and exploitation of *ager publicus* in Italy under the Roman Republic', in *Tâches publiques et enterprise privée dans le monde romain*, ed. J.-J. Aubert. Neuchâtel: 135–78.

Rich, J. W. (2007a) 'Warfare and the army in early Rome', in *A Companion to the Roman Army*, ed. P. Erdkamp. Malden: 7–23.

(2007b) 'Tiberius Gracchus, land and manpower', in *Crises and the Roman Empire*, eds. O. Hekster et al. Leiden and Boston: 155–66.

(2008) 'Lex Licinia, Lex Sempronia: B.G. Niebuhr and the limitation of landholding in the Roman Republic', in *People, Land and Politics. Demographic Developments and the Transformation of Roman Italy 300 BC – AD 14*, eds. L. de Ligt and S. Northwood. Leiden and Boston: 519–72.

(2015) 'Appian, Polybius and the Romans' war with Antiochus the Great: a study in Appian's sources and methods', in *Appian's Roman History: Empire and Civil War*, ed. K. Welch. Swansea: 65–123.

Roselaar, S. T. (2010) *Public Land in the Roman Republic*. Oxford.

Santalucia, B. (2012) 'Le clausole autoprotettive delle leges', in *Leges publicae. La legge nell'esperienza giuridica romana*, ed. J.-L. Ferrary. Pavia: 115–37.

Shatzman, I. (1975) *Senatorial Wealth and Roman Politics*. Brussels.

Skydsgaard, J. E. (1974) 'Transhumance in ancient Italy', *ARID* 7: 7–36.

Smith, C. J. (2006) *The Roman Clan: The Gens from Ancient Ideology to Modern Anthropology*. Cambridge.

Tan, J. (2017) *Power and Public Finance at Rome, 264–49 BCE*. New York.

Terrenato, N. (2001) 'The Auditorium site in Rome and the origins of the villa', *JRA* 14: 5–32.

From Licinius Stolo to Tiberius Gracchus

(2012) 'The enigma of "Catonian" villas: the *De agri cultura* in the context of second-century BC Italian architecture', in *Roman Republican Villas: Architexture, Context and Ideology*, eds. J. A. Becker and N. Terrenato. Ann Arbor: 69–93.

Terrenato, N. and Becker, J. A. (2009) 'Il sito del Monte delle Grotte sulla via Flaminia e lo sviluppo della villa nel suburbio di Roma', in *Suburbium II: il suburbio di Roma alla fine dell'età monarchica alla nascita del sistema delle ville (V–II secolo a. C.)*, eds. V. Jolivet et al. Rome: 394–401.

Tibiletti, G. (1948) 'Il possesso dell'*ager publicus* e le norme *de modo agrorum* sino ai Gracchi', *Athenaeum* 26: 173–236.

(1949) 'Il possesso dell'*ager publicus* e le norme *de modo agrorum* sino ai Gracchi (cont.)', *Athenaeum* 27: 1–41.

(1950) 'Ricerche di storia agraria romana', *Athenaeum* 28: 183–266.

Toher, M. (2005) 'The Tenth Table and the conflict of the orders', in *Social Struggles in Archaic Rome*, 2nd edn., ed. K.A. Raaflaub. Oxford: 268–92.

Torelli, M. R. (1978) *Rerum Romanarum fontes ab anno CCXCII ad annum CCLXV a. Ch.n.* Pisa.

Viglietti, C. (2011) *Il limite del bisogno. Antropologia economica di Roma arcaica.* Milan.

Vigourt, A. (2001) 'M'. Curius Dentatus et C. Fabricius Luscinus: les grands hommes ne sont pas exceptionnels', in *L'Invention des grands hommes de la Rome antique*, eds. M. Coudry and T. Späth. Paris: 117–29.

Wiseman, T. P. (2009) *Remembering the Roman People: Essays on Late-Republican Politics and Literature.* Cambridge.

CHAPTER 3

FRUGALITY AS A POLITICAL LANGUAGE IN THE SECOND CENTURY BCE: THE STRATEGIES OF CATO THE ELDER AND SCIPIO AEMILIANUS*

LAURE PASSET

A concern with luxury starts to register in Roman political discourse from the end of the third century BCE onwards. The *Lex Oppia* against women's luxury was passed during the Second Punic War.[1] It did not outlast the end of the war by much, but the belief that 'luxury' endangered the political balance within the ruling oligarchy and internal peace more generally continued to hold sway. The second century BCE saw the passing of a range of sumptuary laws and use of the censorship to enforce moderation in the lifestyle of the senatorial elite.[2] This development had a correlate: the emergence of a habitus and a rhetoric diametrically opposed to the indulgence in luxury or the ostentatious expenditure of wealth and grounded in the virtue of self-restraint, in other words 'frugality'. Those who endorsed frugality as a value to live by did so in explicit or implicit contrast to behavioural patterns they classified as luxurious – and they gave the distinction a polemic charge by embedding it within a civic ethics: indulgence in *luxuria*, so the discourse of frugality tended to maintain, was the characteristic of men only concerned with their personal interests, whereas 'frugal' members of the elite by definition manifested great dedication to the commonwealth. The posture of frugality also afforded the opportunity to detach oneself from the rest of the elite, in the struggle for influence and prestige and to gain an edge in competition for office: new men like Cato attempted to clear a path to upper magistracies by

---

* I would like to thank Professor Yves Roman for his careful re-reading of this article and Héliette Garcia-Fernandez for her expertise in English.
[1] Agati Madeira 2004.   [2] Regarding Cato's censorship, see Astin 1978: 78–103.

192

Frugality as a Political Language in the Second Century BCE

insisting that they possessed exceptional personal qualities;[3] members of the *nobilitas*, like Scipio Aemilianus, tried at least to maintain the rank of their family, and, if possible, to transcend their esteemed ancestors. In this context, the endorsement of a frugal lifestyle became one possible mode of self-promotion among Rome's senatorial elite[4] – a strategic choice in fashioning a public image that was thought to bring distinct advantages in the public spectacle that was Roman politics.

Cato's frugality was an elaborate exercise in self-fashioning, which resonated powerfully at his time and down the centuries. He endowed the ideal of frugality with definitive shape and promoted it in his many writings: he was the first Roman aristocrat who made such extensive use of texts across a wide range of genres to promulgate his views and visions. This continuation of politics by literary means ensured that his advocacy for a specific way of life survived his death and continued to remain an influential point of reference: in fact, most of the information from textual sources we have about the lifestyle of the Roman elite in mid-Republican Rome is mediated for us by Cato the Elder. It is therefore difficult to know if his behaviour was original or if he only took up an attitude shared by others, especially by conservatives like Valerius Flaccus, who was Cato's main political supporter. According to our sources, Cato is the archetype (and pioneer?) of frugality.[5] His name became virtually synonymous with a frugal disposition.[6] It cannot be overstressed that this reputation is to a great extent the result of Cato's own efforts: he used his speeches and writings to disseminate a cleverly constructed, strategic image of himself.

---

[3] Astin 1978: 1–3. Apart from Cato, there is very little evidence of other frugal behaviour in the elite class during the first half of the second century BCE. Plautus describes such an attitude in only one of his play, *Captiui*. Because this play is dedicated to the elite class, it seems that he parodies some discourses of this group. See Passet 2011: 228–34.

[4] Flower 2011: 271–5.

[5] Many anecdotes stress his simple and plain way of life. See in particular V. Max. 4.3.11; Plu. *Cat. Ma.* 1.9–10; 2.3–4; 3.2 and Sen. *Ep.* 87.9–10.

[6] Plu. *Cat. Ma.* 19.7 or Sen. *Ep.* 120.19.

193

Laure Passet

Cato's frugality was not a necessity but a choice – a conscious effort to assimilate his habitus and conduct to the way of life of the common people. Thus in a speech designed to defend his behaviour during his consulate, he declared that on his voyage to Spain as a consul and governor of the province he drank *non aliud uinum quam remiges*, consciously abstaining from the pleasures and comforts of aristocratic privilege and contenting himself with the staple diet of people far below himself in rank and standing.[7] In a similar vein, he prided himself on taking only five slaves with him during his time as governor of Spain.[8] Aulus Gellius reports Cato as saying that even if he was wealthy, *uillas suas inexcultas et rudes ne tectorio quidem praelitas fuisse [...] ad annum usque aetatis suae septuagesimum.*[9]

His frugality was an attitude that set him apart from the majority of the elite, which seems to have followed a policy of displaying moderation (*modus*) that balanced social rank and way of life. Living below one's means was frowned upon just as much as longing for luxury because it could attract the suspicion of originating in *auaritia*, miserliness. Cato the Elder was aware of the problem that his frugal lifestyle could be considered excessive – in violation of moderation. To combat this impression, he advertised his approach to material sobriety as a *tertium quid* that avoided the antipodal extremes of *luxuria* and *auaritia* – grounded as it was in self-control and aiming for a new, more ascetic position that avoided the pitfalls of both luxury and miserliness. This balancing act remained unstable – and Cato the Elder came under attack for trying to sell the vice of *auaritia* as a virtue. In his speech *De Sumptu*

---

[7] 'No other wine but that which was served out to the rowers.' Cato *Dierum dictarum de consulatu suo* fr. 53 M² (Plin. *Nat.* 14.91). See also Plu. *Cat. Ma.* 4.4. This speech postdates the end of 191 BCE: Fraccaro 1956: 191–2 and Scullard 1951: 258.

[8] Cato *Dierum dictarum de consulatu suo*, fr. 51 M² (Apul. *Apol.* 17.9). See also V. Max. 4.3.11. Cato left his house with three slaves, but when he arrived at the *Villa Publica* on the Field of Mars, he began to think it wasn't enough and ordered his servants to buy two other slaves.

[9] 'His country-seats were plain and unadorned, and not even whitewashed, up to the seventieth year of his age' (Gel. 13.24.1). In a later speech *Ne quis iterum consul fieret* fr. 185 M² (Fest. 14), Cato denounces the luxurious *uillae* of his opponents decorated with lemon tree wood, ivory and Numidian marble.

Frugality as a Political Language in the Second Century BCE

Suo, Cato defended himself against opponents who had tried to bring him into disrepute by putting his frugality into the same category as *auaritia*:[10] *uitio uertunt, quia multa egeo; at ego illis, quia nequeunt egere.*[11] Highlighting prudent management of material wealth thus carried certain reputational risks – of appearing greedy, miserly or poor. To validate frugality as a desirable norm and value, Cato turned it into an integral component of Roman identity. Put differently, he gave the Roman discourse on values an ethnic inflection. Instead of the (abstract) vices of *luxuria* and *auaritia*, he associated *luxuria* with 'the other', in particular the Greek East, a decadent and foreign lifestyle that had recently been introduced to Rome and manifested itself in the urban scene; conversely, he endorsed a frugal habitus (which found discursive articulation in such lexemes as *parsimonia*) as rustic, ancestral and quintessentially Roman.

In his speeches and writings Cato tried hard to endow frugality with rustic connotations and lay claim to personal experience with the lifestyle of the smallholding farmer. In his treatise *de Agri Cultura*, he insists on the benefits of country food, produced by the work of local peasants. Cabbage (*brassica*) comes in for particular praise towards the end of the work (*Agr.* 156–8), as the best vegetable of a sturdy and frugal diet.[12] The image of the hands-on farmer content with the basics of life also informs the self-fashioning in his speeches. In the speech *de suis uirtutibus contra <L.> Thermum post censuram* he famously highlighted his tough upbringing in the Sabine countryside:[13]

Ego iam a principio in parsimonia atque in duritia atque industria omnem adolescentiam meam abstinui agro colendo, saxis Sabinis, silicibus repastinandis atque conserendis.

---

[10] According to Plutarch (*Cat. Ma.* 5.1), Cato was accused of μικρολογία (miserliness).

[11] 'They find fault with me, because I lack many things; but I with them, because they cannot do without them.' Cato, *De sumptu suo*, fr. 174 M^2 (Gel. 13.24.1).

[12] Cf. Dalby 1998: 227 who considers this section a later addition.

[13] Cato, *De suis uirtutibus contra <L.> Thermum post censuram*, fr. 128 M^2 (Fest. p. 350 Lindsay). The translation is based on A. Savagner, *Sextus Pompeius Festus: De la signification des mots*. Paris, 1846: 501. Cf. Astin 1978: 1–3.

195

Laure Passet

From the very beginning, I spent the entire period of my youth in thrift, in hardship and in diligent labour, cultivating fields, clearing out the grounds filled with Sabine rocks and boulders, and sowing on this soil.

According to Cato, then, toiling in the fields produces a frugal habitus. The phrase *adolescentiam meam abstinui* implies that his tough upbringing protected him from temptations and the corrupting pleasures of city life. The countryman trained in austerity by hard work on the farm thus came to embody frugality. This rural connotation of frugality is not particular to Cato. In his play *Mostellaria*, Plautus laughed at his contemporaries who linked virtuous austerity to the countryside by showing the sordid reality of country life.

Cato also linked frugality with ancestral custom (*mos maiorum*). In his *Origines*, he contrasted the simplicity of the way of life of former Romans with the luxury of his time in such areas as food or conspicuous expenditure by women.[14] He claimed, self-servingly, that the Romans had gained their frugality by merging with and then imitating the Sabines, a people they had defeated at the beginnings of the city.[15] According to Cato, frugality thereby became a collective quality of the Roman people, but manifested itself above all in those Romans of Sabine stock (like himself). The frugal man was a genuine Roman (and vice versa) and respected the *mos maiorum*.

Cato did not invest in frugality as an end in itself. For him, the cultivation of a frugal disposition assumed strategic importance in processes of societal reproduction, with a particular focus on the ruling elite. According to a saying of his (or ascribed to him) preserved by Plutarch, 'it was not the part of a man, but of a widow woman, to lessen his substance' (οὐκ ἀνδρός, ἀλλὰ χήρας γυναικὸς εἶναι τὸ μειῶσαι τι τῶν ὑπαρχόντων).[16] These words, whether genuine or not, link an

---

[14] The *antiqui*, for instance, took only two dishes for dinner: Cato *Orig.* 7.12 (Serv. *Commentarii in Vergilii Aeneidos libros* 1.726); female luxury: Cato *Orig.* 7. 9. Cato's *Carmen de moribus* was also built on an opposition between past and present: Gel. 11.2.1 and 5; Letta 1984: 10–11.

[15] Cato *Orig.* 2.22 (Serv. *Commentarii in Vergilii Aeneidos libros* 8.638).

[16] Plu. *Cat. Ma.* 25. See Villa 1952: 102–3.

Frugality as a Political Language in the Second Century BCE

interest in the accumulation of wealth to the role of *paterfamilias* and his responsibility for the wellbeing of the family across generations: a significant fortune was necessary for a man and his son to have successful careers in politics. The frugal management of material resources enabled members of the elite class to preserve their inheritance and their estate – and hence the wealth qualification (a high *census*) requisite for public office. The plentiful recommendations in the *de Agri Cultura* of how to increase the value of one's property ought to be understood in this context. And it is hardly surprising that in 169 BCE Cato supported the *Lex Voconia*, which limited the inheritance rights of women: the law, which forbade women to be named as heirs by testators belonging to the first property-class, was seemingly designed to prevent the dispersal of the family fortune.[17] For Cato, then, frugality was not simply a matter of personal virtue, but of strategic value in perpetuating a family's estate and the rank and standing of its members in society.

The qualities of character inculcated by a frugal approach to the use of material resources ensured further benefits for the commonwealth. Cato's *uir bonus*, that is the good citizen devoted to the *res publica*, was neither rich nor poor because either poverty or wealth led a man to worry only about his own interest and to wallow in *auaritia*, the desire of riches.[18] By contrast, frugal men acted in a civic spirit, not least in their ability to fight for their country – to show martial prowess (*uirtus*) and a hardy disposition willing to undergo hardship and toil (*labor*) on the battlefield. In one of his speeches, Cato draws an explicit link between a frugal outlook and *uirtus*.[19]

---

[17] Cic. *Sen.* 5.14; Liv. *Per.* 41, Gel. 6.13.3; 17.6.1. See further Evans 1991: 71–83.

[18] Villa 1952: 99–103.

[19] *magna [...] cura cibi, magna uirtutis incuria* ('When there is great care about food, there is very little care about manly excellence'): Cato, *Ne lex Orchia derogaretur dissuasio* (?) fr. 146 M² (Amm. Marc. 16.5.2). According to Galletier and Fontaine 1968: 269, Ammianus Marcellinus probably borrowed these words from a collection of *Dicta Catonis* 'in vogue among all persons of letters in the fourth century AD' (Jerome and Augustine mentioned these *dicta*). For the semantics of *uirtus*, see McDonnell 2006. As he points out, Cato uses *uirtus* in the sense of 'martial prowess' three times in his *Origines* (50): 4.7, 7.1, 7.14. But while 'martial prowess' and 'courage in battle' were key manifestations of manliness, *uirtus* had a broader

197

Laure Passet

And in the preface of the *De Agri Cultura*, he declared that countrymen were the best soldiers:[20] their way of life taught frugality, and a frugal lifestyle will result in strong bodies, suited to fighting.[21] The frugal man was thus a good soldier and therefore a good citizen, devoted to the public good – all qualities that Cato claimed for himself.[22] According to Plutarch, Cato showcased his frugality while on campaign as a form of military training in the interest of the commonwealth (*Cat. Ma.* 4.3–4):[23]

Ἐσθῆτα μὲν γὰρ οὐδέποτέ φησι φορέσαι πολυτελεστέραν ἑκατὸν δραχμῶν, πιεῖν δὲ καὶ στρατηγῶν καὶ ὑπατεύων τὸν αὐτὸν οἶνον τοῖς ἐργάταις, ὄψον δὲ παρασκευάζεσθαι πρὸς τὸ δεῖπνον ἐξ ἀγορᾶς ἀσσαρίων τριάκοντα, καὶ τοῦτο διὰ τὴν πόλιν, ὅπως ἰσχύοι τὸ σῶμα πρὸς τὰς στρατείας·

He says that he never wore clothing which cost more than a hundred drachmas; and that, when he was general and consul, he drank the same wine as his slaves; and that the meat or fish bought in the public market for his dinner did not cost above thirty asses – and this too for the city's sake, so that his body might be all the hardier for warfare.

According to Cato, a frugal outlook not only enhanced military prowess but also ensured ethically principled conduct. In the speech that Cato delivered to condemn Minucius Thermus' comportment while on campaign against the Ligurians, he stressed that an oversized interest in food and luxury was the main characteristic of a tyrannical leader, devoted to his own interests. Cato blamed Thermus for having flogged Italian magistrates because they did not take sufficient care of his food[24] – an outrage that violated *fides*, the trust in good leadership that linked Romans to their allies. According to

---

remit, comprising other forms of excellence as well. See Roman and Roman 2007: 92, drawing on Hellegouarc'h 1972: 244: *uirtus* 'means the civic and military qualities of a *uir*, that is a soldier and first of all a leader'.

[20] Cato *Agr.* praef. 4. McDonnell 2006: 55.

[21] Cato *De suis uirtutibus contra <L.> Thermum post censuram* fr. 128 M² (Festus p. 350 Lindsay).

[22] McDonnell 2006: 55–6.

[23] According to Malcovati 1953: 72, this fragment may belong to *De sumptu suo*, a speech delivered by Cato in 164 BCE.

[24] Hellegouarc'h 1972: 244.

Frugality as a Political Language in the Second Century BCE

Cato, then, the frugal man was honest and concerned about the commonwealth, and hence an effective leader and magistrate. Put differently, the frugal man epitomises Roman manliness (*uirtus*).

This construct was part of a personal strategy to make up for his status as a 'new man' (*homo nouus*) and to defend himself against attacks from members of the *nobilitas* while canvassing for the censorship, though he probably was the target of such criticism throughout his career.[25] Whereas the nobility claimed to have gained *uirtus* by birth, which in turn justified their political dominance,[26] Cato argued that *uirtus* had to be acquired through the hardships and the self-discipline that come with the kind of frugal lifestyle he experienced and internalised during his upbringing in the hard Sabine countryside – a world unknown to the *nobiles*, yet imbued with respect for traditional Roman values.[27] Glorious ancestors, then, were not the only way of proving oneself worthy of election to upper magistracies. His aggressive self-fashioning as the positive embodiment of ancestral excellence found its negative counterpart in polemics against contemporary decadence and corruption. As Earl notes, 'the long line of ancestors boasted by a corrupt noble was of no account beside Cato's own youth spent in learning the harsh lessons of abstinence, thrift and hard work in the Sabine country'.[28] Cato thereby turned his obscure background and undistinguished pedigree into a badge of honour and thereby staked out a position of strength from which he was able to reject the criticism he received for his uncommon behaviour.[29] He portrayed himself as a magistrate apart from the others, as the

---

[25] Liv. 39.40.9 and 41.1–2.

[26] *Virtus* is mentioned several times in the epitaphs of the Scipios: *uir [. . .] quoius forma uirtutei parisuma fuit*, *CIL* I² 6.7 (epitaph of Scipio Barbatus, consul in 298 BCE); *nunquam uictus est uirtutei*, *CIL* I² 11 (epitaph of L. Cornelius Scipio, brother of Cn. Hispanus). This quality is also highlighted along with honour, reputation, glory and talent in the epitaph of P. Cornelius Scipio, son of P., in order to offset the lack of magistracy: *CIL* I² 10.

[27] Blösel 2000: 53–9 and Reay 2005: 334–5.   [28] Earl 1970: 47.

[29] Cato *De sumptu suo* fr. 174 M² (Gel. 13.24.1).

199

Laure Passet

only honest man in a world gone corrupt[30] – a paragon of virtue to be admired and imitated as a living *exemplum*.[31]

As Villa notes, Cato gave in to the fashion of the century: the emphasis on charismatic political leaders. During the Second Punic War some generals, especially Scipio, began to be seen as providential men, that is men predisposed by their remarkable character to play a key role in the history of Rome.[32] The trend was not entirely new: it picked up on and amplified the rhetoric of the *optimus ciuitatis* that pervade the eulogies of the *nobiles* of the third century BCE.[33] Cato, of course, disapproved of the endeavours of other outstanding aristocrats to pretend to a societal standing over and above the rest of Rome's ruling elite – which raises the question of how he reconciled his own efforts at charismatic self-promotion with critiquing those of his peers. The emphasis on service for the commonwealth alone, however pronounced it was in Cato, proved insufficient for this purpose: every other aristocrat would also argue that his elevated status was in accordance with the interests of the *res publica* – and reflected his own merit within and achievements on behalf of the commonwealth. The idea of frugality as an ancestral norm enabled Cato to engage in a special kind of self-elevation designed to avoid the divisive self-promotion he despised in others: unlike his peers who claimed to be superior to the norm, Cato pretended to embody what had been the norm in the past but no longer was – since in his own time many, if not most, members of the ruling elite had started to fall short of it. Put differently, he set himself apart from the rest not by elevating himself upwards, but by demoting everyone else downwards.[34] This

---

[30] See e.g. *De sumptu suo* fr. 173 M² (Fronto *ad M. Ant.* 1. 11), where he imagined himself talking with one of his servants who was publicly reading one of his speeches. Every time this servant mentioned his upright behaviour, Cato ordered him to keep quiet because 'they don't want to hear it' (*nolunt audire*) – an ingenious way of highlighting how uncommon his behaviour was in the Rome of his time.

[31] See Agache 1980: 85.   [32] Villa 1952: 107.

[33] Villa 1952: 107, referring to the epitaph of the son of Scipio Barbatus, L. Scipio, consul in 259 BCE (*CIL* I² 9) and to the *elogia* of A. Atilius Calatinus, consul in 258 and 254 BCE (Cic. *Sen.* 61; *Fin.* 2.116).

[34] Villa 1952: 107 notes that Cato was 'convinced of his being an exceptional moral personality'.

Frugality as a Political Language in the Second Century BCE

rhetorical strategy, which aligned well with his *nouitas*, helped to ensure a brilliant career: despite his undistinguished origins, he reached the top of the *cursus honorum*. The patronage of some *nobiles* like Valerius Flaccus is not enough to explain this success. His political and oratorical skills and the careful cultivation of a specific image of himself also played a vital role. Peter Brunt has shown that the nobles of the second century BCE were not able to use the 'ties of clientship' to 'keep the mass obedient' in order to control Roman political life and elections.[35] Patronage was one source of political influence amongst others: *homines noui* could rise to the top if they were able to appeal to the people.

According to A. Bell, political life in Rome had to be spectacular. He explains that 'the eyes as well as the ears of a crowd were attentive to men gesticulating in the Forum, sacrificing and praying to the gods, presiding at the games, advertising personal, national, and divine might in triumph and to the commemorations of men through statues, coins, funeral processions, and monuments.'[36] Lifestyle and discoursing on ways of life can be added to this list. Cato's frugality was spectacular because it contrasted with the usual way of life of the elite class. It was meant to demonstrate that he was a true and valuable member of Rome's ruling elite, that is, a man destined to govern. As H. I. Flower notes, recent studies on the nature of Roman politics have highlighted that 'the political life of Ancient Rome relied very heavily on communication within the city of a particular set of elite self-representations'.[37] Cato's strategy to present himself as an *exemplum* of frugality ensured that, despite the opposition of the nobility, the citizens, 'inflamed' by his speeches against luxury, elected him censor.[38] The people should not be regarded as a passive spectator of the acts and the speeches of the elite. Claude Nicolet notes that there was 'a subtle dialectic' between politicians and the people: 'the people [. . .] react in an intended or

---

[35] Brunt 1988: 415–24. [36] Bell 2004: 20. See also Nicolet 1976: 460–72.
[37] Flower 2011: 275. [38] *accensi*: Liv. 39.41.4. See also Plu. *Cat. Ma.* 16.6–8.

Laure Passet

unexpected manner, and take part [...] in the continuity of the spectacle.'[39] How people saw senators and magistrates influenced the attitudes of the latter. It explains in particular Scipio Aemilianus' choice of broadcasting his commitment to frugality: he, too, opted for a rhetoric of frugality as a means of increasing his popularity.

According to Polybius, our main source for Scipio's youthful self-fashioning and obviously to be used with caution, he cultivated simplicity and temperance from early on (31.25.8):[40]

Πλὴν ὅ γε Σκιπίων [...] πάσαις ταῖς ἐπιθυμίαις ἀντιταξάμενος καὶ κατὰ πάντα τρόπον ὁμολογούμενον καὶ σύμφωνον ἑαυτὸν κατασκευάσας κατὰ τὸν βίον ἐν ἴσως πέντε τοῖς πλώτοις ἔτεσι πάνδημον ἐποιήσατο τὴν ἐπ' εὐταξίᾳ καὶ σωφροσύνῃ δόξαν.

Scipio, however, ... combating all his appetites and molding his life to be in every way coherent and uniform, in about the first five years established his universal reputation for strictness and temperance.

Polybius was of course not a neutral observer. He wanted to show that Scipio Aemilianus, trained in Greek *paideia*, was the only Roman able to stop the moral decadence of Rome and the decline of its imperial regime.[41] However, it is not likely that Polybius entirely invented Scipio's frugality.[42] Other sources confirm the temperance of Scipio. According to Aulus Gellius, he rose up against the loose morals that spread in the city, especially at banquets. He lashed out at Publius Sulpicius Galus, a man he considered too refined.[43] According to Livy, eight years later, during the siege of Numantia, Scipio tried hard to restore the strictest discipline in an army corrupted by licence and luxury.[44] Accentuating his image as an austere man, he especially showed his refusal to indulge in luxury

---

[39] Nicolet 1976: 459–60.
[40] I cite the Loeb translation by W. R. Paton, revised by F. W. Walbank and C. Habicht.
[41] Ferrary 1988: 543 and Terwagne 2007: 372–4.
[42] Astin 1967: 27 admits that 'doubtless Polybius has exaggerated both the amount of time Scipio spent hunting and the extent to which his exploits in the chase won him a reputation for courage; on the other hand his account cannot conceivably be without a substantial element of truth'.
[43] Gel. 6.12.4–5.   [44] Liv. *Per.* 57.

202

Frugality as a Political Language in the Second Century BCE

during his censorship in 142 BCE: in a speech at the beginning of his magistracy, he urged the people to follow the frugal customs of their forefathers.[45] In possible imitation (or emulation) of Cato's strict censorship, he demoted the knight Claudius Asellus to the lowest class of citizens, the *aerarii*, because he spent most of his paternal wealth on luxurious presents for a courtesan. In a later speech against Asellus, he used the same kind of arguments as Cato: he deplored that Asellus used his funds to satisfy his personal and scandalous desires instead of worrying about his family's interests; and contrasted the value of the equipment of Asellus' estate in the Sabine country and the considerable sums spent on his prostitute.[46] The comparison between countryside and urban luxury, between inheritance and excessive spending, closely resembles the one used by Cato to condemn Rome's luxury: Cato compared the high sums spent on luxurious food or pretty young slaves and the value of a field or of ploughmen.[47] In all probability, Scipio modelled his rhetoric of frugality on that of Cato, which shows that Cato's strategy had evidently been successful.[48]

Yet Scipio also tweaked Cato's approach to public self-fashioning in decisive ways. Whereas the wholesale and xenophobic rejection of anything Greek was a key facet of Cato's public persona, Scipio managed to accommodate a (partial) embrace of Greek culture within an overall image of Roman austerity by highlighting engagement with those cultural artifacts that resonated particularly well with his frugal outlook. Thus he professed a liking for the writings of Xenophon, an author who sang the praises of a simple and austere lifestyle. He advertised being on familiar terms with Panaetius of Rhodes, a Stoic philosopher who maintained that temperance was one facet of the practical virtue required of the wise man.[49]

---

[45] Gel. 4.20.10 and 5.19.15.

[46] Scip. Aem. *Pro se contra Tiberium Asellum* fr. 19 M² (Gel. 6.11.9): *[...] si tu in uno scorto maiorem pecuniam absumpsisti quam quanti omne instrumentum fundi Sabini in censum dedicauisti* ('[...] you have squandered more money on one harlot than you reported for the census as the value of all the equipment of your Sabine estate').

[47] Plb. 31.25.5–6.

[48] On the relation between Cato and Scipio Aemilianus, see Astin 1956: 159–80.

[49] Cic. *Off.* 1.15–17.

Laure Passet

Scipio invited this philosopher to come with him during a diplomatic mission in the East in 140 BCE. This anecdotal evidence suggests that Polybius' account, however idealised, picked up on elements of Scipio's self-fashioning. This of course does not mean that, as Polybius maintains, Scipio tried to be frugal during his youth to stop the moral decadence of Rome and the decline of its ruling elite.[50] Likewise, we ought not to assume that his protestations of austerity derived from his interest in Stoicism. On the basis of the sources, it is impossible to ascertain to what extent Panaetius' teaching influenced Scipio's public action – if it did so at all. As Astin notes, 'the fact that among all the numerous references to Scipio and his learning he is nowhere said to have been a Stoïc' does not speak in favour of his being guided by Panaetius' philosophy.[51] Rather, we should see Scipio's predilection for an austere way of life as part of a political strategy.

An anecdote concerning an incident during Scipio's campaign in Spain, related by Plutarch and Frontinus, illustrates how he used his commitment to an austere way of life to gain political leverage (Plu. *Apopht.* 201c–d):[52]

Μεμμίου δὲ τινος χιλιάρχου λαβὼν ὑποζύγια ψυκτῆρας διαλίθους παρακομίζοντα καὶ Θηρικλείους, "Ἐμοὶ μέν, εἶπεν, ἡμέρας τριάκοντα καὶ τῇ πατρίδι, σαυτῷ δὲ τὸν βίον ἅπαντα τοιοῦτος ὢν ἄχρηστον πεποίηκας σεαυτόν'.

He detected in the baggage carried by the pack-animals of Memmius, a military tribune, wine-coolers set with precious stones, the work of Thericles, and said to him, 'By such conduct you have made yourself useless to me and your country for thirty days, but useless to yourself for your whole lifetime.'

Just like Cato, Scipio here contrasts private luxury with public utility. By stressing Memmius' worthlessness, he suggests that a taste for luxury was an obstacle to personal achievement – for a member of the ruling elite that means a distinguished political career. A reputation of frugal conduct was a useful asset in politics – and it is worth emphasising that combatting appetites

[50] See Astin 1967: 290 and also 282–7.
[51] Astin 1967: 298 and also 296–306; Morford 2002: 23.
[52] Here and below I cite the Loeb translation of Plutarch's *Roman Sayings* by F. C. Babbitt. See also Fron. *Str.* 4.1.1.

204

Frugality as a Political Language in the Second Century BCE

and exercising self-restraint do not conflict with aristocratic competitiveness. On the contrary, this kind of 'virtue signalling' could be one way of distinguishing the individual concerned from all others. We capture a reflex of this dynamic in Polybius, who praises Aemilianus for trying to establish a reputation for temperance (31.25.8: ἡ ἐπὶ σωφροσύνῃ δόξα) through the suppression of appetites in his youth, while simultaneously acknowledging his desire for socio-political distinction, if not uniqueness (31.25.9). The cultivation of a specific image of himself was designed to ensure popularity both within aristocratic circles and the populace at large. An anecdote transmitted by Plutarch highlights Scipio's interest in 'recognisability' (Plu. *Apopht.* 200d):

Ἀππίου δὲ Κλαυδίου περὶ τῆς τιμητικῆς ἀρχῆς ἁμιλλωμένου πρὸς αὐτὸν καὶ λέγοντος ὅτι πάντας ὀνομαστὶ Ῥωμαίους αὐτὸς ἀσπάζεται Σκιπίωνος ὀλίγου δεῖν ἀγνοοῦντος ἅπαντας, 'Ἀληθῆ λέγειν', εἶπεν· 'ἐμοὶ γὰρ οὐκ εἰδέναι πολλοὺς ἀλλ᾿ ὑπὸ μηδενὸς ἀγνοεῖσθαι μεμέληκεν'.

When Appius Claudius was his rival for the censorship, and asserted that he greeted all the Romans by name, while Scipio knew hardly one of them, Scipio said, 'You are quite right; for I have not taken such pains to know many as to be unknown to none.'

Scipio's retort suggests that a candidate for upper magistracies could not exclusively rely on personal networks, the base of clients (however large) or active, ingratiating canvassing to guarantee success at elections. What might be even more important was a striking image that ensured the kind of charismatic reputation and renown that translated into votes at election time.[53] As Astin notes, 'Scipio Aemilianus [...] exploited popular appeal more intensively, more unscrupulously, and with greater success than any other leader since the Senate had established its overwhelming ascendancy during the Second Punic War; and in this way he compensated – in certain fields – for his comparative neglect of more traditional methods.'[54] Certainly, Scipio benefited from his

---

[53] Astin 1967: 28–9.
[54] Astin 1967: 29. See also his gloss on 'popular appeal' as 'a broad and imprecise expression, which may embrace many methods of influencing the voter: the sheer magnetism of a brilliant and powerful personality, or the recommendation of men

205

Laure Passet

being a member of a great noble family, but he also exploited his popularity. He managed to obtain a second consulship and the leadership of the war against Numantia in 134 BCE by appealing to the people, thus overcoming the reluctance of the senate.[55]

The Tomb of the Scipios suggests that over time the cultivation of a frugal image became part of a family strategy. F. Coarelli observes that the more prominent the family became, the less epitaphs and sarcophagi were executed with care and refinement.[56] The richest burial was that of Scipio Barbatus (*cos.* 298), the founder of the Tomb. Only his sarcophagus was decorated. That of his son (*cos.* 259), also of the third century BCE, was without decoration, but, as for Barbatus, it was a fine monolithic sarcophagus in *peperino*. Their epitaphs, dating to the third century or, at the latest, the first years of the second century BCE (for Barbatus), are regular and refined.[57] The subsequent burials were, according to F. Coarelli, 'plain stone slabs in tuff, with inscriptions poorly incised'. He stresses the 'nonstandard rudeness' of the graves that were added in the course of the second century BCE.[58] This chronology can be further refined. The inscription on the sarcophagus of L. Cornelius Scipio,[59] son of Scipio Hispallus, who died prematurely at the age of twenty around 180 or 170 BCE, and that of P. Scipio, who died probably in the 170s or 160s BCE still manifest efforts at regularity;[60] the inscription of the latter even features the lines drawn by the engraver to guide his hand. The epitaph of L. Cornelius Scipio, quaestor in 167 and deceased around 160 BCE, shows a shift in the culture of display: it was drawn without any care of parallelism

---

themselves distinguished in public life. Military ability was likely to count for something, especially in times of crisis [...]. But other things less rational and less reputable, also had a great impact' (28–9).

[55] Astin 1967: 135–6 and 183–4, followed by Hackl 1982: 102–5 and Rosenstein 1993: 316.

[56] Coarelli 1970–71: 85.

[57] On these burials, see Zevi 1970: 65–7; 1999: 284–5; Coarelli 1994: 113–16; 1996: 183–8 and 217–23; Flower 1996: 171–5; Etcheto 2008: 495, 513–22 and 535–43.

[58] Coarelli 1970–71: 85.   [59] *CIL* I² 11 (= *ILLRP* I. 312).

[60] *CIL* I² 10 (= *ILLRP* I. 311). On these burials, see Coarelli 1994: 113–16; 1996: 186–7; Etcheto 2008: 545–53 and 558–9.

Frugality as a Political Language in the Second Century BCE

between the lines or of alignment of letters.[61] The apparent carelessness in execution increases further in the inscription of Cn. Cornelius Scipio Hispanus, who probably died shortly after his praetorship of 139 BCE.[62] The lack of attention to detail in the carving of these inscriptions was not due to the family's lack of interest in these two men. The epitaphs carved on their sarcophagi – listing their magistracies and, in the case of L. Scipio, mentioning his father's victory over Antiochus[63], or, in case of Hispanus, the insistence on his *uirtutes*, on the *honor* he gained for his line and on the praises he got from his ancestors[64] – demonstrate that, on the contrary, the members of the family tried hard to glorify these men and to prove that they were worthy of the great Scipionic family. An explanation for the apparent decline in the standards of ostentatious display has therefore to be sought elsewhere. According to F. Coarelli, a link exists between the deliberate poverty of their burials and contemporary public discourse in praise of the *rusticitas* of the *antiqui*: 'it is a very specific ideological fact: *prisca rusticitas* is the unavoidable instrument of political struggle.'[65]

The evolution of the external appearance of the graves and epitaphs of the family members buried in this monument over the course of the second century BCE testifies to the increasing strength of the ideal of frugality among the Scipios and the probable use of this ideal for political purposes. Flower stresses that 'such family burial sites were placed to attract public attention and to serve as advertisements for the family's rank, and perhaps even their politics'.[66] Even if the sarcophagi with the inscriptions were placed inside the tomb and were seen only by the family and their friends and clients who could enter the grave, this did not prevent the epitaphs from being more widely known and enhance the prestige of the Cornelii

---

[61] *RE* 324. *CIL* I². 12 (= *ILLRP* I. 313). Coarelli 1996: 185–7 (n. 27).

[62] *RE* 347. *CIL* I². 15 (= *ILLRP* I. 316). Coarelli 1996: 197.

[63] *CIL* I². 12 (= *ILLRP* I. 313): *Patrem regem Antioco(m) subegit.*

[64] *CIL* I². 15 (= *ILLRP* I. 316): *Virtutes generis mieis moribus accumulaui, progeniem genui, facta patris petiei maiorum optenui laudem ut sibei me esse cretum laetentur, stirpem nobolitauit honor.*

[65] Coarelli 1970–71: 85.   [66] Flower 1996: 159.

Scipiones.[67] As Flower notes, 'the close connections between family traditions and public self-representation suggested by the Scipionic inscriptions reveal the lack of distinction between public and private inherent in aristocratic culture.'[68]

The epitaph of L. Scipio, which postdates 167 BCE (the date of his quaestorship), falls into the period that followed the victory over Macedonia at Pydna, when Rome's imperial success in the Greek East caused significant tensions at home since the increasingly unequal distribution of material resources and symbolic capital put basic principles of oligarchic equality in jeopardy.[69] The ruling elite tried to regulate the transformation of imperial plunder into political influence by passing various sumptuary measures, such as the *senatus consultum* that tried to limit expenditure during the feasts of the elite during the *Ludi Megalenses* or the *Lex Fannia*, both in 161 BCE.[70] L. Scipio's heirs may have deemed it a good idea to highlight the moderation and the frugal tastes of this man by giving his burial a plain and rustic inscription – not least because L. Scipio was the son of Scipio Asiaticus, a man suspected of having misappropriated money during his campaign against Antiochus.[71] They tried to show the selflessness, and so the honesty, of this branch of the family.[72]

It is significant that the least regular inscription in the Tomb is that of Scipio Hispanus, a man particularly praised in his epitaph in order to compensate for his short career in comparison with his ancestors.[73] As Hölkeskamp notes,

---

[67] Flower 1996: 160 and Massaro 1997: 103. [68] Flower 1996: 160 n. 6.

[69] Plb 31.25.6–8.

[70] Plin. *Nat.* 10.71.139; Gel. 2.24.2–6; Macr. 3.16.14 and 3.17.3–4, 6.

[71] Plb 23.14; Cic. *de Orat.* 2.249; *Prov.* 18; Liv. 38.50.4–60.10; V. Max. 3.7.1; 4.1.8; Gel. 6.19; *vir. ill.* 49.15–18 and 53.2.

[72] The son of this L. Scipio (quaestor in 167 BCE), named Cornelius Scipio Asiagenus Comatus (*RE* 339), dead between 164 and 144 BCE at the age of sixteen was also provided with a rough inscription. *CIL* I² 13 (= *ILLRP* I. 314). On this man, see Coarelli 1996: 186 and 196; Etcheto 2008: 564.

[73] His father Cn. Scipio Hispallus, his grandfather Cn. Scipio Calvus, his great-grandfather L. Scipio and the father of this L. Scipio, L. Scipio Barbatus had all be consul, respectively in 176 BCE, 222 BCE, 259 BCE and 298 BCE. On this epitaph, see Flower 1996: 169–70.

208

Frugality as a Political Language in the Second Century BCE

it is not a coincidence if Scipio Hispanus almost apologized in his epitaph in highlighting the fact that he had 'imitated' the feats of his father, that he had himself descendants and that the eminent *maiores* of his *gens* should not be ashamed of him [. . .] because despite the excessively exhaustive enumeration of all these *honores*, something was missing: this son and grandson of consuls, who was related to the first Africanus and Scipio Aemilianus, only reached the praetorship.[74]

The *rusticitas* of his inscription may have contributed to counterbalance this fact, because it was proof of the high moral value of this man, contemptuous of luxury, concerned only with *honores*, that is service on behalf of the *res publica*, and the *dignitatis gradus* of his line.

Was this family strategy inspired by Scipio Aemilianus, who used his frugality as a political tool? Admittedly, he was only a distant cousin of Hispanus; but they probably were on campaign together in Africa in 149 BCE, during the Third Punic War.[75] Massaro suggests that the epitaph of Hispanus may have been written by Scipio Aemilianus, but no certain proof supports this hypothesis.[76] It might be better to suppose that there was a climate favourable to temperance inside the Scipionic family in the middle of the second century BCE, a climate that Scipio Aemilianus may have greatly helped to develop. It is also possible that his frugality was encouraged by the ideas widespread in his adoptive family. The strategy of these Scipios reveals that, in the middle of the second century BCE, public opinion seems to have been more favourably disposed towards a show of frugality on the part of members of Rome's ruling elite than ostentatious consumption ('luxury').

In conclusion, during the second century BCE the manifestation of a frugal *habitus* became one way in which elite Romans could lay claim to being exceptional individuals.[77]

---

[74] Hölkeskamp 2008: 105.

[75] Massaro 1997: 97 n. 1. Hispanus was military tribune or quaestor in Africa. App. *Pun.* 80. 375. On his being in the military camp in front of Carthago, see *RE* 347; Astin 1967: 54 and Etcheto 2008: 571. Scipio Aemilianus military tribune in the same camp: Cic. *Rep.* 6.9; App. *Pun.* 98 and 112; *vir. ill.* 58.4; Astin 1967: 54.

[76] Massaro 1997: 105–8 and 121–4. Against this hypothesis, see Etcheto 2008: 575 and 578, referring to Botteri 1980: 77–8 and 86–7.

[77] See further Passet 2010.

Cato the Elder and Scipio Aemilianus demonstrate the success of this strategy in the court of public opinion. The popular appeal of this form of self-promotion can be explained in part by the symbolic connection between personal self-restraint and public service in the interest of the community. Scipio was most likely influenced by Cato's achievement. There is, however, a profound difference between their respective approaches. According to Polybius, Scipio displayed frugality in order to be worthy of his family.[78] He behaved as a member of the *nobilitas*, bound by tradition to equal or surpass his ancestors. Conversely, Cato did not come from a clan that had distinguished magistrates in the family tree. He therefore tried his best to show that a commitment to the frugal management of material resources was the heritage of a glorious Roman past that belonged to the Roman people as a whole (and especially those with Sabine roots). The entire populace, and not just the *nobilitas*, could in principle identify with Cato's notion of what it is to be quintessentially Roman: in his rhetoric, frugality was a common denominator of the SPQR, and not the prerogative of the elite. There is another difference, but less pronounced. Unlike Cato, Scipio did not mind showing his taste for Greek literature and philosophy – just as his father did. But he did not aim to be a wise man in a philosophical sense. Rather, he tailored his interest in Greek culture to the pursuit of a stellar political career (not unlike Cato), just as certain philosophers such as Panaetius seem to have formed their philosophical ideas in interaction with the principles and protocols of Roman public life.

It is difficult to know to what extent Cato inspired other aristocrats to adopt frugality as a strategy of self-promotion. His later image as an archetype of austerity suggests that he soon became a model and an inspiration. During the last third of the second century the positive resonances of frugality became a *topos* and were widely used by both *populares* and politicians dedicated to the interest of the senatorial elite.

---

[78] Plb 31.23.12 and 24.4–5; 10.

Frugality as a Political Language in the Second Century BCE

Bibliography

Agache, S. (1980) 'Caton le censeur ou les fortunes d'une légende', in *Colloque Histoire et historiographie*, ed. R. Chevallier. Paris: 71–107.

Agati Madeira, E. M. (2004) 'La *lex Oppia* et la condition juridique de la femme dans la Rome républicaine', *Revue internationale des droits de l'Antiquité* 51 (3rd series): 71–107.

Astin, A. E. (1956) 'Scipio Aemilianus and Cato Censorius', *Latomus* 15: 159–80.

(1967) *Scipio Aemilianus*. Oxford.

(1978) *Cato the Censor*. Oxford.

Bell, A. (2004) *Spectacular Power in the Greek and Roman City*. Oxford and New York.

Blösel, W. (2000) 'Die Geschichte des Begriffes *Mos Maiorum* von den Anfängen bis zu Cicero', in *Mos Maiorum: Untersuchungen zu den Formen der Identitätsstiftung und Stabilisierung in der römischen Republik*, eds. B. Linke and M. Stemmler. Stuttgart: 25–97.

Botteri, P. (1980) 'Diodore de Sicile, 34–35, 33: un problème d'exégèse', *Ktéma* 5: 77–87.

Brunt, P. A. (1988) *The Fall of the Roman Republic and Related Essays*. Oxford.

Coarelli, F. (1970–71) 'Discussione sull'articolo di C. Ampolo "Su alcuni mutamenti sociali nel Lazio tra l'VIII e il V secolo"', *DArch* 4–5: 84–6.

(1994) *Guide archéologique de Rome*. Paris.

(1996) 'Il sepolcro degli Scipioni', in *Revixit Ars: Arte e ideologia a Roma. Dai modelli ellenistici alla tradizione repubblicana*. Rome: 179–238.

Dalby, A. (trans.) (1998) *On Farming*. Blackawton.

Earl, D. C. (1970) *The Moral and Political Tradition of Rome*. London.

Etcheto, H. (2008) *Les Cornelii Scipiones. Famille et pouvoir à Rome à l'époque républicaine*. Doctoral thesis. Bordeaux.

Evans, J. K. (1991) *War, Women and Children in Ancient Rome*. London and New York.

Ferrary, J.-L. (1988) *Philhellénisme et impérialisme. Aspects idéologiques de la conquête romaine du monde hellénistique, de la seconde guerre de Macédoine à la guerre contre Mithridate*. Rome.

Flower, H. I. (1996) *Ancestor Masks and Aristocratic Power in Roman Culture*. Oxford.

(2011) 'Elite self-representation in Rome', in *The Oxford Handbook of Social Relations in the Roman World*, ed. M. Peachin. Oxford: 271–85.

Fraccaro, Pl. (1956) *Opuscula. 1. Scritti di carattere generale, Studi Catoniani, I processi degli Scipioni*. Pavia.

Galletier, É. and Fontaine, J. (eds.) (1968) *Ammien Marcellin Histoire*. Tome I (livres XVI–XVII). Paris.

Hackl, U. (1982) *Senat und Magistratur in Rom von der Mitte des 2. Jahrhunderts v. Chr. bis zur Diktatur Sullas*. Kallmünz.

Laure Passet

Hellegouarc'h, J. (1972) *Le vocabulaire latin des relations et des partis politiques sous la République.* Paris.

Hölkeskamp, K.-J. (2008) *Reconstruire une République. La 'culture politique' de la Rome antique et la recherche des dernières décennies.* Nantes (French translation by C. Layle, made in association with F. Hurlet, of *Rekonstruktionen einer Republik: Die politische Kultur des antiken Rom und die Forschung der letzten Jahrzehnte.* Munich. 2008).

Letta, C. (1984) 'L'"Italia dei *mores Romani*" nelli *Origines* di Catone', *Athenaeum* 72 (1-2): 3–30.

McDonnell, M. (2006) *Roman Manliness: Virtus and the Roman Republic.* Cambridge.

Malcovati, E. (1953) *Oratorum Romanorum fragmenta liberae rei publicae.* I. Textus. Turin.

Massaro, M. (1997) 'L'epigramma per Scipione Ispano (CIL, I², 15)', *Epigraphica* 59: 97–124.

Morford, M. (2002) *The Roman Philosophers: From the Time of Cato the Censor to the Death of Marcus Aurelius.* London and New York.

Nicolet, C. (1976) *Le métier de citoyen dans la Rome républicaine.* Paris.

Passet, L. (2010) 'Frugalité et banquet offert au peuple à l'occasion de funérailles: la vaisselle de terre et les peaux de bouc de Quintus Aelius Tubéron', *Ktéma* 35: 51–67.

  (2011) *Refus du luxe et frugalité à Rome: Histoire d'un combat politique (fin du IIIe siècle av. J.-C. – fin du IIe siècle av. J.-C.),* https://tel.archives-ouvertes.fr/tel-01168050 (last accessed 9 February 2020).

Reay, B. (2005) 'Agriculture, writing, and Cato's aristocratic self-fashioning', *ClAnt* 24: 331–61.

Rosenstein, N. (1993) 'Competition and crisis in mid-Republican Rome', *Phoenix* 47: 313–38.

Roman, D. and Roman, Y. (2007) *Aux miroirs de la Ville: Images et discours identitaires romains (IIIe s. avant J.-C. – IIIe s. après J.-C.).* Brussels.

Savagner, A. (1846) *Sextus Pompeius Festus: De la signification des mots.* Paris.

Scullard, H. H. (1951) *Roman Politics, 220–150 B.C.* Oxford.

  (1960) 'Scipio Aemilianus and Roman politics', *JRS* 50: 59–74.

Terwagne, O. (2007) 'Interpréter l'ambassade des trois philosophes en 155: Mise au jour de nouveaux fragments de Polybe', in *LEC* 75: 347–79.

Villa, E. (1952) 'Attualità e tradizione nell'ideale politico e sociale di *uir bonus* in Catone', *Rivista di studi classici* 3: 96–115.

Zevi, F. (1970) 'Considerazioni sull'elogio di Scipione Barbato', *Studi miscellanei: Omaggio a Ranuccio Bianchi Bandinelli. Rome:* 65–73.

  (1999) 'Sepulcrum (Corneliorum) Scipionum', in *Lexicon topographicum urbis Romae IV, P-S (Sepulcrum),* ed. E. M. Steinby. Rome: 284–5.

CHAPTER 4

SMALLHOLDING, FRUGALITY AND MARKET ECONOMY IN THE GRACCHAN AGE*

MATTIA BALBO

Introduction

In the third chapter of his *Considérations* (1734), Montesquieu briefly wonders how the Romans, while not being 'men of another breed than ourselves' – as he notes with subtle irony – were able to maintain a very high proportion of soldiers (1:8) with respect to the population over a long period of time: a proportion which appeared unrepeatable in eighteenth-century Europe, but which led to the rise of Rome from a small town to a great empire. For Montesquieu equity was the sole explanation for such a high military participation in the ancient republics: the equal repartition of land was the foundation of a powerful state and an efficient army since soldiers were motivated to defend their own properties and their interest coincided with that of the state.[1] He even quotes Tiberius Gracchus' renowned speech stressing the importance of small landowners in Roman society:[2]

'Tell me,' said Tiberius Gracchus to the nobles, 'who is worth more: a citizen or a perpetual slave; a soldier, or a man useless for war? In order to have a few more acres of land than other citizens, do you wish to renounce the hope of conquering the rest of the world, or to place yourselves in danger of seeing these lands you refuse us snatched away by enemies?'

Later, in his masterpiece *De l'esprit des lois* (first published in 1748), Montesquieu returns to and further substantiates an argument of great relevance not only to modern scholarship,

---

* I would like to thank Tana de Zulueta for having kindly helped me to revise the English version of this text.
[1] Montesquieu 1734: 21.
[2] Montesquieu 1734: 23–4. English translation by D. Lowenthal: Montesquieu 1965: 41. Ancient source: App. *BC* 1.11.44 (cf. Plu. *TG* 9.5).

213

but also to the political debate in antiquity.[3] The notion that citizen-soldiers constituted the strength of Rome's social system during the Middle Republic (300–100 BCE) dates to the second century BCE. Cato the Elder summarises this concept when he states that a perfect Roman citizen must be first of all a good farmer.[4] In his view a good farmer means also a frugal man, who avoids wasting money and works his estate in the most efficient way, independently of its size.[5] After the defeat of Carthage and the conquest of Greece, when the Roman economy underwent a momentous change of scale, politics began to reflect upon the place of small landowners in the new setting. This chapter aims to reconsider the transformation of smallholding in the late second century BCE, when the Republic starts paying attention to the plight of poor peasants and adopts strategies to revive an economy based on small farms in Central Italy. My discussion will chiefly focus on some aspects concerning landholding during the Gracchan Age (133–121 BCE): the recurrence of some aspects of the notion of frugality in the political debates arising from the Gracchan reforms and the role of smallholdings in the development of a market oriented agriculture, not least in relation to the measures put in place by the Republic to help poor peasants with meeting the means of subsistence. Therefore, I focus on the ideologies of frugality that date back to the political context of the Sempronian laws. Furthermore, this chapter discusses what impact the market economy might have had on smallholdings and reconnects the Gracchan concept of frugality with the practice of agrarian allotment in Italy.

Gracchan Ideology

Frugality appears to have played a key role in the debate around the passing of the *lex Sempronia agraria* in 133 BCE. Several aspects concerning this notion recur among the

---

[3] Montesquieu 1768: V.5, VII.2, XXVI.15, well discussed by Rich 2008: 528–9.
[4] Cato *Agr.* praef.
[5] On the meaning of Cato's frugality see Chapter 3 (Passet) in this volume.

Smallholding, Frugality and Market Economy in the Gracchan Age

arguments of both sides, for and against the law. The very scarce fragments of Tiberius Gracchus' speeches, most of them transmitted by Plutarch and Appian, testify to the great relevance that the tribune attributed to small landowners within the Roman social structure. Gracchus' main concern was the supposed decline in the numbers of *assidui* in the fifth census class, which, as a medium term consequence, might undermine the military recruitment system, and ultimately destroy the supremacy laboriously established by Rome over the previous 50 years.[6] Modern scholars still debate the reliability of Gracchus' statement about the manpower shortage in Italy, the ultimate causes that might have produced such an effect and the social-economic background of Roman Italy in the second century BCE. Among the various positions, I here follow the hypothesis that in the Middle and Late Republic there was no general decrease of the free population in Italy (as stated for example by Brunt and Hopkins),[7] but that the reason of Gracchus' anxieties should be sought in the gradual impoverishment of peasants due to the high competition for arable land in Central and Southern Italy: such competition may have been affected by several factors, such as a probable (though hard to prove) demographic growth, a wider diffusion of large market-oriented estates and the subsequent increase of land prices.[8]

Tiberius seems to ascribe the origin of the serious problems facing small landowners in the agrarian setup of Central Italy to an uncontrolled growth of *latifundia*.[9] These problems were

---

[6] App. *BC* 1.9.35; 11.45; Plu. *TG* 9.4 (= *ORF*⁴ 149–50, frs. 13–15). The chronological boundaries for the rise of the Roman empire, as they were conceived in the second century BCE, are defined in Polybius' *incipit* (1.1.5).

[7] Brunt 1971; Hopkins 1978: 1–98; 1995/1996; and of course Toynbee 1965. A good historiographical discussion can be found in Launaro 2011: 1–7 and de Ligt 2012: 1–39.

[8] Lo Cascio 1994; 2008. For further discussion, see Balbo 2013: 21–42 with further bibliography. A very interesting explanation is that proposed by Rich 1983: 299–305, who, although rejecting Brunt's model, supposes that Gracchus' fear concerns a misunderstood decline, due to failure to rear children. On the competition for land in Italy see especially Roselaar 2010: 180–200.

[9] The notion of *latifundium* has been fundamentally reconsidered by modern scholarship: here I refer to the proper meaning of a large estate, with no allusion to the eighteenth-century Italian 'latifondo'. See *Latifundium* 1995.

215

Mattia Balbo

of two, complementary, kinds, and over the long term could have contributed to a considerable impoverishment of the *assidui* belonging to the fifth class: the illegal occupation of public lands and the absorption of resources on the part of a few speculators – i.e. the 'rich' (πλούσιοι) mentioned by Appian[10] – to the detriment of small farmers; and the massive employment of slave labour in Roman villas instead of wage-earning manpower. The latter aspect recurs often and seems to occupy a very important place in Gracchan propaganda.[11] The anti-slave polemic is perhaps not only the result of the emergency triggered by contemporary revolts in Sicily, though the climate of fear provoked by those events may have played a relevant role in the debate and given greater appeal to Gracchus' arguments. However, we are informed that seasonal labour represents an essential element for the functioning of the Roman villa model, as described by Varro.[12] Moreover, the recruitment pool of free, wage-earning labourers was not only the towns and the urban plebs who could, on demand, move to the countryside, but also and especially the rural plebs already present in the surroundings of the villas. Small land-owners often supplemented their revenues with seasonal labour on neighbouring farms; thus most current studies on the late-Republican *uilla rustica* consider the existence of an adequate level of rural population indispensable to the good

---

[10] App. *BC* 1.7.29: 'The rich gained possession of most of the undistributed land (τῆς ἀνεμήτου γῆς) and after a while were confident that no one would take it back from them. They used persuasion or force to buy or seize property which adjoined their own, or any smallholdings belonging to poor men, and came to operate great ranches instead of single farms (πεδία μακρὰ ἀντὶ χωρίων).' On this passage see also Gargola 2008; Balbo 2013: 11–13; and, more recently, Roselaar 2015.

[11] App. *BC* 1.9.36; 11.44; Plu. *TG* 9.4 (= *ORF*⁴ 149–50, frs. 13–15).

[12] Var. *R.* 1.17.2: 'All agriculture is carried on by slaves, or by freemen, or both. By freemen, when they till the ground themselves, as many poor people do with the help of their families (*pauperculi cum sua progenie*); or hired hands (*mercennariis*), when the heavier farm operations, such as the vintage and the haying, are carried on by the hiring of freemen [...]. In this regard here is my personal opinion: it is more profitable to work unwholesome lands with hired hands than with slaves; and even in wholesome places it is more profitable thus to carry out the heavier farm operations, such as storing the products of the vintage or harvest'. On this passage see esp. de Neeve 1984: 11; 179–83, and Lo Cascio 2009: 71–89. For further and recent discussion on the labour in the villa-system cf. Marzano 2007: 125–53; Capogrossi Colognesi 2012: 139–65; Launaro 2015: 183–5.

Smallholding, Frugality and Market Economy in the Gracchan Age

functioning of this kind of large farm.[13] Indeed, the reckless recourse to low-cost slave manpower on *latifundia* – Tiberius Gracchus seems to say (in Appian) – deprives the poor free peasants and small landowners of an important source of revenue.

We must reaffirm that the Gracchan polemic does not imply direct blame of the *latifundium* or the villa-system itself, but of the consequences of a *latifundium* built according to premises that were socially unsustainable: exclusive occupation of common lands and massive employment of slave labour. This is the picture sketched by Gracchan propaganda, regardless of its historical authenticity, which is debated by several current scholars, and with a number of convincing arguments. And it is on this picture that I would like to dwell a moment.

According to our sources, Tiberius Gracchus proposed an agrarian reform aiming to recover *ager publicus* in Central and Southern Italy, in order to achieve a large-scale viritane redistribution to be followed by grants for the agricultural exploitation of the new lots created in this way.[14] The recovery was to be effected by enforcing an ancient limit on landholding (*modus agrorum*), which restricted individual holdings to 500 *iugera*, a provision traditionally ascribed to the so-called *lex Licinia de modo agrorum* of 367 BCE. This original 'Licinian' limit has long been generally supposed to have applied only to holdings of public land (*ager publicus*). However, recent research has challenged this consensus, and in my view has convincingly shown that, when originally instituted, the limit applied to holdings of all land, private as well as public. The case is discussed in detail by John Rich in this volume, with an interesting attempt to provide a reliable historical context for the pre-Gracchan limit.[15] It has often been argued that the

---

[13] See discussion in Launaro 2011: 149–82; Balbo 2017: 361–4.

[14] App. *BC* 1.9.37–38; *vir. ill.* 64.3; Liv. *Per.* 58; Plu. *TG* 14.1. I have discussed the terms of the *lex Sempronia agraria* in Balbo 2013: 83–104.

[15] See further Rich 2008; Balbo 2010; 2014. In my earlier papers I dated the Licinian law to the end of the fourth century, namely some years before the first reliable mention of a conviction made under this provision, in 298 BCE (Liv. 10.13.14). On the contrary, Rich cautiously accepts the 'traditional' dating around 367 BCE. Although the question is open, a general limit on land fits better with the fourth

217

Mattia Balbo

limit of 500 *iugera* was only introduced in the early second century, but, once it is understood that the limit applied to all forms of landholding, there is no reason to doubt the fourth-century dating implied by our sources. By the second century the limit appears to have become obsolete, even if some indications allow us to suppose that it was not totally abandoned.[16] Gracchus' enactment provided for the enforcement of the limit, but with important modifications: his law was not a mere resumption of the archaic *modus*, but a significant reform with different aims from the original provision. Under the Sempronian law the limit was doubled, and applied only to the public lands, and, instead of (as before) merely imposing a fine for infringements, his law prescribed that public land held in excess of the limit should be recovered and used to make land allotments to new beneficiaries among the Roman plebs. It may well be that the application only to *ager publicus*, legally stated by the *lex Sempronia*, followed a practice de facto undertaken from the third century BCE, when public land became more and more relevant in the Roman economy.[17]

As Rich's chapter shows, the original Licinian limit was at least in part the product of a contemporary ideology of frugality. Gracchus' land recovery programme too assumes many ideological features in some way related to the concept of frugality. Gracchan propaganda seems to stress the importance of a limit to the expansion of economic exploitation – a topic not completely new and connected with the notion of *modestia*, recently studied by Cristiano Viglietti.[18] Of course, it is a limit on some particular conditions: it serves to recover *ager publicus* and is connected with the actual ability of the

---

than with the second century. Rathbone 2003 holds that the limit applied only to private land, but this alternative is less plausible.

[16] See below, n. 34 and 35.

[17] Balbo 2013: 73–83. On the contrary, Rich 2008: 557–60, 565 (and in this volume) supposes as an alternative possibility that, while the Licinian limit was still being enforced, it was applied to all types of land, but it probably stopped being enforced altogether after the early third century BCE.

[18] Viglietti 2011: 121–3, 206–7; 2014: 248. See also his contribution in this volume.

Smallholding, Frugality and Market Economy in the Gracchan Age

holder to exploit the amount of land under his control effectively.

This aspect is explicitly mentioned in the following reference to Gracchan land legislation by Siculus Flaccus, one of the Roman writers on land surveying: 'Gracchus passed a law to prevent anyone in Italy from occupying more than two hundred *iugera*, for he realized that it was a harmful custom for anyone to possess more land than could be cultivated by the occupier himself.'[19] In a celebrated paper, Gianfranco Tibiletti used this text, in conjunction with a confused passage of Columella (1.3.11), to infer the existence of an archaic customary rule (*mos*) forbidding anyone to possess more (public) land than he was able to exploit.[20] However, Tibiletti's hypothesis has been decisively refuted in a fundamental essay by Dario Mantovani, who shows that the term *mos* in these passages does not have a real juridical sense; they should rather be taken as extempore statements by the authors, who, at least in Siculus Flaccus' case, may have been influenced by the ideological background of the Gracchan laws.[21] This passage of Siculus Flaccus is not free of flaws: it is not altogether clear whether the reference is to Tiberius Gracchus or to his brother Gaius, and the eccentric figure of 200 *iugera*, instead of 500 or 1000, may be either a mistake due to the manuscript tradition or a personal interpretation of the writer. Nonetheless, it seems likely that Siculus Flaccus is here reproducing a genuine item of Gracchan propaganda. The link with Tiberius Gracchus' arguments is explicitly stated: the state should (re)introduce a restriction on holdings of public land because it is immoral that some occupiers hold more land than they can really cultivate (*contrarium morem*: the reference to *mos* serves as an ideological legitimation of the restriction). In the historical

---

[19] Sic. Fl. *agrim.* 3 (p. 136 L. = 100 Th. = 102–3 Campbell): *praeterea legem tulit, nequis in Italia amplius quam ducenta iugera possideret: intellegebat enim contrarium esse morem, maiorem modum possidere quam qui ab ipso possidente coli possit.*

[20] Tibiletti 1948: 218–25, followed by Tibiletti 1949: 20–7. His essays on Rome's agrarian history are now collected in Tibiletti 2007. See also the excellent study by Forsén 1991.

[21] Mantovani 1997. See also Rich 2008: 558; 564 n. 120; Tarpin 2014: 186.

219

Mattia Balbo

form in which it had reached him, Siculus Flaccus is recording the Gracchan *modus agrorum*: a measure aiming to encourage the exploitation of the *fundus* by the occupier himself. Indeed we may suggest that Gracchan ideology theorised an ideal model of landholding, which was built upon the following principles: extent directly related to exploitation, if possible farming by the owner, expense reduction and economic efficiency.

Frugality and *Sumptus*

Another aspect related to the concept of frugality that stands out in the story of the Gracchi concerns sumptuary ideology. Aversion to luxury and immoderate expenses in both public and private life – for the two aspects are inseparable according to the Roman *nobilitas* – is a topic of much relevance in the politics and culture of the second century BCE. Tiberius Gracchus resorts to it in several ways: Plutarch informs us that normally, in everyday life, he was 'frugal' (εὐτελής) and 'simple' (ἀφελής).[22] Of course Tiberius follows the model of his first mentor, Scipio Aemilianus: indeed he grew up under Scipio's influence and took from him a number of attitudes as well as methods for managing propaganda and in the dealing with the *populus*. As Laure Passet emphasises well in this volume, Scipio makes use of frugality and austerity in lifestyle as an instrument for acquiring consensus: the success of this behaviour is demonstrated by the enormous popular favour that he enjoyed until a few months before his death, when his attempt to stop the reform process seems to have turned a part of the plebs against him. We may thus assume that when Tiberius appears on the public scene, though choosing Scipio's rival, Appius Claudius Pulcher, as a new mentor,[23] he nevertheless uses the same political instruments refined by Scipio.

---

[22] Plu. *TG* 2.4: 'So likewise in their way of living and at their tables, Tiberius was frugal and simple' (cf. below, n. 24).

[23] Plu. *TG* 4. On the presumed rivalry between Claudius and Scipio see Plu. *Aem.* 38; *praec. ger. reip.* 14; cf. Astin 1967: 111–13; Badian 1972: 674; Briscoe 1974: 125–7.

220

Smallholding, Frugality and Market Economy in the Gracchan Age

A different discourse, but no less interesting, involves Gaius. Again Plutarch affirms that in this regard, as in many others, he was the opposite of his brother (*TG* 2.4):[24]

> Gaius, compared with other men was temperate and even austere (σώφρων καὶ αὐστηρός), but in contrast with his brother was extravagant and over-wrought (νεοπρεπής καὶ περίεργος), as it appears in Drusus' charge against him for having bought some silver dolphins, to the value of twelve hundred and fifty drachmas for every pound weight.

The striking thing here is the precise reference to an accusation of *sumptus* – meaning an immoderate and unjustified waste of money – levelled at him by his opponents: a widespread political tactic in the second century BCE. Beyond the propaganda, this may signal that something has changed in the public's perception of the Gracchi during the 120s BCE. As a mere conjecture, we may assume that this different attitude follows the rupture with Scipio's entourage after the death of Tiberius and, more openly, after the attempt by Scipio to stop the agrarian reform: his own death in suspicious circumstances gave rise to an exchange of accusations between supporters and opponents of the Gracchi.[25] Perhaps the members of the aristocracy that identify themselves with the 'Scipionian' model blame the Gracchi for being spendthrifts, in order to stress the distance between them and the *mos maiorum*. On the other hand, Gaius Gracchus publicly emphasises his own *parsimonia* on at least one occasion: in the speech held after his return from Sardinia (124 BCE) he affirms he has maintained a very moderate conduct in the province, unlike most of his colleagues (*ORF*⁴ fr. 26 = Gel. 15.12.2):

> I conducted myself in my office, as I thought would be to your advantage, not as I believed would contribute to my own ambitions. There was no tavern at my establishment, nor did beautiful slaves wait upon me, and at a

---

[24] See also *comp. Agid. Cleom. Gracch.* 1.6.

[25] The rupture between Tiberius and Scipio's group still puzzles scholars: usually it is dated back to the Attalus affair (Astin 1967: 212; Badian 1972: 714). Apart from that, Scipio, after his return from Spain in 132 BCE, publicly disowns his former pupil and leads the opposition to the agrarian commission (Vell. 2.4.4; Plu. *TG* 21.7–8; cf. App. *BC* 1.19.78–82); cf. Santangelo 2019: 161–2.

221

Mattia Balbo

banquet of mine your sons were treated with more modesty than at their commander's tent.

Here Gaius seems to emulate his elder brother's attitude, to whom tradition ascribes indifference toward the symbols of material wealth. Furthermore, in the words of Gaius frugality is not an end in itself: it has immediate practical implications for the behaviour of magistrates. A frugal office-holder is, in fact, immune to the lure of corruption (*ORF*[4] frs. 27–8 = Gel. 15.12.3–4):

> I so conducted myself in my office that no one could truly say that I received an *as*, or more, as a gift, or that anyone has wasted money (*sumptum fecisse*) on my account. I spent two years in office: if any prostitute entered my house or anyone's slave was bribed on my account, consider me the lowest and basest of mankind. Since I conducted myself so continently towards their slaves, you may judge from that on what terms I lived with your sons. Then, citizens, when I left for Rome, I brought back empty from the province the purses which I took there full of money. Others have brought home overflowing with money the jars which they took to their province filled with wine.

We do not know at which point in his speech Gaius made this statement; however, the causal link between frugality in the private sphere and honesty in the public domain appears evident: *parsimonia* is the best antidote against corruption, against which the future tribune will take measures with the *lex repetundarum*. The same theme occurs again in the *Dissuasio legis Aufeiae* (123 BCE), which contains some first-hand information on Gaius' economic policy. Here, besides reaffirming his indifference to money, he states his intention (as in a political manifesto) to act to increase the financial revenues of the state. An increase in revenues, so he says, will improve the administration of the empire[26] – a particularly interesting declaration of intent, given that the opponents to

---

[26] *ORF*[4] fr. 44 = Gel. 11.10.2–6: 'I myself, who am now recommending to you to increase your taxes (*uectigalia*) in order that you may the more easily serve your own advantage and administer the Republic, do not come here for nothing; but I ask of you not money, but honour and your good opinion. Those who come forward to persuade you not to accept this law are not seeking honour from you but money from Nicomedes. Those who persuade you to accept are also not seeking a good opinion from you but money and profit from Mithradates for themselves'. Cf. Lo Cascio 1982: 94–5; Kay 2014: 77.

Smallholding, Frugality and Market Economy in the Gracchan Age

the reform programme of 123–122 BCE often criticise Gaius for dissipating the public treasury. In particular, the project to control grain prices through the *lex frumentaria*, which required the sale of wheat at lower than market prices, brought on criticism of damaging the public purse. It is likely, however, that the Gracchan *frumentationes*, instead of using fiscal grain, required the purchase by the state of goods intended to be resold at a lower price.[27] The magnitude of the outlay may be better understood if we consider that the same law also provides for an attempt to stabilise supplies by the building of public *horrea*.[28] The main opponent to the *lex Sempronia frumentaria* was the consul of 133 BCE and annalist L. Calpurnius Piso Frugi, who provoked Gaius by presenting himself to claim his own ration.[29] These elements suggest that, during Gaius' career, frugality, though reaffirmed by him, is chiefly utilised by his antagonists in an anti-Gracchan perspective. Thus, we may assume that frugality is a shared theme among the Roman elite, but its application becomes a battlefield for opposing factions. Moreover, it appears that only during the first century BCE are the *populares* able to rediscover the anti-*sumptus* ideology for their own ends, and combine it with the contents of Gaius' measures.[30]

Modus and Confiscation

Having outlined the ideological framework that defined smallholding in the Gracchan age, I shall now consider the possible practical consequences of the concepts of *modus* and frugality. Chiefly I wonder whether the notion of frugality that, as we have seen, played a relevant role in second-century political debate remained by and large confined to the level of discourse

---

[27] The origin of the grain sold in accordance with the Sempronian law (whether fiscal or not) is very debated; however, scholars generally agree that it was sold to the recipients at much lower than market price, perhaps even at half price: Virlouvet 1994: 18; cf. Balbo 2013: 108–10, with further bibliography.
[28] Plu. *CG* 6.3; cf. Garnsey and Rathbone 1985: 20. [29] Cic. *Tusc.* 3.48.
[30] For discussion see Zecchini 2012; 2016; on *popularis* tradition cf. Arena 2012: 116–69.

Mattia Balbo

or whether it also had identifiable practical implications: was it mere propaganda or did reformers actually make some attempts to apply it? How did frugality affect the reform strategies? What impact did Gracchan ideology have on the contemporary social and economic setting? Starting from these questions we can advance some hypotheses. As far as the notion of *modus* is concerned, we do not face too many problems: scholars generally agree that setting a limit to the large estates corresponds to the direct aim of recovering *ager publicus* for reassignment. Ancient sources explicitly attest that the renewal of the 'Licinian' restriction was designed to justify a full-scale regulation of landholdings and a subsequent distribution of land in the agricultural territory of Roman Italy (*terra Italia*).[31]

In the Middle Republic several investigations took place on the initiative of magistrates who were specifically instructed to restore the boundaries between public lands and *agri priuati*. Most of these interventions concerned a specific area, namely the *ager Campanus*, whose nominal public status is often reaffirmed by Rome: these include, for example, the missions led in Campania by the consul Postumius (173 BCE) and by the praetor Lentulus (165 BCE), in order to prevent the illegal occupation of public lands.[32] Moreover, in Italy many stockbreeders (*pecuarii*) are fined for misuse of land: in this case it is difficult to establish the nature of the violations, for it is not reported whether the *pecuarii* simply evaded the payment of *scripturae* or de facto privatised some public land. Some scholars even argue that fines to stockbreeders are inflicted according to the *lex de modo agrorum*.[33] In all these episodes the senate shows the explicit will to reaffirm the public

---

[31] Sic. Fl. *agrim.* 3 (above, n. 19); cf. *lex agraria*, ll. 1–4 (= Crawford 1996: I 113); cf. Vell. 2.2.3 (about the range of Gracchan legislation).

[32] Liv. 42.1.6; 9.7; 19.1–2 (Postumius); Cic. *Agr.* 2.82–83 and Granius Licinianus 28.29–37 Criniti (Lentulus).

[33] Liv. 10.23.13 (296 BCE); 10.47.4 (293 BCE); Ov. *Fast.* 5.279–294; Var. *L.* 5.158; Fest. p. 238.62–66 Lindsay; Vell. 1.14.8; Plin. *Nat.* 18.286; Tac. *Ann.* 2.49 (about 241 BCE); Liv. 33.42.10–11 (196 BCE); Liv. 35.10.11–12 (193 BCE); for the relationship between these episodes and the *lex de modo agrorum* see Rich in this volume. On the possible interpretations of *pecuarius* as 'stockbreeder' or even 'contractor of public pastoral land' see Tibiletti 1948: 228–9.

224

Smallholding, Frugality and Market Economy in the Gracchan Age

ownership of *ager publicus*. Such an intent does not seem to pose many problems from a political point of view, as Cato the Elder appears to confirm when he mentions in passing the *modus agrorum* as a historical example.[34] However, one aspect should be underlined: over and above some possible contextual disputes, of which we have no surviving record, the *patres* of the senate were quite in agreement when it came to restoring the nominal ownership of the Republic over its lands – particularly if this attempt concerned only a well-defined, specific area like the *ager Campanus* mentioned above. If the 500 *iugera* law was recalled in such cases – provided that this rule had not completely fallen into disuse, as Plutarch and Appian instead say – it was only for this purpose. On the contrary, when Tiberius Gracchus proposed his reform, he faced strong opposition among the same *patres* that supported the previous land recoveries. Such opposition might be explained by two complementary hypotheses. First, we may assume that in the lapse of time between the interventions quoted above and the *lex Sempronia* (about 30 years) the occupation of *ager publicus* in Italy increased exponentially, so that a new wide investigation, though necessary, became a burning political problem. Briefly, this is the picture traced by Appian, but concentrated in a much shorter time span than is generally supposed. Secondly – and this explanation seems to me more convincing, although I cannot exclude the first possibility – we could consider that the aims of the Sempronian reform were substantially different. In fact, the land recoveries attested in the first half of the second century BCE did not necessarily dispossess the previous occupiers of their fields: reaffirming the nominal ownership of *ager publicus* in many cases allowed a subsequent regulation of land use by the payment of a specific *uectigal*, which ratified the prior occupation.[35] And, if we also assume that in many cases – such

---

[34] Cato *Rhod.* 5 (*ORF*⁴ fr. 167 = Gel. 6.3.37). See also Balbo 2014: 86–8.

[35] E.g. Liv. 27.7.8; 27.11. Even the *agri* recovered in 173 BCE (above, n. 32) are leased out by the censors (Liv. 42.19.1–2); however it is uncertain whether this implies that the Campanian parcels are granted to new occupiers, or the state simply recognises the existing possessions through a *uectigal* (both solutions are possible). For a juridical history of *ager Campanus* cf. Sacchi 2006: 385–91.

Mattia Balbo

as those in the *ager Campanus* – those affected by the decisions were often Italic *possessores*, we have a further element for explaining the lack of opposition to these measures in the Roman senate (which might have existed, but has not reached us in senatorial sources). The *lex Sempronia*, on the other hand, aimed to restrict land possession and confiscate the excess, in order to carry out a new viritane distribution. Therefore, the chief political problem arose from the range of this reform, which was applicable to all of Roman Italy and not limited to certain areas. It therefore needed strong ideological support, which it derived as we have seen from the notion of *modus/ modestia* and perhaps also that of frugality.

Frugality and Land Allotments

The last point, concerning the application of Gracchan 'frugal' ideology, is more complex. In fact, if Tiberius Gracchus acted as a frugal man, following Scipio's model, this amounts to appropriate conduct on the part of a politician within a general debate on luxury. On the other hand, what does frugality in resource allocation mean in practical terms? From a hypothetical standpoint, I will consider whether the ideological defence of smallholding and the idea of 'frugal farming' finds some correspondence in the practice of assigning land undertaken by the Gracchi. In my opinion, the main problem lies in understanding what meaning we can give to this attempt to preserve smallholdings within the general transformation of the economy in the Late Republic. In other words, should we understand the Sempronian law as a mere agricultural subsidy in support of a declining class, actually irremediably attached to an obsolete means of production? I here refer to the supposedly leading role played by citizen-soldiers in the mid-republican economy. Or, on the contrary, should we interpret this reform as an instrument designed to modify the place of smallholders in the Roman economy? The first hypothesis, which presupposes the gradual disappearance of smallholdings from the Italian agrarian scene during the second century BCE, was widely believed

226

Smallholding, Frugality and Market Economy in the Gracchan Age

by twentieth-century historians.[36] However, this theory rests on two important inferences: that the crisis of smallholding followed a demographic decline of the free population during the Late Republic and the early empire;[37] and that a drastic change occurred in the juridical conditions of farming, through the near-linear development of the slave villa first, and of tenancy and colonate afterwards.[38]

These assumptions have been challenged by several scholars over the past 30 years. It has been amply demonstrated, in my opinion, that smallholding does not disappear with the Gracchi, but continues to survive through the following centuries, and that small farms existed alongside other forms of agricultural exploitation.[39] These different models should not be conceived as following on each other in a chronological sequence; most likely they coexisted in a more complex agrarian setup than previously assumed. Without entering into the details of this long debate, I would like to dwell, however, upon a single point that deserves attention in this chapter. The idea that the second century BCE is characterised by an irreparable decline of smallholding presupposes, from a theoretical point of view, a functional dichotomy between subsistence farming and a market economy. The main economic consequence of the rise of Rome to a Mediterranean-wide empire after the Second Punic War was the expansion of an integrated market for agricultural products, even in areas less affected by this phenomenon in earlier times. Some centuries later Aelius Aristides celebrates this commercial *oikoumene* as one of the most significant impacts of Roman rule.[40] The social and economic changes in rural areas in Italy should thus be seen in relation to the considerable expansion of the market economy. It goes without saying that the first to take advantage of the new market opportunities was the villa, with

---

[36] Esp. Toynbee 1965; Gabba 1973 = Gabba 1976; Gabba 1977.

[37] Beloch 1886; Brunt 1971; Hopkins 1978.

[38] Finley 1976; see discussion in Capogrossi Colognesi 2012: 31–59 with references.

[39] Good discussion in Rathbone 2008 and Launaro 2011: 158–64.

[40] Aristid. *Eis Rom.* 7; 11; 13 (= Jebb p. 199–201); cf. Lo Cascio 2013; Maiuro 2017: 146.

its access to major capital. The origins of the villa-economy are now dated back to the third century BCE, though it typically became widespread in the second century BCE.[41]

But what about smallholding? The traditional view would suggest that small farms were only subsistence enterprises. This would imply a dichotomy, as I mentioned above, between large market-oriented estates (growing thanks to the creation of an integrated market) and small farmsteads, characterised by owner farming (like Varro's renowned *pauperculi*)[42] and of course self-consumption (on the decline, engulfed by the larger *uillae* and unable to withstand the competition). In other words, the market economy is believed to have irreparably damaged small farms, which were no longer competitive. According to this view, the Gracchan defence of *ciues-milites* arrived too late. This interpretation should, however, be reconsidered for a number of reasons. Granted, smallholding probably did suffer as a result of the expansion of a market economy, conceivably causing major problems for poor peasants in central Italy. But we may assume that smallholding also adapted to the market economy, becoming in some ways more market-oriented. Otherwise we would not be able to explain its survival in later times – unless we also assume it only survived in marginal areas with low market penetration, such as mountain territories or places lacking access to a widespread urban network. This seems improbable, and it is equally unlikely that the market involved only the elites and the urban plebs, and excluded the rural population. So we should consider what changes may have affected smallholding when it became, even partially, market-oriented, and whether such changes may be among the causes of the impoverishment of free peasants, together with the pressure on resources that turned into a competition for *ager publicus*. Such a question can only be posed here in general terms, omitting at present the likely regional variations: the various areas of Italy could of course have had different agrarian setups and did not

---

[41] De Nardis 2009; Capogrossi Colognesi 2012: 127–34.
[42] Var. *R.* 1.17.2 (see above, n. 12).

Smallholding, Frugality and Market Economy in the Gracchan Age

necessarily develop a uniform market system.[43] At a macro-level, it would seem that the agrarian landscape of central Italy showed a widespread 'hunger for land', arguably the combined outcome of demographic growth and the impact of a market economy. Where this phenomenon was more widespread – for example in Etruria, Latium and Campania – it could determine the trends in land prices and reduce access of poor peasants to this resource. We may also ponder whether the agrarian reforms took shape against this background, as an attempt to remedy the imbalances at the root of social discontent.

On this point, a hypothesis may be advanced, albeit with caution: when the Gracchan reformers proposed their measures for poor peasants, what they likely had in mind was market-oriented agriculture. We can find a hint of this in the Pergamon affair of 133 BCE: Livy's *Periocha* says that when the agrarian law was approved its authors noticed that in Italy there was less *ager publicus* already available for cultivation than expected.[44] So Tiberius Gracchus proposed to use Attalus' treasure to provide the beneficiaries with starting capital: Plutarch clearly attests to this, when he affirms that such funds were conceived to start farming (i.e. to cover the expenses for equipment and seed).[45] Therefore, some scholars have proposed that allotments chiefly concerned lands that were not already agricultural, but could be reconverted to agricultural use – which mostly happened after the death of Tiberius, as he did not live to see the application of his law. Emilio Gabba, indeed, assumes that the *lex Sempronia* aimed to reconvert into farming many pastoral lands in the Central and Southern Apennines: several Gracchan boundary-stones come from the areas that are presumed – this is a

---

[43] Roselaar 2008.

[44] Liv. *Per.* 58: 'Then, since there was less land than he could divide without incurring the wrath of the plebs, for he had so excited their greed of having large amounts, he announced that he would promote a law to divide the money left by king Attalus among those who expected to receive land according to his first law'.

[45] Plu. *TG* 14.1 (πρὸς κατασκευὴν καὶ γεωργίας ἀφορμήν).

Mattia Balbo

hypothesis – to have been mainly used for transhumance during the second century BCE.[46]

If so, reconverting pastures into agricultural land was a measure to increase productivity: grain farming can support a larger population than extensive cattle-farming. This may be regarded both as a measure to help poor peasants and as a sort of 'frugal farming', with the aim to achieve greater efficiency: grain farming may be a poorer form of exploitation but it supports a higher population. Therefore, we are dealing with a resource reallocation in order to improve yields, which seems to correspond to the ideological defence of smallholding as outlined in Gracchan propaganda. Substituting cattle-breeders with farmers is a measure for supporting a growing population, by means of resource redistribution.

Furthermore, our sources attest that the reform did not simply aim to feed a larger population (according to a subsistence model, we might say in modern terms), but also to increase the number of *assidui* available for military recruitment. It seems clear that the reformers foresaw, or feared, a drop of recruits during the worst military crisis of the second century BCE, due to the serious troubles caused by the Celtiberian War and the slave revolt in Sicily. Such a shortage, whose deeper causes are not known to us, was perhaps considered by Tiberius Gracchus to be the effect of the impoverishment of peasants, who were struggling as a result of the increased competition for land in central Italy. Thus the agrarian reform did not aim to make the population grow, but rather to improve its economic standing by increasing the number of *assidui*, or even just to support an already growing population. In other words, this law may be interpreted as a

---

[46] For example Lucania, Samnium and Daunia. See Gabba 1979: 38–46; 1990: 677–8. A very interesting reference to this practice is contained in the *elogium* from Polla, which seems to be connected with the Gracchan context and comes from an area affected by Gracchan activity (*CIL* I² 638 = *ILS* 23, l. 12–14: 'I was the first one to make shepherds give way to ploughmen on public land'). Cf. Gabba 1990: 678. According to some sources, Cato the Elder sometimes considered cattle-breeding a much better investment for rich men than agriculture since it was more advantageous in terms of costs and gains (Cic. *Off.* 2.89; Col. 6. *praef.* 4–5). This may even allude to a context in which stock-raising was growing and attracting capital.

230

Smallholding, Frugality and Market Economy in the Gracchan Age

measure to increase the number of people who might qualify to register in the fifth census class. We should also recall (again as a conjecture) that the minimum threshold necessary to comply with this class appears not to have been reduced during the second century BCE, as was assumed by Gabba.[47] Or rather, the adoption of one or more supposed reductions is not confirmed by our sources. If this is the case, we may consider the Gracchan policy of allotments as a measure intended to produce revenue sufficient not just for the subsistence of the beneficiaries, but for them to reach an annual census of 11,000 uncial *asses*.[48] Therefore, we can say that the reformers did not act in terms of a subsistence economy. Their objective was a general improvement of economic conditions, to be achieved through the distribution of agricultural land.

These considerations lead us to think about the role of smallholding in the market economy, and the practice of land allotments. There is little evidence regarding the size of lots granted according to the *lex Sempronia*. It is very likely that there was no standard measure, but local variations determined by different factors, such as the ratio between available land and the number of beneficiaries, local productivity, the quality of land and – I may add – their monetary value. Some scholars have estimated the existence of lots of 30 *iugera* at least (7.5 ha), if not more, as in the doubtful case of Luceria studied by Dominic Rathbone.[49] Such a size, if confirmed, would have considerably exceeded the one deemed standard for the owner-farmed smallholding, namely 7 *iugera* (2 ha).[50]

---

[47] Gabba 1973: 10–14 = Gabba 1976: 5–7; cf. Brunt 1971: 402–3. *Contra* Lo Cascio 1988 with broad discussion.

[48] Liv. 1.43.7. Lo Cascio 1988: 282; 289–90; Lo Cascio 2008: 247.

[49] The epigraphic *lex agraria* (l. 13–14 = Crawford 1996: I 114) refers to plots of 30 *iugera*: for the usual identification of this size with the typical Gracchan allotment, see e.g. Carcopino 1929: 10; Badian 1972: 704; and Richardson 1980: 1. However, Gabba 1990: 674 doubts this figure, and Roselaar 2010: 232–3 rejects it: she prefers to trace back Gracchan allotments to the ancient practice of Roman colonies that traditionally provided to *ciues Romani* no more than 10 *iugera* each. On Luceria cf. Rathbone 2008, esp. 308–9, with plots of 80 to 90 *iugera*. See also Guariglia and Panebianco 1937: 89–90, who calculate plots of 50 *iugera* in Lucania.

[50] The conventional standard of 7 *iugera* occurs e.g. in Liv. 5.30.8; V. Max. 4.4.7; 11. See discussion in Capogrossi Colognesi 2012: 73; 114–19. For the problems posed

Mattia Balbo

We can speculate about this. First, the Gracchan lots seem to conform with the colonial model of allotments (especially that of Latin colonies), rather than that provided by the smaller viritane distributions. We know that the foundation of colonial settlements (*ex nouo*) required larger allotments than the traditional 7 *iugera*; for in a new foundation the state had to encourage people to migrate, and colonists starting anew also needed more land than the standard smallholding, in order to include non-agricultural usages, such as grazing, firewood collection and woodland harvesting. Normally common land served these purposes, and in well-established agricultural communities they provided an important supplement. New colonies also had common land for similar uses (*subseciua*), but in recently established settlements their management may have proven difficult. This explains why, circumstances permitting, the state preferred to allot more land to colonists. On the contrary, viritane distributions usually completed the extant situation and supported prior landholdings. Thus, the policy led by the agrarian *tresuiri* seems to have followed the colonial model also because, in the 130s and 120s BCE land allotments were made in areas far from Rome, where there might have been more recoverable *ager publicus* (to the detriment of Italians until 125 BCE, at least). Therefore, as soon as possible, Gaius connected the agrarian reform to a *lex coloniaria*, giving fresh impulse to further colonisation in the late second century BCE.

However, according to what I have argued above about the role of the market economy, can we assume that the Republic was redefining smallholding? If the Gracchan allotments aimed to increase the wealth of beneficiaries in a market economy perspective, we might find here another reason for granting more than 7 *iugera*. Perhaps such a small amount of former pastoral land, though sufficient to sustain a peasant family, was not considered enough to produce a *census* suitable

---

by the occurrence of *septem /septena iugera* in two passages by Varro (*R.* 1.2.9) and Columella (1.3.10), cf. Tibiletti 1950: 236–9; Rich 2008: 552 n. 94 and his chapter in this volume.

232

Smallholding, Frugality and Market Economy in the Gracchan Age

to remain or become *assiduus*. Although this is merely conjecture, we can spot a slight difference between the ideological standard and the practice of land allotments, and this difference can be explained by the intervening changes in the social and economic background as well as the purposes of the agrarian reform. The Gracchi supported the ideal of citizensoldiers and recalled the traditional model of land allotments, which sprung from contemporary culture, but at the same time they updated the practice in order to adapt to new circumstances. And the same change occurred with the 'Licinian' *modus*, which indeed the *lex Sempronia* doubled, applying the general principles that were supposed to have inspired it to new circumstances.

Bibliography

Arena, V. (2012) *Libertas and the Practice of Politics in the Late Roman Republic*. Cambridge.

Astin, A.E. (1967) *Scipio Aemilianus*. Oxford.

Badian, E. (1972) 'Tiberius Gracchus and the beginning of the Roman revolution', *ANRW* I.1: 668–731.

Balbo, M. (2010) 'La *Lex Licinia de modo agrorum*: riconsiderazione di un modello storiografico', *RFIC* 138(3–4): 265–311.

    (2013) *Riformare la res publica. Retroterra sociale e significato politico del tribunato di Tiberio Gracco*. Bari.

    (2014) '*Lex tam acerba:* la sanzione per i trasgressori del *modus agrorum* nella Roma repubblicana', *RFIC* 142(1): 75–90.

    (2017) 'Attività economiche e popolamento rurale nella Cisalpina occidentale in età romana', in *Popolazione e risorse nell'Italia del Nord dalla Romanizzazione ai Longobardi*, eds. E. Lo Cascio and M. Maiuro. Bari: 357–69.

Beloch, K. J. (1886) *Die Bevölkerung der griechisch-römischen Welt*. Leipzig.

Briscoe, J. (1974) 'Supporters and opponents of Tiberius Gracchus', *JRS* 64: 125–35.

Brunt, P. A. (1971) *Italian Manpower 225 BC–AD 14*. Oxford.

Capogrossi Colognesi, L. (2012) *Padroni e contadini nell'Italia repubblicana*. Roma.

Carcopino, J. (1929) 'Les Lois agraires des Gracques et la guerre sociale', *BAGB* 22: 3–23.

Crawford, M. H. (ed.) (1996) *Roman Statutes*. London.

de Ligt, L. (2012) *Peasants, Citizens and Soldiers: Studies in the Demographic History of Roman Italy 225 BC–AD 100*. Cambridge.

Mattia Balbo

De Nardis, M. (2009) 'Plauto, Catone e la "villa schiavistica"', in *Agricoltura e scambi nell'Italia tardo-repubblicana*, eds. J. Carlsen and E. Lo Cascio. Bari: 141–55.

de Neeve, P. W. (1984) *Colonus: Private Farm-Tenancy in Roman Italy during the Republic and the Early Principate*. Amsterdam.

Finley, M. I. (1976) 'Private farm tenancy in Italy before Diocletian', in *Studies in Roman Property*, ed. M. I. Finley. Cambridge: 103–21.

Forsén, B. (1991) *Lex Licinia Sextia de modo agrorum – Fiction or Reality?* Helsinki.

Gabba, E. (1973) *Esercito e società nella tarda repubblica romana*. Firenze.
(1976) *Republican Rome, the Army and the Allies*, trans. P. J. Cuff. Berkeley and Los Angeles.
(1977) 'Considerazioni sulla decadenza della piccola proprietà contadina nell'Italia centro-meridionale del II sec. a.C.', *Ktema* 2: 269–84.
(1979) 'Sulle strutture agrarie dell'Italia romana fra III e I sec. a.C.', in *Strutture agrarie e allevamento transumante nell'Italia romana (III-I sec. a.C.)*, eds. E. Gabba and M. Pasquinucci. Pisa: 15–73.
(1990) 'Il tentativo dei Gracchi', in *Storia di Roma*, II.1, eds. G. Clemente, F. Coarelli and E. Gabba. Torino: 671–89.

Gargola, D.J. (2008) 'The Gracchan reform and Appian's representation of an agrarian crisis', in *People, Land and Politics: Demographic Developments and the Transformation of Roman Italy, 300 BC–AD 14*, eds. L. de Ligt and S. Northwood. Leiden: 487–518.

Garnsey, P. and Rathbone, D. (1985) 'The background to the grain law of Gaius Gracchus', *JRS* 75: 20–5.

Guariglia, E. and Panebianco, V. (1937) 'Termini graccani rinvenuti nell'antica Lucania', *RSS* 1: 58–91.

Hopkins, K. (1978) *Conquerors and Slaves*. Cambridge.
(1995/1996) 'Rome, taxes, rents and trade', *Kodai* 6/7: 41–75.

Kay, P. (2014) *Rome's Economic Revolution*. Oxford.

Latifundium (1995) = *Du latifundium au latifondo. Un héritage de Rome, une création médiévale ou moderne? Actes de la table ronde internationale (17–19 décembre 1992)*. Paris.

Launaro, A. (2011) *Peasants and Slaves: The Rural Population of Roman Italy (200 BC to AD 100)*. Cambridge.
(2015) 'The nature of the villa economy', in *Ownership and Exploitation of Land and Natural Resources in the Roman World*, eds. P. Erdkamp, K. Verboven and A. Zuiderhoek. Oxford: 173–86.

Lo Cascio, E. (1982) 'Spesa militare, spesa dello stato e volume delle emissioni nella tarda repubblica', *AIIN* 29: 75–97.
(1988) 'Ancora sui censi minimi delle cinque classi "serviane"', *Athenaeum* n.s. 66: 273–302.
(1994) 'The size of the Roman population: Beloch and the meaning of the Augustan census figures', *JRS* 84: 23–40.

Smallholding, Frugality and Market Economy in the Gracchan Age

(2008) 'Roman census figures in the second century BC and the property qualification of the fifth class', in *People, Land and Politics. Demographic Developments and the Transformation of Roman Italy, 300 BC – AD 14*, eds. L. de Ligt and S. Northwood. Leiden: 239–56.

(2009) *Crescita e declino. Studi di storia dell'economia romana*. Roma.

(2013) 'Roma come "mercato comune del genere umano"', in *Elio Aristide e la legittimazione greca dell'impero di Roma*, eds. P. Desideri and F. Fontanella. Bologna: 185–201.

Maiuro, M. (2017) 'Il monte dei cocci', in *Storia mondiale dell'Italia*, ed. A. Giardina. Roma–Bari: 146–9.

Mantovani, D. (1997) 'L'occupazione dell'*ager publicus* e le sue regole prima del 367 a.c.', *Athenaeum* 85(2): 575–98.

Marzano, A. (2007) *Roman Villas in Central Italy: A Social and Economic History*. Leiden and Boston.

Montesquieu, C. de Secondat, Baron de (1734) *Considérations sur les causes de la grandeur des Romains et de leur décadence*. Lausanne.

(1768) *De l'esprit des lois*, rev. edn. London.

(1965) *Considerations on the Causes of the Greatness of the Romans and their Decline*, trans. D. Lowenthal. New York and London.

Rathbone, D. (2003) 'The control and exploitation of *ager publicus* in Italy under the Roman Republic', in *Tâches publiques et entreprise privée dans le monde romain*, ed. J.-J. Aubert. Neuchâtel: 135–78.

(2008) 'Poor peasants and silent sherds', in *People, Land and Politics. Demographic Developments and the Transformation of Roman Italy, 300 BC–AD 14*, eds. L. de Ligt and S. Northwood. Leiden: 305–32.

Rich, J. (1983) 'The supposed Roman manpower shortage of the later second century B.C.', *Historia* 32: 287–331.

(2008) '*Lex Licinia, Lex Sempronia*: B.G. Niebuhr and the limitation of landholding in the Roman Republic', in *People, Land and Politics. Demographic Developments and the Transformation of Roman Italy, 300 BC–AD 14*, eds. L. de Ligt and S. Northwood. Leiden: 519–72.

Richardson, J.S. (1980) 'The ownership of Roman land: Tiberius Gracchus and the Italians', *JRS* 70: 1–11.

Roselaar, S. T. (2008) 'Regional variations in the use of the *ager publicus*', in *People, Land and Politics. Demographic Developments and the Transformation of Roman Italy, 300 BC – AD 14*, eds. L. de Ligt and S. Northwood. Leiden: 573–602.

(2010) *Public Land in the Roman Republic: A Social end Economic History of Ager Publicus in Italy, 396–89 BC*. Oxford.

(2015) 'Italian allies and access to *ager Romanus* in the Roman Republic', *MEFRA* 127(2), http://mefra.revues.org/3055 (last accessed 9 February 2020).

Mattia Balbo

Sacchi, O. (2006) *Regime della terra e imposizione fondiaria nell'età dei Gracchi. Testo e commento storico-giuridico della legge agraria del 111 a.C.* Napoli.

Santangelo, F. (2019) *Roma repubblicana. Una storia in quaranta vite.* Roma.

Tarpin, M. (2014) 'Strangers in Paradise. Latins (and other non-Romans) in colonial context: a short story of territorial complexity', in *Roman Republican Colonization: New Perspectives from Archaeology and Ancient History*, eds. T. D. Stek and J. Pelgrom. Rome: 161–91.

Tibiletti, G. (1948) 'Il possesso dell'*ager publicus* e le norme *de modo agrorum* sino ai Gracchi', I–III, *Athenaeum* n.s. 26: 173–236.

(1949) 'Il possesso dell'*ager publicus* e le norme *de modo agrorum* sino ai Gracchi', IV–VI, *Athenaeum* n.s. 27: 3–42.

(1950) 'Ricerche di storia agraria romana', *Athenaeum* n.s. 28: 183–266.

(2007) *Studi di storia agraria romana*, ed. A. Baroni. Trento.

Toynbee, A. J. (1965) *Hannibal's Legacy: The Hannibalic War's Effects on Roman Life.* London.

Viglietti, C. (2011) *Il limite del bisogno: Antropologia economica di Roma arcaica.* Bologna.

(2014) 'Economia', in *Con i Romani: Un'antropologia della cultura antica*, eds. M. Bettini and W. M. Short. Bologna: 215–48.

Virlouvet, C. (1994) 'Les lois frumentaires d'époque républicaine', in *Le ravitaillement en blé de Rome et des centres urbains des débuts de la République jusqu'au Haut Empire.* Rome and Naples: 11–29.

Zecchini, G. (2012) 'L'evoluzione della élite popularis dai Gracchi a Cesare', in *Del municipio a la corte. La renovación de las élites romanas*, ed. A. Caballos Rufino. Sevilla: 19–35.

(2016) 'Ideologia suntuaria romana', *MEFRA* 128(1), http://mefra.revues.org /3168 (last accessed 18 July 2017).

CHAPTER 5

FRUGALITAS, OR: THE INVENTION OF A ROMAN VIRTUE

INGO GILDENHARD

Introduction

Philologists tend to be a fractious bunch. When it comes to Roman frugality, however, remarkable consensus prevails. From the Renaissance onwards, Latinists have remained enthralled by those ancient Roman self-definitions that place a premium on *frugalitas* – whether as a cultural (or even innate) disposition towards the prudent management of material resources or (at least) a discursive ideal that captures behavioural norms – if, perhaps, in a counterfactual spirit. Belief in *frugalitas* as an arch-Roman quality also continues to hold sway in the context of the classical tradition: Roman characters distinct for their commitment to peasant parsimony, such as Cincinnatus at the plough or turnip-roasting M'. Curius Dentatus, continue to shape the way in which the popular imagination envisions the authentic Romans of yore – and have often been deemed to offer important lessons for personal conduct in public and private life. The intertwining of imperial grandeur and personal moderation found in our ancient sources such as Cicero has indeed resonated down the centuries, often in a pronounced didactic key.[1] A representative voice from the early modern period is that

---

[1] See e.g. Cic. *S. Rosc.* 50: *maiores nostri ... ex minima tenuissimaque re publica maximam et florentissimam nobis reliquerunt; suos enim agros studiose colebant, non alienos cupide adpetebant; quibus rebus et agris et urbibus et nationibus rem publicam atque hoc imperium et populi Romani nomen auxerunt* ('our ancestors ... have left us a supremely powerful and prosperous commonwealth, which had been very small and poor: they diligently cultivated their own fields and did not greedily desire those of others; thereby they added lands, cities and nations and thus magnified our commonwealth and this empire and the name of the Roman people').

237

Ingo Gildenhard

of Pino della Tosa in Leonardo Bruni's (1370–1444) *History of Florence*, exhorting his compatriots to be adventurous in public affairs and international politics while practising moderation and self-restraint in private – just like the Florentines' imaginary forbears, the Roman people (*History of Florence* 6.6):

> Populus romanus, parens noster, numquam orbis imperium nactus esset, si suis rebus contentus nova coepta impensasque refugisset. nec sane idem propositum est homini publice et privatim. nam publice quidem magnificentia proposita est, quae in gloria amplitudineque consistit; privatim vero modestia et frugalitas.

> The Roman people, our ancestors, never would have obtained dominion of the world if they, content with their own affairs, had avoided new undertakings and expenses. Man's purpose differs sharply in public and private affairs. In public affairs the aim is magnificence, which consists in glory and grandeur; in private affairs it is moderation and frugality.

The habit to wax lyrical about the old-school morality that supposedly made Rome great survived well into the twentieth century. Especially among those invested in the supposed value of Roman morality for educational purposes, *frugalitas* was thought to form an essential part of the *mos maiorum*, as one of the ancestral Roman virtues and a key enabling factor of Rome's imperial might that one would do well to emulate. To pick out just one voice among many: 'But there was a time when the virtues ruled and reigned in the city by the Tiber; Rome's greatness cannot be explained upon any other hypothesis. *Pietas, gravitas, simplicitas, honos, fides, pudicitia, industria, frugalitas, probitas,* taught around the family altar, made Rome what she was – laid in solid rock a foundation upon which was erected a glorious edifice that for a thousand years defied all the winds of earth and heaven.'[2] As always, there are exceptions.[3] But the belief in the self-evident status of

---

[2] Poteat 1938: 522.

[3] Thus *frugalitas* is notably (though without explanation) absent from the otherwise rather comprehensive catalogue of Roman virtues compiled by Litchfield 1914: 9. He lists *iustitia (aequitas)*; *fides*; *pietas erga deos, patriam, parentes, ceteros*; *seueritas (disciplina militaris)*; *fortitudo*; *constantia (et in morte propinquorum)* = *patientia*; *continentia*; *paupertas (v. luxuria)*; *clementia*; *moderatio (v. ambitio/petulantia)* as

Frugalitas, or: The Invention of a Roman Virtue

frugalitas as a time-honoured Roman virtue remains widespread today, if in a more muted rhetorical key.[4]

The frequency with which scholars have blithely embraced *frugalitas* as a Roman virtue since time immemorial, however, stands in inverse proportion to critical studies devoted to the concept. Most champions of Roman *frugalitas* take its illustrious place in the Roman constellation of values simply for granted, without seeing any need for argument or evidence. Unlike other Roman value terms, such as *uirtus* or *pietas,* which have generated a mountain of (frequently controversial) secondary literature, studies of *frugalitas* with a lexical focus have been few and far between. One of the more sustained discussions (itself a model of compression) can be found in Gian Biagio Conte's *Latin Literature: A History.* It is worth citing in full, as a convenient synopsis of the *communis opinio* on *frugalitas* in ancient Rome – as well as the rhetorical moves designed to endow this view with plausibility:[5]

The term [sc. *frugalitas*], which derives from *frux,* properly indicates the style of life of the diligent farmer who lives from the fruits of his own harvest. As the early rural traditions grew more remote from Rome and as society was transformed by the influx of wealth and luxury goods, the concept of *frugalitas* came to form part of the *mos maiorum.* People began to see in it

---

well as *amicitia* (*concordia*); *gratia; obseruantia; grauitas;* and, interestingly, *munificentia* (*liberalitas*) (*v. auaritia*). Likewise, Lind 1979, building on Litchfield, singles out *exempla uirtutis, gloria, magnitudo animi, dignitas, auctoritas, grauitas, honos* and *nobilitas* as constitutive elements of *mos maiorum* in his discussion of 'Roman moral conservatism' without listing *frugalitas,* despite characterising the ancestral ideal at the outset as 'a frugal way of life, hardy, simple, plain' (according to Posidonius).

[4] Random examples include Goddard 1994: '*Frugalitas* was conceived as a cornerstone of the Romans' achievement, a distinguishing quality responsible for their surpassing military vigour, their industry, concord and piety' (from the abstract); Ceaicovschi 2009: 29 n. 8: 'Cato himself carefully crafted his public image through his writings that was based on such traditional Roman values as *parsimonia, dignitas, gravitas,* and *frugalitas*'; and Goldschmidt 2013: 158, who speaks of 'the traditional Roman virtues of *fortitudo* and *frugalitas*'. See also Walsh 1955: 370, who gives the impression that *frugalitas* is a key virtue in Livy, or Cordier 2006: 184. An extreme case is Zanda 2011: 10, who proclaims '*labor, industria, parsimonia, frugalitas, disciplina, contentia* [sic] and *gravitas* were the main values of Roman society before *luxuria* and *avaritia* transformed them into *desidia, socordia, inertia, lubido, avaritia* and *superbia*' with reference to Sal. *Cat.* 12 and Liv. 34.4.2, though *frugalitas* occurs in neither passage.

[5] Conte 1994: 797.

239

Ingo Gildenhard

the model that needed to be restored if the crisis of the *res publica* was to be resolved; they celebrated the example of commanders such as Cincinnatus, who went from plowing to warfare and then returned to plowing. While the *homo frugi ac diligens* acquired normative character in legal literature as a criterion by which to evaluate someone's ability to administer an estate, Cicero in his philosophical work strove to modernize the concept of *frugalitas* by assimilating it to Greek ethical concepts. *Frugalitas* slowly became primarily an inner attitude, retaining only a dim echo of its rural origins and no longer designating a concrete style of life, a process brought to completion in certain passages of Seneca's *Epistles*.

Embedded in this paragraph is an elegant little history of our concept that sketches its alleged semantic evolution along the following four stages:

Stage 1:

Originally (or 'properly'), so the story goes, *frugalitas* had a simple and straightforward referent or indeed embodiment – the lifestyle of the prudent, self-sufficient farmer. We do not get much help in fixing a date when life was simple and the semantics of *frugalitas* were straightforward and precise, but the second sentence, with its telltale invocation of 'rural traditions' growing ever more remote while Roman society underwent a transformation through the corrupting influx of wealth and luxury, suggests that Conte has in mind the years conventionally referred to as the early and middle republic (roughly c. 510–c. 180 BCE).[6]

Stage 2:

In the subsequent period of transformation, so the story continues, *frugalitas* as originally conceived disappeared from Roman society as a style of life; instead, it entered the *mos maiorum* as a counterfactual ideal. Put differently, while more and more Romans ceased to enact *frugalitas* and abide by the principles of prudent husbandry, the notion retained its validity as an ancestral value (or, to formulate the point a bit more cautiously, a value *projected back onto* the ancestors), designed to combat 'the crisis of the *res publica*'. It is left unclear what this crisis was; and again, we miss precise chronological indicators of what centuries are at issue. But it is possible to infer from the

---

[6] For a reconsideration of 'periods' in Roman history see Flower 2010, who proposes 'thirteen chronological periods, including six republics' (33) to replace the conventional labels 'early', 'middle' and 'late': the time-span covered by Stage 1 comprises her pre-republican transitional period (c. 509–494), her proto-republic (494–451/0) and her Republics 1–3 (450–180).

240

Frugalitas, or: The Invention of a Roman Virtue

reference to 'the influx of wealth and luxury goods' that the period in question covers the years after the Second Punic War, which saw Rome's successful expansion into the Greek East and a vast increase in the import of (plundered) wealth. In the years of c. 180–c. 100 BCE, then, *frugalitas* is said to have become, in what is only an apparent paradox, simultaneously irrelevant in practice and a much-invoked ancestral value.

Stage 3:

Until now, the protagonists of Conte's story have been 'the term (or concept) of *frugalitas*', 'rural traditions' and 'people' ('they'); now, for the first time, an identifiable individual enters the historical stage: Cicero. His appearance certainly facilitates dating: we are in the late republic (c. 100–c. 31 BCE), where two further developments in the semantics of our noun are said to have taken place: in Cicero's *philosophica*, the concept is deemed to have undergone 'an update' (i.e. away from the now presumably outdated 'early rural traditions') with the help of Greek ethical thought; and the figure of the *homo frugi ac diligens* appears as a point of reference in legal literature.[7]

---

[7] The reference is presumably to Gaius, *dig.* 21.1.18 pr., perhaps via the Italian translation of Fraenkel 1922, who gestures to this passage in a discussion of the 'catechism of the duties of a good servant' that gets rehearsed in various Plautine slave-monologues. See Fraenkel 1960: 234/430 (= 2007: 167/416): 'for the bases of these rules in real life compare Gaius, *Dig.* 21.1.18 pr.' – an extract from the edict of the curule aediles, the language of which is, so Fraenkel, 'a sure sign of the great antiquity of these formulas': *si quid uenditor de mancipio adfirmauerit idque non ita esse emptor queratur, aut redhibitorio aut aestimatorio (id est quanti minoris) iudicio agere potest: uerbi gratia si constantem aut laboriosum aut curracem uigilacem esse, aut ex frugalitate sua peculium adquirentem adfirmauerit, et is ex diuerso leuis proteruus desidiosus somniculosus piger tardus comesor inueniatur* : 'If the vendor makes some assertion about a slave and the purchaser complains that things are not as he was assured that they were, he can proceed by the action for rescission or that for a diminution in which an assessment is made. Suppose that the vendor says that the slave is loyal or hard-working or diligent or vigilant or that through his thrift, he has acquired a peculium and, on the contrary, he is fickle, wanton, slothful, sluggish, idle, tardy, or a wastrel' (translation by A. Watson). The precise 'antiquity' of the phrase *ex frugalitate sua* is impossible to determine. For leads, see Kaser 1951 on edictorial style and Jakab 1997: 124–39. For future reference, it is worth noting that the *frugalitas* at issue is that of a slave trying to save up money to buy his freedom. Cf. further Ulp. *dig.* 21.1.19 (*Curule Aediles' Edict*, book 1): *sciendum tamen est quaedam et si dixerit praestare eum non debere, scilicet ea, quae ad nudam laudem serui pertinent: ueluti si dixerit frugi probum dicto audientem* ('we have, however, to realise that there are statements that a vendor might make which he does not have to validate, namely, those which simply extol the slave; for instance, that he is thrifty, upright and obedient' – trans. A. Watson).

241

Ingo Gildenhard

Stage 4:

The ethical nuancing and semantic enrichment continued during the early imperial age (c. 30 BCE–120 CE), finding a certain culmination in the writings of Seneca the Younger, where *frugalitas* refers first and foremost to a mental disposition or attitude towards (the use of) material wealth (rather than a prudent way of life grounded in agricultural pursuits).

In Conte's story, *frugalitas* appears to have a solid presence throughout Roman history, while undergoing some novel semantic inflections under the influence of Greek culture during the late republic and early empire. The way he tells it, one could be tempted to assume the availability of a substantial amount of data also for those stages where he does without a featured representative. Yet upon inspection, the vague formulations Conte uses for the early periods ('people began to see ...', 'they celebrated ...') obfuscates an irritating lack of evidence – and the chilling fact that someone like Cicero, notorious as he is for his conceptual creativity, happens to be the first Roman cheerleader of *frugalitas* on record. Conte is not alone in relying on rhetorical sleights of hand to endow *frugalitas* with an ancestral pedigree. Myles McDonnell does the same:[8]

> If there was a native Roman idea that had been traditionally thought to embrace all the virtues, it was *frugalitas... reliquas etiam virtutes frugalitas continet, ... tres virtutes, fortitudinem, iustitiam prudentiam frugalitas complexa est. – '... indeed frugalitas* does embrace the rest of the virtues ... *frugalitas* therefore comprised the three virtues – courage, justice, prudence.'

Yet again, the one who actually does the 'traditional thinking' here is none other than – and exclusively – Cicero. The only pieces of evidence McDonnell cites in support of his contention that the Romans 'traditionally thought' of *frugalitas* as the virtue of all virtues are the *Tusculan Disputations* (3.16–17, from which he quotes, and *Tusc.* 4.36), written in 45 BCE, and the speech on behalf of king Deiotarus (*Deiot.* 26), dating to the same year. Not that he could have done better: the notion

---

[8] McDonnell 2006: 134 n. 90.

242

Frugalitas, or: The Invention of a Roman Virtue

that *frugalitas* is a super-virtue comprising all the others comes straight out of *Tusculan* 3, but finds no backing in any earlier (or other!) source.[9] McDonnell pounces on Cicero's singular promotion of *frugalitas* for a reason: a key aim of his monograph on Roman manliness is to show that the original semantic core of *uirtus* was 'martial prowess' first and foremost, with other aspects of excellence (ethical, political) being later accretions, under the influence of Greek thought.[10] For this project, Cicero's assertion that *frugalitas* had the comprehensive sense of polyvalent excellence that he wishes to keep away from *uirtus* comes in handy. To turn Cicero into a straightforward source for ancestral realities, however, violates one of McDonnell's well-taken principles for the study of *uirtus*: 'Using works written during the last decades of the Republic's existence to demonstrate that a value was traditional is a hazardous procedure, because it risks overlooking important cultural changes that occurred in Rome over the course of the third and second centuries.'[11] And what is methodological sauce for the goose (*uirtus*) is even more so for the gander (*frugalitas*). In fact, the gander's situation is significantly more precarious: whereas it is quite easy to trace the presence of *uirtus* in the Latin lexicon back to the middle republic (whatever its precise range of meaning might have been), search engines and

---

[9] McDonnell also refers to Eisenhut 1973: 64–5, who cites no additional passages either. Lind 1992: 33–4 is more perceptive: 'This experiment [in *Tusc.* and *Deiot.*] in search of an all-inclusive word was later abandoned by Cicero; *frugalitas* could not compete with *uirtus* as an equivalent of ἀρετή.' At *De Beata Vita* 4.31 Augustine claims: *merito etiam uirtutum omnium matrem multi frugalitatem esse dixerunt*; but he names none of the many and proceeds to cite *Deiot.* 26. His co-option of Cicero's notion of *frugalitas* in *Tusc.* and *Deiot.* is part of the wider conceptual and theological agenda in this particular treatise, in which he redefines the innovative conception of *frugalitas* Cicero advances in these two works (and these two works only) in a Christian key: see Introduction 103–07 and Barbone 1994.

[10] For the ethical aspects of excellence (*uirtus*) in late-republican times see Noreña 2011: 80. Among the many concepts he surveys – including *prudentia, iustitia, temperantia, aequitas, humanitas, integritas, probitas, constantia, sapientia – frugalitas* is conspicuous by its absence.

[11] McDonnell 2006: 134. The use of Cicero's *oeuvre* to reconstruct the traditional semantics of a notion such as *frugalitas* is widespread – despite the methodological dangers inherent in taking specific instances as representative of more general usage.

Ingo Gildenhard

dictionaries turn up precisely nothing for *frugalitas* before the first century BCE. It occurs once each in Publilius Syrus and Varro;[12] and there are sixteen occurrences of the noun in Cicero. Numbers only take off in the (early) imperial period: *frugalitas* occurs five times each in Seneca the Elder and Valerius Maximus; and becomes something of a buzzword in Seneca the Younger (30), Quintilian (including declamations) (21); and Pliny the Younger (12).

Neither Conte nor McDonnell (nor anyone else for that matter who keeps hailing *frugalitas* as a traditional virtue) seems to be aware of, or is keen to acknowledge, this spotty record of attestations from republican times. What compounds the problem of *frugalitas*' scanty presence before the middle of the first century BCE (which, one could argue, owes itself in part to significant gaps in our literary record) is its no-show in texts where, according to the traditional story, it ought to figure left, right and centre. Yet one looks in vain for *frugalitas* in Cato the Elder's *de Agri Cultura*, replete though it is with talk about *fruges*. The *phenomenon* of frugality (in the sense of prudent husbandry aimed at generating a surplus or maximising profit and a concomitant rejection of conspicuous consumption) figures prominently in his argument;[13] but the *lexeme frugalitas* does not occur either here or elsewhere in his (transmitted) writings. Even in those places where Cato fashions himself as embodying an ancestral ideal of hardy self-sufficiency, his rhetoric relies on other concepts – such as *parsimonia*, *duritia* or *industria*.[14] Strikingly, *frugalitas* does not even make an appearance in Cicero's re-imagining of Cato Maior in the *de Senectute*, despite the fact that he had just praised *frugalitas* as the arch-Roman value of old in the

---

[12] See below 253 and Introduction 13 n.37.

[13] See e.g. *Agr.* 1.6: *scito idem agrum quod hominem, quamuis quaestuosus siet, si sumptuosus erit, relinqui non multum.* However productive a field or a person might be, the expense of high maintenance will quickly cut into profit or surplus.

[14] Cato, *De suis uirtutibus contra <L.> Thermum post censuram*, fr. 128 M⁴. In the vernacular, the slippage from *parsimonia* to frugality is easy and tempting. See Coffee 2017, who notes 'Cato's staunch commitment to thrift, grounded in the archaic ideal [read: what *Cato* asserts to be an archaic ideal] of *parsimonia*' on page 48 and then turns him into one of the 'paragons of frugality' on page 50.

244

Frugalitas, or: The Invention of a Roman Virtue

Tusculan Disputations. Opportunities existed: when, for instance, Cicero's Cato tells the anecdote of the Samnites offering gold to M'. Curius Dentatus, whom Valerius Maximus later hails as *exactissima norma Romanae frugalitatis idemque fortitudinis perfectissimum specimen* (4.3.5), he only admires his *continentia* and the *temporum disciplina* (*Sen.* 56). At least in this respect, then, Cicero's portrait of Cato the Elder seems historically accurate![15] In short, for the alleged heydays of *frugalitas*, i.e. the years of the early and middle republic, the word seems to have gone AWOL.

The same is not the case for the corresponding adjective *frugi*, a little lexical weirdo with a complex pedigree: as the dative of the noun *frux, frugis* (f.), *frugi* seems to have originally occurred in such phrases as '*esse frugi bonae*', i.e. 'to be capable of giving a good crop' or (when applied to persons) 'to be a reliable and useful chap'. Over time, the predicative final dative also became a self-standing attribute in its own right; and 'eventually *bonae frugi* was abbreviated to *frugi*, which functioned as an indeclinable adjective'.[16] As such, *frugi*, in the moral sense of 'reliable and useful', is fairly widespread in New Comedy, where it does duty as a Latin equivalent of the Greek χρήσιμος (akin to *utilis*).[17] Plautus in particular but also Terence use *frugi* frequently. The adjective also features as the *cognomen* of Lucius Calpurnius Piso Frugi (*cos.* 133 BCE); and it occurs regularly in late-republican authors such as Cicero and Varro. But even the statistical presence of *frugi* in the surviving corpus of Latin literature contains some

---

[15] Cf. also *Parad.* 1.12: *quid continentia C. Fabrici, quid tenuitas uictus M'. Curi sequebatur?*, where *frugalitas* could have served as a possible alternative for *tenuitas uictus* – even though this formulation and related phrases, such as *tenuis uictus* (see e.g. *Tusc.* 3.49 and 5.89 both times with reference to Epicurus), also had an interesting career: Introduction 12.

[16] Palmer 1988: 70, comparing similar semantic developments for *laetus, felix, almus* and *probus*.

[17] Lindsay 1900: 336 (*ad Capt.* 956 *Frugi bonae*): '*Frux* in the Singular had this metaphorical sense in various old phrases, e.g. *Pseud.* 468 *tamen ero frugi bonae, Poen.* 892 *erus si tuos uolt facere frugem, Trin.* 118 *quin ad frugem conrigis?*, 270 *Certa res est ad frugem adplicare animum,* but most frequently in the predicative or attributive use of the Dat., *homo frugi* or *homo frugi est.* Hence the later survival of *frugi* as an Adjective.'

Ingo Gildenhard

striking oddities: like *frugalitas*, it makes no appearance in the writings of Cato the Elder.[18]

If one takes our sources seriously (meagre as they are), it is difficult not to conclude that there is virtually no evidence for the early history of *frugalitas* as sketched out by Conte and presupposed by others, at least as far as the relevant lexemes are concerned. *Frugalitas* does not occur at all, and *frugi*, despite its etymology, has no particular association with farming or a rural style of life. There is no evidence whatsoever that *frugalitas* was ever part of the *mores maiorum* before Cicero – however one wishes to define this far from straightforward phenomenon.[19]

Put differently, the history of the term *frugalitas* begins for all intents and purposes with Cicero – a writer and thinker renowned for his creative use of Latin and conceptual innovations and with an established reputation for bamboozling his readers into thinking that what he says is factually or historically accurate.[20] He is the earliest author in whom *frugalitas* has a statistically significant presence. But on inspection, even the Ciceronian evidence turns out to be far from straightforward: the distribution of *frugalitas* across his *oeuvre* as a whole is distinctly uneven – and decidedly odd. While the noun makes an occasional appearance in a handful of speeches in the 60s (*pro Fonteio*) and 50s (*pro Plancio, pro Sestio, pro Flacco*) all discussed in more detail below, most instances occur at two particular moments in Cicero's career: the *Verrines* (5), which date to 70 BCE; and the *Tusculan Disputations* (7) along with the contemporaneous *pro rege Deiotaro* (2), both of which

---

[18] As noted by Coffee 2017: 226 n. 4: 'The hyperfrugal elder Cato does not use either term [sc. *frugi* or *frugal–*], showing his *frugalitas* through deeds rather than words.' The distinction between discourse and practice is of course a good one, though does not apply here: like no other Roman before (and very few thereafter) Cato promoted himself and his frugality in deeds *and* words (see Gotter 2001) – he just did not use the lexemes *frugi* or *frugalitas* for this purpose. The question thus remains whether Cato ever heard of the abstract noun *frugalitas* or, indeed, was keen to be associated with the attribute *frugi*.

[19] For insightful discussion see e.g. Bettini 2000 and Blösel 2000.

[20] For examples see Gildenhard 2011, with further bibliography.

246

Frugalitas, or: The Invention of a Roman Virtue

Cicero wrote in 45 BCE.[21] Moreover, what startles just as much as this clustering is the glaring absence of *frugalitas* in places where, again, those beholden to the traditional story should surely expect the noun to appear.

Thus, in his two earliest surviving defence speeches, the *pro Quinctio* and the *pro Sexto Roscio Amerino*, Cicero typecasts his defendants as farmers (in the case of Sextus Roscius picking up on and re-evaluating the characterisation of the prosecution) who embody the full slate of peasant values – whereas their accusers emerge as despicable city slickers with all the attendant vices.[22] The lexical scope for these exercises in 'ethical syncrisis' is broad;[23] but *frugalitas* is conspicuous by its absence: the first time Cicero brings it forcefully into play for his character-profiling are the *Verrines*. *Frugalitas* is also conspicuously left out of the rather comprehensive portfolio of qualities that distinguish the *summus imperator* of the *pro lege Manilia*, delivered in 66 BCE, i.e. not long *after* the *Verrines*. One of the key conceptual operations in his discussion of Pompey's *uirtus* – together with *scientia militaris*, *auctoritas*, and *felicitas* one of the four basic qualities that make up the perfect general – is the transformation of the singular *uirtus*

---

[21] As Eisenhut 1973: 65 n. 65 notes, Cicero's use of *frugalitas* in the *pro Deiotaro* 'dürfte ein Reflex aus der Beschäftigung mit *frugalitas* in den *Tusculanen* sein.'

[22] For the technique see Klodt 2012: 64–9, with further bibliography.

[23] In *Quinct.* Cicero associates his defendant with *sanctimonia, diligentia, officia boni uiri* (55), *rusticana illa atque inculta parsimonia, pudor, sanctimonia, officium, fides, diligentia, uita omnino semper horrida atque arida, uirorum bonorum disciplina* (92–4) and his accuser Naevius with *luxuries, licentia, cupiditas, petulantia, profusis sumptibus uiuere, magnifice splendideque conuiuium ornare, uoluptates, quaestum et sumptum Galloni sequi, audacia* and *perfidia* (92–4). In *S. Rosc.* he characterises his client as a *homo imperitus morum, agricola et rusticus* (143), who, at his father's behest, lived his whole life in the countryside, preoccupied with the cultivation of land (39: *ruri habitare*; *in agro colendo uiuere*); and far from being a reason to hate his father, as the prosecution alleges, this way of life ensured that Roscius developed the moral fibre of the Romans of old: in support of his claim, Cicero evokes the time of the ancestors when everyone tilled their own fields, did not seek to enrich themselves greedily, and therefore enabled Rome's rise to imperial greatness (50, cited above note 1; cf. Dyck 2010: 119: 'Cicero contrives to allow some of the ethos of early Rome to rub off on his client') – as opposed to the vices (in particular *luxuria, auaritia, audacia* and *improbitas*) that prevail in Sulla's coterie. Again, the lexemes *frugi, frugaliter* and/or *frugalitas* would seem to fit perfectly into the picture that Cicero here paints of his defendant, dedicated as he is to the cultivation of *fruges*, but they do not occur in the speech.

247

Ingo Gildenhard

into a plurality of *uirtutes* (not in the sense of 'deeds' but 'virtues'). This move enables Cicero to subdivide the set of qualities into those narrowly focused on martial prowess, the so-called *uirtutes imperatoriae* (*labor in negotiis, fortitudo in periculis, industria in agendo, celeritas in conficiendo, consilium in prouidendo*: *Man.* 29) and those to do with personal and civic ethics, not least in the context of imperial warfare and provincial administration, viz. *innocentia, temperantia, fides, facilitas, ingenium* and *humanitas* (*Man.* 36).[24] In the context of the speech, the basic rationale of this ploy is twofold: it is supposed to render Pompey an attractive appointment in the war against Mithridates; and it assimilates Pompey to Cicero, who could not plausibly claim a large share in *uirtutes imperatoriae* but considered himself an embodiment of the ethical *uirtutes* he enumerates, in particular of course *ingenium* and *humanitas*.[25] Given that he had just cast himself as a figure of *frugalitas* in the *Verrines*, where the notion also figures as a quality that renders Rome attractive to its allies, his failure to include *frugalitas* in the *pro lege Manilia* baffles: if the traditional story were true, it ought to have been an attractive term to choose.

Likewise, after talking up *frugalitas* as the virtue of all virtues in the *Tusculans*, Cicero does not mention *frugalitas* even once in his great *summa* of Roman civic ethics, the *de Officiis* (44 BCE), written only a year after the *Tusculans* – despite the fact that he again operates with a Stoicising set of four cardinal virtues. Yet instead of subsuming *fortitudo, iustitia* and *prudentia* under *frugalitas* as he does in *Tusc.* 3.17, he now identifies *iustitia, sapientia, magnitudo animi* and *temperantia* as the four aspects of the honourable at the beginning of the treatise (1.12–15) and then, towards the end of book 1, elevates *decorum* to the virtue with the same overarching function as *frugalitas* in the *Tusculans* (1.93).[26] There are

---

[24] In *Tusc.* 3.16, Cicero identifies *innocentia* and *temperantia* as lesser synonyms of *frugalitas*.

[25] See Gildenhard, Hodgson et al. 2013: 108–9.

[26] See Schofield 2012: 50–3 for discussion of *decorum* as the fourth virtue in *de Officiis*. With reference to *frugalitas* in the *Tusculans* he notes: 'The passage in which this

248

Frugalitas, or: The Invention of a Roman Virtue

thus some striking shifts in terminology from the *Tusculans* to the *de Officiis*: *frugalitas* ceases to be the overriding virtue; and the (standard) *temperantia* (often linked with *moderatio* or *modestia*) reappears as the preferred Latin equivalent of σωφροσύνη ('temperance'). Cicero's experimentation with *frugalitas* in the *philosophica* was thus nothing more than a flash in the pan (even though it helped to set off the shooting star career of *frugalitas* in later authors) – and thus hardly supports the idea that his one-off assertion in *Tusculan* 3 that it was the virtue of all Roman virtues reflects a long-standing certainty within Rome's cultural imaginary (as opposed to a quirky authorial decision on his part). Indeed, the *Tusculans Disputations* are Cicero's only theoretical writing in which the noun occurs.[27]

The clusters and the silences raise two key questions. First, why does *frugalitas* not play a greater role in Cicero's thinking? And second, why does he invest in *frugalitas* at two particular moments in his career, i.e. the *Verrines* and the *Tusculans* (and the *pro rege Deiotaro*)? To make headway here, we need to explore the semantics of *frugi* in pre-Ciceronian

> discussion [of the interconnectedness of all virtues in Stoic theory] is set (*Tusc.* 3.16–18) expends a lot of energy on finding a good Roman name for the fourth virtue. Perhaps surprisingly (and certainly uniquely in his philosophical writings) Cicero opts for *frugalitas*, which he wants us to take not in the usual narrow sense of "being economical," "good control of resources".'

[27] Other noteworthy silences – inexplicable if Cicero's pronouncement that *frugalitas* is a Roman value-term in *Tusc.* 3 had any basis in reality – include the opening of *de Republica*, where he claims that any valuable insight achieved by (Greek) philosophers is only the retrospective articulation in discourse of what (Roman) statesmen had long enacted in practice: *nihil enim dicitur a philosophis, quod quidem recte honesteque dicatur, quod <non> ab iis partum confirmatumque sit, a quibus ciuitatibus iura discripta sunt. unde enim pietas, aut a quibus religio? unde ius aut gentium aut hoc ipsum ciuile quod dicitur? unde iustitia fides aequitas? unde pudor continentia fuga turpi<tu>dinis adpetentia laudis et honestatis? unde in laboribus et periculis fortitudo?* If there was anything to the traditional story, *frugalitas* cries out for inclusion here, especially in light of the ethnic and polemical edge that Cicero claims for the noun in the *Tusculans* – though it of course may have featured in portions of the work now lost. (Augustine, in retrospect, finds the work full of praise of *frugalitas* and *continentia*. See *Ep.* 91.3: *intuere, obsecro te, et cerne quantis ibi* [= the *de Republica*] *laudibus frugalitas et continentia praedicetur et erga coniugale uinculum fides castique honesti ac probi mores, quibus cum praepollet ciuitas uere florere dicenda est*). Cf. also *Cat.* 2.25 (another ethical syncrisis), where Cicero's antonym of choice for *luxuria* is *temperantia*.

Ingo Gildenhard

times, distinguishing a semantic strand that can be traced back to New Comedy from one that has its origin in the Roman magistrate and annalist Lucius Calpurnius Piso Frugi.

The Slaves and the *Nobilis*: From the *Homines Frugi* of New Comedy to L. Calpurnius Piso Frugi

While the noun *frugalitas* is unattested before the first century BCE, the same is not the case for the adjective *frugi*, which registers frequently, if selectively, in our literary record from the late third century BCE onwards. From a socio-linguistic point of view, however, its discursive habitat looks schizophrenic: in the comedies of Plautus and Terence as well as elsewhere, it tends to figure as an attribute of persons with low social standing (in particular slaves and freedmen); but it then also appears, somewhat surprisingly and seemingly incongruously, as the second *cognomen* (*agnomen*) of L. Calpurnius Piso Frugi, who belonged to the senatorial elite, holding the consulship in 133 and the censorship in 120 BCE. Both aspects of *frugi* are key to understanding Cicero's deployment of *frugalitas*.

The Homines Frugi *of New Comedy*

The semantics of *frugi* in New Comedy cover a fairly wide range, with two particular foci, i.e. 'usefulness' and (if the emphasis is on morality) 'sound character' (Ramsay 1869: 229–30):

The true meaning of *frugi* is clearly indicated by the etymology – it is used to denote that a person is 'profitable' or 'useful' either to himself or to others. ... When used with reference to one who is profitable to himself it may signify 'economical' or 'thrifty,' ... and generally, 'of good moral character' ... also, however, 'discreet' or 'worldly wise,' without implying moral rectitude...; in *As.* 1.3.23 it is applied to a *lena* who attends to her own interests. ... *Frugi* may be used also with reference to one who is profitable to others, and hence it is the characteristic epithet for an honest, steady, thrifty, respectable slave, who studies his master's interest.[28]

---

[28] See also Treggiari 2007: 42: 'The word is untranslatable, but was applied, not exclusively, to well-behaved, useful, sober, thrifty, and profitable slaves.'

250

Frugalitas, or: The Invention of a Roman Virtue

Therefore *frugi* can be applied without consideration of social status;[29] but there is a clear sense that 'being *frugi*' is a quality associated above all with persons belonging to lower social ranks, such as slaves or freedmen – and not just in comic scripts.[30] The exchange between the incensed Hegio and Stalagmus, his runaway slave and kidnapper of his son, in Plautus' *Captiui* is a case in point (954–57):

HEGIO:	Age tu illuc procede, bone uir, lepidum mancupium meum.
STALAGMUS:	Quid me oportet facere, ubi tu talis uir falsum autumnas?
	Fui ego bellus, lepidus: bonus uir numquam, neque frugi bonae,
	Neque ero umquam; ne \<in\> spem ponas me bonae frugi fore.
HEGIO:	'Go on, step forward, good man, my charming piece of property.'
STALAGMUS:	'What ought I do when a man like you tells lies? I used to be pretty and charming: a good man? Never! Nor beneficial nor will I ever be; so don't get your hopes up that I'll be beneficial in future.'

In addressing his truant slave, Hegio combines the deeply ironic use of exalted aristocratic idiom (*bone uir*) with the brutal legalism *mancupium meum* ('my property'), rendered more offensive by the attribute *lepidum*, which hints at Stalagmus' former role as a 'sexual plaything of his pederastic master'.[31] In turn, Stalagmus first deflates Hegio's sarcasm by taking the words at face value and disowning the label *uir bonus*, of which a *nobilis* would be proud, as laughingly inappropriate; and then proceeds to reject the standard quality label applied to slaves (*frugi bonae*) as well (picking up on *mancupium*), a point he

---

[29] For *frugi* describing members of the social elite in comic scripts, see the passages collected by Stewart 2012: 186 n. 86: '*Asin.* 856, joined with *continens*; *Men.* 579, contrasting with *nequam*; *Most.* 133, joined with *probus*; *Persa* 453–454, contrasting with *malus* and *nequam*; *Trin.* 321–322, joined with *probus*.'

[30] For freedmen see Mouritsen 2011: 59–64 or MacLean 2018: 52–3: 'In Latin epigraphy..., tradesmen who receive epithets like *honestus, bonus, frugi*, and *fidelis* are often, though not always, freedmen or probable freedmen.'

[31] Leigh 2004: 91 with reference to *Capt.* 966. See further Stewart 2012: 76: 'The term *mancipium* designated a legal category of property including land, horses, and other valued commodities of an agrarian economy (Gai. *Inst.* 1.120)' with references to Watson 1975: 85–6 and Bradley 1994: 18.

251

Ingo Gildenhard

re-emphasises through repetition.[32] Stalagmus, a criminal to boot (and proud of it), is neither good nor useful.

Elsewhere, comic playwrights use *frugi* to explore the ambiguity – or rather the possibility of non-coincidence – between morality and utility when it comes to the conduct of slaves. Frequently, the moral sense of the attribute becomes relative, or, in Stewart's words, 'contingent' upon the interest of his master. She notes with reference to *Bacch.* 651–60 that '. . . the trickster slave Chrysalus asserts that the *frugi* slave must accommodate himself to changing moral circumstance and mirror the morality of a situation, whether it is good or bad' and generalises (2012: 185–6):[33]

> The passages – whether or not they represent a humorous and comfortable denigration of slave behavior for a Roman audience – presume a recognized, independent slave subjectivity and underscore the slave's contingent morality as a necessary skill for survival. The use of the word *frugi* to describe slaves elsewhere in Plautus corroborates the slave's contingent morality as a skill of accommodation. *Frugi* occurs to describe the judgment of the slave by others, particularly the master, and seems to designate an upright slave (e.g., *Cas.* 255, contrasting with *nequam*; *Cas.* 268, contrasting with *improbus*; *Cas.* 283, joined with *probus*). Yet when the slave uses it of himself, it describes the capacity to recognize and mirror the different emotional states of the master (*Amph.* 958–961). . . . The catechism of good behavior in slaves and the usage of *frugi* offer parallels for the trickster's behavior and identify the behavior as an extreme use of the set of behaviors enjoined by slavery.

The semantics of *frugi*, ranging from 'useful' to 'morally sound', encapsulate the hybrid status of a slave as a 'thing' with 'character' – a possession endowed with human qualities, an instrument with morals; and it is a lexeme firmly rooted in the slave-milieu.[34] *Frugi*, then, is not an attribute bound to

---

[32] See further the discussion by Stewart 2012: 75–6. There might be a joke here about Stalagmus' Sicilian background (see Leigh 2004: 90–1 with reference to *Capt.* 887–9), Sicily being the island of *bonae fruges*.

[33] See also Stewart 2012: 184 on *Aul.* 587–91 and 599–602: 'So the slave Strobilus asserts that the *frugi* slave needs to perform useful actions for the master, to subordinate his own interest to the master's will, and to recognize the master's will from his very expression.'

[34] *frugi* also functions as the positive of *frugalior, frugalissimus*, though Quint. *Inst.* 1.6.17 suggests the existence of a positive **frugalis*, which, unlike the comparative (*frugalior*) and superlative (*frugalissimus*), is unattested in archaic and classical Latin. See Ax 2011: 256–8. *frugalior* is used rarely in New Comedy, but seems

252

Frugalitas, or: The Invention of a Roman Virtue

make a member of Rome's ruling elite swell with pride. And indeed, as Santoro L'Hoir observes, someone like 'Cicero does not use *frugi* of senatorial *viri*.'[35] That stands to reason: while typically aristocratic markers of distinction may travel downwards to lift someone of lower social standing up, complimentary attributes typically applied to freedmen and slaves do not easily travel upwards: this would be dragging exalted personages down, damning them with subaltern praise.

The association of *frugi* (and *frugalitas*) with a slave-milieu appears to be born out by the evidence of mime, scanty as it is. The two most famous representatives of this dramatic genre both conjoin the notion of thriftiness with misery. One of the *sententiae* of Publilius, a Syrian who arrived in Rome enslaved but was freed for his wit and went on to a stellar, pan-Italic career as composer and performer of mimes (Macrobius 2.7.6–10) runs: *Frugalitas miseria est rumoris boni* ('Frugality is wretchedness with a good name'); and the one line surviving from the mime *Carcer* by his rival Decimus Laberius seems to express a similar sentiment: *homo frugi, quod tibi relictumst, retines miserimonium* ('thrifty fellow, you retain the wretchedness that was left to you').[36]

There is, however, one notable exception: at some point in his career Lucius Calpurnius Piso decided to co-opt the term into his very name, calling himself Lucius Calpurnius Piso Frugi and bestowing this *agnomen* also on his descendants. In the light of our findings so far, this is a rather puzzling move, yet of tremendous consequences for further developments in the historical semantics of *frugi* and (by extension) *frugalitas*.

---

slightly more classy than *frugi*. See e.g. Plaut. *Trin.* 609–10 or Ter. *Hau.* 681, where it is used with reference to freeborn citizens who commit themselves to a greater degree of thrift or material sobriety. The superlative *frugalissimus* is not attested before Cicero's *Verrines* (where it occurs with considerable frequency: see below). The adverb *frugaliter* occurs once with reference to a slave (Plaut. *Epid.* 565–6: ... *ille eam rem adeo sobrie et frugaliter | accurauit ut ... ut ad alias res est impense improbus*); once as part of a gnomic truth (Plaut. *Persa* 449–50, the slave Toxilus speaking: *si quam rem accures sobrie aut frugaliter, | solet illa recte sub manus succedere*).

[35] Santoro L'Hoir 1992: 17 n. 45.

[36] For text, translation and commentary, see Panayotakis 2010: 164–8.

Ingo Gildenhard

Lucius Calpurnius Piso Frugi[37]

Piso (c. 180–118 BCE) first made a splash when, as one of the tribunes of the plebs in 149 BCE, he saw through the *Lex Calpurnia de pecuniis repetundis*, the first piece of legislation at Rome designed to curtail provincial exploitation: it enabled the prosecution of former magistrates for theft or extortion after their time in office. After holding the praetorship some time between 138 and 136 BCE, which may have involved participation in a campaign against rebellious slaves in Sicily, he reached the consulship in 133 BCE, which he held together with Publius Mucius Scaevola. During his consulship, he was in command of the First Sicilian Slave War, capturing Morgantina and moving on to attack Henna, the origin and centre of resistance, which, however, only fell the following year to his consular successor. Back in Rome, he became a vocal opponent of the Gracchi and their measures, offering forceful opposition to Gaius Gracchus' grain laws in 123 BCE. In 120 BCE he was elected censor. He also authored an annalistic history towards the end of his life.

A good starting point for getting a purchase on Piso's idiosyncratic epithet is Forsythe's discussion (1994: 25):

> At some time during his life Piso's upright and austere behavior earned him the nickname Frugi. No other Roman is known to have ever received this appellation. Consequently, his descendants proudly retained his name as a standard part of the family's nomenclature, and on several occasions ... Cicero found it useful to parade Piso and his virtuous name before his listening or reading audience to serve as a paragon of moral rectitude. It would be interesting to know who first bestowed this name upon Piso and whether he did so out of genuine admiration of the man's character or as a sophisticated sneer at his old fashioned conservatism.

An invective pedigree is nothing unusual in the context of Roman nomenclature.[38] Derogatory *cognomina* are legion:[39]

---

[37] See Forsythe 1994; Oakley 2005: 573–4; Pobjoy 2013.

[38] On Roman names see e.g. Kajanto 1965; Matthews 1973; Nicolet 1977; Salway 1994; Salomies 2008; Rosillo-López 2017; Solin 2017.

[39] For the Roman *cognomen* ('this odd third name'), see Corbeill 1996: 57–98, with reference to earlier literature.

254

Frugalitas, or: The Invention of a Roman Virtue

'The originally negative meanings of *cognomina* did not deter families who used them later with pride because such *cognomina* expressed familial status and were therefore effective weapons in the political competition between prominent families.'[40] The argument that families used these names as an asset in the competition for rank and standing goes back to Mommsen.[41] Corbeill situates the rise of pejorative *cognomina* more specifically in the increasingly competitive political culture of the second century BCE when some families became so powerful as to threaten the oligarchic equilibrium and attracted negative labels designed to keep their ambition in check.[42] Partly for this reason, it seems to have been a phenomenon confined to the ruling elite: in republican times such *cognomina* 'were applied almost exclusively among males of the senatorial class ... the few examples attested for freedmen and lower-class free persons were, so far as our sources tell us, not hereditary'.[43] The choice of *frugi* therefore shows several signs of caustic wit: first, given that it is a quality associated primarily with slaves and freedmen, it seems particularly ill-suited as an aristocratic epithet; and secondly, *Frugi* joins Piso, which 'apparently derives from agriculture' as a second *cognomen*, causing an ironic reinforcement of the initial slur (it is hardly surprising that someone called 'Peasant' turns out to be 'Frugi').[44]

---

[40] van der Blom 2010: 99 n. 84, in a more general discussion of the transmission of family characteristics across generations, also with reference to Piso Frugi and his descendants.

[41] Corbeill 1996: 61–2, with reference to Mommsen 1864: 59–60.

[42] Corbeill 1996: 63.   [43] Corbeill 1996: 59 with reference to Thylander 1952: 100.

[44] Corbeill 1996: 79 n. 76. For punning on the putative rusticity of the Pisones see also *Laus Pisonis* 14–17: ... *nam quid memorare necesse est,* | *ut domus a Calpo nomen Calpurnia ducat* | *claraque Pisonis tulerit cognomina prima,* | *humida callosa cum 'pinseret' hordea dextra?* ('What need to record how the Calpurnian house derives its name from Calpus and won its first famous surname of Piso for pounding (*pi(n)seret*) the moist barley with hard-skinned hand?'). Peirano 2012: 150 notes that the information the anonymous poet provides about Piso's family 'relates not to the Calpurnii's *tituli*, but to a detail that evokes their rustic origin. The detail about the preparation of barley is a curious choice at the very least. Etymological wordplays were considered acceptable topics of praise, provided, as Aelius Theon tells us, that one could stay away from the vulgar (πάνυ φορτικόν) and laughable (καταγέλαστον), which one might feel has not happened with the author of the

Ingo Gildenhard

When and how did the name originate? An anecdote to do with Piso's opposition to C. Gracchus' *lex frumentaria* in 123 BCE transmitted by Cicero would seem to provide a *terminus ante quem* – and confirm that he acquired the *agnomen* during his lifetime (Cic. *Font.* 39):

Exstat oratio hominis, ut opinio mea fert, nostrorum hominum longe ingeniosissimi atque eloquentissimi, C. Gracchi; qua in oratione permulta in L. Pisonem turpia ac flagitiosa dicuntur. at in quem uirum! qui tanta uirtute atque integritate fuit ut etiam illis optimis temporibus, cum hominem inuenire nequam neminem posses, solus tamen Frugi nominaretur. quem cum in contionem Gracchus uocari iuberet et uiator quaereret, quem Pisonem, quod erant plures: 'cogis me,' inquit, 'dicere inimicum meum Frugi.' Is igitur uir quem ne inimicus quidem satis in appellando significare poterat, nisi ante laudasset, qui uno cognomine declarabatur non modo quis esset sed etiam qualis esset, tamen in falsam atque iniquam probrorum insimulationem uocabatur.

There is an extant oration of a man, Caius Gracchus, in my opinion by far the most talented and eloquent of our countrymen. In this oration Lucius Piso is accused of many a shameful and criminal deed. What a man to be so accused! A man who was of such excellence and integrity, that even in those stellar times, when it was impossible to find anyone morally worthless, still only he was called Frugi. And when Gracchus ordered him to be summoned before the assembly, and his lictor asked him which Piso, because there were many of the name, he said: 'You are compelling me to call my enemy "Thrifty".' That very man then, whom even his enemy was unable to single out with sufficient clearness without first praising him, whose surname by itself pronounced not only who he was, but what sort of man he was – that very man was, nevertheless, exposed to a false and unjust accusation of disgraceful conduct.

Within the context of the speech, Cicero exploits the anecdote as evidence that even persons of high moral character, such as Piso Frugi or his present client Fonteius, may find themselves accused of shameful doings; but in Piso's case the slander results in an onomastic paradox: as his opponent Caius Gracchus has to concede, a eulogy of Piso's sound morals is built

Laus.' See also Plin. *Nat.* 18.10: *Pisonis a pisendo.* The connection to 'pea' is controversial – rejected by Fraenkel 1935: 1653 ('Daß *Piso* nichts mit *pisum* "Erbse", frz. *pois*, zu tun haben kann, folgt aus der Quantitätsverschiedenheit der *i* in beiden Wörtern'), it is still considered possible by Ernout and Meillet 1959. Cf. Di Brazzano 2004: 161 n. 34.

256

Frugalitas, or: The Invention of a Roman Virtue

into his very *agnomen* Frugi.[45] Another piece of evidence proves that this particular L. Calpurnius Piso was the first in the family to integrate the attribute into his nomenclature. In a comment on Cicero's speech *pro Flacco*, the scholiast Bobiensis notes that many members of the family bear the cognomen (*plurimi quidem ex hac familia cognomentum frugalitatis habuerunt*), but the first one who merited it was the L. Piso who passed the law against provincial exploitation and was the main enemy of Gaius Gracchus: *sed enim primus hoc meruit L. Piso, qui legem de pecuniis repetundis tulit et fuit C. Graccho capitalis inimicus*.[46] When and why he did so is impossible to determine; but various 'trigger-events', which are by no means mutually exclusive, suggest themselves:

First, the *agnomen* may have had something to do with his authorship of the first ever *lex de repetundis* during his tribunate in 149 BCE. The scholia comment just cited does not necessarily imply that the author thought Piso acquired the attribute *frugi* because of the law or his opposition to Gracchus, two events that are anyway decades apart. And as *pro Fonteio* 39 (cited above) makes clear, when Piso clashed with C. Gracchus over a grain law in 123/2 BCE, Frugi seems to have already been part of his nomenclature. Still, his most notable act as tribune easily falls under the rubric of aristocratic self-restraint (Forsythe 1994: 13):

> The only known act of Piso's tribunate was his passage of the *Lex Calpurnia de pecuniis repetundis*, a major landmark in the development of Roman criminal law. ... Piso's bill established for the first time a standard legal procedure by which Roman magistrates could be prosecuted for misappropriating property. It fixed the penalty as simple restitution and ordained that a senatorial jury would hear the case and assess the amounts involved. Though modified by a *Lex Junia* and replaced by the *Lex Acilia* of C. Gracchus, the Calpurnian law on extortion formed the original precedent for subsequent criminal legislation during the late republic.

Cicero labels the standing court that Piso established, in which cases of provincial exploitation could be heard, a 'citadel of the

---

[45] van der Blom 2016: 85–6.   [46] *in Cic. Flacc.* fr. 10 p. 96 Stangl.

Ingo Gildenhard

allies'.[47] But the main motivation for setting up a permanent *quaestio de repetundis* was most likely the desire of the senatorial oligarchy to impose limits on enrichment by its members. The courts did not put an end to the system of exploitation below the governing class (the *publicani*); it thus belongs into the same orbit as sumptuary legislation.[48] The attribute 'thrifty' goes well with the individual who legally enforced a certain measure of self-restraint among his peers.

Second, Piso might have earned his epithet while being in command during the slave-war in Sicily (the land of *fruges*), perhaps again as a sarcastic quip on his insistence on austerity and (military) discipline in the land of plenty.

And third, the attribute *frugi* might have been initially deployed to mock his personal outlook or lifestyle – and Piso himself then embraced the label. That *frugi* can function both as a slur and a badge of honour has to do with its traditional semantics and ideological connotations: as we have seen, it is the kind of praise one would extend to a useful and trustworthy slave or upright and honest freedman, who leads a (necessarily) thrifty existence and has a parsimonious outlook that could be considered dishonourable in someone who belonged to the ruling elite, of whom one could expect a certain degree of generosity – *liberalitas* was after all a virtue in its own right. If the slur was: 'You behave like a slave (or freedman)!', Piso's reply might have been: 'Indeed! And I am proud of it' (playing off the idea that a *homo frugi* is not just niggardly-thrifty but also a 'person of good character', the humble equivalent of a *uir bonus*) – so proud indeed that he integrated the attribute into his nomenclature.[49] For our concerns, at any rate, the original impetus behind, and the precise socio-political function of, pejorative *cognomina* in Roman

---

[47] *Diu. Caec.* 18.

[48] The extensive bibliography includes Lintott 1981; 2008; Hofmann-Löbl 1996: 68–73, and Prag 2013.

[49] A similar strategy of taking the sting out of a slur by embracing it is adopted by Horace, who 'faces full on the *inuidia* attaching to his presumptuous friendship by repeating an abusive formulation of his pedigree, *libertino patre natum*' (Gowers 2012: 217 on *S.* 1.6). On Horace, see further below 295–8.

Frugalitas, or: The Invention of a Roman Virtue

aristocratic culture matter less than the fact that the practice existed and that such nominal slurs had the potential to be integrated as a sign of distinction into the official nomenclature of a (branch of a) *gens*.

In his *Annals*, most likely composed around or after his censorship in 120 BCE, Piso seems to have used the medium of historiography with not inconsiderable wit to explore the potential of the epithet for purposes of self-promotion, thereby amplifying its value as a marker of a specific kind of aristocratic distinction. The fragments, however meagre, suggest that the overall vision of Roman history Piso expressed in his *Annals* accords perfectly with the ideology of prudent self-restraint in various spheres of life and with the emphasis on thrift and merit, virtue and discipline across and beyond distinctions of class and rank that manifests itself in his embrace of Frugi as *agnomen*: the surviving bits are replete with moralising rhetoric and rebukes of the depravities of the young.[50] The authorial posture that Piso adopts thus fits his epithet: he tells a story of decline caused by the weakening of frugal values among a new generation of degenerate Romans who are – as he puts it, perhaps programmatically in his preface – devoted to the penis.[51]

His historiographical work offers evidence that Piso fully understood the humble milieu in which his chosen epithet was at home, more specifically its association with slaves and freedmen – and that he nevertheless embraced it as a way to signal virtue. One episode in particular merits a more detailed look in this context: under the heading *quonam igitur modo utilissime colentur agri?* (*Nat.* 18.39), the Elder Pliny reports

---

[50] Pobjoy 2013: 232: 'It is likely that the *agnomen* was already familiar by the time that Piso's history was published, but references of this sort in the work might have helped to solidify its associations.'

[51] Cic. *Fam.* 9.22.2 = F 42 *FRHist*. The fragment is not placeable with any certainty. For Piso's view of Roman history and, more generally, the Roman discourse of decline see Biesinger 2016. If the self-fashioning of his offspring Piso Frugi, one of the consuls of 58 BCE, is anything to go by, he may also have expressed his values in his demeanour. In his speech *in Pisonem*, Cicero therefore faced the challenge to transform what appear to be positive qualities into their negative counterparts, arguing that what seems to be an index of old-fashioned, ancestral virtue is in fact just a dirty and foreign countenance. See Edwards 1993: 201 for discussion.

Ingo Gildenhard

that Piso recorded the following incident in his narrative (*Nat.* 18.41–3 = F 35 *FRHist*; trans. Rackham/Loeb):

C. Furius Cresimus e seruitute liberatus, cum in paruo admodum agello largiores multo *fructus* perciperet, quam ex amplissimis uicinitas, in inuidia erat magna, ceu *fruges* alienas perliceret ueneficiis. (42) quamobrem ab Spurio Albino curuli aedile die dicta metuens damnationem, cum in suffragium tribus oporteret ire, instrumentum rusticum omne in forum attulit et adduxit familiam suam ualidam atque, ut ait Piso, bene curatam ac uestitam, ferramenta egregie facta, graues ligones, uomeres ponderosos, boues saturos. (43) postea dixit: ueneficia mea, Quirites, haec sunt, nec possum uobis ostendere aut in forum adducere lucubrationes meas uigiliasque et sudores. omnium sententiis absolutus itaque est.

Gaius Furius Chresimus, a liberated slave, was extremely unpopular because he got much larger returns from a rather small farm than the neighbourhood obtained from very large estates, and he was supposed to be using magic spells to entice away other people's crops. He was consequently indicted by the curule aedile Spurius Albinus; and as he was afraid he would be found guilty, when the time came for the tribes to vote their verdict, he brought all his agricultural implements into court and produced his farm servants, sturdy people and also according to Piso's description well looked after and well clad, his iron tools of excellent make, heavy mattocks, ponderous ploughshares, and well-fed oxen. Then he said: 'These are my magic spells, citizens, and I am not able to exhibit to you or to produce in court my midnight labours and early risings and my sweat and toil.' This procured his acquittal by a unanimous verdict.

The passage offers evidence for the history of magic;[52] studies in social mobility in mid-republican Rome;[53] Roman legal procedures;[54] and the history of emotions[55] – even though

[52] Graf 1997: 62–5 and 107–9; Gordon 1999: 253–4, who tries to explain this as a situation where the larger landowners do not make the profit from modern, rational agricultural techniques and were looking for someone to blame for their disappointment; Rives 2002; Ogden 2009.

[53] Treggiari 1969: 109 discusses the anecdote in the context of freedmen acquiring wealth, not least through hard labour, including the improvement of farmland; see also Rawson 1976: 94 (on the upward social mobility of intelligent freedmen who made enthusiastic farmers, with Cresimus functioning as 'the ideal industrious smallholder'). The phenomenon is of course much older. Hostility among the ruling elite toward upwardly mobile freedmen already registers in our sources for the end of the fourth century: see note 57 below.

[54] Liebs 2012: Ch. 2.

[55] See Kaster 2005: 101, who analyses the two types of *inuidia* at work in the anecdote: 'the charge of magic is obviously a way for the neighbors to put a decent face on their own naked envy, as they measure Cresimus' crops against their own and find

260

Frugalitas, or: The Invention of a Roman Virtue

certain aspects of the text remain elusive.[56] It is, for instance, impossible to identify the curule aedile in question, one Sp. (Postumius) Albinus, with certainty. Most opt for the consul of 186 (and date his aedileship to 191); but as Kunkel and Wittmann note, the *fasti* feature Sp. Albini already for the fourth century, which makes it at least possible that we are dealing with a carrier of this name from an earlier period who did not reach the consulship and is therefore otherwise unknown.[57] Some scholars maintain that Piso invented the entire episode.[58] And it is at any rate our one and only mention of Furius Cresimus.[59]

Be all of this as it may, for our purposes the only thing that matters is that the name of the freedman happens to be Gaius Furius *Cresimus*, which is the Greek equivalent of *frugi*.[60] This fact turns the anecdote into a parable on Piso's *agnomen* – and as such was perhaps even written up as a wry response to the slur that the attribute *frugi* might have been designed to be. Piso acknowledges the associations of *frugi* with the milieu of slaves and freedmen, but then turns the fault into a feature,

---

the assessment painful. From this point of view, the anecdote reminds us that slander is the tribute that malice pays to shame.'

[56] For extensive discussion see Forsythe 1994: 376–84 and Pobjoy in *FRHist*.

[57] Kunkel and Wittmann 1995: 502 n. 111. In many ways, the fragment complements Piso's treatment of Cn. Flavius, who, having been born of a freedman father (*patre libertino natus*) held the office of *scriba* and then got elected to the curule aedileship – much to the discomfiture of some *adulescentes nobiles* (F 31 *FRHist*). According to Plin. *Nat.* 33.17 and Pompon. *dig.* 1.2.2.7, this Flavius was the *scriba* of Appius Claudius Caecus, *qui senatum primus libertinorum filiis lectis inquinauerat* (Liv. 9.46.10): see Woodman 2009: 159–60. Cf. Cornell 2000: 84–5; Bernard 2018: 11–12.

[58] See e.g. Latte 1960/1968, who also notes that in Piso's own time, Sp. Postumii Albini held the consulship in 186, 174, 148, and 110 (840 n. 5); Kierdorf 2003: 28 ('Ungeschichtlichkeit' of the anecdote because of the name, even though it was frequent in the Greek East); or Ogden 2009: 277: 'This tale, apocryphal and moralizing as it evidently is, provides an example of how it was envisaged that the law against crop-charming might be put into use.'

[59] Münzer 1910: 351.

[60] Pobjoy 2013: 232 n. 12: 'from his cognomen, it can be deduced that C. Furius as a slave had been called "Cresimus" or "Chresimus": according to Cicero (*Tusc.* 3.16)... that is the Greek equivalent of "Frugi" (though somewhat narrower in scope).' For similar bi-lingual play, see *L'Année épigraphique*, Année 2010, No. NA1 (2013), inscription Nr. 330 (156–7), dating to the early empire and concerning a slave with the name Chrestes, who is praised *frugalitatis causa*. On the naming of slaves see further Bruun 2013.

Ingo Gildenhard

casting Cresimus as an equivalent of the *uir bonus* of Cato's *de Agri Cultura*, whereas his adversaries emerge as decadent. Our Mr. Joe Frugi, a former slave from the Greek East, embodies Piso's ancestral values to a higher degree than entitled members of the established Roman elite. He is therefore a more successful farmer, who, on account of his personal qualities (in particular being *frugi*) manages to transform his ability for agricultural *labor* into plentiful *fruges* and therefore wealth – but (given the times) does not attract admiration for his efforts, but envy or even hatred (*inuidia*) from his social superiors who dislike his success. *frugi* thereby turns from an indicator of low social status into a marker of outstanding moral qualities that operate independent of class distinctions.[61] Even if this kind of allegorical hide-and-seek is more familiar to us from sophisticated poetry such as Virgil's *Eclogues*, it is thus tempting to assume that Piso embedded this character in his *Annals* not least because Cresimus exemplifies (and gives a positive spin to) his *agnomen*.

In Piso, then, the epithet *frugi* (and the notion of *frugalitas*, arguably *avant la lettres*) found a powerful advocate: as legislator, military commander in Sicily, conservative politician and moralising historiographer, he helped to ennoble the attribute. With Piso's adoption of the *agnomen* Frugi, the lexeme had arrived in the upper echelons of Roman society: in addition to the meanings found in Plautus and Terence, *frugi* here for the first time features in an act of aristocratic self-promotion. Whatever the context, rationale and rhetorical thrust of this act of onomastic creativity, it increased the ideological range of *frugi* significantly. In addition to a slave-attribute, it now also came to epitomise a specific set of elite values, revolving around the notions of thrift, prudence, self-restraint, successful husbandry and ancestral discipline. In promoting these values in his *Annals*, he operated with the

---

[61] Cf. Graf 1997: 62: 'Pliny's account does not come from book XXX, his history of magic, but from a context concerned with the virtues of the ancestral Roman farmers; his interest here is not sorcery, but *mores maiorum*, the agricultural virtue of the ancient farmers whom the Romans were proud of having once been.'

262

Frugalitas, or: The Invention of a Roman Virtue

idea of selective, cross-generational continuity, asserting that only very few untimely individuals (such as he himself) managed to embody the excellence of old, whereas decadence prevailed among his contemporaries. The ensuing semantic expansion, which reconfigured qualities looked-for in slaves in an aristocratic key, removed or at least diminished some of the social stigma from the attribute *frugi* and thereby opened the door for the career of the abstract noun *frugalitas* as an ancestral virtue in Cicero.

Cicero

Before considering in detail the clustering of *frugalitas* in the *Verrines* and the *Tusculan Disputations* (as well as the *pro rege Deiotaro*) and why the noun does not figure more prominently elsewhere in Cicero's *oeuvre*, it will be useful to take a glance at his use of *frugi* in the light of our findings so far.

Cicero's Homines Frugi

Cicero continues to apply the adjective *frugi* in the two basic senses attested for the second-century BCE: in line with the usage found in New Comedy, he employs the attribute as a characteristic epithet for an honest slave or freedman; and following in the tradition established by Lucius Calpurnius Piso Frugi, the consul of 133 BCE, he uses the lexeme to refer to this distinguished *nobilis* and some of his (often less distinguished) descendants.

Across all genres – letters, speeches, dialogues – *frugi* is first and foremost associated with slaves or freedmen, though it also keeps company with other nondescript individuals, such as Fabius Luscus, Nicias Talna, one Bruttius, or C. Nasennius, a townsman of Suessa.[62] In his correspondence with Publius

---

[62] *Att.* 4.8a.3 = 82 SB (Fabius Luscus): *satis enim acutus et permodestus ac bonae frugi* with Santoro L'Hoir 1992: 17 n. 17; *Att.* 13.28.4 = 299 SB (Nicias Talna): *ille de ingenio nihil nimis, modestum et frugi; Fam.* 16.21.4 = 337 SB (Bruttius): *cuius cum frugi seueraque est uita tum etiam iucundissima conuictio; ad Brut.* 1.8.2 = 15 SB

Ingo Gildenhard

Sestius, for instance, Cicero has occasion to appraise his secretary Decius, who was probably one of Sestius' freedmen, as a *homo frugi* and a *homo prudens*.[63] Likewise, in a letter of recommendation, he calls the freedman of T. Ampius Balbus a *hominem frugi et modestum et patrono et nobis uehementer probatum*.[64] For our purposes, Cicero's eulogy of a freedman of Atticus, Marcus – so named at the moment of his manumission in honour of Cicero: *Att.* 4.15.1 = 90 SB; 27 July 54 BCE – Pomponius Dionysius, is particularly telling:[65] it includes explicit reflections on the social connotations of *frugi* (*Att.* 7.4.1 = 127 SB):[66]

> quem quidem cognoui cum doctum, quod mihi iam ante erat notum, tum sanctum, plenum offici, studiosum etiam meae laudis, frugi hominem, ac, ne libertinum laudare uidear, plane uirum bonum.

> I have found him not only a good scholar, which I already knew, but upright, serviceable, zealous moreover for my good name, an honest fellow, and in case that sounds too much like commending a freedman, a really fine man.

After emphasising Dionysius' learnedness (*doctum*), his moral qualities (*sanctum*) and his sense of duty, including in particular his devotion to Cicero (*plenum offici, studiosum etiam meae laudis*: the arrangement of the items is clearly climactic), Cicero concludes his 'ordinary' praise by calling Dionysius a *frugi homo*. At this point, he could have stopped.[67] Instead, he takes his praise one step further – because he is worried that

---

(C. Nasennius): *fortem uirum, Brute, tibi commendo, frugi hominem et, si quid ad rem pertinet, etiam locupletem.*

[63] *Fam.* 5.6.1 = 4 SB: *Cum ad me Decius librarius uenisset egissetque mecum ut operam darem ne tibi hoc tempore succederetur, quamquam illum hominem frugi et tibi amicum existimabam, tamen, quod memoria tenebam cuius modi ad me litteras antea misisses, non satis credidi homini prudenti tam ualde esse mutatam uoluntatem tuam.* See Park 1918: 66 n. 5: 'He receives the typical freedman's adjective *frugi*, and is probably a freedman and in Sestius' employ' and Shackleton Bailey 1977: 281.

[64] *Fam.* 13.70.1 = 298 SB, to Servilius Isauricus, Rome, 46–44 BCE.

[65] For Dionysius (and his – up and down – relationship with Cicero) see Christes 1979: 107–15, further Santoro L'Hoir 1992: 17–18.

[66] For Cicero's letters I cite the text and translation by D. R. Shackleton Bailey in the Loeb Classical Library.

[67] Christes 1979: 114: 'Mit *frugi hominem*, das einer zusammenfassenden Würdigung, gewissermaßen einer Gesamtnote im Zeugnis, gleichkommt, könnte die Würdigung abschließen.'

264

Frugalitas, or: The Invention of a Roman Virtue

the label *frugi homo* situates Dionysius too forcefully within his social milieu. To avoid the impression that his appreciation of him is qualified (along the lines of 'a jolly talented and upright fellow – for a freedman'), Cicero concludes by calling him a *uir bonus* (with a slight hedge in *plane*), an unequivocally high form of praise.[68] 'Hier', as Jürgen Blänsdorf puts it, 'scheinen alle Standesgrenzen durchbrochen.'[69] In fact, the social uplift is arguably less pronounced than Christes and Blänsdorf make it out to be. From Cato the Elder onwards (and certainly in Cicero), we capture efforts to endow *uir bonus* with ethical significance, independent of social background.[70] Cicero might simply have wished to situate his praise of Dionysius above the slave/freed vs. free divide (*servus/libertus v. ingenuus*). But precisely because he breaks class boundaries in his praise of Dionysius, he highlights their existence, also in terms of linguistic registers. His progression from *homo frugi* to *uir bonus* presupposes a clear sense of social scaling, and both the nouns (*homo > uir*) and the attributes (*frugi > bonus*) take a distinctive step upwards.[71] *homo frugi*, the passage makes clear, is a label conventionally attached to a useful and honest slave or

---

[68] Christes 1979: 114: 'Mit *vir bonus* bezeichnet der Römer den Mann, der im öffentlichen und private Leben den Anforderungen des herrschenden Lebensideals gerecht wird.'

[69] Blänsdorf 2016a: 585 ('Here all status boundaries seem broken'). For slaves and slavery in Cicero more generally see Blänsdorf 2016b.

[70] Cato the Elder, in the preface to the *de Agri Cultura*, notoriously claims: *et uirum bonum quom laudabant, ita laudabant, bonum agricolam bonumque colonum. amplissime laudari existimabatur qui ita laudabatur.* And the *uir bonus* ('an honest man') is a pervasive presence throughout the treatise (cf. 148, 149: disputes are to be settled *uiri boni arbitratu* 'according to the decision of an honest man') – it is this tradition of Cato the Elder, in which the emphasis on moral worth (however defined) challenges the social elitism of inherited privilege, that Cicero tabs into, though the passage also indicates that the moral definition of *bonus*, while more inclusive and operating according to universalising criteria of merit, only drops so far down the social scale: the distinction between free citizen and (former) slave remains very much in place. See Cicero's ethical redefinition of the *uir bonus* or *optimus quisque*, as referring to ethical perfection independent of social status, not least in the *pro Sestio*: Gildenhard 2011: 149–56.

[71] For the connotations of *homo* see Santoro L'Hoir 1992: 18–20 ('*Homo*: Laudation for the Less-Distinguished') and 21: 'Its use in reference to slaves, freedmen, foreigners, and even the dimmer lights of the municipal aristocracy, renders it a likely word for political invective. To call a member of the upper classes, who would normally be termed a *vir*, a *homo*, is an effective way of diminishing his status.'

Ingo Gildenhard

freedman or other person of low social standing; *uir bonus*, by contrast, conveys without a doubt that Cicero genuinely appreciates Dionysius as a person of remarkable quality, talent and moral fibre, above and beyond his low-ranking position in Roman society. And it does of course not affect the fundamental point that calling a Roman aristocrat a *homo frugi* would be damning with faint praise.

The speeches yield a similar picture. A particularly striking passage for our concerns occurs in the speech Cicero delivered on behalf of Gnaeus Plancius, who stood accused of *ambitus* for his canvassing as candidate for the aedileship in 55 BCE. To reject the claim of the prosecution that Plancius' lack of skills in public speaking and the law renders his electoral success suspicious, Cicero argues that the public does not assess candidates with reference to their specialist competences but the general excellence and integrity of their character (*uirtus, probitas, integritas in candidato, non linguae uolubilitas, non ars, non scientia requiri solet*) – and proceeds to illustrate the point by means of an analogy involving the slave market (*Planc.* 62; trans. N. H. Watts):

ut nos in mancipiis parandis quamuis frugi hominem si pro fabro aut pro tectore emimus, ferre moleste solemus, si eas artis quas in emendo secuti sumus forte nesciuerit, sin autem emimus quem uilicum imponeremus, quem pecori praeficeremus, nihil in eo nisi frugalitatem, laborem, uigilantiam esse curamus, sic populus Romanus deligit magistratus quasi rei publicae uilicos; in quibus si qua praeterea est ars, facile patitur, sin minus, uirtute eorum et innocentia contentus est.

In purchasing slaves, however honest (*frugi*) a man may be, if we have bought him as a carpenter or plasterer we happen to be annoyed if he turns out to be ignorant of the skills we had in mind when we bought him. But if we buy a slave to occupy the post of steward or shepherd, the only qualities we care about in him are frugality (*frugalitas*), industry (*labor*) and vigilance (*uigilantia*). This is how the Roman people select their magistrates, for they are, as it were, stewards of the republic. If, in addition to the requisite moral qualities, they are experts in anything, the people are well pleased; if not, they are content with uprightness (*uirtus*) and integrity (*innocentia*).

For some tasks involving handicraft, proficiency in a specialist skill (*ars*) is indispensable – and its absence cannot be compensated for by moral integrity; conversely, certain positions of

266

Frugalitas, or: The Invention of a Roman Virtue

authority that entail oversight of others and administrative competence do not require any particular kind of manual expertise – but demand qualities of character.[72] Thus anyone in need of a carpenter or plasterer would be justifiably irritated if he were sold a slave without the necessary skill-set – even if his acquisition turned out to be a person of sound character (a *frugi homo*); by contrast, in procuring a steward (*uilicus*), sound character (so Cicero claims) is the only quality that truly matters.[73] When Cicero then pivots from the slave market to the commonwealth via the figure of the *uilicus* (retained in a metaphorical sense: just as *patresfamilias* appoint stewards to oversee the administration of their households, so the Roman people elect magistrates to oversee the governance of the *res publica*), the same principles apply – though Cicero subtly shifts the emphasis: in the second half of the analogy, there is no equivalent to the figure of the inept if morally sound slave. Instead, he focuses right away on the aristocratic counterpart to the *uilicus*, for whom excellence of character is a sufficient condition of success in public elections – any additional skill (*ars*) is of course welcome, but ultimately an inessential asset, mere gravy on top.[74] Against the (unwelcome) assimilation of *uilici* and *magistratus* that the analogy entails, Cicero is keen to uphold social distinctions.[75] Thus he chooses a different set of terms when identifying the basic attributes of each type of person: in an outstanding steward the essential hallmarks are *frugalitas*, *labor* and *uigilantia*; in a magistrate, *uirtus* and *innocentia*. The divide – as

---

[72] The argument here has interesting affinities with passages in Plato, though Cicero of course refrains from making any such pedigree explicit, following the tenet of *obfuscatio doctrinae*.

[73] This rhetorical claim does not match reality. A good *uilicus* had considerable expertise in agricultural matters, precisely because his main responsibility consisted in the efficient management of the estate to maximise profit. See Knoch 2005: 167–8 and Menner 2006: 153–4, with further literature.

[74] For comparable instances see *Rep.* 5.5, where he compares the knowledge and insight of his ideal statesman to that of an outstanding *uilicus* and *Sest.* 137 with Kaster 2006: 380. As Carlsen notes, good bailiffs were difficult to obtain (1995: 61 n. 171 with further literature).

[75] Compare and contrast the simile in *de Republica* 5 that figures the *rector rei publicae* as a *uilicus* of the *res publica*. See Nelsestuen 2014 for discussion.

Ingo Gildenhard

we shall see shortly – is not particularly pronounced. Piso Frugi 'ennobled' *frugalitas*, and all three terms that are here used with explicit reference to slaves Cicero elsewhere opts for to hail the special qualities of *homines noui*. But in this particular passage, *frugi* and *frugalitas* emerge as positive qualities specifically of those situated at the lowest ranks of the social hierarchy – in comparison and contrast to the idiom Cicero employs to speak of the civic sphere and aristocratic milieu.

The particular association of *frugi* with slavery also helps Cicero to articulate the perverse scenario of a senate enslaved in *Philippic* 8 (32):[76]

> etenim, patres conscripti, cum in spem libertatis sexennio post sumus ingressi diutiusque seruitutem perpessi, quam captiui frugi et diligentes solent, quas uigilias, quas sollicitudines, quos labores liberandi populi Romani causa recusare debemus?[77]

> Indeed, senators, now that after a period of six years we have begun to entertain the hope of liberty again, having endured slavery longer than well-behaved (*frugi*) and conscientious (*diligentes*) prisoners of war customarily do, what watchfulness, what anxieties, what exertions ought we to shrink from for the sake of liberating the Roman people?

The strong link between slavery and *frugi* also registers in Cicero's theoretical writings (*de Orat.* 2.248):[78]

> Sed hoc mementote, quoscumque locos attingam, unde ridicula ducantur, ex eisdem locis fere etiam grauis sententias posse duci: tantum interest, quod grauitas honestis in rebus seuerisque, iocus in turpiculis et quasi deformibus ponitur, uelut eisdem uerbis et laudare frugi seruum possimus et, si est nequam, iocari.

> You should remember, however, that each and every commonplace that I may touch upon as a source for the humorous can, generally speaking, also serve as a source for serious thoughts. The only difference is that seriousness depends on matters that are honorable and earnest, joking on things that are

---

[76] When Cicero says of Antony *frugi factus est* at *Phil.* 2.69 as a comment on Antony's decision to part company with his mistress, the mime-actress Cytheris, the irony is palpable – and arguably also downgrades Antony to the status of slave or freedman, especially since it comes after lavish praise for the house of Pompey (which Antony turned into a brothel) and the man himself.

[77] For the text and commentary see Manuwald 2007: 1029.

[78] I cite the translation of J. M. May and J. Wisse, *Cicero On the Ideal Orator*, Oxford 2001. Cf. *de Orat.* 2.287.

268

Frugalitas, or: The Invention of a Roman Virtue

a bit dishonourable and, in a sense, ugly. For instance, we can use the same words for praising a slave who is deserving (*frugi*), and for ridiculing one if he is bad (*nequam*).

In the main, then, Cicero continues to operate with the traditional semantics of *frugi* that we also capture in New Comedy and elsewhere. There are, however, distinct moments when he makes use of the 'elite' variant of *frugi* that Piso brought into being.

Piso Frugi and the Verrines

At various places in his *oeuvre*, Cicero mentions Piso Frugi or one of his descendants, often with a comment on the disciplined self-restraint implied by the *agnomen*.[79] The earliest surviving instances of this practice occur in the *Verrines*, where such references are part of a full-blown ideology of *frugalitas*, which he uses as a means of attacking Verres. Thus at *Ver.* 2.1.101 he dismisses the idea of associating the defendant with *frugalitas* as absurd:

> Homo scilicet aut industria aut opera probata aut frugalitatis existimatione praeclara aut denique, id quod leuissimum est, adsiduitate, qui ante quaesturam cum meretricibus lenonibusque uixisset ...

> As if he were a man of proven diligence and hard work with an excellent reputation for uprightness and thrift (*frugalitas*) or at the least reliable application – he, who had lived before his quaestorship with prostitutes and pimps ...

The reference to Verres' sexual incontinence in particular (... *cum meretricibus lenonibusque uixisset*) might allude obliquely to the harangue against the free-wheeling love-lives of the present generation that seems to have formed part of Piso Frugi's *Annals*.[80] A similar slur occurs at *Ver.* 2.2.110 when

---

[79] See e.g. *Fam.* 9.22.2 = 189 SB: *at uero Piso ille Frugi in annalibus suis queritur adulescentis 'peni deditos' esse*; *Att.* 1.3.3 = 8 SB: *Tulliolam C. Pisoni L. f. Frugi despondimus*; or *Fin.* 2.90: *sed qui ad uoluptatem omnia referens uiuit ut Gallonius, loquitur ut Frugi ille Piso, non audio nec eum, quod sentiat, dicere existimo.*

[80] Sexual misdemeanour is a standard invective charge – as we can gather from C. Gracchus' self-promotion who identifies indulgence in illicet sexual acts as one of the areas in which he exercised self-restraint. See Introduction 63. The allure of

269

Ingo Gildenhard

he identifies an ill-advised invitation extended to Verres as the only blemish on the otherwise faultless record of Sthenius (from the Sicilian town Thermae), whom Verres had prosecuted on drummed-up charges of forgery:

> nihil aliud in eo quod reprehendi possit inuenio, nisi quod homo frugalissimus atque integerrimus te hominem plenum stupri flagitii sceleris domum suam inuitauit.

> I can find nothing in him that provokes criticism except that a man of such outstanding uprightness and honesty invited to his house a man like you – brimming with sexual trangression, scandal and crime.

And at *Ver.* 2.2.192, Cicero again dismisses the notion of praising Verres for his *frugalitas* as absurd:

> nunc uero quid faciat Hortensius? auaritiaene crimina frugalitatis laudibus deprecetur? at hominem flagitiosissimum libidinosissimum nequissimumque defendit.

> But now what can Hortensius do? Can he argue against the charges of avarice by praising Verres' frugality? After all, he is defending a man who is the physical embodiment of profligacy, lust and wickedness.

This policy of disassociation culminates in two passages in which Cicero contrasts Verres with Piso Frugi – the one who instituted the kind of court in which Verres now stands trial (*Ver.* 2.3.195):

> cum tibi senatus ex aerario pecuniam prompsisset et singulos tibi denarios adnumerasset quos tu pro singulis modiis aratoribus solueres, quid facere debuisti? si quod L. Piso ille Frugi, qui legem de pecuniis repetundis primus tulit, cum emisses quanti esset, quod superaret pecuniae rettulisses.

> When the senate had given you money from the state treasury, and, for every measure, had paid you a denarius that you were to pay the farmers, what should you have done? If you had wanted to do what Lucius Piso Frugi, who first carried a law about extortion, would have done, once you had bought the corn at the regular price, you would have returned whatever money remained.

Verres, so Cicero goes on to argue, pocketed the money he had received from the senate and extorted further cash from the

---

the topic has resulted in a correspondingly vast amount of secondary literature: for a recent discussion, see Gildenhard 2018: 29–33 with much further bibliography.

270

Frugalitas, or: The Invention of a Roman Virtue

farmers. Piso Frugi thus offered the perfect foil: he was, as Coffee puts it, 'no philosopher's fiction, but a real man of the generation before Cicero, who acted out of principle in proposing a provincial anticorruption law and seeing it ratified by the Senate. The times had already changed, perhaps, but his brand of frugality, which in this case meant looking out for the Roman treasury, remained a model that any noble Roman could choose to emulate, not just the flinty younger Cato.'[81] Cicero's contrastive treatment of Verres and Piso Frugi culminates in the onomastic showdown at *Ver.* 2.4.57. After recounting an anecdote to illustrate the conscientiousness of Lucius Piso, the son of the Lucius Piso who first carried a law about extortion (*... qui primus de pecuniis repetundis legem tulit*), Cicero continues:

ridiculum est me nunc de Verre dicere, cum de Pisone Frugi dixerim; uerum tamen quantum intersit uidete. ... nimirum ut hic nomen suum comprobauit, sic ille cognomen.

It is ridiculous for me to speak about Verres now, given that I have just been speaking about Piso Frugi. Still, note what a difference there is between the two ... The one for sure lived up to his name, the other to his epithet.

The figure of Piso Frugi and his legislative track-record enable Cicero in the *Verrines* to formulate a 'socioeconomic ethic' that allows him to skewer the piggish profiteer Verres.[82] As a Roman magistrate he should have lived up to the standards of *frugalitas* that Piso Frugi enshrined in law. Instead, Cicero identifies *frugalitas* as a hallmark of the Sicilians, both collectively and individually. Early on in the second speech of the second *actio*, Cicero elaborates this point in programmatic detail by contrasting the positive qualities of the Sicilians with the contemptible rest of the Greeks while simultaneously assimilating them to the Romans of old – as opposed to the current generation of Romans which has fallen under the spell of Greek idleness and luxury (*Ver.* 2.2.7):[83]

---

[81] Coffee 2017: 100–1.   [82] The term is Coffee's 2017: 100.
[83] Cf. *Flacc.* 71 (in praise of the people of Apollonis – the most frugal in all of Asia in their satisficing devotion to agricultural toil): *Homines sunt tota ex Asia frugalissimi, sanctissimi, a Graecorum luxuria et leuitate remotissimi, patres familias suo*

Ingo Gildenhard

iam uero hominum ipsorum, iudices, ea patientia uirtus frugalitasque est ut proxime ad nostram disciplinam illam ueterem, non ad hanc quae nunc increbruit uideantur accedere: nihil ceterorum simile Graecorum, nulla desidia, nulla luxuries, contra summus labor in publicis priuatisque rebus, summa parsimonia, summa diligentia. sic porro nostros homines diligunt ut iis solis neque publicanus neque negotiator odio sit.

And then again, the hardiness, the excellence, the *frugalitas* of the inhabitants is such that it almost matches our own way of life – that ancestral one not the one that has come to prevail in our generation. In nothing do they resemble the rest of the Greeks: they know no sloth, no luxury – only supreme effort in public and private affairs, supreme thrift, supreme diligence. Moreover, they hold us Romans in such high regard that, uniquely, they dislike neither the tax-collector nor the businessman.

Patientia, *uirtus*, *frugalitas*, *disciplina*, *labor*, *parsimonia* and *diligentia* here face off against *desidia* and *luxuries* across ethnic and generational fault lines: Cicero pushes Verres, as a representative of the current generation of Roman politicians that has lost the ancestral ways, into a Greek corner, while turning the Greeks of Sicily into honourable Romans because of their commitment to old-fashioned virtues (and amiable embrace of Roman rule).[84] At various moments throughout the set of speeches, he reinforces this positive image of the Sicilians, either by praising them collectively as *frugi* or singling out individuals who hail from the island for their *frugalitas*.[85]

Most strikingly, the 'frugality coalition' Cicero marshalls against Verres also includes himself – and *homines noui* more generally. After complaining about the fact that someone like Verres, of certified worthlessness (*nequitia*) and criminal daring

---

contenti, aratores, rusticani; agros habent et natura perbonos et diligentia culturaque meliores.

[84] For discussion see Petrocheilos 1974: 46–7; Pittia 2004: 20.

[85] Collective: *Ver.* 2.3.67: *sunt omnes Siculi non contemnendi, si per nostros magistratus liceat, sed homines et satis fortes et plane frugi ac sobrii, et in primis haec ciuitas de qua loquor, iudices*; individuals: *Ver.* 2.4.39: *Diodorus, homo frugi ac diligens, qui sua seruare uellet, ad propinquum suum scribit ut iis qui a Verre uenissent responderet illud argentum se paucis illis diebus misisse Lilybaeum* (for the construction of the phrase *homo frugi ac diligens* see Spevak 2014: 305–6); *Ver.* 2.5.30: *non defendam Apolloni causam, amici atque hospitis mei, ne tuum iudicium uidear rescindere; nihil de hominis frugalitate, uirtute, diligentia dicam.*

272

Frugalitas, or: The Invention of a Roman Virtue

(*audacia*), enjoys ease of access to and friendship with members of the senatorial elite (*homines magni atque nobiles*) such as Hortensius in striking contrast to the contempt suffered by new men like himself despite their outstanding qualities (*uirtus et integritas*), he lets rip against the perverse preferences of the established nobility, which is hostile to new men of excellent character while courting a scoundrel such as Verres (*Ver.* 2.3.7):[86]

> odistis hominum nouorum industriam, despicitis eorum frugalitatem, pudorem contemnitis, ingenium uero et uirtutem depressam exstinctamque cupitis: Verrem amatis!

> You resent the industry of new men, you look down on their frugality, you scorn their sense of decency, you yearn to see their talent and excellence thwarted and squashed. Yet Verres you love!

Why would they cultivate a relationship with a person who lacks, as Cicero goes on to detail, any kind of excellence (*uirtus*), industry (*industria*), integrity (*innocentia*), sense of decency (*pudor*), sense of shame (*pudicitia*), conversational wit (*sermo*), literary culture (*litterae*) and civilised manners (*humanitas*) and who is the living embodiment of shamefulness (*dedecus*) and disgrace (*turpitudo*), stupidity (*stultitia*) and uncivilised manners (*inhumanitas*) – while rejecting other persons of the highest integrity and prudence (*frugalissimi homines*), who, so Cicero implies, possess all those admirable qualities that Verres so conspicuously lacks? The reason, he submits, is that Verres depends on them for protection – for a corrupt establishment he is a useful minion (2.3.8). Put differently, Cicero here delivers a blast of 'new-man' rhetoric that operates with the countervailing principles of '*homo nouus* = *prisca uirtus*' and 'established *nobilis* = current vice'.[87]

In the *Verrines*, then, the tactical deployment of *frugalitas* serves several interrelated purposes: it is marshalled to contrast the degenerate Verres (and the current *nobilitas* more

---

[86] See also *Ver.* 2.1.71: *homo autem ordinis sui frugalissimus qui tum accensus C. Neroni fuit P. Tettius*; 2.1.137: *M. Iunius patruus pueri frugalissimus homo et castissimus*.

[87] Wiseman 1971.

273

Ingo Gildenhard

generally) with the *maiores*, using the same generational contrast that Calpurnius Piso Frugi, the first *de-repetundis* legislator, frequently draws in his *Annals* (and which ultimately goes back to the *homo nouus* Cato the Elder). On this basis Cicero can draw up a united front against Verres, consisting of the respected *consularis* and censor Calpurnius Piso *Frugi*, Cicero himself in his capacity as *homo nouus* (who embodies ancestral excellence), and the Sicilians, who are cast as honourable Romans, but are also *frugi* (in the sense of useful and subservient allies) and inhabitants of the island of *fruges*. Poised in-between, awkwardly, are the oligarchic power-brokers of the established nobility who have to make up their minds with whom to side, Cicero or the discredited defendant. The specific context of the trial against Verres thus explains the investment Cicero here makes in *frugi* and the abstract noun *frugalitas* (his earliest attested use of it). Adding *frugalitas* to the list of qualities that distinguish the new man proved an attractive move for the purpose of this particular set of speeches, enabled by Piso Frugi, who is repeatedly hailed as the legislator who brought the *repetundae* courts into being.

In speeches delivered after the *Verrines*, Cicero occasionally invokes the ideology of *frugalitas* he configured here, though never again with such elaborate programmatic force. Thus he uses *frugi* and Piso Frugi at *pro Fonteio* 39–40, again in the context of a trial *de repetundis*. This time, however, he acts on the side of the defence and argues that even such an upright individual as Piso Frugi, the very same who set up this type of court and was known for his self-restraint as signalled by his *agnomen*, was at times wrongly accused. As part of this argument Cicero recounts the anecdote that Gaius Gracchus baulked at identifying his adversary by his *agnomen* Frugi (see above 256–7), which serves him as basis for assimilating Fonteius to Piso Frugi: there is not a trace of *libido, petulantia, crudelitas* or *audacia* in his client; rather, the judges see before themselves a prudent and honest man, moderate and self-controlled in every aspect of his life, with a pronounced sense of decency, fully committed to his social and civic obligations

274

Frugalitas, or: The Invention of a Roman Virtue

and profound respect for the gods.[88] As we have seen, *frugi* as such is hardly a proper attribute for a person of high social standing, and it takes the presence of Piso Frugi to make this lexical choice attractive and compelling.[89] The notion of *frugalitas* also makes a cameo appearance in a third trial *de repetundis*. In 59 BCE, Cicero defended Flaccus and, in a rehearsal of his *curriculum uitae*, noticed service under the propraetor M. Pupius Piso Frugi Calpurnianus. The scholiast Bobiensis preserves a fragment, in which Cicero praises Piso for living up to his inherited *cognomen*, the implication being that the defendant manifests similar qualities as his erstwhile superior.[90] And we might also capture a whiff of the '*Frugi*-complex', though without explicit reference, in the *pro Caelio*. The term seems to have played some role in Caelius' self-defence, as attested by Quintilian (*Inst.* 1.6.28–9):[91]

> Haec [sc. Etymologia] habet aliquando usum necessarium, quotiens interpretatione res de qua quaeritur eget, ut cum M. Caelius se esse hominem frugi uult probare, non quia abstinens sit (nam id ne mentiri quidem poterat), sed quia utilis multis, id est fructuosus, unde sit ducta frugalitas.

> Etymology is sometimes of the utmost use, whenever the word under discussion needs interpretation. For instance Marcus Caelius wishes to prove that he is *homo frugi*, not because he is abstemious (for he could not even pretend to be that), but because he is useful to many, that is *fructuosus*, from which *frugalitas* is derived.

If one reads Cicero's biographical trajectory of the defendant with Piso in mind, he gradually matures from someone 'dedicated to the penis' (cf. n. 79 above) into a properly restrained and useful member of Roman society. And Cicero marks this transformation at programmatic moments with reference to *fruges* and *fructus*.[92]

---

[88] *Font.* 40: *frugi igitur hominem, iudices, frugi, inquam, et in omnibus uitae partibus moderatum ac temperantem, plenum pudoris, plenum officii, plenum religionis uidetis.*

[89] Citroni Marchetti 1995: 27. By glossing *frugi* here with *moderatus* and *temperans*, he also endows the term with proto-philosophical qualities reminiscent of Greek σώφρων – a nexus that fully comes into its own in the *Tusculans* (see below).

[90] *M. Pisone, qui cognomen frugalitatis nisi accepisset, ipse peperisset* (Stangl, p. 96, 22–3).

[91] For Quintilian, I cite the text and translation of D. A. Russell in the Loeb Classical Library.

[92] *Cael.* 28, 76, 80.

Finally, he also uses the founder of this branch of the Piso family as a benchmark against which to measure lesser members – such as L. Calpurnius Piso Frugi, one of the consuls of 58, whom he held responsible for his exile. Given his impressively unkempt and sober appearance and a *cognomen* 'that seems to testify that frugality was a hereditary quality of the family' (... *quod erat eo nomine ut ingenerata frugalitas uideretur* ...), people thought – wrongly as it turned out – that he would live up to the high standards set by his ancestors (*Sest.* 21).

To sum up this part: in the *Verrines*, Cicero employs Piso's public persona and his caché as inventor of the *repetundae* courts to discredit Verres. The references to Piso Frugi and *frugalitas* in the *pro Fonteio* and *pro Flacco* also seem motivated primarily by Piso's association with this particular court setting. But, as we have seen, it was not a sufficiently compelling virtue to be consistently used for eulogistic self-labelling, let alone for praising other members of Rome's senatorial elite *without* this particular Piso in the picture. In Cicero's orations, *frugalitas* thus figures as a quality primarily associated with a specific individual (and his *gens*) and hence of limited applicability – rather than a generally accepted ancestral ideal. It is not until the *Tusculan Disputations* in 45 BCE, when *frugalitas* suddenly pops up as the virtue of all Roman virtues. Upon inspection, this second moment of heavy investment also owes itself to a particular set of circumstances and a bubbling creativity (rather than the rehearsal of a generally accepted piece of cultural knowledge).

Tusculan Disputations *(and* Pro Rege Deiotaro*)*

Scholars interested in *frugalitas* tend to start with Cicero's extended discussion of the lexeme in *Tusculan* 3.15–18, where he proposes *frugalitas* as one possible (indeed the best) translation of the Greek term σωφροσύνη and goes on to suggest that it comprises all other *uirtutes*. With appeal to the 'authority' of Cicero, many are then happy to generalise on the basis of this particular passage, positing *frugalitas* as a key value in

276

Frugalitas, or: The Invention of a Roman Virtue

Rome's cultural imaginary since time immemorial. Cicero (one assumes) would have been just as proud and bemused by the success of this conceptual sleight of hand as he was by the jury he misled with his speech on behalf of Cluentius.[93] But there is really no reason why one should fall for his fabulations hook, line and sinker. The text offers sufficient clues for anyone who does not positively *want* to be hoodwinked that his account of *frugalitas* is tailor-made for the thematic economy of the *Tusculans* – and should therefore not be invested with sweeping representative value for Roman thinking on the subject more generally.

Cicero's disquisition on *frugalitas* is part of a (Stoicising) argument that the wise man (*sapiens*) does not experience mental distress (*aegritudo*). At the end of 3.15, Cicero articulates the claim that the wise man is able to use his *ratio* in such a perfect way as to keep his *animus* free of any disorder; and since distress is a disorder of the soul (*aegritudo perturbatio est animi*), the wise man will never experience it (*semper igitur ea sapiens uacabit*). This tenet receives further discussion, which involves the semantics of *frugi* and *frugalitas* (§§ 16–18). In the course of it *frugi* and *sapiens* emerge as virtual synonyms. Cicero concludes this section by revisiting the opening claim: *aberit igitur a sapiente aegritudo* (§ 18). This brief survey shows that for the purpose of his *philosophical* argument *stricto sensu* there was no need to bring *frugalitas* into play at all. We are, rather, dealing with a detour, which Cicero syntactically marks as such (*Tusc.* 3.16):[94]

ueri etiam simile illud est, qui sit temperans – quem Graeci σώφρονα appellant eamque uirtutem σωφροσύνην uocant, quam soleo equidem tum temperantiam, tum moderationem appellare, non numquam etiam modestiam; sed haud scio an recte ea uirtus frugalitas appellari possit, quod angustius apud Graecos ualet, qui frugi homines χρησίμους appellant, id est tantum modo utilis; at illud est latius; omnis enim abstinentia, omnis innocentia (quae apud Graecos usitatum nomen nullum habet, sed habere potest ἀβλάβειαν;

---

[93] Quint. *Inst.* 2.17.21.
[94] For Cicero's *Tusculan Disputations*, I cite the translation of J. E. King in the Loeb Classical Library, with adjustments.

Ingo Gildenhard

nam est innocentia adfectio talis animi quae noceat nemini) – reliquas etiam uirtutes frugalitas continet.

It is also probable that the temperate man – the Greeks call him σώφρων, and they apply the term σωφροσύνη to the virtue which I usually call, sometimes temperance (*temperantia*), sometimes self-control (*moderatio*), and occasionally also discretion (*modestia*); but possibly the virtue could rightly be called *frugalitas*, which has a narrower semantic range with the Greeks, who call 'frugal' men χρήσιμοι, that is to say simply useful; our term has a wider semantic range: all abstinence and all inoffensiveness (which with the Greeks has no customary label, though it is possible to use ἀβλάβεια, harmlessness; for inoffensiveness is a disposition of the soul to injure no one) – *frugalitas* embraces all other virtues as well.

Tellingly, the passage begins with an anacoluthon. What Cicero seems to want to say in the opening sentence is that not just the wise man, but also someone who is *temperans*, is (by and large?) free from mental distress – but then, as King puts it, 'the argument loses itself in a long disgression on terminology written in the *conversational* irregular style which Cicero often adopts in his dialogues'.[95] Whether the argument truly loses itself remains to be seen – but what follows can indeed be labelled a digression of sorts, pegged on to Cicero's use of *temperans* and the corresponding Greek term (σώφρων), which leads to *frugi* and *frugalitas* coming into play. Cicero is up front about the fact that *frugalitas* is anything but an orthodox translation of σωφροσύνη.[96] On previous occasions (cf. *soleo*), he went for a range of alternative possibilities to render the concept into Latin, such as *temperantia, moderatio* or *modestia*. All three offer a better fit – and indeed continue to serve him nicely as Latin equivalents of σωφροσύνη in any text but the *Tusculans*, such as the *de Officiis*, composed a year later. Here, however, he wonders whether *frugalitas* is not suited best – even though he has to concede that any such suggestion runs into problems. After all, the well-established Greek lexical equivalent to Latin *frugi* is χρήσιμος, in the

---

[95] King 1927: 242.

[96] On the difficulties of translating σωφροσύνη see North 1966 and Malherbe 2013: 466–72. Conversely, there *is* a Greek equivalent to *frugalitas*, i.e. φειδώ/φειδωλία, which has no particular philosophical force.

278

Frugalitas, or: The Invention of a Roman Virtue

narrow sense of 'useful'. To validate the felicity of *frugi/frugalitas* as Latin glosses on Greek σώφρων/σωφροσύνη, Cicero insists, rightly, that *frugi* has a somewhat wider semantic range than χρήσιμος: as we have seen, in addition to 'useful', 'serviceable' (the core meaning of χρήσιμος), it can also have moral connotations ('of sound character').[97] But he exaggerates when he claims that the concept of *frugalitas*, especially as articulated in the attribute *frugi*, comprises *omnis ... abstinentia, omnis innocentia*: given that *frugi* is an attribute primarily associated with slaves and other persons of low social standing, there is a potential tension between its two principal meanings 'useful' and 'morally sound': as discussed, the two qualities may coincide – but also be at variance with one another. Yet his emphatically anaphoric continuation with *omnis enim abstinentia, omnis innocentia* would seem to suggest that every kind of abstinence and harmlessness is a natural quality of a *homo frugi* – even though Cicero never spells this out, perhaps because he realised that such an assertion would have been a step too far. Instead, he offers up a parenthetical dig at the Greeks and the moral deficiencies of their lexicon, homing in on an apparent semantic void for 'harmlessness' in Greek, which has no directly corresponding equivalent to Latin *innocentia* – it would be, so Cicero suggests, ἀβλάβεια, which he proffers as a neologism of his own coinage. The insidious subtext here is that the lexical void signals the absence of the phenomenon – implying that all Greeks are somehow morally compromised. After the parenthesis, we get a restart of the sentence – which means that the nominative phrases *omnis enim abstinentia, omnis innocentia* are left hanging in another anacoluthon.[98] Out of this syntactic rupture

---

[97] Cicero glosses over the fact that the adjective χρηστός offers a better Greek match for *frugi* than χρήσιμος in that it also combines the two aspects of 'serviceable', 'useful' and 'good', 'honest', 'worthy'.

[98] See Pinkster 2015: 1211: 'the sentence starts with two constituents in the nominative. After the parenthesis the sentence continues with *reliquas enim virtutes* in the accusative, as object of *continet*. This is clearly a failed construction (an "anacoluthon"), for which sometimes the term NOMINATIVUS PENDENS is used.'

279

Ingo Gildenhard

comes Cicero's monumental pronouncement that *frugalitas* comprises all other virtues as well.

In light of the previous history of the lexeme, this claim is as grandiose as it is counterintuitive. Cicero knows this – and tries to muster evidence to endow his contention with some credibility (*Tusc.* 3.16–17):

quae nisi tanta esset, et si is angustiis, quibus plerique putant, teneretur, numquam esset L. Pisonis cognomen tanto opere laudatum. sed quia, nec qui propter metum praesidium reliquit, quod est ignauiae, nec qui propter auaritiam clam depositum non reddidit, quod est iniustitiae, nec qui propter temeritatem male rem gessit, quod est stultitiae, frugi appellari solet, eo tris uirtutes, fortitudinem iustitiam prudentiam, frugalitas complexa est (etsi hoc quidem commune est uirtutum; omnes enim inter se nexae et iugatae sunt): reliqua igitur et quarta uirtus sit ipsa frugalitas. eius enim uidetur esse proprium motus animi adpetentis regere et sedare semperque aduersantem libidini moderatam in omni re seruare constantiam. cui contrarium uitium nequitia dicitur.

Had the meaning [sc. of *frugi*] not been so comprehensive and been confined to the narrow limits of common usage, it would never have become the much eulogised surname of L. Piso. But because neither the man who through fear has deserted his post (a characteristic of cowardice), nor the man who through avarice has failed to restore a deposit privately entrusted to him (a characteristic of injustice) nor the man who through rashness has mismanaged a business transaction (a characteristic of imprudence), are usually called 'frugal', 'frugality' has come to include the three virtues of courage, justice and prudence (though this is a feature common to the virtues; for they are all mutually linked and bound together). So let frugality itself be the remaining, fourth virtue: it seems to be its special function to guide and compose the eager impulses of the soul and, by a constant opposition to lust, to preserve on every occasion a tempered consistency. The vice which is its opposite is called 'worthlessness' (*nequitia*).

The paragraph advances two inconclusive (if not outright flawed) arguments before concluding with the grand fiat (*sit ... frugalitas*) that turns *frugalitas* into the fourth virtue. First, against those who maintain that the semantic range of *frugalitas* is too narrow in scope for it to function as an umbrella-virtue, Cicero summons the *agnomen* of Piso Frugi. Yet while it is true that Piso's adoption of the epithet into his nomenclature significantly broadened its meaning and appeal, the allegation that he adopted *frugi* because of its broad

Frugalitas, or: The Invention of a Roman Virtue

meaning and positive connotations is (as we have seen) clearly false, and even the semantic rewiring of *frugi* by Piso never managed to endow the concept of *frugalitas* with the kind of comprehensive centrality in Rome's universe of values that Cicero claims for it here. In a second argument, Cicero, implicitly operating with the Platonic and Stoic notion of four cardinal virtues, notes that someone who is a coward, greedily unjust or foolish in economic matters would not be called *frugi*, and on this basis posits that *frugalitas* also comprises the qualities of *fortitudo*, *iustitia* and *prudentia*.[99] The reasoning is dubious – and ultimately beside the point: exactly the same kind of argument could be made for the other Latin equivalents for σωφροσύνη, i.e. *temperantia, moderatio* and *modestia*. The slippage into the Stoic doctrine that (a) all virtues are interrelated and (b) that there are four cardinal ones and the inclusion of *frugalitas* within the set enables Cicero to assert what he needed to prove, namely that *frugalitas* is a better Latin term for (Stoic) σωφροσύνη than any of the well-established alternatives.

Cicero goes on to explore the etymological implications of *frugalitas* and its antonym *nequitia* in a ludic spirit possibly inspired by Varro;[100] and returns, via a series of conceptual associations (*frugi > moderatus et temperans > constans > quietus > perturbatione omni/aegritudine uacuus > sapiens*), to the thesis of the third *Tusculan Disputation*, namely that the wise man does not experience distress (*Tusc.* 3.18):

frugalitas, ut opinor, a fruge, qua nihil melius e terra, nequitia ab eo (etsi erit hoc fortasse durius, sed temptemus: lusisse putemur, si nihil sit) ab eo, quod nequicquam est in tali homine, ex quo idem 'nihili' dicitur. – qui sit frugi igitur uel, si mauis, moderatus et temperans, eum necesse est esse constantem; qui autem constans, quietum; qui quietus, perturbatione omni uacuum,

---

[99] For the (complex) Roman reception of the Greek canon of four cardinal virtues see Classen 2010: 320–31 ('Plato's virtues in Rome').

[100] Cf. Gellius in his disquisition on *leuitas* and *nequitia* (6.11.8): *M. Varro in libris De Lingua Latina, 'ut ex "non" et ex "uolo",' inquit, '"nolo", sic ex "ne" et "quicquam", media syllaba extrita, compositum est "nequam".'* Cf. also 6.11.2 about the 'classical' semantics of *nequam*: *'nequam' hominem nihili rei neque frugis bonae, quod genus Graeci fere* ἄσωτον *uel* ἀκόλαστον *dicunt.*

Ingo Gildenhard

ergo etiam aegritudine. et sunt illa sapientis: aberit igitur a sapiente aegritudo.

'Frugality', I think, is derived from 'fruit' (*frux*) and nothing better comes from the earth: 'worthlessness' is derived – this may well be a bit of a stretch, but let me try it out: consider it a joke if it should come to nothing – from that which is *nequicquam* ('no thing') in such a person; hence he is also said to be 'good-for-nothing'. The man therefore who is 'frugal' or, should you prefer it, self-restrained and temperate must be consistent; the consistant man must be calm; the calm man must be free from all disturbance, therefore free from distress as well. All these are characteristics of the wise man. Therefore distress will keep far away from the wise man.

Put differently, he here retraces in inverse order the lexemes that he started out with. If at 3.15–16 he moved from *sapiens* to *temperans/moderatus* to *frugi*, he here moves from *frugi* to *moderatus/temperans* to *constans* and *quietus* and ends with *sapiens*. Overall, then, the 'digression' has a clear purpose, namely the assimilation, indeed identification, of the (Roman) *homo frugi* with the (Stoic) figure of the *sapiens*, via the translation of σωφροσύνη with *frugalitas* – even though the arguments proffered in favour of this proposition are tenuous or contrived. This raises two questions. First, why does Cicero go to such trouble to establish the identity of 'being wise' and 'being frugal'? And second, why, in the *Tusculans*, is he so keen on endowing *frugalitas* with such central importance and comprehensive remit?

To make headway with the second question, i.e. how we are to explain Cicero's – soon abandoned – experiment with and investment in *frugalitas*, we need to get the overall rationale of his philosophical writings into view. In a nutshell, his *point of departure* is the political crisis of the 50s (Cicero, the saviour of Rome, exiled and marginalised; the city in crisis) and 40s (an autocrat in charge); his *mission* is the recovery of perceived ancestral wisdom and excellence in personal conduct and civic affairs with the help of Greek (philosophical) thought and intellectual techniques; and the enabling *premise* is the ultimate identity of the nomological knowledge evolved and enacted by the Roman ancestors and the theoretical knowledge that the best of the Greek thinkers later (!) codified in philosophical

282

Frugalitas, or: The Invention of a Roman Virtue

discourse. Within this framework, Cicero's writings have a twofold purpose: (a) to help solve the current political malaise of the Roman *res publica*, not least through investment in education: Cicero construes the reason for the breakdown of the ancestral commonwealth (hailed as the historical realisation of the most perfect of all possible civic communities, the instantiation, in Roman history, of a Platonic ideal) as a failure in traditional educational discipline, which he set out to remedy both within and by means of his literary works; and he achieves this by (b) articulating a philosophy in Latin that is based on but ultimately superior to its Greek counterpart. Put differently, Cicero's theoretical enterprise and its political thrust can be summarised as follows: he employs Greek philosophical thought to reform Roman political practice – and (ancestral) Roman political practice (and the cultural knowledge which it enacts) to critique and outclass Greek philosophical thought.[101]

How does the disquisition on *frugalitas* in *Tusculan* 3 fit into this overarching agenda? On the most basic level, he domesticates key tenets of Stoic doctrine by relating them to familiar Roman concepts. Relating the potentially unfamiliar to the familiar is good pedagogy – and highlights the benefits to be derived from a more systematic study of Greek philosophical thought. Arena puts it well:

in his attempt to show that early Latin speakers adopted a language and a norm on mental derangement that were in tune with later Stoic thinking, Cicero, one may suggest, appears to be engaged in an important cultural operation. He seems to provide the members of the political elite, not so versed in philosophy, with a compendium of philosophical systems that lie at the foundations of their political language and, as such, remind them of the role that the study of philosophy should play in the political conflicts of the time.[102]

But this apparent embrace of Greek cultural resources captures only half of the dialectic movement Cicero performs

---

[101] For a more detailed exposition of Cicero's philosophical project, with particular emphasis on the *Tusculan Disputations*, see Gildenhard 2007a.

[102] Arena 2011: 309.

283

Ingo Gildenhard

whenever he engages with Greek philosophy, as a passage in Book 4 illustrates (*Tusc.* 4.36–7):

> atque ut haec tabificae mentis perturbationes sunt, aegritudinem dico et metum, sic hilariores illae, cupiditas auide semper aliquid expetens et inanis alacritas, id est laetitia gestiens, non multum differunt ab amentia. ex quo intellegitur, qualis ille sit, quem tum moderatum, alias modestum temperantem, alias constantem continentemque dicimus; non numquam haec eadem uocabula ad frugalitatis nomen tamquam ad caput referre uolumus. quodnisi eo nomine uirtutes continerentur, numquam ita peruolgatum illud esset, ut iam prouerbii locum optineret, 'hominem frugi omnia recte facere'. quod idem cum Stoici de sapiente dicunt, nimis admirabiliter nimisque magnifice dicere uidentur. (37) ergo hic, quisquis est, qui moderatione et constantia quietus animo est sibique ipse placatus, ut nec tabescat molestiis nec frangatur timore nec sitienter quid expetens ardeat desiderio nec alacritate futili gestiens deliquescat, is est sapiens quem quaerimus, is est beatus, cui nihil humanarum rerum aut intolerabile ad demittendum animum aut nimis laetabile ad ecferendum uideri potest.

Moreover, just like these corroding disorders of the mind, i.e. distress and fear, so those more cheerful emotions – desire always greedily coveting something and empty eagerness, that is, exuberant delight – are not far different from aberration of mind. This illustrates the character of the person whom I describe as 'self-controlled' (*moderatum*) or 'disciplined' (*modestum*) or 'temperate' (*temperantem*) or 'consistent and self-contained' (*constantem continentemque*). At times, I am inclined to subsume all of these terms under the concept of frugality as their prime source. For unless the virtues had been comprehended in this term it would never have come so widely into common use that by now it passes for a proverb that 'the frugal man does everything aright,' exactly what the Stoics say of the 'wise man,' but when they do so, their language is held to be too high-flown and grandiloquent. (37) Therefore the man, whoever he is, whose soul is tranquillised by restraint and consistency and who is at peace with himself, so that he neither pines away in distress, nor is broken down by fear, nor consumed with a thirst of longing in pursuit of some ambition, nor maudlin in the exuberance of meaningless eagerness – he is the wise man whom we seek, he is the happy man who can think no human occurrence insupportable to the point of dispiriting him, or unduly delightful to the point of rousing him to ecstasy.

In this follow-up to the disquisition at the outset of *Tusculan* 3, Cicero claims in the spirit of 3.16 that *frugi/frugalitas* encompass related terms such as *moderatus* (~ *moderatio*), *modestus* (~ *modestia*), *temperans* (~ *temperantia*), *constans* (~ *constantia*), *continens* (~ *continentia*) and establishes *frugi* as a down-

284

Frugalitas, or: The Invention of a Roman Virtue

to-earth and thoroughly Roman equivalent to the grandiloquent (Stoic) *sapiens*. What matters here is not so much Cicero's renewed effort to marshall further (dubious) evidence for the proto-philosophical significance of *frugi*, which he does with sly humour.[103] It is, rather, the explicit attack on the Stoics, whom he censures for their conceit. Embedded within this explicit identification of the Roman *homo frugi* with the Stoic *sapiens* is a threefold assertion of Roman superiority. First, the fact that *frugalitas* is an ancestral value implies chronological priority over Stoic theorising. Second, the proverb proves wide dissemination and demotic appeal: by projecting Stoic idiom, figures of thought and conceptual parameters back into Rome's ancestral cultural imaginary, Cicero promotes the Romans as always already committed to proto-Stoic ideals. And third, the dismissal of the Stoics for their rhetorical grandstanding feeds right into Roman prejudices about voluble and boastful Greeks in general and the rhetorical-didactic ineptitude of the Stoics in particular.[104]

So Cicero's point is decidedly not that the Romans need to study philosophy per se – his point is rather that they ought to use philosophy to re-discover and revalidate an ethics that sustained Rome's commonwealth in the past. Philosophy is a Greek heuristic device for recapturing and valorising anew the quintessence of ancestral Rome. This wisdom continues to register in pre-philosophical (ordinary) language. If in the preface to *de Republica* he advances the claim that statesmen anticipated in practice what philosophers later on articulated in discourse (following Dicaearchus),[105] in the *Tusculans* he takes this approach a decisive step further: the enacted ideals, he now claims, also found decisive discursive codification within the Latin language. His syncrisis of Greek and Roman value terms is designed to prove that, at least from the point of view of ethics, Latin is the superior language in which to do

---

[103] For *non numquam* ('on occasion') read: 'precisely once before, in the previous book'; and the proverbial saying he cites is so common that it is transmitted nowhere else.

[104] See e.g. Wardy 1996; Atherton 1988.

[105] For Cicero and Dicaearchus see McConnell 2012.

Ingo Gildenhard

philosophy. Conversely, of course, it is precisely this polemic drubbing of the Stoics that enables Cicero to ground the ideal figure of Stoic philosophy firmly within Roman common sense: the correction buttresses (partly by obfuscating) the cooption.

But why did Cicero, in the *Tusculans* but nowhere else, deem it advantageous to centre his system of ancestral-philosophical values in *frugalitas*? He seems to have passed over the term in the *de Republica* (where he advances a very similar argument about the proto-philosophical qualities of the Roman people as here); and in the (also Stoicising) *de Officiis, frugalitas* again disappears from view. To make headway here (and therefore also set up his use of *frugalitas* in the contemporary speech on behalf of king Deiotarus), a more detailed look at changes in historical context – and how they inflect Cicero's writings – may pay dividends. Within his philosophical *oeuvre*, it is possible to distinguish three phases: (i) the 50s BCE, when the *res publica* was (still) more or less extant (*de Orat.*, *Rep.* and *Leg.*); (ii) 46 until the Ides of March 44 BCE, when (in Cicero's pregnant formulation) the *res publica* was 'lost' (*amissa*) (*Brut.*, *Hort.*, *Tusc.* etc.); and (iii) 44/43 BCE, after the murder of Caesar led to the revival (however brief) of the republican common-wealth. Cicero's writings in phases (i) and (iii) manifest a somewhat different profile of priorities and preferences from those that date to phase (ii). In works dating to (i) and (iii), for instance, Cicero ranks oratory over philosophy (or, put differently, active participation in civic life over *cognitio ueri*); in phase (ii), he *seems* to prefer philosophy to oratory.[106] This should not surprise – or be considered a contradiction: in a situation where active participation in civic life has become impossible, the pursuit of theoretical insight and individual self-sufficiency enabled by philosophy rises in importance. It is of course crucial to appreciate that Cicero reshuffles his priorities only under political duress: his ranking of philosophy above oratory stands as an indictment of Caesar's autocratic

[106] Gildenhard 2007a: 152–5.

Frugalitas, or: The Invention of a Roman Virtue

erasure of the public sphere and hence the option to partake meaningfully in the administration of the commonwealth.

The same logic manifests itself also in different conceptions of *uirtus*: in works dating to phases (i) and (iii), Cicero insists, unequivocally, that *uirtus* must be applied in practice: *in usu sui tota posita est* (*Rep.* 1.2); in phase (ii) he is much invested in the self-sufficiency of *uirtus*, which does not *require* application in socio-political practice.[107] More generally, Cicero foregrounds a different set of virtues in phases (i) and (iii) in comparison and contrast to phase (ii). In the former, the principal virtue is *iustitia* as enacted by a philosophically trained *gubernator ciuitatis* in a civic context. In the latter, we get a privileging of such virtues as *grauitas*, *constantia* or *frugalitas* – embodied by a philosophically trained *sapiens*, who could (and ought to) make a meaningful contribution to a functioning republican commonwealth but is also able to exist happily under a tyrannical regime such as Caesar's, owing to the self-sufficient supremacy of his *uirtus*. Put differently, Cicero's *philosophical* investment in *frugalitas* belongs to phase (ii) of his theoretical writings, when he had specific reasons for validating Roman notions of self-restraint and self-sufficiency as a means of coping with tyranny.

In the *Tusculans*, Cicero's investment in *frugalitas* thus has a triple thrust: (a) by comparing and contrasting the Latin term to equivalent Greek ones, Cicero illustrates the proto-philosophical qualities of the Latin language and its superiority to Greek for articulating profound ethical truths, thereby challenging the prevailing *communis opinio* that Greek was better suited to philosophy than Latin;[108] (b) the sense of self-restraint, moderation and self-discipline built into *frugalitas* – along the Greek virtue of σωφροσύνη – contrasts sharply with the boundless desire and excessive passions of the tyrant and conversely, as a quality that enables proto-philosophical

---

[107] Gildenhard 2007a: 128–30.
[108] Cf. Lucretius' complaints about the limits of the Latin lexicon (esp. 1.136–9 and 3.258–61) or Sen. *Ep.* 58.1: *quanta uerborum nobis paupertas, immo egestas sit, numquam magis quam hodierno die intellexi*, further Fögen 2000.

Ingo Gildenhard

self-sufficiency, offers an antidote to the pathologies of the soul (*aegritudines*) bound to affect those forced to live under a tyrannical regime like that of Caesar; and (c) as an ancestral virtue *frugalitas* evokes a period in Roman history when a republican system of government flourished and thereby forms a basis not just for coping with, but resisting autocratic power.

In the *pro rege Deiotaro*, a speech delivered in the same year he composed the *Tusculan Disputations*, Cicero puts this proto-philosophical conception of *frugalitas* to use on behalf of his client, the Galatian king Deiotarus, who stood accused of trying to poison Caesar. Caesar himself sat in judgement – a scenario Cicero manipulates to construe the dilemma that the verdict on the defendant is simultaneously a verdict on the judge: if Caesar decides in favour of the prosecution, he is a savage tyrant; if he decides in favour of the defendant, he is a 'good' *king* – like Deiotarus. Towards the end of the speech, Cicero brings *frugalitas* into play to repudiate the claim that Deiotarus was overjoyed when he received the news that Caesar's underling Domitius had perished in a shipwreck and Caesar was beset with difficulties during his African campaign (*Deiot.* 26):[109]

quid deinde? furcifer quo progreditur? ait hac laetitia Deiotarum elatum uino se obruisse in conuiuioque nudum saltauisse. quae crux huic fugitiuo potest satis supplici adferre? Deiotarum saltantem quisquam aut ebrium uidit umquam? omnes sunt in illo rege uirtutes, quod te, Caesar, ignorare non arbitror, sed praecipue singularis et admiranda frugalitas. etsi hoc uerbo scio laudari regem non solere. frugi hominem dici non multum habet laudis in rege; fortem iustum seuerum grauem magni animi largum beneficum liberalem – hae sunt regiae laudes, illa priuata est. ut uolet quisque, accipiat. ego tamen frugalitatem id est modestiam et temperantiam, uirtutem maximam iudico. haec in illo est ab ineunte aetate cum a cuncta Asia, cum a magistratibus legatisque nostris, tum ab equitibus Romanis qui in Asia negotiati sunt, perspecta et cognita.

And what next? What is the next assertion of this villain? He says that Deiotarus, elated by the glee this news inspired, fuddled himself with wine and danced naked at a banquet. Can crucifixion inflict adequate punishment upon this runaway? Has anyone ever seen Deiotarus either drunk or

---

[109] I cite the (adjusted) translation of N. H. Watts in the Loeb Classical Library.

288

Frugalitas, or: The Invention of a Roman Virtue

dancing? This king is an exemplar of all the virtues, as I think you, Caesar, know well enough; but in nothing is he more remarkable and more admirable than in his sobriety (*frugalitas*), even though I know that kings are not commonly praised in such terms. To be called a sober person does not convey much commendation to a king. Bravery, justice, earnestness, dignity, magnanimity, liberality, kindliness, generosity – these are the qualities we commend in a king; sobriety in a subject. Everyone is free to put what construction he pleases upon my words; none the less I pronounce sobriety (*frugalitas*), by which I mean self-discipline and temperance, to be the highest virtue. His possession of this virtue from his earliest youth was recognised and attested not only by the whole of Asia and by our magistrates and ambassadors, but also by the Roman knights who carried on business in Asia.

There are several points to note here, especially with reference to the *Tusculans*. To begin with, it is telling that Cicero conceptualises the universe of values differently: while Deiotarus may share in all virtues (*omnes sunt in illo rege uirtutes*), all *uirtutes* are here not subsumed under *frugalitas* – even though *frugalitas* is singled out as the highest virtue and the one virtue in which Deiotarus is most distinguished. Cicero concedes (again in implicit contrast to the *Tusculans* where he pointedly ignored the humble milieu in which *frugi* was initially – and continued to be primarily – at home) that praising a king of all people as *frugi* is counterintuitive: *fortitudo, iustitia, seueritas, grauitas, magnitudo animi, largitio, beneuolentia* and *liberalitas* are obvious aristocratic-royal virtues; just as obviously, *frugalitas* is not. And he 'rescues' *frugalitas* from all-too negative associations with slavery by calling it a *uirtus priuata*, i.e. a virtue that manifests itself above all not in magistrates and kings, but in the generally sound disposition of individuals that do not hold public office or are subjects. Cicero does not deny that Deiotarus possesses all the *uirtutes regiae* that he enumerates; but he elevates *frugalitas*, which he identifies, in a clarifying gloss, with the philosophical qualities of *modestia* and *temperantia* (in Greek σωφροσύνη), into the highest of the virtues (*maxima uirtus*).

This surprising operation, which draws on the conceptual work on *frugalitas* Cicero had done in the *Tusculans* but tweaks the semantic and rhetorical profile of the term to the

289

Ingo Gildenhard

exigencies of the occasion, helps to exculpate Deiotarus and put pressure on Caesar. The argument here is subtle and insidious. First, Cicero, by establishing a category of virtues he calls 'royal' and including among the so-called *uirtutes regiae* a number of qualities for which Caesar too is known, he assimilates the Roman dictator to a foreign potentate: 'The *imperatoris uirtutes* [of the *pro Marcello* and the *pro Ligario*] turn into *regiae laudes*. The Roman commander is compared to a foreign king.'[110] Then, in a second step, he claims that this particular king is not your stereotypical king at all. The quality of *frugalitas*, which is not primarily grounded in the sphere of politics, but refers to a proto-philosophical and arch-Roman disposition along the lines developed by Cicero in the *Tusculans*, emerges as the most distinctive hallmark of Deiotarus. A cross-transference turns the Roman Caesar into someone resembling a foreign king/tyrant and the foreign king Deiotarus into an upright (ancestral) Roman. The quality of *frugalitas*, understood in the sense of proto-philosophical self-restraint, squashes any implication of excessive ambition or other forms of incontinence such as alcoholism or exhibitionism. Deiotarus is more a philosopher than a king, and hence hardly a threat to Caesar. And if Caesar wishes to avoid associations with tyranny, he would be well advised to practice some moderation himself – starting with a verdict of innocence for Deiotarus.

The sense of *frugalitas* in the *pro rege Deiotaro* thus builds on its equation with σωφροσύνη in the *Tusculans* and develops the concept further by positioning it explicitly within an autocratic context: its labelling as a *uirtus priuata* brings to mind its early career as a quality associated with slaves and other low-ranking individuals who had no share in the Roman field of power. In a situation of autocracy, this condition of disempowerment potentially included everybody, even (other) kings: all are ultimately subservient to the reigning potentate. Because of its peculiar history *frugalitas* could articulate an

---

[110] Peer 2008: 200; further Classen 2010: 326.

Frugalitas, or: The Invention of a Roman Virtue

ethics of self-sufficiency that retained some aristocratic-republican prestige but could also accommodate a withdrawal from socio-political life – and as such was a mental disposition ideally suited to ensure survival under tyrannical regimes, while also drawing attention to a situation of virtual enslavement. The career of the term in the early empire bears out this inbuilt duplicity: members of the (senatorial) elite hail *frugalitas* as an aristocratic value that brings to mind both (philosophically informed) self-restraint and ancestral (republican) discipline and therefore constitutes a perfect quality for the empowered subaltern who wants to signal, to equal degrees, both accommodation to a system in which a monarch is in charge (implying a condition of servitude for everyone else – as Caligula saw fit to spell out) and independence.[111] The great irony for Cicero (and those classicists who believe in the tales he tells) is that, rather than looking back to the heydays of the republic with his definition of *frugalitas* in *Tusculans* and the *pro rege Deiotaro*, he is looking forward to the realities of the imperial period. The semi-depoliticised, philosophical understanding of *frugalitas*, suitably ennobled by its labelling as ancestral in Cicero's oeuvre, makes it a *uirtus priuata* ideally suited for an aristocracy that needs to redefine itself in relation to the *princeps* – from whose own perspective, however, everyone else may well appear the equivalent of a slave.

In the light of the discussion so far, it is worth returning briefly to a question posed at the outset, namely why Cicero does not use *frugalitas* where one would expect the term to appear if the orthodox understanding of the concept were true. The first thing to note is that until the *Tusculans* the only context in which Cicero operates with the notion at all are, apart from the odd invocation of Piso Frugi as a positive foil for his degenerate descendants, orations that have to do with *repetundae* cases, where again Piso Frugi, in his role as author of the legislation that established this particular *quaestio*, accounts for its presence. Until the *Tusculans*, then, *frugalitas*,

[111] For Caligula see Introduction 80–2

291

Ingo Gildenhard

at least within Rome's aristocratic milieu, was a value tied to a specific individual, *gens* and court and avoided in other contexts – which ought not to surprise given its original and primary association with slaves and freedmen. Even Piso's caché was apparently insufficient to justify its deployment as a general value-term outside the *repetundae* courts. This explains (for instance) why Cicero steered clear of *frugalitas* in the long list of virtues he marshalls in praise of Pompey in the *pro lege Manilia* – where *frugalitas* in the sense Cicero develops for the first time in the *Tusculans* would have made a perfect fit.

Only in the *Tusculans* does *frugalitas* feature as the Roman virtue par excellence, as the Latin equivalent of σωφροσύνη – a seemingly perplexing rise to prominence best explained with reference to the peculiar political circumstances at the time of writing: Cicero here further ennobles an original slave-value that enabled him to combine ancestral discipline (and hence commitment to a nostalgic republicanism) with the inner disposition necessary to cope with conditions of tyranny. The transformation of *frugalitas* into the virtue of all virtues, however, rested on shaky arguments and evidence. Accordingly, Cicero dispensed with *frugalitas* when the political situation changed drastically yet again on the Ides of March 44 BCE. With the dictator dead, he could return to conceptual choices better aligned with the traditional semantics of the republican commonwealth, where *frugalitas* only ever featured marginally. After Caesar's assassination and the concomitant revival of the *res publica*, Cicero abandons the experiment with *frugalitas* and the investment in *uirtus* as primarily an inner disposition and reverts to a conception of *uirtus* grounded in its practical application, above all in politics. As a treatise in civic ethics, the *de Officiis* has a lot to say about the responsible use of material resources in the public sphere;[112] but Cicero's operational categories are *beneficentia*, *liberalitas* and *magnificentia* or *largitio*, *cupiditas*, *auaritia* and *inliberalitas*, among

---

[112] See e.g. *Off.* 1.68 or 2.56–64.

292

Frugalitas, or: The Invention of a Roman Virtue

others – and decidedly not *frugalitas*. Yet his conceptual creativity under Caesar set the stage for the stellar career of the term in the early imperial period when the lexeme *frugalitas* finally comes fully into its own.

Further Developments: The Early Principate

To review the results of our discussion so far: there is no evidence at all that the Roman elite cultivated *frugalitas* as one of its virtues before the second half of the second century BCE, when Piso Frugi decided to turn a slur into a slogan and elevate the attribute *frugi* into a label that signified thrift and self-restraint across a wide range of activities and settings, such as sexual urges, the use of (public) wealth or consumption of food and drink. Piso's social uplift of what was originally a slave-characteristic proved enabling for Cicero's conceptual innovations. His writings (a) continue the traditional use of *frugi* as a desirable quality in persons of low social status, but also (b) significantly strengthen the semantic strand brought into being by Piso Frugi, not least by (c) endowing the abstract noun *frugalitas* with proto-philosophical significance by turning it into a novel Latin equivalent of σωφροσύνη and (d) promoting its use as a *uirtus* that fuses republican nostalgia (via Piso Frugi) with the principled self-restraint that behooves an ethically upright member of the ruling elite, especially in autocratic regimes.

As a result, by the end of the republic *frugalitas* had joined other terms signifying thrift, austerity, self-restraint and diligence, such as *diligentia, industria, moderatio, modestia, modus, parsimonia* or *temperantia*. But unlike its quasi-synonymous brethren, with their comparatively narrow scope of meanings and rather bland semantics, *frugalitas*, as a specifically Roman mode of self-restraint, possessed a stunning degree of what one might label 'interstitial complexity'. Owing to the decisive interventions of Piso Frugi and Cicero, who radically expanded the traditional semantics of *frugi* and *frugalitas*, the noun now encompassed a range of frequently conflicting associations. It could be used with reference to

Ingo Gildenhard

diverse social milieux and types (from slave to freedman to senator to king), blended Greek philosophy with Roman (agricultural) realities, coordinated republican pasts with the autocratic present and mingled ethics with economics – but all in rather loose and ambiguous ways, with several inbuilt and unresolved contradictions that could accommodate a wide range of attitudes towards wealth in particular: *frugalitas* in the sense of thrift could be a strategy for maximising profit, but in the sense of 'self-restraint' it could also signify a 'satisficing' approach towards resource management and lifestyle. And as an economic and/or ethical *habitus* it did not conflict with a great, indeed even an obscene, amount of wealth.[113]

One should of course beware of falling into the trap of the 'pansemantic fallacy', i.e. the assumption that in any given use of a specific word all of its meanings listed in a dictionary are (equally) in play.[114] At the same time, in the case of *frugalitas* we should reckon with the possibility that authors found the term appealing precisely because of its ideological polyvalency.[115] In fact, its Janus-faced, interstitial nature (slave/freedman/senator/autocrat, Greek/Roman, ethics/economics, republican past/imperial present) has an analogue in the complex position of various elites in the socio-political and cultural fields of power of the principate: as empowered subalterns, senators and other high-ranking and well-educated individuals partook in ruling the world and were yet beholden to the emperor and were equally steeped in Greek (philosophical)

---

[113] For the terms see Osborne 2009: 103: 'Peasants tend to be modelled as pursuing "satisficing" rather than "maximizing" strategies, and effectively content with their economic lot.'

[114] See West 1995a: 13; 1995b: 160–1; 1998: 65–6. Cf. Gaskin 2013: 190.

[115] Cf. Citroni Marchetti 1995: 27 n. 23: 'La *frugalitas* può apparire virtù più privata che pubblica [with reference to *Deiot.* 26]... Ma essa può anche essere considerata alla base dell'assenza di passionalità [with reference to *Tusc.* 3.18]... È in quanto la *frugalitas* garantisce la resistenza agli impulsi [~ *Tusc.* 3.17] che può considerarsi particolarmente idonea per definire un magistrato corretto. Nella *Pro Fonteio* essa è chiamata a colorare l'ambito romano in quanto opposto alla *libido* dei barbari.' We should not assume, however, that the notion of *frugalitas* possessed the semantic range we find in Cicero's *oeuvre* independent of it. Cicero does not simply employ the term in senses already established; rather, it is he who re-defines and expands the semantic range of *frugalitas* in innovative ways.

294

Frugalitas, or: The Invention of a Roman Virtue

culture and Roman historical traditions. These agendas often interlock with the posture of self-restrained omnipotence and its faux-republican credentials adopted by those *principes* interested in being deemed *ciuilis* – as a particular brand of autocratic ideology and its occasional rejection.[116] It should therefore not surprise that authors of the triumviral and early imperial period accorded *frugi*, *frugalitas* and related lexemes a salient role in their literary projects and their authorial self-fashioning. Horace, Valerius Maximus, Seneca the Elder, Petronius, Seneca the Younger, Quintilian and Pliny the Younger (to list those considered below in rough chronological order) all brought **frug*–terms into play for a range of reasons: to position themselves or their characters in socio-political space; to define what it is to be Roman; to flesh out a (specifically Roman) ethics of self-restraint, for educational purposes in rhetoric or philosophy; to comment on aspects of the economics of status, in particular to gain conceptual purchase on the phenomenon of social mobility and the fluid interface of wealth and power; or to negotiate the imperial present while evoking ancestral-republican values.

Horace

In *Annales* 8, Ennius included within an overall appreciation of the distinguished *nobilis* Geminus Servilius a portrait of a good companion, with whom Servilius is said to have spent those few hours of leisure not taken up by matters of state and warfare.[117] He imagines an individual who is low of rank but makes up for lack of pedigree with a rich portfolio of personal qualities: he is trustworthy (280: *fidelis*) and pleasant (280: *suauis*, *iucundus*; 281: *commodus*), full of good social sense and tact (he knows when to talk and when to remain silent), deeply knowledgeable about antiquarian matters both civic

---

[116] On the figure of the *princeps ciuilis* see the classic study by Wallace-Hadrill 1982; further Introduction 75–101.

[117] *Ann.* 8.268–86 Skutsch. For discussion see e.g. Scheidle 1993: 49–51; Gildenhard 2003: 110–11; Hardie 2007.

Ingo Gildenhard

and religious, and entirely content with his lot in life (280: *suo contentus, beatus*).[118] The passage maps out a space for a relatively novel social type within Rome's aristocratic milieu, with the help of Greek conceptual resources: 'The sketch, purported by Aelius Stilo to describe Ennius himself, draws upon Hellenistic descriptions of "the king's confidant".'[119] Its transposition to Rome, with its patronage networks centred in powerful *nobiles* who operated as 'quasi-kings', was relatively straightforward and acquired even further point and poignancy when Rome's socio-political structures during the late republic and early imperial period began to resemble the royal courts of the Hellenistic age. Intellectuals and artists who found themselves in the vicinity of influential powerbrokers needed to justify their privileged position: their enjoyment of close proximity to those at the top of the socio-political hierarchy was bound to trigger social envy and potentially carried disreputable connotations of spineless opportunism and immoderate ambition in an effort of social climbing. To counter the suspicion that he was a pushy careerist without an ounce of moral scruples who was reaping material and immaterial rewards he did not deserve, Ennius highlights moral probity, which manifests itself not least in modesty and lack of ambition, and genuine usefulness in a relationship of beneficial reciprocity.

This apologia for the intellectual subaltern at the top of the socio-political pyramid served Horace to think through and broadcast his own position in Roman society as a friend of Maecenas, which entailed membership in the circle around the triumvir Octavian and the *princeps* Augustus.[120] Like Ennius, he justifies upward social mobility by insisting that he is not interested in social advancement: 'being content' with one's lot in life is the keynote to Horace's first book of *Sermones*.[121] The

---

[118] Cf. Scheidle 1993: 50: '*Suo contentus* (280) verrät einen einfachen und bescheidenen Lebensstil ganz im Sinne der *frugalitas*, der trotzdem das Gefühl höchster Zufriedenheit (ibid.: *beatus*) aufkommen läßt.'

[119] Freudenburg 2010: 279.

[120] Labate 1996: 437–41 (on *S.* 2.6), cited by Freudenburg 2010: 279; Hardie 2007.

[121] *S.* 1.1.1–3: *Qui fit, Maecenas, ut nemo, quam sibi sortem | seu ratio dederit seu fors obiecerit, illa | contentus uiuat, laudet diuersa sequentis?* with Gowers 2012: 177 ('the central motto of *Satires* I'). Horace poses a good question in an age of social

Frugalitas, or: The Invention of a Roman Virtue

lexeme *contentus* then recurs throughout the collection before dwindling in his subsequent works.[122] In the fourth *sermo*, Horace is most upfront about its autobiographical significance, in a passage that also features the adverb *frugaliter* (*S.* 1.4.105–8):[123]

> insueuit pater optimus hoc me,
> ut fugerem exemplis uitiorum quaeque notando,
> cum me hortaretur, parce frugaliter atque
> uiuerem uti contentus eo quod mi ipse parasset.

My excellent father accustomed me to this by labelling each of the vices by example so that I would escape them. When he exhorted me to live thriftily, frugally, and content with what he had saved for me.

The way of life Horace's father exhorts his son to adopt might be considered typical of a freedman of good character and thus hints at Horace's passive-aggressive self-identification as the son of a freedman (*libertino patre natum*).[124] It is likely that the emphatic embrace of his non-flattering background obscures a more complex story. As Williams has plausibly argued, when Horaces uses this 'metrically discordant phrase', 'the words do not present the poet's own description of himself, but that used derisively by others' – arguably a reference to the fact that his father was captured and sold into slavery in the course of the Social War (before then being registered as a full Roman citizen after manumission).[125] And the rationale for 'owning up' to the fact that his father was (at one point) deprived of *libertas* is perhaps similar to that which motivated

---

mobility owing to political upheavals, including his own rollercoasting up and down the social ranks. Cf. MacLean 2018: 89: 'Horace presents himself as the son of a freedman for rhetorical reasons, to deflect the charge of unreserved social-climbing and to establish moral grounds for his advancement' with reference to Oliensis 1998: 34.

[122] *S.* 1.1.3, 118; 3.15; 4.108; 6.93; 10.56, 72. The only occurrences outside of *S.* 1 are *S.* 2.2.108; 7.15; *Ep.* 1.16.49; *Epod.* 14.13; and *AP* 202.

[123] Horace uses *frugaliter* nowhere else; his use of *frugi* is also limited and restricted to persons of low social standing or women: *AP* 202; *Ep.* 1.16.49 (*sum bonus et frugi*); *S.* 1.3.49 (*parcius hic uiuit: frugi dicatur*) 2.5.76 (*Penelope frugi*), 81; 2.7.2.

[124] *S.* 1.6.6, 45, 46; *Ep.* 1.20.19–22.

[125] Williams 1995: 297–8; see Moles 2007: 166–7 and Freudenburg 2010: 281–2 for more on the Greek background (Bion of Borysthenes identifying himself as 'the son of a freed slave' to Antigonos Gonatas, D. L. 4.46) and its implications.

Piso to adopt Frugi as *agnomen*: an attempt to take the sting out of a slur and turn it into a positive source of value by fully embracing and redefining it as a badge of honour. Horace uses his loss (or lack) of elite status as a means to endow his moral teachings with paternal authority. With *parce, frugaliter* and *contentus*, he lists quintessential qualities of the thrifty freedman and the good farmer – and thus also harks back to the agricultural ethos of ancient Rome that links economic prudence with moral fibre.[126] It was a peculiar, paradoxically brilliant *persona* to adopt for an author of satires – traditionally a genre of excess and glut, overstuffed (or so Horace makes out) with food-talk or, self-referentially, overflowing with verses, verbiage and excessive outspokenness (*libertas*). Horace redefines the genre in his own image – rejecting the generic excess of the *eques* Lucilius on moral, socio-political and aesthetic grounds. His self-elevation through commitment to moderation enables him to cast a critical glance on society – in a posture akin to that adopted by republican historiographers who also diagnosed moral failings in the surrounding culture, while tending to exempt themselves from the general picture, a posture that in Horace of course always comes with a moderating (self-)ironic tinge in line with his subservient status.[127]

Valerius Maximus

In its patchwork ways, Valerius' collection of memorable deeds and sayings recapitulates an Augustan conception of history.[128] Many of his *exempla* register a concern with decadence and decline, but Valerius does not plot his material as showing an irrevocable descent into moral chaos (along the

---

[126] See e.g. Cic. *de Orat.* 2.287: *cum optimus colonus, parcissimus, modestissimus, frugalissimus esset* with Astin 1988: 22 or Sal. *Cat.* 9.2: *domi parci, in amicos fideles erant.*

[127] Cf. Woodman 2009: 157–60, who argues that Horace invokes the *Annals* of Calpurnius Piso Frugi, specifically the episode of Cn. Flauius, who is also tagged as *patre libertino natus.* See above 261 n.57.

[128] See Introduction 76–8; Lucarelli 2007; Langlands 2008 and 2018; Itgenshorst 2017.

Frugalitas, or: The Invention of a Roman Virtue

lines of Sallust), which would have ill suited the propaedeutic purpose of the collection. The very existence of *exempla bona* selectively reaffirms the republican past as a source of value for the imperial present – which is extolled as the period that has seen the culmination of Rome's historical mission. Valerius Maximus is one of the proponents of the plot of Rome rising from humble beginnings ('the hut of Romulus') to an empire that spanned the world – a progressive view of history insofar as the current generation has been able to arrest the self-destructive tendencies of the recent past.[129]

In line with the imperial ideology of the early principate, he identifies *disciplina militaris* as the one stable variant in Roman history; and after Cicero's conceptual efforts, *frugalitas* joins more traditional terms to capture the virtuous disposition of 'the ancients' (*antiqui*), whom he celebrates for their dietary plainness (*simplicitas*) and self-restraint (*continentia*) across all social strata, a humbleness linked to efficacious piety.[130] As a result of their moderation in matters of food, drink and sex and their rejection of luxury they enjoyed rude health – the mother of which he identifies as *frugalitas* (2.5.6):[131]

ceterum salubritatem suam industriae certissimo ac fidelissimo munimento tuebantur, bonaeque ualitudinis eorum quasi quaedam mater erat frugalitas, inimica luxuriosis epulis et aliena nimiae uini abundantiae et ab immoderato ueneris usu auersa.

But they guarded their health with the most certain and reliable protection of careful living, and frugality was a kind of mother to their well-being; inimical to luxurious banquets, a stranger to excess of wine, averse to immoderate sexual indulgence.

Previous paragraphs noted 'firsts in extravagance' (concerning games, items of clothing, table ware, consumption of food and wine) very much in the spirit of identifying watersheds in the

---

[129] V. Max. 2.8 *praef.*
[130] V. Max. 2.5.5: *fuit enim illa simplicitas antiquorum in cibo capiendo humanitatis simul et continentiae certissimus index: nam maximis uiris prandere et cenare in propatulo uerecundiae non erat. ... primitiis enim et libamentis uictus sui deos eo efficacius quo simplicius placabant.*
[131] For Valerius Maximus I cite the text and translation by D. R. Shackleton Bailey in the Loeb Classical Library.

299

Ingo Gildenhard

rise of decadence in the spirit of Piso Frugi and other republican historiographers.

In addition to being a general characteristic of the 'exemplary' ancients, in Valerius *frugalitas* also enters the Roman *exempla*-discourse *stricto sensu*, insofar as it became part of the triangulation of a named figure, a striking deed and a value term.[132] The first such instance occurs at 4.3.5:[133]

> M'. autem Curius, exactissima norma Romanae frugalitatis idemque fortitudinis perfectissimum specimen, Samnitium legatis agresti se in scamno adsidentem foco eque ligneo catillo cenantem – quales epulas apparatus indicio est – spectandum praebuit: ille enim Samnitium diuitias contempsit, Samnites eius paupertatem mirati sunt.

> M'. Curius was the consummate pattern of Roman frugality and at the same time a clearly established model of bravery. He showed himself to the gaze of Samnite envoys seated by the fire on a rustic stool eating out of a wooden dish – what kind of fare can be deduced from these concomitants. For he despised the riches of the Samnites, whereas the Samnites wondered at his poverty.

Valerius here combines the generalising notion of exemplarity pioneered by Cato the Elder, where 'the ancients' collectively function as benchmarks of excellence (cf. *exactissima norma*) with the more conventional conception of the *exemplum*, in which a named figure is linked to an exemplary deed or saying (in this case, Curius' austere reception of the Samnites). The attribute *Romana* (here employed to underscore the contrast to the Samnites) endows *frugalitas* with a quasi-ethnic or at least

---

[132] See *Rhet. Her.* 4.62, further Hölkeskamp 1996: 310–15; Stemmler 2000: 151–68.
[133] See also 4.3.7 (about Q. Aelius Tubero and/or Sex. Aelius Paetus Catus, cos. 198: for the confusion see the discussion by Patterson below 355): *quam bene Aetolicis domestica praetulerat, si frugalitatis eius exemplum posterior aetas sequi uoluisset!* ('How right he was to prefer domestic articles to the Aetolian, if only later times had chosen to follow the example of his frugality!'); 4.3.11 (on Cato's austere lifestyle while on campaign): *atqui ista patientissime superior Cato tolerauit, quia illum grata frugalitatis consuetudo in hoc genere uitae cum summa dulcedine continebat* ('And yet the elder Cato tolerated all this quite uncomplainingly because the frugal habits he loved kept him in this way of life which he thoroughly enjoyed'); and 6.9.3 (on Valerius Flaccus' change in outlook after being made a Flamen): ... *usus duce frugalitatis religione, quantum prius luxuriae fuerat exemplum, tantum postea modestiae et sanctitatis specimen euasit* ('using religion as his guide to good conduct, earlier an example of dissipation, he later became no less a pattern of propriety and purity').

300

Frugalitas, or: The Invention of a Roman Virtue

culturally distinctive emphasis, continuing Cicero's project in the *Tusculans* where he identifies the very lexeme as distinctively and uniquely Roman, and perhaps also tapping into the new emphasis on Roman ethnic identity promoted by Virgil in particular – an approach that underwrites Valerius' basic organising principle of dividing his material into domestic and foreign *exempla*.[134]

Seneca the Elder

Frugalitas features prominently in two of Seneca the Elder's *Controversiae*, 2.1 and 2.6. Both pieces contain debates that involve the potential contingency of virtues – 2.1 with reference to social mobility (and attendant issues of moral worth and social status), 2.6 with reference to age.

The scenario of *Contr.* 2.1 features a rich man, who, after disinheriting three sons of his own, wishes to adopt the son of a poor man. The poor father is happy to oblige – but his son flat out refuses. This act of filial disobedience gets him disinherited. The case for the son includes hymns to the virtues of poverty that some of the declaimers embed within wider historical vistas. Porcius Latro, for instance, blends a celebration of Rome's humble origins and rustic virtues that enabled her rise to imperial greatness with a celebration of present peace and prosperity after decades of moral decline and civil discord (2.1.1). Others take a more ahistorical approach. In pleading the case of the son to his father, Arellius Fuscus Senior starts by attacking the moral depravity of the rich man and his household and insists that the qualities the poor son cultivated by growing up in virtuous deprivation, such as *frugalitas*, would go unappreciated, or even count as vices in his new surroundings (2.1.4). He argues that the transplantation of someone poor into a setting defined by wealth will inevitably result in some misalignment of behaviour and context (2.1.4: *aliquid in domo locupleti non agendum agam*). What counts as

---

[134] For Virgil's investment in the notion of *gens Romana* see Gildenhard 2007b.

Ingo Gildenhard

(praiseworthy) *frugalitas* among the poor will look like (ignominious) *humilitas* among the rich: *quae apud nos frugalitas est, apud illos humilitas est* (2.1.4).

Arellius Fuscus thus advances the idea that frugality is a virtue that behooves the poor – those who have to exercise prudent husbandry in order to get by; for those better off, practising the same thrift and humbleness would be out of kilter with their socio-economic status and be regarded as improper and debasing. According to this view, *frugalitas* is a milieu-specific virtue and hence also a milieu-specific vice – or, rather, material sobriety and prudent husbandry may attract either a positive (*frugalitas*) or a negative (*humilitas*) label dependent on external circumstances. This view fits in with Roman notions of *noblesse oblige*, i.e. that those who enjoy a certain socio-economic status are expected to engage in degrees of expenditure, not least to fund acts of *liberalitas*, above the means of the poor who have to be frugal out of necessity. But it does not align well with the historical *exemplum* of Tubero that Arellius Fuscus goes on to invoke, who illustrates the possibility of poverty (*paupertas*) amounting to excellence (*uirtus*) (2.1.8). And it contrasts sharply with the radical view on the inverse correlation of wealth and virtue that the philosopher Fabianus endorses (2.1.25):[135]

'etiamsi sustinerem alicui tradi, at diuiti nollem', et in diuitias dixit, non in diuitem: illas esse quae frugalitatem, quae pietatem expugnassent, quae malos patres, malos filios facerent.

'Even if I could stand being handed over to another, I should not want to be handed over to a rich man.' And he inveighed, not against the rich man but against wealth. It was wealth that had taken frugality and natural affection by storm, wealth that made bad fathers and bad sons.

Unlike the notion of *frugalitas* brought into play by Arellius Fuscus, which is contingent upon socio-economic circumstances, Fabianus seems to endorse an idea of *frugalitas* grounded in moral absolutism: *frugalitas* and *pietas* are *always* virtues – and they stand in opposition to vice fostered by

---

[135] I cite the translation of M. Winterbottom in the Loeb Classical Library.

Frugalitas, or: The Invention of a Roman Virtue

wealth, which is *always* corrosive of virtue. The views on *frugalitas* Seneca here collected thus span the spectrum from Roman pragmatism to the uncompromising absolutism of Greek philosophy. The notion that frugal living does not constitute an absolute value but is relational to the status of a person recurs in *Contr.* 2.6, which explores the scenario of a father who joins his spendthrift son in indulging in debauchery (perhaps with the intention to cure him of it?) – only to be declared insane by his offspring. One target of this cross-generational satire is the double standard of the young: they are bound to find it abhorrent if their parents engage in the same prodigial style of life they like to affect. This is hardly surprising: children prefer their parents to be economically prudent and abide by conventional morality, keeping their patrimony together, getting married, raising children and ensuring a good reputation.[136] Hispo Romanius, adopting the father's point of view, sums it up elegantly in the paradox that nothing of the morally upright things he has achieved in life is more upright (*frugalius*) than his son's admiration for his *frugalitas*.[137] At the heart of the case is fun with the standard trajectory from the freewheeling licence of youth (which may include dabbling in various forms of vice) to a meaningful contribution to society expected of grown-ups, which involves a return *ad frugalitatem* (2.6.8) and the acceptance of roles as husband and father that include serious socio-economic obligations and responsibilities incompatible with a life of debauchery[138] – i.e. the plot of maturation that underwrites many comic scripts and that Cicero imagines his client to have undergone in the *pro Caelio*.

[136] Cf. the funerary epitaph for 'most frugal' Sempronius Donatus, *ILS* 8435: *Sempronio Donato homin.* | *frugalissimo, ...* | *cuius frugalitati heres ma\ximas gratias aget, amplius mere\nti heres honorabit.*
[137] *Contr.* 2.6.13: *placet uobis frugalitas mea, quod patrimonium seruaui, quod adquisiui, quod uxorem mature duxi, semper dilexi, quod ab omni me tutum fabula praestiti. illud adfirmo, nihil tota uita frugalius feci.*
[138] Rufus Vibius, arguing the case for the son, imagines him quoting his father as saying, in an effort to solicit outrage: *'rusticum iuuenem! Praematura seueritas non est frugalitas sed tristitia: quid tu senex facies?'*, which he believes will solicit outrage in the audience – and counter the suggestion that his father was acting intentionally (intead of having lost his mind).

Ingo Gildenhard

Petronius

Petronius, best known for his programmatic celebration of immoderation and extravagance of every kind, seems an odd author in whom to look for *frugalitas*. And yet, the concept turns out to be central for his novel. The *Satyrica* feature a smorgasboard of characters, ranging from delicious to revolting, many of whom belong 'to the large class of educated freedmen, of undetermined ethnic background',[139] all out to make a living, find love and get ahead in society. The surviving portion of the work, however, is dominated by a character who has managed to do just that despite being an *un*educated freedmen of determinable ethnic background: Trimalchio. He is the physical embodiment of upward social mobility on account of economic smarts alone. Because of his elevated status in terms of wealth, he holds up a distorting mirror to members of the upper classes who read this text, including perhaps the emperor himself, if we identify the author with T. Petronius Niger, one of the consuls of 62 CE and, according to Tacitus, Nero's *arbiter elegantiae*.[140] For while elite snobbery is very much part of the fun, the complexities of the text are such that any feeling of superiority ultimately remains precarious. Deft use of the **frug–* lexicon constitutes one of the ways in which Petronius situates his characters in society, captures their moral qualities and socio-economic aspirations and brings into focus standards (and their perversion) in the spheres of rhetoric, sex and food (which in Petronius, as elsewhere, are suggestively homologous)[141] – but also undercuts upperclass pretensions.

The concept first occurs in the opening scene of the surviving text: set in a school of rhetoric, it features a debate between Encolpius and Agamemnon about the history of oratory, current developments (not least the influence of *declamatores* and

---

[139] Courtney 2001: 41.
[140] *Ann.* 16.18. Prag and Repath 2009: 5–10 offer a good discussion of the question of the author and its implication.
[141] On the metaphorics of food in Latin literature, in particular Petronius, see Gowers 1993; Rimell 2002.

304

Frugalitas, or: The Invention of a Roman Virtue

doctores) and the virtues and vices of various oratorical styles. Once Encolpius has squarely put the blame for the verbal flatulence that passes for eloquence these days on the teachers of rhetoric, Agamemnon, one such, shifts it onto the students and especially their parents, who in their ambition and stupidity reject the *seuera lex* of arduous educational discipline for their children, hothousing them into a public career before they are ready (4). The lack of a proper bootcamp in rhetorical training in their youth, so he argues, will stunt their oratorical efforts throughout the rest of their lives. He elaborates his point with an improvised poem in the humble style of Lucilius (*schedium Lucilianae humilitatis*) that begins as follows (5):[142]

Artis seuerae si quis ambit effectus
mentemque magnis applicat, prius mores
frugalitatis lege poliat exacta.

Anyone who aspires to mastery of a serious professional skill and applies his mind to great endeavours should first perfect his character by scrupulous adherence to the principle of frugality.

After Encolpius' invective blast against the excess of Asia with its vacuous rhetorical bombast,[143] Agamemnon here upholds the old-school value of hard work as a necessary precondition for success in any meaningful and demanding endeavour, such as mastery of the art of eloquence. The phrase *lex frugalitatis* ('the principle of frugality') covers a wide range, from commitment to thrift and material sobriety (and the rejection of luxury and easy gratification) to the formation of a sound character through serious effort and a high degree of self-discipline. The poem goes on to extol the virtue of self-restraint and moral integrity in matters both social and literary and advises the aspiring orator to give the dinner-parties of the licentious (*cenas impotentium*) a pass and buckle down instead

---

[142] The point can be read as an oblique commentary on Nero and his premature accession to the throne, for which see Gowers 1994.

[143] See esp. Petr. 2: *nuper uentosa istaec et enormis loquacitas Athenas ex Asia commigrauit animosque iuuenum ad magna surgentes ueluti pestilenti quodam sidere afflauit...*

305

Ingo Gildenhard

to a syllabus consisting of the classics in Greek and Latin literature.[144]

We here get an elite variant of *frugalitas* that combines old-school morality with intellectual values in an educational setting, covering such issues as character formation by means of self-control in matters of food consumption, sexual ethics, pedagogical discipline and training in oratory – a variant of which we will see again in Seneca the Younger and Quintilian.[145] But this high-cultured ideal of *frugalitas* as a virtuous disposition that enables intellectual brilliance stands very much in contrast to the *lex frugalitatis* that dominates in the *Cena Trimalchionis*. The key stretch for our concerns are §§ 73–6. The point of departure is Trimalchio's announcement that one of his slaves, whom he describes as a *homo praefiscini frugi et micarius* ('a frugal and crumbs-picking fellow, meaning no evil') is today celebrating his first shave, which he considers an occasion for unrestrained partying.[146] The onset of manhood was indeed a momentous occasion for a slave, especially since it was supposed to bring the period of his sexual exploitation by his master to an official end.[147] That sex is indeed in the air becomes apparent when Trimalchio starts fondling another slave boy who serves his table, much to the annoyance of his wife Fortunata.[148] He justifies his behaviour as follows (Petr. 75):

---

[144] For discussion see Connors 1998: 11–12.

[145] Breitenstein 2009: 75 compares Sen. *Ep.* 17.5 and Quint. *Inst.* 10.3.26, for which see below 321–2 and 326. For *frugalitas* as an aesthetic category to capture a specific mode of oratory see also Macr. 5.1.5: *oratorum autem non simplex nec una natura est, sed hic fluit et redundat, contra ille breuiter et circumcise dicere adfectat; tenuis quidam et siccus et sobrius amat quandam dicendi frugalitatem, alius pingui et luculenta et florida oratione lasciuit* ('But the nature of orators is not a single, simple thing: this one is fluent and overflowing while that one aims to speak briefly and concisely, the spare, dry, and sober sort likes a certain austerity of speech, another frolics with a rich, flashy, flowery style' – trans. R. A. Kaster).

[146] Petr. 73: *Tum Trimalchio: 'Amici, inquit, hodie servus meus barbatoriam fecit, homo praefiscini frugi et micarius. itaque tangomenas faciamus et usque in lucem cenemus.'*

[147] Richlin 2009: 90. For the sexual exploitation of slaves of both sexes by their Roman masters see further Cantarella 1992: 99; Fantham 2011: 118.

[148] Petr. 74: *cum puer non inspeciosus inter nouos intrasset ministros, inuasit eum Trimalchio et osculari diutius coepit.*

306

Frugalitas, or: The Invention of a Roman Virtue

Puerum basiaui frugalissimum, non propter formam, sed quia frugi est: decem partes dicit, librum ab oculo legit, thraecium sibi de diariis fecit, arcisellium de suo parauit et duas trullas. non est dignus quem in oculis feram?

I kissed this most frugal boy not because of his beauty but because he is *frugi*: he is good at basic maths, knows how to read a book on sight, has acquired for himself Thracian armour from his daily allowance, bought a round-backed chair with his own money and two ladles. Surely he deserves to be the apple of my eye?

Here we have a freedman extolling a slave in the idiom of slavery. The qualities captured by *frugalissimus* and *frugi* are those of a useful slave with personal ambition: basic skills in numeracy and literacy and a knack for financial transactions. Trimalchio kisses the boy out of narcissism: he is the spitting image of his younger self – a point that becomes clear when he turns to his guests and regales them with tidbits about his past (Petr. 75):[149]

uos rogo, amici, ut uobis suauiter sit. nam ego quoque tam fui quam uos estis, sed uirtute mea ad hoc perueni. Corcillum est quod homines facit, cetera quisquilia omnia. bene emo, bene uendo; . . . sed ut coeperam dicere, ad hanc me fortunam frugalitas mea perduxit. tam magnus ex Asia ueni, quam hic candelabrus est. ad summam, quotidie me solebam ad illum metiri, et ut celerius rostrum barbatum haberem, labra de lucerna ungebam. tamen ad delicias ipsimi annos quattuordecim fui. nec turpe est, quod dominus iubet. ego tamen et ipsimae satis faciebam. scitis quid dicam: taceo, quia non sum de gloriosis.

Please, my friends, make yourselves comfortable. I was once just what you are, but through my innate excellence I have come to this. A bit of sound sense is what makes men; the rest is all rubbish. 'I buy well and sell well'. . . . Well, as I was just saying, frugality has brought me into this fortune. When I came from Asia I was about as tall as this candle-stick. In fact I used to measure myself by it every day, and grease my lips from the lamp to grow a beard the quicker. Even so, for fourteen years I was my master's toyboy. No disgrace in obeying your master's orders. Well, I used to amuse my mistress too. You know what I mean; I say no more, I am not a conceited man.

---

[149] I cite the (adjusted) translation of M. Heseltine and W. H. D. Rouse as revised by E. H. Warmington in the Loeb Classical Library.

Ingo Gildenhard

Trimalchio here boasts of his *uirtus* and *frugalitas* as the enabling factors of his rags-to-riches story: *frugalitas* entails (good) *fortuna* in the sense of (inordinate) wealth.[150] But he manages to compromise these qualities with countervailing imagery. To begin with, he highlights Asia, well known as a place of excess and luxury, as his region of origin. Then he casually lets drop that his period of sexual enslavement was inordinately long: 'his 14-year span of sexual service would have carried him well past the normal 12-to-18 eligibility period.'[151] And in addition to being the passive victim of his master's sexual urges, he acted as seducer of his mistress. In terms of geography and sexual behaviour – to say nothing about the consumption of food and drink – Trimalchio is the exact opposite of frugality.[152] In other words, he is the physical embodiment of <u>both</u> *libido/luxuria* <u>and</u> *frugalitas*. Paradox defines him: he is a virtuous abomination and a conceptual monstrosity.

At one level of reading, Trimalchio thus undercuts his own claims to certain elite forms of *uirtus* and *frugalitas* and reveals himself as beholden to the freedman's variant. At another level, however, the text turns the joke on the elite reader. First,

---

[150] In line with the rule of paradox, Petronius later on in the novel has *frugalitas* undone by (bad) fortune. See § 115 (upon discovering Lichas drowned, Encolpius reflects upon the unpredictability of fortune in human affairs, noting among other absurdities the scenarios of food choking the glutton and frugality the abstemious (...*cibus auidum strangulauit, abstinentem frugalitas*).

[151] Richlin 2009: 90. This raises the question whether the days of suffering sodomy are over for the *homo frugi* of §73. But the fact that Trimalchio celebrates the shave and then acts out his erotic passions on another boy seems to indicate that his restraint in sexual matters is superior to that of his former master.

[152] Petronius associates *frugi* and *frugalitas* with self-restraint in sexual matters also later on. See § 84 ('*uellem, tam innocens esset frugalitatis meae hostis, ut deliniri posset. nunc ueteranus est latro et ipsis lenonibus doctior*') with Schmeling and Setaioli 2011: 358: '**frugalitatis** here would have nothing to do with *paupertas*, but reflect E.'s belief that he has treated Giton properly while Ascyltos has not.' Cf. Habermehl 2006: 89–91. At § 116 a *uilicus* informs the travellers about the customs of Croton, a city whose inhabitants he characterises as single-minded fornicators without concern for *litterarum studia, eloquentia, frugalitas* or *sancti mores*. Cf. also § 140 (part of the Philomela-episode who prostitutes her children for financial gains): *Eumolpus, qui tam frugi erat ut illi etiam ego puer uiderer, non distulit puellam inuitare ad pygesiaca sacra*. For suggestions of how we are to imagine the scene to unfold (who is where, when, on top of whom, for what purposes) see Panayotakis 1995: 182–9.

Frugalitas, or: The Invention of a Roman Virtue

the passage just cited ends with a gnomic reflection that agency is a requisite for meaningful morals. Without agency, there is no virtue and no turpitude: obeying the command of a master is therefore void of moral implications. Trimalchio flatly denies that his past as the passive victim of sexual aggression has any morally incriminating implications or consequences for his character. And the narrative has already shown that in terms of sexual morals he is superior to his master: unlike his own extended period of sexual enslavement, his own slaves are released from sexual bondage as soon as they reach manhood: the very fact that Trimalchio gives erotic attention to another *homo frugi* (indeed *frugalissimus*) at the very party of the slave boy who has just come of age reconfirms the point.

Secondly, the passage comes embedded with gestures to frugal norms and their opposite that concern the highest echelon of Roman society. The reference at 73.5 to 'tables made of solid silver and pottery cups inlaid with gold' (*mensas totas argenteas calcesque circa fictiles inauratos*) constitutes a cheeky allusion to a senatorial sumptuary regulation that solid gold vessels are not to be used for dinning purposes.[153] Excess, in other words, is not just the preserve of freedmen. Again, the joke is double-edged: at one level, the socio-political elite know how to consume conspicuously in proper style, with the right dishes and the correct display of literary learning; but at another level, they are a mirror-image of Trimalchio, not least in terms of (lack of) self-restraint, lavish expenditure and conspicuous consumption.

And thirdly and most importantly, Trimalchio continues his autobiographical flashback with a brief account of his business career, recounting how he started with an inheritance, ventured into commerce, lost his first fleet of five trading vessels, had his wife sell her jewellery to fund a second bigger attempt, struck it lucky, used the profit to buy up the entire estate of his former master and adopted the lifestyle of a senatorial landowner. This meant retiring from active business, building a

---

[153] Schmeling and Setaioli 2011: 308 with reference to Tac. *Ann.* 2.33.

Ingo Gildenhard

villa, and starting to act as financial patron of adventurous freedmen (Petr. 76). In the course of his business career he transformed himself from a *homo frugi*, a former slave pursuing commerce as *mercator* and *negotiator*, into someone resembling a landholding aristocrat cultivating *fruges* but continuing to be commercially active as a financier and middle-man – a Cato Maior Rediuiuus as he really was, bringing to mind the old-fashioned ideology of *industria* and *parsimonia*.[154] But in a literary universe where Cato the Elder and Trimalchio look the same, any sense of moral distinction and socio-political differentiation instantly implodes.

At closer inspection, then, Trimalchio turns out to be superior to his master across the board – in moral, social and economic terms. Put differently, his personal qualities, the *uirtus* and *frugalitas* he claims for himself, enable him to outperform their elite counterparts. As a result he utterly upends any sense of social order – very much in the spirit of the Saturnalia that animates the narrative. *Frugalitas* above all, in the sense of thrift and financial smarts, fuels the socio-economic mobility that produces freedmen who can eventually lord it over their former masters also in real life. Looking at Trimalchio, Petronius' elite readers may well wonder how *frugi* they want their slaves to be. *Frugalitas*, then, plays a pivotal, if paradoxical role in the topsy-turvey world of the *Satyrica* – as the paradoxical catalyst that brings into being the most striking forms of excess, moral disorder and social inversion, of all of which the figure of Trimalchio is the living embodiment.

Seneca the Younger

Seneca recognised the potential of the lexeme *frugalitas* – especially in the Graeco-Roman, historico-philosophical sense developed by Cicero – for providing help with imbricating

---

[154] D'Arms 1981: 101, cited by Schmeling and Setaioli 2011: 317, who also review the earlier literature that tended to divide Trimalchio's business career into two stages, the first centred in trade, the second in landownership.

Frugalitas, or: The Invention of a Roman Virtue

Roman culture and Greek, specifically Stoic, doctrine, i.e. the two worlds that he brings into synergetic dialogue throughout his *oeuvre*. In his writings, *frugalitas* figures prominently as (a) an ancient ideal and traditional Roman virtue of (b) particular relevance, once suitably redefined with the help of Stoic philosophy, in the present imperial context and (c) ideally suited to articulate central aspects of Stoic philosophy in a quintessentially Roman guise. The following survey will look in turn at these three variants of *frugalitas* in Seneca (one could call them *frugalitas antiqua et rustica*; *frugalitas imperatoria uel ciuilis*; and *frugalitas philosophica*), even though assignment of any one instance to any one category is often arbitrary – and ought not obfuscate the point that it was precisely the polyvalence of *frugalitas* with its interstitial potency that made it such a valuable concept for Seneca.[155]

(a) Exceptionally, Seneca associates *frugalitas* with drudging labour beneath the social rank and standing of the imperial elite. Thus in the *de Breuitate Vitae*, he encourages his addressee Paulinus, who was *praefectus annonae* at the time (48–55 CE) and thereby responsible for the distribution of corn to the populace, to retire from public life to devote himself to the more fruitful pursuit of philosophy:[156] stepping down is easy since there are many others of exacting frugality able to take over the task (18.4: *non deerunt et frugalitatis exactae*

---

[155] By contrast the adjective *frugi* occurs only four times: *Apoc.* 11.5 (cognomen); *Ep.* 51.3 (*boni mores* – as opposed to luxury); and *Ep.* 120, in which Seneca uses the term twice (19; 22) to establish a scale that ranges from *frugi/grauis/contentus* on the one hand to *prodigus/uanus* on the other, to illustrate unsteady and fickle characters. His ready use of the noun and his rare and unremarkable use of the adjective suggest that he deemed the former properly 'ennobled' in both philosophical and socio-political/historical terms, but not the latter. The situation is similar with Pliny the Younger: see below 332–3 n.209.

[156] *DBV* 18.4: *istum animi uigorem rerum maximarum capacissimum a ministerio honorifico quidem sed parum ad beatam uitam apto reuoca et cogita non id egisse te ab aetate prima omni cultu* studiorum liberalium *ut tibi multa milia* frumenti *bene committerentur: maius quiddam et altius de te promiseras* ('Recall that keen mind of yours, which is most competent to cope with the greatest subjects, from a service that is indeed honourable but hardly adapted to the happy life, and reflect that in all your training in liberal studies, extending from your earliest years, you were not aiming at his – that it might be safe to entrust many thousand pecks of corn to your charge; you gave hope of something greater and more lofty' – trans. J. W. Basore).

Ingo Gildenhard

homines et laboriosae operae). frugalitas here picks up on both the agricultural term *frumentum* and the phrase *studia liberalia* in the previous sentence (cited in n. 156): it situates the *homines* in a low social milieu of rusticity and manual labour and affiliates them with useful and honest slaves or freedmen, i.e. as *frugi* in the traditional sense, as opposed to a member of the social elite and its intellectual aspirations such as Paulinus, to whom he refers with a significantly more ambitious idiom.[157]

But such a dismissive use of *frugalitas*, motivated, as it seems to be, by Paulinus' daily dealings with *fruges* and Seneca's desire to dissociate his addressee from this sphere of activity as both below his status and stymying his philosophical potential, is the exception. Elsewhere in Seneca, *frugalitas* carries powerfully positive connotations, not least as a virtue of the past. Thus in *Ep.* 95 he argues that moral decline and depravity have vastly increased over the years, culminating in the present state of utter moral madness, not just on the individual level but society at large (30: *non priuatim solum, sed publice furimus*); in earlier times, no great effort was necessary to return the deviant to the desired state of virtue since the failing tended to be minor (32: *non erat animus ad frugalitatem magna ui reducendus, a qua paullum discesserat*); nowadays, however, general *peruersitas* prevails (33–4). His philosophical project, as it turns out, is all about reinvigorating this virtue, not least for its practical benefits: *antiqua frugalitas* is one of the qualities that the injustice, violence and cruelty of Fortuna is said to disregard at *Consolatio ad Polybium* 3.5 – together

---

[157] See the superlative phrase *rerum maximarum capacissimum* and the comparatives *maius* and *altius*, further Duff 1915: 161 cited by Williams 2003: 239. The use of *frugalitas* at *Ep.* 114.17, where L. Arruntius, a historiographer affecting a prose style modelled on Sallust (for attempts at identification and dating see the entry by Levick in *FRHist* 1.448–50), is described as a *uir rarae frugalitatis*, seems similarly motivated by the wider thematic context: it arguably anticipates Seneca's use of the language of luxury and corruption after a list of excessive redeployments of Sallust's stylistic idiosyncrasies: *haec ergo et eiusmodi uitia, quae alicui impressit imitatio, non sunt indicia luxuriae nec animi corrupti* (20). As Edwards 2019: 301 notes, Seneca here endows the process of imitation itself with agency, though leaves it unclear 'what makes the imitator liable to follow a faulty model', esp. since he seems to have pre-emptively cleared Arruntius from personal responsibility by praising him for his *frugalitas*.

Frugalitas, or: The Invention of a Roman Virtue

with 'blamelessness put to the test by every law' (*innocentia ad omnem legem exacta*), 'persistent self-restraint despite unlimited opportunities to acquire unlimited wealth' (*felicitatis summae potentia summa conseruata abstinentia*), 'a sincere and safe love of literature' (*sincerus et tutus litterarum amor*) and 'a mind free from any stain' (*ab omni labe mens uacans*).

(b) *Frugalitas* is a standard entry in Senecan catalogues of virtues.[158] He employs them to define what to look for in the best specimens of humanity – whether the person under consideration is his own brother or a potential emperor.[159] Far from being only confined to subservient settings, *frugalitas* can also be found at the very top of the socio-political hierarchy: it is one of the qualities of Marcellus, Augustus' one time heir apparent.[160] But Seneca stops short of praising Nero for *frugalitas* – the single occurrence of the noun in the *de Clementia* rather identifies it as an essential quality for the subaltern to prosper under an autocratic regime (1.23.2):

> in qua ciuitate raro homines puniuntur, in ea consensus fit innocentiae et indulgetur uelut publico bono. putet se innocentem esse ciuitas, erit; magis irascetur a communi frugalitate desciscentibus, si paucos esse eos uiderit. periculosum est, mihi crede, ostendere ciuitati, quanto plures mali sint.

---

[158] Examples include *Ep.* 49.12; *Ep.* 88, which is devoted to redefining the meaning of liberal studies: rejecting the conventional understanding of *studia liberalia* as comprising grammar, music, geometry, arithmetic, astrology, rhetoric and dialectic (the Greek *egkuklios paideia*), Seneca argues that they are mere stepping stones towards the study of philosophy, which alone qualifies for the label *studium liberale*; in answer to the rhetorical question whether the basic syllabus teaches any of the virtues, he answers in the negative, considering *fortitudo, fides, temperantia, humanitas, simplicitas, modestia, moderatio, frugalitas, parsimonia, clementia* (29–30); and *Ep.* 115.3: what would one see if one were able to peer into the *animus* of a *uir bonus*? *iustitia, fortitudo, temperantia, prudentia, frugalitas, continentia, tolerantia, liberalitas, comitas, humanitas, prouidentia cum elegantia, magnanimitas, pondus, grauitas, auctoritas.*

[159] *Nat.* 4a *praef.* 10: *frugalitas* is one of the qualities with whom he could flatter his older brother Annaeus Novatus unsuccessfully (together with a god-like *ingenium, comitas, suauitas, bonitas* and *prudentia*, among others).

[160] *Consolatio ad Marciam* 2.3: Seneca brings Octavia into play as an *exemplum malum*, one deaf to consolation after the death of Marcellus who was mature beyond his years: *adulescentem animo alacrem, ingenio potentem, sed frugalitatis continentiaeque in illis aut annis aut opibus non mediocriter admirandae, patientem laborum, uoluptatibus alienum, quantumcumque imponere illi auunculus et ... inaedificare uoluisset, laturum ... frugalitas* and *continentia* here figure as qualities that delimit power and sustain excellence by controlling desire and enabling labour.

313

Ingo Gildenhard

In a civic community in which humans are rarely punished, uprightness becomes customary and is allowed to flourish as a common good. Let a state think it is upright and it will be. It will be angrier with those who deviate from common standards of sober and upright living (*frugalitas*) if it sees that such persons are few. Believe me, it is dangerous to show to the civic community in how great a majority the evil are.

As commentators have noted, Seneca here gives the notion of *frugalitas* a novel twist: in the *de Clementia*, 'it contributes a new element to the theme of self-control that pervades the treatise. The combination with *communis* is found only here.'[161] Essentially, Seneca brings *frugalitas* into play as the civic counterpart to and equivalent of imperial *clementia*: the former refers to the self-restraint ordinary citizens ought to exercise; the latter to an important manifestation of the self-restraint that behooves the emperor. Cicero prefigured this notion of *frugalitas* as essentially a *uirtus priuata* (where *priuatus* = everyone but the *princeps*: cf. Plin. *Ep.* 2.1 with Whitton 2013: 70) in an imperial context in the *Tusculan Disputations* and, especially, his *pro rege Deiotaro* (26). What Cicero there identified as a desirable quality of a subordinate king in the face of the autocratic might of Caesar, Seneca here extends to the entire citizen-body under Rome's imperial regime (hence the attribute *communis*). The passage thus brings to mind Caligula's pronouncement that only the emperor is free and unrestrained – and everyone else better be *frugi*.[162] One of the aims of *de Clementia* is of course precisely to prevent Nero from turning into another Caligula; and the treatise encourages him to restrain himself, exercising *clementia*, even when his subjects fail to do so (defaulting from *frugalitas*). The passage deftly interrelates the *clementia* of the emperor and the *frugalitas* of his citizens: practice of the former encourages the latter, whereas lack of *clementia* will advertise the (already significant) lack of *frugalitas* within the civic community and will lead to accelerated decline in morals. Put differently, for the propaedeutic purposes of the *de Clementia* Seneca sees fit

---

[161] Braund 2009: 365, with reference to *Tusc.* 3 and *Deiot.* 26.
[162] Suet. *Cal.* 37. See Introduction 80–2.

314

Frugalitas, or: The Invention of a Roman Virtue

to suggest that the fish does not always rot from the head down; but if the head rots, the rest is sure to follow quickly.[163] (c) The best way to keep the *frugalitas* of the citizens in proper shape is through the education that Seneca offers in and through his writings. In a nutshell, his pedagogy applies the resources of Greek philosophy to regain ancestral standards of excellence in personal conduct (*antiqua frugalitas*). In this respect, Seneca's philosophical project is identical to that of Cicero: both use Greek thought to recover Roman historical excellence – and use Rome's historical excellence to advertise their intellectual efforts as superior to Greek precedents.[164] Like Cicero, Seneca understood the pedagogical benefits of defining the philosophical perfection he strives after as identical to a historically already realised, hence achievable and specifically Roman disposition.

At *de Beneficiis* 6.24.1, Seneca explicitly conceives of *frugalitas* as a form of traditional educational discipline (*disciplina*) that shapes and tempers the force of youth and enables children to grow up properly (overcoming *libertas immatura*). But in the main he is interested in *frugalitas* as the dispositional and behavioural *outcome* of such discipline. In its 'popular' variant frugality does not require training in philosophy. Seneca praises several individuals for frugal habits, which he considers conducive to good health based on a modest diet and, if fortune so wishes, a long life.[165] More generally, those who have incorporated *frugalitas* and *boni mores* into their

---

[163] The passage thus has affinities with the idea that the best *regimen morum* an emperor can practise is to lead by example. See Tac. *Ann.* 3.55; Plin. *Pan.* 45–6 and Introduction 84–6.

[164] See above 282–3.

[165] *Ep.* 58.32: *potest frugalitas producere senectutem, quam ut non puto concupiscendam, ita ne recusandam quidem. iucundum est secum esse quam diutissime, cum quis se dignum, quo frueretur, effecit.* 101.3: even a man like Cornelius Senecio, a Roman knight, and on the verge of becoming rich because of his economic prudence, his knowledge of making and keeping money (*et quaerendi et custodiendi scientia*), known for his *frugalitas* and taking care of his body and his wealth (*hic homo summae frugalitatis, non minus patrimonii quam corporis diligens ...*) passed suddenly away stricken by angina. Cf. *Ep.* 108.21, involving a disquisition in which Pythagoras argues for the advantages of vegetarianism, with reference to the doctrine of metempsychosis: *si uera sunt ista, abstinuisse animalibus innocentia est; si falsa, frugalitas est.*

315

Ingo Gildenhard

outlook on life prefer modest clothing as better suited to their values than ostentatious apparell – and choose to stay away from certain locations: Baiae, with its reputation for *luxuria*, is not a good fit.[166] But those who only profess commitment to *frugalitas* and *parsimonia* without truly embracing material sobriety and self-restraint will inevitably yield to *luxuria* and *uoluptates*, who do their evil ways even more effectively behind a frugal veneer.[167] And multifarious voices of temptation exist, ready to lead those astray who are not properly fortified: they also inveigh against the philosophical life and issue a Siren-call to indulge in pleasure whenever and how much as possible, inviting anyone willing to listen to stop thinking about the future, heirs and patrimony – and to reject *frugalitas*.[168] Very few ever reach a completely frugal state of mind. In fact, perfect *frugalitas* is the preserve of the Stoic figure of the *sapiens*. At key moments in his *oeuvre*, in particular the *Letters to Lucilius*, Seneca suggests a coincidence between the mental outlook of the Romans of yore and that of the Stoic sage – an identification that *frugalitas*, in its Ciceronian variant, enables and furthers at the lexical level.

One of the key obstacles that prevents Seneca's audience from achieving genuine *frugalitas* and hence also the *uirtus* and the *felicitas* of the *maiores* and the *sapiens* is the prevailing ideology of wealth. And he therefore devotes significant effort to rethink ordinary understandings of wealth and poverty and

---

[166] *Ep.* 51.2–3.

[167] *Ep.* 56.10: *idem de luxuria dico, quae uidetur aliquando cessisse, deinde frugalitatem professos sollicitat atque in media parsimonia uoluptates non damnatas, sed relictas petit, et quidem eo uehementius, quo occultius* ('And so also with luxury, which sometimes seems to have departed, and then when we have made a profession of frugality, begins to fret us and, amid our thrift, seeks the pleasures we left but did not renounce. Indeed, the more stealthily it comes, the greater is its force' – trans. R. M. Gummere, slightly adjusted).

[168] *Ep.* 123.10–11. The Sirens are mentioned at 12. For someone beholden to a life of luxury, *frugalitas* is anyway a form of punishment: *Ep.* 71.23: *luxurioso frugalitas poena est.* The philosophical point under discussion here is that *uirtus*, understood as a mental disposition of the agent, is the only criterion by which to assess an action. This can lead to counterintuitive results – but they are only counterintuitive to those stuck in common sense without philosophical wisdom. To illustrate this point Seneca lists scenarios in which a good thing will look abhorrent to someone weak of mind.

316

Frugalitas, or: The Invention of a Roman Virtue

its quotidian consequences. At the outset of *de Tranquilitate Animi*, for instance, the dedicatee Serenus, a young prefect of Nero's nightwatch, of humble background but poised for a career in politics, spells out how difficult it is to maintain a frugal outlook in contemporary Roman society. He professes the greatest love of frugality (1.5: *summus amor parsimoniae*), which manifests itself in homely and inexpensive furniture and food, modest apparell and special liking for a single unskilled slave and silverware fit for purpose but without pedigree (1.5–7). But when exposed to the razzle-dazzle of luxury (sumptuously clothed slaves in great numbers, the palatial splendour of a house and the attention this wasteful use of patrimony attracts from the people) he feels his commitment to *frugalitas* under siege.[169] He knows he should not be attracted by material splendour, but cannot help feel saddened (*recedo itaque non peior, sed tristior*).

To combat such weakness of good intention (cf. 1.15: *bonae mentis infirmitas*) when it comes to the ostentatious display of affluence, Seneca sketches out a pragmatic middle ground: after evoking Diogenes the Cynic as an unattainable ideal or rather as contrastive foil since unnecessarily extreme, he suggests that the best measure of wealth is not a state of poverty but a state or disposition not far removed from poverty[170] – before shifting the focus to what really matters: a mental disposition that renders material possessions irrelevant since it is satisficing and ideally self-sufficient and therefore able to transform even a state of apparent poverty into wealth (9.1):

placebit autem haec nobis mensura si prius parsimonia placuerit, sine qua nec ullae opes sufficiunt nec ullae non satis patent, praesertim cum in uicino remedium sit et possit ipsa paupertas in diuitias se, aduocata frugalitate, conuertere.

---

[169] *Tranq.* 1.9: *circumfudit me ex longo frugalitatis situ uentientem multo splendore luxuria et undique circumsonuit.*

[170] *Tranq.* 8.9: *optimus pecuniae modus est, qui nec in paupertatem cadit nec procul a paupertate discedit.*

Ingo Gildenhard

Moreover, we will embrace this measure if we have already embraced thrift, without which no riches are enough or ever available to a sufficient degree, especially since the cure is near and poverty itself with the aid of frugality can turn itself into wealth.

No new *exempla* are required for the important lesson that where material riches are concerned the road to *felicitas* begins with the embrace of *parsimonia* and *frugalitas*. All one needs to do is imitate the ancestors.[171] Their style of life is the epitome of self-sufficiency and self-restraint – they teach us to increase our self-control and control our extravagance, to moderate our desire for glory, to mollify our anger, to face poverty with equanimity and to cultivate frugality.[172] Put differently, Seneca employs *frugalitas* and its association with ancestral virtue to suggest that the path to self-improvement, firmness of mind and happiness that he invites Serenus to pursue boils down to something as arch-Roman and straightforward as imitation of the ancestors (*imitatio maiorum*). Frugality emerges as the bridge between the counterintuitive obscurities of Greek thought and Roman realities, rendering the important insights of Stoic doctrine readily understandable, relateable and applicable to Seneca's Roman readers.

Similar scenarios play themselves out in and across the *Letters to Lucilius*. The discourse of wealth (*diuitiae*) and poverty (*paupertas*) that Seneca gradually transforms into a discourse of *frugalitas* first registers in *Letter* 2, triggered by a citation from and critique of Epicurus, i.e. his dictum that 'contented poverty is an honourable estate' (*Ep.* 2.6: *honesta res est laeta paupertas*). Seneca objects that *laeta paupertas* is a *contradictio in adiecto*: a mental state of contentment (*laeta*) is incompatible with the notion of poverty. He elaborates: *non qui parum habet, sed qui plus cupit, pauper est* ('Not he who has too little but he who craves more is poor'). And he concludes by getting at the same issue from the point of view of wealth: in

---

[171] *Tranq.* 9.2: *discamus membris nostris inniti, cultum uictumque non ad noua exempla componere, sed ut maiorum mores suadent.*

[172] *Tranq.* 9.2: *discamus continentiam augere, luxuriam coercere, gloriam temperare, iracundiam lenire, paupertatem aequis oculis aspicere, frugalitatem colere.*

318

Frugalitas, or: The Invention of a Roman Virtue

response to the question of what the proper limit to wealth is (2.6: *quis sit diuitiarum modus, quaeris?*), Seneca specifies first to have what is necessary and second to have what is enough (*primus habere quod necesse est, proximus quod sat est*). In his philosophical take on the wants and needs of material riches, he thus (a) redefines poverty as not being about external circumstances but a matter of internal disposition; and (b) imposes a measure on wealth with reference to external criteria, though he distinguishes between the basic necessities of subsistence, the minimum amount of calories to stay alive (*quod necesse est*) and some unspecified surplus on top (*quod sat est*).[173] In his discussion of both poverty and wealth, Seneca imperceptibly edges away from an extreme: an existence below the bare necessities can hardly be described as 'contented', i.e. genuine poverty does exist. Conversely, a hardline philosopher such as Diogenes the Cynic might well consider having the bare necessities a sufficient measure of wealth: by moving from the necessary (*necesse*) to the sufficient (*sat*), Seneca gains some wriggle room for a less rigorous take on the proper limit to wealth (*diuitiarum modus*).[174] As a result, an as yet ill-defined middle ground opens up: with reference to poverty, Seneca disowns the paradoxical nonentity *laeta paupertas* by way of adumbrating a mental state of contentment with subsistence, which he leaves unlabelled here (*laeta* 'something' – just not *paupertas*); with reference to wealth, he broaches a philosophically informed sense of what 'sufficient' might consist in – above and beyond, that is, the abject squalor of the (sub-)subsistence level. As subsequent letters show, this middle ground, which avoids both the paradoxical obscurities (Epicurus) and the extremes (Diogenes) of Greek philosophy, has a simple Roman name: *frugalitas*.

---

[173] Unless we want to equate the necessary with the sufficient. In places Seneca also configures the sufficient as an absolute standard (if less easily definable than the necessary). See e.g. *Ep.* 17.10: *saeculum muta, nimis habes. idem est autem omni saeculo, quod sat est.* Seneca might here assimilate the *sat* to the *necesse*, moving beyond his distinction in *Ep.* 2 into more rigorous philosophical territory.

[174] Extremists may well *equate* (a) *laeta paupertas*, (b) *modus diuitiarum* and (c) *quod necesse est*.

319

Ingo Gildenhard

In *Letter* 5 *frugalitas* defines the perfect middle ground that (again) avoids two extremes: unenlightened investment in material riches (the problem of Roman society) and the antisocial squalor affected by certain (Greek) intellectuals, which needlessly puts people off philosophy (a tough sale as it is) (5.2) and, worse, even violates the first principles of philosophy, including the doctrine that one ought to live according to nature (5.4). Seneca objects to both – the former is a sign of luxury, the latter of madness.[175] What he endorses instead is a form of existence that combines a philosophically informed inner disposition (which is radically different from that found in society at large) with a reasonably cultivated, socially acceptable outward appearance and style of life that ensures full and functional participation in society: *intus omnia dissimilia sint, frons populo nostra conueniat* (5.2). We should cultivate *frugalitas* as an inner disposition, not an outward affectation – which implies that we can dress well and, if we so happen to possess it, also use tableware made of precious metal.[176] In short, philosophy calls for *frugalitas*, nothing more and nothing less – and *frugalitas* does not have to be squalid: *frugalitatem exigit philosophia, non poenam, potest autem esse non incompta frugalitas* (5.5). As a mental disposition that amounts to indifference to material wealth, *frugalitas* operates independently of the external circumstances we find ourselves in and is of equal relevance to the poor and the rich.[177]

In Letter 5, i.e. quite early in the collection, Seneca thus implies that the *frugalitas* philosophy demands need not, indeed should not, lead to any (radical) adjustment in the

---

[175] *Ep.* 5.5: *quemadmodum desiderare delicatas res luxuriae est, ita usitatas et non magno parabiles fugere dementiae.*

[176] *Ep.* 5.3: *non splendeat toga, ne sordeat quidem. non habeamus argentum, in quod solidi auri caelatura descenderit, sed non putemus frugalitatis indicium auro argentoque caruisse.*

[177] As Seneca goes on to note, both a person who uses earthenware dishes as if they were silver and a person who uses silver as if it were earthenware should be considered great. If anything, the challenge the rich man faces is the greater one: *infirmi animi est pati non posse diuitias* (5.6); it is at any rate the side of the challenge Seneca himself and his primary audience face …

320

Frugalitas, or: The Invention of a Roman Virtue

lifestyle of the rich. While he does express his disapproval of *luxuria* (a form of conspicuous consumption widely practised among his Roman readers), his main target is the conspicuous squalor put on display by those who have a perverse conception of what philosophy entails. The emphasis is propaedeutic: his aim is decidedly not to turn his addressee Lucilius or his readers into versions of Diogenes the Cynic – quite the contrary.[178] Yet whereas he emphasises here that inner disposition and outward appearance are distinct, later on in the collection he suggests that a commitment to philosophical *frugalitas* also has consequences for how one lives one's external life and operates in society.[179]

Thus in *Letter* 17, Seneca argues that poverty and wealth (*paupertas* and *diuitiae*) are both sources of mental illness. The solution to the pathologies of obsession with material possession, with having too little and acquiring ever more, is a frame of mind that is content with essentials – *frugalitas*. Against the objection that a wholesale dedication to the philosophical life might result in poverty (*paupertas*) Seneca argues that *paupertas* is not to be feared, but to be embraced – even the wise rich man behaves as if he were poor (*Ep.* 17.4–5):

paupertas contenta est desideriis instantibus satis facere: quid est ergo, quare hanc recuses contubernalem, cuius mores sanus diues imitatur? si uis uacare animo, aut pauper sis oportet aut pauperi similis. non potest studium salutare fieri sine frugalitatis cura; frugalitas autem paupertas uoluntaria est.

Poverty is content with fulfilling pressing needs. Why, then, should you reject philosophy as a comrade? Even the rich man copies her ways if he is sound of mind. If you want to have mental freedom, you either have to be a poor man or resemble a poor man. Study cannot become a source of wellbeing unless you embrace frugality; yet frugality is voluntary poverty.

---

[178] For Roman interactions with Cynicism see Billerbeck 1982. Cf. Martial 4.53 with Moreno Soldevila 2006: 373.

[179] Seneca applies this approach not just to the reassessment of material wealth. See Gloyn 2017: 203 (who uses *Ep.* 5 as her case in point): 'Yet despite his apparent willingness to accommodate Roman social norms, Seneca outlines a radical path of action that requires his Stoic *proficientes* to completely reconstruct how they understand the family, our place within it, and its relationship to the wider world.'

Ingo Gildenhard

The prospect of poverty (and hence the need for further enrichment as insurance) is therefore no excuse to put off complete devotion to philosophy, in the form of practised *frugalitas* in the sense of *paupertas uoluntaria* – and Seneca now suggests that the inner frugal disposition he is interested in cultivating does benefit from a frugal style of life. While in *Letter* 5, he insisted on the greatest possible degree of difference between the mental outlook of *frugalitas* and outward appearance, here he recommends a conscious assimilation: the life of the frugal rich man ought to *resemble* that of the poor.[180]

As *Letter* 87 shows, within Roman society, this coincidence of frugal disposition and frugal lifestyle is a tough ask – even for Seneca himself. He gives an account of a journey undertaken with a friend in the most frugal of circumstances, in terms of the attendant number of slaves, the amount and kind of food consumed (just the barest necessities: 3: *de prandio nihil detrahi potest*) and the cart used (powered by old and malnourished mules guided by a barefoot driver). He notes his blissful state of mind – happy, prosperous, productive, at peace with itself, disinterested in anything external and inessential – until an outside observer enters the scene. Then shame kicks in: *uix a me obtineo ut hoc uehiculum uelim uideri meum* (4) – and even though Seneca realises that his sense of shame (*uerecundia*) is perverse (*peruersa*), he blushes unwillingly whenever they encounter a more luxurious party (*quotiens in aliquem comitatum lautiorem incidimus, inuitus erubesco*: 4).[181] Put differently, he here reimagines for himself a variant of the scenario that Serenus rehearsed at the outset of the *de Tranquilitate Animi*.[182] Seneca's self-diagnosis is harsh: he has made some

---

[180] He comes back to this idea even more explicitly at *Ep.* 18.5–6: as a lesson, Seneca recommends to his charge to live *as if* he were poor – to exercise the mindset that poverty all but enforces, but that someone in pursuit of *sapientia* should adopt voluntarily and willingly: *contentus minimo ac uilissimo cibo, dura atque horrida ueste*. See further Rosivach 1995.

[181] For the entourage of a travelling senator see Amm. Marc. 14.6.17; his picture of 'social status on the move' nicely illustrates why more frugal travellers of similar standing in society might feel a sense of shame and humiliation.

[182] For the connection between *Tranq.* and *Ep.* 87 see Inwood 2005: 348–9, arguing that the parallels help to establish the special epistolary, dialogic qualities of this particular treatise.

322

Frugalitas, or: The Invention of a Roman Virtue

progress towards realising the philosophical life – he lives frugally; but like Serenus, he has not yet made sufficient progress to dare professing his frugality openly: *parum adhuc profeci. nondum audeo frugalitatem palam ferre* (5). He still cares about the opinion of random fellow travellers he happens to meet on the road. This shows continued belief in the erroneous – yet ubiquitous – notion that material wealth is an indicator of moral worth. Seneca proceeds to contest this correlation, first with reference to the exemplary conduct of Cato the Elder (9–11), which grounds Stoic philosophy in Roman history, then by means of philosophical argumentation, though not without a supporting quotation from Virgil's *Georgics*, to give the Greek discourse a Roman flavour (20).

He returns to the problem that the wrong company (society) encourages wrong conduct in *Letter* 94. A status-conscious audience compromises frugal philosophical commitments. With judging onlookers removed, it is easy to revert to a simple philosophically focused life. The countryside is a place of *frugalitas* not because of its association with agriculture and peasant values – but because it is a place of solitude, away from the judging eyes of onlookers.[183] Even at this stage, however, Seneca does not advocate the conspicuous austerity of the cynic who preens himself by virtue of his squalor in public – rather, for reaching a perfect match between internal and external *frugalitas* (as it were), Seneca recommends withdrawal from public life altogether.[184] In fact, some passages in his *oeuvre* suggest that such withdrawal from society might be the first step towards divinity.

Not content with identifying *frugalitas* with the disposition of the Stoic sage, Seneca in places elevates it even further, developing a notion of what one could label 'sublime frugality', insofar as he associates the concept with the

---

[183] *Ep.* 94.69: *non est per se magistra innocentiae solitudo nec frugalitatem docent rura, sed ubi testis ac spectator abscessit, uitia subsidunt, quorum monstrari et conspici fructus est.*

[184] *Ep.* 94.71: *ambitio et luxuria et impotentia scaenam desiderant; sanabis ista, si absconderis.*

Ingo Gildenhard

supernatural sphere. Thus at *de Beneficiis* 4.8.4 he lists *frugalitas* alongside *iustitia, probitas, prudentia* and *fortitudo* as one of the good qualities of the cosmic divinity, the one divine mind that pervades the universe – seemingly drawing a parallel between 'the doctrine of the unity of the virtues: whoever has one, has them all' and 'the idea of aspects of the divine reason'.[185]

Even more strikingly, in *Letter* 73 he identifies *frugalitas* as the quality that enables human beings to rise to the level of the gods. To get this remarkable ascent underway, Seneca notes that the philosopher owes much to those in charge of the commonwealth since they generate the *pax* and the *libertas* (8) as well as the *otium* (10) to pursue philosophy – which opens up a personal path to heaven.[186] He then proceeds to argue that the wise man is superior even to the supreme divinity (Jupiter). In his attempt to bolster this bold claim, he notes that while both Jupiter and the wise man survey and scorn all the possessions of others with equal equanimity, the wise man will esteem himself more highly: whereas Jupiter, who laid down responsibility for the world, is unable to make use of any possession (hence it is not a matter of volition in his case), the wise man could but does not want to – in his case, the abstinence is voluntary. Unlike Jupiter, the sage has it within his power to want successfully – or not to want. He therefore enjoys a greater degree of freedom and autonomy than the supreme divinity in the sphere of material self-restraint: Jupiter has no choice; the sage does.[187] Seneca concludes this section with a citation from Sextius (73.15):

---

[185] Griffin 2013: 238. The fact that Cicero uses *frugalitas* (instead of the rather more standard *temperantia*) might owe itself to the influence of *Tusc.* 3.16–17 and *Deiot.* 26, where Cicero hails *frugalitas* as the *maxima uirtus* that comprises all others.

[186] *Ep.* 73.11: *quanti aestimamus hoc otium, quod inter deos agitur, quod deos facit? ita dico, Lucili, et te in caelum compendiario uoco.*

[187] On the importance of freedom and autonomous agency for Seneca see further Inwood 2005: 302–21 and Edwards 2009, both without reference to *Ep.* 73, which should perhaps play a larger role in scholarly discussion of volition, agency and the politics of freedom in Seneca.

324

Frugalitas, or: The Invention of a Roman Virtue

Credamus itaque Sextio monstranti pulcherrimum iter et clamanti: 'hac "itur ad astra" [= *Aen.* 9.641], hac secundum frugalitatem, hac secundum temperantiam, hac secundum fortitudinem.'

Let us therefore believe Sextius when he shows us that most beautiful path and exclaims: '"This is the way to the stars" – according to frugality, temperance and courage.'

Frugalitas, in other words, understood in the Stoic sense of freedom from wants and desires, helps pave the way to apotheosis – to a state of being akin to that of the gods.[188] In Seneca's world, then, *frugalitas* informs consideration of what to have for dinner no less than our drive towards deification.

In all, then, *frugalitas* in Seneca has a truly stunning scope and is of cardinal importance: it speaks to such themes as the self and self-sufficiency, volition (and autonomy), internal dispositions and their outward enactment, poverty and wealth, society and solitude, the Greek and the Roman, extremes and golden means, self-restraint and virtue, the abject and the sublime. It is one of the ways in which Seneca establishes an interface between Roman realities and the philosophical outlook he advocates: his approach to the teaching of philosophy includes concession to Roman common sense especially in the earlier letters, where he lures his readers into philosophical discourse, encourages them to enter his literary worlds, making them look non-threatening – before working up to more radical insights, more difficult, more counterintuitive lessons. In this project, the semantic scope of the lexeme *frugalitas* and Roman *exempla* offer welcome support, suggesting that what he advocates for philosophical reasons constitutes (lost) Roman cultural knowledge, an ancestral ideal, enacted by exemplary figures in the distant past (very much according to the plot of societal decline formulated by Cato the Elder and other Roman historiographers); and the coincidence of ancestral and philosophical *frugalitas* renders the ideal real.

---

[188] Note that the arch-Roman pair of *fortitudo* and *frugalitas* (cf. V. Max. 4.3.5 cited above 300) brackets the Greek-flavoured *temperantia* = σωφροσύνη (a virtual synonym of *frugalitas*, of course, at least according to Cic. *Tusc.* 3.15–17).

Ingo Gildenhard

Quintilian[189]

Quintilian shows interest in the etymology and the semantics of *frugi* and *frugalitas*[190] – as well he might: in the *Institutio*, *frugalitas* (as antonym of *luxuria*) is a self-evident virtue (5.10.73: *frugalitas bonum, luxuria enim malum*) and an indispensable enabling factor and intrinsic characteristic of his perfect orator.[191] In two places, he identifies a frugal way of life – including abstention from sex and a healthy diet – as essential for cultivating the health and physique that an orator has to have to undergo the rigorous training that will ensure a virile performance.[192] The identification of *frugalitas* as a prerequisite for reaching perfection in oratory prepares for the key role that the noun plays in the final, climactic book of the work.

Quintilian opens *Institutio Oratoria* 12 by defining the orator in the tradition of Cato as 'a good man skilled in speaking' – a definition anticipated by allusive references to the Catonian conception, which Quintilian 'updates' with the help of Stoic philosophy, throughout the work from 1 pr. 9

---

[189] For Quintilian, I cite the text and translation of D. A. Russell in the Loeb Classical Library. For the project of the *Institutio* (and its influence on Pliny) see now Whitton 2019.

[190] See *Inst.* 1.6.17, 29.

[191] Quintilian is sufficiently aware of cross-cultural differences to realise that not every audience (an all-important consideration for the orator) will see eye to eye on the matter of self-restraint. See *Inst.* 3.7.24: *frugalitas apud Sybaritas forsitan odio foret, ueteribus Romanis summum luxuria crimen.* The emphatic *ueteribus* and the superlative *summum* suggest that the Romans of Quintilian's time remain in principle committed to *frugalitas* even if they have adopted a somewhat more tolerant attitude towards luxury (they no longer consider *luxuria* the *worst* possible crime). At the same time, the passage reinforces the special affinity of *frugalitas* with Rome and her cultural superiority.

[192] *Inst.* 10.3.26; 11.3.19. With the identification of *frugalitas* as prerequisite for a robust physique and manly voice (as opposed to the feeble and shrill voice of eunuchs, women and the sick) compare and contrast 12.10.21 where Quintilian uses *frugalitas* in an aesthetic-stylistic sense in reference to writers who are 'content with a certain frugality of eloquence' (*quadam eloquentiae frugalitate contentos*). He considers this form of eloquence a lightweight *variant* of Atticism, though not representative of the phenomenon as such. Put differently, the *orator* should be frugal, not his *eloquentia*: the *frugalitas* of the man ensures that his eloquence will rise above it.

326

Frugalitas, or: The Invention of a Roman Virtue

onwards.[193] He then sharpens the requirement of moral soundness: not only does the orator have to be a good man; in fact, no one can become an orator unless he *is* a good man.[194] Any form of vice or wickedness will inevitably result in failure to achieve this goal. Part of his justification for this seemingly counterintuitive proposition (history shows – and Cicero knows – that the ability to speak well and persuasively is by no means limited to men with sound morals) comes from the fact that becoming an orator requires a tremendous amount of effort and application. Even honourable activities if pursued excessively will compromise the requisite regimen of study – to say nothing of desire, avarice and envy and the other negative emotions that haunt an evil mind (*mala mens*), rendering it incapable of meaningful study of literature and any other *bona ars*. Instead, the arduous path towards becoming an orator presupposes, above all, *frugalitas*: 'is not frugality', Quintilian asks rhetorically, 'essential for enduring the labours of study' (12.1.8: *age, non ad perferendos studiorum labores necessaria frugalitas*)? Only a frugal way of life provides the fertile ground for the seeds of intellectual activities (assimilated to *fruges* via a simile in the previous sentence) to flourish. Given the centrality of *frugalitas* to the development of the orator, lust and luxury need not apply: *quid ergo ex libidine ac luxuria spei* (12.1.8)?

Towards the end of 12.2, Quintilian gives this elevation of *frugalitas* into a key ingredient of supreme eloquence historical depth and a cross-cultural edge. The section is ostensibly devoted to the question which school of philosophy can contribute to eloquence most (12.2.23: ... *quaestio exoritur, quae secta conferre plurimum eloquentiae possit*). In fact, Quintilian implies after briefly considering and dismissing various possibilities that none of the schools has much to contribute to the

---

[193] *Inst.* 12.1.1: *sit ergo nobis orator quem constituimus is qui a M. Catone finitur uir bonus dicendi peritus.* For discussion of Quintilian's notion of the *orator* and its Catonian affiliations see Winterbottom 1964; Reinhardt and Winterbottom 2006: xlvi–l.
[194] *Inst.* 12.1.3: *neque enim tantum id dico, eum qui sit orator uirum bonum esse opportere, sed ne futurum quidem oratorem nisi uirum bonum.*

Ingo Gildenhard

study of eloquent articulation; at the same time, some philosophical schools have formulated sound ethical precepts that the aspiring orator will choose to form his character, as the most direct road to *uirtus*.[195] He does not name the philosophers who provide these *honestissima praecepta*, but his phrasing makes it clear that he is thinking of Plato and the Stoics in particular.[196] His refusal to identify potentially inspirational Greek intellectuals by name is deliberate. More important than the ethical precepts articulated by anonymous philosophers, however admirable they might be, are the deeds and sayings of historical action-figures, an area in which the Romans excel above all others (12.2.29–30):

> magis etiam quae sunt tradita antiquitus dicta ac facta praeclare et nosse et animo semper agitare conueniet. quae profecto nusquam plura maioraque quam in nostrae ciuitatis monumentis reperientur. an fortitudinem, iustitiam, fidem, continentiam, frugalitatem, contemptum doloris ac mortis melius alii docebunt quam Fabricii, Curii, Reguli, Decii, Mucii aliique innumerabiles? quantum enim Graeci praeceptis ualent, tantum Romani, quid est maius, exemplis.

> even more important are the records of the notable sayings and actions of the past. Nowhere is there a larger or more striking supply of these than in the history of our own country. Could there be any better teachers of courage, justice, loyalty, self-control, frugality, or contempt for pain and death than men like Fabricius, Curius, Regulus, Decius, Mucius, and countless others? Rome is as strong in examples as Greece is in precepts; and examples are more important.

Just as any author worth his salt, Quintilian selects those value terms of particular relevance to his literary project and the historical circumstances of composition. Starting with the

---

[195] *Inst.* 12.2.27: *quare in exemplum bene dicendi facundissimum quemque proponet sibi ad imitandum, moribus uero formandis quam honestissima praecepta rectissimamque ad uirtutem uiam deliget* ('Thus, as a model of oratory, he will pick the most eloquent for imitation, but for forming his character he will choose the noblest possible precepts and the most direct road to virtue').

[196] See esp. *Inst.* 12.2.28: *haec sunt quibus mens pariter atque oratio insurgant: quae uere bona, quid mitiget metus, coerceat cupiditates, eximat nos opinionibus uulgi animumque caelestem <cognatis sideribus admoueat>?* ('Here are themes to elevate mind and language alike: "What things are truly good?" "What can calm fear, restrain desire, free us from common misconceptions, and <bring> the heavenborn soul <into contact with its starry kindred>?"')

Frugalitas, or: The Invention of a Roman Virtue

conventional *fortitudo* (bravery in battle), he moves on to qualities that sustain socio-political life (*iustitia, fides*) and the satisficing self-restraint of individuals (*continentia, frugalitas*), before concluding with the philosophising notion of contempt for pain and death (*contemptus doloris ac mortis*), which harks back to *fortitudo* at the outset but also brings to mind works of theoretical reflection such as Cicero's *Tusculan Disputations* (in particular books 1 and 2) that validate this quality as an essential element not just for warfare but also life under an autocratic regime. And like Cicero, he brings Rome's record of ancestral achievements into play to demote Greece in the context of cross-cultural rivalry – while assigning a significant, if seemingly subsidiary role to Greek philosophy within his own intellectual enterprise. *frugalitas,* as a shining star in the firmament of ancestral *Roman* virtues in the tradition of Cicero and Valerius Maximus (cf. *dicta ac facta*), is perfect for advancing this agenda: for Quintilian, it constitutes a mental and ethical disposition informed equally by hands-on discipline and moral precepts gleaned from, yes, Greek philosophy but above all Roman history that manifests itself in a way of life reminiscent of the most distinguished republican ancestors and finds physical embodiment in Cato the Elder's *uir bonus* and his own *orator perfectus.* Put differently, Quintilian centres Romanness and its epitome, the supreme orator, in *frugalitas.*

Pliny the Younger

At the most basic level, *frugalitas* for Pliny is a necessity to meet his social obligations. The maintenance of the senatorial rank he has achieved, so he concedes, is a costly business, which in *Epistle* 2.4 he captures in the neat formulation *dignitas sumptuosa*; but his thrift and material sobriety, his *frugalitas,* enable him to live up to his socio-political status and the expectation of expenditure in the tradition of communal *liberalitas* it entails.[197] The combination of manifold

---

[197] *Ep.* 2.4.3: *sunt quidem omnino nobis modicae facultates, dignitas sumptuosa, reditus propter condicionem agellorum nescio minor an incertior. sed, quod cessat ex reditu,*

Ingo Gildenhard

responsibilities and limited resources enhance the generosity of the financial support he offers to Calvina at a level he can barely afford. In a sense, Pliny here employs a variant of 'enforced frugality':[198] the element of compulsion diminishes the degree of personal credit he can take for his frugal style of life, though in the context of this particular letter his emphasis that he strives hard to make ends meet of course serves a particular rhetorical purpose.[199] And he manages to transform his seemingly moderate means, which 'require' him to be frugal, into a badge of honour, literally making a virtue out of necessity and broadcasting his *frugalitas* as (also) a matter of choice and as such a manifestation of a specific kind of moral superiority grounded in the exercise of self-restraint.

The strategy that turns *frugalitas* into a disposition to be proud of is three-pronged: Pliny (a) valorises the tradition of thought that sees in *frugalitas* a quality of the Romans of old and locates its continuing existence in the very region of Italy from which he hails himself – as well as individuals who have the ear of the reigning *princeps*; (b) validates voluntary moderation as a virtuous alternative to the orthodox economics of status, not least in arenas conventionally defined by extreme forms of conspicuous consumption such as banquets; and (c) aligns his self-promotional commitment to *frugalitas* in his *Letters* with the imperial image he fashions for Trajan in the *Panegyricus*.

---

frugalitate suppletur, ex qua uelut fonte liberalitas nostra decurrit ('True, on the whole my financial resources are rather limited and my rank and standing in society are expensive to maintain; my income is dependent on returns from my estate and hence smallish and rather precarious. But any shortfall is made up by frugality: it is the source or, if you will, spring from which our generosity flows'). For Pliny's use of his letters to self-promote (and immortalise) his *liberalitas* see the excellent discussion by Whitton 2013: 103; on senatorial obligations more generally Talbert 1984: 54–66 (cited by Whitton 2013: 108) and now also Hartmann 2016: 173–8 ('Die Nöte der traditionellen Elite').

[198] See Introduction 15.

[199] Cf. Shelton 2013: 100: 'As one of the wealthiest landowners in the area and one who had competed successfully in Roman politics, he was expected to help the citizens of his hometown with advice and, more importantly, with financial support for community projects.'

330

Frugalitas, or: The Invention of a Roman Virtue

(a) In various places, Pliny connects *frugalitas* with the satisficing sobriety and other virtues of the imaginary small-scale farmer of old – an effect he achieves like Seneca and his uncle Pliny the Elder through the simple expedient of attaching the attribute *antiqua* to the noun.[200] The diachronic perspective the temporal descriptor opens up also enables him to imply that this variant of ancestral sobriety has given way to novel and lesser forms in the meantime or has disappeared altogether – except in certain regions of Italy that preserve the old traditions, such as Brescia in the North, which, of course, is not far from Comum, Pliny's own city of origin.[201] The reign of Trajan is particularly conducive for these traditions to flourish anew: *prisca frugalitas*, manifesting itself in both food consumption and austere living quarters, is one of the many qualities of Titius Aristo, a legal expert and adviser of the emperor.[202] Pliny, then, is right at home in the new regime – especially since *frugalitas* is a quality he shares with other members of his household and his circle of friends, such as his 'ideal' third wife Calpurnia;[203] his freedman Zosimus;[204] and his boyhood friend Atilius Crescens.[205]

---

[200] See above 312 and Plin. *Nat.* 1, summary of Book 33: *de luxuria in uasis argenteis; frugalitatis antiquae in argento exempla.*

[201] *Ep.* 1.14.4: as part of recommending Minicius Acilianus as prospective husband for the niece of his addressee Iunius Mauricus he notes his favourable origins: *patria est ei Brixia ex illa nostra Italia, quae multum adhuc uerecundiae, frugalitatis atque etiam rusticitatis antiquae retinet ac seruat.* As Carlon 2009: 160 n. 32 points out, with his 'topography of frugality' Pliny plays the same game of recentring traditional Roman virtues in the periphery as Cato the Elder: 'Pliny's homeland is certainly even further removed from Rome and its enticements than Cato's Sabine land. Its distance helps it to retain the same revered and ancient virtues of moderation and restraint that Cato highlights in his *De Agricultura.*'

[202] *Ep.* 1.22.4: *ad hoc quam parcus in uictu, quam modicus in cultu! soleo ipsum cubiculum eius ipsumque lectum ut imaginem quandam priscae frugalitatis adspicere.*

[203] *Ep.* 4.19.2 (about his third wife Calpurnia, who hailed from the same frugal region of northern Italy as he himself): *summum est acumen, summa frugalitas: amat me, quod castitatis indicium est.* For Calpurnia and her thriftiness, also in the wider context of Pliny's oeuvre, see Carlon 2009: 158–65 and Shelton 2013: 97–104 and 111–15.

[204] *Ep.* 5.19.9: *est enim tam parcus et continens, ut non solum delicias, uerum etiam necessitates ualetudinis frugalitate restringat.*

[205] *Ep.* 6.8.5: *homo est alieni abstinentissimus, sui diligens, nullis quaestibus sustinetur, nullus illi nisi ex frugalitate reditus.*

Ingo Gildenhard

(b) But for Pliny *frugalitas* is not just an ancient quality; its proper enactment amounts to a social philosophy that challenges key social conventions in the name of a virtue ethics centred in humanity and moderation. Thus in *Epistle* 2.6 Pliny 'describes a counter-exemplary dinner at which the host served different grades of food to different guests: an occasion that should be defined by communality became the site of offensive hierarchy.'[206] When Pliny mentions to his host, who manages to be 'extravagant and mean at once',[207] that his own policy is to serve up the same menu to everyone, including freedmen, his host walks right into the trap. Since it never crosses his mind that Pliny might compromise on lavish hospitality at the upper end of the social scale, he naively asks him how he manages to afford such profligacy – opening himself up for Pliny's chiastic *coup de grâce*: *liberti mei non idem quod ego bibunt, sed idem ego quod liberti* ('my freed-men don't drink the same wine I do – *I* drink what *they* do').[208] In the rest of the letter, Pliny more generally criticises the extravagance (*luxuria*) at some men's tables 'under the guise of frugality' (*specie frugalitatis*); instead of faking the virtue, members of the elite ought properly restrain themselves – at least when it comes to the consumption of food and drink. His host, by scrimping on expenditure for his freedmen while indulging himself and his peers, practises a mean and hence wrong-headed kind of thriftiness, whereas Pliny continues in the tradition of elite moderation established by Piso Frugi, while also subtly acknowledging that *frugalitas* traditionally belongs into a humble social milieu by using the treatment of freedmen to make his point.[209] Overall, then, Pliny (according to Pliny)

---

[206] Whitton 2013: 120.   [207] Whitton 2013: 121.

[208] Deliberate downscaling of food and drink consumption to the level of ordinary people is a trope of self-promotional elite frugality since Cato the Elder, who boasted that on his voyage to Spain as consul and governor he quaffed the same wine as his rowers (*non aliud uinum quam remiges*): Cato, *Dierum dictarum de consulatu suo* fr. 53 M[4] (Plin. *Nat.* 14.91). See Chapter 3 (Passet).

[209] Despite the fact that the noun *frugalitas* obfuscates differences in social status insofar as it assimilates the lifestyle of the prudent senator to that of a slave or a freedman of modest means within an overall ideology of thrift and moderation, Pliny, just like Seneca, is squeamish about applying the attribute *frugi* to any of his upperclass acquaintances – though he is less concerned when it comes to buildings

Frugalitas, or: The Invention of a Roman Virtue

manages to balance and combine perfectly the two virtues of *priuata frugalitas* and *publica magnificentia* (to put it in the terms Cicero adumbrates in the *pro Murena*).

(c) In the *Panegyricus* Pliny upscales *frugalitas* yet further by turning it into the trademark of the self-restraint omnipotence and civic virtue of the current *princeps*. Like no other lexeme it captures the shift in imperial ideology (as formulated not least by Pliny himself) after the death of Domitian. The 'adoptive emperorship' put in place by Nerva and Trajan in and of itself invited renewed investment in Augustan ideas of ultimate equality between the *princeps* and the rest of the governing class. Whereas a 'bad' emperor like Caligula enforced an unbridgeable divide between himself and all of his subjects, including those of the highest rank, those emperors or their eulogists who wanted to promote themselves as a *primus inter pares* or *princeps ciuilis* would emphasize commitment to a set of values shared by all members of the ruling elite, moderating the exercise of their autocratic power and reviving proto-republican notions of *libertas*.[210] Pliny's ideal emperor manages to square the circle of imperial flamboyance and personal humility in a novel 'recombination of opposites'.[211] Under

---

and food. Of the six occurrences of the adjective in the letters, two refer to good-quality slaves (*Ep.* 1.21.2; 3.19.7) and two to the golden mean in the context of conspicuous display or consumption (*Ep.* 2.17.4: the *atrium* of his Laurentian villa is *frugi nec tamen sordidum*: see Whitton 2013: 229 and xii–xiii; the 'moralizing equation of building and man' goes back to Cato the Elder: see Bloomer 2011: 32; *Ep.* 3.1.9: the *cena* at Spurinna's was *non minus nitida quam frugi*). Just once does Pliny use *frugi* with reference to someone of high social standing and then only to indicate a generic type as opposed to singling out a specific individual: at *Ep.* 2.17.26 he mentions that, while the resources required for bathing (wood and water) are abundant within the vicinity of his Laurentian villa, the provisions in the close-by village would be sufficient for a thrifty person (*frugi quidem homini sufficit etiam uicus*). Whitton 2013: 251 glosses the opening phrase with 'but for a person of moderation', noting that *homo* could refer to either Pliny himself or a potential visitor (or both). Cf. *Ep.* 3.9.33 (reference to Libo Frugi).

[210] Gowing 2005: 120–31; Connolly 2009. Endeavours to define what *libertas* might mean in autocratic times are of course co-extensive with the principate – and indeed the triumviral period. See e.g. Strunk 2017 or most recently Wolstencroft 2019 (on how Horace conceived of freedom in his first book of *Satires*).

[211] See *Pan.* 4. 4–7 with Feldherr 2019: 392–4 (quotation from 394); for the 'imperial paradox' of flamboyance and self-restraint see Dench 1998: 145–6, cited at Introduction 76.

333

Ingo Gildenhard

those conditions, *frugalitas* advances to a leitmotif in Pliny's *Panegyricus*.[212]

With the disappearance of coded hypocrisy, says Pliny at the outset, eulogy can be straightforward and honest – there is no longer any danger that anyone would interpret praise of an emperor's *frugalitas* as an indictment of his *luxuria*.[213] And that is precisely what Pliny does: in § 41, he praises Trajan's self-restraint when it comes to filling the imperial coffers as *frugalitas principis*. Very much like Tacitus' Vespasian with his *parsimonia*, the *princeps* sets an example – and in so doing, he shapes the rest of the citizen body, which may lack the moral fibre to pursue good and shun evil if it sees the reward for *labor, uigilantia* and *frugalitas* go to *inertia, somnus* and *luxuria* (44.8).[214] When Trajan holds table the two positive values of *frugalitas* and *humanitas* vie with each other, generating a perfect balance.[215] The theme of Trajan's *frugalitas* culminates in § 88, which begins (not coincidentally) with Pliny noting that most of the emperors, though lording it over everyone else as masters of their subjects, were themselves the slaves of their freedmen, at the mercy of their counsels and their whims (88.1: *plerique principes, cum essent ciuium domini, libertorum erant serui: horum consiliis horum nutu regebantur*). Trajan, by contrast, while holding his freedmen in high esteem, does not empower them unduly at the expense of the senatorial elite – the highest honour they have any right to expect is a reputation for being honest and of good character (88.2: *tu libertis tuis summum quidem honorem, sed tamquam libertis habes*

---

[212] Two recent treatments, both with excellent discussion of the text's curious gestation history and further bibliography, are Geisthardt 2015: 83–219 and Feldherr 2019. See also the papers in Roche 2011.

[213] 3.4: *Non enim periculum est, ne, cum loquar de humanitate, exprobrari sibi superbiam credat; cum de frugalitate, luxuriam; cum de clementia, crudelitatem; cum de liberalitate, auaritiam; cum de benignitate, liuorem; cum de continentia, libidinem; cum de labore, inertiam; cum de fortitudine, timorem.* On Pliny and 'truth-speaking' see e.g. Bartsch 1994: 148–87 and, with further nuance, Geisthardt 2015: 119–28 ('Das Problem der Ernsthaftigkeit des Lobredners'), who deftly links the matter of truth to the text's history of composition.

[214] Cf. Tac. *Ann.* 3.55. See Introduction 85.

[215] 49.6: *non ipsum tempus epularum tuarum, cum frugalitate contrahat, extendit humanitas?*

334

Frugalitas, or: The Invention of a Roman Virtue

abundeque sufficere his credis, si probi et frugi existimentur). The attribute *frugi* puts the freedmen in their proper place: 'the monarch's autonomy and self-restraint are configured through his ability to preserve domestic hierarchies, which had come to bear on the public sphere more consequentially in the empire than ever before.'[216]

Yet after evoking the 'Plautine' strand of the semantics of *frugi* as a quality associated with the milieu of (former) slaves, Pliny proceeds to recall the rise of *frugalitas* up the social scale through the intervention of Piso Frugi. Trajan's approach to the management of human resources earns him the epithet 'best' as a cognomen, or so Pliny notes in a rhetorical act of 'meta-terminological *optimization*' (88.4–6):[217]

Iustisne de causis Senatus Populusque Romanus OPTIMI tibi cognomen adiecit? paratum id quidem, et in medio positum, nouum tamen. scias neminem ante meruisse, quod non erat excogitandum, si quis meruisset. an satius fuit, FELICEM uocare? quod non moribus, sed fortunae datum est: satius, MAGNUM? cui plus inuidiae, quam pulchritudinis inest. adoptauit te optimus princeps in suum, senatus in OPTIMI nomen. hoc tibi tam proprium, quam paternum; nec magis definite distincteque designat, qui TRAIANUM, quam qui OPTIMUM appellat: ut olim frugalitate Pisones, sapientia Laelii, pietate Metelli monstrabantur. quae simul omnia uno isto nomine continentur. nec uideri potest optimus, nisi qui est optimis omnibus in sua cuiusque laude praestantior.

Is there not just reason for the title bestowed on you by the Senate and people of Rome – the title of *Optimus*, Best? It may seem ready-made and commonplace, but in fact it is something new. No one is known to have merited it before, though it was there to be used if someone proved worthy. Would it have been better to call him 'Fortunate'? This is a tribute to his luck, not his character. What about 'the Great'? This has a ring of envy rather than renown. In adopting you, the best of emperors gave you his own name, to which the Senate added that of *Optimus*, to be as much your personal name as the one your father gave. Thus you are as clearly designated and defined by the name of *Optimus* as by that of Trajan; just as formerly the family of Piso was known for frugality, and that of Laelius and Metellus for wisdom and filial piety. All these virtues are contained in the

---

[216] MacLean 2018: 116.
[217] Henderson 2011: 170. I cite the translation of Betty Radice in the Loeb Classical Library.

Ingo Gildenhard

single name which is yours, for 'the Best' can only refer to the man who outstrips all others who are best in their own distinctive ways.

After recalling the 'aristocratic' variant of *frugalitas* associated with Piso Frugi and his descendants, Pliny ends with a move reminiscent of Cicero's *Tusculans*: just as in *Tusculan* 3 all virtues are subsumed in *frugalitas*, so here *frugalitas*, *sapientia* and *pietas* are aspects of Trajan's epithet *optimus*.[218] Put differently, in this remarkable paragraph Pliny, in what amounts to a brief history of the concept, retraces the semantic evolution of *frugi* from slave-value to the badge of honour of a specific republican *gens* to Cicero's philosophising play with the unity of virtues, which here come together in the superlative *optimus*. His evocation of the complex history of *frugi/frugalitas* in republican times carries a programmatic charge: it feeds into the association of the adoptive emperorship with the renewal of republican virtues. Put differently, Pliny promotes *frugalitas* as a (new) 'imperial ideal', as one key strand of his *princeps-ciuilis* ideology.[219]

Conclusion

In a sense, Pliny's synoptic reconfiguration of *frugi/frugalitas*, which takes in the entire prehistory of the lexemes, has brought us full circle – and we can conclude with another look at the passage from Bruni cited at the outset. The antithesis between public and private Bruni draws is reminiscent of Cicero's famous pronouncement at *pro Murena* 76 that the Roman people hate private luxury (*priuata luxuria*) but love public splendour (*publica magnificentia*),

---

[218] The importance he accords *frugalitas* here might explain why Pliny does not use the noun to praise Trajan's wife Plotina at *Pan.* 83.7 as one might have expected. Plotina is of course exemplary in her self-restraint (see Shelton 2013: 111, who notes in a discussion of the *frugalitas* of Pliny's wife Calpurnia that 'in the *Panegyricus*, he pointed out that Plotina had imitated the simple lifestyle of her husband, Trajan'), but Pliny chooses other lexemes to make this point.

[219] It did not catch on: see Noreña (2011), who does not index the term. It did, however, inspire the late-antique panegyrist Pacatus Drepanius: Introduction 95–100.

336

Frugalitas, or: The Invention of a Roman Virtue

though Cicero does not use *frugalitas* either here or elsewhere in the *pro Murena*.[220] The notion of *frugalitas* as a *uirtus priuata*, as thrift and/or moderation in private life, first finds articulation in the *pro rege Deiotaro* – and then recurs in early imperial authors. But Bruni of course has no interest in such historical nuances. Rather, he mixes and matches texts and ideas, coopting and adjusting various sources in his endeavour to fabricate a reified image of the ancient Romans *tout court* that foregrounds two distinct desirables: the pursuit of imperial grandeur in public affairs and commitment to a frugal ethics in private life. The essential and timeless character of his construct implies the possibility of ethnic continuity: he considers the *populus Romanus* the ancestor of contemporary Florence (*parens noster*). But while Bruni evokes the possibility of lineage in terms of blood-kinship, he simultaneously breaks with classical modes of thought at the conceptual level: whereas his ancient sources tend to conceive of *priuata frugalitas* and *publica magnificentia* as working in unison and synergy, in Bruni the pairing features within a larger polemic that contrasts two opposing mentalities in contemporary Florence, 'one political and public, the other mercantile and private' and is part of a 'blame-game about Florence's failure to grab Lucca in 1329': Bruni's character Pino argues that the city wasted this opportunity for aggressive statescraft because the spirit of lily-livered mercantilism prevailed in the public sphere.[221] Put differently, here we get the paradox of *priuata frugalitas* out of control, of moderation in need of moderation, so that it does not transgress its proper remit and thereby undermine the heroic quest for *publica magnificentia*![222]

---

[220] On *Mur.* 76 see further Introduction 65–70, also Adamietz 1989: 226–9; La Penna 1989: 18–23; Berno 2014: 370–2.

[221] Ianziti 2012: 127. Cf. Struever 1970: 137–8 and Hörnqvist 2004: 62–3.

[222] This line of reasong is reminiscent of Cicero's attack on the austerity of Tubero and Cato the Younger in the *pro Murena*, as being at variance with Rome's imperial stature. But Cicero gives no positive expression to the notion of private moderation.

Ingo Gildenhard

Bibliography

Adamietz, J. (1989) *Cicero, Pro Murena*. Darmstadt.

Arena, V. (2011) 'The Consulship of 78 BC. Catulus versus Lepidus: an optimates versus populares affair', in *Consuls and Res Publica: Holding High Office in the Roman Republic*, eds. H. Beck, A. Duplá, M. Jehne and F. Pina Polo. Cambridge: 299–318.

Astin, A. E. (1988) '*Regimen Morum*', *JRS* 78: 14–34.

Atherton, C. (1988) 'Hand over fist: the failure of Stoic rhetoric', *CQ* 38: 392–427.

Ax, W. (2011) *Quintilians Grammatik (Inst. Orat. 1,4–8): Text, Übersetzung und Kommentar*. Berlin and Boston.

Barbone, S. (1994) '*Frugalitas* in Saint Augustine', *Augustiniana* 44: 5–15.

Bartsch, S. (1994) *Actors in the Audience: Theatricality and Doublespeak from Nero to Hadrian*. Cambridge: 148–87.

Bernard, S. (2018) 'The social history of early Roman coinage', *JRS* 108: 1–26.

Berno, F. R. (2014) 'In Praise of Tubero's Pottery: A Note on Seneca, Ep. 95.72–73 and 98.13', in *Seneca Philosophus*, eds. J. Wildberger and M. L. Colish. Berlin and Boston: 369–91.

Bettini, M. (2000) '*Mos, mores und mos maiorum*: Die Erfindung der "Sittlichkeit" in der römischen Kultur', in *Moribus antiquis res stat Romana: Römische Werte und römische Literatur im 3. und 2. Jh. v. Chr.*, eds. M. Braun, A. Haltenhoff and F.-H. Mutschler. Munich and Leipzig: 303–52.

Biesinger, B. (2016) *Römische Dekadenzdiskurse: Untersuchungen zur römischen Geschichtsschreibung und ihren Kontexten (2. Jahrhundert v. Chr. bis 2. Jahrhundert n. Chr.)*. Stuttgart.

Billerbeck, M. (1982) 'La réception du cynisme à Rome', *L'Antiquité Classique* 51: 151–73.

Blänsdorf, J. (2016a) 'Ciceros Werke über das Leben der Sklaven und Freigelassenen im spätrepublikanischen Rom', *Gymnasium* 123: 569–95.

(2016b) *Das Thema der Sklaverei in den Werken Ciceros*. Stuttgart.

Bloomer, W. M. (2011) *The School of Rome: Latin Studies and the Origins of Liberal Education*. Berkeley, Los Angeles, London.

Blösel, W. (2000) 'Die Geschichte des Begriffes *mos maiorum* von den Anfängen bis zu Cicero', in *Mos Maiorum: Untersuchungen zu den Formen der Identitätsstiftung und Stabilisierung in der römischen Republik*, eds. B. Linke and M. Stemmler. Stuttgart: 25–97.

Bradley, K. (1994) *Slavery and Society at Rome*. Cambridge and New York.

Braund, S. (2009) *Seneca, De Cementia: Edited with Text, Translation, and Commentary*. Oxford.

Breitenstein, N. (2009) *Petronius, Satyrica 1–15: Text, Übersetzung, Kommentar*. Berlin and New York.

Frugalitas, or: The Invention of a Roman Virtue

Bruun, C. (2013) 'Greek or Latin? The owner's choice of names for *vernae* in Rome', in *Roman Slavery and Roman Material Culture*, ed. M. George, Toronto, Buffalo, London: 19–42.

Cantarella, E. (1992) *Bisexuality in the Ancient World*. New Haven.

Carlon, J. M. (2009) *Pliny's Women: Constructing Virtue and Creating Identity in the Roman World*. Cambridge.

Carlsen, J. (1995) *Vilici and Roman Estate Managers Until AD 284*. Rome.

Ceaicovschi, K. (2009) 'Cato the Elder in Aulus Gellius', *Illinois Classical Studies* 33–4: 25–39.

Christes, J. (1979) *Sklaven und Freigelassene als Grammatiker und Philologen im antiken Rom*. Wiesbaden.

Citroni Marchetti, S. (1995) 'Lo spazio straniato: Percorsi psicologici e percezione del tribunale nelle orazioni di Cicerone *pro Fonteio, pro Q. Roscio comoedo, pro Cluentio* I', *MD* 35: 9–57.

Classen, C. J. (2010) *Aretai and Virtutes: Untersuchungen zu den Wertvorstellungen der Griechen und Römer*. Berlin and New York.

Coffee, N. (2017) *Gift and Gain: How Money Transformed Ancient Rome*. Oxford.

Connolly, J. (2009) 'Fear and freedom: a new interpretation of Pliny's *Panegyricus*, in *Ordine e sovversione nel mondo greco e romano*, ed. G. Urso. Pisa: 259–78.

Connors, C. (1998) *Petronius the Poet: Verse and Literary Tradition in the Satyricon*. Cambridge.

Conte, G. B. (1994) *Latin Literature: A History*, trans. by J. B. Solodow, revised by D. Fowler and G. W. Most. Baltimore and London.

Corbeill, A. (1996) *Controlling Laughter: Political Humor in the Late Roman Republic*. Princeton.

Cordier, P. (2006) 'L'ethnographie romaine et ses primitifs: Les paradoxes de la "préhistoire" au présent', *Anabases* 3: 173–93.

Cornell, T. J. (2000) 'The Lex *Ovinia* and the emancipation of the senate', in *The Roman Middle Republic: Politics, Religion and Historiography c. 400–133 BC*, ed. C. Bruun. Rome: 69–89.

Courtney, E. (2001) *A Companion to Petronius*. Oxford.

D'Arms, J. (1981) *Commerce and Social Standing in Ancient Rome*. Cambridge, MA.

Dench, E. (1998) 'Austerity, excess, success, and failure in Hellenistic and early imperial Italy', in *Parchments of Gender: Deciphering the Bodies of Antiquity*, ed. M. Wyke. Oxford: 121–46.

Di Brazzano, S. (2004) *Laus Pisonis: introduzione, edizione critica e commento*. Pisa.

Dowling, M. (2006) *Clemency and Cruelty in the Roman World*, Ann Arbor.

Duff, J. D. (1915) *L. Annaei Senecae Dialogorum libri x, xi, xii*. Cambridge.

Dyck, A. R. (2010) *Cicero, Pro Sexto Roscio*. Cambridge.

Edwards, C. (1993) *The Politics of Immorality in Ancient Rome*. Cambridge.

Ingo Gildenhard

(2009) 'Free yourself! Slavery, freedom and the self in Seneca's Letters', in *Seneca and the Self*, eds. S. Bartsch and D. Wray. Cambridge: 139–59.

(2019) *Seneca: Selected Letters*. Cambridge.

Eisenhut, W. (1973) *Virtus Romana: Ihre Stellung im römischen Wertsystem*. Munich.

Ernout, A. and Meillet, A. (1959) *Dictionnaire étymologique de la langue latine*. Paris.

Fantham, E. (2011) '*Stuprum*: public attitudes and penalties for sexual offences in republican Rome', in *Roman Readings: Roman Responses to Greek Literature from Plautus to Statius and Quintilian*. Berlin and New York: 115–43.

Feldherr, A. (2019) 'Out of the past: Pliny's *Panegyricus* and Roman historiography', *Maia* 71: 380–411.

Flower, H. I. (2010) *Roman Republics*. Princeton and Oxford.

Fögen, T. (2000) *Patrii sermonis egestas: Einstellungen lateinischer Autoren zu ihrer Muttersprache*. Munich and Leipzig.

Forsythe, G. (1994) *The Historian L. Calpurnius Piso Frugi and the Roman Annalistic Tradition*. Lanham, New York and London.

Fraenkel, E. (1922/2007) *Plautine Elements in Plautus: (Plautinisches im Plautus)*, trans. by T. Drevikovsky and F. Muecke. Oxford. [= *Elementi Plautini in Plauto*. Florence, 1960].

(1935) 'Namenwesen', *RE* 16.2: 1611–70.

Freudenburg, K. (2010) '*Horatius Anceps*: persona and self-revelation in satire and song', in G. Davis (ed.) *A Companion to Horace*. Chichester: 271–90.

Gaskin, R. (2013) *Language, Truth, and Literature: A Defence of Literary Humanism*. Oxford.

Geisthardt, J. M. (2015) *Zwischen Princeps und Res Publica: Tacitus, Plinius und die Senatorische Selbstdarstellung in der Hohen Kaiserzeit*. Stuttgart.

Gildenhard, I. (2003) 'The "annalist" before the annalists: Ennius and his *Annales*', in *Formen römischer Geschichtsschreibung von den Anfängen bis Livius*, eds. U. Eigler et al. Darmstadt: 93–114.

(2007a) *Paideia Romana: Cicero's Tusculan Disputations*. Cambridge.

(2007b) 'Virgil vs. Ennius – or: the undoing of the Annalist', in *Ennius perennis: the Annals and beyond*, eds. W. Fitzgerald and E. Gowers. Cambridge: 73–102.

(2011) *Creative Eloquence: The Construction of Reality in Cicero's Speeches*. Oxford.

(2018) *Cicero, Philippic 2, 44–50, 78–92, 100–119: Latin Text, Study Aids with Vocabulary, and Commentary*. Cambridge.

Gildenhard, I., Hodgson, L., et al. (2013) *Cicero, On Pompey's Command (De Imperio), 27–49. Latin Text, Study Aids with Vocabulary, Commentary, and Translation*. Cambridge.

Frugalitas, or: The Invention of a Roman Virtue

Gildenhard, I., Gotter, U., Havener, W. and Hodgson, L. (eds.) (2019a) *Augustus and the Destruction of History: The Politics of the Past in Early Imperial Rome*. Cambridge.

(2019b) 'Introduction', in *Augustus and the Destruction of History: The Politics of the Past in Early Imperial Rome*, eds. I. Gildenhard et al. Cambridge: 1–36.

Gloyn, L. (2017) *The Ethics of the Family in Seneca*. Cambridge.

Goddard, J. P. (1994) *Moral Attitudes to Eating and Drinking in Ancient Rome*. Diss. Cambridge.

Goldschmidt, N. (2013) *Ennius' Annales and Virgil's Aeneid*. Oxford.

Gordon, R. L. (1999). 'Imagining Greek and Roman magic', in *Witchcraft and Magic in Europe 2: Ancient Greece and Rome*, ed. V. Flint et al. London: 159–275.

Gotter, U. (2001) *Griechenland in Rom? Die römische Rede über Hellas und ihre Kontexte (3.–1. Jh. v. Chr.)*. Habil. Freiburg.

Gowers, E. (1993) *The Loaded Table: Representations of Food in Roman Literature*. Oxford.

(1994) 'Persius and the decoction of Nero', in *Reflections of Nero: Culture, History and Representation*, eds. J. Elsner and J. Masters. London: 131–50.

(2012) *Horace: Satires, Book 1*. Cambridge.

Gowing, A. (2005) *Empire and Memory*. Cambridge.

Graf, F. (1997) 'How to cope with a difficult life: a view of ancient magic', in *Envisioning Magic*, eds. P. Schäfer and H. G. Kippenberg. Leiden, New York, Cologne: 93–114.

Griffin, M. T. (2013) *Seneca on Society: A Guide to De Beneficiis*. Oxford.

Habermehl, P. (2006) *Petronius, Satyrica 79–141: Ein philologisch-literarischer Kommentar, Bd. 1: Sat. 79–110*. Berlin and New York.

Hardie, P. (2007) 'Poets, patrons, rulers: the Ennian traditions', in *Ennius Perennis: The Annals and Beyond*, eds. W. Fitzgerald and E. Gowers. Cambridge: 129–44.

Hartmann, E. (2016) *Ordnung in Unordnung: Kommunikation, Konsum und Konkurrenz in der stadtrömischen Gesellschaft der frühen Kaiserzeit*. Stuttgart.

Henderson, J. (2011) 'Down the pan: historical exemplarity in the Panegyricus', in *Pliny's Praise: The Panegyricus in the Roman World*, ed. P. Roche. Cambridge: 142–74.

Hofmann-Löbl, I. (1996) *Die Calpurnii*. Frankfurt a. M.

Hölkeskamp, K.-J. (1996) 'Exempla und mos maiorum: Überlegungen zum kollektiven Gedächtnis der Nobilität', in *Vergangenheit und Lebenswelt: Soziale Kommunikation, Traditionsbildung und historisches Bewußtsein*, eds. H-J. Gehrke and A. Möller. Tübingen: 301–38.

Hörnqvist, M. (2004) *Machiavelli and Empire*. Cambridge.

Ianziti, G. (2012) *Writing History in Renaissance Italy*. Cambridge, MA.

341

Ingo Gildenhard

Inwood, B. (2005) *Reading Seneca: Stoic Philosophy at Rome*. Oxford.

Itgenshorst, T. (2017) 'Au-delà d'une fabrique de la norme: l'oeuvre de Valère Maxime', in *La norme sous la République romaine et le Haut-Empire*, eds. T. Itgenshorst and P. Le Doze, Bordeaux: 517–31.

Jakab, É. (1997) *Praedicere und cavere beim Marktkauf: Sachmängel im griechischen und römischen Recht*. Munich.

Kajanto, I. (1965) *The Latin Cognomina*. Helsinki.

Kaser, M. (1951) 'Zum Ediktsstil', in *Festschrift Schulz II*, Weimar: 21–70.

Kaster, R. A. (2005) *Emotion, Restraint, and Community in Ancient Rome*. Oxford.

(2006) *Cicero: Speech on behalf of Publius Sestius*. Oxford.

Kierdorf, W. (2003) *Römische Geschichtsschreibung der republikanischen Zeit*. Heidelberg.

Klodt, C. (2012) 'Prozessparteien und politische Gegner als *dramatis personae*: Charakterstilisierung in Ciceros Reden', in *Studium declamatorium: Untersuchungen zu Schulübungen und Prunkreden von der Antike bis zur Neuzeit*, eds. B.-J. Schröder and J.-P. Schröder. Leipzig: 35–106.

Knoch, S. (2005) *Sklavenfürsorge im Römischen Reich*. Hildesheim.

Kunkel, W. and Wittmann, R. (1995) *Staatsordnung und Staatspraxis der römischen Republik: Die Magistratur*. Munich.

Labate, M. (1996) 'Il sermo oraziano e i generi letterari', in *Zeitgenosse Horaz: der Dichter und seine Leser seit zwei Jahrtausenden*, eds. H. Krasser and E. A. Schmidt, Tübingen: 424–41.

Langlands R (2008) '"Reading for the moral" in Valerius Maximus: the case of *severitas*', *CCJ* 54: 160–87.

(2018) *Exemplary Ethics in Ancient Rome*. Cambridge.

La Penna, A. (1989) 'La leggitimazione del lusso privato da Ennio a Vitruvio: momenti, problemi, personaggi', *Maia* 41: 3–34.

Latte, K. (1960/1968) 'Der Historiker L. Calpurnius Piso Frugi', in *Kleine Schriften*. Munich: 837–47.

Leigh, M. (2004) *Comedy and the Rise of Rome*. Oxford.

Liebs, D. (2012) *Summoned to the Roman Courts: Famous Trials from Antiquity*, trans. R. L. R. Garber and C. G. Cürten. Berkeley.

Lind, L. R. (1979) 'The tradition of Roman moral conservatism', in *Studies in Latin Literature and Roman History I*, ed. C. Deroux. Brussels: 7–58.

(1992) 'The idea of the republic and the foundations of Roman morality: second part', in *Studies in Latin Literature and Roman History VI*, ed. C. Deroux. Brussels: 5–40.

Lindsay, W. M. (1900) *The Captivi of Plautus: edited with Introduction, Apparatus Criticus and Commentary*. London.

Lintott, A. (1981) 'The *leges de repetundis* and associate measures under the Republic', *Zeitschrift der Savigny-Stiftung für Rechtsgeschichte, Romanistische Abteilung* 8: 162–212.

(2008) *Cicero as Evidence: A Historian's Companion*. Oxford.

Frugalitas, or: The Invention of a Roman Virtue

Litchfield, H. W. (1914) 'National *exempla virtutis* in Roman literature', *HSCP* 25: 1–71.

Lucarelli, U. (2007) *Exemplarische Vergangenheit: Valerius Maximus und die Konstruktion des sozialen Raumes in der frühen Kaiserzeit*. Göttingen.

MacLean, R. (2018) *Freed Slaves and Roman Imperial Culture: Social Integration and the Transformation of Values*. Cambridge.

Malherbe, A. J. (2013) *Light from the Gentiles: Hellenistic Philosophy and Early Christianity: Collected Essays, 1959–2012*. Boston.

Manuwald, G. (2007) *Cicero, Philippics 3–9, ed.* with Introduction, Translation and Commentary, 2 vols. Berlin and New York.

Matthews, V. J. (1973) 'Some puns on Roman *cognomina*', *Greece & Rome* 20: 20–4.

McConnell, S. (2012) 'Cicero and Dicaearchus', *Oxford Studies in Ancient Philosophy* 42: 307–49.

McDonnell, M. (2006) *Roman Manliness: Virtus and the Roman Republic*. Cambridge.

Menner, J. (2006) 'D. 33, 7, 18, 4 – *vilicus und vilica* als Objekte eines Erbschaftsstreites', in *Sklaverei und Freilassung im römischen Recht: Symposium für Hans Josef Wieling zum 70. Geburtstag*, ed. T. Finkenauer. Heidelberg: 153–87.

Moles, J. (2007) 'Philosophy and ethics', in *The Cambridge Companion to Horace*, ed. S. Harrison. Cambridge: 165–80.

Mommsen, T. (1864) *Römische Forschungen*. Berlin.

Mouritsen, H. (2011) *The Freedman in the Roman World*. Cambridge.

Moreno Soldevila, R. (2006) *Martial, Book IV: A Commentary*. Leiden and Boston.

Münzer, F. (1910) 's.v. Furius (53)', *RE* 7.1: 351.

Nelsestuen, G. A. (2014) 'Overseeing *res publica*: the *rector* as *vilicus* in *De Re Publica 5*', *CA* 33: 130–73.

Nicolet, C. (1977) 'L'onomastique des groupes dirigeants sous la République', in *L'onomastique latine. Actes du colloque international, 13–15 octobre 1975*, Paris, 45–61.

Noreña, C. F. (2011) *Imperial Ideals in the Roman West: Representation, Circulation, Power*. Cambridge.

North, H. F. (1966) *Sophrosyne: Self-Knowledge and Restraint in Greek Literature*. Ithaca, NY.

Oakley, S. P. (2005) *A Commentary on Livy Books VI–X, Volume III: Book IX*. Oxford.

Ogden, D. (2009) *Magic, Witchcraft, and Ghosts in the Greek and Roman Worlds: A Sourcebook*, 2nd edn. New York.

Oliensis, E. (1998) *Horace and the Rhetoric of Authority*. Cambridge.

Osborne, R. (2009) 'Economic growth and the politics of entitlement', *CCJ* 55: 97–125.

Ingo Gildenhard

Palmer, L. R. (1988) *The Latin Language*. Norman.

Panayotakis, C. (1995) *Theatrum Arbitri: Theatrical Elements in the Satyrica of Petronius*. Leiden, Boston, Cologne.

(2010) *Decimus Laberius: The Fragments*. Cambridge.

Park, M. E. (1918) *The Plebs in Cicero's Day: A Study of Their Provenance and of Their Employment*. Cosmos Press.

Peer, A. (2008) 'Cicero's last Caesarian speech: the *Pro Rege Deiotaro* as a final warning before the Ides of March', in *Studies in Latin Literature and Roman History XIV*, ed. C. Deroux. Brussels: 189–208.

Peirano, I. (2012) *The Rhetoric of the Roman Fake: Latin Pseudepigrapha in Context*. Cambridge.

Petrocheilos, N. (1974) *Roman Attitudes to the Greeks*. Athens.

Pinkster, H. (2015) *Oxford Latin Syntax: Volume 1: The Simple Clause*. Oxford.

Pittia, S. (2004) 'Les élites Siciliennes au miroir du plaidoyer cicéronien contre Verrès', in *Autocélébration des élites locales dans le monde romain*, ed. M. Cébeillac-Gervasoni, L. Lamoine and F. Trément. Clermont-Ferrand: 15–31.

Pobjoy, M. P. (2013) 'L. Calpurnius Piso Frugi', *The Fragments of the Roman Historians, vol. 1: Introduction*, eds. T. J. Cornell. Oxford: 231–9.

Poteat, H. (1938) 'Some reflections on Roman philosophy', *CJ* 3.9: 514–22.

Prag, J. R. W. (2013) 'Provincials, patrons, and the rhetoric of repetundae', in *Community and Communication: Oratory and Politics in Republican Rome*, eds. C. Steel and H. van der Blom. Oxford: 267–83.

Prag, J. and Repath, I. (2009) 'Introduction', in *Petronius: A Handbook*, eds. J. Prag and I. Repath. Malden and Oxford: 1–15.

Ramsay, W. (1869) *The Mostellaria of Plautus, with Notes Critical and Explanatory Prolegomena and Excursus*. London.

Rawson, E. (1976) 'The Ciceronian aristocracy and its properties', in *Studies in Roman Property: By the Cambridge University Research Seminar in Ancient History*, ed. M. I. Finley. Cambridge: 85–102.

Reinhardt, T. and Winterbottom, M. (eds.) (2006) *Quintilian, Institutio Oratoria: Book 2*. Oxford.

Richlin, A. (2009) 'Sex in the *Satyrica*: outlaws in literatureland', in *Petronius: A Handbook*, eds. J. Prag and I. Repath. Malden and Oxford: 82–100.

(2017) *Slave Theater in the Roman Republic: Plautus and Popular Comedy*. Cambridge.

Rimell, V. (2002) *Petronius and the Anatomy of Fiction*. Cambridge.

Rives, J. (2002) 'Magic in the XII Tables revisited', *CQ* 52: 270–90.

Roche, P. (ed.) (2011) *Pliny's Praise: The Panegyricus in the Roman World*. Cambridge.

Rosillo-López, C. (2017) 'Popular public opinion in a nutshell: nicknames and non-elite political culture in the late republic', in *Popular Culture in the Ancient World*, ed. L. Grig. Cambridge: 91–106.

344

Frugalitas, or: The Invention of a Roman Virtue

Rosivach, V. J. (1995) 'Seneca on the fear of poverty in the *Epistulae Morales*', *L'Antiquité Classique* 64: 91–8.

Salomies, O. (2008) 'Choosing a *cognomen* in Rome: some aspects', in *A Roman Miscellany: Essays in Honour of Anthony R. Birley on his Seventieth Birthday*, eds. H. M. Schellenberg, V.–E. Hirschmann and A. Krieckhaus. Gdansk: 79–91.

Salway, B. (1994) 'What's in a name? A survey of Roman onomastic practice from c. 700 BC to AD 700', *JRS* 84: 125–45.

Santoro L'Hoir, F. (1992) *The Rhetoric of Gender Terms: 'Man', 'Woman', & the Portrayal of Character in Latin Prose*. Leiden, New York, Cologne.

Scheidle, K. (1993) *Modus optumum: Die Bedeutung des 'rechten Maßes' in der römischen Literatur (Republik – frühe Kaiserzeit), untersucht an den Begriffen 'Modus – Modestia – Moderatio – Temperantia'*, Frankfurt a. M.

Schmeling, G. and Setaioli, A. (2011) *A Commentary on the Satyrica of Petronius*. Oxford.

Schofield, M. (2012) 'The fourth virtue', in *Cicero's Practical Philosophy*, ed. W. Nicgorski. Notre Dame: 43–57.

Shackleton Bailey, D. R. (1977) *Cicero: Epistulae ad Familiares, Vol. I: 62–47 B.C.* Cambridge.

Shelton, J.-A. (2013) *The Women of Pliny's Letters*. London and New York.

Solin, Heikki (2017) 'Zur Entwicklung des römischen Namensystems', in *Politische Kultur und soziale Struktur der Römischen Republik: Bilanzen und Perspektiven* (= Akten der internationalen Tagung anlässlich des 70. Todestages von Friedrich Münzer, Münster, 18.–20. Oktober 2012), eds. M. Haake and A.-C. Harders. Stuttgart: 135–54.

Spevak, O. (2014) *The Noun Phrase in Classical Latin Prose*. Leiden.

Stemmler, M. (2000) '*Auctoritas exempli*: zur Wechselwirkung von kanonisierten Vergangenheitsbildern und gesellschaftlicher Gegenwart in der spätrepublikanischen Rhetorik', in *Mos Maiorum: Untersuchungen zu den Formen der Identitätsstiftung und Stabilisierung in der römischen Republik*, eds. M. Stemmler and B. Linke. Stuttgart: 141–205.

Stewart, R. (2012) *Plautus and Roman Slavery*. Chichester.

Struever, N. S. (1970) *The Language of History in the Renaissance: Rhetorical and Historical Consciousness in Florentine Humanism*. Princeton.

Strunk, T. E. (2017) *History after Liberty: Tacitus on Tyrants, Sycophants, and Republicans*. Ann Arbor.

Talbert, R. J. A. (1984) *The Senate of Imperial Rome*. Princeton.

Thylander, H. (1952) *Étude sur l'épigraphie latine*. Lund.

Treggiari, S. (1969) *Roman Freedmen During the Late Republic*. Oxford.

(2007) *Terentia, Tullia, and Publilia: The Women of Cicero's Family*. Abingdon.

van der Blom, H. (2010) *Cicero's Role Models: The Political Strategy of a Newcomer*. Oxford.

345

Ingo Gildenhard

(2016) *Oratory and Political Career in the Late Roman Republic.* Cambridge.

Wallace-Hadrill, A. (1982) '*Civilis princeps*: between citizen and king', *JRS* 72: 32–48.

Walsh, P. (1955) 'Livy's preface and the distortion of history', *AJP* 76.4: 369–83.

Wardy, R. (1996) *The Birth of Rhetoric: Gorgias, Plato and their Successors.* London and New York.

Watson, A. (1975) *Rome of the XII Tables.* Princeton.

West, D. A. (1995a) *Cast out Theory: Horace Odes 1.4 and 4.7.* Presidential Address, Classical Association.

(1995b) *Horace Odes I: Carpe Diem.* Oxford.

(1998) *Horace Odes II: Vatis Amici.* Oxford.

Whitton, C. (2013) *Pliny the Younger: Epistles Book II.* Cambridge.

(2019) *The Arts of Imitation in Latin Prose: Pliny's Epistles/Quintilian in Brief.* Cambridge.

Williams, G. D. (2003) *Seneca: De Otio. De Breuitate Vitae.* Cambridge.

Williams, G. W. (1995) '*Libertino patre natus*: true or false?', in *Homage to Horace*, ed. S. J. Harrison. Oxford: 296–313.

Winterbottom, M. (1964) 'Quintilian and the *vir bonus*', *JRS* 54: 90–7.

Wiseman, T. P. (1971) *New Men in the Roman Senate, 139 B.C.–A.D. 14.* Oxford.

Wolstencroft, S. (2019) 'From ferocity to friendship: how Horace changed satire', *Omnibus* 78: 10–12.

Woodman, A. J. (2009) 'Horace and historians', *CCJ* 55: 157–67.

Zanda, E. (2011) *Fighting Hydra-like Luxury: Sumptuary Regulation in the Roman Republic.* Bristol.

CHAPTER 6

FRUGALITY, BUILDING, AND HEIRLOOMS IN AN AGE OF SOCIAL MOBILITY*

JOHN R. PATTERSON

Luxury, in many of its manifestations anyway, is comparatively easy to detect in the archaeological record.[1] Seneca, reflecting on the character of Augustus' close associate Maecenas, provides us with a kind of checklist of the different forms of luxury at Rome and the sequence in which they spread. 'When good fortune has spread luxury far and wide,' he says, 'men begin to show a greater interest in their personal appearance. Then they develop an enthusiasm for furniture. Next they devote attention to their *domus*, so that they become as extensive as rural estates, their walls shine with marble that has been carried across the seas, and the roofs are adorned with gold, so that the gleam of the inlaid floors may match that of the ceiling. After that their sumptuous taste is transferred to banquets, where distinction is achieved by novelty and reorganizing the traditional sequence of dishes ...'.[2] While it is difficult archaeologically to trace fine items of dress, or the sequence of dishes on a menu, exotic marbles are easily identified, as is house-building on a monumental scale, or amphorae containing some forms of expensive food and drink; while

---

* I am very grateful to Christopher Berry, Tiziana d'Angelo, Alina Kozlovski, Astrid Van Oyen, and Andrew Wallace-Hadrill for bibliographical suggestions and other advice.

[1] On the topic in general, see Berry 1994 esp. 63–86, and Wallace-Hadrill 2008: 316–55; on the phenomenon of female luxury in particular, and measures to contain it, see e.g. McClintock 2013. Recent discussions of luxury in material culture include Lapatin 2008; 2014; 2015.

[2] *Ep.* 114.9, with the discussion in Berry 1994, 6–8. While Seneca's writings are a valuable source of insight into one particular Roman's attitudes to both luxury and frugality, it is worth bearing in mind the exceptional scale of that author's personal wealth: Tacitus (*Ann.* 13.42) and Dio (61.10.3) estimate it at 300 million sesterces. See Griffin 1976: 286–94, with 299–300 on frugality; Garnsey 2007: 123–5.

347

John R. Patterson

evidence from Pompeii and Herculaneum gives us – though no doubt on a more modest scale – some idea of the furniture and tableware in precious metals that would have been on display in a wealthy Roman house of the early Principate.[3]

On the other hand, it is very hard to identify frugality, which Seneca describes as a kind of 'voluntary poverty',[4] in the archaeological record, and in particular to distinguish it from meanness, cost-cutting, or lack of resources. For example Seneca and Martial allude to *cellae pauperum*, 'chambers of the poor', which appear to be rooms in a wealthy house deliberately designed as if they were the homes of the poor, as a location for (temporary) simple living:[5] it is hard to see how such a room could be distinguished archaeologically from, say, a slave's quarters, except perhaps in terms of its position within the house.

Now this is not to say that the study of the archaeological record in this kind of enquiry is unfruitful, and the corresponding problem with starting from the literary evidence, as we will see, is that it is very difficult to disentangle the treatment of frugality from that of luxury. Indeed in a study of storage buildings in rural villas in Italy of the first century BCE, Astrid Van Oyen has recently demonstrated how moral concerns and material culture can and should be inter-related in our understanding of these structures. As well as practical requirements, the scale and design of storage facilities can be seen to reflect the broader moral contexts within which the villa-owners were operating: these include admiration for the virtue of self-sufficiency, and the need conspicuously to display resources produced at the villa, with the implicit message that these might be used to help clients and supporters.[6] The approach I am adopting here is to set the relationship of frugality and material culture in a specific but broader framework, namely that of social mobility in Roman society of the late Republic

---

[3] On furniture: see Mols 1999, esp. 139-42; Allison 2004: 139–40; De Carolis 2007; and more generally, Wallace-Hadrill 2011: 211–19. On tableware: see esp. Painter 2001.

[4] *Ep.* 17.5.   [5] Sen. *Ep.* 18.7; 100.6; Mart. 3.48.   [6] Van Oyen 2015, esp. 97–100.

348

Frugality, Building, and Heirlooms in an Age of Social Mobility

and early Principate. This approach isn't an entirely new one – Catharine Edwards for example has convincingly couched her analysis of luxury at Rome in the context of elite anxieties about status,[7] and Van Oyen, in discussing the relationship of morality and villa-architecture, observes more generally that in the late Republic 'social mobility, the extension of citizenship, and new riches brought into question what it meant to be a member of the elite'.[8] Nevertheless, it is I think worth looking at how attitudes to *frugality* in particular can also be related to patterns of social mobility. I want to focus on those aspects of frugality which most closely relate to the built environment and material culture more generally, concentrating in particular on elite housing, but also discussing silver plate for the table, in the last two centuries of the Republic and the early Principate.

Two Electoral Surprises

I begin with two stories concerning elections at Rome in the second century BCE. The first relates to Q. Aelius Tubero and his involvement in the funeral banquet held, probably in 129 BCE, in memory of Scipio Aemilianus, the destroyer of Carthage. The story is preserved in Cicero's speech defending L. Licinius Murena on a charge of electoral bribery in 63 BCE, but also in Valerius Maximus and Seneca. Tubero was asked by the organiser of the banquet, Q. Fabius Maximus Allobrogicus, to provide coverings for the couches. In keeping with his Stoic beliefs he used goatskins instead of fine cloths on (plain) wooden Punic-style benches, and instead of silver cups provided *uasa Samia* which Cicero describes as 'more appropriate if Diogenes the Cynic had died than for the commemoration of the death of the great Africanus'. The Roman people took this very badly, and as a result Tubero was unsuccessful

---

[7] Edwards 1993: 138. See also the discussion of links between sumptuary legislation and fluidity in the social order in Berry 1994: 80–2, and Wallace-Hadrill 2008: 327–8.

[8] Van Oyen 2015: 122.

John R. Patterson

in the elections when he stood for the praetorship, 'ousted by the goatskins', as Cicero puts it. The orator's conclusion is that 'the Roman people hate private *luxuria*, but they love public *magnificentia*'.[9]

One of the most interesting aspects of the story is the way in which it is cast in terms of political failure contrary to expectation. Cicero introduces Tubero as '*uir eruditus* ... *et honestus homo et nobilis*' while Valerius' version is set within a collection of anecdotes 'on electoral defeats'. The latter observes that Tubero was 'otherwise an excellent man', and had been well-placed as a candidate because of his distinguished family relationships: he was grandson of L. Aemilius Paullus (who had defeated Perseus, king of Macedon) as well as being nephew of Scipio Aemilianus. The point of the story for Cicero was that despite all the advantages of his family background, this *homo integerrimus* and *ciuis optimus* was unexpectedly defeated in the election, because of the *sordes* and *inhumanitas* displayed at the banquet. Seneca, himself a Stoic, takes a more positive view, suggesting that Tubero's pottery vessels 'will last throughout all eternity', unlike the gold and silver of his rivals.

The second anecdote is really more about luxury than frugality, and again comes from Cicero, who in his *de Officiis* recounts how Cn. Octavius – who in 165 BCE was the first of his family to be elected consul – was notable for having built on the Palatine an attractive and imposing house. 'When everyone went to look at it, the house was thought to have supported its owner, a new man, in his campaign for the consulship.'[10] Octavius, who was subsequently killed while on a diplomatic mission in Asia Minor and honoured with a statue on the Rostra, is also mentioned in the *Ninth Philippic* as 'a great and distinguished man, who was the first to bring a consulship into a family which was afterwards rich in brave men'. So here we have the opposite scenario to the

---

[9] Cic. *Mur.* 75–6 with Fantham 2013: 181–2; V. Max. 7.5.1; Sen. *Ep.* 95.72–3. For the suggestion that *uasa Samia* are to be identified with black-gloss ware (the shiny surface of which might be thought to mimic the appearance of silver) see Wallace-Hadrill 2008: 407–11.

[10] *Off.* 1.138.

Frugality, Building, and Heirlooms in an Age of Social Mobility

unsuccessful *nobilis* Tubero: the achievement of a *nouus homo* in gaining the consulship is explained in terms of the impressiveness of his house.[11]

Unsurprisingly, both of these stories turn out on closer investigation to be more complicated than the accounts preserved in Cicero and Valerius Maximus would suggest. The orator has a particular reason for bringing up the story about Aelius Tubero in defence of Murena, as he wants to compare the prosecutor Cato, also a Stoic, with Tubero, and in the process to bracket the two together in terms of their rigid and impractical adherence to philosophical principles. Murena, by contrast, with his strong military background, is just the kind of practical man the Roman state needs as consul in 62 BCE, given the ongoing threat posed by Catiline's conspiracy, which is repeatedly emphasised during the speech.[12] Other issues, in fact, may have contributed to Tubero's lack of electoral success – we hear in Cicero's *Brutus*, for example, that Tubero had an even more severe character than his philosophical beliefs would demand, and while serving as triumvir he had ruled in court against his own uncle Scipio Aemilianus, whose funeral he would subsequently be involved in organising. Besides 'like his life, his oratorical style was harsh, uncultivated, and uncouth, so he did not achieve the distinction of his ancestors as regards public office'.[13] So there may in reality have been a range of reasons why the voters rejected Tubero's candidature for the praetorship, not just the episode of Aemilianus' funerary banquet; indeed the discovery at Rome of ceramic bowls with a reddish-brown slip bearing scratched slogans in support of the younger Cato's (successful) campaign in 63 BCE for the tribunate of the *plebs,* and Catiline's in the same year for the consulship, suggests that the use of pottery vessels at such public events – perhaps associated with a distribution of food – was not unfamiliar in the late Republic, at

---

[11] *Phil.* 9.4 with Manuwald 2007: 1058. The reference to 'brave men' here may be an allusion to the young Octavian – the speech was delivered in 43 BCE – but the latter's family link with Cn. Octavius was in reality very doubtful: see Dyck 1996: 316. For a recent discussion of *noui homines* and their houses, see Jones 2016.
[12] Cic. *Mur.* 48–53; 78–85.   [13] *Brut.* 117.

John R. Patterson

least in an electoral context.[14] Similarly, though Octavius was evidently the first man in his family to reach the consulship, Wiseman suggests that he was the son of a praetor, and Octavius had already had an extremely successful career, culminating in his defeating Perseus of Macedon in a sea-battle during his own praetorship in 168 BCE.[15] Given the demographic and financial constraints identified by Hopkins and Burton, it is clear that a continuous influx of new blood into the Roman senate was essential if that body was to continue to exist,[16] but it is striking that it was felt necessary to find explanations for the success of *noui homines* and the failure of *nobiles*, and both luxury and frugality formed part of that explanatory framework. The paradox here is that while frugality in the first century BCE often tended to be associated with *noui homines* (at least by themselves),[17] in these stories the *nobilis* Tubero displays *frugalitas* and the *nouus homo* Octavius displays *magnificentia*.

Houses and Heirlooms

With Sulla's substantial expansion of the Senate, and a corresponding increase in the number of quaestors elected annually to 20, it is clear that the intensity of political competition increased significantly in the post-Sullan period, even beyond the already high levels apparent during the century since the end of the Second Punic war.[18] Pliny the Elder highlights the increased competition in house-building during this period: 'The most reliable accounts agree that in the consulship of M. Lepidus and Q. Catulus (i.e. 78 BCE), there was no finer house in Rome than that of Lepidus himself – but, by

---

[14] Panciera 1979 (re-published as Panciera 2006: 1059–72 with some further observations on the bowls at 1068); for the texts see *AE* 1979: 63–4, and *CIL* VI 40897 and 40904. The vessels are now in the Museo Nazionale alle Terme di Diocleziano at Rome. See also Giovagnoli 2012a; 2012b.

[15] Wiseman 1971: 3 n. 2, with Broughton 1951: 428.   [16] Hopkins 1983: 31–119.

[17] Gildenhard, Chapter 5 in this volume.

[18] Steel 2013: 109–10; 138–9. Santangelo 2006: 8–11 argues that the membership of the Senate after Sulla is more likely to have been in the region of 450–500 than the 600 often envisaged.

352

Frugality, Building, and Heirlooms in an Age of Social Mobility

Hercules, within 35 years the same house was not among the first hundred.' Even before then, we find anecdotes suggesting that rivalry between aristocrats over the grandeur of their houses was already a familiar scenario: Pliny records that at the beginning of the first century BCE, the finest house in Rome was considered to be that on the Viminal belonging to the *eques* and expert in civil law C. Aquilius, which surpassed even that of Q. Lutatius Catulus on the Palatine. Also very distinguished, and notable for being decorated with marble columns which had originally been used in the temporary theatre he had constructed during his aedileship, was that of the celebrated orator L. Licinius Crassus. Evidently there was an informal 'league table' of the finest residences in Rome; and politicians, and observers of the political scene, had a clear idea of the ranking.[19]

Pliny and Valerius Maximus highlight a quarrel between this Crassus and Cn. Domitius Ahenobarbus – both of them from very high-profile noble families, so the issue of *nouitas* was not a consideration in this case. The two men were colleagues as censors in 92 BCE. Domitius, who according to Pliny was notorious for his bad temper and was 'inflamed by that particularly bitter sort of hatred which originates in rivalry', denounced Crassus for living in a grandiose mansion while overseeing the morals of other Romans as censor. Pliny and Valerius Maximus give different accounts of what happened next – the sums of money mentioned by Valerius being significantly larger, as well as the number of trees involved – but according to Pliny's version, Domitius offered to pay one million sesterces for Crassus' house, which Crassus accepted, apart from demanding an additional payment for six exotic nettle-trees which stood in the house. Domitius then refused to buy the property at all without the trees, whereupon Crassus retorted 'am I the one who is setting a bad example ... I who live quite pleasantly (*comiter*) in the house that came to me by inheritance (*mihi hereditate obuenit*), or is it you, who

---

[19] Plin. *Nat.* 36.109–10 and 17.1–6 with Wallace-Hadrill 2000: 185.

John R. Patterson

value six trees at a million sesterces?'[20] It is worth mentioning in passing that Domitius (whose house has been identified by some scholars with structures discovered underneath the entrance-way of the Golden House built by his descendant the emperor Nero)[21] and Crassus (who lived in a house above the Forum close to that subsequently occupied by M. Aemilius Scaurus, and excavated in the 1990s) were neighbours as well as rivals.[22] But the point I particularly want to stress here is that Crassus defended himself from criticism by emphasising that he had received the house as an *inheritance*. Recent scholarship has tended to stress the lack of attachment of the elite of Republican Rome to their urban houses, and the rapid turnover in the market for such properties, but this picture may be unduly influenced by the rivalries of Cicero's time, given the importance of his letters as a source of information, and this passage shows that a man might well distinguish between a property he had purchased and one he had inherited, even if he was in fact willing to sell it.[23]

We can find the same sorts of allegations and arguments deployed by those who owned, or were accused of owning, excessively large quantities of silver plate. Alongside the more general increase in disposable wealth in Rome related to the expansion of Roman power in the Greek world in the decades after the Hannibalic War, and then the destruction of Carthage and Corinth in 146 BCE, Pliny tells us that there was a significant growth in the practice of collecting silver after Rome's acquisition of the kingdom of Pergamum in 133 BCE, and the sale of the king's possessions.[24] As with luxury in housing, we can map out this trend using a series of anecdotes preserved in Pliny and Valerius Maximus. For example we are told by Valerius that P. Cornelius Rufinus, an ex-consul and

---

[20] Plin. *Nat.* 17.3–4; V. Max. 9.1.4.
[21] Domitius' house: Carandini 1988: 370–1; Carandini, Bruno and Fraioli 2010: 71–4; more cautiously, Papi 1995a; Carlsen 2006: 98–9.
[22] Crassus' house: Papi 1995b.   [23] Rawson 1976; Guilhembet 2006: 92–3, n. 7.
[24] Plin. *Nat.* 33.148–9. See Strong 1966: 109–10 for two silver bowls, found at Civita Castellana, which may have been among the Pergamene vessels brought to Rome in 133 BCE.

Frugality, Building, and Heirlooms in an Age of Social Mobility

former dictator, was expelled from the Senate in the early third century BCE for having collected 10 lbs of silver plate.[25] Scipio Aemilianus in 129 BCE bequeathed to his heir 32 lbs of silver, but his nephew Q. Fabius Maximus Allobrogicus was thought to have owned 1000 lbs of silver, and M. Livius Drusus, tribune of the plebs in 91 BCE, 10,000 lbs.[26] Meanwhile L. Licinius Crassus (the owner of the nettle-trees) allegedly spent 100,000 HS on a pair of cups by the renowned silversmith Mentor, though Pliny tells us he was too ashamed actually to use them.[27] Restrained behaviour in relation to silver could conversely be seen as an indication of frugality, as a rather garbled story transmitted by Valerius Maximus and Pliny demonstrates. Valerius records how a Roman commander called Q. Tubero Catus was offered some fine silver vessels by ambassadors of the Aetolian League who had previously seen him eating off pottery, but he refused the offer, saying that *continentia* should not be assumed to need help as *paupertas* did. Valerius goes on to exclaim rhetorically 'if only later times had chosen to follow the example of his *frugalitas*!'[28] Pliny tells the same story about someone called Catus Aelius, and it is generally assumed that it is Sex. Aelius Paetus Catus, consul in 198 BCE, who is being referred to in both cases, although there is evidently some confusion with an Aelius Tubero who was the father of the frugal but unsuccessful candidate for the praetorship mentioned earlier.[29] Pliny also says that Catus Aelius 'until the last day of his life never owned any silver apart from the two bowls given to him by his wife's father L. Aemilius Paullus'; but it was Q. Aelius Tubero who in reality was the son-in-law of Aemilius Paullus, serving with him in his campaigns against Perseus of Macedon.[30] Regardless of the identity of the protagonist in the story, it is worth underlining that to claim silver cups had been a family gift, or inherited from one's forebears, was evidently a strategy

---

[25] V. Max. 2.9.4, with Plin. *Nat.* 33.142.   [26] Plin. *Nat.* 33.141.
[27] Plin. *Nat.* 33.147.   [28] V. Max. 4.3.7.   [29] Plin. *Nat.* 33.142.
[30] Plutarch also provides a version of the story which stresses the modest lifestyle of Tubero's family, and describes the gift as being a single five-pound bowl of silver: see Plu. *Aem.* 28.7 and *Mor.* 198 b–c.

John R. Patterson

which could be deployed when one was accused of, or felt at risk of an allegation of, this kind of *luxuria*. According to Valerius Maximus even C. Fabricius, who as censor in 275 BCE had expelled Cornelius Rufinus from the Senate, and his censorial colleague Q. Aemilius Papus, each possessed a silver *patella* (a dish for ritual use) and a silver salt-cellar: Papus justified his possession of these objects by saying that since he inherited them, they should not leave his possession.[31] More than 300 years later, we find Seneca's friend (and perhaps relative) Annaeus Serenus, who claims to be possessed by *summus amor parsimoniae,* portrayed as explaining that his silver is 'my rustic father's – heavy plate bearing no maker's name' (and hence inherited, and not the work of particularly distinguished craftsmen).[32] Archaeologically retrieved assemblages of silver tend to be composed of a range of older and more recent pieces, suggesting that silver collections might be assembled over several generations,[33] and literary texts show how silver artefacts might be acquired either by purchase or by inheritance. Several anecdotes in Cicero and Plutarch record how silver vessels might be specially commissioned by an individual,[34] while a passage in Petronius' *Satyricon* suggests that some of the items in the lavish silver collection of the fictional freedman Trimalchio (including vessels depicting Cassandra killing her sons and Daedalus enclosing Niobe in the Trojan Horse – the joke is about Trimalchio's ignorance of classical mythology – as well as the fights of famous gladiators) were chosen or commissioned by him, but others were bequeathed to him as legacies.[35] The emperor Vespasian, Suetonius tells us, was particularly fond of a little silver cup which had formerly belonged to his grandmother, and he

---

[31] V. Max. 4.4.3.   [32] Sen. *Tranq.* 1.7.   [33] Strong 1966: 133.
[34] Cic. *Div.* 1.79; Plu. *Cic.* 1.6; *Mor.* 204e–f.
[35] Petr. 52. Unfortunately the text here is corrupt but the word *reliquit* is indicative of inheritance, whether from Mummius, the conqueror of Corinth in 146 BCE (Bücheler's conjecture) or from Trimalchio's own patron (Müller's suggestion of *patronus meus*). See Schmeling 2011: 214. The scenes on the vessels are humorously garbled allusions to Medea's murder of her sons and Daedalus' enclosing Pasiphae in a wooden cow.

Frugality, Building, and Heirlooms in an Age of Social Mobility

was in the habit of drinking out of it on days of family celebration.[36]

Two assemblages of silver plate of particular interest in this context are the hoard of 109 silver vessels found in a cistern in the wine-cellar of a villa at Boscoreale near Pompeii, and a similar assemblage of 118 silver artefacts found under the bath-suite of the Casa del Menandro in the town of Pompeii itself, both of which were evidently deposited before the eruption of Vesuvius in AD 79. One silver kylix, apparently (but not certainly) from the Boscoreale hoard and preserved in the British Museum, was produced around 300 BCE by craftsmen in southern Italy, and thus would have been an heirloom of some antiquity;[37] otherwise the Boscoreale collection comprised artefacts assembled over some 75 years, including a pair of vessels, depicting scenes from what appears to have been an Augustan monument at Rome, which had been much used, to judge by their state of wear.[38] The Casa del Menandro hoard similarly contains items dated between the mid-first century BCE and mid-first century CE.[39] The scale of these hoards (72 lbs of silver at the Casa del Menandro, 92 lbs at Boscoreale) would have been modest by comparison with the silver collections attested at Rome itself, but are nevertheless indicative of the way in which assemblages in the capital might have been built up over time.[40] The discovery in the House of Julius Polybius at Pompeii of a bronze *hydria* dated to 460–450 BCE, and originally awarded as a prize in athletic contests held in honour of the goddess Hera at Argos in Greece, also illustrates how other kinds of heirlooms might be preserved in private houses for long periods: Zevi suggests that the vessel may have earlier been used as a container for ashes in a grave and subsequently looted (as we know from literary sources to have happened at Corinth and Capua, for example) before becoming part of the householder's private collection.[41]

---

[36] Suet. *Ves.* 2.1, with Allen 1958: 2.
[37] Walters 1921, no. 15; Ward-Perkins and Claridge 1976, no. 336.
[38] Kuttner 1995, with discussion of the hoard in general at 6–9.
[39] Painter 2001: 21.
[40] For general discussion of silverware from the Vesuvian sites, see Künzl 1984.
[41] Str. 8.6.23 and Suet. *Caes.* 81.1 with Lazzarini and Zevi 1988–1989.

John R. Patterson

If the fact of owning pieces of silver plate given by relatives, or a house inherited from one's ancestors, could be used as a strategy for justifying one's position to the censors or other critics, this would help explain why allegations of luxury and claims to frugality together formed a significant component in the language of rivalry between *noui homines* and *nobiles*. *Noui homines* were potentially at a disadvantage in this respect, but frequently had the resources to acquire silver or fine houses by purchasing them. We hear in one of Cicero's letters to Atticus, for example, that his rival Clodius had sneered at Cicero for having bought a house in the city: Clodius himself by contrast would have inherited his residence on the Palatine from his ancestors.[42] It may also help to explain why, even though the censors might criticise members of the elite for lavish building, the Republican sumptuary laws concerned themselves primarily with restricting the cost of banquets (*luxus mensae*). Other factors played a part too – Roman aristocratic houses were public as well as private spaces, although naturally considered part of an aristocrat's estate. The sumptuary laws were concerned to discourage members of the elite from consuming their patrimony, which extravagant eating achieved much more definitively than extravagant building, where the embellished property at least remained in the owner's possession; and the ancient families of Rome would have been disproportionately affected by any attempt to clamp down on luxurious houses.[43] In fact Roman legislation about the size of houses, such as the *Lex Tarentina* from southern Italy, was more concerned to express the *minimum* size of a house to be occupied by a city-councillor (defined in terms of the number of tiles on the roof), rather than banning undue ostentation in building.[44] Similarly, the exemplary expulsion from the Senate of Cornelius Rufinus for possessing silver was not (so far as we know) regularly repeated by later censors:[45] it was the *display*

---

[42] *Att.* 1.16.10.   [43] Clemente 1981; Gabba 1988: 38–40; Zanda 2011: 18.

[44] *Lex Tarentina* 26–9 with Crawford 1996: 310. On the absence of sumptuary legislation relating to houses, see Wallace-Hadrill 2008: 336–7.

[45] Zanda 2011: 43–4.

358

Frugality, Building, and Heirlooms in an Age of Social Mobility

at a banquet of more than 100 lbs of silver, rather than owning such an amount, that was banned by the *Lex Fannia* of 161 BCE and subsequently the *Lex Didia* of 143: the silver, unlike the food consumed at a banquet, could in due course be bequeathed to one's heirs.[46]

Social Mobility and Frugality in the Civil Wars and Under the Principate

If in general the scope for upward social mobility in the Roman Republic was limited, one period in which there was significant change in this respect was during, and after, the civil wars of the first century BCE.[47] Anxieties about luxury and frugality were well to the fore at this time. Civil war, and the subsequent proscriptions, which involved the condemnation and murder of many leading citizens, had as their consequences not only the seizure of booty by the victorious soldiers, but also the allocation of property to veterans as a reward for their service in the civil war armies. This redistribution of wealth might be expressed in the ostentatious use of precious metals, as among the traditional elites of the previous generations: Pliny preserves a striking story of a veteran from the army of Mark Antony, later settled at Bononia, who served dinner to the emperor Augustus on a golden platter. This, it turned out, had been made from gold melted down from the legs of a statue of the goddess Anaitis pillaged by Antony's forces during their campaign against the Parthians.[48] If the civil wars had a direct impact on the wealth and status of the rank-and-file soldiers, the same was even more true of those higher up the social scale. Many men of noble families perished fighting at Philippi – where Brunt estimates casualties

---

[46] Gel. 2.24.2. Fannius' original law related to the banquets hosted in turn by *principes ciuitatis* on the occasion of the *Ludi Megalenses*. The speech given by Livy to the tribune L. Valerius in support of the proposed repeal in 195 BCE of the *Lex Oppia* (a law which had been introduced to restrict female luxury after the battle of Cannae) notes that the loss involved in turning gold into jewellery was limited to the costs of manufacture (Liv. 34.7.4, with Zanda 2011: 116–17).

[47] For further discussion see Patterson 1993: 101–4.   [48] *Nat.* 33.83.

John R. Patterson

on both sides to amount to 40,000 men – or in the proscriptions which followed;[49] conversely, Augustus on seizing power discovered that during the civil wars the membership of the senate had risen from 600 to over 1000, and in his *Res Gestae* he records that he reviewed that body three times in order to eject the more dubious newcomers.[50] Equestrians too benefited from the upheavals of the civil war era: Augustus' close associate Maecenas himself was one example, and another was P. Vedius Pollio, best known to posterity for his habit of throwing his slaves to be eaten alive by lampreys in his fishponds.[51] Vedius' origins are obscure, but he seems to have been the son of a freedman, and acquired a large fortune, in Asia apparently, during the civil war years.[52] When he died in 15 BCE, he bequeathed his property to the *princeps* in the hope and expectation that Augustus would use it to build some kind of monument commemorating him. Augustus accepted the bequest of Vedius' maritime villa at Posillipo on the Bay of Naples, but demolished his house on the Oppian Hill at Rome, and subsequently used the site to build a portico in honour of his wife Livia.[53] Ovid alludes to the tradition that in early Rome those aiming for kingship were punished by having their houses destroyed,[54] but comments that in this case, damaging *luxuria* was the cause of the demolition: the house 'occupied a space larger than many towns enclose within their walls.'[55] Listing the various disasters and political crises of Augustus' reign at the beginning of his *Annals*, Tacitus refers to *Vedii Pollionis luxus*.[56] The limited archaeological investigations so far undertaken at the site do seem to confirm that the house, which appears to have been terraced and had entrances at more than one level on the Oppian hill, was immense in size

---

[49] Tac. *Ann.* 1.2; D.C. 52.42.5; Brunt 1971: 487–8. For further discussion of the decline of the nobility, see Patterson 2016.

[50] *RG* 8.2; Suet. *Aug.* 35.1; D.C. 52.42.1; 54.13–14.

[51] Sen. *Ira* 3.40.2; *Clem.* 1.18.2; Plin. *Nat.* 9.77; D.C. 54.23.2.   [52] Syme 1961.

[53] D.C. 54.23. On the story of Vedius' house and its relation to Augustus' broader moral programme, see in particular Boudreau Flory 1984, esp. 325–30; Edwards 1993: 164–7.

[54] For this practice, see Mustakallio 1994; Flower 2006: 47–51.

[55] Ov. *Fast.* 6. 639–44.   [56] *Ann.* 1.10.

Frugality, Building, and Heirlooms in an Age of Social Mobility

(estimated at about 8,400 m²),[57] and Ovid sees its destruction as an example to others.[58] Presumably we should see this episode alongside the allusions to frugality in Augustus' house on the Palatine: according to Suetonius he 'lived there in a house notable neither for its size nor its elegance [...] its rooms lacking marble decoration or fine pavements'. The couches and tables from Augustus' house, notable for their *parsimonia*, were apparently still visible in Suetonius' own time.[59] The destruction of Vedius' villa can thus be seen in terms of Augustus seeking to re-assert the importance of frugality, despite Vedius, as several ancient authors emphasise, having been a personal friend of the *princeps*.[60] We know that Vedius established a Caesareum in Beneventum;[61] and the discovery to the NE of that city, at Pietrelcina, of a fragmentary relief depicting Apollo, Diana, Latona and Victoria in front of a temple, may indicate the location of one of his rural villas, where he produced wine for export.[62] If so, his loyalty to the ideology of the *princeps* was reflected in its decoration: the relief is known also from other examples, one of which came from Augustus' villa at Capri, and may allude to Octavian's temple of Apollo, or that of Victory on the Palatine.[63]

Reviewing efforts by the emperor Claudius to give additional powers to his procurators in the provinces, Tacitus alludes briefly to the excessive powers assigned to equestrians in previous times, one of those named being Vedius Pollio, before going on to highlight the even more inappropriate authority given to imperial freedmen under that emperor.[64] All autocracies tend to promote social mobility, as loyal individuals of comparatively low status gain influence and rank due to the personal support of the monarch,[65] and just as Vedius, Maecenas and others did under Augustus, so imperial freedmen such as Pallas, Narcissus and Callistus gained

---

[57] Panella 1987, esp. 624 for a pavement associated with Vedius' house; Zanker 1987: 477–83; Panella 1995; 1999.
[58] Ov. *Fast.* 6.647.   [59] Suet. *Aug.* 72–3.   [60] Sen. *Ira* 3.40.4; Plin. *Nat.* 9.77.
[61] *CIL* 9.1556 = *ILS* 109.
[62] Adamo Muscettola 1996; Torelli 2002: 172–4; Iasiello 2004: 40–3.
[63] Zanker 1988: 62–5.   [64] *Ann.* 12.60.   [65] Andreski 1998, 137.

John R. Patterson

influence and wealth under Claudius.[66] Luxury and frugality again became focal points of the traditional elite's hostility to these groups. After alluding to various (comparatively modest) examples of extravagance in relation to silver plate under the Republic, Pliny goes on to comment that Drusillanus, a slave of Claudius, owned a silver dish of 500 lbs in weight, and eight accompanying side dishes of 250 lbs each.[67] In an admiring account of the modesty and restraint of the baths at the villa of Scipio Africanus which he had visited at Liternum in Campania, Seneca compares these with the baths of the present day, with their marble from Alexandria and Thasos, mosaics of Numidian stone, and silver taps, before revealing that he is actually referring to *plebeiae fistulae* (baths for the *plebs*) and hasn't yet talked about *balnea libertinorum* which were by implication even more ostentatious.[68] Elite disapproval of the undue advancement of these ex-slaves is again couched in terms of a contrast between luxury and frugality. Similarly, Pliny notes that the four small onyx columns in the theatre of L. Cornelius Balbus at Rome, regarded as miraculous in the reign of Augustus, were easily outshone by Claudius' freedman Callistus, who had 30 such columns in his dining room.[69] Tacitus alludes ironically to the *antiqua parsimonia* displayed by the imperial freedman Pallas, who possessed a personal fortune of 300 million sesterces: he had suggested to the emperor that women who married slaves should be penalised, and was offered by the senate the insignia of a praetor and the sum of 15 million sesterces, but turned down the financial reward, 'content with the honour alone'.[70]

It is Tacitus too who provides us with a key text on the phenomenon of frugality under the principate, in a discussion of the emperor Tiberius' approach to the problem of luxury, which had become an issue of particular concern in 22 CE,

---

[66] On the rise of imperial freedmen: Hopkins 1974, 113–114; Weaver 1972 esp. 259–266; Weaver 1974; Millar 1992, 69–83; Mouritsen 2011, 93–96. On their wealth see esp. Plin. *Nat.* 33.134; Suet. *Cl.* 28.
[67] *Nat.* 33.145.   [68] Sen. *Ep.* 86.6–7.   [69] Plin. *Nat.* 36.60.
[70] Tac. *Ann.* 12.53. For further (adverse) comment on this episode by the younger Pliny, see Plin. *Ep.* 7.29; 8.6.

362

Frugality, Building, and Heirlooms in an Age of Social Mobility

following an earlier series of sumptuary measures on the part of the Senate in 16 CE, prohibiting the manufacture of gold dinner-plate, and the wearing of garments of oriental silk by men.[71] It was thought that Tiberius, perceived as *princeps antiquae parsimoniae*, would take a severe line on this, but in the event he concluded that efforts to suppress luxury were likely to be counterproductive, and that these matters were best left to the conscience of individual citizens. Tacitus then goes on to observe that during the hundred years between the Battle of Actium and the accession of Galba in 68 CE, *luxus mensae* tended to go out of fashion. He argues that early in the principate, 'formerly wealthy aristocratic families [...] were ruined by a passion for magnificence [...] the more impressive the fortune, the *domus*, and the trappings of a man, the more distinguished his reputation and his *clientela*. After the cruel time of the executions' (views differ as to whether the reference is to the rule of the Julio-Claudians or the civil wars of 68–69 CE and the reign of Domitian) 'when a famous reputation meant death, those who survived turned to wiser practices. At the same time, the *noui homines*, brought repeatedly into the Senate from the municipalities and colonies and even from the provinces, introduced their own parsimonious habits (*domestica parsimonia*) [...] but the chief promoter of this stricter moral code was Vespasian, himself a man of old-style virtue in his dress and lifestyle (*antiquo ipse cultu uictuque*). Thereafter [...] deference to the emperor and the love of emulating him proved more powerful than fear of the law and its penalties'. Tacitus concludes by observing that 'not all things were better in the old days; but our own age too has produced many instances of artistic excellence for imitation by posterity', a phrase which appears to relate to contemporary literary production (perhaps including that of the author himself).[72]

This is a very interesting passage for various reasons, and not only because of the optimistic tone suggesting the

---

[71] For the initiatives in 16 CE, see Tac. *Ann.* 2.33; on Tiberius' concern with the problem of luxury, Suet. *Tib.* 34.
[72] Tac. *Ann.* 3.52–5 with Woodman and Martin 1996: 376–413.

363

John R. Patterson

possibility of moral improvement, so different from what we find in Livy's preface, for example.[73] The stress on the *noui homines*, whether from the regions of Italy or the provinces, and their contribution to this new climate of *parsimonia,* is particularly striking, and ties in with the persona that the younger Pliny creates for himself in his *Letters.* This should perhaps not surprise us, given the similarities between Pliny's origins in Comum in north Italy and Tacitus's, either in Cisalpine or Narbonese Gaul, and their shared membership of the same intellectual and social circle. Pliny proudly relates to a correspondent how at the races recently Tacitus was engaged in intellectual conversation by a Roman knight, before being asked whether he came from Italy or the provinces, and then whether he was Tacitus or Pliny.[74] In his *Panegyricus,* Pliny himself praises the frugality of Trajan and his predecessor Nerva: at banquets, for example, it is 'not gold or silver, or the exquisitely ingenious dishes, which we admire, but the agreeable charm of the emperor' (i.e. Trajan). Earlier in this passage, however, Pliny has noted that 'when *frugalitas* might have cut short a dinner, the emperor's *humanitas* extended it': Trajan avoids the disagreeable consequences of excessive frugality.[75] But Pliny in his correspondence is also keen to stress his own personal restraint in these matters. He particularly admires the lifestyle of T. Vestricius Spurinna, consul of 98 CE, on which he intends to model his own old age: dinner with Spurinna is a simple (*frugi*) meal, but elegant (*nitida*), and brought in on dishes of solid antique silver (*in argento puro et antiquo*).[76] We are also told that 'Corinthian' bronze vessels – made from a bronze alloy of particularly high quality, if not necessarily from Corinth itself – were also in general use in the house of Spurinna, recalling the antique hydria in the House of Julius Polybius at Pompeii.[77] This apparent paradox recalls the willingness to use antique (and especially ancestral) silver

---

[73] Rutherford 1989: 77–8.   [74] Plin. *Ep.* 9.23.2–3.
[75] Plin. *Pan.* 49.5–7. For the frugality of Nerva, see *Pan.* 51.   [76] Plin. *Ep.* 3.1.9.
[77] For the high reputation of 'Corinthian' vases, see Plin. *Nat.* 34.6–8. Tiberius was concerned about the high prices being paid for these: Suet. *Tib.* 34. Petronius' Trimalchio gives a characteristically idiosyncratic account of the origin of the alloy:

364

Frugality, Building, and Heirlooms in an Age of Social Mobility

plate in the Republic even among those who claimed to be frugal; elsewhere in the *Letters* there are numerous examples of the properties of Pliny himself or of his friends being referred to proudly or admiringly as *frugi*. He describes the *cubiculum* of the distinguished lawyer Titius Aristo and its bed as 'an image of traditional frugality (*imago priscae frugalitatis*)', for example.[78] Pliny's own villa on the Laurentine coast to the south-west of Rome, has an *atrium frugi, nec tamen sordidum*, while the *uicus* near the villa is 'enough for a frugal man'.[79] There are also numerous references to Pliny's ties with northern Italy: for example he recommends a friend called Minicius Acilianus as a husband for another friend's niece, noting that he comes from Brixia, 'one of the towns in our part of Italy which still retains intact much of its moderation and *frugalitas*, along with its ancient rustic virtue' in a phrase which echoes Tacitus' observations on the decline of *luxus mensae*.[80]

In this context, then, we can see an enthusiasm for *frugalitas*, and disapproval for luxury, as again related to the mobility of outsiders into the ruling class of Rome: now, however, it is men like Pliny and Tacitus who themselves are providing the narrative of their own advancement, and their frugality is implicitly contrasted with the excessive behaviour of 'bad' emperors like Caligula, who notoriously claimed that 'a man needs to be either frugal or a Caesar'.[81] Their model does indeed seem to be Vespasian, as we can see from Pliny's account of a typical day on his own Tuscan estate – and indeed that of his uncle the Elder Pliny – both of which closely resemble Suetonius' description of a typical day in the life of that emperor.[82]

But is the supposed decline in luxury to which Tacitus refers reflected in reality as well as ideology? A few considerations suggest that it might be. In the Julio-Claudian period

---

see *Sat.* 50 with Schmeling 2011: 210–11. On 'Corinthian' vases more generally, see Emanuele 1989; Wallace-Hadrill 2008: 373–5.
[78] *Ep.* 1.22.4. [79] Plin. *Ep.* 2.17.4 and 26.
[80] *Ep.* 1.14.4 with Tac. *Ann.* 3.55 and 16.5. See also D'Arms 1984: 460–2 for more examples of these ties.
[81] Suet. *Cal.* 37.1.
[82] Plin. *Ep.* 9.36; 3.5.8–13; Suet. *Ves.* 21, with Crook 1955: 27–8.

365

John R. Patterson

ostentation in the city of Rome was liable to attract unwanted attention. Following the death of Germanicus, public opinion was alienated when his supposed murderer, Cn. Piso, celebrated his return to Rome with festive decorations and a banquet at his house, which was situated in a particularly visible location overlooking the Forum: 'in that populous quarter, nothing was hidden', as Tacitus puts it.[83] There was also the risk that the emperor's hostility might be attracted by the ownership of a lavish house, which the emperor might covet for himself. However, one consequence of the great fire of 64 CE, which devastated the Palatine and surrounding areas, and the subsequent construction of Nero's Golden House, was that as Suetonius puts it 'the houses of generals of old were burned, still decorated by spoils taken from the enemy.'[84] The result was that the aristocracy tended to move to the periphery of the city: after the great fire, the main centres of elite residence were the Esquiline, the Quirinal, the Aventine, the Viminal and the Caelian.[85] Whether their new houses were really more frugal than their predecessors around the Forum and Palatine had been is hard to assess, but they were certainly less high-profile. At the same time, and for the same reasons, the tombs of the senatorial aristocracy under the early and middle empire tended, with a few notable exceptions like the Pyramid of Cestius on the road leading to Ostia,[86] to be more modest and located further from the centre of Rome, and thus less visible in the urban context than those of their late-Republican predecessors: for example the tomb of the Licinii and Calpurnii, dated to the mid-first century CE and located close to the later Aurelianic walls on the Via Salaria,[87] or that of the historian Tacitus, close to the Via Nomentana.[88]

Conclusion

Frugality, then, as well as being a moral ideal, was an ideological battleground in the ongoing struggle in Roman society

---

[83] *Ann.* 3.9.   [84] Suet. *Nero* 38.2.   [85] Eck 1997; Guilhembet 2001: 232–4.
[86] Ridley 1992.   [87] Boschung 1986.   [88] Alföldy 1995; Birley 2000.

366

Frugality, Building, and Heirlooms in an Age of Social Mobility

between those who saw themselves as members of a traditional elite and those who were perceived as newcomers; as with luxury, we find the ideal being most debated at times when social mobility was most apparent and most controversial. In Roman society of the second century BCE, the scope for mobility was in reality limited, but exceptional luxury or frugality contributed to a greater visibility in public life, which might work to the benefit or the detriment of an individual's political career. Ostentatious private building and the collection of silver plate were a particular focus of contention, but sumptuary laws were drafted in such a way as not to penalise the family homes or the antique silver collections of the aristocracy. The upheavals of the civil wars led to the rise of morally dubious individuals like Vedius Pollio, and Augustus as *princeps* reasserted the virtue of *parsimonia* in part through the destruction of Vedius' house, but also by means of the frugality of his own residence. The rise of imperial freedmen in subsequent years, and the wealth they amassed, aroused the antagonism of the senatorial elite, who in turn reasserted the ideal of frugality; one consequence of the upheavals of 69 CE was an increased presence in the Senate of men from North Italy and the provinces, who modelled themselves on the Sabine emperor Vespasian, and have provided for posterity the predominant elite voice of the high empire (we should remember that a rather different view of luxury is presented by e.g. Statius, who praises the use of silver and fine decorations in the baths of Claudius Etruscus).[89] But at the end of the day we need to remember that the ideal of frugality was a relative one: Seneca was able to reassure his readers that *frugalitas* could be displayed in making a journey accompanied by only one carriage-load of slaves.[90]

Bibliography

Adamo Muscettola, S. (1996) 'Un rilievo deliaco da Pietrelcina: sulle tracce di Vedio Pollione', *La Parola del Passato* 51: 118–31.

[89] *Silv.* 1.5, with Edwards 1993: 142.   [90] *Ep.* 87.2–5.

John R. Patterson

Alföldy, G. (1995) 'Bricht der Schweigsame sein Schweigen? Eine Grabinschrift aus Rom', *MDAIR* 102: 251–68.

Allen, W. (1958) 'Imperial mementoes in Suetonius', *CB* 35.1: 1–4.

Allison, P. (2004) *Pompeian Households: An Analysis of Material Culture.* Los Angeles.

Andreski, S. (1998) *Military Organisation and Society*, 2nd edn. London.

Berry, C. J. (1994) *The Idea of Luxury: A Conceptual and Historical Investigation.* Cambridge.

Birley, A. R. (2000) 'The life and death of Cornelius Tacitus', *Historia* 49: 230–47.

Boschung, D. (1986) 'Überlegungen zum Liciniergrab', *JDAI* 101: 257–87.

Boudreau Flory, M. (1984) 'Sic exempla parantur: Livia's shrine to Concordia and the Porticus Liviae', *Historia* 33: 309–30.

Broughton, T. R. S. (1951) *The Magistrates of the Roman Republic*, vol. 1. New York.

Brunt, P. A. (1971) *Italian Manpower 225 BC–AD 14.* Oxford.

Carandini, A. (1988) *Schiavi in Italia. Gli strumenti pensanti dei Romani fra tarda Repubblica e medio Impero.* Rome.

Carandini, A., Bruno, D. and Fraioli, F. (2010) *Le case del potere nell'antica Roma.* Bari.

Carlsen, J. (2006) *The Rise and Fall of a Roman Noble Family: The Domitii Ahenobarbi 196 BC–AD 68.* Odense.

Clemente, G. (1981) 'Le leggi sul lusso e la società romana tra III e II secolo a.C.', in *Società romana e produzione schiavistica, vol. 3. Modelli etici, diritto e transformazioni sociali*, eds. A. Giardina and A. Schiavone. Bari: 1–14.

Crawford, M. H. (ed.) (1996) *Roman Statutes.* London.

Crook, J. A. (1955) *Consilium principis.* Cambridge.

D'Arms, J. (1984) 'Upper-class attitudes towards *viri municipales* and their towns in the early Roman empire', *Athenaeum* 62: 440–67.

De Carolis, E. (2007) *Il mobile a Pompei ed Ercolano: letti, tavoli, sedie e armadi.* Rome.

Dyck, A. R. (1996) *A Commentary on Cicero, De Officiis.* Ann Arbor.

Eck, W. (1997) 'Cum dignitate otium: senatorial *domus* in imperial Rome', *SCI* 16: 162–90.

Edwards, C. (1993) *The Politics of Immorality in Ancient Rome.* Cambridge.

Emanuele, D. (1989) 'Aes Corinthium: fact, fiction, and fake', *Phoenix* 43: 347–57.

Fantham, E. (ed.) (2013) *Cicero's Pro L. Murena oratio.* New York.

Flower, H. I. (2006) *The Art of Forgetting: Disgrace and Oblivion in Roman Political Culture.* Chapel Hill.

Gabba, E. (1988) *Del buon uso della ricchezza: saggi di storia economica e sociale del mondo antico.* Milan.

368

Frugality, Building, and Heirlooms in an Age of Social Mobility

Garnsey, P. (2007) *Thinking about Property: From Antiquity to the Age of Revolution*. Cambridge.

Giovagnoli, M. (2012a) 'Coppetta per l'elezione di Catone', in *Terme di Diocleziano: la collezione epigrafica*, eds. R. Friggeri, M. G. Granino Cecere and G. L. Gregori. Milan: 203.

(2012b) 'Coppetta per l'elezione di Catilina', in *Terme di Diocleziano: la collezione epigrafica*, eds. R. Friggeri, M. G. Granino Cecere and G. L. Gregori. Milan: 204.

Griffin, M. (1976) *Seneca: A Philosopher in Politics*. Oxford.

Guilhembet, J.-P. (2001) 'Les résidences aristocratiques de Rome, du milieu du Ier siècle avant n.è. à la fin des Antonins', in *La ville de Rome sous le haut-empire: nouvelles connaissances, nouvelles reflexions* (= Pallas 2001): 215–41.

(2006) 'Acquérir, louer ou négocier des biens immobiliers de prestige à Rome à la fin de la république et aux premiers siècles de l'empire', in *Sur la ville de Rome* (= Cahiers de la MRSH-Caen 46): 91–197.

Hopkins, K. (1974) 'Elite mobility in the Roman Empire' in M. I. Finley (ed.) *Studies in Ancient Society*. London: 103–20. (= *Past and Present* 32, 1965, 12–26.)

(1983) *Death and Renewal*. Cambridge.

Iasiello, I. M. (2004) *Dall'IRAP all'Archeoclub: Quarant'anni di ricerche archeologiche in Pietrelcina*. Pietrelcina.

Jones, L. (2016) 'Memory, nostalgia and the Roman home', in *Ruin or Renewal? Places and the Transformation of Memory in the City of Rome*, eds. M. García Morcillo, J. H. Richardson and F. Santangelo. Rome: 183–212.

Künzl, E. (1984) 'Le argenterie', in *Pompei 79: raccolta di studi per il decimonono centenario dell'eruzione vesuviana*, ed. F. Zevi. Naples: 211–28.

Kuttner, A. (1995) *Dynasty and Empire in the Age of Augustus: The Case of the Boscoreale Cups*. Berkeley.

Lapatin, K. (2008) 'Luxus', in *Pompeii and the Roman Villa: Art and Culture around the Bay of Naples*, ed. C. Mattusch. New York: 31–51.

(2014) 'Roman luxury from home to tomb and sanctuary' in *The Berthouville Silver Treasure and Roman Luxury*, ed. K. Lapatin. Los Angeles: 127–47.

(2015) *Luxus: The Sumptuary Arts of Greece and Rome*. Los Angeles.

Lazzarini, M. L. and Zevi, F. (1988–1989) 'Necrocorinthia a Pompei: una idria bronzea per le gare di Argo', *Prospettiva 53/56. Scritti in ricordo di Giovanni Previtali*, vol. 1. 133–48.

McClintock, A. (2013) 'The *Lex Voconia* and Cornelia's jewels', *Revue internationale des droits de l'antiquité* 60: 183–200.

Manuwald, G. (2007) *Cicero's 'Philippics' 3–9 Edited with Introduction, Translation and Commentary*. Berlin.

John R. Patterson

Millar, F. (1992) *The Emperor in the Roman World*, 2nd edn. London.

Mols, S. T. A. M. (1999) *Wooden Furniture in Herculaneum: Form, Technique and Function*. Amsterdam.

Mouritsen, H. (2011) *The Freedman in the Roman World*. Cambridge.

Mustakallio, K. (1994) *Death and Disgrace: Capital Penalties with Post mortem Sanctions in Early Roman Historiography*. Helsinki.

Painter, K. S. (2001) *The Insula of the Menander at Pompeii vol. IV: The Silver Treasure*. Oxford.

Panciera, S. (1979) 'Catilina e Catone su due coppette romane', in *Φιλίας χάριν: miscellanea di studi classici in onore di Eugenio Manni*, vol 5. Rome: 1636–62.

(2006) *Epigrafi, epigrafia, epigrafisti: Scritti vari editi e inediti (1956–2005)*. Con note complementari e indici. Rome.

Panella, C. (1987) 'L'organizzazzione degli spazi sulle pendici settentrionali del Colle Oppio tra Augusto e i Severi', in *L'Urbs: espace urbain et histoire (Ier siècle av. J.C. – IIIe siècle ap. J.-C.)*. Rome: 611–54.

(1995) 'Domus: P. Vedius Pollio', in *Lexicon Topographicum Urbis Romae* 2, ed. E. M. Steinby. Rome: 211–12.

(1999) 'Porticus Liviae', in *Lexicon Topographicum Urbis Romae 4*, ed. E. M. Steinby. Rome: 127–9.

Papi, E. (1995a) 'Domus: Cn. Domitius Ahenobarbus', in *Lexicon Topographicum Urbis Romae* 2, ed. E. M. Steinby. Rome: 93.

(1995b) 'Domus: L. Licinius Crassus', in *Lexicon Topographicum Urbis Romae* 2, ed. E. M. Steinby. Rome: 128.

Patterson, J. R. (1993) 'Military organization and social change in the later Roman Republic', in *War and Society in the Roman World*, eds. J. Rich and G. Shipley. London: 92–112.

(2016) 'Imperial Rome and the demise of the imperial nobility', in *Ruin or Renewal? Places and the Transformation of Memory in the City of Rome*, eds. M. García Morcillo, J. H. Richardson and F. Santangelo. Rome: 213–42.

Rawson, E. (1976) 'The Ciceronian aristocracy and its properties', in *Studies in Roman Property*, ed. M. I. Finley. Cambridge: 85–102.

Ridley, R. T. (1992) 'The praetor and the pyramid: the tomb of Gaius Cestius in history, archaeology and literature', *Bollettino di Archeologia* 13–15: 1–30.

Rutherford, R. B. (1989) *The Meditations of Marcus Aurelius: A Study*. Oxford.

Santangelo, F. (2006) 'Sulla and the Senate: a reconsideration', *Cahiers Gustave-Glotz* 17: 7–22.

Schmeling, G. (2011) *A Commentary on the Satyrica of Petronius*. Oxford.

Steel, C. (2013) *The End of the Roman Republic, 146 to 44 BC: Conquest and Crisis*. Edinburgh.

Strong, D. E. (1966) *Greek and Roman Gold and Silver Plate*. London.

370

Frugality, Building, and Heirlooms in an Age of Social Mobility

Syme, R. (1961) 'Who was Vedius Pollio?', *JRS* 51: 23–30.

Torelli, M. R. (2002) *Benevento romana*. Rome.

Van Oyen, A. (2015) 'The moral architecture of villa storage in Italy in the 1st c. BC', *JRA* 28: 97–124.

Wallace-Hadrill, A. (2000) 'Case e abitanti a Roma', in *Roma imperiale: una metropoli antica*, ed. E. Lo Cascio. Rome: 173–220.

(2008) *Rome's Cultural Revolution*. Cambridge.

(2011) *Herculaneum: Past and Future*. London.

Walters, H. B. (1921) *Catalogue of the Silver Plate (Greek, Etruscan, and Roman) in the British Museum*. London.

Ward-Perkins, J. B. and Claridge, A. (1976) *Pompeii AD 79*. London.

Weaver, P. R. C. (1972) *Familia Caesaris: A Social Study of the Emperor's Freedmen and Slaves*. Cambridge.

(1974) 'Social mobility in the early Roman empire: the evidence of the imperial freedmen and slaves', in *Studies in Ancient Society*, ed. M.I. Finley. London: 121–40. (= *Past and Present* 37, 1967: 3–20.)

Wiseman, T. P. (1971) *New Men in the Roman Senate, 139 BC–AD 14*. Oxford.

Woodman, A. J. and Martin, R. H. (eds.) (1996) *The Annals of Tacitus Book 3. Edited with a Commentary*. Cambridge.

Zanda, E. (2011) *Fighting Hydra-Like Luxury: Sumptuary Regulation in the Roman Republic*. London.

Zanker, P. (1987) 'Drei Stadtbilder aus dem Augusteischen Rom', in *L'Urbs: espace urbain et histoire (Ier siècle av. J.C. – IIIe siècle ap. J.-C.)*. Rome: 475–89.

(1988) *The Power of Images in the Age of Augustus*. Ann Arbor.

CHAPTER 7

FROM POVERTY TO PROSPERITY: THE RECALIBRATION OF FRUGALITY

CHRISTOPHER J. BERRY

According to Seneca, successful study requires *frugalitas*, that is, a simple life of voluntary poverty.[1] From the middle Stoa into Christian teaching and on into the early modern period, it was, in Cicero's formulation, dishonourable [*turpe*] to sink into luxury and to live a soft life but, in contrast, it was honourable [*honestum*] to live frugally, simply, soberly and with self-restraint [*parce, continenter, seuere, sobrie*] (*de Officiis* 1.106). The idealised family of values here portrayed was overturned. This *bouleversement* was, of course, the product of many causes over at least a couple of centuries. Taking that as given, this account has to be limited. To give focus I concentrate on the work of Hume and Smith, who provide two of the most notable expressions of this recalibration of frugality. Frugality for them is not a moral bulwark against the invasive corruptions of bodily appetites and social degradation but a practice or pattern of behaviour that serves to enhance social well-being, including the rightful enjoyment of material benefits by all. The thrust of my argument is that their recalibration or re-evaluation is central to their enterprise of defending the modern world of commerce. I emphasise their justificatory intent because I am not claiming that their animus toward the classical view is without precedent.[2]

---

[1] Sen. *Ep.* 17.5: *non potest studium salutare fieri sine frugalitatis cura; frugalitas autem paupertas uoluntaria est* ('Study cannot be helpful unless you take pains to live simply; and living simply is voluntary poverty' – trans. R. M. Gummere/Loeb).

[2] Hans Baron (1988: Ch. 9), for example, claimed that Leonardo Bruni and his generation rejected the Stoic idea of *paupertas* and links that to the revival of (pseudo) Aristotelian *Oeconomica* on which Bruni wrote a commentary. It is, however, central to my argument that Hume and Smith also reject the Aristotelian perspective and represent a break from Renaissance humanism (see further below).

372

From Poverty to Prosperity: The Recalibration of Frugality

I

In the classical (and neo-classical tradition), *frugalitas* meant living simply, in accordance with the requirements of natural needs. These requirements were limited. The body has needs which must be satisfied but there is also a natural or rational limit to this satisfaction – hence only drink when thirsty and only have sex for the sake of conception and only wear on one's feet what is functionally needed. As Epictetus (*The Manual* § 39) admonished, to desire gilded or embroidered slippers is to forsake those limits, is to lose control. A frugal or simple life is thus one where reason controls desires. Cicero captured the common or shared core by explicitly associating *frugalitas* with the virtue of self-command, as especially manifested by control of (bodily) appetites and desires (*libidines*).[3] Those who exercise that control cannot, as Seneca affirmed, experience poverty;[4] it is only those who are governed by desire who judge they are poor when they cannot attain what they want.

By the same token once limits are over-ridden then those who are rich are never rich enough; the seeker of the pleasures of luxury can never be satisfied. Not only does luxury corrupt manly virtue (it emasculated and was uniformly associated with 'feminine' qualities of softness, weakness and irresolution) (see Edwards 1993: Ch. 2) it also – and not coincidentally – undermined societal strength and cohesion. Hence on a general level, Livy (1 *Praef.* 11) attributed Rome's decline to it falling away from virtuous frugality (*paupertati ac parsimonae*) and falling into the embrace of luxury, avarice and desire, occasioned by imports from 'the East'. While, on a more particular level, Sallust (*War with Catiline* 5.8; 12.2) similarly judged Catiline's conspiracy to be symptomatic of the contemporary corruption of civic virtue by the evils of luxury and avarice while, conversely, poverty (*paupertas*) was seen at that

---

[3] Cicero, *Tusc.* 3.15–17. He openly identifies *frugalitas* with the Greek σωφροσύνη. For a detailed examination of this passage plus a wide-ranging thorough, and detailed lexicological, treatment see Chapter 5 (Gildenhard).

[4] *Consolatio ad Helviam* 11.3. Cf. *Ep.* 2.6.

373

Christopher J. Berry

time as disgraceful because honour was now (alas) accorded to riches. The moral story encapsulated here, and of course told by many others from the satires of Juvenal to the natural history of Pliny, maintained a powerful hold; the Fall of Rome, up to and including the eighteenth century, was deemed by neo-Stoics and neo-republicans to hold a profound lesson for their own time.

II

To illustrate this persistence and help provide a more proximate context for Hume and Smith I note briefly a work of another Scot. (Sir) George Mackenzie (1636 or 1638–1691) was a Scottish Parliamentarian and Lord Advocate. Best known for his authoritative *Institutions of the Laws of Scotland* (1684) he was the author of other works. These include *The Moral History of Frugality* written in 1691 but published in 1711.[5] The essay self-consciously enjoins 'us [to] embrace ancient Frugality, under whose empire Vice was of old curbed with great success.' Avarice and luxury are identified as the two 'Capital Enemies' of the 'friendly wise and convenient Virtue of Frugality' (Mackenzie, 1716: 143). As we have seen, this is the argument of Sallust and others. Indeed, Mackenzie reproduces familiar themes. Hence frugality 'harden'd Men into a Temper of being Soldiers', while the luxurious 'become effeminate and soft unable to defend and improve their Native Country' (1716: 147, 162; cf. 164). There are limits to our 'natural Necessities' in contrast to 'Imaginary fantastick Necessities' (1716: 144, 143) which, as both avarice and luxury exhibit, 'can never be satisfied nor bounded' (1716: 162). Reminiscent of Seneca's comment on the quality of the flour in the bread being nothing to Nature, since what matters is that the stomach is filled not flattered [*delectari*] (*Ep.* 119.3), for Mackenzie a 'Frugal and Temperate Man can by Fasting till a convenient time make any food pleasant' (1716: 162).

---

[5] Mackenzie's essay is briefly discussed in Allan 2000: 202–5.

From Poverty to Prosperity: The Recalibration of Frugality

Mackenzie identifies reason and Nature ('man's chief Rule') as the defence against luxury and avarice (1716: 148, 160), since they enable our 'Senses and other inferior Faculties' to be our servants and not our 'wild Masters' (1716: 163). Hence a life of luxury manifests 'a great defect in our Reason' (1716: 160). He makes the to-be-expected references to Roman, and Spartan, history. The world, he declares, was 'debauched by Roman luxury as that was fed by their Spoils' despite their sumptuary legislation (1716: 146, 147, 148) and he refers to Cato being more celebrated for his 'frugal Severity' than were Caesar or Pompey for their conquests (1716: 146). He quotes Lucan to that end and later cites Horace (1716: 157), but, despite his vocabulary and argument echoing that of the Roman moralists, his direct 'classical' citations are few. This paucity is a consequence of Mackenzie viewing frugality through a Christian lens. It is God who has 'imprinted an Abhorrence upon our Minds' against avarice, luxury and other vices and has 'enamoured us of Frugality' (1716: 144), which is 'the true Mathematick of Christian morality' (1716: 144). Of course this does not discount the contribution of heathen philosophers; indeed God thought it 'fit' to send them into the world 'little before his Son to convince Men that the vices which he was to curb by his Gospel were abhorr'd by those whom they Honoured with the Names of Wise Men and Lovers of Virtue' (1716: 149).

Mackenzie's language reflects a prevalent strand in early modern thought whereby, among the educated, Christianity and Stoicism were intertwined, if not always seamlessly.[6] Not that this symbiosis was absent earlier, as both Clement of Alexandria and Tertullian clearly exhibit in their terminology (Mackenzie references the latter [1716: 146]).[7] It continued

---

[6] For the Jansenist/Augustinian antipathy to Stoicism see Brooke 2012: Ch. 4. He also brings out the role of Stoicism as the major source of the critique of luxury (152). This not to say Stoicism had a monopoly but Cicero, Seneca and Epictetus were all heavily cited in the sixteenth century, see Tilmouth 2007: Ch.1.

[7] Clement's *Paedagogus* for example is a catalogue of the dangers of excess and luxury, with the judgment Πλοῦτος δὲ ἄριστος ἡ τῶν ἐπιθυμιῶν πενία (2.3.39.4: *uerae autem diuitiae sunt, paupertas cupiditatum*: 'true wealth is dearth of desires'). Tertullian's *De Cultu Feminarum* echoes, though even more resoundingly, Clement's misogyny as he

375

Christopher J. Berry

into the eighteenth century, where published sermons and pamphlets associated frugality with Christian living and lamented the luxury of the times.[8]

There is another, albeit subdued, strand in Mackenzie's essay that in the context of this chapter is worth observing. The only contemporary 'state' he refers to is Holland. He maintains that the Hollanders originally practised frugality out of necessity rather than choice but later recommended it as the best means to 'enlarge their Trade' (1716: 147).[9] This, as we shall see, becomes a key feature of Hume and Smith's recalibration but, in line with the tenor of his essay, Mackenzie does not take that step. He adverts to the defence of luxury that it sustains 'many poor Artisans and others who would starve without its assistance' (1716: 159) but rejoins that there would be no poor were it not for avarice and luxury (163). Indeed echoing long-established prejudice, he adds most artisans are unnecessary (such as those involved in the production of perfume, lace, embroidery and 'such things which Frugality contemns as Baubles' [1716: 159]). Here is a clear demarcation. Hume and Smith commend frugality because it produces industry (productive artisanal employment) of which a key incentive is the desire to possess baubles.

---

inveighs against transgressing limits and strikingly refers to the manliness of faith being unmanned (*fidei uirtus effeminari*) by *deliciae* (2.13.3).

[8] See for example, Edward Watkinson 1776: 26: '[Christ] gave sanction to frugality by his own Practice'; William Adams 1770: 20: '[frugality] is a prudent and virtuous use of that which through the Blessing of God is gained by your Labour and Industry. And this is the more necessary to be mentioned at a time when Luxury ... has deeply affected all degree of men amongst us'.

[9] The Dutch, as England's great trading rivals, acted as a touchstone and this produced many analyses to account for their success. One example of this literature is Sir William Temple's influential *Observations upon the United Provinces* (1668). He noted, among the causes of this Dutch success, their frugality and parsimony and the lack of shame attached to such behaviour but he detects signs (evidenced by the introduction of sumptuary laws) of a growth in 'luxury, idleness and excess' which, he conventionally judges, would undermine their 'habitual industry, parsimony and simplicity', the very foundations of their trade. Like Mackenzie, Temple also surmises that Dutch frugality was originally a matter of necessity (1754: vol. I, 124, 138, 92). Hume cited Temple several times, Smith owned this edition of Temple's works and, in passing, testifies to the commonplaceness of the association between Holland and frugality (1982a: 209).

376

From Poverty to Prosperity: The Recalibration of Frugality

III

How do we account for the recalibration? Two background conditions or developments stand out. These can be stated with necessary brevity. The first is the post-Galilean 'revolution' in physics and the associated but fundamental re-thinking of epistemology and ethics. Reason's controlling and motivating force was rejected in favour of that role being played by passions or desires. Both Hume and Smith accept broadly John Locke's empirical version of this re-thinking, in that they reject, on the one hand, the Cartesian strand of modern rationalism while, on the other, depart from the egocentric individualistic implications of the work of Thomas Hobbes. That departure, though, did not contest Hobbes' basic proposition that humans are motivated by the passions (their appetites and aversions) so that reason's role is subordinately instrumental. Hence, in a direct reversal of Mackenzie's attribution of master/servant roles, in one of Hume's most famous/notorious declarations, 'Reason is and ought only to be the slave of the passions, and can never pretend to any other office than to serve and obey them'.[10] Smith expresses a similar sentiment (1982a: 320).

The second development was a defence of commerce. This was defensive because it too had to combat the assumptions and prejudices of the Greek and Roman moralists who saw implicit in commerce conduct and values antipathetic to *antiqua frugalitas*. *Hoi kapeloi* or *mercatores* were suspect not only because they were weak, making them unfit for military duty, but also because their devotion to private pursuits rendered them inferior, necessarily ill-equipped for the commitments of citizenship. From the Stoic and teleological view it was not that men could not adopt the commercial life but that such a life was unworthy, it was (as Cicero, Seneca and others had observed) the inferior, sub-human/sub-masculine, concern of animals, slaves and women. The defence had begun in the

---

[10] Hume 1978: 415. See also the unambiguous judgement that 'the chief spring or actuating principle of the human mind is pleasure or pain' (1978: 574).

377

Christopher J. Berry

seventeenth century in pamphlets on 'trade'. These writings were typically *pièces d'occasion* (such as defending the private operations of the East India Company) but employed the rhetoric of the national or public interest. The rhetoric betrayed the defensiveness. It can be detected, for example, in Thomas Mun's *England's Treasure by Forreign Trade* (published 1664 but probably written earlier). Therein Mun defends what he calls the 'noble profession' of the merchant, whose private endeavours will, when properly conducted, accompany the public good. However, in his text he still feels he has to criticise 'Piping, Potting, Feasting, Fashion' which 'hath made us effeminate ... declined in our Valour' (that is to say he is rehearsing the stock ingredients of the Livian/Sallustian legacy).[11] The legacy began to weaken, so in 1690 Nicholas Barbon, while side-stepping the still opprobrious term 'luxury', produces a defence of trade without Mun's prevarication (indeed he explicitly criticises him). In addition, Barbon, by openly commending 'fashion' and 'wants of the mind', signals his divergence from the standard neo-Stoic position, since he identifies these wants as comprising anything that satisfies desire such as those goods that 'can gratifie his Senses, adorn his Body and promote the Ease, Pleasure and Pomp of Life'.[12] It is this gradual shift that Mandeville notoriously represented in the increasingly elaborate iterations of the *Fable of the Bees* (1721–32) when he produced a more open if still oblique defence of luxury (and critique of frugality) (Mandeville 1988: I, 107–123).

Hume provides one of the key texts in this defence. His ostensible strategy in 'Of Refinement in the Arts' (original title [1752] 'Of Luxury') is to correct the extreme positions of those who, on the one hand, decry and those, on the other, who

---

[11] Mun 1664: I, 72–3. While he advocates domestic frugality to increase the quantity of 'natural wealth' that can be exported, he also counsels that this frugality should not be so extensive (some pomp can be indulged) that few foreign goods are purchased with the consequence that England is unable to sell its exports (1664: 9, 60). Mun was another who used the Dutch as a comparator.

[12] Barbon 1905: 11, 14. Not surprisingly Barbon is critical of 'frugality'. I discuss Barbon in Berry 1994: 108–25. For a subsequent discussion from a somewhat different perspective, see Kellow 2011.

378

From Poverty to Prosperity: The Recalibration of Frugality

praise luxury tout court. While Mandeville (unnamed) is criticised as an example of the latter position, in practice, it is the former, whom he calls 'severe moralists' (Sallust is named as an example), who are his main target. These moralists associate poverty and virtue (Hume 1985: 275). Hume dissociates them. For him there is nothing ennobling or redemptive about poverty; it is a debasement (Hume 1985: 198).[13]

One consequence of this is that Hume rejects the Senecan notion of frugality or poverty as a voluntary state. This idea passed easily into Patristic and then mainstream Christian teaching and practice. Hence for St Thomas Aquinas, poverty is commendable because it frees a man from 'worldly solicitude'.[14] It was acknowledged that not all poverty was voluntary. The canon lawyer Huguccio (of Pisa), in his commentary (1188) on Gratian's *Decretum* (1140), elaborated upon this by dividing the poor into three categories. There were those who while born poor willingly endured it as an expression of their love of God, and also there were those who deliberately surrendered their possessions that they might live a virtuous Christian life. Both of these exemplified voluntary poverty. The third category, however, comprised those who were destitute and liable to be inhibited from achieving the higher moral values. This was involuntary poverty. However, the thrust here is on the involuntary poor being inhibited; as the first category intimates, the dominant sensibility was that poverty was not of itself an evil to be extirpated. Indeed, Stoic echoes can still be heard in Huguccio's explicit identification of this third category with those who are poor because they are filled with the 'voracity of cupidity'.[15]

For the Reformation theologians, voluntary poverty was a 'popish conceit' as William Perkins called it (1612: II, 148).

---

[13] I discuss Hume's argument in Berry 2018: Ch. 11 (originally published in 2008).

[14] Aquinas (*Summa contra gentiles* III-2-133/141-2). The Dominicans took a less austere view of the demands of a Christian life than the Franciscans for whom 'voluntary poverty' was a central ideal. I here, and in the following paragraph, follow my earlier account (Berry 2013: Ch. 3).

[15] Huguccio, 'Sunt alii pauperes sola cupiditatis habendae voracitate' quoted in Tierney 1959: 11.

Christopher J. Berry

Yet poverty was still seen as providential and even those whose 'calling' requires the performance of 'poore and base duties' will not be base in the sight of God, if they undertake those duties in obedient faith to His glory (1612: I, 757–8). These theologians continued the assault on luxury and enjoined a worldly asceticism but there was a change of emphasis.[16] While justification was indeed *sola fide*, so 'good works do not make a good man' yet 'a good man does good works' (Luther 1961: 69), these theologians associated salvation with industry and, in consequence, linked indolence with lack of virtue. While this applied to the 'idle', consumption-orientated, rich (see Booth 1993: 162) it also encompassed 'beggars and vagabonds' whose poverty became presumptive evidence of their wickedness (see Hill [1968: 215], Tawney [1938: 229]).

Hume and Smith retain a positive valuation of industry and a negative valuation of indolence but they shift the basis of the valuation as they recalibrate frugality. The Ciceronic idealisation of the severe virtues (quoted above) means that 'frugality' is swept up in Hume's broad-brush critique of the debasement suffered by the poor. However, the argument is nuanced. Whereas the compass of 'poverty' is effectively re-described, and its moral qualities effaced, by identifying it with impoverishment, 'frugality' is understood more narrowly as it undergoes a more subtle re-evaluation.

IV

Hume typically associates, though not exclusively, industry with frugality (1975: 243, 277, 313). The association itself is not novel. It can be found in Cicero (*de Officiis* 1.92) [*diligentia, parsimonia*] as well as in eighteenth century

---

[16] The now classic exposition of this is Max Weber's. He identifies what he calls 'die innerweltliche protestantische Askese' as an outlook that restricted consumption (especially luxuries) while freeing acquisition of goods from the inhibitions of traditionalistic ethics (1904: 20, 75; cf. 1930: 170–1).

380

From Poverty to Prosperity: The Recalibration of Frugality

homiletic literature (see note 8). The point, however, is not the association itself but the 'work' it does in Hume's overall argument.[17] For Hume, industry is one leg of an 'indissoluble' trio alongside 'knowledge and humanity' which, he declares, is 'peculiar to the more polished and ... the more luxurious ages' (1985: 271). (We will meet this trio again.) An industrious life is an active life and 'action', for Hume, is a key component in human happiness (1985: 269–70); in general terms, to be happy is to enjoy life (1975: 247).[18] This enjoyment includes indulging in luxury, defined by him as 'great refinement in the pleasures of sensory gratification of the senses' (1985: 266). This has two relevant negative implications. First, it distances him from the typical Puritan emphasis on industry (or diligence) as a Christian virtue and as bulwark against lasciviousness, as it inhibits those 'exuberant Spirits which are otherwise apt to break forth in unlawful flames' (Steele 1684: 79; cf. Luther 1961: 68). Second, action in the form of industry is to be distinguished from Cicero's *negotia publica* (*de Officiis* 1.69), the involvement in public or political affairs. Humean industry is a private endeavour.

Hume employs the term 'frugality' against the background of his account of the emergence of commerce out of the collapse of feudalism causally triggered by the availability and diffusion of luxuries (Mackenzie's 'baubles'), initially from abroad. But rather than being malicious *semina* as Livy (39.6.9) would have it, they are positively transforming. His *History of England* provides the narrative but his earlier analytical *Political Discourses* (published 1752), in which 'Of Luxury' appeared, prefigure the argument. In his essay *Of Interest* in that collection, he argues that where, as in the late feudal era, there is nothing but

---

[17] Compare Quentin Skinner's notion of 'strategy' (including what he terms 'rhetorical manipulation') in persuasive argumentation. However, in that same piece he rather strangely cites 'frugality' – without any direct evidence – as a novel evaluative term toward the end of the sixteenth century to describe behaviour for which approval was sought (2002: 145–57).

[18] For Hume's view of happiness see Berry 2018: Ch. 15, where his view is contrasted with that of Aristotle and the Stoics.

Christopher J. Berry

'a landed interest' there will be 'little frugality' because landlords are 'prodigal'.[19]

But with the development of commerce there is an increase in industry. This he declares 'encreases frugality' because it gives rise to merchants. In sharp contrast to the 'classical' prejudice, and without any of Mun's defensiveness, Hume describes merchants as 'one of the most useful races of men' whose passion, he identifies without censure, is love of gain (1985: 300). They are not inclined to dissipate this 'gain' on selfish pleasure. Indeed in a reversal of the classical association their activities work to the benefit of all. The explanation for this is that merchants 'beget industry' as they distribute resources through society. This sets in train a process whereby competition among traders reduces profits which causes a willing acceptance of low interest rates which makes commodities cheaper thus encouraging consumption and thereby 'heightening the industry' (1985: 302–3). This marks a clear advance on an agricultural, as well as *oikos*-based, 'economy'.

Moreover, since merchants 'covet equal laws', the concomitant of this is that commerce begets liberty, understood by both Hume and Smith as the freedom to live under equitable laws. This for them is the hallmark of modern liberty and is self-consciously distinguished from ancient liberty. Smith (1982b: 185) professed in his Glasgow lectures that modern liberty, alongside opulence, were 'the two greatest blessings enjoyed by mankind'. I will return to liberty at the end of my discussion but here I pursue the notion of prosperity or opulence.

What does it mean to be 'blessed' by opulence? The crucial fact is that members of a commercial society are able to enjoy a far better standard of living than those in earlier ages. In material terms their basic needs of food, shelter and clothing are better and more adequately met (respectively Smith 1981: 90, 74, 87). This enhanced 'quality of life' also incorporates

---

[19] Hume 1985: 298–9. They are prodigal because they do little with their revenue other than consume it (it is their 'way of life'). Smith 1981: 339 contrasts the 'frugal man' with the 'prodigal' who 'encroaches upon his capital'.

382

From Poverty to Prosperity: The Recalibration of Frugality

relationships, such as being able to care for the vulnerable (see the Introduction to the *Wealth of Nations*). The obverse of the blessing of opulence is the misery of poverty, as Smith explicitly describes it (1981: 10). As in Hume, this 'poverty' lacks any redeeming features. Again, like Hume, Smith too develops nuanced recalibration of the role played by 'frugality'.

We mentioned above that Cicero in *Tusculan Disputations* linked frugality with the virtue of self-command but he also acknowledged that it has come to incorporate the other three cardinal virtues of courage or fortitude, justice and prudence. We can see in Smith a recalibration of all four of these virtues thus indicating how far-reaching is the difference in perspective between that represented by moralised Roman *frugalitas* and that represented by a modern commercial world, where as he says 'every man becomes in some measure a merchant' (1981: 37). Smith of course is not denying that the cardinal virtues are virtues but he re-casts them to make them apt for the modern world. There are of course no sharp edges; there is no sudden transition from Mackenzie to Smith. George Blewitt (1725: 37–8, 40), for example, in his critique of Mandeville, is at one with Mackenzie in affirming the virtuousness of frugality while consciously linking trade with the 'real source of a national Wealth'.[20]

But at the risk of being overly schematic I now outline Smith's reconstruction of each of the cardinal virtues with the aim of indicating how the treatment of frugality is not some discrete re-evaluation but part of a wider change in moral/social theory of which Smith is a significant representative.[21]

V

Smith links approbatively frugality and prudence in the *Moral Sentiments* because both are directed at the 'acquisition of

---

[20] See Joyce Appleby 1978: 276, who notes that in theories of trade as they developed in the seventeenth century, 'frugality and industry' were defended on purely economic grounds and that there were no religious obstacles to the argument that 'frugality and restraint impeded economic development'.

[21] I have given a fuller account of Smith's reconstruction, some of which I here draw upon, in Berry 2018: Ch. 19.

Christopher J. Berry

fortune' (1982a: 190). The immediate implication of this is that fortune or opulence is not a corruption but is, we recall, a blessing. This 'acquisition' is the result of the desire in human nature (from womb to grave) of 'bettering our condition' and this is what prompts saving; the 'principle of frugality', he says, predominates 'very greatly' in the greater part of men across the whole course of their life (1981: 341). This is the context for the vast majority of the references to 'frugality' in the *Wealth of Nations* and provides an often remarked upon link between Smith's two major works.[22] Alongside the extent of a market the other key factor in the growth of societal prosperity or 'public opulence' is the accumulation of capital, the source of which is saving. Here differing from Hume,[23] for Smith parsimony has priority over 'industry' (1981: 337). 'Industry' Smith does regard as a virtue but, now like Hume, he detaches it from its penitential moorings that remain clearly still present in the numerous homiletic works.[24] Against this backcloth how does Smith link frugality with prudence?

He declares that of all the virtues prudence is the one most useful to ourselves (1982a: 189); its 'proper business' is care for one's health, fortune, rank and reputation (1982a: 213). The prudent man's conduct is approved of by Smith's moral benchmark, the Impartial Spectator or the internalised standard by which all conduct, including one's own, is judged (1982a: 215). More precisely, this approval is granted because through the steadiness of this prudent man's 'industry and frugality' present advantage (that is, incurring some current pain, such as postponing consumption) is foregone in favour of greater return in the future (that is more pleasure later, such as having

---

[22] Jeffrey Young 1997: 45 is representatively typical when he calls the parallel between prudence in *TMS* and frugality in *WN* 'obvious'. The limited discussion by commentators of 'frugality' in Smith is invariably in the context of prudence.

[23] For a somewhat exaggerated account of their different views of frugality see Gordon Davis 2003. Nevertheless, Smith and Hume do – and this is what is at stake here – share a perspective that differentiates their account from that of the classical and neo-classical thinkers.

[24] Steele 1684 typically cites Genesis 3.19 ('in the sweat of thy face') as well as the Ninth Commandment.

384

From Poverty to Prosperity: The Recalibration of Frugality

more fortune for consumption if that is desired).[25] Although, as this calculus suggests, prudence is not the 'most ennobling of virtues' it fits the circumstances of a commercial society. The disposition or virtue of this prudent man of commerce, and contrary to the civic republican ideal whether in its classical Ciceronic/Livian mode or the early modern form of, say, Algernon Sydney or Andrew Fletcher,[26] is not to agitate or to involve himself in public service or in the pursuit of 'solid glory' (1982a: 216). (I will return to glory.)

A society where every man is to some extent implicated in exchange, is, it follows, characterised by inter-dependence. With respect to a particular manufacture, Smith illustrates this with the famous example of pin-making (1981: 14–15) and with respect to societal inter-dependence with the example of a coarse woollen coat. Indeed he truncates an enumeration of the various trades involved in the latter's manufacture by declaring that 'many thousands' are implicated in this 'humble product' (1981: 22–3). Each individual, he declares, 'stands at all times in need of the co-operation and assistance of great multitudes' (1981: 26) but very few of those are personally known to any participant. Hence Smith likens a commercial society to an 'assembly of strangers' (1982a: 23). Later I will pick up the bearing of this on the virtue of justice but first there is more to say about prudence.

When Cicero linked frugality with prudence he also, as we saw above, linked it to the virtue of moderation or

---

[25] Gloria Vivenza 2001: 55 holds that this view of prudence was described by Cicero, *de Finibus* 1.32–3, but this view is presented there in the voice of an Epicurean. Regardless of the fact that some scholars have identified Epicurean strands in Smith, the force of this identification (and also that of Stoicism – see below) must not be exaggerated. Smith (and Hume) of course knew their 'classics' but their engagement is one of recalibration so locating precedents is of limited utility.

[26] According to Sydney, 'men can no otherwise be engaged to take care of the publick than by having such a part in it' (1990: 196); this involves liberty as independence (1990: 17) and civic equality (1990: 452) which are lost when 'pride, luxury and vice' is held 'more profitable to a nation than the virtues upheld by frugality' (1990: 196, 17, 350). He typically attacks mercenaries (1990: 153, 210) and in this Machiavellian trope he was echoed by Fletcher where having disparaged 'a perpetual change of fashions in clothes, equipage and furniture' commends the 'frugal and military way of living' that militias represent (1979: 5).

385

Christopher J. Berry

self-command. Just as Smith dismisses frugality as poverty so he distances himself from Cicero's prudence in the form of self-command. Notwithstanding Cicero's eclecticism, it is Stoic philosophy that is his touchstone here. That Smith subscribes to Stoic tenets is a claim that is often made. It would not be surprising if he did subscribe since that was a common stance. However, there are good grounds to doubt Smith's affiliation (see, for example, Bee and Paganelli 2019). He flatly declares that, 'the plan and system which Nature has sketched out for our conduct seems to be *altogether different* from that of the Stoical philosophy' (1982a: 292 my emphasis). But more significantly these grounds can be seen to stem from his account of the modernity of commercial society.

The basis of Smith's moral theory lies in the dynamics of social life. In a well-known analogy he likens society to a mirror, in which we see reflected the effect of our behaviour on others (1982a: 110). We learn how to behave by gauging these effects. Though this is to short-circuit an intricate discussion, for Smith, morality is a matter of socialisation. Social intercourse teaches individuals what behaviour is acceptable and, in due course, these social judgements are internalised as conscience as represented by the Impartial Spectator. Smith knows full well this is contrary to classical Stoicism in its pristine formulation with its depiction of a 'sage', who in the expression of his complete independence truly knows what is in his control. For example, Epictetus (*The Manual* § 1), who though chronologically a 'late Stoic' adhered to the austere position of the School's founders, makes a point of declaring that the 'free man' is indifferent to the opinions (*doxai*) of others. In sharp contrast, Smith declares that 'respect for ... the sentiments of other people is the *sole* principle which, upon most occasions, overawes all those mutinous and turbulent passions' (1982a: 263 my emphasis). For the Stoics the virtue of self-command derives from the rational will; in Smith its source is social interaction.

Given this source then Smith can argue that the exercise of this virtue improves as a consequence of the requirements of living among strangers. This hinges on Smith's account of

From Poverty to Prosperity: The Recalibration of Frugality

sympathy. In outline terms, when confronted by the behaviour of another, we imagine how we would act in that situation. If we think the behaviour apt we approve (and disapprove if inapt). Since for Smith actors want the approval of the spectators (it pleases) they adjust their behaviour accordingly. This adjustment requires greater effort in an anonymous setting and that added effort serves to strengthen character. This enables an actor in a commercial society to attain a greater degree of moderation and exhibit more consistently the virtue of self-command than is possible in more tribal or clannish times (1982a: 146). In this way individuals in a commercial society are (in general terms) able to act 'according to the dictates of prudence, justice and proper beneficence' (1982a: 241).

I will turn to justice and beneficence shortly but there remains an additional point to make about self-command which will lead us to consider another recalibration. Smith refers to these requirements of commercial living as 'gentler exertions of self-command', as giving 'lustre' to the distinctively commercial (or 'respectable' [1982a: 242]) virtues of 'industry and frugality'. In contrast to the severe demands of the Stoics, they are 'gentle' in two respects. He observes that the 'condition of human nature' would be 'peculiarly hard' if the affections (such as, say, those characteristic of family life) which naturally affect our conduct, could 'upon no occasion appear virtuous' (1982a: 305). It is I think clear he has the severe Epictetean posture in mind. Elsewhere to overall similar effect, in a passage critical of those who would decry it, he refers, in a telling phrase to 'the natural joy of prosperity' (1982a: 139). Prosperity or opulence rather than a negative subject of moral disapproval is positively joyous (a blessing) and, by extension, its provision through the activities of merchants is morally unwritten.

The other respect in which Smith's use of 'gentle' is noteworthy is that it also adverts to his approach to the cardinal virtue of courage. Smith does not include courage in his dedicated section on virtue in the *Moral Sentiments* but the omission of this definitionally masculine virtue is not surprising. Smith does not question that command of fear is virtuous

387

Christopher J. Berry

(and does refer to the decline in 'martial virtue' as a damaging effect of the division of labour [1981: 787]) but, as an instance of the recalibration I am exploring, he effectively replaces it with the virtue of 'humanity'.

Smith ties the expression of humane sentiments to a heightened sensitivity to the feelings of others. Significantly, and in line with Hume's association of his indissoluble trio of industry, knowledge and humanity with luxurious or polished ages, this sensitivity is subject to social and moral development. A 'humane and polished people', Smith says, have 'more sensibility to the passion of others' (1982a: 207). This is the case most emphatically when set against the infanticide practised by the Greeks (and condoned by its most eminent philosophers) but also when set against the 'hardiness demanded of savages', as manifest in their resistance to, and infliction of, torture. But, he says, this behaviour 'diminishes their humanity' (1982a: 209). While this hardiness might look like an exemplary exhibition of the virtue of self-command this is misleading. This savage (Stoic) self-command, when compared to that exercised by civilised peoples, is more a matter of repression. Its supposed exemplary status is further undermined because it is rather the civilised than the savage man who exhibits 'the most exquisite humanity [and] is naturally the most capable of acquiring the highest degree of self-command' (1982a: 152).

The savage's behaviour is all the more unedifying given its association with 'falsehood and dissimulation', when compared to the 'frank, open and sincere' habits of a 'polished people' (1982a: 208). This point can be extended to note a similar negative comparison to Cicero (and classical thought in general). We noted above the derogation of merchants and their way of life as not fitting pursuits for free men. As Cicero (*de Officiis* 1.150) put it, merchants do not exhibit *liberalitas* but, more revealing in the current context, he further asserts that they have to tell lies to make a living. In direct contrast Smith observed that 'when the greater part of the people are merchants they always bring probity and punctuality into fashion' so that these are 'the principal virtues of a commercial nation' (1982b: 539).

388

From Poverty to Prosperity: The Recalibration of Frugality

There is no room here for 'glory'; a status typically won on the battlefield by exhibiting courage. In contrast to the gentleness Smith associates with self-command, Mackenzie, we can recall, declared that 'frugality hardened Men into the Temper of being soldiers' (1716: 303–4). Since Roman virtue, its military prowess, was a concomitant of its commitment to a frugal life then the 'modernity' of Smith and Hume, with their recalibration of frugality as well as of courage, had its counterpart in a disparagement of this picture of military success reposing on 'hard men'. If following classical precedent, hardiness is supposed vital to national greatness, as measured by military strength, then it is important to the argumentative success of Hume and Smith's defence of a commercial society that they undermine this view of 'greatness' and its associated virtues. In this defence Hume appeals to the evidence (a ploy also adopted by Mandeville [1988: I, 122–3]). The supposed causal link between luxury and military weakness fails the test of constant conjunction, as manifest by the cases of France and England, that is, the two most powerful *because* most polished and commercial societies (Hume 1985: 275; cf. Hume 1894: II, 598–9).

This combination is made possible by the very 'superfluity' that industry in the pursuit of luxury has created. In times of peace this superfluity goes to the maintenance of manufactures and the 'improvers of liberal arts' (hallmarks of civilisation), but when an army is needed the sovereign levies a tax, the effect of which is to reduce expenditure on luxuries. This frees up, for the military, those who were previously employed in luxury-good production; they constitute a sort of 'storehouse' of labour (Hume 1985: 272; cf. 1985: 261–2). Nor does it follow that these will be inferior troops. On the contrary, recalling the 'indissoluble chain' that links industry and humanity with knowledge, these fighters will benefit not only from the technology that a commercial society can command but also from the overall higher level of intellectual competence.[27]

---

[27] In his *History* (1894: I, 498) Hume implicitly connects the development of artillery with humanity (the third link in the chain) when he observes that, though 'contrived

Christopher J. Berry

Rome's military triumphs were supposed to be due to its citizen-soldiers, who living frugally and thus not yet corrupted by avarice and ambition, were committed (unto death) to their *patria*. For Smith, as professed in his Glasgow classroom, and reiterated in the *Wealth of Nations*, militias are outmoded; standing armies 'must be introduced' (1981: 703; 1982b: 543). What counts (and in practice always has) is 'regularity, order and prompt obedience to command', something more appropriately achieved by professional soldiers than by a contingently collected group of uneducated amateurs (1981: 699). Despite the superiority of a standing army its presence was a cause for apprehension. The fear was that a professional or standing army, as supposedly evidenced by the last years of the Roman Republic, could be used to suppress domestic liberties. Smith addresses this fear directly. In explicit repudiation of the position of 'men of republican principles' (such as Fletcher), he claims this army can, under particular conditions, 'in some cases be favourable to liberty' (1981: 706).[28]

Hume acknowledged that courage and love of glory are species of heroic virtue and which are on the face of it 'much admir'd' but then proceeds to observe that those of 'cool reflection' are inclined to regard heroism as mischievous and only a 'suppos'd virtue' (1978: 599–601).[29] The time for heroes has passed; they cause disorder and they would be out of place in a commercial society where order is premised on reliable expectations or predictability (see below). He gives this view a clear historical perspective. Referring to sixteenth century Scotland, he claims that when 'arms' prevail over 'laws' then 'courage preferably to equity or justice was the virtue most valued and respected' (1894: II, 81; cf. I, 115 on the Anglo-Saxons).[30] Smith too observed that 'the most intrepid valour

for the destruction of mankind,' it has 'rendered battles less bloody and has given greater stability to civil societies'.

[28] The requisite condition is that the chief officers in the army are drawn from the 'principal nobility and gentry', who have, in consequence, 'the greatest interest in the support of the civil authority' (Smith 1981: 706).

[29] For helpful comment see Baier 1991: 210.

[30] He generalised this in the *Enquiry Concerning the Principles of Morals*, 'it is indeed observable that among all uncultivated nations who have not as yet had full

From Poverty to Prosperity: The Recalibration of Frugality

may be employed in the cause of the greatest injustice' and because it can be used to equal effect to good or bad ends then it can be 'excessively dangerous' (1982a: 241; cf. 264). The references by both Hume and Smith to justice here are indicative of the large role that this virtue plays in their thought. This is not the place to develop their expositions. All that it is appropriate to do is pick out a couple of aspects. For Hume, 'without justice society must immediately dissolve' (1978: 497; cf. 1975: 199) and for Smith, 'justice is the main pillar that upholds the whole edifice. If it is removed, the great, the immense fabric of human society ... must in a moment crumble into atoms' (1982a: 86). This functional necessity, as such, is not novel and Cicero (*de Officiis* 2.40) by linking *iustitia* with *negotiis* had established an influential precedent.[31] Nonetheless Hume and Smith re-assess it. Hume's is the most radical as he denies the 'naturalness' of justice; it is rather 'artificial' and expresses itself in 'rules' (chiefly with regard to property) (1978: 491). Smith while identifying a natural root to justice in the shape of resentment also links justice with rule-following.

It is a revealing insight into Smith's argument that he chose quite deliberately to illustrate the indispensability of justice with the fact that it makes a society of different merchants possible, that is, one where 'mutual love and affection' are absent (1982a: 86). From this it follows that 'beneficence is less essential to the existence of society than justice' (1982a: 86). Modern societal coherence does not depend on love and affection, including implicitly and arguably the bonds of intense patriotism. You can coexist socially with those to whom you are emotionally indifferent. Smith in this regard refers to justice as a negative virtue because 'we often fulfil all the rules of justice by sitting still

experience of the advantages attending beneficence, justice and the social virtues, courage is the predominant excellence' (1975: 255). One of the implications of this is that Hume thinks the Romans 'uncultivated'.

[31] For Cicero it is a requirement of co-operation and applies not only (if principally) between friends but also between thieves. In line with their view of commerce as interaction between strangers, Hume and Smith deliberately adopt a narrower construction.

391

Christopher J. Berry

and doing nothing' (1982a: 82). It is an outmoded notion of the civic republicans that political virtue requires action on the public stage (or the battlefield).

The premium to act justly in a commercial society, the concern 'not to hurt our neighbour', constitutes the character of a 'perfectly innocent and just man'. And such a character, Smith continues, can 'scarce ever fail to be accompanied with many other virtues, with great feeling for other people, with great humanity and great benevolence' (1982a: 218). Members of a commercial society can thus be both just and benevolent. It is here that the recalibration of the virtue of benevolence can be discerned.

Nowhere does Smith (or indeed Hume [1975: 78ff]) deny the virtuousness of benevolence or imply that a commercial society undermines virtue and morality but the two virtues of justice and benevolence do have a different character and focus. While justice is strict, like grammar, benevolence is 'loose, vague and indeterminate', like literary style (1982a: 327). While justice can be satisfied by inaction, by forbearance and rule-abidingness, benevolence consists in positive action. These actions are typically reserved for those known personally to us and are exercised at our discretion but, as we have seen, in a modern society we coexist among strangers toward whom we have to act impartially on a non-discretionary basis; we treat them in accordance with the rules of justice.

Smith's reference to the strictness of justice has its counterpart in Hume's emphasis on the rigidity or inflexibility in the application of its rules. This, Hume argues, is necessary to sustain predictable behaviour, to underwrite the ability of individuals to act 'in expectation that others are to perform the like' (1978: 498). Such expectations are required for the interdependency exemplified by Smith's woollen coat. For Smith it is only through living under the rule of law, or system of justice, that individuals will have 'confidence' in the 'faith of contracts' and 'payment of debts' (1981: 910). This confidence reposes on the reliable certitude that default will be punished.

This speaks to another difference between justice and benevolence. In line with jurisprudential conventions,

392

From Poverty to Prosperity: The Recalibration of Frugality

questions of justice are enforceable (obeying the law is not discretionary), while the obligations attending benevolence are matters of degree and open to a discretionary judgement, as in charitable actions. We can see here, once more, the fit between the notion of justice as rule-following and the requirements of living among strangers. This relies on social stability and security, the source of which is the 'protection of the magistrate' together with the administration of government which, as Hume says, 'must act by general laws that are previously known to all the members'.[32]

In Smith the administration of justice is one of the three duties he assigns to government (the other two are the provision of external security and public works). This enumeration is prefaced by the dictum that 'according to the system of natural liberty ... every man, as long as he does not violate the laws of justice is left perfectly free to pursue his own interest his own way'. Government polices any such violations but is 'completely discharged from a duty ... of superintending the industry of private people and of directing it towards the employments most suitable to the interest of society' (1981: 687). While Smith's prime target is the mercantilist endeavour to force trade into a particular channel (1981: 506, 516), the principle of government non-involvement has a wider remit.

A telling case in the current context is his scornful dismissal of sumptuary laws. This legislation he condemns as 'the highest impertinence and presumption' whereby 'kings and ministers ... pretend to watch over the economy of private people and to restrain their expense' (1981: 346). Hume is equally dismissive. Given that government has 'no other object or purpose but the distribution of justice' (1985: 37) then he judged restrictions on consumption, as purposed by sumptuary legislation, as ineffectual (1894: I, 535; cf. II, 231; II, 602). But beyond that they were detrimental to the happiness and pleasure that all men desire (1985: 276), central to which is the

---

[32] Hume 1985: 41 remarks that it is the hallmark of the 'best civil constitution' that therein 'every man is restrained by the most rigid laws' (see also 1985: 31).

Christopher J. Berry

enjoyment of material things, of 'a more splendid way of life than what their ancestors enjoyed' (1985: 264).

Sumptuary laws were a recurrent feature of the Roman republic and empire, where the focus was typically to restrict the cost of banquets (as in *Lex Orchia*) or, to a lesser extent, clothing (as in *Lex Oppia*).[33] They were a persistent feature of medieval and early modern Europe (and beyond) as they went into great detail to regulate apparel, especially of women.[34] The underlying philosophy was Stoic and *frugalitas* functioned implicitly as a norm of proper consumption. Given this provenance and function, it is no surprise to see that Mackenzie (1716: 148, 161) supported them but so, too, did Mun (1664: 7) as part of his defensiveness while Barbon (1905: 11) was dismissive.

These laws sought to enforce the 'limits' that nature/reason prescribes. Alternatively put, they attempted to police desires in the light of a supposedly rational, objectively valid, account of the 'good life' or constituents 'good and politic order'.[35] In practical or realistic terms they were attempts at control and stabilisation in the face of fluidity occasioned by social change.[36] At their heart was an attempt to sustain some rank order by regulating permissible apparel by social status, while also incorporating the aim of countering political corruption (particularly in Rome) and, to a greater or lesser extent, the furthering of mercantilist principles. These laws failed and they gradually atrophied, even if at different rates, and though this legislation died out earlier in England than elsewhere it still had its advocates in the eighteenth century.[37]

[33] Subsequent to my limited treatment (Berry 1994: Ch. 3), see for a contextual overview, Wallace-Hadrill 2008: Ch. 7. From a narrower analytical focus see Arena 2011 and Dauster 2003, who relegates the significance of *luxuria* and emphasises rather the role of control of patronage by the elite. Now see Zanda 2011 for the most systematic overview.

[34] There is an extensive literature on sumptuary legislation as it was enacted in different and specific sites across Europe. For a recent survey see Muzzarelli 2009.

[35] Preamble to the English Act of Apparel (1553) quoted in Harte 1976: 139.

[36] Compare Alan Hunt's 1996: 396 argument that this legislation sought to secure a stable connection between appearance and entitlement.

[37] See moralists, like Watkinson 1766: 26: 'The Romans had Sumptuary Laws, we seem to be much of want of them'. Bishop Berkeley also advocated sumptuary legislation and citing the Romans (and Persians and Lacedaemonians), he juxtaposes 'frugality'

394

From Poverty to Prosperity: The Recalibration of Frugality

What lurks here is Smith and Hume's view of liberty which I adumbrated earlier. Their subscription to the principles of modern liberty is a concomitant of their recalibration of frugality and the other virtues. The nub of this modern liberty is captured by Smith's sense of individuals being left to pursue their own desires within the framework of the rule of law/ justice. This is inclusive; it is enjoyed by all because all have desires that they have a right to pursue and all equally enjoy the protection of law. This contrasts with the idea of liberty implicit in *frugalitas*, which was exclusive. This exclusivity characterised both strands of ancient liberty.[38] In the preeminently Stoic strand, liberty was a state of *apatheia* or tranquillity, as bodily desires are firmly controlled by the rational will, and whence as a consequence of its exactingness only an exclusive few, or sages, were able to achieve it. While in the 'civic' or republican strand of Livy, Cicero and others liberty consisted of activity in the political world to realise the public good but which was only enjoyed by those who had leisure and that was made possible, as Smith pointed out, by the presence of a class of slaves (1982b: 410; cf Hume 1985: 257, 383). Hence just as regarding opulence as a blessing, and prosperity as joyous, overturned the negativity they possessed as the counterparts to the virtue of frugality, so this modern liberty overturned the negativity associated with bodily desires and the disparagement of a commercial life that was implicated in the severe ideals that a frugal life embodied.

VI

There are, of course, innumerable ways to chart the differences between the 'ancient' and the 'modern' world. This chapter has

as the 'strength of Bodies politic' and Luxury as their corruption (1953: VI, 7, 31). While in the extensive debate on commerce, Charles Davenant, for example, in 1704, regarded frugality as 'general good oeconomy' and elsewhere a little earlier (1698) had argued that sumptuary laws should restrain (albeit that will be 'very difficult') 'our luxury and depraved manners' (1771: IV, 428; I, 347). That the very frequency of the Roman laws (Zanda 2011 provides a list) was testimony to their inadequacy was not lost on contemporaries, see Tacitus, *Ann.* 3.52.

[38] See further Berry 2013: 125–9.

Christopher J. Berry

simply illustrated one particular strand. It has outlined the shift from frugality as the meritorious eschewing of opulence and excess, or poverty as a virtue, to the benefits of prosperity for the material well-being of individuals in an inclusively free and just society. If the view is taken that systems of morality reflect (which is not to say they are passive recipients) their social ethos then Roman *frugalitas* and Smithian frugality inhabit a different constellation of values. But this should not be taken to mean that these are mutually opaque. I chose the term 'recalibration' to highlight the fact that Smith and Hume (my two modern representatives) are engaged in a dialogue as they re-interpret, and thus re-evaluate, their classical legacy. As even a casual perusal of their work bears out, they do not undertake this engagement from a position of ignorance. But the engagement is fuelled by their wider concern to identify, and vindicate, the values of commercial society, as a novel and superior mode of social living.

The fact that this is indeed a vindication testifies to the potency still possessed by the legacy. This is manifest in their contemporaries who were in various ways critical of these commercial values. Albeit typically fortified by Christian commitment, this criticism is drawn from the classical storehouse of virtues and the trope of the 'Fall of Rome' to which end invoking *frugalitas* was seen as a helpful ally. Its absence, according to these critics, in contemporary society given over as it is to luxury and self-interest underwrote its continuing significance. While it might seem Hume and Smith's arguments won the day, the form of society they in principle vindicate has hardly been immune from criticism. Indeed amid the swelling literature on sustainability, there has been an injunction to live simply; a stress on an 'ethic of sufficiency' that re-invokes voluntary poverty and the virtue of living frugally.[39] On this line of argument there is a need to recalibrate anew the passage from poverty to prosperity.

---

[39] For a survey of some of these arguments see Berry 2016.

396

From Poverty to Prosperity: The Recalibration of Frugality

Bibliography

Adams, W. (1770) *The Duties of Industry, Frugality and Sobriety*. Shrewsbury.

Allan, D. (2000) *Philosophy and Politics in Later Stuart Scotland*. Edinburgh.

Appleby, J. (1978) *Economic Thought and Ideology in Seventeenth-Century England*. Princeton.

Aquinas, T (1928) *Summa Contra Gentiles*, trans. English Dominican Fathers. London.

Arena, V. (2011) 'Roman sumptuary legislation: three concepts of liberty', *European Journal of Political Theory* 10: 463–89.

Baier, A. (1991) *A Progress of Sentiments*. Cambridge, MA.

Barbon, N. (1905) *A Discourse of Trade* (1690), ed. J. Hollander. Baltimore.

Baron, H. (1988) *In Search of Florentine Civic Humanism*. Princeton.

Bee, M. and Paganelli, M. (2019) 'Adam Smith, anti-Stoic', *History of European Ideas* 45: 572–84.

Berkeley, G. (1953) 'Essay toward preventing the ruin of Great Britain', in *Works* 9 vols., eds. A. Luce and T. Jessop. Edinburgh.

Berry, C. (1994) *The Idea of Luxury*. Cambridge.

(2013) *The Idea of Commercial Society in the Scottish Enlightenment*. Edinburgh.

(2016) 'Luxury: a dialectic of desire?', in *Critical Luxury Studies*, eds. J. Armitage and J. Roberts. Edinburgh: 47–66.

(2018) *Essays on Hume, Smith and the Scottish Enlightenment*. Edinburgh.

Blewitt, G. (1725) *An Enquiry whether a general Practice of Virtue tends to the Wealth or Poverty, Benefit or Disadvantage of a People*. London.

Booth, W. (1993) *Households: On the Moral Architecture of the Economy*. Ithaca.

Brooke, C. (2012) *Philosophic Pride: Stoicism and Political Thought from Lipsius to Rousseau*. Princeton.

Dauster, M. (2003) 'Roman Republican sumptuary legislation: 182–102' in *Studies in Latin Literature and Roman History XI*, ed. C. Deroux. Brussels: 65–93.

Davenant, C. (1771) *Works*, 5 vols., ed. C. Whitworth. London.

Davis, G. (2003) 'Philosophical psychology and economic psychology in David Hume and Adam Smith', *History of Political Economy* 3: 269–304.

Edwards, C. (1993) *The Politics of Immorality in Ancient Rome*. Cambridge.

Fletcher, A. (1979) 'A Discourse of Government with relation to Militias' (1698) in *Fletcher of Saltoun: Selected Writings*, ed. D. Daiches. Edinburgh.

Harte, N. (1976) 'State control of dress and social change in pre-industrial England' in *Trade, Government and Economy in Pre-Industrial England*, eds. D. Coleman and A. John. London: 132–65.

Christopher J. Berry

Hill, C. (1968) *Puritanism and Revolution*. London.

Hume, D. (1894) *History of England* (1757–63) in 3 volumes. London.

(1975) *Enquiry Concerning the Principles of Morals* (1751), eds. A. Selby-Bigge and P. Nidditch. Oxford.

(1978) *A Treatise of Human Nature* (1739/40), eds. A. Selby-Bigge and P. Nidditch. Oxford.

(1985) *Essays: Moral, Political and Literary*, ed. E. Miller. Indianapolis.

Hunt, A. (1996) *Governance of the Consuming Passions: A History of Sumptuary Law*. London.

Kellow, G. (2011) 'Strength and riches: Nicholas Barbon's new politics of commerce', *Erasmus Journal of Philosophy and Economics* 4: 1–22.

Luther, M. (1961) 'Freedom of a Christian' in *Martin Luther: Selections from his Writings*, ed. J. Dillenberger. Garden City, NY: 42–85.

Mackenzie, G. (1716) *Works*, vol.1. Edinburgh.

Mandeville, B. (1988) *The Fable of the Bees* (1732), 2 vols., ed. F. Kaye. Indianapolis.

Mun, T. (1664) *England's Treasure by Forraign Trade*. London.

Muzzarelli, M. G. (2009) 'Reconciling the privilege of the few with the common good: sumptuary laws in Medieval and early Modern Europe', *Journal of Medieval and Early Modern Studies* 39: 587–617.

Perkins, W. (1612) *Works*, 2 vols. Cambridge.

Skinner, Q. (2002) 'Moral principles and social change' reprinted in *Visions of Politics*, vol. 1. Cambridge: 145–57.

Smith, A. (1981) *An Inquiry into the Nature and Causes of the Wealth of Nations* (1776), eds. R. Campbell and A. Skinner. Indianapolis.

(1982a) *The Theory of Moral Sentiments* (1759/1790), eds. A. Macfie & D. Raphael. Indianapolis.

(1982b) *Lectures on Jurisprudence*, eds. R. Meek, D. Raphael and P. Stein. Indianapolis.

Steele, R. (1684) *The Tradesman's Calling*. London.

Sydney, A. (1990) *Discourses concerning Government* (1698). Indianapolis.

Tawney, R. (1938) *Religion and the Rise of Capitalism*. London.

Temple, W. (1754) *Works* 4 vols. Edinburgh.

Tertullian (1869) *De Cultu Feminarum*. Edinburgh: Ante-Nicene Christian Library. Vol. 11.

Tierney, B. (1959) *Medieval Poor Law*. Berkeley.

Tilmouth, C. (2007) *Passion's Triumph over Reason: A History of the Moral Imagination from Spenser to Rochester*. Oxford.

Vivenza, G. (2001) *Adam Smith and the Classics*. Oxford.

Wallace-Hadrill, A. (2008) *Rome's Cultural Revolution*. Cambridge.

Watkinson, E. (1766) *Frugality and Diligence Recommended and Enforc'd from Scripture*. York.

Weber, M. (1904) 'Die protestantische Ethik und der Geist des Kapitalismus', *Archiv für Sozialwissenschaft und Sozialpolitik* 20.1: 1–54.

From Poverty to Prosperity: The Recalibration of Frugality

(1930) *The Protestant Ethic and the Spirit of Capitalism*, trans. T. Parsons. London.

Young, J. (1997) *Economics as a Moral Science*. Cheltenham.

Zanda, E. (2011) *Fighting Hydra-like Luxury: Sumptuary Regulation in the Roman Republic*. Bristol.

INDEX LOCORUM

XII Tables
  3.4–5: 141
  5.2: 137 n.42
  5.4–5: 177
  6.1: 137 n.42
  6.5b: 137 n.42
  7.11: 137 n.42
  8.18a–b: 140
  10.1–10: 133
Ammianus Marcellinus
  14.6.17: 322 n.181
  21.16.5–6: 94 n.237
  25.4.4: 12, 94
Appian
  BC
    1.7.26–8.34: 168–9
    1.7.29: 216
    1.8.33–4: 175–6
    1.9.35: 215 n.6
    1.9.36: 216 n.11
    1.9.37: 185
    1.9.37–8: 217 n.14
    1.11.44: 213 n.2, 216 n.11
    1.11.45: 215 n.6
    1.11.46: 185
    1.19.78–82: 221 n.25
Augustine
  De Beata Vita: 103–7
    4.31: 243 n.9
  Ep.
    36.23: 102 n.267
    85.2: 102–3 n.267
    91.3: 249 n.27
    189.7: 102–3 n.267
    211.9: 102–3 n.267
Augustus
  RG
    8.2: 360
    15–23: 75

Calpurnius Piso Frugi, Lucius
  F 31: 261 n.57
  F 35: 260–2
  F 42: 259
Cassius Hemina
  F 41: 178 n.39
Cato Maior
  Agr.
    praef. 4: 198 n.20, 214, 265 n.70
    1.6: 244 n.13
    2.7: 18 n.48
    56–8: 142 n.67
    148–9: 265 n.70
    156–7: 195
  orat.
    51 M: 194
    53 M: 194, 332 n.208
    98 M: 52 n.122
    124 M: 137 n.43
    128 M: 151 n.101, 195–6, 198,
      244 n.14
    146 M: 197 n.19
    163 M: 61 n.146
    167 M: 163–4, 225
    173 M: 61 n.145, 200 n.30
    174 M: 151 n.102, 194–5, 199 n.29
    185 M: 194 n.9
  Orig.
    2.22: 196 n.16
    7.9: 196
    7.12: 196
Cicero
  Agr.
    2.10: 170 n.19
    2.82–3: 224 n.32
  Amic.
    96: 173–4 n.26
  Att.
    1.3.3 = 8 SB: 269 n.79

400

Index Locorum

1.16.10 = 16 SB: 358
4.8a.3 = 82 SB: 263 n.62
4.15.1 = 90 SB: 264
7.4.1 = 127 SB: 264
13.28.4 = 299 SB: 263 n.62
Brut.
  117: 351
ad Brut.
  1.8.2 = 15 SB: 263–4 n.62
Cat.
  2.25: 249 n.27
Deiot.
  26: 105–6, 242, 288–90, 314,
    324 n.185
de Orat.
  2.248: 268–9
  2.249: 208 n.71
  2.287: 268 n.78, 298 n.126
Diu.
  1.79: 356 n.34
Diu. Caec.
  18: 257–8.
Fam.
  5.6.1 = 4 SB: 264 n.63
  9.22.2 = 189 SB: 269 n.79
  13.70.1 = 298 SB: 264 n.64
  16.21.4 = 337 SB: 263 n.62
Fin.
  2.90: 269 n.79
  2.116: 200 n.33
Flacc.
  fr. X: 275
  71: 271 n.83
Font.
  39: 256–7
  39–40: 274–5
Leg.
  2.58: 133 n.25
  2.62: 133 n.25
Man.
  29: 248
  36: 248
Marc.
  1: 91–2
Mur.
  48–53: 351 n.12
  74–7: 66–72, 336–7
  75–6: 349–50

78–85: 351 n.12
Off.
  1.12–15: 248
  1.15–17: 203 n.49
  1.68: 292 n.112
  1.69: 381
  1.92: 380
  1.93: 248
  1.106: 372
  1.138: 350
  1.150: 388
  2.40: 391
  2.56–64: 292 n.112
  2.87: 151 n.101
  2.89: 230 n.46
Parad.
  1.12, 12, 245 n.15
  6.49: 151 n.102
  6.51: 151 n.102
Phil.
  8.32: 268
  9.4: 350–1
Planc.
  62: 266–8
Prov.
  18: 208 n.71
Quinct.
  55: 247 n.23
  92–4: 247 n.23
Rep.
  1.2: 249 n.27, 287
  2.39: 136 n.37
  6.9: 209 n.75
Sen.
  14: 197 n.17
  56: 245
  61: 200 n.33
Sest.
  21: 276
  72: 31 n.81
S. Rosc.
  37–9: 38 n.95, 247 n.23
  50: 31 n.81, 77 n.178, 237 n.1, 247
    n.23
  74–5: 38
  143: 247 n.23
Tusc.
  3.15: 277

401

Index Locorum

Cicero (cont.)
  3.15–17: 373
  3.16–17: 242, 248, 277–81,
    324 n.185
  3.16–18: 104–5
  3.18: 281–2
  3.48: 223 n.29
Ver.
  2.1.56: 32 n.83
  2.1.71: 273 n.86
  2.1.101: 269
  2.1.137: 273 n.86
  2.2.7: 271–2
  2.2.110: 269–70
  2.2.192: 270
  2.3.7–8: 273
  2.3.67: 272 n.85
  2.3.112: 145 n.77
  2.3.195: 270–1
  2.4.39: 272 n.85
  2.4.57: 271
  2.5.30: 272 n.85
  4.36–7: 284–5
Clement of Alexandria
Paed.
  2.3.39.4: 375 n.7
Columella
  1 praef. 14: 148 n.88
  1.3.10–11: 173–4 n.26, 184 n.60, 231–2
    n.50
  1.3.11: 166 n.12, 180 n.43, 181 n.49,
    219
  1.9.4: 13 n.37
  6 praef. 4–5: 230 n.46
  10 praef. 1: 13 n.37
  11.1.19: 13: 13 n.37
CIL
  I² 6.7: 199 n.26
  I² 9: 200 n.33
  I² 10: 199 n.26, 206
  I² 11: 199 n.26, 206
  I² 12: 206–7
  I² 13: 208 n.72
  I² 15: 207
  I² 638: 230 n.46
  6.11602: 19 n.52
  6.26192: 19 n.52
  6.40897: 352 n.14

  6.40904: 352 n.14
  8.9520: 19 n.52
  8.11294: 19 n.52
  9.1556: 361 n.61

Dio Cassius
  fr. 29: 173 n.25
  fr. 36.22: 183 n.56
Diodorus Siculus
  14.102.4: 178 n.40
Dionysius of Halicarnassus
  4.14–22: 136 n.37
  13.4: 148 n.91
  14.12: 181 n.49
  17/18.4.3: 183 n.56
  20.13: 184 n.58

Ennius
Ann.
  8.268–86 Sk: 295–6
  456 Sk: 31 n.82
Epictetus
Ench.
  1: 386
  39: 373

Fannius, C.
  6–7 M: 64–5 n.155
Festus
  47.1–2L: 144 n.73,
    180 n.47
  89.1L: 146 n.80, 148 n.90
  238.62–6L: 224 n.33
  276L: 182 n.53
Florus
  1.10.2–3: 184 n.60
Fronto
Ant.
  1.5.3: 174 n.28
Str.
  4.1.1: 204 n.52
  4.3.12: 184 n.60

Gaius
Inst.
  1.192: 137 n.42
dig.
  21.1.18 pr.: 241 n.7

402

Index Locorum

Res cottidianae
2.3: 137 n.42
Gellius
2.1.1: 34 n.87
2.24.1: 12 n.35, 34 n.87
2.24.2–6: 208 n.70, 359 n.46
4.8: 49 n.119
4.20.10: 203 n.45
5.19.15: 203 n.45
6.3: 163–4
6.11.2: 281 n.100
6.11.8: 281 n.100
6.12.4–5: 202
6.13.3: 197 n.17
6.19: 208 n.71
11.2.1: 196 n.14
11.2.5: 196 n.14
13.24: 151 n.102, 194 n.9
17.6.1: 197 n.17
20.1.23: 166 n.11
20.1.45–7: 141
Gracchus, C.
23 M: 63
26–8 M: 63, 221–2
44 M: 222
Granius Licinianus
28.29–37: 224 n.32

Horace
S.
1.1.1: 296 n.121
1.4.105–8: 297
1.6: 258 n.49
2.8: 34 n.86

Jerome
Dialogi contra Pelagianos
3.11, 35: 102 n.266
in Zachariam
3.12, 187: 102 n.266
Julian
or.
6.202a: 94–5 n.240
Juvenal
3.182–3: 75
5: 34 n.86
9.6–8: 75 n.171
11: 34 n.86

11.1–26: 75 n.171
11.43: 75 n.171
14.86–95: 75 n.171

Laus Pisonis
14–17: 255 n.44
Livy
1 praef. 11: 373
1.43.1–9: 136 n.37
1.43.7: 231 n.48
2.47.6: 144 n.73
3.31.1: 148 n.91
4.25.13: 50
5.30.8–9: 148 n.88, 178 n.40,
   231 n.50
5.31.5: 148 n.91
6.4.4–5: 178 n.40
6.5.8: 178 n.40
6.16.6–7: 144 n.73
6.21.4: 179 n.42
6.35–42: 164–5
6.35.4–5: 173
6.36.11: 144 n.73
6.37.2: 167
6.39.9: 167
6.41.11: 167
7.15.11: 179 n.42
7.16.9: 164–5, 175, 181 n.49
8.11.14: 144 n.73
8.21.11: 144 n.73, 180 n.48
9.46.10: 261 n.57
10.13.14: 165, 181
10.23.13: 182 n.53, 224 n.33
10.47.4: 224 n.33
33.42.10–11: 184 n.62, 224 n.33
34.4–7: 61 n.147
34.4.2: 239 n.4
34.4.8: 165–6
34.7.4: 359 n.46
35.10.11–12: 184 n.62, 224 n.33
38.50.4–60.10: 208 n.71
39.55.7–9: 148 n.88
39.6: 56 n.134, 381
39.40.9: 199 n.25
39.41.4: 201 n.38
40.29.1–2: 148 n.88
41.1–2: 199 n.25
41.13.4–5: 148 n.88

403

Index Locorum

Livy (cont.)
42.1.6: 224 n.32
42.4.3–4: 144 n.73
42.9.7: 224 n.32
42.19.1–2: 224 n.32
Per.
11: 183 n.56
14: 148 n.88, 184 n.58
41: 197 n.17
57: 202
58: 170 n.20, 217 n.14, 229 n.44

Macrobius
2.5.8: 76 n.174
2.7.6–10: 253
3.16.14: 208 n.70
3.17.3–4: 208 n.70
3.17.6: 208 n.70
5.1.5: 306 n.145
Martial
3.48: 348 n.5

New Testament
Lk
6:21–2: 101
18:25: 101
Mk
10:25: 101
Mt
6:24: 101
11:5–6: 101–2
19:24: 101

Ovid
Fast.
5.279–94: 182 n.53, 224 n.33
6.639–47: 360–1
Met.
8.611–724: 18 n.48

Panegyrici Latini
II.4.5: 95–6
II.7.3: 97 n.248
II.9: 97
II.10–12: 96–7
II.13: 97–8
II.14: 99–100
II.20.5–6: 100
II.26–7: 100

III.10–12: 93–4
IV.3.3: 92 n.231
IV.31.3: 92
IV.35.1: 93
IV.35.4: 93 n.236
V: 93 n.236
VI.6.1: 92
VI.16.3: 92 n.232
VII.3.4–4.1: 92
VIII.19.3: 92
IX.8.2: 92
XI.5.4: 92
Petronius
2–5: 304–6
26–78: 34 n.86
50: 364–5 n.77
52: 356 n.35
73–6: 306–10
84: 308 n.152
115: 308 n.150
116a: 308 n.152
140: 308 n.152
Plautus
Bacch.
651–60: 252
Capt.
954–57: 251
956: 245 n.17
Poen.
892: 245 n.17
Pseud.
468: 245 n.17
Trin.
118: 245 n.17
270: 245 n.17
1028–9: 151 n.102
1028–45: 59–60
Pliny the Elder
Nat.
7.139–40: 53–5
10.139: 133 n.27, 208 n.70
17.1–6: 353 n.19
17.3–6: 353–4
18.7: 144 n.73, 146 n.80
18.11: 137 n.43
18.7: 180 n.47
18.17: 166 n.12, 181 n.49
18.18: 148 n.88, 173 n.26, 184 n.60
18.41: 18 n.48

404

Index Locorum

18.286: 224 n.33
19.52: 146 n.80, 148 n.90
33.83: 359
33.141: 355 n.26
33.142: 355 n.25, 355 n.29
33.145: 362
33.147: 355 n.27
33.148–9: 354
34.6–8: 364 n.77
36.109–10: 353 n.19
Pliny the Younger
Ep.
1.14.4: 331, 365 n.80
1.21.3: 332–3 n.209
1.22.4: 331, 365 n.78
2.1: 86
2.4: 329–30
2.6: 332–3
2.17.4: 332–3 n.209, 365 n.79
2.17.26: 332–3 n.209, 365 n.79
3.1.9: 332–3 n.209, 364 n.76
3.5.8–13: 365 n.82
3.9.33: 332–3 n.209
3.19.7: 332–3 n.209
4.19: 19 n.53, 331
5.19.9: 331
6.8.5: 331
9.23.2–3: 364
9.36: 365 n.82
Pan.
2.7: 96 n.244
3.4: 334 n.213
4.4–7: 333 n.211
9: 96 n.245
41: 334
44–6: 85 n.208
44.8: 334
45: 99–100, 315 n.163
49.5–7: 364
49.6: 334 n.215
51: 364 n.75
83.7: 336 n.218
88: 334–6
Plutarch
Aem.
28.7: 355 n.30
38: 220 n.23
Apopht.
200d: 205

201c–d: 204
Cam.
39.5–6: 166 n.10, 173 n.25, 181 n.49
Cat. Ma.
1.9–10: 193 n.5
2: 31 n.82
2.3–4: 193 n.5
3.2: 193 n.5
4.3–4: 198
4.4: 194 n.7
5.1: 195 n.10
16.6–8: 201 n.38
19.7: 193 n.6
21.5–8: 185
25: 196 n.16
CG
6.3: 223 n.28
Cic.
1.6: 356 n.34
comp. Agid. Cleom. Gracch.
1.6: 221 n.24
Crass.
2.9–10: 184 n.60
Mor.
194E: 184 n.60
198b–c: 355 n.30
204e–f: 356 n.34
praec. ger. reip.
14: 220 n.23
Publ.
21.10: 144 n.73
TG
2.4: 220–1
4: 220 n.23
8.1–4: 168–9
9.2: 185
9.4: 216 n.11
9.5: 213 n.2
10.4: 185
14.1: 217 n.14, 229 n.45
21.7–8: 221 n.25
Polybius
1.1.5: 215 n.6
23.14: 208 n.71
31.23.12: 210
31.24.4–5: 210
31.24.10: 210
31.25.5–6: 203 n.47
31.25.6–8: 208 n.69

405

Index Locorum

Polybius (cont.)
  31.25.8: 202, 205
  31.25.9: 205

Quintilian
  Decl.
    261: 19 n.50
    298: 15 n.42
  Inst.
    1 pr. 9: 326–7
    1.6.17: 252 n.34, 326 n.190
    1.6.28–9: 275, 326 n.190
    2.17.21: 277 n.93
    3.7.24: 326 n.191
    4.2.123–4: 34 n.86
    5.10.73: 326
    10.3.26: 326 n.192
    11.3.19: 326 n.192
    12.1.1–8: 326–7
    12.2.23–30: 327–8
    12.10.21: 326 n.192

Sallust
  Cat.
    5.8: 373
    6.3: 40
    9.2: 298 n.126
    12: 239 n.4
    12.2: 373
  Hist.
    1.11 M: 178 n.39
    2.70 M: 34 n.86
Scholia Bobiensia
  in Cic. Flacc. fr. 10 Stangl: 257
Scipio Aemilianus
  19 M: 203
  32 M: 81 n.190
Scriptores Historiae Augustae
  Alex. Sev.
    37.1: 89–90
  Ant. Pius
    7: 88
  Did. Jul.
    3.7–10: 89
  M. Ant.
    7.5: 88–9
  Pert.
    8.9–11: 89
    12.2–6: 89 n.221

  Sev.
    17.6: 89
  Verus
    1.4: 89
    5.6–7: 89
Seneca the Elder
  Contr.
    1.6.4: 77 n.179
    2.1: 77 n.179, 301–3
    2.6: 303
Seneca the Younger
  Ben.
    4.8.4: 324
    7.7.5: 184 n.60
  Clem.
    1.23.2: 313–15
  DBV
    18.4: 311–12
  Ep.
    2.6: 318–19
    5: 320–1
    17.4–5: 321–2
    17.5: 16, 348, 372
    17.10: 319 n.173
    18.5–6: 322 n.180
    18.7: 348 n.5
    49.12: 313 n.158
    51.2–3: 316
    56.10: 316
    58.32: 315 n.165
    71.23: 316 n.168
    73: 324–5
    86.6–7: 362 n.68
    87: 322–3
    87.2–5: 367
    87.9–10: 193 n.5
    88: 313 n.158
    94: 323
    95: 312
    95.72–3: 350 n.9
    101.3: 315 n.165
    108.21: 315 n.165
    114: 312 n.157, 347
    115.3: 313 n.158
    119.3: 374
    120.19: 193 n.6
    123.10–12: 316
  Helv.
    11.3: 373 n.4

406

Index Locorum

Marc.
  2.3: 313 n.160
Nat.
  4a praef. 10: 313 n.159
Polyb.
  3.5: 312–13
Tranq.
  1.5–7: 317
  1.7: 356 n.32
  1.15: 317
  8.9–9.2: 317–18
Siculus Flaccus
  102.31–3 Campbell: 169–70 n.17, 180
    n.43, 219 n.19, 224 n.31
Statius
  Silv.
    1.5: 367
Strabo
  8.6.23: 357 n.41
Suetonius
  Aug.
    28.3: 75
    72–3: 361
    72.1: 76
  Caes.
    81.1: 357 n.41
  Cal.
    37.1: 81, 314 n.162, 365 n.81
  Cl.
    16: 82
    35.1: 82
  Gal.
    9.1: 83 n.198
    12–13: 83
    14.2: 83 n.198
    16: 83
  Jul.
    42.1: 176
  Nero
    30.1: 82–3
    38.2: 366
  Otho
    3.2: 83
  Tib.
    28: 80 n.187
    34: 363 n.71, 364 n.77
    42–4: 80 n.187
  Ves.
    2.1: 356–7

21: 365 n.82
Vit.
  11–14: 83

Tacitus
  Ann.
    1.4–15: 80 n.186
    1.10: 360
    2.33: 362–3
    2.49: 224 n.33
    3.9: 366
    3.52–5: 363 n.72
    3.52.2: 133 n.27
    3.52.2–54.5: 80 n.187
    3.53.1–4: 133 n.27
    3.54.3: 151 n.102
    3.55: 84–5, 315 n.163, 334 n.214,
      365 n.80
    3.55.2–3: 56 n.133
    3.55.4: 85 n.208
    3.56.1: 80 n.188
    3.56.3: 85 n.208
    12.53: 362
    16.5: 365 n.80
  Hist.
    1.1: 86
Tertullian
  de Cultu Feminarum
    2.13.3: 375–6 n.7
Thucydides
  7.87.1–3: 143

Ulpian
  dig.
    21.1.19: 241 n.7
    27.19.1: 137 n.44
  Tituli ex corpore
    12.2: 137 n.44
    19.1: 137 n.42
    19.7: 137 n.42

Valerius Maximus
  1.1.1b: 40
  2.5.5–6: 299–300
  2.8 praef.: 77 n.179,
    299 n.129
  2.9.4: 355 n.25
  3.7.1: 208 n.71
  4.1.8: 208 n.71

Index Locorum

Valerius Maximus (cont.)
4.3.5: 13 n.37, 148 n.88, 183, 184 n.60,
    245, 300, 325 n.188
4.3.7: 300 n.133, 355 n.28
4.3.11: 193 n.5, 194 n.8, 300 n.133
4.4: 97 n.247
4.4.3: 356 n.31
4.4.5: 31 n.81
4.4.7: 231 n.50
4.4.11: 36 n.91, 97 n.247, 231 n.50
6.9.3: 300 n.133
7.5.1: 350 n.9
8.6.3: 166 n.10, 181 n.49
9.1.4: 354 n.20
Varro
L.
  5.158: 224 n.33
R.
  1.2.9: 164, 231–2 n.50
  1.10.2: 144 n.73, 180 n.47
  1.17.2: 216 n.12, 228 n.42

1.22: 18 n.48
1.44: 145 n.77
3.3.6: 13
Velleius Paterculus
1.14.7: 148 n.88
1.14.8: 224 n.33
2.2.3: 224 n.31
2.4.4: 221 n.25
2.6.3: 166 n.10, 169 n.17
de Viris Illustribus
  20.3–4: 166 n.10, 173 n.25,
    181 n.49
  33.5–6: 184 n.60
  49.15–18: 208 n.71
  53.2: 208 n.71
  58.4: 209 n.75
  64.2: 169–70 n.17
  64.3: 217 n.14

Zonaras
  7.24.7–13: 173 n.25

GENERAL INDEX

A note on Roman names: for reasons of accessibility, emperors, authors and other well-known figures are indexed under their commonly used names, e.g. Augustus, Caesar, Caligula, Cato (the Elder and the Younger), Cicero, Gracchus (Gaius and Tiberius) or Sulla; other individuals under their *nomen gentile*, e.g. Quintus Caecilius Metellus under Caecilius, Metellus Q.; Lucius Calpurnius Piso Frugi under Calpurnius Piso Frugi, L.

abstention, collective, 27, 53, 61
abstinentia, 11, 83, 277, 279, 313
Aelius Paetus Catus, Sex., 355
Aelius Tubero, Q., 66, 89, 300, 302, 337, 349–52, 355
Aemilius Papus, Q., 356
Aemilius Paullus, L., 350, 355
Aemilius Scaurus, M., 354
ager Campanus, 224–5
Ager Pomptinus, 178
ager publicus, 4, 159–87, 217–18, 224, 228, 232
agriculture, 4, 11–18, 37, 128, 145, 164, 214, 216, 229–30, 255, 323
agronomists, 13
allotment, 34, 167, 178, 184, 213–33
ambitio, 11, 16, 59–60, 65, 238, 323
ambitus, 50, 64–5, 68, 71, 96, 266
Ammianus Marcellinus, 94, 101, 197
ancestor, 337
ancestral, 1–2, 9, 13, 32, 44, 46, 51, 58, 60, 62, 65, 67, 69–71, 195–6, 199–200, 238, 240, 242–4, 259, 262, 272, 274, 276–93, 295, 315, 318, 325, 329, 331, 364
anthropology, 8, 143
Antiochus III, 207–8
Antoninus Pius, 88
Antony, Mark (Antonius, M.), 268, 359
Appian, 160, 168–71, 175–6, 185–6, 215–16, 225
Aquilius, C., 353

archaeology, 14–15, 40–2, 129–32, 139, 145–6, 149, 172, 347–8, 360
Aristides, Publius Aelius, 227
assidui, 215–16, 230
Atilius, 31
Attalus, 221, 229
auaritia, 11, 38, 83, 194, 197, 239, 247, 292
audacia, 38, 247, 273–4
Augustine, 102–8, 197, 243, 249
Augustus, 18, 75–80, 82, 84, 296, 313, 347, 359–62, 367
Aurelius Severus Alexander, M., 89
Aurelius, Marcus, 88
austerity, 5, 15, 29, 31–3, 35, 49, 62, 65–72, 76, 100, 128, 196, 202–4, 210, 220–1, 254, 258, 293, 300, 306, 323, 331, 337, 379, 386

Baiae, 316
banquet, 25, 66, 69, 74–5, 89, 107, 221, 247, 288, 349–51, 359, 366
Barbon, Nicholas, 378
Bion of Borysthenes, 33, 297
Blewitt, George, 383
Boscoreale hoard, 357
bribery, 23, 50, 55, 59, 65, 70, 349
Bruni, Leonardo, 238, 336–7, 372

Caecilius Metellus, L., 53–5
Caecilius Metellus, Q., 53–5
Caesar, Julius (Iulius Caesar, C.), 72, 87, 91, 176, 286–8, 290, 292, 314, 375

409

General Index

Caligula, 76, 81–2, 291, 314, 333, 365
Callistus (freedman of Claudius), 361
calories, 15, 34, 143, 319
Calpurnia (3rd wife of Pliny the
  Younger), 19, 331, 336
Calpurnius Piso Frugi, L., 31, 63, 72, 81,
  223, 245, 249–76, 298, 332, 335–6
Calpurnius Piso, Cn., 366
Campania, 224, 229, 362
capital, 3, 16, 21, 26, 37, 43–4, 78, 140,
  208, 228–30, 357, 382, 384
Carthage, 67, 128, 214, 349, 354
Carvilius Maximus, Sp., 52
Casa del Menandro, 357
Cassius, Sp., 47
Cato the Elder (Porcius Cato,
  M. 'Censorius'), 12, 17, 20, 30, 32,
  49, 51–2, 57, 61–3, 65, 67, 76, 84, 86,
  163, 184, 192–210, 214, 225, 230,
  244, 246, 262, 265, 274, 300, 310,
  323, 325, 329, 331–2
Cato the Younger (Porcius Cato,
  M. 'Uticensis'), 65–72, 89, 337
censorship, 27, 79, 82, 85, 98–9, 192, 199,
  203, 205, 250, 259
census, 22–3, 34, 36, 41, 49, 79, 136, 138,
  149, 175, 177, 197, 203, 215, 231–2
chrêsimos/χρήσιμος, 245, 278
Christianity, 96, 101–8, 243, 374–6, 379,
  381, 396
Cicero (Tullius Cicero, M.), 5, 12–13, 29,
  31–2, 37, 63, 65–72, 75, 77, 84,
  89–92, 102–8, 133, 136, 163, 170,
  233–6, 349–52, 354, 356, 358, 372–3,
  375, 377, 380, 383, 385, 388, 391, 395
Cincinnatus, 28, 30, 32, 47, 127, 129–30,
  237, 240
civil war, 73, 77, 359–62
Claudius (emperor), 82, 361–2
Claudius Asellus, 203
Claudius Caecus, App., 30, 261
Claudius Marcellus, M. (42–23 BCE),
  313
Claudius Pulcher, App., 220
clementia, 92, 238, 313–14, 334
Clodius, P., 358
Columella, 13, 151, 166, 179, 219, 232
commerce, 3, 5, 17, 37, 51–2, 127–8, 227,
  309, 372–96

commercial society, 382, 385, 387,
  389–90, 392
Commodus, 89
conspicuous consumption, 10, 23, 27, 34,
  41, 44, 58, 74, 80, 87, 102, 131–2,
  134–6, 244, 309, 321, 330
Constantine, 92–3
continentia, 11–12, 92, 238, 245, 249, 284,
  299, 313, 329, 334, 355
Corinth, 354, 356–7, 364
Cornelius Balbus, L., 362
Cornelius Lentulus, P., 224
Cornelius Rufinus, P., 49, 183, 354, 356
Cornelius Scipio Aemilianus, P., 62, 81,
  192–210, 220, 349–52, 355
Cornelius Scipio Africanus, P., 200
Cornelius Scipio Asiaticus, L., 208
Cornelius Scipio Barbatus, L., 206
Cornelius Scipio Hispallus, Cn., 206
Cornelius Scipio Hispanus, Cn., 207
Cornelius Scipio, L., 206
Cornelius Scipio, L. (cos. 259 BCE), 206
Cornelius Scipio, L. (q. 167 BCE), 206
Cornelius Scipio, P., 206
corruption, 1, 27, 199, 222, 312, 373, 384,
  394
cultural imaginary, 6, 15, 17, 65, 73, 75,
  249, 277, 285
culture, political, 20–8
cupiditas, 11, 247, 284, 292
cupido, 11, 165
Curius Dentatus, M'., 12–13, 28, 30–1,
  49, 174, 183, 237, 245
Cynic, 67, 70, 94, 317, 319, 321, 349

decadence, 5, 9, 33–4, 46, 56, 66, 76–7,
  199, 202, 204, 263, 298, 300
decline, 1, 5–6, 33–4, 45–6, 56, 60, 76–7,
  85, 202, 204, 207, 215, 227–8, 259,
  298, 301, 312, 314, 325, 360, 365,
  373, 388
demographics, 4, 34, 41
demoralisation, 2, 372–96
Dicaearchus, 285
Didius Julianus, 89
diet, 7, 12, 81, 89, 94, 99, 103, 128, 141,
  143–4, 146–7, 194–5, 203, 299, 304,
  315, 317, 326, 332, 374
dignitas, 44, 81, 100, 209, 239, 329

410

General Index

diligentia, 11–12, 38, 88, 247, 272, 293, 380
Diogenes the Cynic, 67, 70, 94, 317, 319, 321, 349
disciplina, 11–12, 19, 48, 96, 238–9, 245, 247, 272, 299, 315
Domitian, 86, 95, 333, 363
Domitius Ahenobarbus, Cn., 353
Drusillanus, 362

East India Company, 378
economics of status, 20–8, 34, 39, 43–4, 53, 56–7, 73–4, 79, 82, 295, 330
economy, 2–6, 14, 127–51
  imperial, 75
  market, 4, 64, 213–33
  oikos-based, 382
  political, 14, 20–8, 39–40, 51, 57, 63, 72–3, 93, 100
  villa, 228
emmer, 40, 141, 145
empire, 1–2, 52, 57, 67, 72–3, 75, 77–8, 87–8, 93, 99, 107, 147, 213, 215, 222, 227, 237, 242, 261, 291, 299, 335, 366–7, 394
Ennius, 31, 295–6
Epictetus, 373, 375, 386
Epicurean, 33, 108, 385
Epicurus, 33, 245, 318
Etruria, 131, 229

Fabius Maximus Allobrogicus, Q., 66, 349, 355
Fabricius Luscinus, C., 31, 49, 127, 183, 328, 356
fiscal regimes, 21, 25, 34
Fletcher, Andrew, 385, 390
Foucault, Michel, 7
freedmen, 14, 18–20, 23, 34, 37–8, 63, 72, 75, 249–53, 255, 259–61, 292, 304–10, 312, 332, 334, 361, 367
French Revolution, 160
frugalitas, 86
  Latin equivalent of σωφροσύνη, 103–4, 278, 292, 373
  semantics of, 7, 13, 16, 102–8, 233–6, 373
frugaliter, 13, 72, 247, 253, 297–8

frugality
  ancestral, 9, 12, 32, 36, 40, 76, 88, 127, 129, 196, 200, 365
  and aesthetics, 12, 306
  as a Christian virtue, 102–8, 374–6
  as a divine quality, 323
  as a Roman trait/virtue, 3, 9, 13, 29, 61–2, 72, 195–6, 210, 300, 329
  as attitude to wealth, 1, 10, 16, 35–9, 136
  as the mother of health, 299
  as wretchedness with a good name, 253
  enforced, 15, 34, 147, 330, 376
  ethos of, 3, 11, 16, 51, 159, 180, 184, 194
  excessive, 65–72, 89–90, 364
  in Buddhist tradition, 108
  in Islamic tradition, 108
  in Jewish tradition, 108
  legislated, 24, 27–9, 34
  of the subaltern, 18–20, 23, 81, 141–51, 307
  rhetoric of, 11, 28–34, 202–3
  v. luxury, 2, 5, 38, 73, 81, 192, 220, 305, 348, 352, 358–9, 362, 367, 378
  voluntary, 15, 97, 139, 194
frugi, 13, 18–20, 37, 63, 72, 81, 86, 364
  semantics of, 233–6
Furius Cresimus, C., 260

Galba, 83, 363
Gellius, Aulus, 12, 34, 49, 141, 163–4, 166, 179, 194, 202, 281
gender, 1, 5, 20, 25, 48, 61, 198, 297, 359, 375, 377, 394
Germanicus (Iulius Caesar, Germanicus), 366
gladiatorial games, 45
gloria, 56
gold, 31, 76, 81, 93, 129, 134, 245, 309, 347, 350, 359, 363–4
golden mean, 65, 90, 106, 333
Gracchi, the, 9
Gracchus, Gaius (Sempronius Gracchus, C.), 63, 169–70, 213–33, 254, 257, 274
Gracchus, Tiberius (Sempronius Gracchus, T.), 47, 50–1, 159–87, 213–33

411

General Index

Gratian, 379
Greece, 30, 32–5, 48, 56–7, 59–63, 65–72,
  82, 101, 181, 195, 202–3, 208, 210,
  214, 240–3, 245, 249, 261, 271–2,
  275–94, 296–7, 303, 306, 310–25,
  328–9, 354, 357, 373, 377, 388
greed, 1, 29, 38, 51, 62, 136, 165, 179,
  195, 229

Hannibal, 55
historiography, 1, 33, 45, 76, 186, 259
Hobbes, Thomas, 377
homiletic literature, 381
homo nouus, 31, 44, 75, 84, 183, 192, 199,
  201, 268, 272–4, 350
homo oeconomicus, 3, 16, 21
Horace, 12, 72, 258, 295–8, 333,
  375
House of Julius Polybius, 364
housing, 41, 74, 127–51, 233–6, 349, 351,
  358, 360, 366
Huguccio (of Pisa), 379
humanitas, 70, 91, 96, 100, 243, 248, 273,
  313, 334, 364
Hume, David, 108, 130, 372–96
husbandry, 1, 14–15, 17, 24, 34–5, 48, 62,
  240, 244, 262, 302

imagines, 43–4, 46, 53
improbitas, 11, 247
industria, 11, 13, 62, 195, 238–9, 244,
  248, 269, 273, 293, 310
innocentia, 38, 81, 248, 266–7, 273, 277,
  279, 313, 315
integritas, 11, 243, 266, 273
invective, 35, 61, 82, 87–8, 90–1, 254,
  265, 269, 305
Iron Age, 145
iugera, 34, 36, 50, 140, 144–8, 159–87,
  213–33

Jerome, 197
Julian, 12, 93–4
Juvenal, 75, 88, 99, 374

Laberius, Decimus, 253
landownership, 4–5, 159–87, 310
largitio, 11, 64, 70–1, 289, 292
latifundia, 169, 215

Latium, 17, 115, 129, 131–2, 135, 138,
  145, 229
Latium Vetus, 129, 131–2, 135
Law of the Twelve Tables, 25, 44, 133,
  137–8, 140–2, 144, 177, 180
laws, 24–8
leges agrariae, 25, 167
leges cibariae, 25
leges de ambitu, 26, 50, 58
leges de repetundis, 25, 58, 257–8,
  274–5
leges fenebres, 25
leges Liciniae, 26
leges sumptuariae, 25, 44, 48, 58, 61,
  79–80, 133, 136, 140, 149, 166, 180,
  192, 208, 220, 258, 309, 349, 358,
  363, 367, 375–6, 393–4
Lex Agraria of 111 BCE, 176
Lex Calpurnia de pecuniis repetundis,
  254, 257
Lex Claudia. See plebiscitum Claudianum
Lex Fannia, 208, 359
Lex Genucia, 26
Lex Iulia et Papia Poppaea, 79
Lex Licinia de modo agrorum, 50,
  159–87, 217
Lex Oppia, 61, 165, 192, 359, 394
Lex Orchia, 394
Lex Poetelia, 50, 182
Lex Sempronia agraria, 214, 217
Lex Villia Annalis, 26
Lex Voconia, 197
Libanius, 94
liberalitas, 11, 49, 64, 70–1, 73, 75, 84, 90,
  93–4, 102, 239, 258, 289, 292, 302,
  313, 329, 388
libido, 11, 93, 100, 274, 294, 308
libra farris, 141–2
licentia, 11, 60, 247
Licinius Crassus, L., 353
Licinius Murena, L., 65–72, 349–52
Licinius Stolo, C., 50–1, 159–87
Livius Drusus, M., 355
Livy, 61, 109, 136, 159–87, 202, 229, 239,
  359, 364, 373, 381, 395
Locke, John, 377
Ludi Megalenses, 208, 359
Lutatius Catulus, Q., 353
Luther, Martin, 380

412

General Index

luxuria, 1, 11, 13–14, 19, 33, 38, 45,
64–72, 78, 81, 83–4, 90, 94, 97, 99,
102, 151, 192, 194, 238–9, 247, 249,
271, 308, 316–17, 321, 323, 326–7,
331–2, 334, 336, 350, 356, 360, 394
luxuries, 11, 38, 58, 102–3, 247, 272, 381, 389
luxury, 1, 65–72, 136, 347, 362, 376, 378,
381, 395
luxus, 11, 97, 99, 358, 360, 363, 365

Mackenzie, George (Sir), 374–7, 381, 383
Maecenas, 296, 347, 360–1
Maelius, Sp., 47
Mamertinus, Claudius, 93–5
Mandeville, Bernard, 2, 378, 383, 389
Manlius Capitolinus, M., 47
Martial, 321, 348
Mentor (silversmith), 355
methodology, 13–14, 31, 40–1, 50, 85, 243
Metrodorus, 33
mobility, social, 21–3, 26, 34, 73, 260,
295–6, 301, 304, 310, 348, 359, 361,
365, 367
moderatio, 11, 71, 75, 80, 82–3, 86, 88,
90, 96, 104, 238, 249, 278, 281, 284,
293, 313
modestia, 11, 75, 82, 86, 92, 106, 218,
226, 238, 249, 278, 281, 284, 289,
293, 313
modus, 11, 83, 103, 106, 170, 194, 217,
220, 223, 233, 293, 317, 319
modus agrorum, 159–87
monetisation, 21, 53, 57
Montesquieu, 2, 160, 213
mos maiorum, 32, 59, 65, 196, 221,
238–40, 246, 262
Mun, Thomas, 378

Narcissus (freedman of Claudius), 361
nequitia, 11, 103–4, 107, 272, 280–1
Nero, 82, 101, 304, 354
Nerva, 85–6, 96, 333, 364
nobilitas, 33, 39, 42–72, 78, 182, 193, 199,
201, 210, 220, 239, 273–4, 360
nostalgia, 2, 9, 35, 46, 292–3

orator perfectus, 329
Otho, 83
Ovid, 18, 116, 182, 360

Pacatus Drepanius, 15, 95–101
Palladius, 13
Pallas (freedman of Claudius), 361
Panaetius, 203, 210
Pantaleoni, Maffeo, 3
Papirius Cursor, L., 52
parsimonia, 10–12, 38, 45, 60, 62, 65, 80,
85–6, 88–90, 93–4, 99–102, 105–6,
151, 183, 195, 221–2, 239, 244, 247,
272, 293, 310, 313, 316–17, 334,
361–4, 367, 380
patrimony, 16, 19, 22, 24, 26–7, 34, 41–3,
52, 54, 80, 137–8, 150–1, 303,
316–17, 358
paupertas, 11, 16, 75, 77, 105, 238, 287,
302, 308, 317–19, 321, 355, 372–3,
375
peasant, 2, 14–16, 20, 32, 62, 78, 84, 232,
237, 247, 323
pecuarii, 182, 224
Perkins, William, 379
Perseus of Macedon, 163, 350, 352, 355
Pertinax, 89
Petronius, 72, 99, 295, 304–10, 356, 364
Philippi, 359
pietas, 92–3, 238–9, 249, 302, 336
Plautus, 59–60, 193, 196, 245, 250–2, 262
plebiscitum Claudianum, 52, 185
Pliny the Elder, 166, 331, 352, 355, 374
Pliny the Younger, 13, 72–3, 85–6, 88,
95–101, 107, 244, 295, 311, 329–36
Plutarch, 160, 168–71, 185–6, 195–6,
198, 204–5, 215, 220–1, 225, 229,
355–6
Polybius, 202, 204–5, 210, 215, 357
Pompeii, 348, 357, 364
Pompey (Pompeius Magnus, Cn.), 91,
247, 268, 292, 375
Popilius Laenas, M., 164
populares, 223
Postumius Albinus, L., 224
Postumius Megellus, L., 183
poverty, 7, 10, 16, 18, 34, 49, 77, 97, 105,
128–9, 143, 148, 178, 183, 197, 207,
300–2, 316–18, 321–2, 325, 348,
372–3, 379–80, 383, 386, 396
praefectus morum, 79
princeps ciuilis, 75, 87, 92, 95–101, 295,
333

413

General Index

productivity, 2, 230–1
profit, 3, 17, 21, 222, 244, 260, 267, 294, 309
prosperity, 3, 40, 46–7, 128, 301, 382, 384, 387, 395–6
Publilius Syrus, 244
Pydna, 208

Quintilian, 72, 244, 275, 295, 306, 326–9

Reformation, the, 379
reification, 1, 5, 8, 35, 337
res mancipi, 137–9, 150
revenues, 12, 21, 34, 61, 216, 222
revolution, literary, 28–34
rhetoric, 9, 11, 14, 17–18, 26, 28–34, 49, 54, 57, 63–4, 84, 91, 93, 192, 200–3, 210, 239, 242, 244, 259, 262, 267, 273, 285, 289, 295, 297, 304–5, 313, 330, 335, 378, 381
Rhodians, 61, 163, 174, 184
Romulus, 40, 78, 180, 299
rustic, 40, 78, 127, 129, 195, 208, 255, 300–1, 356, 365
rusticitas, 37, 76, 207, 209

Sabine, 31, 61, 84, 148, 184, 195–6, 199, 203, 210, 331, 367
Sallust, 105
Samnite, 172, 175, 182, 300
satisficing, 16–17, 28, 32, 34, 36, 47, 271, 294, 317, 329, 331
Second Punic War, 1, 192, 200, 352
self-fashioning, 9, 14, 28, 30, 34, 48, 61, 193, 195, 199, 202–3, 259, 295
self-restrained omnipotence, 75, 82, 92, 295
self-sufficiency, 1, 18, 28, 32, 34, 36–7, 94, 128, 240, 244, 286–7, 291, 317–18, 325, 348
senate, 23, 36, 49, 74–5, 79–80, 85, 87–8, 183, 206, 224, 268, 270, 352, 360, 362
Seneca the Elder, 72, 244, 295, 301–3
Seneca the Younger, 13, 16, 72, 242, 244, 295, 306, 310–25, 347, 372
Septimius Severus, L., 89

sex, 12, 19, 38, 63, 87, 92, 180, 251, 269–70, 293, 299, 304, 306, 308–9, 326, 373
Sextius, L., 160, 164–5, 167, 173, 176, 179, 181
Siculus Flaccus, 169, 180, 219
silver, 12, 22, 36, 49, 73, 129, 133, 183, 221, 309, 320, 349–50, 354–5, 357–8, 362, 364, 367
simplicitas, 11, 238, 299, 313
slaves, 13–14, 18–20, 34, 36–8, 55, 60, 63, 72, 81, 133, 137, 142, 182, 194, 198, 203, 216, 221–2, 249–55, 259, 261, 263, 279, 290, 292, 304–10, 312, 317, 322, 333–4, 360, 362, 367, 377, 395
smallholding, 17, 64, 213–33
Smith, Adam, 108, 372–96
sobrietas, 11, 103, 105
Socrates, 34
sôphrôn/σώφρων, 221, 275, 278–9
sôphrosunê/σωφροσύνη, 103–4, 107, 205, 249, 276, 278, 281–2, 287, 289–90, 292–3, 325, 373
Spain, 95, 204
Sparta, 35, 65–72, 98
Stoicism, 33, 37, 65–6, 108, 203, 249, 281–6, 310–25, 349–51, 374–6, 385–8, 394–5
subsistence, 15, 17, 34, 36, 42, 141–51, 214, 227–8, 230, 319
Suetonius, 76, 81–3, 88, 356, 361, 365
Sulla (Cornelius Sulla Felix, L.), 79, 91, 247, 352
Sulpicius Galus, P., 202
Sulpicius Rufus, Ser., 65–72
sumptus, 10–11, 90, 93, 133, 221, 223
superbia, 1, 61, 100, 239
surplus, 3, 15–16, 18, 21, 34, 42, 55, 148, 244, 319
sustainability, 108
Sydney, Algernon, 385

Tarquinius Superbus, 46
taxes, 93, 222
tax-farming, 64
technology, 3, 128, 130, 138, 389
temperantia, 11, 91, 104, 106, 243, 248–9, 278, 281, 284, 289, 293, 313, 324–5
Temple, William (Sir), 376

414

General Index

tenuitas, 11–13, 245
Terence, 245, 250, 262
Theodosius, 92, 95–101, 107
thrift, 2, 7, 15–16, 19, 37–8, 46, 58, 62,
  67, 79, 89, 99–100, 102, 105, 196,
  199, 241, 244, 253, 259, 262, 269,
  272, 293, 302, 305, 310, 316, 318,
  329, 332, 337
Tiberius, 83, 362
Tiro, 163–5, 173
Titius Aristo, 365
Tomb of the Scipios, 206
trade, 4, 52, 130, 132, 135, 310, 376, 378,
  383, 393
Trajan, 85–6, 95–101, 330, 333–5, 364
transhumance, 15, 175, 230
Trimalchio, 304–10, 356, 364
triumph, 51
Tubero Catus, Q., 355

urbanitas, 37, 76

Valerius Flaccus, L. (*cos.* 195 BCE), 201
Valerius Maximus, 13, 40, 72, 181,
  183–4, 244–5, 295, 298–9, 329, 349,
  351, 353–4
Varro, 13, 164–5, 173, 216, 228, 232,
  244–5, 281
Vedius Pollio, P., 360

Verginius Rufus, L., 86
Verres, C., 72, 116, 269–74, 276
Vespasian, 84–5, 99, 334, 356, 363, 365,
  367
Vestricius Spurinna, T., 364
villa, 140, 172, 177, 216–17, 227, 310,
  333, 348, 357, 360, 362, 365
Villa delle Grotte, 172
viritane redistribution, 217
uir bonus, 20, 197, 212, 251, 258, 262,
  265, 313, 327, 329
uirtus, 66, 71, 92, 100–1, 104, 197,
  199, 239, 243, 247, 266–7, 272–3,
  277, 280, 287, 289–90, 292–3,
  302, 308, 310, 314, 316, 324,
  328, 337
visual, 42, 48, 84
Vitellius, 83–4
uoluptas, 11, 69, 71, 247, 316

warfare, 40, 47–8, 51, 54, 172, 178,
  181, 198, 213, 240, 248, 295,
  329
wealth, 40, 88, 93, 100, 180, 362
Weber, Max, 380
wife, wives, 14, 18–20, 34, 142, 145–6,
  173, 331, 336

Xenophon, 37, 203